The book of
Football
Obituaries

The book of
Football
Obituaries

Ivan Ponting

This edition first published by Pitch Publishing 2012

Pitch Publishing
A2 Yeoman Gate
Yeoman Way
Durrington
BN13 3QZ
www.pitchpublishing.co.uk

A CIP catalogue record is available for this book from the British Library

ISBN 978-1-908051-47-9

Typesetting and origination by Pitch Publishing.

Printed in Great Britain by TJ International.

Contents

Foreword by James Lawton

Few obituary pages run wider in their scope than those of *The Independent;* radical rabbis have to take their chances along with distinguished academics, military stalwarts and aboriginal folk heroes. But for those who love football, who feel a special wave of nostalgia when one of the gilded players of their youth lines up finally on the playing fields of eternity, there is invariably a point of certainty to go along with the sense of loss. They do not go without honour and a proper accounting.

This is provided unerringly by Ivan Ponting, whose feeling for and knowledge of the national game, and the men who down the years have made it such an integral part of so many lives, is superbly illustrated in this collection.

There is nothing mawkish or inflated about the work of Ponting. He is too diligent a researcher and clean and unsentimental a writer to provide his readers with anything less than a rounded picture of every football life he is so regularly asked to record.

The result in these pages is more than a series of perfectly formed cameos of notable football lives, satisfying though these are in themselves, but also a deeply personalised guide to the history of a game which, under the influence of celebrity and wealth that would have been unimaginable in the youth of some of the men who re-emerge so colourfully here, sorcerers like Raich Carter, Wilf Mannion and Len Shackleton, is sometimes hard to recognise today.

One of his few regrets – which we can only share on our own behalf – is that such icons as Sir Matt Busby and Bobby Moore died before Ponting changed from becoming a casual contributor to one of the pillars of the widely saluted *Indy* Obit pages.

His craft, however, has not gone short of opportunities for the achievement of great distinction, and no one could have put down his accounts of the lives of such poignant heroes as George Best and Alan Ball without being both deeply moved and perfectly informed.

Ponting's touch has also served brilliantly in acknowledging the lives of less famous players, but ones who contributed magnificently to the texture and the depth of their profession. A classic example came with the death in 2007 of Bill Perry, the South African-born winger who was responsible for confirming the status of one of the most memorable and romantic days in the history of English football when he scored the winning goal so dramatically in the Stanley Matthews final of 1953.

Perry's fine career, and three appearances for England, were warmly acknowledged – alongside the lives of a hard-line rabbi, an Italian banker and racehorse owner, and Miss Lois Maxwell, the fabled Miss Moneypenny in 14 James Bond films.

Ponting wrote: "On a sunlit May afternoon in 1953 the Blackpool winger's injury-time strike was in a category of glory entirely of its own." Deftly, the writer made a permanent record of Perry's moment in the sun. It is just another reason to applaud the decision to grant similar recognition to the enduring work of Ivan Ponting.

James Lawton,
Chief Sports Writer,
The Independent

Introduction

Since the first edition of this book in 2008, a procession of truly illustrious names have been added to the contents list. Such men as Sir Bobby Robson, Malcolm Allison, Nat Lofthouse and the tragic young Gary Speed from these shores, and titans of the world game such as Socrates, the flamboyant Brazilian, and Florian Albert, the sublimely talented Hungarian, have all passed away.

Whenever a famous football man dies, there is an inevitable degree of public grief, depending on the age of the individual and the circumstances of his demise. But newspaper obituaries, in the majority of cases, are not about mourning. They are about the celebration of the lives of often remarkable characters who have loomed large in the collective consciousness of their countless supporters, people who have admired them week by week, season by season; been touched by them, perhaps outraged by them, maybe even loved them in that special way which fans reserve for their sporting heroes. There is so much to remember, so many emotions to stir, and I hope this book goes some way towards achieving both.

I have been contributing obituaries to *The Independent* since 1991, when the great Arsenal winger Cliff Bastin died and the newspaper's regular writers were busy elsewhere. Clearly in a tight corner, the editor of the Gazette section, which contained the obituaries at that time, took a punt on a call to an obscure freelance from the depths of Somerset, and since then I have attempted to capture the essence of some of the most eminent names ever to grace our national game.

Between these covers are my takes on the likes of Alan Ball, Sir Stanley Matthews, Sir Alf Ramsey, Brian Clough, Bob Paisley, John Charles, Johnny Haynes, Ferenc Puskas and many other famous individuals, as well as some who are not as well known but who still left their own indelible mark on football history and in the minds of their followers.

As a personal reflection, into this last-mentioned category falls Alfie Biggs, primarily of Bristol Rovers, known widely and affectionately in the West Country as 'The Baron'. He loomed large in my childhood and provided regular thrills and countless hours of diversion for myself and my friends. My memories of Alfie are cherished dearly.

The obituaries are presented chronologically, in the order that their subjects died, with one exception. I have elected to begin with George Best, whom I grew up watching at every opportunity and who was the most completely captivating footballer of the age. Despite the obvious regrets about the turbulent Irishman's off-the-field troubles, the scope of his achievement was truly uplifting, and as is the case with every life recalled in these pages, I trust I have done him justice.

In most cases there has been no updating of the circumstances which prevailed at the time of writing, so it is intended that any topical reference provides an authentic flavour of the relevant era. Most of all, though, I hope the accumulated joy afforded by the men featured here firmly outweighs the melancholy at their passing.

Ivan Ponting,
August 2012

Acknowledgements

Ivan Ponting would like to thank the following: Andy Cowie of Colorsport, who provided the pictures; James Lawton for his inspiration and support; Graham Hales for his beautifully clean design, his patience and his unfailingly good-hearted enterprise; Dean Rockett, truly a gem of a copy editor; Chris Maume, Diana Gower, Jamie Fergusson, Sarah Quarmby, Warren Howard, Lewis Jebb and Annabel Freyberg, *The Independent* obituaries team present and past, for humouring this country bumpkin for so long; Simon Lowe, who proposed the book, and Paul Camillin, who ran with it again; Melanie Michael-Greer for looking after business; Les Gold for his enthusiasm and contacts; and, as ever, Pat, Rosie and Joe Ponting.

Author's Note

The obituaries which appear in this collection, all 246 of them, were written individually for a daily newspaper, *The Independent*, and therefore each one is sufficient unto itself, in its original incarnation having to bear no relation to anything else. However, when all the pieces are gathered together between the covers of a book, it is inevitable that issues, incidents and sometimes phraseology can crop up more than once. For this circumstance, the author humbly craves the readers' indulgence.

George Best

'Genius' is a term so chronically overused in conjunction with sport that it is in danger of being comprehensively devalued. It should be rationed scrupulously, reserved for the truly sublime rather than being squandered on the merely remarkable. However, there should be no hesitation in dusting down the 'g' word for a rare fitting recipient, and such a man was George Best.

Look beyond the lurid, fast-living image and set aside, for a moment, the alcoholism which was destined to transform his life so tragically. Like Stanley Matthews before him, Best was the symbol of footballing excellence for a whole generation. There were other magnificent players, including Bobby Charlton and Denis Law at his own club, Manchester United; but the mercurial Irishman was on a pedestal of his own and rightly so.

As Matt Busby, his Old Trafford mentor, put it: 'George had more ways of beating a player than anyone I've ever seen. He was unique in his gifts.' Unfortunately, he was singular, too, in that he was the first 'pop-star' footballer whose every off-field action was scrutinised by the media. Relevant advice was scant, there being no precedent to his situation, and eventually the ceaseless attention, in which he revelled at first but subsequently reviled, goaded him inexorably towards self-destruction.

Best was born the first of six children of an iron-turner at the Harland and Wolff shipyard in Belfast. A Protestant, though not in the political sense, he was brought up on the Cregagh housing estate and was crazy for kicking a football from the age of nine months.

Though his prodigious natural talent became evident early in his childhood, he was a skinny specimen, verging on the puny and embarrassed by his lack of stature, and his family considered him too small to tilt at a future in the professional game. Neverthless Best was fanatical about football and idolised the mid-1950s Wolverhampton Wanderers side, then the epitome of sporting glamour through their exploits in a series of continental friendlies in the days before formal European competition.

An intelligent boy, he passed the 11-plus examination only to find that his grammar school majored in rugby. His reaction – and how typical this would seem, later in life – was truancy, partly because he had been split from former friends and partly to play in soccer matches. Soon he was transferred to a secondary modern which catered for his obsession and he progressed, though not enough to earn selection for Northern Ireland Schoolboys. However, Best's breathtaking ability was spotted by Bob Bishop, Manchester United's chief scout in Ulster, who rang Matt Busby and proclaimed: 'I think I've found a genius.'

Even then, the path to stardom was to be tortuous for the seemingly frail wisp of a 15-year-old who crossed the Irish Sea to Old Trafford in 1961. Having barely left his home city before, he travelled on an overnight ferry with the similarly unworldly Eric McMordie – later to enjoy success with Middlesbrough and Northern Ireland – and was distinctly underwhelmed by his reception in Manchester. Little was done to welcome the painfully shy duo and soon they succumbed to homesickness, returning to Belfast and, in Best's case, to a likely future as a printer. Soon, though, he changed his mind and went back to Old Trafford where, before long, he was to stand the established order on its head in spectacular fashion.

He announced his limitless potential in training sessions, sparkling against star performers such as goalkeeper and fellow Ulsterman Harry Gregg, whom he duped too repeatedly for beginner's luck to have been a factor. Still only 17, Best tasted senior action for the first time in September 1963 and by December he was a fixture in Busby's side, one of the final elements, and surely the most crucial, in the painstaking reconstruction process which had been under way since the Munich air disaster five years earlier.

Operating alongside fellow world-class forwards in Law and Charlton, Best was incandescent, a magical manipulator of a football and an entertainer supreme. Positioned nominally on the wing but roaming at will, he was capable of going past opponent after opponent, able and frequently eager to make brutal assailants look like clumsy buffoons, and he was as clinical a finisher as any in the land.

Much is made of his heavenly fusion of skill and speed, balance and timing, which made him virtually unplayable at times. In addition, though, Best was immensely brave and, in his early twenties, attained a resilient strength and an unshakeable self-belief which enabled him to laugh in the face of the vicious physical punishment to which he was routinely subjected. Enhancing his worth still further, he was mentally acute, which allowed him to apply his instinctive flair to maximum advantage. In short, in a footballing sense he was flawless, possessing the assets to excel in any role.

True, there were times when team-mates would scream in exasperation, when the Irishman, having dribbled past three defenders, would teeter on the verge of losing possession to a fourth. The chances were, though, that in the next breath they would be hailing a wonder goal, created from a seemingly impossible position.

Performing in this vein, Best contributed monumentally to League championships in 1965 and 1967 and to the attainment of United's so-called holy grail, the European Cup, in 1968. Indeed it was during the exhilarating pursuit of that elusive prize that George Best the footballer made the quantum leap to Georgie Best the pop icon.

Early in 1966, the Red Devils had defeated mighty Benfica, the Portuguese champions, by three goals to two in the first leg of a European Cup quarter-final at Old Trafford. The second leg in Lisbon's Stadium of Light was a daunting prospect and Busby, with uncharacteristic caution, had urged his men to play it safe for the first 20 minutes.

Best had other ideas. Running at the Eagles' formidable rearguard with swashbuckling abandon, he scored two fabulous goals in the opening 12 minutes and inspired a scintillating 5-1 victory. His display was greeted rapturously but the impact was magnified still further when he donned a sombrero to descend from the plane's steps on his return to England. With his good looks, flowing locks and, now, his sense of the flamboyant away from the pitch, he was enshrined as 'El Beatle'.

Duly, his life took on a different dimension. Now he was public property as never before and he delighted in the advantages thus accrued. Commercial opportunities abounded, beautiful girls prostrated themselves before him and the attraction of alcohol became gradually more insistent. For a long time, though, despite dire warnings from Busby that he was going down the wrong road, that was not a problem to a young and exceptionally fit athlete.

Inklings that difficulties were brewing for Best surfaced after 1968, during which he was voted both English and European Footballer of the Year after contributing an opportunist's goal to United's European Cup final defeat of Benfica at Wembley.

In the wake of that longed-for triumph, a perhaps understandable sense of complacency emanated from Old Trafford, where a 59-year-old manager with an ageing team might have been excused a little weariness after battling back from the horror of Munich.

Best, though, had a different agenda. He was still young and hungry for more honours, becoming increasingly frustrated at what he saw as lack of ambition around him. Not surprisingly, a gradual decline set in at the club, and the fact that it was largely masked by Best's individual splendour – he was top scorer in five successive campaigns from 1967/68 to 1971/72 and once netted six times in an FA Cup tie against Northampton Town – did little to placate United's principal asset.

Sadly, there was to be no consolation on the international front, where Best turned in occasional inspirational displays – notably in a stirring win over Scotland at Windsor Park, Belfast, in 1967 – but usually was hamstrung by the poor overall standard of the team. As a result, he would refer to his Northern Ireland efforts as 'recreational football', a slight which reflected overweening gall at his unavoidable absence from the world's great tournaments rather than genuine malice.

Back in Manchester, his disillusionment was heightened when Busby refused to make him captain, citing his growing irresponsibility as the reason, and there followed a succession of disciplinary spats and absences without leave as he turned ever more frequently towards the bottle. In addition, he fell out with Bobby Charlton, being sickened by what he perceived as the older man's holier-than-thou attitude over his playboy lifestyle. For his part, Charlton believed, with simple logic, that Best was letting the side down.

Meanwhile the Belfast boy's sexual conquests were spread regularly across the newspapers – he admitted that he saw most attractive women as a challenge – and his goldfish-bowl existence intensified when he moved into a custom-built, ultra-modern house in Bramhall which became a mecca for rubberneckers.

After Busby's retirement, Best led his two successors as manager – first Wilf McGuinness and then Frank O'Farrell – a merry dance with his unscheduled absences, and by the spring of 1972 his situation was approaching crisis point. Though still playing superbly at times, and carrying an otherwise mediocre team, he could no longer shoulder the responsibility and his drinking spiralled dangerously out of control.

That May, unable to cope, he announced his retirement and decamped to Marbella, only to return for the start of the new season. But more strife was in store. By December he was transfer-listed after further indiscretions, only to be lured back by yet another new manager, Tommy Docherty. It was a dubious rapprochement which ended in acrimony when the team hit the skids, quickly followed by Best himself, who played his last game for relegation-doomed Manchester United as a distinctly portly 27-year-old on New Year's Day 1974.

What followed was largely irrelevant to what made George Best special in the first place, his football career continuing for a further ten years but playing second fiddle to drink, sex and gambling, and it constitutes a tale more edifying in summary than gruesome detail.

At various junctures he ran the Slack Alice nightclub in Manchester and Bestie's Bar at Hermosa Beach, California. There was a spectacular fall-out with one Miss World,

Marjorie Wallace, which resulted in Best being charged with theft before being released without a stain on his character, and a fling with another holder of that title, Mary Stavin.

There were marathon benders without number and sundry brawls; a Christmas spent in prison for drink-driving; various hospitalisations for alcoholism; divorce from Angela Macdonald Janes, the long-suffering mother of his son, Calum; and admitted guilt over the emotional neglect of his own mother, who died an alcoholic at the age of 54.

Post United, the pick of Best's footballing travels included three summers with Los Angeles Aztecs, during which he faced the likes of Pele and Franz Beckenbauer and intermittently rediscovered the old flair, fitness and enthusiasm. Also there was an initially exhilarating but eventually unsatisfying brief stint with Second Division Fulham in harness with his fellow showman, Rodney Marsh. Then came turbulent sojourns with Fort Lauderdale Strikers and Hibernian, and fleeting service with San Jose Earthquakes, during which he contrived one goal of divine quality, which saw him mesmerise four defenders before beating the goalkeeper.

After his divorce from his first wife, there were long-term liaisons with model Angie Lynn and with Mary Shatila, who also guided his business affairs as he earned a living through personal appearances. In 1995, still fighting alcoholism, he arranged to marry Alex Pursey, a Virgin flight attendant half his age, but failed to turn up for his own wedding because he had gone drinking with another girl. The ceremony took place a week later and an intermittently turbulent relationship lasted for some years, though it was to founder in the end. Meanwhile Best continued to thrive as a professional celebrity, an after-dinner speaker and soccer pundit who was engagingly witty when sober, sometimes obnoxious when not.

In 2002 he underwent a liver transplant, and his subsequent inability to give up alcohol despite being offered the chance of a new life finally affected the broadly sympathetic way in which he was viewed by large swathes of the public. Hitherto many people had a twinkle in their eyes when they spoke of George Best; afterwards there was a widespread feeling that he had acted with a selfish disdain for which he deserved contempt.

At that point, he spoke movingly of his plight, which he recognised fully: 'I didn't decide one day that I would drink myself to death. It is as a result of alcoholism. Alcoholism is a disease. It's the same with drugs. You can't suddenly decide "I'll be a drug addict."'

Despite that, despite everything, the game he illuminated so brilliantly remained his defining passion to the last. He was addicted to alcohol and he was addicted to women. But most of all he was addicted to football.

Best leaves unanswerable questions behind him. How great might he have become but for the bottle? Had Matt Busby been younger, less scarred by past trauma, might he have imposed sufficient discipline to inspire the most naturally gifted player of modern times to scale even loftier peaks?

At this distance, it doesn't matter. For seven or eight seasons George Best gave untold pleasure to countless fans all over the world, created so much that was beautiful and left a hoard of deathless memories. And that is enough.

George Best: born Belfast, 22 May 1946; played for Manchester United 1963-74, Stockport County 1975, Cork Celtic 1976, Los Angeles Aztecs 1976-78, Fulham 1976-77, Hibernian 1979-80, Fort Lauderdale Strikers 1979, San Jose Earthquakes 1980-81, Golden Bay 1981, Bournemouth 1983, Tobermore 1984; capped 37 times by Northern Ireland 1964-77; died London, 25 November 2005.

Cliff Bastin

If the videos and T-shirts, posters and pillowcases, and the rest of the infernal paraphernalia that now tumbles tackily from the shelves of football souvenir shops had been abroad in the 1930s, then a fair percentage of it would have been adorned by the placid features of Cliff Bastin.

The richly-gifted Devonian was a soccer star who served Arsenal and England in an era when such beings were lauded without being ever deified or exploited in the modern way. Indeed, even his nickname, 'Boy', referred to precocity of talent rather than personality – had he been born half a century later, might we have been inflicted with the cult of 'Bazza'? – and he exuded the dignity and level-headedness then expected of leading sportsmen. Sometimes Bastin was criticised, by those who did not know him, for aloofness, but that was unjust; in fact, he suffered from deafness, which proved a severe social handicap until an operation improved matters after his retirement from the game.

Though it is notoriously difficult to judge the merits of a performer whose glory days were so long ago, both the testimony of Bastin's peers and the evidence of the record books proclaim that he was special. Something of a boy wonder in his home town of Exeter, he rose quickly through the local school team to join Exeter City, graduating to their senior side at the prodigiously early age of 15. Yet his breakthrough into the big time owed something to good fortune. Arsenal's Herbert Chapman – who many still maintain was the greatest of all club managers – was interested in signing another Exeter man and, accordingly, arrived to watch City in action. When the game started, however, the prospective target barely got a look-in as Chapman was captivated by the skill and calmness of the young Bastin, then playing at inside-forward.

Chapman wasted no time in making his approach and Bastin, after much phlegmatic consideration – footballers were not overpaid in those days, and he had trained as an electrician – committed his future to the Gunners. What a momentous decision it turned out to be, although not before the callow rookie, on arriving at his new place of work, had been turned away by a commissionaire who mistook him for an autograph-hunter.

Soon Bastin had switched to the left wing, the position in which he was to find fame, and in which an avalanche of honours was to descend on his neat, well-oiled head. He finished that 1929/30 season with an FA Cup winner's medal, and it speaks volumes for a sincere nature that he sent it to his former teacher in Exeter. The following term, having established a productive partnership with the brilliant Alex James, he played a major part in the club's first League championship triumph and, as a decade of Arsenal domination unfolded, his achievements piled up.

By November 1931, he was an England international, thus winning every top honour the game had to offer while still in his teens. Further title-medals were garnered in 1933, 1934 and 1935 – the Gunners' much celebrated treble – and yet another in 1938, with a second FA Cup victory being added in 1936. During the 1932/33 campaign he netted 33 times, still a League record for a winger, and no Arsenal player has ever topped his 176 goals for the club.

Bastin excelled for England too, winning 21 caps and contributing some breathtaking performances, one of the most famous coming against soon-to-be-crowned World Champions Italy in 1933, in Rome, where the partisan fans, sick of seeing their heroes tantalised by the Englishman, chanted 'Basta Bastin' ('Enough of Bastin'). His success was based on magnetic ball-control, a savage shot and the intelligence to make the most of

Chapman's innovative tactical acumen. Instead of hugging the touchline in the manner of traditional wingers, he would cut inside frequently, scoring almost as many goals as he made for others. Bastin's career was curtailed by the war. Due to his deafness, he could not join the forces, and he spent most of the conflict manning an air-raid post on top of Highbury's main stand; afterwards he played only a few games at right-half before retiring.

On departing the game, he wrote a column for the *Sunday Pictorial* and ran a restaurant in Edgware, before returning to Exeter as landlord of the Horse & Groom pub. He left that trade in 1977, since when he had lived a quiet life in his native city, rarely visiting the stadium where his reputation was forged. As long as there's an Arsenal, though, the name of Cliff Bastin will be revered.

Clifford Sydney Bastin: born Exeter, Devon, 14 March 1912; played for Exeter City 1927-29, Arsenal 1929-47; capped 21 times by England 1932-38; died Exeter, 3 December 1991.

Jack Kelsey

Jack Kelsey was a sporting hero of the tall, quietly-spoken, clean-cut variety, the type they used to write about in children's comics. But Kelsey was for real. Throughout most of the 1950s and the early 1960s, he kept goal for Arsenal and Wales with a presence that bordered on omnipotence. It was an era when Britain was richly blessed with accomplished custodians – the likes of Gil Merrick and Bert Williams, Ted Ditchburn and Harry Gregg – but few would dispute that Kelsey was the finest of his day.

Yet in terms of medals and trophies, his reward was surprisingly scant. Admittedly, he would not have expected to win many international prizes in a Welsh team that never remotely matched his own quality, but at club level he was a victim of dismal fortune. For much of his heyday, the Arsenal side was one of the most mundane in Highbury history. He was the club's sole world-class player, and week after week was called upon to perform near miracles between the posts, merely to maintain his employers' mid-table status in the First Division.

In character with the man, he was not a flashy keeper, his positional ability as vital to his craft as his agility and strength. Like Pat Jennings years later, Kelsey had hands like shovels which seemed to swallow up the ball with an inevitability that made attackers despair. Invariably, he exuded calmness and confidence, plucking a swirling cross from the brow of some dreadnought centre-forward or hurling himself head first among flailing size-12 feet as if it were the simplest thing in the world.

Kelsey, who had been a steelworker before joining Arsenal from the Welsh amateur team Winch Wen in 1949, needed every ounce of self-belief following a traumatic senior debut. He let in five goals against Charlton Athletic in February 1951, and was derided by a local music-hall comedian. The Gunners' manager, Tom Whittaker – a decent man and a protective father figure to callow youngsters living away from home for the first time – was furious, extracting a promise from the theatre that the destructive jibes would not be repeated, and affirming his faith in the boy. Whittaker compared Kelsey to a pilot shot down, through no fault of his own, on his first mission, and swiftly relaunched the fledgling career with marked success.

Thus, in the 1952/53 season, Kelsey was ready to take advantage of a lucky break, playing enough games as deputy for the injured George Swindin to earn a League championship medal, his only major club honour. But although Arsenal would never fill his trophy cabinet, he did not lack recognition. He played for Great Britain against the Rest of Europe in 1955, and after he had performed majestically in Wales' gallant progress to the quarter-finals of the 1958 World Cup, the Brazilians nicknamed him 'The Cat with Magnetic Paws'.

Ironically, it was in a friendly international against Brazil in May 1962 that Kelsey suffered the injury that ended his playing days at the premature age, for a goalkeeper, of 32. That day in Rio de Janeiro, while winning his 41st cap – more than any British custodian before him – he dived at the feet of the centre-forward Vava and jolted his back severely.

Protracted efforts to regain fitness ended in failure, and the following year he started a new job with Arsenal, taking charge of the club's lottery and shop. Kelsey approached this new challenge with the same enthusiasm that had infused his football, and he excelled, eventually retiring as commercial manager in 1989, 40 years on from his arrival at Highbury. It was not long after that I met Jack, who had agreed to help my research for a book on Arsenal. I came to know a hospitable, honest and intelligent man to whom family and close friends were of paramount importance. A widower with two sons, he doted on his one-year-old grandson, and lived quietly in north London until his death following a short illness.

Though he kept a close eye on the football world through television and the newspapers, he was not obsessed by the game and his visits to Highbury had become rare. One of his greatest joys was woodwork, for which he had shown aptitude throughout his adult life, and in retirement he fashioned doll's houses of enormous intricacy and beauty.

Jack Kelsey exhibited not a trace of ego but he knew his worth. He was a true and talented sportsman.

Alfred John Kelsey: born Swansea, Glamorgan, 19 November 1929; played for Arsenal 1949-62; capped 41 times by Wales 1954-62; commercial manager Arsenal 1963-89; died London, 18 March 1992.

John Atyeo

John Atyeo was the best-known, best-loved and most accomplished player in the history of West Country football.

'Big John' to all who knew him, he merited the epithet for more than his strapping six-foot stature: five strikes in six games for England, more goals scored for one club (his beloved Bristol City) than by any star of any era, the extraordinary record of never being cautioned by a referee in more than 650 senior matches – all that tells only part of the story. The full measure of the man was evident in an engagingly open personality, combining the lively intelligence that made him a successful and enlightened schoolteacher with the unadorned simplicity of a true countryman.

From his boyhood in Wiltshire, Atyeo was an outstanding all-round sportsman but, though his talents at rugby and cricket were enviable enough, it was at football that he excelled. For a centre-forward, he lacked nothing: big-framed and brawny, majestic in the air, he possessed both skill and power in either foot and the acumen to apply those gifts to optimum advantage. Indeed, so colossal was his potential that he was coveted by the reigning League champions, Portsmouth, who gave him two first-team outings as an amateur in 1950/51 and made strenuous attempts to secure his signature.

But Atyeo's roots were deep in home soil and he opted for the more familiar surroundings of Ashton Gate, where pretty soon he was selling eggs from his mother's hens to his new City team-mates. Before long, too, he was scoring prolifically for the Robins and in the mid-1950s offers poured in from the likes of Arsenal, Spurs, Liverpool and even Internazionale, the great Milan club. The fee mentioned was £50,000 – at today's inflated valuations, the equivalent of many millions – but he was not to be tempted, even in an era when players were limited to a niggardly maximum wage.

Atyeo's decision was influenced by the need for more mental stimulus than any game could provide. Throughout most of his career he played part-time, first working as a quantity surveyor, then training as a teacher, and but for that semi-professional status must have represented his country more often.

Even with an international strike-rate close to a goal a game, even after scoring the goal that won England qualification for the 1958 World Cup finals in Sweden, even though he never finished on the losing side, he was discarded, the only conceivable explanation being that the selectors (there was no all-powerful manager then) objected to his part-time status. No matter, between 1951 and 1966 he served City royally, scoring 350 goals, helping them win the Division Three (South) title in 1955, and captaining them to promotion to Division Two ten years later.

Off the pitch, Atyeo's life was equally fulfilling. On retirement from football he threw himself into teaching and went on to become head of mathematics at a school in Warminster, where he lived with his wife and five children. He was utterly dedicated and on exam days would rise early to offer pupils last-minute revision sessions at 7am – he reckoned there was more satisfaction in helping youngsters than in all his footballing glory and to the last he was unstinting with his time and effort.

A perceptive columnist for the Plymouth-based *Sunday Independent*, John Atyeo was open-minded and astute, modest and humorous, qualities enhanced by old-fashioned family values yet tempered by a certain disarming naivety that never left him. His death at home, following a heart attack, leaves the football scene immeasurably the poorer.

Peter John Walter Atyeo: born Westbury, Wiltshire, 7 February 1932; played for Portsmouth 1951, Bristol City 1951-66; capped six times for England 1955-57; died Warminster, Wiltshire, 8 June 1993.

Jim Holton

Traditionally, Manchester United's footballing idols tend towards the glamorous and spectacular; where once Best, Law and Charlton captivated audiences at the Old Trafford 'Theatre of Dreams' now Cantona and Giggs hold centre stage. But in between, during a period when the Red Devils' fortunes were at a low ebb, Jim Holton emerged as a cult hero with a difference.

The soccer cliche 'rugged Scot' might have been fashioned for the giant central defender. Well-nigh unbeatable in the air and abrasive in the tackle, he exerted a truly formidable physical presence which, on balance, compensated amply for an undeniable clumsiness when it came to the game's finer points. In some quarters he was criticised for his rumbustious methods, but he was devoid of malice and it was significant that any vilification came from outraged spectators rather than his opponents on the pitch.

Having been an amateur with Celtic, then failed to make the grade at West Bromwich Albion, Holton was rebuilding his confidence with lowly Shrewsbury Town when United – struggling at the foot of the First Division in January 1973 – gambled £80,000 on his raw promise. His vigorous approach made him an instant darling of the Stretford End – itself no longer with us, having fallen casualty to the modern move towards all-seater stadiums – and soon the affectionate chant of 'Six foot two, eyes of blue, Big Jim Holton's after you' became a familiar refrain.

Though unable to prevent United's relegation in 1974, Holton became an increasingly effective and influential player, winning international recognition and playing a stirring part in Scotland's 1974 World Cup campaign. Sadly, after helping to set his club on course for an immediate return to the top flight, he suffered a broken leg in December 1974, thus beginning a sequence of ill-fortune that was to dog him for the remainder of his career.

On the comeback trail in the reserves, he shattered his leg again and – with others prospering in his absence and United riding high once more – there seemed little alternative but to seek a fresh start elsewhere. Accordingly Holton joined Sunderland in 1976 and then Coventry, but a series of injuries limited his progress; indeed at his final club, Sheffield Wednesday, his fitness problems were so severe that he never played a senior match.

However, Holton was a personable fellow, tailor-made for the licensing trade, and he became a successful publican in Coventry, where he lived with his wife and two teenage children until his death of a suspected heart attack after a fitness training session.

James Allan Holton: born Lesmahagow, Lanarkshire, 11 April 1951; played for West Bromwich Albion 1968-71, Shrewsbury Town 1971-72, Manchester United 1973-76, Sunderland 1976-77, Coventry City 1977-81; capped 15 times for Scotland 1973-74; died Warwick, 4 October 1993.

Danny Blanchflower

If the 20th century is going to throw up a more original, eloquent, free-thinking football man than Danny Blanchflower, then it has little time to lose. The intellectual Ulsterman played the game as inspiringly as he spoke about it, making him a priceless asset in a field not noted for such heady combinations.

Blanchflower left an indelible mark on the history of British football with his often innovative captaincy of Tottenham Hotspur in 1960/61, the season in which the north London club became the first since Victorian times to achieve the coveted League and FA Cup double. It was a fittingly glorious zenith to a remarkable career.

For all his excellence, Blanchflower was not a spectacular footballer, more a subtle, all-pervasive influence from his position at right-half (a midfielder in modern parlance). In his prime, between 1957 and 1962, he was one of the most creative players in the game, capable of dictating the tempo of a match like few others.

Neither quick nor muscular, though endowed with a wiry strength, Blanchflower had an instinct for slipping into space at crucial moments. Having seized the initiative while less thoughtful performers milled around unproductively, he would impose his presence with his remarkable passing skills. One moment Blanchflower was shackled, the next free and bellowing for possession; then, an instant later, the ball was nestling in the opponents' net, probably deposited there by Jimmy Greaves, Bobby Smith or Cliff Jones, but all courtesy of their skipper's exquisite vision.

Though his mother played for a local ladies' team, the Belfast-born Blanchflower did not hail from a sporting family. But he fell in love with football at an early age, excelled at junior level and in 1945 signed for a leading Irish side, Glentoran. Four years later he crossed the water to sign for Barnsley, and before long was celebrating his first full international cap.

Blanchflower did well for his new club and attracted the attention of the more fashionable Aston Villa, whom he joined in 1951. At the age of 25, and maturing into a very fine player, he seemed ready-made for stardom. But soon he became disenchanted with the unimaginative, inflexible tactics employed at Villa Park and, in typically outspoken manner, made his feelings known.

Come 1954, he seemed set to break the British transfer record with a £40,000 move to Arsenal. But the Gunners appeared to get cold feet over the fee and instead Blanchflower joined Tottenham Hotspur for £30,000. It was the turning point of his professional life.

At White Hart Lane, he was managed by Arthur Rowe, whose exhilarating push-and-run Spurs side of the early 1950s was in need of rebuilding. Together the two men set about the task of creating a team in a traditionally stylish Tottenham mould, but the partnership was split when illness precipitated Rowe's retirement in 1955. The new Spurs manager, Jimmy Anderson, though he made Blanchflower his captain, was not on the same wavelength and the pair clashed after the eloquent Irishman made tactical changes during an FA Cup semi-final and the side lost. The fact that similar enterprise had paid dividends before was overlooked.

However, despite being deprived of the captaincy, Blanchflower grew ever more influential and in 1957/58 completed what was arguably his most brilliant individual campaign, which he climaxed by leading Northern Ireland to the last eight of the World Cup in Sweden. Deservedly, he was named Footballer of the Year by the game's writers, an accolade repeated in 1961.

Yet still Spurs were not winning trophies and their new manager, Bill Nicholson, dropped Blanchflower, whom he described as being invaluable in a good side but a luxury in a bad one because of his inadequate defensive input. By now Blanchflower was 33 and the end might have been imminent, but the astute Nicholson had none of it. He turned down a transfer request and reinstalled his elder statesman as captain – to fabulous effect.

With wonderful new players, such as the Scots Dave Mackay and John White, added to the team, Spurs improved markedly during the following term, the prelude to the all-conquering exploits of 1960/61. In 1961/62 they let the League slip away to the unfancied Ipswich Town, but retained the FA Cup, then became the first British team to claim a European trophy, lifting the Cup Winners' Cup in 1963.

By this time Blanchflower was at the veteran stage, often playing through the pain of a debilitating knee condition, but his overall contribution seemed ever more important. By now he was taking an increasingly prominent role in training and as liaison man between manager and players. When a combination of injury and age (he was 38) forced him to quit in 1964, Tottenham lost a guiding light.

Many, including Nicholson himself, reckoned that Blanchflower would be ideal as Spurs' next boss, and when Nicholson stepped aside in 1974 he recommended his former skipper as his successor. But the board of directors, presumably cringing at the prospect of appointing such a forthright character, refused the advice and Blanchflower continued the successful journalistic career – he wrote an incisive column for the *Sunday Express*, frequently railing in articulate fashion against what he saw as unjust authority – that he had begun after hanging up his boots.

In fact, Blanchflower did sample management later, taking charge of Northern Ireland and briefly running a lacklustre Chelsea team at the end of the 1970s. By then, perhaps, he had been absent from day-to-day involvement in football for too long and the results were poor; in any case, he professed himself disillusioned with values in the modern game.

Blanchflower – whose brother Jackie played for Manchester United until he was seriously injured in the Munich air disaster of 1958 – continued with the *Sunday Express* until 1988. After that his slide into infirmity grieved all who had known him as a superb player, canny tactician, incurable romantic and maverick sage, a magnetic personality who dominated any room into which he walked.

True, he was never 'one of the lads', preferring to go his own way, as on the day he dismissed Eamonn Andrews by refusing, on live television, to take part in the *This Is Your Life* programme. Indeed, there were times when his undeniable ego upset people around him. But every successful man must know his own worth – and Danny Blanchflower's was immense.

Robert Dennis Blanchflower: born Belfast, 10 February 1926; played for Glentoran 1945-49, Barnsley 1949-51, Aston Villa 1951-54, Tottenham Hotspur 1954-64; capped 56 times by Northern Ireland 1949-62; manager of Northern Ireland 1976-79, Chelsea 1978-79; died Cobham, Surrey, 9 December 1993.

Roy Vernon

Roy Vernon was a colourful, at times tempestuous Welshman blessed with a vivid talent for football and an ebullient, buccaneering character in which there was no trace of false modesty. Thus, when asked at the height of his career, in the mid-1960s, to name the outstanding goal-scorers in the land, he replied, in a tone of cool certainty: 'There's Denis Law, there's Jimmy Greaves and then there's me.'

Those privileged to witness the quicksilver Scot and the predatory Englishman in their spectacular prime may be disinclined to include Vernon in such illustrious company. Yet the very comparison speaks volumes for Vernon's credentials as one of the most lethal marksmen of the post-war era.

To those who knew him as a teenager, there was little doubt that he was headed for the heights. Vernon's sportsmaster at Rhyl Grammar School, who helped nurture the gifts of many a prospective professional footballer, reckoned he could teach him nothing. As he excelled in local football, Vernon proved a magnet to the big clubs. But, ever one to go his own way, he rejected the overtures of Everton – whom he would one day lead to glory – and Manchester United, signing instead for Blackburn Rovers, reasoning that he would encounter less keen competition at Ewood Park. Thereafter Vernon's progress was rapid. He made his top-flight debut in 1955 and some 18 months later, not yet 20, he won the first of 32 full caps for Wales. In 1957/58 he was an integral part of the Rovers side that won promotion to the First Division, and then crowned his season by appearing in the World Cup finals in Sweden.

But Vernon was a headstrong young man prone to question authority, and after a succession of rows with the Rovers manager, Dally Duncan, he was sold to Everton for £27,000 plus the Toffees' striker Eddie Thomas.

At Goodison Park his game matured and Vernon blossomed into a magnificent taker and maker of goals with a delightful range of skills, one minute silky and subtle, the next venomously incisive. Striking up a potent partnership with the Scot Alex Young, Vernon topped Everton's scoring chart in each of his four complete seasons with the club, eventually netting 110 times in 200 senior games. His finest hour came in 1962/63 when he captained Everton to the League championship and it was fitting that he scored a hat-trick against Fulham on the day the title was clinched.

However, controversy continued to dog his footsteps. On Merseyside he came under the iron disciplinary rule of the Everton manager, Harry Catterick, who could not accept Vernon's free-wheeling, rather sardonic outlook, and Vernon was once sent home from a United States tour for breaking a curfew. But Catterick was determined to make the most of him. He gave Vernon the captaincy in the hope that responsibility would have a mellowing effect – an imaginative move which met with some success.

Clearly, though, the two men were not compatible in the long term and in 1965 Vernon joined Stoke City for £40,000, still only 28 and with plenty left to give. During five years in the Potteries he contributed impressively if fitfully, a niggling knee injury reducing his effectiveness all too often. Eventually, after a brief sojourn with Halifax Town, Vernon wound down his career in South Africa before returning to Lancashire to play football for fun in the amateur ranks.

If his pace had departed, his skill was as sharp as ever, and so was his sense of humour. Once told by an earnest non-League boss that his midfield couldn't find him because he was standing still, Vernon responded: 'If they can't find me when I'm standing still, how the hell do you expect them to find me if I'm running around?'

Thomas Royston Vernon: born Ffynnongroyw, North Wales, 14 April 1937; played for Blackburn Rovers 1955-60, Everton 1960-65, Stoke City 1965-70, Halifax Town 1970; capped 32 times for Wales 1957-67; died Blackburn, Lancashire, 5 December 1993.

Johnny Hancocks

There wasn't much of the footballer Johnny Hancocks, but what there was tended to make an explosive impact. Standing 5ft 4in and wearing size-two boots, Hancocks was a right-winger whose dashing style and savage shot typified the all-action Wolverhampton Wanderers side assembled by their manager, Stan Cullis, after the Second World War.

Hancocks was a leading light of the gold-and-black combination that finished the 1940s as a major power, then vied for supremacy with Manchester United's Busby Babes during the next decade.

Having impressed steadily in local amateur circles, the tiny teenager turned professional with Walsall in 1938 and showed high promise with the Saddlers, who were then struggling in the nether regions of the Third Division South. Hancocks' burgeoning career was placed on hold by the outbreak of war, though he put his athleticism to effective use, serving as a PT instructor in the Army and excelling in services football. Come 1946 his potential was recognised by Wolves, who signed him for £4,000, and pitched him straight into their senior ranks.

He was an instant hit, his strength and determination compensating amply for lack of inches, but it was his ability to strike the ball crisply that took the eye. Thunderous shots, especially from free-kicks, were his speciality – his final tally of 158 goals in 343 League games was remarkable for a flankman – and his expertise in delivering long, raking crosses was another telling factor in the team's success.

Sometimes the home crowd at Molineux might grow impatient if he appeared to hold on to the ball too long but, in general, they took him warmly to their hearts. Indeed, it was not hard to see why as he took a key role in the FA Cup final triumph over Leicester City in 1949, performed rousingly as Wolves finished runners-up in the League the following season and helped them blaze the British trail into Europe in a series of stirring friendlies against top-quality opposition from behind the Iron Curtain.

But best of all was his contribution as the club lifted the League championship for the first time in 1954.

That season the 34-year-old Hancocks finished joint top scorer with 25 goals, as well as laying on many more for the likes of Dennis Wilshaw and Roy Swinbourne. Thereafter he continued as buoyantly prolific as ever, topping the Wolves strike chart in two more campaigns before, in 1956, Cullis decided younger blood was needed.

Hancocks' path to international stardom was barred by such luminaries as Stanley Matthews and Tom Finney, and he played only three times for England, but acquitted himself with spirit, especially on his debut when he netted twice against Switzerland at Highbury in 1948. He completed his playing days with non-League clubs, later working in an iron foundry in his home town of Oakengates, in Shropshire, before retiring in 1979. Despite suffering a long illness which left him partially paralysed he endeavoured to keep in touch with the football scene he had bestrode so excitingly and for so long. He will go down as one of the Wolves' very finest; Johnny Hancocks would not ask for more than that.

John Hancocks: born Oakengates, Shropshire, 30 April 1919; played for Walsall 1938-46, Wolverhampton Wanderers 1946-56; capped three times for England 1948-50; died 18 February 1994.

Tony Waddington

The amiably wily Tony Waddington was an admirably sound, widely respected football manager over almost two decades, during which he earned two claims to undying fame.

In 1972, he led 104-year-old Stoke City to their first major honour, the League Cup; but even more vividly inscribed in the Potteries' sporting annals is Waddington's part in one of the most romantic tales in football folklore.

In October 1961 Stoke were a side on the skids, languishing near the foot of the Second Division and on the verge of bankruptcy. Recognising that something extraordinary was needed, Waddington re-signed the city's favourite son, the 46-year-old Stanley Matthews, from Blackpool, for a token £3,500.

There had been a deafening outcry throughout the Potteries some 14 years earlier when Matthews, then recognised as the world's leading player, had left Stoke to join the Seasiders. Now, the majority of Stoke's supporters acclaimed Waddington for his boldness, but there were those who denounced the deal as nostalgic folly. But how well Waddington, at 36 one of the youngest managers in the League and nearly ten years Matthews' junior, had gauged both public opinion and the capabilities of the old maestro. Inspired by the incomparable 'Wizard of Dribble', City finished the season in a respectable eighth place. Crucially, too, attendances at the Victoria Ground soared, bringing in much-needed extra cash.

Waddington recruited other experienced players – the likes of Jimmy McIlroy from Burnley and Dennis Viollet from Manchester United – who melded so well with the magic of Matthews that Stoke finished 1962/63 as Second Division champions, with the future Sir Stan scoring the goal that clinched the title.

During the remainder of the 1960s, several successful relegation battles notwithstanding, Waddington established the club as a fixture in the top flight. As a bonus, in 1964 City reached the League Cup final but were defeated over two legs by Leicester City. During this period, too, Waddington pulled off another transfer coup, signing the magnificent goalkeeper Gordon Banks from Leicester.

Yet while Stoke endeavoured to serve up entertaining football, there was rarely a sign of a trophy until the early 1970s. City reached two consecutive FA Cup semi-finals, losing them both to Arsenal after replays, but made amends by defeating Chelsea at Wembley to win the League Cup in 1972, the winning goal coming from yet another veteran, George Eastham.

Using that triumph as a platform, Waddington put together his finest team, in which Alan Hudson and Jimmy Greenhoff were outstanding, and in both 1974 and 1975 they finished fifth in the First Division, a splendid result for an unfashionable club.

All the while the shrewd Mancunian operated skilfully within a tight budget. But when key men were sold, apparently for reasons of economy, the team slid and in March 1977, two months before Stoke were relegated, he resigned, citing too much pressure on his family as his reason.

There followed two years out of football before he took over lowly Crewe Alexandra, and spent two seasons in a vain effort to keep them away from the nether regions of the Fourth Division. In both terms Crewe were knocked out of the FA Cup by non-League opposition and it came as little surprise when Waddington left them, and professional management, in 1979.

Waddington's career in senior football had begun in 1941 as an amateur wing-half with Manchester United, for whom he played briefly in wartime competition before serving as a radio telegraphist on HMS *Hound*, a minesweeper which took part in the D-Day landings.

After the war, he was told he would never play again because of a knee injury, but he went on to confound the experts by making some 200 senior appearances for Crewe. In 1952 he joined Stoke as youth coach, graduating to assistant manager in 1957, then taking the senior post three years later when his mentor, Frank Taylor, was sacked.

Surprisingly in the light of his subsequent espousal of attacking methods, in his first season as manager he was criticised for over-cautious tactics, his defence being dubbed 'The Waddington Wall'. And then came Stanley Matthews.

Anthony Waddington: born Manchester, 9 November 1924; played for Manchester United (as amateur) 1941-46, Crewe Alexandra 1946-52; coached Stoke City 1952-60; managed Stoke City 1960-77, Crewe Alexandra 1979-81; died Crewe, Cheshire, 29 January 1994.

Terry Hibbitt

Terry Hibbitt was a footballer of cunning, often beguiling artistry. At his peak in the early and middle 1970s, during the first of two spells with Newcastle United, the slender little midfield general was beloved of the passionate Tyneside fans. They hailed him for the immaculate, imaginative service he provided for goal-scoring cult hero Malcolm Macdonald, and warmed to him for his perky, plucky demeanour. Occasionally his name would be mentioned as an England possible but international recognition never materialised, even at a time when a number of less talented individuals were being honoured by their country.

The Yorkshireman Hibbitt entered the professional game as a school-leaver, joining Leeds United in the season after Don Revie had led the Elland Road club to promotion from the Second Division. For the next ten years Leeds were a mighty power in the land, and the opportunity was there for the gifted Hibbitt to excel. But such were the playing riches at Revie's disposal that the Bradford-born left-footer could never claim a regular place, understandably being unable to oust Eddie Gray from his flank role or Johnny Giles from his berth as chief play-maker.

Uncowed by the situation – he was known to venture an impudent rejoinder to his magisterial manager, something no one else would dare – Hibbitt battled on as a classy reserve. However, after scoring with his first kick of his first senior match in 1966, he started fewer than 50 games over the next five years, and though he helped Leeds lift the Inter Cities Fairs Cup (now the UEFA Cup) in 1968, he missed out on their other triumphs.

Clearly he needed a change and in August 1971 a £30,000 transfer took him to Newcastle, where he fulfilled his potential at last. Hibbitt made his Magpies debut on the same day as Macdonald and immediately the two men struck up a rapport. The schemer's sweeping, perceptive passing offered ready ammunition for the explosive 'Supermac' to fire and the upshot was half a decade of memorably exhilarating entertainment.

Together they starred in Newcastle's progress to the 1974 FA Cup final, being especially irresistible in the semi-final victory over Burnley, only for the big day at Wembley to bring bitter disappointment. In one of the most one-sided finals of modern times, they were outclassed 3-0 by Liverpool, though it is significant that the match was still goalless when Hibbitt's mobility was reduced drastically by a wrenched knee just before the interval. Until then he had represented United's most likely hope of upsetting the rampant Merseysiders.

After missing much of the subsequent term through injury, Hibbitt joined Birmingham City for £100,000 in August 1975 and gave the Blues, then in the First Division, three years of admirable service before returning to Newcastle in an exchange deal involving the winger Stewart Barrowclough.

Now, though fractionally past his peak, the mature midfielder resumed effectively as the brains of the Magpies' attack and became captain. But in the summer of 1981 he was forced by knee problems to retire from top-grade football. He remained close to the game, though, and made a brief comeback as player-coach with non-League Gateshead in 1986, while making his living as a newsagent in Newcastle.

Hibbitt will be remembered as a player of subtlety and skill who, on his day, was a pure pleasure to watch.

Terence Hibbitt: born Bradford, Yorkshire, 1 December 1947; played for Leeds United 1965-71, Newcastle United 1971-75 and 1978-81, Birmingham City 1975-78; managed Gateshead 1986-87; died Newcastle-upon-Tyne, 4 August 1994.

Billy Wright

If Billy Wright had been trotted out as a comic-strip hero, he would have been ridiculed as being too good to be true. Blond and handsome, personable and clean-living, he was England's football captain and the first man from any country to win a century of international caps; he led the mighty Wolverhampton Wanderers, one of the most successful sides of the 1940s and 1950s, to all the top domestic honours and he captivated Britain by marrying one of its best-loved pop stars, the flaxen-haired beauty Joy Beverley (the one in the middle of the Beverley Sisters).

Wright was a paragon of sporting and family virtue. He exuded wholesome, uncomplicated enthusiasm, was a slave to the work ethic and modest to a fault. And, to burnish the spotless persona still further, he had risen to eminence only after overcoming two heart-tugging early setbacks: being reduced to tears when written off as 'too small' at the age of 15, and later bouncing back from an injury which had threatened to end his career almost before it had begun.

In fact, though they could hardly be described as blots on his escutcheon, there were certain differences between the genial Salopian and Roy of the Rovers. For a start, Wright was a defender, and therefore not natural headline fodder as a spectacular match-winner. But more tellingly, and rather surprisingly in view of his immense achievements, he was not blessed with outstanding natural talent. Indeed, his ability to control and pass a ball were distinctly mediocre, and as a right-half in his twenties his positional play was questionable, too.

Despite his mastery of the fierce, perfectly timed tackle and a prodigiously spring-heeled leap that lifted his solid 5ft 8in frame high above towering opponents in aerial duels, those defects might have reduced Wright to the crowded ranks of soccer's also-rans. But what gave him his edge – particularly at his best, after his mid-1950s conversion to centre-half – was a keen footballing brain which enabled him to read the game, putting him one move ahead of most men around him. He would break up countless attacks through intelligent interceptions, rescue stricken colleagues by perceptive covering and remain cool in the most frenzied of crises.

As a skipper, he was no bullying martinet, eschewing unseemly exhortation in favour of quiet motivation, declaring that 'captaincy is the art of leadership, not dictatorship', invariably setting an impeccable personal example in terms of both effort and sportsmanship.

Wright, whose father worked in an iron foundry and was a useful amateur player, had supported Arsenal as a boy, but went for a trial with his local club, Wolves, in 1938 in response to a newspaper advertisement. Though taken on as an apprentice, the stocky kid with the shock of fair hair – 'Snowy' to his new Molineux workmates – made so insignificant an early impression that the team's manager, Major Frank Buckley, sent him packing, telling the tearful teenager he wasn't big enough to make the grade. Even when Wright heard, 20 minutes later, that Buckley had changed his mind, the relief was tainted by the news that the managerial U-turn had been inspired more by the industrious apprentice's prowess with broom and scrubbing brush (in his secondary role as groundsman's helper) than by his aptitude for football.

However, Wright worked hard and progressed, playing his first senior game in 1939 and then, having picked up valuable experience guesting for Leicester City when Wolves withdrew temporarily from wartime competition, he turned professional in 1942. A bright future beckoned but then came near-calamity when he suffered a badly broken ankle. Buckley, for one, thought Wright would not play again, but he confounded the doubters to make a swift recovery and see out the balance of the war as an Army PT instructor.

He found time to excel in services football, too, and come January 1946 he was chosen for England in an unofficial Victory celebration international against Belgium. Though selected at inside-left, after an injury to Frank Soo he was moved to right-half, the position he filled on his full England debut later the same month.

Now Wright came into his own. By the age of 24 he was skippering both club and country; in 1949 he led Wolves to triumph in the FA Cup final against Leicester and a year later he took England into the first of three consecutive World Cup tournaments. That was in Brazil, where the team performed badly, especially in a humiliating 1-0 defeat by the United States, but Wright, at least, survived with reputation intact. Though his form dipped in the 1950/51 season, he proved so resilient that he was named Footballer of the Year in 1952, then in 1954 captained Wolves to their first League championship.

That summer brought a turning-point in the Wright career when he switched to the centre of defence during the World Cup finals in Switzerland, following an injury to Syd Owen. It was apparent that he had found his true niche, his new role making light of his ball-playing limitations and emphasising his more solid qualities. In addition, it conserved the 30-year-old's energy and, no doubt, lengthened his playing span considerably.

During mid-decade Wolves, now managed by Stan Cullis, were challenged only by Manchester United's Busby Babes as England's finest, and Wright's contribution was enormous, notably in several high-profile friendlies with crack Continental clubs which helped to blaze the British trail into Europe.

Two more League titles followed, in 1958 and 1959, the last-mentioned year providing Wright with a memorable swansong. That April, on the day his daughter Victoria was born, he was picked for his 100th international; six weeks later, the world's sole cap-centurion made his 105th and final appearance for his country, the last 70 of them consecutive; in June he was appointed CBE; in August he retired, aged 35 but still at the pinnacle of his profession.

The decision to stop playing, made only after he struggled to keep up with younger team-mates during pre-season training, unleashed an avalanche of public acclamation for one of English football's favourite sons. Indeed, more than 20,000 fans turned up for Wolves' early-August trial match that was his farewell appearance in the gold-and-black colours he had graced for so long.

Now Wright found himself in great demand. Wanderers offered him a job for life, initially as assistant to Cullis, and other clubs were willing for him to become their boss with immediate effect. However, he opted instead for the international arena, taking charge of England's youth and under-23 teams, with an unspoken understanding that one day he would assume command of the senior side in succession to his friend Walter Winterbottom.

But that was never to be. When his boyhood favourites, Arsenal, offered him the Highbury hot-seat in 1962 he could not resist, and he took on the onerous task of reviving the north Londoners' flagging fortunes. Wright made a promising start, too, buying the star centre-forward Joe Baker and guiding the Gunners to seventh and eighth places in the First Division during his first two campaigns.

But this encouraging progress could not disguise underlying problems. It seemed that Wright was simply too nice for the job, lacking the necessary ruthlessness to make hard decisions, and he suffered a consequent decline in respect from some of his staff. Inevitably, results suffered and, after two finishes in the bottom half of the table, the unthinkable happened – Billy Wright was sacked.

Yet his spell at Highbury should not be viewed as a complete flop. He was a beneficial influence on a generation of Arsenal youngsters and much of the talent he nurtured – the likes of Charlie George and John Radford – came through as Bertie Mee led the Gunners to the League and FA Cup double in 1971.

Thereafter, understandably rather disillusioned, Wright left football to build a successful new career in television, first as a front-man on such programmes as *Junior Sportsview*, then as an imaginative administrator. He became head of sport for both the Midlands-based ATV and its successor, Central TV, before retiring in 1989. During his media sojourn he fell prey to alcohol problems, which he faced and conquered, later describing that process as his greatest victory.

But it is as England's golden-haired captain, he of the Boy Scout image on and off the pitch, that Billy Wright claims a special place in the annals of British sporting history.

William Ambrose Wright: born Ironbridge, Shropshire, 6 February 1924; played for Wolverhampton Wanderers 1938-58; capped 105 times for England 1946-58 (captain 90 times); CBE 1959; managed Arsenal 1962-66; Head of Sport and Outside Broadcasts, ATV Network Ltd 1966-81; Controller of Sport, Central Television Ltd 1982-85, consultant 1985-89; died Barnet, London, 3 September 1994.

Raich Carter

Raich Carter, 'The Great Horatio', was by common consent the finest English inside-forward of his generation. But for the Second World War which sliced his footballing career in two, he would have won many more than his 13 full international caps, though that relatively meagre total – relative, that is, to his immense talent – might have had a bit to do with an impatient, abrasive side to his character.

Carter was that rare being, a magnificent maker and taker of goals, and were he playing today his transfer valuation would surely be astronomical. During his peak years and beyond, when his black hair had turned prematurely to a distinguished silver, he cut an imperious figure, radiating self-confidence as he strutted around the pitch, invariably dictating the course of a game. Some would (and did) call him arrogant, but there was no denying the Carter class. He shot thunderously with either foot, especially his left; his ball control was impeccable and his body-swerve little short of sublime; and, crucially, he possessed the intelligence to put these natural gifts to maximum use.

He could roll immaculate passes through the tiniest of gaps, sometimes seeming to shred defences at will, and much of his work alongside Stanley Matthews, when the two formed a right-wing pair for England, was breathtaking. Indeed, few men appreciated the footballing needs of 'The Wizard of Dribble' as Carter did, and, certainly from this distance, the reluctance of the selection committee (this was well before the days of the all-powerful team boss) to use them in tandem more regularly appears incomprehensible.

The Wearsider Raich, the son of a professional footballer, exuded all-round sporting ability from an early age, his magnificent athleticism making light of a lack of physical stature. By 1927 he was playing for England Schoolboys and in 1930 he joined Leicester City on trial, only to be released because he was 'too small'.

His home-town club, Sunderland, had no such qualms, and earlier thoughts of an engineering career were jettisoned as he progressed rapidly to first-team status. Thereafter Carter's rise became positively meteoric. In 1934 he made his full England debut, against Scotland at Wembley; two years on he inspired an essentially ordinary Sunderland team to the League championship, becoming the youngest title-winning skipper in the process; in 1937 he was the star turn as the Rokerites beat Preston North End to lift the FA Cup. Thus, at 23, Raich Carter had won every honour then available to a footballer.

Nevertheless, his international appearances were spasmodic and it was not until 1943, when that other splendid inside-forward Wilf Mannion was drafted into the army, that Carter was recalled to the England side on anything like a regular basis.

Having joined the RAF and been stationed at a pilot rehabilitation centre at Loughborough, it was convenient for Carter to guest for nearby Derby County while the conflict continued, and when peace resumed the Rams had seen enough of him to make the arrangement permanent. Accordingly they paid some £8,000 for his services, a transaction of which Carter, not a man renowned for false modesty, remarked later: 'Sunderland were silly to sell me and Derby were lucky to get me.'

At the Baseball Ground, he linked up with the brilliant Irishman Peter Doherty, and together they helped Derby win the first post-war FA Cup final. That same year, 1946, Carter furnished further proof of his all-round prowess by appearing in three first-class cricket matches for Derbyshire and might have flourished in the summer game but for his football commitments. As it was, having won his last cap in 1947 at the age of 33, he moved to comparatively humble Hull City for a £6,000 fee in 1948, initially as player-assistant boss but within a month as fully fledged player-manager. A year later, while still taking an active part on the pitch – 'I am determined to play on as long as I can raise a gallop,' he said – he led his charges to the Third Division North championship, and what seemed likely to be a successful management career was under way.

Carter upset some followers when he declared: 'My aim is to play high-class football and let the result take care of itself.' But his acquisition of high-quality performers such as Neil Franklin and Don Revie signalled that he would not be content to linger idealistically in the Second Division. However, having not achieved the promotion he had expected, Carter, ever the perfectionist, resigned in September 1951.

He returned for the second half of the season as a player only, showing much of his old flair, and when he made his final Football League appearance that spring he had scored 216 goals in 451 outings. Those creative feet were still itchy, however, and in 1953, his 40th year, he spent half a season with Cork Athletic, helping them to win the Irish equivalent of the FA Cup. Clearly Carter had more to contribute and later that year he took over the reins of Leeds United, guiding them to promotion to the top flight in 1956. Nevertheless, his intolerance of lesser talents ruffled plenty of feathers at Elland Road and after his best player, John Charles, had departed for Italy, results declined and he was dismissed.

Come 1960 Carter was back in circulation as manager of Mansfield Town, whom he led out of the Fourth Division in 1963, after which he moved up to Middlesbrough. Sadly, at Ayresome Park he experienced the leanest time of his life in soccer and with the club on the brink of relegation to the Third Division, he was sacked in 1966.

Thereafter Carter worked in the sports department of a Hull store and then ran a business in the town before retiring to nearby Willerby, suffering a severe stroke in 1993. During his latter years he was disdainful of modern trends in the game, but once, looking back, he admitted there could be no finer life than a footballer's. He could have added, with truth, that there had been few finer footballers than he.

Horatio Stratton Carter: born Sunderland, 21 December 1913; played for Sunderland, 1931-45, Derby County 1945-48, Hull City 1948-52, Cork Athletic 1953; capped 13 times for England 1934-47; managed Hull City 1948-52, Leeds United 1953-58, Mansfield Town 1960-63, Middlesbrough 1963-66; died Willerby, Humberside, 9 October 1994.

Geoff Bradford

Football in general, and Bristol Rovers in particular, could do with more men like Geoff Bradford. He was the most prolific goal-scorer in that homely club's history; he remains the only Pirate to win a full England cap; and, were it possible to hold a cross-generation poll of fans to determine the finest player ever to wear Rovers' distinctive blue-and-white quarters, the odds would be heavily in favour of the gentle, acutely unassuming Bristolian coming out on top.

When Bradford was in his bountiful 1950s prime, he was accorded a sporting celebrity in the West Country exceeded only by that of his close friend and rival, the late John Atyeo of Bristol City; meanwhile at grounds around the country, he was often the only Rovers player of whom the local supporters had heard.

The acclaim, however, never turned his head, and when the two men were together at a function, invariably Bradford would ask the more outgoing (though also modest) Atyeo to deal with the demands of press and public.

Yet for all his self-effacing nature, there was a deep vein of steel running through the Bradford character, as he demonstrated forcibly at the dawn of the 1960s when professional footballers were threatening to strike in a bid to do away with the outdated maximum wage rule.

The rest of his Eastville comrades were ready to take industrial action, but he stood firm despite hurtful jibes that he was a blackleg, believing passionately that although pay needed to be improved, abolition of the widely despised restriction would be detrimental to the wider game.

Happily, after the players' union won the day without needing to withdraw their labour, there appeared to be no residual ill will from his colleagues. He was far too nice a man for that.

Bradford's impressive playing record – 260 goals in 511 senior outings – owed much to a sharp-edged technical talent which contrasted vividly with his unthrusting personality. He was as clean, accurate and powerful a striker of the ball with either foot as could be found outside the game's top division, in which, sadly, he never played. His touch was subtle and certain, his timing in the air was intuitive.

To these gifts were added a natural resilience which saw him return in triumph from two fearful leg injuries which might have put him out of football for good. His critics called him lazy, but Bradford, known as 'Rip' (Van Winkle) to team-mates because of his knack for sleeping before a match, could justifiably refer them to his goal tally.

His England chance came in October 1955, against Denmark in Copenhagen, when he scored once and made another for Tom Finney in a 5-1 victory. It seemed enough to warrant a second call but this never arrived and Bradford returned uncomplainingly to bread-and-butter duty with Rovers, who had plucked him from local amateur ranks in 1949 and who remained his only professional club.

The highlight of Bradford's 15 years at Eastville – the much-loved home of the Pirates until a controversial move to Bath in 1986 – came in 1952/53 when his club record of 33 goals did much to secure the Division Three (South) championship. Had his peak years not coincided with football's controversial wage restraint, it is reasonable to suppose that such a talent would have moved on to more lucrative fields, but all who revelled in his exploits as a Rover would find it hard to imagine their faithful spearhead in the colours of another club.

After his retirement in 1964, Bradford became a petrol tanker driver, continuing to live quietly in the city of his birth.

Geoffrey Reginald William Bradford: born Bristol, 18 July 1927; played for Bristol Rovers 1949-64; capped once for England 1955; died Bristol, 30 December 1994.

Vic Buckingham

Vic Buckingham was something of a footballing romantic. The teams he managed in England, the Netherlands, Greece and Spain reflected his own natural elegance and flamboyant personality – they were entertaining and aesthetically pleasing even if, certainly in his homeland, where he spent the bulk of his career, they did not achieve consistent success.

Buckingham's greatest glory on the domestic scene came in 1954 when he guided West Bromwich Albion to triumph in the FA Cup and came close to becoming the first man this century to preside over the much-coveted League and Cup double. After that, there seemed no limit to the heights such an enterprising, articulate and deep-thinking individual might scale, but somehow the summits, at least in England, eluded him. However, his efforts in the foothills brought a welcome dash of verve to the domestic game.

As a footballer, Buckingham had been a stylish but unremarkable defender who rose through the junior sides of Tottenham Hotspur, the only professional club for which he played. He made his senior debut in 1935, when Spurs were in the Second Division, as a centre-half, later settling at left-half before the Second World War interrupted his progress. After the conflict, the emergence of the outstanding wing-halves Ronnie Burgess and Bill Nicholson enforced a switch to left-back, where Buckingham performed efficiently until his retirement in 1949.

Though he had never tested his talent in the First Division, his attractive blend of eloquence and intelligence made him a prime candidate for coaching. Soon he was instructing Spurs' juniors, Middlesex FA and Oxford University, the latter niche leading to his appointment as boss of the Oxbridge team Pegasus.

Surrounded by like-minded, bright and adventurous spirits, Buckingham was in his element and he led the team to victory in the 1951 Amateur Cup final. Clearly, he had learned much from his mentor, the innovative Tottenham boss Arthur Rowe, and Pegasus played the exhilarating, fast-moving football that was to become the hallmark of Buckingham's teams down the years.

Inevitably, this success attracted professional interest and in the summer of 1951 he became manager of Bradford Park Avenue, showing enough promise in the prosaic surroundings of the Third Division North to be called to higher office in February 1953.

His new employers were West Bromwich Albion, an ambitious First Division club who seemed perfectly tailored to Buckingham's emerging ability. Accordingly, he saw them to fourth place in the League and in the 1953/54 campaign he came close to making history. The Throstles finished four points behind the champions, Wolverhampton Wanderers, but they overcame Preston North End – the great Tom Finney et al – to win a rousing FA Cup final by three goals to two. Orchestrated by the majestic wing-half Ray Barlow and spearheaded by the skilful Ronnie Allen, the team promised even better things to come but, sadly, they never materialised, though West Bromwich continued to entertain fitfully for the remainder of the 1950s.

By 1959, perhaps feeling he had gone as far as he could at the Hawthorns, Buckingham opted for what in those days was seen as a dramatic change, going continental with Ajax of Amsterdam. In the less frenetic world of Dutch football, Buckingham's preference for pure skill paid rich dividends, and the club who would one day rule Europe topped the League in 1960, then won their domestic cup the following season.

In addition, Buckingham discovered and encouraged a young man, Johan Cruyff, who would mature into one of the greatest footballers Europe has ever produced. The innovative coach's future in Holland appeared enviable.

However, the call of his native land proved too strong and, after coming close to joining Plymouth Argyle, he took over at Sheffield Wednesday in the spring of 1961.

Having finished the season as League runners-up, the Hillsborough club expected the new manager to catapult them into the very front rank of English clubs. But as Spurs were in their pomp and Everton, Liverpool and Manchester United were all emerging from relative dormancy, it was a task that proved beyond him and he was not offered new terms when his contract expired in 1964. In truth, Buckingham had been no failure. Wednesday had remained in the top six throughout his reign and had reached the quarter-final of the Fairs Cup (now the UEFA Cup) in 1962, losing only by the odd goal in seven to mighty Barcelona. Coincidentally, soon after his departure, the sporting world was rocked by a bribery scandal which, eventually, would see three Wednesday men, Tony Kay, Peter Swan and David Layne, banned from the game. When the full facts emerged, Buckingham was mortified that any players of his could be caught up in such dishonesty.

Though understandably disillusioned, he re-entered soccer in January 1965, as boss of struggling Fulham. Clearly changes were needed urgently and Buckingham instituted them on a sweeping scale. However, he dispensed with too many experienced players for the liking of most pundits – who were particularly critical of his failure to get on with, and his subsequent knock-down sale of, the gifted Rodney Marsh – and after three years of travail he was dismissed in January 1968.

Fulham were relegated four months later, but Buckingham's stock remained high in Europe and soon he took charge of the Greek club Ethnikos. The locals loved his outgoing nature and generosity of spirit and he did well; this success leading to coaching posts with Barcelona, whom he led to Spanish Cup glory in 1971, and Seville.

Vic Buckingham never managed again in England, but he had done enough to be remembered warmly as one of the more colourful and original members of the British and European footballing fraternities.

Victor Frederick Buckingham: born London, 23 October 1915; played for Tottenham Hotspur 1935-49; managed Bradford Park Avenue 1951-53, West Bromwich Albion 1953-59, Ajax of Amsterdam 1959-61, Sheffield Wednesday 1961-64, Fulham 1965-68, Ethnikos 1968; coached Oxford University 1949-50, Pegasus 1950-51, Barcelona 1970-71, Seville 1972; died 26 January 1995.

Len Goulden

Len Goulden was a captivating footballer, a richly creative inside-forward whose flowing skills earned him a regular place in the England side for two years before the Second World War. But for the conflict, it is probable that the genial Londoner would have added considerably to his tally of 14 caps. Indeed, a telling measure of Goulden's stature is that his international honours were won when he was a player with West Ham United, then in the middle reaches of the Second Division. He specialised in switching the point of attack, suddenly and dramatically, with raking left-foot passes that could render helpless several opponents at a stroke.

Born in Hackney and raised in Plaistow, Goulden progressed rapidly as a teenager, winning selection for England schoolboys in 1926 and joining the Hammers as an amateur five years later. As was then the custom, he was farmed out to gain experience with local non-League clubs, in his case Chelmsford and Leyton, before turning professional at Upton Park in the spring of 1933. So eyecatching was Goulden's talent that he was pitchforked immediately into senior action, emerging as his team's star performer for the remainder of the decade.

Yet despite Goulden's frequently brilliant efforts, West Ham failed to gain promotion, and his only club honour was a Football League wartime cup medal, received for his part in victory over Blackburn Rovers at Wembley in 1940. There was stirring consolation in his country's colours, beginning with a scoring debut in the 6-0 thrashing of Norway in Oslo in 1937 and ending prematurely with the outbreak of war in 1939.

After the hostilities, during which he served in the police force, the 33-year-old Goulden realised that if he was to sample life in the First Division he would have to forsake the Hammers. Accordingly in 1945 he joined Chelsea in a £5,000 deal.

At Stamford Bridge, Goulden spent five largely fulfilling seasons, including a two-year stint fashioning bullets for the great centre-forward Tommy Lawton to fire and a later productive spell as a wing-half. Sadly, though, his trophy cabinet remained devoid of medals, the nearest he came to glory being an FA Cup semi-final defeat by Arsenal in 1950.

That year Goulden retired as a player, joining the Chelsea coaching staff before becoming boss of Watford in 1952. Alas, despite guiding the Hornets to fourth place in the Third Division South in 1954, he proved too easy going for management and was dismissed in 1956. There followed three years as a sub postmaster before a three-season return to Watford as part-time coach, two years passing on his knowledge in Libya and a spell in charge of non-league Banbury Town. A final coaching post with Oxford United in 1969 signalled his farewell to the game.

Thereafter he worked on a United States Air Force base in Northamptonshire before retiring to Cornwall. Goulden, whose son Roy played briefly for Arsenal and Southend United, will be remembered as one of England's most cultured schemers and a humorous, immensely popular man.

Leonard Arthur Goulden: born London, 16 July 1912; played for West Ham United 1933-45, Chelsea 1945-50; managed Watford 1952-56; died London, 14 February 1995.

Johnny Nicholls

In the spring of 1954, the boots of the footballer Johnny Nicholls seemed to be sprinkled with stardust. In April, on his 23rd birthday, he made his debut for England, scoring with a brilliant diving header that silenced the famous Hampden Roar and helped to pave the way to victory over Scotland. A month later the young inside-left's stage was Wembley, where he helped his club, West Bromwich Albion, beat Preston North End – Tom Finney and company – to lift the FA Cup.

Nicholls was part of a vibrant, attacking Throstles combination which, under their manager Vic Buckingham, had failed only narrowly to become the first side this century to win the double of the League championship and the Cup.

He had finished the season as Albion's top League scorer with 28 strikes in 38 outings, just ahead of his club and country team-mate Ronnie Allen, and when he was picked for England's next game, against Yugoslavia, a glittering future appeared to beckon.

But, sadly, that match in Belgrade was to prove Nicholls' final bow at full international level and he never scaled the giddy heights which had once appeared possible.

Despite his knack of cracking the ball cleanly with either foot, admirable aerial ability and a typical goal-poacher's instinct of being in the right place at the right time, Nicholls did not progress as anticipated, his cause not helped by a series of niggling injuries. Also, competition for places, both with Albion and England, grew distinctly warmer.

Come May 1957, Buckingham judged Nicholls surplus to requirements and the striker, who at 26 should have been approaching his peak, moved to Second Division Cardiff City.

However, he did not flourish at the lower level, failing to hold a regular place at Ninian Park, and that November dropped another division to link up with humble Exeter City. Again, he faced injury problems, but made a favourable early impression with a hat-trick in the Devon derby against Plymouth Argyle.

After a knee operation Nicholls recovered something of his early form and played a leading role in Exeter's stirring if unsuccessful bid for promotion from the Fourth Division in 1958/59. The following summer, with a doubt remaining over his fitness, he left the Football League to serve Worcester City, then Wellington Town, Oswestry Town and several amateur clubs in the Midlands.

Memories of Nicholls, who had unsuccessful trials with both Albion and Wolverhampton Wanderers before turning professional with West Bromwich in 1951, will evoke in some fans a certain poignancy for what might have been. But that should never obscure his achievements as an integral part of the Throstles' most compelling side since the Second World War.

John Nicholls: born Wolverhampton 3 April 1931; played for West Bromwich Albion 1951-57, Cardiff City 1957, Exeter City 1957-59; died Wolverhampton 1 April 1995.

Ted Drake

Ted Drake was one of London football's favourite adopted sons, and little wonder. As a fearless, rampaging centre-forward in the 1930s, he contributed an avalanche of goals to the cause of all-conquering Arsenal; and two decades later he guided less fashionable Chelsea to the high-point in their history, their sole League championship to date.

But there was more to the popular Hampshireman's appeal than his professional accomplishments, impressive though they were. Ted Drake was blessed with an infectiously sunny outlook on life in general and football in particular. As a player he was dashingly courageous, thrillingly bold; as a manager he was committed, perhaps a trifle idealistically at times, to that same positive approach; and throughout more than half a century spent in and around the game he was a modest, cheerful and unfailingly gentle man.

But for a relatively minor injury which forced him to miss a schoolboy trial, Drake might never have taken his place in Highbury folklore as arguably the Gunners' greatest ever marksman, certainly until Ian Wright came along. That trial had been organised by Arsenal's north London rivals, Tottenham Hotspur, who had been keen on the all-action youngster, but needed a little more evidence before signing him. Thus the opportunity passed by and Drake slipped into non-League soccer with Winchester City, while making his living as in apprentice gas-meter inspector.

Soon a Southampton scout spotted his potential and he became a Saint in November 1931, wasting little time in establishing himself as a dynamic performer. Drake's method was direct: fast, immensely strong and immeasurably determined, he packed a ferocious shot in either 'peg', was combative in the air and, while his approach was not overburdened with subtlety, he could control the ball with commendable dexterity. Thus equipped, he netted 48 times in 72 League outings for Second Division Southampton before joining Arsenal for £6,500 in March 1934.

On acquiring Drake at the second attempt – the player had refused to leave the south coast for the capital a year earlier – George Allison, Arsenal's manager, described his purchase as 'the best centre-forward in the world'; a bit steep perhaps, though before long the broad-shouldered marksman was proving that the description might not be entirely fanciful.

That spring he contributed seven strikes in ten games to help secure the League title, then scored 42 (including seven hat-tricks) as the championship was retained in 1934/35 (Arsenal's third in succession), overcame injury to snatch the only goal of the 1936 FA Cup final against Sheffield United and top-scored yet again as the Gunners garnered their fifth League triumph of the decade in 1937/38.

Memorable individual performances were many during this golden sequence, but two stand out with deathless clarity. He began the first, at Villa Park in December 1935, as an unlikely hero, having been out of form and nursing a heavily strapped knee; he ended it having scored all the Gunners' goals in a 7-1 victory – still a joint record for a single match in the English top division – and having hit the post with one of only two other shots.

If that encounter offers the most vivid illustration of Drake's hunger for goals, then a game at Brentford in April 1938 surely serves as the most telling example of another characteristic: bravery to the point of foolhardiness. That afternoon he broke two bones in his wrist, received nine stitches to a head wound and was carried off the pitch twice – the second time unconscious, slung over the shoulder of trainer Tom Whittaker.

Indeed, many believed that it was this very whole heartedness which shortened Drake's career. Often he played on in pain and it was a back injury sustained on an Army PT course, and later exacerbated on the football pitch, that forced him out of the game in 1945. He retired having netted 139 times in 182 League and FA Cup outings for Arsenal and six times in five matches for his country, his future with England having been curtailed by the emergence of the brilliant Tommy Lawton.

After the Second World War, in which he served in the RAF as a flight lieutenant, Drake turned to management, beginning with non-League Hendon before taking over at Reading in 1947. He proved an uplifting leader of men, moulding the Royals into an entertaining, free-scoring side which missed out narrowly on promotion from the Third Division South in both 1949 and 1952.

On the strength of that achievement, Drake took over as manager of Chelsea in June 1952, breezing into a rather staid Stamford Bridge to invigorating effect. One of his first acts was to banish the Chelsea Pensioner from the club badge, thus removing joke-fodder for a generation of music-hall comedians, and soon the club was transformed from First Division strugglers to title contenders.

The culmination of the revolution came in 1954/55 when Chelsea upset all known odds by outstripping mighty Manchester United and Wolves to win the championship, making Drake the first man to earn that particular honour as both player and manager. Few had believed that Drake would inspire what was mainly a combination of rookies and shrewd but inexpensive transfer-market acquisitions into such a force, and the elated boss declared that it meant more to him than all his own playing successes.

As champions, Chelsea were entitled to a place in the newly launched European Cup but, sadly for the ebullient Drake, the League and the Football Association forbade entry and the Stamford Bridge board accepted the ruling. A year later Manchester United were to ignore similar opposition, a decision which offered a fascinating insight into contrasting degrees of vision and ambition at two leading clubs.

In fact, the Londoners might have proved ill-fitted to face continental opposition. In the second half of the 1950s, despite the hyperbole surrounding the so-called Drake's Ducklings – highly promising young players such as Jimmy Greaves, Terry Venables and Peter Bonetti – results fell away alarmingly.

The board, having tasted success, wanted more. Tension grew between directors and manager and in September 1961, following a disagreement over the appointment of Tommy Docherty as a coach, Drake was sacked. Disillusioned, he left the game to become a bookmaker, but later he regretted the decision and in 1965 he returned to the game to assist the Fulham manager Vic Buckingham. That lasted only until Buckingham himself was dismissed in 1968, after which Drake returned to the betting business before serving a six-month term as assistant manager of Barcelona in 1970.

There followed a spell as an insurance salesman before he went back to Fulham, running the reserves before becoming chief scout in 1975, and then a life president of the Craven Cottage club.

Ted Drake, a gifted all-round sportsman who played county cricket for his native Hampshire in the 1930s, retained a lively interest in football into his eighties, though excursions from his Wimbledon home to watch matches became increasingly rare as his health deteriorated. Unlike some of his contemporaries, Drake betrayed no trace of bitterness that he had played in an era when material rewards were meagre, a telling measure of a fine footballer and a delightful man.

Edward Joseph Drake: born Southampton 16 August 1912; played football for Southampton 1931-34, Arsenal 1934-1945; capped five times for England 1934-38; managed Hendon (non-League) 1946, Reading 1947-52, Chelsea 1952-61, Barcelona (assistant) 1970; played cricket for Hampshire 1931-36; died 30 May 1995.

Johnny Carey

Johnny Carey was a thoroughbred footballer who exuded class and calmness as Manchester United's first post-war captain and one of the most accomplished full-backs the British game has produced.

A soft-brogued Dubliner who earned the epithet 'Gentleman John' for his scrupulous fairness and unruffled demeanour no matter how dire the circumstances, Carey won every domestic prize available to him. His collection of honours included the Footballer of the Year award in 1949, an accolade underlined by the identity of the only previous holder, Stanley Matthews.

Carey had his moments, too, as an enterprising club manager, but without matching the degree of excellence he achieved as a player after crossing the Irish Sea to Old Trafford in 1936. That journey to find fortune, which became a familiar one over the years as United established strong links with both the Republic and Northern Ireland, owed plenty to chance. The Red Devils' chief scout, Louis Rocca, was in Dublin to evaluate another rookie, but found his eye riveted to the young Carey, whose skill and elegance were readily apparent.

The shrewd talent-spotter wasted no time in agreeing a £200 fee with St James' Gate, the boy's club, yet after the elation of signing for the Reds came a temporary deflation for Carey, over which he chuckled later. On arrival in Manchester, the impressionable 17-year-old spied a newspaper hoarding which proclaimed 'United sign star', and he jumped to the uncharacteristically immodest conclusion that he must be the subject of the story. But on buying a paper he found that the 'star' in question was Blackburn Rovers' Ernie Thompson, and a mere two lines at the bottom of the page were devoted to the acquisition of one J Carey. What happened to Thompson? He disappeared into obscurity after three games.

For Carey, then an inside-forward, the 1937/38 season proved momentous. Still only 18, he broke into the United side, helping to secure promotion from the Second Division, and also won the first of his 29 caps for the Republic of Ireland.

But just as his career was gathering momentum, the Second World War intervened and he was faced with an agonising decision. Hailing from neutral Ireland, he had the right to go home if he wished, but the highly principled youngster reckoned that 'a country that gives me my living is worth fighting for' and he joined the British Army. His service took him to North Africa and Italy, where he guested for several clubs, delighting the locals who dubbed him 'Cario', with both his personality and his ability.

By 1945, when something like normal football service was resumed, United had acquired a new and visionary manager, Matt Busby, who recognised in Carey's quiet authority and integrity the makings of a natural leader, and duly made him club captain. He was impressed, too, by the Irishman's versatility – over the years he played in every position for United except outside-left, even excelling as stopgap goalkeeper – and, being well blessed for forwards, converted him to right-back.

It was an inspired decision. Carey's immaculate ball control and constructive passing ability melded with his clever positional play and crisp tackling to create what was something of a novelty at the time, a constructive defender. He found himself in charge of an exhilarating side which included such scintillating attackers as Charlie Mitten, Stan Pearson and Jack Rowley and there are those who maintain it was the most entertaining in United's history.

Perhaps, though, the firm accent on offence left a little to be desired at the back and United's League record between the 1946/47 and 1950/51 seasons was the impressive but frustrating one of second, second, second, fourth and second. The title arrived at last in 1951/52, with Carey now employed as a polished wing-half, proving enormously influential in his more advanced role.

Meanwhile consolation for the championship near-misses had been found in 1948 when Carey lifted the FA Cup after Blackpool, Stanley Matthews et al, had been beaten 4-2 in a glorious exhibition of fluent football. The skipper could take much of the credit: as well as his customarily smooth display on the pitch, he had contributed a quietly stirring half-time pep-talk when the Reds were 2-1 in arrears.

On the international front, too, Carey prospered. Thanks to his British Army service, he was eligible until 1949 to play for Northern Ireland as well as the country of his birth, and he did so with distinction. His most memorable achievement with the Republic was leading them to a 2-0 victory over England in 1949, a further personal highlight being his captaincy of the Rest of Europe against Great Britain two years earlier.

Carey retired as a player in 1953, turning down a coaching post at Old Trafford to manage Second Division Blackburn Rovers. Like Busby, he favoured positive passing football and he assembled a young side which narrowly missed promotion four times before achieving it in 1958. But he did not guide them on their top-flight adventure, instead accepting the challenge of reviving Everton, a big club languishing among the First Division's also-rans.

He inherited a poor team, and could take much credit for lifting them to fifth place by the spring of 1961, but it was not to be enough. The chairman, the pools magnate John Moores, ran out of patience and sacked Carey, relaying the decision in the back of a London taxi. Moores felt a tough disciplinarian was needed and, clearly, that was not 'Gentleman John'. In fairness to the chairman, his chosen man, Harry Catterick, led Everton to the title two years later; equally, in fairness to Carey, his part in building the team should be stressed.

By common consent, the pipe-smoking Carey had been unlucky at Goodison, a view he reinforced in his next job, in charge of Leyton Orient. In his first full season at Brisbane Road, and operating on a shoestring, he led the Londoners into the First Division for the first time in their history. Sadly, he did not have the financial resources to keep them there more than one season, but his reputation remained high when he moved on to Nottingham Forest in 1963. Staying true to his belief in attacking play, he presided over a resurgence at the City Ground, culminating in a thrilling 1966/67 campaign which saw Forest finish runners-up in the title race and reach the FA Cup semi-finals.

Thereafter, though, the team faltered alarmingly and in December 1968, after half a season without a home win, he was dismissed. The following year he returned to Blackburn, at first in charge of administration but then as team boss, an arrangement terminated by the club when Rovers were relegated to the Third Division in 1971. That was Carey's last active involvement in football and he went on to work for a textiles company, then in the treasurer's office of Trafford Borough Council. A drily humorous raconteur, after retiring in 1984 he would recall his playing pomp with modesty and speak of his managerial days without a hint of bitterness. He was 'Gentleman John' to the last.

John James Carey: born Dublin, 23 February 1919; played for Manchester United 1936-53; capped 29 times by Republic of Ireland 1937-53, seven times by Northern Ireland 1946-49; managed Blackburn Rovers 1953-58, Everton 1958-61, Nottingham Forest 1963-68, Blackburn Rovers 1969-71; died Macclesfield, Cheshire, 22 August 1995.

Harold Shepherdson

As the confidant and foil of Alf Ramsey, Harold Shepherdson played an integral part in English football's finest hour, the lifting of the World Cup in 1966. He served the national side longer than any player or manager, being team trainer from 1957 to 1974, and worked under three bosses: first Walter Winterbottom, then Ramsey and finally Joe Mercer.

During an era of dramatic change which stretched from the twilight of Tom Finney's international career to the dawn of Kevin Keegan's, Shepherdson applied cold sponges and tended strained groins through a record 171 matches, including four World Cup tournaments.

The equable Shepherdson was the ideal aide for the rather aloof Ramsey, in particular, and their contrasting personalities were illustrated aptly at their moment of supreme triumph. When the final whistle signalled that it was all over against West Germany at Wembley in 1966, 'Shep' leapt from his seat to cavort in joy while the manager sat stone-faced and, at least outwardly, emotionless.

After rising through the ranks of local junior football, Shepherdson had joined Middlesbrough as an amateur in 1932, turning professional four years later. A burly centre-half, he made his senior debut at West Bromwich in May 1937 but found the

Scottish international stopper Bob Baxter too classy a performer to oust permanently from the first team, and he remained on the fringe of the side until the outbreak of the Second World War.

After serving as an army physical training instructor during the conflict, Shepherdson found it no easier to claim a regular place and was transferred to Southend United in 1947. Sadly, his playing days were ended abruptly by a knee injury before he had made a League appearance for the Shrimpers.

But within a few months he had returned to Ayresome Park as assistant trainer. Exhibiting a winning mixture of shrewdness and approachability, he rose to become chief trainer two years later and was recruited to do the same job for England (while retaining his Middlesbrough post) in 1957. Thereafter Shepherdson helped Winterbottom prepare his teams for World Cup final tournaments in Sweden (1958) and Chile (1962), then slotted smoothly into the Ramsey regime, which began in 1963.

The affable Teessider was just what Ramsey needed: an old-style trainer who would not concern himself too much with tactics, but who could look after the players' fitness expertly while bringing to his work a natural humour, easy diplomacy and appealing accessibility, none of which was the manager's forte.

Shepherdson stayed for the rest of Ramsey's reign, which encompassed the 1970 World Cup finals in Mexico and ended when England failed to qualify for the 1974 tournament. After that, Shepherdson assisted Joe Mercer through his seven-match stint as caretaker, stepping aside when Don Revie took over later that year.

Through all this, Shepherdson had been busy at Middlesbrough, too, first in his capacity as trainer, then in four spells as caretaker-manager – after the departures of Raich Carter in 1966, Stan Anderson in 1973, Jack Charlton in 1977 and Bobby Murdoch in 1982 – and finally as chief executive (football) until his retirement in 1983.

Subsequently, he remained on the football scene by covering matches for BBC Radio Cleveland, and never lost his sense of humour. When one national newspaper mistakenly announced that he was dead, in 1993, he laughed: 'Like Mark Twain before me, reports of my death have been exaggerated.'

Harold Shepherdson: born Middlesbrough, 28 October 1918; played for Middlesbrough 1932-47, Southend United 1947; assistant trainer, trainer, caretaker-manager and chief executive (football), Middlesbrough 1949-83; trainer, England 1957-74; MBE 1969; died Marton, Cleveland, 13 September 1995.

Albert Johanneson

Albert Johanneson was the first black footballer to achieve true prominence in the English professional game. Others before him, such as Roy Brown of Stoke City, and Doncaster Rovers' Charlie Williams (who became better known as a comedian), enjoyed worthy careers just after the Second World War, but the personable South African's dashing exploits with Leeds United in the 1960s gave him a far higher public profile.

Johanneson was a left winger whose explosive pace, bewitching sidestep and knack of scoring goals made him one of the most effective early contributors to the revival at Elland Road inspired by Don Revie.

Having been recommended to the then Second Division club by a teacher in his home town of Johannesburg, the 21-year-old Johanneson impressed on a three-month trial with Leeds, and then became one of Revie's first signings in April 1961. Conditioned by a life of rigid apartheid, Johanneson was understandably unsure of himself initially, not even knowing if he was allowed to join his white colleagues in the team bath. They responded by stripping him of his kit and plunging him in; a rough-and-ready welcome but a warm one which he appreciated.

Thereafter, Johanneson settled well both on and off the pitch, winning promotion to the senior side, and became a favourite with the Elland Road fans. They, like the vast majority of other supporters, judged him purely on his merits as a footballer, and he stood out as one of the few entertainers in an essentially dour team.

Incidents of racism were extremely rare, though on one occasion he complained that an Everton defender, whom he didn't name, had called him a 'black bastard' during the heat of a particularly bitter match. Revie's advice was to 'call him a white bastard back.'

Johanneson distinguished himself in the latter stages of Leeds' successful battle against relegation in 1961/62, then became firmly established in the side and was the joint top scorer with 13 League goals as they won the Second Division championship two years later.

He was especially effective in tandem with the club's skipper, Bobby Collins. As the effervescent little Scottish schemer put it: 'Albert could fly and I could put the ball on the spot for him. When he was in his stride there weren't many who could catch him.'

Johanneson's performing peak came, perhaps, in 1964/65, when the newly promoted Leeds were pipped for the title only on goal average by Manchester United, then lost the FA Cup final to Liverpool. In retrospect, that Wembley defeat – Johanneson was the first black player to appear in a final, but made disappointingly little impact – marked something of a watershed in his career. It was as though his self-belief, always rather fragile, had taken a severe knock and he was never quite the same again.

Soon after that he lost his place to the England international Mike O'Grady, and then became increasingly peripheral through a combination of niggling injuries and the rise of the brilliant Eddie Gray. Accordingly, Johanneson was no more than a bit player as Revie's Leeds matured into a mighty footballing force and it was no surprise when he left to join York City, of the Fourth Division, in the summer of 1970.

Though in his 31st year, he had much to offer the Minstermen and in his one full season at Bootham Crescent, he helped them gain promotion. He continued to be dogged by fitness problems, however, and retired in 1971.

In the years that followed, Johanneson fell on hard times and his health suffered as he became dependent on alcohol. A gentle fellow, he had been popular with his team-mates, some of whom attempted to help him over his difficulties. Poignantly, though, he died alone in a tiny council flat in a Leeds tower block, aged only 55, and had reportedly been dead for several days before his body was discovered. It was a pitiful end for a man who, in his pomp, had thrilled huge crowds and earned their affection.

Albert Johanneson: born Johannesburg, 12 March 1940; played for Leeds United 1961-70, York City 1970-71; died Leeds, c24 September 1995.

Dave Bowen

Through the best of times and those less memorable, the cause of Welsh football had no more devoted, passionate and inspirational champion than Dave Bowen.

Wales has never boasted a team likely to conquer the world, but in 1958, with Arsenal's Bowen excelling as skipper and motivator supreme, the Red Dragon fluttered more proudly than at any other time in its football history.

Unfancied Wales, deemed fortunate to reach the World Cup finals in Sweden, were expected to bow out humbly. But the wing-half Bowen – with the likes of John and Mel Charles, Cliff Jones, Ivor Allchurch and Jack Kelsey performing nobly alongside him – had not read that particular script. After drawing three games, against the majestic Hungarians, Mexico and Sweden (eventual finalists), Wales gave a titanic performance to defeat the Magyars in a play-off for a quarter-final place. Bowen, in particular, was brilliant, his tackling ferocious, his passing perceptive and his strength of will immense, yet he still had plenty left for an even bigger challenge.

That was against Brazil in the next round, and the Welsh captain's immediate opponent was a 17-year-old named Pele, who was in the process of earning acclaim as the world's best player. In fact, the young master netted the only goal of the game for a magical side destined to lift the trophy, but not before Bowen and company had covered themselves in glory by their gallant display.

That campaign provided an appropriate zenith to the 30-year-old Welshman's career, much of which had been played out in a lower key than many observers believed his ability warranted. Bowen grew up in the South Wales rugby heartland and was a comparatively late starter in the round-ball game. Indeed, when he contracted rheumatic fever as a boy it seemed unthinkable that he would make a living from sport. However, a pair of football boots won in a raffle gave him the impetus to try and Bowen went on to make football his life. After he had trained as a surveyor at the South Wales Colliery, he moved with his family to Northampton and joined the local League club in 1947. A handful of senior outings followed, though the versatile youngster was no overnight star. Bowen's big break came when he met Pat Whittaker, son of the Arsenal manager George, during his National Service in the RAF. Prompted by the enthusiasm of Whittaker junior, the Gunners took a close look at the intelligent, articulate Welshman and in July 1950 parted with £1,000 to sign him from Northampton.

After scoring twice on his debut on the wing for Arsenal reserves Bowen settled at left-half, and earned his First Division call-up in 1951. However, a combination of injuries and the presence at Highbury of Joe Mercer kept the younger man on the sidelines until a broken leg ended Mercer's career in 1954.

Now Bowen came into his own; he played more games for the Gunners than he missed, and won a place in the Welsh team, becoming captain of his country after just three internationals. He was a storming, passionate performer – team-mates reckoned he made more noise on the pitch than any dozen fans – and it was no surprise when he took over as club skipper in 1957/58. But come the summer of 1959, Bowen accepted a £7,000 move back to Northampton. The job description was player-boss but after one season in the dual role he opted to concentrate on management, with spectacular results. Over the next few terms he led the Cobblers from the Fourth Division to the First, where they spent only one campaign, 1965/66, before sliding back to the basement.

In fact, by the time of the final relegation, from Third to Fourth Division, Bowen had changed roles to become general manager, leaving Tony Marchi in charge of the team; but the game's folklore credits Bowen as the first man to guide a club all the way up one side of the Football League mountain, then all the way down the other.

The upswing, which included the Third Division championship in 1962/63, represented a phenomenal achievement, but Northampton possessed neither the support nor the resources to maintain it. In 1969, with the club at a low ebb, Bowen resumed charge of team affairs, keeping the reins until 1972. Thereafter he continued as general manager and club secretary until 1985, before a spell as a director preceded retirement.

As if not busy enough at Northampton between 1964 and 1974, Bowen was also part-time manager of Wales, struggling to make an impact with his tiny pool of players and winning only eight games out of 40 played. Bowen, whose son Keith played for Northampton, Brentford and Colchester United, later went into business as a bookmaker and reported on football for the *People* newspaper.

Various contemporary pundits reckoned he possessed the potential to become a top-rank manager; some even said he should have been offered the Arsenal job that went to Billy Wright in 1962. Such an opportunity never fell his way, but Dave Bowen could look back proudly on a distinguished and varied contribution to the game he loved.

David Lloyd Bowen: born Natyffyllon, near Maesteg, South Wales, 7 June 1928; played for Northampton Town 1947-50, 1959-60, for Arsenal 1950-59; capped 19 times by Wales 1954-59; managed Northampton Town 1959-67 and 1969-72, Wales 1964-74; died Northampton, 25 September 1995.

Eddie Clamp

The name of Clamp was a byword for ferocity in British football during the late 1950s. In his ruthless pomp as a ball-winner for Wolverhampton Wanderers, and, briefly, for England, 'Chopper Eddie' was accorded a lurid reputation akin to that enjoyed today by Vinnie Jones.

Indeed, had Eddie Clamp risen to prominence in the tabloid age, it is likely that he would have eclipsed the ostentatious Wimbledon bruiser in the notoriety stakes, for he was a more complete performer. Though renowned for his physical approach – it would be idle to deny his methods were crude at times – Clamp was no one-dimensional clogger, and, with all due respect to the not untalented Jones, the taciturn Midlander had considerably more to offer in terms of ball control and passing ability.

Having won international honours as a schoolboy, Clamp turned professional with Wolves in 1952, then developed rapidly under the aegis of Molineux's martinet manager, Stan Cullis. He made his senior debut as a 19-year-old wing-half, against Matt Busby's Manchester United at Old Trafford, as Wolves were closing in on the First Division title in the spring of 1954. And although he did not play enough games to earn a medal that season, there was to be no shortage of honours coming Clamp's way.

By 1955/56 he was a regular member of Cullis' all-action, but undeniably skilful team – a hard man in a hard side – and two years later his strength, stamina and all-round efficiency were an important factor in the club's championship triumph.

Clamp was rewarded by a full international call-up on the eve of the 1958 World Cup finals in Sweden, and he formed an all-Wolves half-back line with Billy Wright and Bill Slater. He performed creditably in four consecutive games for his country, all of which were drawn, but widespread disappointment at England's generally sketchy showing in the game's premier tournament cost him his place – which went to the more stylish Ronnie Clayton of Blackburn Rovers – and Clamp was shunted permanently from the international stage at the age of 23.

He continued to prosper at club level, though, helping Wolves to lift a second successive title in 1959 and missing out on a hat-trick when Burnley pipped them by a single point in 1960. That term, however, there was heady consolation in the FA Cup, with

Wolves defeating Blackburn 3-0 at Wembley. Sadly, it was a scrappy encounter, labelled the 'dustbin final' in the Midlands press, a criticism which rankled with Clamp for the rest of his life. Having distinguished himself in the famous gold and black, Clamp accepted a new challenge in September 1961, joining Arsenal in a £34,500 deal. He had been bought to instil steel into what was then a rather languid Gunners combination, but that very combativeness was to prove his undoing.

Six months after Clamp's arrival in London, his former Molineux skipper Billy Wright became Arsenal manager and took exception to 'Chopper Eddie's' aggressive style. The final straw was a brutal tackle on the gentlemanly Aston Villa full-back Charlie Aitken, perpetrated right under Wright's nose, and Clamp was on his way out.

Next stop was Stoke City, whom he joined for £14,000 in September 1962, and that season he assisted a Stanley Matthews-inspired team of veterans to top the Second Division. Two years on, by now aged 30, he served a short stint with Third Division Peterborough United before entering non-League circles, first with Worcester City and then with Lower Gornal.

Clamp retired from regular football in 1969 to run a building and decorating business in Wednesfield, Staffordshire, but continued to turn out in charity matches for the Wolves Old Stars. Opponents reported, often ruefully, that while he had lost his speed, he had retained that characteristic bite.

Harold Edwin Clamp: born Coalville, Leicestershire, 14 September 1934; played for Wolverhampton Wanderers 1952-61, Arsenal 1961-62, Stoke City 1962-64, Peterborough United 1964-65; capped four times by England 1958; died Wednesfield, Staffordshire, 14 December 1995.

Harry Cripps

Countless footballers have been held in esteem, even reverence, by fans enraptured by their heroes' sporting prowess. But few at any club have been loved – if that word seems excessive, it fits the bill here – in the manner of Harry Cripps by followers of Millwall throughout the 1960s and early 1970s.

'Arry Boy, as he was affectionately dubbed, was a rather rotund left-back who tackled ferociously and strove constantly and courageously for a dozen or so seasons as the Lions rose from Fourth Division mediocrity to the brink of the top flight.

But Cripps represented infinitely more to Millwall than his highly respectable tally of 444 senior appearances and 40 goals. A warm, humorous individual, he enjoyed a rich rapport with the toughly self-sufficient denizens of Cold Blow Lane, who saw him as one of their own. He played the game seriously but he revelled in by-play with the crowd.

Other players, many far more gifted than the somewhat ponderous though not unskilful defender, were equally committed to the cause and a few of them were as combative (though that took some doing). But none of them could count on a welcoming roar just for taking the pitch or be allowed such good-natured leeway on making a mistake. Indeed, a significant part of the Cripps appeal was that he could take criticism, and was never a moaner no matter how dire the circumstances.

'Arry Boy had arrived at The Den in June 1961, a 19-year-old reeling with the shock of being rejected by West Ham United. A keen competitor, he soon became established in the first team and played a crucial role in the Lions' two successive promotion campaigns, from the Fourth and Third Divisions, in 1965 and 1966. Thereafter he was a model of consistency, enjoying a stint as skipper, holding the club's appearance record for a spell and still being an important member of the side when Millwall just missed attaining the top flight in 1972. After that the ageing Cripps switched to midfield, where his lack of pace was less exposed, until he moved to Charlton Athletic in October 1974. That term he helped his new club reach the Second Division, subsequently serving them as assistant manager to Andy Nelson. In later years Cripps managed non-League Barking, was number-two to his old friend Bobby Moore at Southend, coached a variety of amateur sides and worked in insurance. But it is as the very epitome of Millwall FC that 'Arry Boy's place in football folklore is assured.

Henry Richard Cripps: born East Dereham, Norfolk, 29 April 1941; played for West Ham United 1956-61, Millwall 1961-74, Charlton Athletic 1974-75; died 29 December 1995.

Bobby Langton

With Tom Finney and the incomparable Stan Matthews bestriding English football so majestically in the immediate post-war years, international prospects for wingmen of less rarefied talents were limited. All credit, then, to Bobby Langton for collecting 11 caps and doing enough to suggest that he might have won many more.

The forthright Lancastrian, who was always ready to stand up for his employment rights during an era when clubs believed that players should be seen and not heard, was a powerful outside-left with a rasping shot. In his early days, he relished cutting in from the flank to create havoc with his direct running, though many maintained he was more effective in later years, when wily tactical acumen compensated for reduced pace.

Langton turned professional with Blackburn Rovers, having been signed for £50 from the non-League Burscough Victoria as a teenager in 1937. Within a year he was in the senior side, becoming top marksman with 14 strikes in 37 games as Rovers won the Second Division title in 1938/39. Then came the war, much of which he spent as an infantryman in India, though for some of it he was a guest with Glentoran, helping them to reach the Irish Cup final.

With Finney preferred fleetingly to Matthews on the right flank, England gave Langton his first cap on the left in their opening peacetime international, against Northern Ireland at Belfast in 1946, and he scored in a 7-2 victory. He retained his place for several matches, thereafter playing intermittently until winning his last honour in 1950.

By then he had changed clubs, having left Blackburn when they were relegated in 1948 and joined Preston North End in a £16,000 deal. Langton scored a goal after only seven seconds of an early game for his new employers, but did not settle at Deepdale, Bolton Wanderers paying a club record £20,000 for his services in 1949.

He served the Trotters well, picking up an FA Cup loser's medal against Blackpool in the famous Stanley Matthews final of 1953, only for a dispute to result in his return to Blackburn that autumn. Though 34, he proved a sound acquisition, contributing fruitfully for three years before a brief spell in Ulster with Ards. There followed service to a succession of non-League clubs, culminating with a stint as boss of his home-town club Burscough Rangers in 1968. Langton epitomised the finest traditional qualities of Lancashire football – down-to-earth realism, spiced with a certain flair.

Robert Langton: born Burscough, Lancashire, 8 September 1918; played for Blackburn Rovers 1938-48, Preston North End 1948-49, Bolton Wanderers 1949-53, Blackburn Rovers 1953-56; died Burscough, 13 January 1996.

Harry Potts

Harry Potts never enjoyed the fame of Busby, Shankly or a dozen other football managers of his era; nor did he court Clough-like controversy or attract headlines for matters unrelated to the game.

Yet, arguably, the achievement of this gentle but passionately committed north-easterner in guiding unfashionable little Burnley to the League championship in 1960 and maintaining the Clarets' stature as a leading power in the land for several seasons afterwards was more remarkable than the tumultuously trumpeted triumphs of his renowned peers. That Potts garnered only limited kudos from the public – although soccer insiders were in no doubt as to his worth – was due partly to his own unassuming personality, but also to the fact that Burnley had a fiery figurehead in its chairman, Bob Lord, who was ever ready to shout the odds on the club's behalf. Their complementary characters melded ideally.

There were two major strands to Potts' success. Firstly, he was an exceptionally shrewd strategist – no one mentioned 4-4-2 in the late 1950s and early 1960s, but often that was the system he employed, enabling a team blessed with few stars to compete with, and frequently outdo, the big-city battalions.

Secondly, his sincerity and genuine concern for the young men in his charge turned Burnley into a family club and fostered a rare team spirit.

The Potts regime was an enlightened one in which sometimes he would ask the opinions of his players, though for all his usual quiet modesty, he could explode with anger when confronted with what he perceived as cheating or laziness.

Certainly he could show steel and take unpopular decisions when he deemed them necessary, for instance the controversial 1963 sale of his brilliant but ageing midfield general Jimmy McIlroy to Stoke City.

Fans condemned him when the deal was mooted – indeed 'Potts Out' graffiti survived on walls in the town for at least two decades after the event – but he did not waver.

Harry Potts had served Burnley as a player, too, arriving as a 17-year-old in 1937. He showed immense promise as a goal-scoring inside-left, only for his momentum to be interrupted by the Second World War, during which he served in the RAF and played in India. There was time, also, to guest for Fulham and Sunderland before resuming at Turf Moor in 1946.

In the first season after the conflict, Potts top-scored as Burnley gained promotion to the First Division and he almost won the FA Cup for them, shooting against the bar at Wembley before Charlton Athletic claimed the trophy in extra time of the final. In 1950 he was sold to Everton for £20,000, but didn't secure a regular place at Goodison Park and retired as a player, having reached his middle thirties, in 1956.

Always a deep and impressive thinker, Potts took a coaching post with Wolverhampton Wanderers later that year, before moving into management with Shrewsbury Town of the Third Division South in the summer of 1957. Immediately it became clear he was in his element and, a mere seven months later, he accepted the boss' chair at Burnley.

The squad he inherited was sound rather than spectacular, though the two main creators, the cultured wing-half Jimmy Adamson and the inspirational inside-forward McIlroy, were outstanding. Potts was quick to recognise, too, the merits of his callow wing man John Connelly, and he laid great emphasis on a youth system which was to pay rich dividends over the coming years.

After two creditable campaigns, Burnley scaled the heights in 1959/60, pipping Wolves for the championship in the final match. Cynics suggested it would be a one-off achievement, and in terms of silverware they were right. But Burnley continued to excel, despite being straitened financially by the abolition of the players' maximum wage, a development which greatly favoured the rich clubs.

In 1960/61 they reached the quarter-finals of the European Cup, going out by a single goal in Hamburg after losing a 3-1 home advantage, they finished fourth in the League table and were semi-finalists in both the FA Cup and League Cup.

The following season they could, and probably should, have lifted the coveted League and FA Cup double, but squandered a championship lead to let in Alf Ramsey's unfancied Ipswich Town at the death, and lost at Wembley to Tottenham Hotspur. Then in 1962/63 they finished third in the First Division.

Thereafter, sadly, money became increasingly short, the team broke up following the departure of McIlroy, and the rest of the decade – save for another third place in 1965/66 – brought relative mediocrity. Attendances fell, talented youngsters such as Willie Morgan were sold to survive, and in 1970 Potts was shifted 'upstairs' to become general manager.

Weary and frustrated in such a peripheral role, he left in 1972 to become boss of Second Division Blackpool, who missed promotion only narrowly in his first term. However, after two more cash-strapped seasons of respectable mundanity, he was sacked in May 1976.

Soon Potts returned to Burnley – by then in the second flight – as chief scout, and took over as manager again in 1977, only to be dismissed after a poor start to 1979/80. It was a poignant exit for the most successful boss in the club's history.

In the 1980s Potts scouted for the non-League Colne Dynamos, but his activities were restricted increasingly by Parkinson's disease.

Harold Potts: born Hetton-le-Hole, County Durham, 22 October 1920; played for Burnley 1937-50, Everton 1950-56; managed Shrewsbury Town 1957-58, Burnley 1958-70, Blackpool 1973-76, Burnley 1977-79; died Burnley, Lancashire, 15 January 1996.

Neil Franklin

Neil Franklin was arguably the finest centre-half the England football team ever had. After losing his early prime to the Second World War, he became an automatic choice for his country, only to scupper an apparently gilded career by one disastrous, if understandable, decision.

When he walked out on Stoke City, turned his back on England's first World Cup campaign, and flew to Bogota in the summer of 1950, Franklin believed he was heading for a pot of gold and securing his family's financial future. No more would he be a slave to the English game's iniquitous system which made players little more than appallingly paid slaves to their clubs.

But the hoped-for El Dorado in Colombia – then acrimoniously outside the jurisdiction of the Federation of International Football Associations – proved to be a sorry illusion, and in less than two months he was back home in the Potteries, chastened, largely ostracised and destined for virtual oblivion for the rest of his time as a player.

Franklin's excellence was never in question from the day in 1939 that he turned professional with First Division Stoke, his home-town club. He didn't make his senior debut before the conflict but was catapulted to prominence by consistent magnificence in wartime football, for City, for the RAF, and, eventually, in England's unofficial Victory matches.

When peacetime competition resumed in 1946, Franklin's full international place was not in doubt, and he cemented it with a then-record 27 consecutive appearances over the next four years.

What made Neil Franklin different as a central defender was his pure skill. Virtually all stoppers of his era were hunky bustlers whose brawn and aggression were their paramount assets, but the Stoke number-five adopted a singularly subtle approach. Though firm in the tackle and competitive in the air – indeed, impressively so for a man of 5ft 11in who weighed just 11 stone – he tended to master his adversaries by shrewd positional sense and almost uncanny anticipation. Then, having gained possession of the ball, he could stroke it with masterful accuracy to whichever colleague he chose. Invariably, Franklin appeared in command of a situation, serenely composed, a born organiser, a delight to the eye.

When his decision to leave Stoke for Santa Fe of Bogota to play in a so-called rebel league became public, bedlam broke out across the soccer world. As he, together with his City team-mate George Mountford, flew to South America to earn reportedly ten times their English wages, they were slated cruelly as 'greedy traitors', some of their most vociferous critics having a vested interest in the British game's maintaining its unfair status quo. Of course, there were sound football reasons why the 27-year-old Franklin should not place himself beyond the pale, and Walter Winterbottom, the gentlemanly England manager, was among those who had implored him not to go.

Sadly for the bold adventurer, his idyll did not last long. Most of Santa Fe's other recruits were Argentinians, with whom the Stoke pair found it difficult to play. There were also problems settling in a strange country for Franklin's pregnant wife and his six-year-old son, and the pressure became too much for him to bear. Accordingly, he flew home to England after less than two months, homesick and disillusioned, leaving Bogota behind him forever. Not surprisingly, he was not made welcome. Suspended for four months by the football authorities and his club, shunned by some of his erstwhile colleagues, the country's most accomplished centre-half spent the winter of 1950/51 in a non-productive limbo which was ended in February by a £22,500 move to Second Division Hull City.

The extent of the widespread feeling against Franklin could be judged by the fact that none of the major clubs tried to acquire his proven talent, but that did not bother Hull's boss, Raich Carter. He had long coveted his former England colleague and reckoned there was no reason why the centre-half should not return to the international reckoning at the same time as providing inspiration for the Tigers.

Unfortunately, neither ambition was achieved. Despite obvious poverty in central defence England never picked Franklin again, preferring to run through no less than a dozen inferior performers over the next four years before shifting Billy Wright to fill the troublesome position. As for his contribution to Hull, it was badly hampered by injuries and promotion was not achieved.

Thereafter, Franklin's playing days petered out in poignant anti-climax. There were brief lower-division interludes with Crewe Alexandra and Stockport County before he moved into non-League circles, serving the likes of Macclesfield and Wellington Town (whom he also coached) before he retired in 1962.

However, Franklin was determined to remain in the game and coached in Cyprus before accepting the manager's seat at Third Division Colchester United in November

1963. He could not prevent their relegation the following season, but led them straight back up, only for another demotion to bring about his dismissal in 1968.

In later years, Franklin ran a pub in Oswaldtwistle, Lancaster. But for that one fateful decision to seek his fortune, there is no telling what glorious tales of soccer achievement he might have had to tell his regulars.

Cornelius Franklin: born Shelton, Stoke-on-Trent, 24 January 1922; played for Stoke City 1939-50, Santa Fe of Bogota 1950, Hull City 1951-56, Crewe Alexandra 1956-57, Stockport County 1957-58; capped 27 times for England 1946-50; coached Apoel, Cyprus 1963; managed Colchester United 1963-68; died Stone, Staffordshire, 9 February 1996.

Bob Paisley

When Bill Shankly astonished the football world by stepping down as Liverpool manager in the summer of 1974, the job of guiding the fortunes of the great Anfield institution was offered to his distinctly diffident deputy, the quiet north-easterner Bob Paisley.

With characteristic modesty, Paisley was reluctant to assume the reins and urged Shankly – an almost Messiah-like figure on Merseyside and a seemingly impossible act to follow – to change his mind and carry on.

But though he regretted it later, Shankly was not for turning and Paisley announced, humbly, that he would do his best. Nine years later, he retired as the most successful boss in English football history, having led the Reds to six League championships, three European Cups, one UEFA Cup and three League Cups.

Paisley didn't ooze charisma like Shankly or court controversy like Brian Clough; he wasn't revered like Matt Busby or held in universal affection like Joe Mercer; but when it came to the pragmatic business of filling trophy cabinets with silverware, he put the lot of them in the shade.

His football life began in his native County Durham where, while still in his teens in 1939, Paisley helped the crack local side Bishop Auckland lift the then-coveted FA Amateur Cup. He was a wing-half of considerable potential and it was inevitable that he would be snapped up by a leading professional club. Sure enough, later that year he headed west for Anfield and the start of a bountiful association that was to last for more than half a century.

After losing six years of his career to the Second World War, Paisley became established in the Liverpool side and played a doughty part in securing the League title in 1947. In keeping with his subsequent managerial style, there was nothing flashy about his play. He was a flintily indomitable performer doing an admirably solid job, his industry and tenacity compensating amply for any marginal shortfall in craft and guile.

Seldom, if ever, did he hit the headlines, but he never let his side down, which made it all the more hurtful when he was axed unexpectedly by manager George Kay from the team which faced Arsenal in the 1950 FA Cup final at Wembley. He had played in all the previous rounds, even contributing a rare goal against local rivals Everton in the semi-final.

He was missed, too, on the big day as the Gunners' Scottish schemer Jimmy Logie, who would have been Paisley's direct opponent, proved vastly influential in their 2-0 victory, but typically there were no histrionics from the Reds' phlegmatic loyalist. Instead he buckled down to regain his slot, and duly he saw out his playing career over four more steady seasons before joining the Anfield coaching staff in 1954.

There followed five doldrum years for Liverpool as they strove to rise from the Second Division, but a new era dawned in 1959 with the arrival of the inspirational Shankly. Paisley, by then a skilled physiotherapist and acknowledged expert in diagnosing injuries, became the Scot's first lieutenant.

Radical change swept Anfield and as promotion to the top flight in 1961/62 was followed by an avalanche of honours – League titles in 1963/64 and 1965/66, the club's first FA Cup in 1965 – Shankly was rightly lauded. But beavering away in the background all the while was Paisley, and the mammoth, if unobtrusive part he was playing in laying the foundations for future glory was not widely recognised at the time.

However, the Liverpool board knew their man well and when Shankly dropped his retirement bombshell after winning the FA Cup in 1974, it was to Paisley they turned.

Most contemporary pundits feared the faithful retainer was on a hiding to nothing: if the Reds continued on their triumphant way, people would say it was all down to the team Shankly had created; but if standards slipped, then the new man would get the flak. There followed an ominously barren season in 1974/75 and there were a few awkward moments when the irrepressible Shankly turned up at the training ground and was addressed as 'Boss' by the players.

But Paisley was made of stern stuff and was not to be drawn into any competition for the affection of his men, nor was he going to ape his wisecracking predecessor in supplying a memorable quote for every occasion. He declared he would let his players do the talking for him on the pitch, and in the years that followed they could hardly have been more eloquent.

After making a few subtle changes to his side – recruiting understated gems such as full-back Phil Neal from Northampton Town and midfielder Terry McDermott from Newcastle United, and converting struggling striker Ray Kennedy into a key contributor on the left flank – Paisley led Liverpool to the League and UEFA Cup double in his second season in charge. Thereafter there were major trophies – including European Cups, which even Shankly had never attained – every term for the rest of his career.

In 1976/77 the rampant Merseysiders retained their championship and were unlucky to lose to Manchester United by a fluke goal in the FA Cup final, but within four days they had made up for that disappointment in unforgettable style with the headiest triumph in the club's history to that point.

On a jewelled evening in Rome, the Anfielders – captained in typical heart-on-sleeve fashion by Emlyn Hughes and featuring England star Kevin Keegan for the last time before his controversial transfer to Hamburg – beat Borussia Moenchengladbach 3-1 to claim the European Cup, thanks to a goal each from Paisley proteges McDermott and Neal, and another from iron-man defender Tommy Smith.

Thus Liverpool had captured the biggest prize in club football for the first time, but it was not to be the last. Paisley's side, which he was developing steadily, mainly by bold but characteristically canny excursions into the transfer market, retained the continental crown in 1978, overcoming the drab Belgians FC Bruges at Wembley through a single goal from his most significant capture, Kenny Dalglish.

There followed further League titles in 1978/79, 1979/80, 1981/82 and 1982/83, a trio of consecutive League Cup triumphs (1981 to 1983) and, most fulfilling of all, Paisley's third taste of European Cup euphoria in Paris in 1981, when fellow north-easterner Alan Kennedy supplied the only goal of a tight final against the mighty Real Madrid. As the honours piled up, it was impossible to charge Paisley with making capital of another man's work. He it was who signed the likes of the magnificent goal-poacher-cum-creator Dalglish, the crunchingly physical but luxuriantly talented play-maker Graeme Souness and the incomparably poised central defensive duo of Alan Hansen and Mark Lawrenson, creating one of the most powerful and entertaining club sides of all time.

A meticulous planner, clever tactician and shrewd judge of a player, he never stopped preaching to his charges the traditional Shankly gospel of passing and movement, controlling the ball and finding space to receive a return dispatch, always supporting the man in possession, and, above all, working until they could barely stand.

Appealingly, too, this essentially shy individual became more outward-going as the years passed, his wry one-liners not as headline-worthy as Shankly's wicked barbs but revealing a keen sense of humour, nevertheless. For example, in 1977 as he took a few minutes off from preparing his men for their climactic contest in the Olympic Stadium, he pronounced drily: 'The last time I was in Rome was 33 years ago. I helped to capture it!'

Paisley was 64 when he elected to step aside in the spring of 1983, making way for the more overtly affable Joe Fagan, his assistant and another long-time Liverpool servant who had paid his dues in the fabled Anfield boot room.

There were those who reckoned that, like Shankly before him, he was leaving prematurely, and Fagan's instant success – completing the remarkable treble of European Cup, League championship and League Cup in his first campaign at the helm – emphasised, with no disrespect to his splendid former assistant, that he could have attained an even more staggering list of honours had he chosen to linger.

But he felt that with a new wave of young footballers pressing for recognition, and with unsettling speculation about his retirement mounting among fans, the time was ripe for departure, and he withdrew gracefully, modestly, the lack of bombast as becoming as it was typical of the man.

Two years on from his retirement, Paisley returned to Anfield in the wake of the Heysel tragedy as consultant to the newly-appointed manager Kenny Dalglish and went on to join the board. Come the early 1990s poor health curtailed his activities and he resigned his directorship, becoming a vice-president of the club he had served so royally.

Though undoubtedly hard when the occasion demanded – as plenty of former Liverpool stars could testify – Paisley was essentially a kind, caring man who, as Brian Clough remarked, proved the fallacy of the myth that nice guys win nothing.

As he had promised so self-effacingly, Bob Paisley had done his best – and it turned out to be better than anyone else's.

Robert Paisley: born Hetton-le-Hole, County Durham, 23 January 1919; player for Bishop Auckland (amateurs) 1937-39; Liverpool 1939-54; second team trainer 1954-59, first team trainer 1959-70, assistant manager 1970-74, manager 1974-83, member of the board 1983-92, team consultant 1985-87, life vice-president 1992-96; OBE 1977; died Liverpool, 14 February 1996.

Alan Brown

It is difficult to imagine any football manager being harder or straighter than Alan Brown. No club in his charge ever lifted a major trophy, yet he remained a hugely respected if somewhat idiosyncratic member of his profession, his name a byword for truth, frankness and rigid discipline. Yet while the 'iron man' image will be forever synonymous with the complex Northumbrian, his contribution as one of soccer's most thoughtful and innovative tacticians should never be overlooked. Neither should his sheer passion for the game, which he once described, with no hyperbole intended, as 'one of the biggest things that's happened in creation'.

The son of a painter and decorator, Brown went to grammar school and had a yen to be a teacher, but as one of a large family during the Depression he did not have the opportunity for further education. However, he was blessed with natural athleticism and, after revealing immense promise as an unyielding centre-half in local football, he joined Huddersfield Town in 1933.

He did not settle contentedly with the Terriers, feeling rather neglected and leaving to spend two years as a policeman before returning to make a few dozen senior appearances for the club before the war.

However, it was after the conflict, having been transferred to Burnley, that Brown made his most significant impact as a player. In 1946/47 he skippered the Lancastrians to promotion from Division Two and led them to Wembley for the FA Cup final, in which they were defeated 1-0 by Charlton Athletic. In 1948 a £15,000 deal took him to Notts County, but the 34-year-old played only a handful of games before ending his playing days.

Thereafter Brown opened a restaurant in Burnley, but returned to the game he loved on the suggestion of Stanley Rous, then Secretary of the Football Association, later to become the world's leading soccer administrator.

In 1954, after three and a half seasons as a coach with Sheffield Wednesday, Brown moved into management with his former employers, Burnley, upsetting several senior players who were not keen on the prospect of being bossed by such a tower of moral rectitude. Unsurprisingly, Brown was unfazed by this undercurrent and set about his new task with evangelistic zeal. To him such virtues as integrity and industry were compulsory and he saw to it that his club espoused them, too. Indeed, when work started on a new outdoor training centre on the edge of town, he helped to dig the foundations himself and 'volunteered' his players to do likewise. A few hands were blistered, and probably a few egos, as well.

However, Brown was never solely a disciplinarian. His deep fascination with strategy was evident in the mesmerising range of free-kick routines he instituted, and in his enterprising use of short corners, both of which were much copied elsewhere. Also, with the Turf Moor club not blessed with bottomless coffers, he was committed to the introduction and development of youngsters, a policy which he was to pursue vigorously elsewhere in later years and which did much to pave the way for future Burnley triumphs.

Brown was not to be part of those, though. After keeping the Clarets in the First Division's top half for three seasons, he left for Sunderland, who had been suffering scandals over illegal payments to players and who were languishing near the foot of the table. He was scathingly contemptuous of such abuse and, despite the Wearsiders being relegated for the first time in their history in 1958, the energetic Brown both ensured that their act was well and truly cleaned up and revitalised their playing fortunes. He spent far more time in a tracksuit than behind his desk and, after several near-misses, led them to promotion in 1964.

To the consternation of many fans, he then left to take over at Sheffield Wednesday, an ambitious club with what was then the most sumptuously appointed stadium in the land.

Brown took the Owls to the 1966 FA Cup final, in which they lost after leading Everton by two goals, but League form tended to be mediocre or worse and in February 1968 he returned to Sunderland. Another relegation in 1970 was followed by two failures to win promotion and the sack in November 1972. After that Brown coached in Norway, a prelude to a retirement blighted by ill health.

He will be remembered as a man who believed that rules, both for football and life, were sacrosanct. For example he refused, always, to sanction material inducements to parents of promising youngsters, at a time when that practice was widespread, even if it meant losing a possible future star. His contempt for the moral bankruptcy that spawned the recent 'bung' scandals must have been total. His career never attained the dizziest heights, but his personal standards did. Emphatically, Alan Brown was not for turning.

Alan Winston Brown: born Corbridge, Northumberland, 26 August 1914; played for Huddersfield Town 1933-46, Burnley 1946-48, Notts County 1948; coached Sheffield Wednesday 1951-54; managed Burnley 1954-57, Sunderland 1957-64, Sheffield Wednesday 1964-68, Sunderland 1968-72; died Barnstaple, Devon, 8 March 1996.

Eric Houghton

When Eric Houghton kicked a football, it was sensible not to stand in its path. Between the wars, as an Aston Villa and England left-winger, he established a reputation as one of the most destructively powerful marksmen the game had seen. Off the pitch, though, the author of those famously violent strikes was a mild and courteous fellow and throughout his subsequent career as a manager, the highlight of which was leading his beloved Villa to FA Cup glory in 1957, he ruled by a quiet strength of character which earned him widespread respect.

Houghton had seemed destined for a life in soccer since his teenage days as a prodigiously prolific centre-forward who revelled in turning out for his school on a Saturday morning, then playing for his village side in the afternoon. After excelling in local non-League circles, notably with Boston Town, he was recommended to Aston Villa by an uncle who had once played for the club, signing amateur forms in 1927 and giving up a bakery job to turn professional a year later.

Having been converted into a flankman – Villa were magnificently served in the centre by the revered Pongo Waring – Houghton gained rapid promotion to the senior side, uncharacteristically missing a penalty on his debut in January 1930 but impressing generally with his dashing style, his slick manipulation of the ball and, above all, his shooting prowess.

Clearly the eager rookie offered immense promise but no one expected the Houghton star to ascend quite so instantly as it did during season 1930/31, in which he scored 30 times as Villa finished as First Division runners-up, and he was rewarded by an England call-up. He netted in that game, too, a 5-1 victory over All Ireland, and could count himself unlucky that his prime coincided with that of Arsenal's Cliff Bastin, whose brilliance ended Houghton's international involvement only two years later.

At club level, however, the Villa man continued to flourish and he played a major part in the Birmingham club's Second Division championship triumph of 1938, two years after suffering the trauma of relegation. All the while the Houghton howitzer grew in renown and he became a dead-ball specialist, many of the 170 senior goals he netted before leaving Villa Park in 1946 having come from penalties and free-kicks.

Houghton's new club was lowly Notts County, for whom he played until 1949 when he took over as manager and, with England centre-forward Tommy Lawton at his disposal, he led the Magpies to the Third Division South title in his first campaign at the helm.

Three terms of unspectacular consolidation followed before he took the job closest to his heart, that of bossing Aston Villa. Quietly but firmly, he set about revitalising a once-great club which had fallen on mediocre times. He gave youngsters their chance and he spent heavily on well-known recruits, but could not achieve his ambition of mounting a realistic championship challenge.

There was uplifting consolation in 1957, though, when the Villans upset the odds to beat newly-crowned League champions Manchester United in the FA Cup final, albeit in controversial circumstances after United's goalkeeper, Ray Wood, was seriously injured. However, hopes that the Wembley victory would inspire a general recovery were dashed and, with his side struggling near the foot of the table, a sad Houghton was sacked in November 1958.

Though he was never to manage another League club, the popular East Countryman was not to lack employment in the game he loved. Thereafter he joined Nottingham Forest as chief scout and bossed non-League Rugby Town in the early 1960s, before serving Walsall in various capacities, including director. Next he enjoyed a second return to Villa Park, pioneering the club lottery before taking a seat on the board for seven years from 1972, and it was fitting when his devotion to the claret-and-blue cause was marked in 1983 by his elevation to senior vice-president.

Houghton – who in his youth had been a sporting all-rounder proficient enough at cricket to play for Lincolnshire at Minor Counties level and Warwickshire Seconds – retained his fervour for football to the end, watching Villa regularly at senior, reserve and youth level until ill health curtailed his activity during the current season. He never tired of reminiscing with supporters, never refused to sign an autograph, was never less than a perfect gentleman. When Eric Houghton died, Aston Villa lost one of their most loyal servants and an ambassador of immeasurable worth.

William Eric Houghton: born Billingborough, Lincolnshire, 29 June 1910; played for Aston Villa 1927-46, Notts County 1946-49; capped seven times for England 1930-32; managed Notts County 1949-53, Aston Villa 1953-58; died Birmingham, 1 May 1996.

Cliff Holton

Only four men since the war have scored more goals in English League football than Cliff Holton, though the big, burly Oxonian never scaled the giddy heights predicted for him as a young Arsenal star during the early 1950s.

In mid-decade, as he stood on the threshold of his prime, he suffered a plateau in his development which saw him converted into a half-back, then dispatched to the lower divisions for the remainder of his career. However, his response was both spirited and emphatic: returning to his striking role, he contributed a further double-century of goals over the subsequent nine years, becoming a cult hero at several clubs in the process.

Surprisingly, Holton had begun his football life as a defender, serving Isthmian League Oxford City as a full-back before joining Arsenal in 1947. It was not until 1950, after National Service in the Army, that he was switched to centre-forward and he earned a place in the Gunners' senior side in the spring of 1951.

Imposing, strong and far quicker than was suggested by a rather ungainly, loping gait, Holton adopted a rampaging style which unsettled opponents. He wasn't a bad passer either, but he was most famous for his thunderous power of shot in either foot, which accounted for many of his goals.

This enviable catalogue of attributes brought encouraging progress in 1951/52, though he disappointed at Wembley as an injury-riven Arsenal lost the FA Cup final to Newcastle. The following campaign ended in glory, though, Holton's 19 goals in 21 outings helping to secure the League championship, and the promising 24-year-old was spoken of as an England international of the future.

Alas, that was not to be. Thereafter the Gunners began to labour and in 1954/55 he lost his berth to the ageing Tommy Lawton. A year later, having been switched to left-half, Holton was restored to the side and became captain for a spell. But despite doughty service in various roles, he was judged surplus to requirements as new manager George Swindin sought to revamp a lacklustre team and he was sold to Watford for £9,000 in October 1958. Holton was 29 by then and many believed his best days were behind him. In fact, he was about to enter his most productive period. After taking a little time to settle at Vicarage Road, he became one of the most revered figures in the Hornets' history, netting a club record for one term of 48 League and FA Cup goals as he skippered them to promotion from the Fourth Division in 1960.

When he left for Northampton in 1961 – Watford reckoned he was spending too much time on business interests, which he denied strenuously – there were protest petitions from outraged fans, whose judgement was soon borne out. Just five hours after joining the Cobblers on a Saturday morning, Holton had scored a hat-trick for his new employers. Watford then struggled unexpectedly for the rest of the season.

Later, Holton's goals helped both Northampton and Crystal Palace gain promotions, and he went on to net regularly in a second spell at Watford, for Charlton Athletic and for Orient, before a gammy knee forced retirement in 1967.

A forthright and articulate individual, he seemed ideal soccer management material but he preferred to concentrate on a precision engineering business, based not far from his home in Hadley Wood in Hertfordshire, which he ran until 1989 before working part-time in sports marketing.

Cliff Holton's tally of 293 League goals in 570 appearances has been bettered by only Arthur Rowley, Jimmy Greaves, John Atyeo and John Aldridge since the war. And but for his infuriating mid-1950s blip, that select list surely would have been significantly shorter.

Clifford Charles Holton: born Oxford, 29 April 1929; played for Arsenal 1947-58, Watford 1958-61, Northampton Town 1961-62, Crystal Palace 1962-65, Watford again 1965-66, Charlton Athletic 1966, Orient 1966-67; died Spain, 30 May 1996.

Bobby Keetch

By no stretch of the imagination could Bobby Keetch be described as an outstandingly gifted footballer, yet he stamped his extrovert personality indelibly on the London soccer scene in the mid-1960s.

A fearsomely abrasive central defender who enjoyed his playing pomp with Fulham, Keetch cut a bold and courageous figure on the pitch, his immaculately coiffured blond thatch and swashbuckling style making him instantly recognisable.

He was not exactly a shrinking violet off duty, either, being renowned at the time for a flamboyant lifestyle in which beautiful girls, fast cars and hectic socialising were de rigueur.

After failing to make the grade with his first club, West Ham United, whom he had joined after leaving school, Keetch revived his career after signing for Fulham in 1959. It was immediately apparent to all at Craven Cottage that they had been joined by a character who was markedly different from the average young footballer.

Though extremely popular with his peers, after training the strikingly confident teenager tended not to accompany them to the local snooker hall, preferring instead to visit art galleries and antique shops, laying the foundations for a lucrative future when his playing days were done.

Keetch won a regular first-team place late in the 1962/63 season, thereafter helping Fulham through several successive (and successful) battles to remain in the First Division, his combative efforts complementing the more skilful input from the likes of Johnny Haynes, Alan Mullery, George Cohen and Bobby Robson. The muscular Londoner relished especially his confrontations with star forwards and it was said that the bigger the reputation of an opponent, the bigger the boots Keetch would wear for the occasion.

He was devastated in May 1966 when manager Vic Buckingham, seeking to establish a more cultured defensive approach, gave him a free transfer. At this stage, having made strides in the art world, he considered leaving football but was persuaded to enlist with Third Division Queen's Park Rangers. It was to prove a fruitful association, as he helped the Loftus Road club rise rapidly to the top flight before bowing out of the English game, still aged only 27, in 1969.

Emigration to South Africa and two years with Durban City followed, along with simultaneous business success. Later Keetch, a family man, moved back to London where he continued to thrive in arts and antiques. Earlier this year he was involved in the launch of a themed West End restaurant, 'Football, Football', and though he no longer took an active part in professional soccer, he remained in touch through his close ties with Terry Venables and other leading figures in the game. The warmth of their tributes, on learning of his premature death, speaks volumes for the impact of Bobby Keetch. He was, most definitely, one of a kind.

Robert David Keetch: born Tottenham, London, 25 October 1941; played for Fulham 1959-66, Queen's Park Rangers 1966-69, Durban City 1969-70; died London, 29 June 1996.

Jimmy Gordon

Without becoming one of football's household names – indeed, he was unknown professionally outside the confines of the game – Jimmy Gordon exercised a profound influence on one of the most remarkable sporting success stories of modern times.

A wise, unfussy, endlessly enthusiastic Scot, he spent the last six years of his long career in soccer as chief coach to Nottingham Forest, playing an unsung but crucial part in the hitherto unfashionable Trentsiders' rise from the ranks of Second Division strugglers to twice-crowned champions of Europe.

Throughout this glorious interlude, between January 1975 and his retirement in May 1981, Gordon's shrewd instruction and skilful preparation of high-quality athletes was admirable, yet arguably it did not represent the most onerous aspect of his duties. No, what made the coach's contribution so special was the manner in which he coped with the club's hugely talented but undeniably eccentric management team of Brian Clough and the late Peter Taylor.

A man of unimpeachable integrity and ever approachable, Gordon was an expert in rebuilding the confidence of young men whose egos had taken a battering from the acerbic

Clough. Though hard in his own way, expecting total dedication and ceaseless effort from his charges, Gordon became a much-respected 'father-confessor' and go-between, without whom Forest would have been immeasurably the poorer.

When the manager and his equally mercurial lieutenant were away from the City Ground, Gordon was left to supervise the day-to-day running of football matters, a task he accomplished with calm efficiency. In 1980 Clough rewarded his loyal retainer by arranging for him to lead Forest out at Wembley before the League Cup final against Wolves. Sadly, they lost that day but by then the popular coach was well acquainted with the taste of triumph.

Having spent the first five years of his working life as a miner in West Lothian, Gordon was familiar with a less glamorous side of life, too, a grounding which served him well during a worthy playing career as an old-fashioned wing-half with Second Division Newcastle United, whom he joined in 1935, and then First Division Middlesbrough after the war.

Though the conflict – during which he served in the Army – had robbed him of what should have been his prime years, he excelled at Ayresome Park, where he became a tenacious ball-winner whose main job was to supply possession to star England inside-forward Wilf Mannion. Gordon didn't quite attain international class himself, but he earned the approbation of his peers, notably the great Bill Shankly, who once said of him: 'If you had to play against Jimmy every week you would never sleep at night.'

He played until he was 38, being so fit that later he regretted not continuing until he was at least 40, before learning his trade as a trainer with Middlesbrough and going on to become chief coach of Blackburn Rovers in the mid-1960s.

However, the most fateful moment in Gordon's professional life still lay ahead. It came in 1969 in the form of a call from Brian Clough, whom he had known as a talented but highly precocious and argumentative footballer at Middlesbrough. Clough was offering the chance to coach Derby County, newly promoted to the top flight, and after some persuasion Gordon accepted.

Thereafter he was an essential part of the Clough bandwagon, contributing to Derby's League title in 1972, accompanying the famous extrovert during his ill-fated 44-day sojourn as boss of Leeds United in 1973 and then, after a brief spell as a storeman with Rolls-Royce, he joined Clough at Forest. There followed promotion to the First Division in 1977, League title and League Cup triumphs in 1978, European Cup final glory against Malmo in 1979 and Hamburg in 1980, as well as another League Cup win in 1979.

Clough – with whom there were to be sad differences over the Scot's contribution to a book on his controversial former manager following his retirement – described his trusty aide as 'dignified, dedicated and charming' and there is no shortage of people in football who would echo those sentiments.

Gordon, whose wife Olive died in 1994, lived in Derby. He had been suffering from Alzheimer's disease, the bane of so many former footballers, for two years.

James Gordon: born Fauldhouse, West Lothian, 23 October 1915; played for Newcastle United 1935-45, Middlesbrough 1945-54; coached Middlesbrough 1954-61, Blackburn Rovers 1961-69, Derby County 1969-73, Leeds United 1973, Nottingham Forest 1975-81; died Derby, 29 August 1996.

Tommy Lawton

Certain footballers straddle their eras like titans, their pre-eminence so palpable that any attempt to place them in a pecking order is meaningless. So it was with Tommy Lawton, the princeliest, the most complete, simply the best centre-forward in Britain as the 20th century approached its half-way mark.

Lawton carried with him the unmistakable aura of stardom, radiating charisma and, even in quiet moments on the field, emitting a wholly distinctive brand of cool menace. Though a powerfully-built six-footer, he combined the physical strength expected of a big man with the nimbleness of a ballet dancer. His movement over the ground was graceful, seemingly languid at times, but that was an illusion. In fact, he was quick, often blindingly so, and he had a habit of pouncing with sudden venom to score goals seemingly out of nothing.

His control of the ball was commendable and the power of his shot was ferocious, but it was in the air that Tommy Lawton attained his full and glorious majesty. Indeed, shrewd contemporary judges assert that no more brilliant header of the ball ever lived. His muscular legs and abdomen enabled him to spring to prodigious heights, and he was blessed with a sense of timing that verged on the uncanny.

Indeed, such was his expertise that at times he appeared to defy gravity, creating the optical illusion of hovering while the ball homed in on that wide forehead, the sleek, dark hair and prominent beak of a nose intensifying the impression of some ravenous raptor closing on its prey. He played fair, too, being a dream to referee despite carrying all that muscle, reserving his occasional moments of tetchiness for less talented team-mates who failed to reach his exacting standards.

Yet, for all his magnificence, Lawton – in common with many gifted contemporaries – suffered a double blight on his career. He lost six years of his prime to the Second World War, and he played at a time when financial rewards for even the top performers were in no way commensurate with their pulling power. Thus while the clubs' coffers bulged as crowds flocked to see the big names, the players were restricted to wages that were risible in comparison.

Lawton, an intelligent fellow with a sharp business brain, railed against such iniquity. He spoke his mind, fell into dispute with various employers and became something of a wanderer from job to job. Thus, while adored by supporters of whichever club he was representing at the time, he never remained in one place long enough to become a folk hero in the manner of, say, Tom Finney at Preston or Billy Wright at Wolves.

The phenomenal sharp-shooting ability of the strapping Lancastrian first became apparent during his schooldays, when he netted some 570 goals in three seasons. Thereafter he started work in a tannery near his Bolton home and joined Burnley as an amateur in 1935, turning professional at Turf Moor a year later. He made his senior debut as a 16-year-old, then underlined his promise with a hat-trick at home to Tottenham Hotspur four days after his 17th birthday in October 1936.

That was more than enough to alert the attention of bigger clubs to such a precocious talent and, sure enough, three months later he joined Everton for £6,500. Now, briefly, Lawton found himself playing alongside Bill 'Dixie' Dean, perhaps the most famous goal merchant of them all. Bill was nearing the end of his prolific career, but he was willing and able to pass on priceless knowledge to the callow colleague who was to inherit his mantle. Accordingly, Lawton became his club's marksman-in-chief in 1937/38, and topped the Football League's scoring chart with 28 goals. The following term brought even richer bounty: his 35 strikes, once again more than anyone else in the country, were hugely instrumental in Everton landing the League championship, and he earned the personal accolade of an England call-up while still in his teens. Lawton strode on to the world stage with stupendous assurance, netting in each of his first six games, and there seemed no limit to what he might achieve.

But then came the war – he served in the Army's Physical Training Corps – and though he shone in unofficial internationals alongside such luminaries as Stanley Matthews and Raich Carter, he was reduced to guesting for the likes of Aldershot, Tranmere Rovers and Morton at club level. Thus his early prime was lost to top-class competition.

When life returned to something like normality in 1945, Lawton found himself at odds with Everton, and he was transferred to Chelsea for £11,500. By then 26 and an awesomely formidable operator, he excelled in his one full season at Stamford Bridge, breaking the club's scoring record with 26 goals and netting twice for Great Britain against the Rest of Europe in 1947.

However, later that year his relationship with his new employers ran into difficulties and an announcement that he was leaving precipitated a hectic chase for his services. There followed one of the sporting shocks of the age when the spearhead of England's attack was sold to Third Division Notts County for a then-record fee of £20,000.

It was an eccentric move, to say the least – a modern equivalent would be Alan Shearer throwing in his lot with, say, Crewe Alexandra – even though the maximum-wage rule then in force meant that he did not lose out financially. Whatever his reasons for accepting such a dramatic drop in status, the great man threw himself into his new club's cause with gusto, and in 1950 helped them lift the Division Three (South) title. By that time, though, he had lost his England place, the selectors unwilling to persist with a player out of touch with top-flight football, and many supporters felt he was doing himself an injustice.

From time to time there were rumours of a transfer back to the big time, yet when Lawton moved on again, for £12,000 in 1952, it was to another unfashionable outfit, Brentford of the Second Division. Come January 1953, when he became player-boss at Griffin Park, the switch began to make more apparent sense, but there was to be no smooth transition to management. Instead Lawton presided over a period of travail. He was booed for the first time in his life, to which he took grave exception, and before long he resigned as manager while continuing as a player.

Then, in September 1953, in the twilight of a remarkable if not entirely satisfying career, came a development as amazing as had been his earlier switch to Notts County. Aged nearly 34, Lawton joined Arsenal, the reigning champions, who had started the season badly and whose largely young, transitional side were sorely in need of his nous and maturity.

It was a bold move which met with only qualified success. It was six months before he scored his first League goal, and he wasn't always sure of his place, but he was able to assist several youthful marksmen in the same way that Bill Dean had once helped him. Ironically, the Gunners had wanted to sign Lawton when he had left Burnley back in 1937, when they were in their all-conquering pomp and he had the world at his feet. Had they done so, club and player might have scaled unimagined heights together.

As it was, Lawton departed Highbury in 1956 to become player-boss of non-League Kettering Town, proving an enlightened and imaginative manager as he led them to the Southern League championship the following year. On the back of that achievement, he took over the reins of Notts County in 1957, but his return to Meadow Lane was ill-fated, County being relegated from the Second Division at the end of his sole campaign in charge.

Perhaps temporarily disillusioned by the game, Lawton spent four years running a village pub near Nottingham, later returning to Kettering for stints as manager and director and to Notts County, as a coach and chief scout, in the late 1960s. Thereafter he worked as a salesman for a grandstand seat firm, and in 1984 began a respected and popular football column for the *Nottingham Evening Post*.

During his playing days Lawton had seemed a serious, sometimes even sombre individual, giving the impression of a man well aware of his own worth but unsure that he was receiving adequate recompense for it. But later he was able to adopt a philosophical attitude, reflecting wryly on the fortune he would have earned had he been born 50 years later.

In any event, he could be content in the knowledge that he was one of the finest footballers Britain has produced. His 231 goals in 390 League games, and his 22 strikes in 23 internationals were enough to prove that.

Yet he was a performer who transcended mere statistics as surely as, in his pomp, he had soared above hapless defenders. He was an entertainer whom people would travel long distances to watch and part with hard-earned cash for the privilege. Above all else, Tommy Lawton was a star.

Thomas Lawton: born Bolton, Lancashire, 6 October 1919; played for Burnley 1935-37, Everton 1937-45, Chelsea 1945-47, Notts County 1947-52, Brentford 1952-53, Arsenal 1953-56, Kettering Town 1956-57; capped 23 times for England 1938-48; managed Brentford 1953, Kettering Town 1956-57, 1963-64, Notts County 1957-58; coach and chief scout, Notts County 1968-70; died Nottingham, 6 November 1996.

Stan Pearson

Stan Pearson was a lovely footballer, a beguiling mixture of subtle visionary and unflashy technician; and he was one of the most satisfyingly complete inside-forwards of his day.

He provided the attacking brains, and a lot of the goals, for the swashbucklingly attractive Manchester United side assembled by Matt Busby after the Second World War; and but for the fact that he numbered Wilf Mannion and the incomparable Raich Carter among his contemporaries, it is reasonable to suppose that the unassuming Lancastrian would have added significantly to his inappropriately meagre total of eight England caps.

A supporter of his local club since the age of seven, Salford-born Pearson rose irresistibly through the ranks of junior football before achieving his boyhood ambition by joining the Red Devils, signing amateur forms as a 16-year-old in 1935 and turning professional 18 months later. There followed a sensational senior debut in November 1937, when he set up four goals in a 7-1 victory at Chesterfield, and by season's end he was a powerfully emerging force in the team that secured promotion to the old First Division.

Then, with the gifted rookie on the threshold of what promised to be a majestic career, the war intervened to consign a whole generation of emerging talent to footballing limbo. However, though Army service took him to India and Burma, there was time to guest for Newcastle, Brighton and Queen's Park Rangers as well as to represent his own club in wartime competitions, and when the conflict ended the unscathed 26-year-old was eager for the game and approaching his prime.

And how he blossomed. Slotting stylishly into one of the most exhilarating of all forward lines – Jimmy Delaney, Johnny Morris, Jack Rowley, Pearson himself and Charlie Mitten – he became a key factor as Busby's buccaneering side enchanted the massive post-war crowds, so hungry for entertainment after six years of being denied top-level soccer.

Pearson scored heavily, 149 times in 345 outings for United, but arguably his greatest worth was in creating opportunities for team-mates through an instinctive awareness of where they would run and a priceless knack of reaching them with adroit first-time distribution. His hallmark was accuracy, whether delivering raking crossfield passes or delightful close-range flicks and glides, and though there was nothing flamboyant about either the man or his method, the supporters loved him for his craftsmanship.

He was never the fastest man afield and his shot was not the most powerful – the majority of his strikes coming from inside the penalty box – but he made up for that in ample measure through his sharp intelligence, masterful ball control and enormous stamina which enabled him to forage ceaselessly for possession.

Yet even though Pearson and his attacking partners could take the breath away, the United side they graced so thrillingly was to endure a nightmare of championship frustration. Indeed, they finished as title runners-up in four out of the five seasons immediately after the war and did not claim the coveted crown until 1952.

However, there was rich compensation in 1948 when they beat Blackpool to win the FA Cup in what was recognised as the most captivating final to that date; in fact, there are shrewd judges who maintain, even now, that Wembley has yet to host its equal. The Seasiders, who included Stanley Matthews in their ranks, led 2-1 at half-time but United fought back to win 4-2, with Pearson supplying the crucial third goal ten minutes from the end. That year, at the age of 29, the Old Trafford stalwart was rewarded for his sparkling form with an overdue international call-up, and he continued to represent his country on an occasional basis for the next four years, his most memorable contribution being the two goals which beat Scotland at Hampden Park in 1952.

Back on the club front, Pearson's consistency became a byword in Manchester and he missed only a handful of games through injury before a combination of age, and the new wave of precocious youngsters known as the Busby Babes, overtook him in 1953/54.

That February he was sold to Second Division Bury for £4,500 and he served the Shakers royally for three years, netting 56 times in 122 League starts, before moving on to Chester of the Third Division North as player-boss in 1957. Still in splendid physical fettle as he approached his 40th birthday, Pearson helped his new club reach the Welsh Cup final in 1958 before retiring as a player in 1959.

He remained at Sealand Road as manager but his team struggled in the League's lower reaches and this charming but quiet fellow did not relish the pressure, so he resigned in November 1961.

Thereafter Pearson, who was twice widowed, ran a newsagent's shop and post-office in Prestbury, Cheshire, until the 1980s. He continued to be an avid fan of his beloved Red Devils and was a season-ticket holder until his health deteriorated in recent years.

Stan Pearson will be remembered at Old Trafford for his bountiful ability and constant loyalty during an uplifting period in the club's history. Manchester United have known finer players . . . but not too many.

Stanley Clare Pearson: born Salford, Lancashire, 11 January 1919; player for Manchester United 1935-1954, Bury 1954-57, Chester 1957-59; capped eight times for England 1948-52; managed Chester 1957-61; died Alderley Edge, Cheshire, 17 February 1997.

Len Millard

Rarely can a nickname have been as unrepresentative of a man's character as that of footballer Len Millard, a stalwart defender with West Bromwich Albion for a dozen seasons after the Second World War.

He was a quiet, unassuming fellow, renowned for his gentlemanly conduct and never booked in his 476 senior games for the club, yet he was dubbed 'The Agitator'.

The sobriquet was coined, perhaps in a spirit of irony, because the wingers who were confronted by the ultra-dependable left-back tended to become agitated by his efficiency, which reduced them to marginal figures on the fringe of the action.

The prime example of the modest Millard's expertise was his subduing of the great Tom Finney in the FA Cup final of 1954. It should be stressed that 'The Preston Plumber', who was the newly-crowned Footballer of the Year and arguably the finest player of his generation, never became remotely agitated, which would have been alien to his own sporting nature. But Finney was starved of the ball comprehensively by the steady Millard, who was man of the match by common consent and richly deserved the honour, as Albion's captain that day, of lifting the famous trophy.

Indeed, but for a late run of defeats, due at least partially to an injury crisis, West Bromwich might have won the League championship, too. Had they done so, Millard would have entered soccer legend as the man who skippered the first team this century to capture the coveted League and FA Cup double. As it was, they finished as runners-up and the amiable Midlander remained an unobtrusive figure, little known outside the game.

Millard had signed for the Throstles as a teenage amateur in 1937, then played in wartime competitions as a centre-forward before converting to wing-half by the time hostilities ceased in 1945. During the subsequent decade he missed only a handful of matches and helped gain promotion from the Second Division in 1949, continuing to hold a regular place in the top flight until his 39th year.

In 1958 Millard moved to non-League Stafford Rangers, whom he served as manager until 1961. After that he continued to shun the limelight, working in the West Midlands until his retirement in the early 1980s.

Leonard Millard: born Coseley, near Wolverhampton, 7 March 1919; played for West Bromwich Albion 1937-1958; died Coseley, 2 March 1997.

Frank Brennan

They called him 'The Rock of Tyneside', and with good reason. When Newcastle United became a footballing power in the land soon after the Second World War, Frank Brennan was the colossus at the heart of their rearguard, standing between the great centre-forwards of the day and the Magpies' goal like a walking seam of granite.

A strapping, raw-boned Scot with an engaging personality, he became an adoptive Geordie and a local cult hero, sharing the limelight with his even more famous team-mates, centre-forward Jackie Milburn and left-winger Bobby Mitchell.

Majestic in the air, a fearsome tackler and deceptively fleet of foot for such a large man, Brennan specialised in winning the ball and passing it on, with a minimum of fuss, to more creative colleagues.

After excelling as a teenager in Scottish junior leagues, he took his first step towards soccer eminence by joining the Airdrieonians club, based to the east of Glasgow, as an amateur in 1941, later turning professional and representing his country in wartime competition.

The turning point of the Brennan career arrived in 1946 when he played brilliantly in a Victory international against England, snuffing out the threat of star spearhead Tommy Lawton and attracting the attention of leading clubs from south of the border.

Both Sunderland and Preston North End pressed their suit, but the race for his signature was won by Newcastle, who paid £7,500 for the privilege of taking the hugely promising 22-year-old to St James' Park. Brennan made an instant impact in the English game, soon making his official international debut – surely he would have won more than his seven caps but for the gifted Willie Woodburn of Glasgow Rangers – and was an ever-present in the United side which gained promotion to the First Division in 1948.

For the next few seasons Newcastle were a top side, always missing out on the League title but making ample amends with successive FA Cup triumphs, a glorious one against Blackpool in 1951 followed by a distinctly fortuitous victory over Arsenal a year later. Brennan played a key role in both, bottling up the effervescent Stan Mortensen in the first and holding firm against the gallant Gunners, who had been reduced to ten men through injury, in the second.

Thereafter he continued to be a bulwark of the team until a financial dispute with the club cost him his place in 1954/55 – he missed United's third Wembley victory in five years in 1955 – and led to his controversial departure in March 1956. It was the era of the iniquitous maximum wage system and the fans pilloried the directors over what was perceived widely as unfair treatment of their favourite. There were public protest meetings and the case was raised at the Trades Union Congress but all to no avail.

Now Brennan joined non-League North Shields as player-coach, serving them enterprisingly for six seasons before spending five years as a globetrotting coach, spreading the soccer gospel to such far-flung outposts as Singapore and Trinidad.

In 1967 he returned to North Shields, inspiring them to FA Amateur Cup glory in 1969, then managing Fourth Division Darlington for a brief spell in the early 1970s. There followed a stint as trainer-coach of part-timers South Shields before he opted to concentrate on his sports outfitters business in Newcastle. Eventually the contentedly exiled Scot retired to nearby Whitley Bay. Frank Brennan will be remembered best for his prime in the black-and-white stripes of Newcastle United. Beyond reasonable dispute, he remains the finest, most dominant defender in the club's history. Given the current Magpies' notorious defensive frailty, what wouldn't manager Kenny Dalglish pay for the modern equivalent of 'The Rock of Tyneside'?

Francis Brennan: born Annathill, near Glasgow, 23 April 1924; played for Airdrieonians 1941-46, Newcastle United 1946-56; capped seven times by Scotland 1946-54; managed Darlington 1971-72; died Newcastle, 5 March 1997.

Eddie Quigley

He never cut the most athletic of figures on the football field, but that didn't stop Eddie Quigley becoming, for a time, the most expensive player in the history of the British game. In fact, the burly Lancastrian belied his ponderous appearance and misleadingly languid air to become one of the most proficient and sought-after goal-scorers of the post-war era, arguably deserving more international recognition than the two England 'B' caps which went his way.

In some ways Quigley was ahead of his time, a deep-lying, deep-thinking marksman blessed with subtle passing skills, the type of operator destined to become fashionable in the mid-1950s, when his playing days were drawing to a close.

He began his career in 1941 with his home-town club, Bury, as a full-back but his destiny became clear one day at Millwall when, switched to centre-forward because of an injury crisis, he scored five goals. Thereafter Quigley remained in the front line – either as spearhead or, more often, as an inside-forward – and soon caught the eye of more fashionable clubs. In October 1947 he joined Sheffield Wednesday for £12,000, going on to score freely for two years, but it was his next move which catapulted Quigley into the headlines. When he switched to Preston North End in December 1949, the fee was £26,500, a British transfer record.

The idea was that he would forge a stylish partnership with the marvellous Tom Finney but, in a footballing sense, the two never gelled. Thus, after helping Preston to lift the Second Division title in 1951, he moved on again, this time to Blackburn Rovers – his fourth Division Two club – for £20,000.

At Ewood Park, Quigley hit prime form, flourishing especially under the attacking regime of manager Johnny Carey, and netting 95 times in 166 senior outings before returning to Bury for his last campaign, as a 35-year-old in 1956.

Always a serious student of the game, Quigley appeared ideal management material and duly he spent six years learning his trade with non-League Mossley. Then, in 1962, he returned to Football League ranks as Bury's youth coach and chief scout, unearthing such talents as Colin Bell and Alec Lindsay, both of whom would go on to play for England.

Quigley's first berth as a boss was at Stockport, where he moved in April 1966, remaining at Edgeley Park for six months during which he did much of the spadework towards County's Fourth Division title triumph of 1966/67. However, by the time the trophy was presented, he had departed to Blackburn, where he became chief coach and assistant manager to Jack Mansell, who was soon to resign.

After a brief spell as caretaker, during which Rovers narrowly missed promotion to the First Division, Quigley was confirmed as fully-fledged boss in April 1967. He had earned a reputation as a shrewd tactician and much was expected of him, but the next two terms proved frustrating, with promising starts followed by springtime fade-outs.

Come 1970, with the team struggling, Quigley swapped jobs with general manager Carey. True, he had responsibility for scouting and the youth system but he was never happy in a mainly administrative role, preferring the day-to-day involvement with the senior side. At the end of 1970/71, against a background of severe financial constraint, Blackburn were relegated to the Third Division for the first time in their history and both Carey and Quigley were sacked.

The latter, who had been criticised for being over-reliant on blackboard theory, returned to the fray as manager of Stockport in 1976 and derived enormous satisfaction when his comparatively humble charges knocked Blackburn out of the League Cup at Ewood Park. Sadly, a slump followed and he was sacked in 1977.

Quigley went on to scout for Blackburn, under Howard Kendall, and Blackpool before retiring in the early 1980s.

Edward Quigley: born Bury, Lancashire, 13 July 1921; played for Bury 1941-47, Sheffield Wednesday 1947-49, Preston North End 1949-51, Blackburn Rovers 1951-56, Bury 1956; managed Stockport County 1966 and 1976-77, Blackburn Rovers 1967-70; died Blackpool, 18 April 1997.

Peter Springett

A transfer deal that was surely unique and a telling role in one of the most astonishing upsets seen at Wembley stadium ensure goalkeeper Peter Springett's niche in English soccer folklore.

The ground-breaking transaction – believed to be the only one in which brothers moved in opposite directions – took place in May 1967 and involved Springett leaving Queen's Park Rangers for Sheffield Wednesday in exchange for £24,000 and his more famous sibling Ron, a fellow net-minder who had played 33 times for England. At the time, 21-year-old Peter was regarded as one of the most promising keepers in the land while Ron, ten years his senior, was approaching his career's end.

That spring the younger brother's stock was particularly high as he had just helped the Londoners to lift the Third Division title and, more sensationally, to come back from two goals down to defeat top-flight West Bromwich Albion in the first League Cup final to be held at Wembley.

With the score at 2-0 Springett made two crucial saves, thus enabling the underdogs, inspired by Rodney Marsh at his extravagant best, to net three times in the last 27 minutes and claim a romantic victory.

After joining the Loftus Road club as an apprentice in 1963, Springett enjoyed rapid progress, making his first-team debut that year and earning a regular place during 1965/66. The move to First Division Wednesday gave him a grander stage, but though he developed into an admirably steady performer and won England under-23 honours, he never managed the quantum leap to full international status.

However, as his contemporaries included such outstanding custodians as Gordon Banks, Peter Shilton and Ray Clemence that can hardly be classed as a failure.

Sadly for Springett, the Owls were on the decline in the late 1960s and were relegated in 1970. Over the three following seasons he lost his berth to Peter Grummitt but recovered it in 1973/74, only for Wednesday to plunge into the Third Division a year later. Thereafter he was freed to join Barnsley, whom he helped to gain promotion from the Fourth in 1978/79, before retiring in 1980 having played in nearly 600 senior matches.

On leaving the game, Springett joined the police, and for a time acted as a liaison officer between the South Yorkshire force and the fans of Sheffield United.

For the last four years he has battled an illness which had confined him to a wheelchair, though only weeks before his death he had declared his determination to walk again.

Peter John Springett: born Fulham, 8 May 1946; played for Queen's Park Rangers 1963-67, Sheffield Wednesday 1967-75, Barnsley 1975-80; died Sheffield, 28 September 1997.

Ray Daniel

Ray Daniel was a footballing thoroughbred and proud of it.

A bulwark of the Welsh game during the 1950s, the most glorious decade of its history, he was one of the original ball-playing centre-halves in an era when brawn tended to outstrip finesse as a defender's chief requirement.

Indeed, he boasted the delicate touch of an inside-forward and, as an extremely self-confident, intensely sociable fellow, there was little he liked better than to demonstrate his dexterity to an admiring audience. A favourite trick was to drop a half-crown coin on to his left foot, flick it to his right, then on to thigh and shoulder before depositing it bewilderingly into his top pocket. Daniel rose to soccer prominence during the early 1940s in Swansea, stepping off a remarkable conveyor-belt of talent which was to include Trevor Ford, John and Mel Charles, Ivor and Len Allchurch, Cliff Jones and Terry Medwin.

Only 15 when he made his first-team debut for the Swans as a full-back in wartime competition, he exhibited such enormous potential that he was snapped up by mighty Arsenal while still an amateur in 1946.

Two months after arriving at Highbury – following in the footsteps of his brother, Bobby, who was killed in the war – Daniel turned professional, but although a starry future was predicted, the young Welshman was to serve a lengthy apprenticeship in the shadow of the influential Les Compton. That did nothing to harm his international prospects, however. He won the first of his 21 full caps against England at Roker Park in 1950 and was called to his country's colours three times while still an Arsenal reserve.

It was not until 1951/52 that he secured a regular club berth, finishing that landmark campaign at Wembley, where the north Londoners lost the FA Cup final to a late goal by Newcastle United. However, though the Magpies took the silverware, the glory went to the Gunners, who battled bravely with ten men for most of the match after losing Walley Barnes to injury. Daniel earned a special mention in dispatches for playing in constant pain, his forearm encased in plaster as a legacy of an accident in a game at Blackpool three weeks earlier.

The disappointment of that defeat was swept away in the most emphatic manner as Arsenal lifted the League championship in 1952/53 with Daniel, now at his imperious peak, missing only one match and excelling in a formidable half-back trio alongside Alex Forbes and skipper Joe Mercer.

Playing glorious football, combining creativity with the solidity which might be expected of a powerful six-footer, he was described as a Welsh equivalent of Neil Franklin, arguably the finest central defender England ever had. Firmly established at Highbury, he seemed likely to consolidate his role as an Arsenal stalwart for the remainder of the decade, but a disagreement over playing styles contributed to a surprise switch. Sunderland, then ensconced in the top fllght and known as the 'Bank of England club', were in the process of assembling a star-studded side and Daniel was persuaded to join his friend and fellow Welsh international, Trevor Ford, on Wearside.

After the £27,500 move – a record for a defender at that time – Daniel gave some of his most polished displays, helping to achieve fourth place in the First Division in 1954/55. But in the long term the so-called team of all the talents never gelled, results were frustratingly poor and when manager Bill Murray experimented with the Welshman at centre-forward it was to little avail.

Matters worsened in 1957 when the club became embroiled in controversy over illegal payments to footballers, several of whom, including Daniel, were briefly suspended.

That year proved a watershed in his career. He lost his place in the Wales team to Mel Charles – thus missing out on the rousing progress to the World Cup quarter-finals the following summer – and he was transferred to Second Division Cardiff City for £7,000. Within a few months he had returned to his first love, Swansea Town, before slipping out of the Football League to join Hereford United. Daniel spent seven years at Edgar Street in the relatively undemanding arena of the Southern League, including a stint as player-boss, before leaving the game in 1967.

Thereafter he worked successively as a publican in Swansea, as a regional manager for the Courvoisier brandy company and as a sub-postmaster in Cockett, a village on the outskirts of his home town. Daniel will be remembered as one of the most gifted and charismatic of all Welsh players, if one whose prime might have lasted a little longer; and as a warm-hearted, wise-cracking fellow who lived his life to the full.

William Raymond Daniel: born Swansea, South Wales, 2 November 1928; played for Swansea Town 1943-46, Arsenal 1946-53, Sunderland 1953-57, Cardiff City 1957-58, Swansea Town 1958-59, Hereford United 1960-67; capped 21 times for Wales 1950-57; died Clevedon, Bristol, 6 November 1997.

David Smith

Reaching the fourth round of the FA Cup represents an improbable proposition for bosses of lower division football clubs. Indeed, to the majority of men in that harassing occupation, the prospect is little more than a fantasy. However, Dave Smith turned it into reality – and he did it twice.

By far the most memorable of the two glorious sequences was the first, in 1958, when his lowly Northampton Town side played host to Arsenal in the third round and overturned the mighty Gunners by three goals to one.

Boosted by a much-trumpeted concoction of sherry, eggs, glucose and orange juice, Smith's courageous Cobblers performed well above their Third Division South station to flummox their illustrious vistors, who included the world-class Welsh goalkeeper Jack Kelsey and the Scottish international marksman David Herd amongst their number. In the fourth round Northampton were ousted, but only after a plucky battle, by Liverpool.

Smith's second remarkable FA Cup run occurred in 1961, when he guided Fourth Division Aldershot to the competition's last 32, where Stoke City of the Second defeated them only after two replays. Those two peaks apart, the diminutive north-easterner's career was of the worthy variety. As a 20-year-old right-winger he had once harboured hopes of success with his local club, Newcastle United, but was released to join non-League South Shields after only one senior appearance.

During the Second World War, he guested for Derby County and Glasgow Rangers before joining Northampton, for whom he scored 30 goals in 128 League matches in the five seasons after the conflict. He coached a little, then became club secretary in 1951, taking over as manager three years later.

In 1959, after five terms spent in mid-table, Smith switched to Aldershot as secretary-boss, remaining in charge of team affairs – best finish seventh in Division Four – until 1967. Four more seasons were spent as secretary-general manager until his dismissal, and retirement from the professional game, in 1971.

David Smith: born South Shields, County Durham, 12 October 1915; played for Newcastle United 1935-36, Northampton Town 1943-50; secretary of Northampton Town 1951-54; managed Northampton Town 1954-59; secretary and manager/general manager of Aldershot 1959-71; died Derby, 26 November 1997.

Ian Moores

There was a time when big, blond and bewhiskered Ian Moores was being touted as an England centre-forward in the making. Indeed, while cutting a dash with his first professional club, Stoke City, in the mid-1970s, he made two international appearances at under-23 level. But somehow, having achieved a seemingly ideal career move to

Tottenham Hotspur, Moores faded disappointingly from the limelight, though he went on to labour worthily at a less rarefied plane.

Moores made his senior debut for the Potters, then a major force in the old First Division and one of the most entertaining sides in the land, in April 1974. The next season, though not a regular member of the team, he learned quickly from such immensely gifted colleagues as Jimmy Greenhoff and Alan Hudson, and played a telling part in the club's impressive League form. In fact, had the City squad been extensive enough to cope with an injury crisis of crippling proportions, the 20-year-old Moores might have been pocketing a championship medal.

As it was he was attracting attention from a host of leading clubs, and after he had played what was to prove the most compelling football of his life during the subsequent campaign, earning his international recognition in the process, he joined Spurs for £75,000 in August 1976.

Now came a period of golden opportunity for Moores and he began ideally with a goal in a stirring victory against Manchester United at Old Trafford. But although his aerial power was fearsome and sometimes he could apply a delicate touch that was surprising in such a strapping fellow, too often he appeared cumbersome and gauche.

Sadly but inevitably, especially with the north Londoners suffering relegation from the top flight at the end of his first term at White Hart Lane, the fans lost patience with him and his star began to fall.

There was one memorable day in the Second Division, when he contributed a hat-trick to Tottenham's 9-0 trouncing of Bristol Rovers, but such bounty was rare. Indeed, his overall tally was poor and he failed to hold his place as Spurs were promoted at the first attempt.

In October 1978, with hopes of full England honours long gone, Moores accepted a £55,000 switch to Second Division Orient (as Leyton Orient were called at the time), whom he served competently for four seasons, usually at centre-forward but occasionally in midfield.

Moores was released when the Brisbane Road club was demoted in 1982, going on to brief stints with Bolton Wanderers and Barnsley (on loan) and a spell with Apoel in Cyprus. Thereafter several non-League clubs and Landskrona Bols of Sweden afforded humble outlets for the talents of a man for whom expectations had once been so high.

Ian Richard Moores: born Chesterton, Staffordshire, 5 October 1954; played for Stoke City 1972-76, Tottenham Hotspur 1976-78, Orient 1978-82, Bolton Wanderers 1982-83, Barnsley on loan 1983; two England under-23 caps 1975; died Stoke-on-Trent, Staffordshire, January 1998.

Jack Marshall

Before a combination of Jack Walker's millions and the inspirational guidance of Kenny Dalglish brought fame and success to Blackburn Rovers in 1995, only one man since the war had given the homely football club from the Lancashire textile town the faintest whiff of championship glory.

His name was Jack Marshall and whereas those modern messiahs had untold financial resources at their disposal, three decades earlier the personable Lancastrian, known throughout the game as 'Jolly Jack', was forced to watch every penny as he led a make-do-and-mend side to the summit of England's premier league.

'Marshall's Misfits' sat proudly, albeit briefly, atop the old First Division on Boxing Day 1963, their presence on that lofty pinnacle a tribute to the manager who had constructed an attractive, attacking team, substantially from erstwhile unconsidered talents.

Sadly, it couldn't last and Rovers were overhauled subsequently by the big-city brigade from Liverpool and Manchester. The unavoidable springtime sale of star centre-forward Fred Pickering to Everton, one of Blackburn's chief rivals, proved the final nail in that season's title aspirations, a situation rendered all the more poignant because Pickering had been converted by Marshall from a plodding reserve full-back, the player's rise to prominence thus personifying his boss' shoestring shrewdness.

Thereafter, with seeming inevitability as the fortunes of most small-town clubs began to nosedive following the abolition of the players' maximum wage limit, Rovers declined during the remainder of Marshall's Ewood Park reign and an exhilarating period of their history was over.

Jack Marshall had entered professional football as a player at Burnley in 1936 and emerged as a capable full-back before injury forced his premature retirement in 1948. He became a coach, serving Bury and Stoke City before joining Sheffield Wednesday in 1954 and assisting national boss Walter Winterbottom with the preparation of the England 'B' team.

In October 1958 Marshall stepped up to management, experiencing relegation from the Third Division with Rochdale in his first season, but performed impressively enough to take charge of top-flight Blackburn, a club riven by internal strife, in September 1960. He embarked on a sorely-needed team-rebuilding job with gusto, disregarding reputations and experimenting boldly while enjoying admirable support from classy stalwarts Ronnie Clayton and Bryan Douglas, with the result that Rovers became one of the most entertaining sides in the land.

However, the slide that followed the comparative euphoria of 1963/64 led to demotion in 1966 and Marshall's resignation in February 1967. Later that year he was appointed assistant boss of Sheffield Wednesday, shifting to the manager's seat in February 1968. He worked hard at Hillsborough but left after a disappointing 1968/69, later taking over at Bury for a brief spell before spending the decade leading up to his 1979 retirement back at Blackburn as club physiotherapist.

It was fitting that Marshall should finish his footballing days at Ewood Park. As Rovers fans with long memories will confirm, when 'the team that Jack built' crops up in conversation, it is not always the Walker version which is being discussed.

John Gilmore Marshall: born Bolton, Lancashire, 29 May 1917; played for Burnley 1936-48; managed Rochdale 1958-60, Blackburn Rovers 1960-67, Sheffield Wednesday 1968-69, Bury 1969; died Rotherham, 1 January 1998.

George Marks

Five thousand pounds would barely buy a day's labour from a top footballer today, yet in 1946 it was enough to make George Marks the world's most expensive goalkeeper.

Yet curiously in such record-breaking circumstances, his transfer from Arsenal to Blackburn Rovers came about because he was no longer wanted by the Gunners, his best years having been lost to the Second World War.

Indeed, Marks' entire soccer career was devastated by the conflict. Though he played only two League games for the north Londoners – whom he had joined from amateur side Salisbury Corinthians in 1936 – he finished season 1938/39 as their first-choice keeper, then went on to help them win the Football League South Cup in 1942/43. Most notably, though, he highlighted his potential by representing England in eight wartime internationals between 1941 and 1943. Official caps were not awarded for these matches, availability of players being something of a lottery at the time, yet the Wiltshireman's selection for his country alongside the likes of Stanley Matthews and Tommy Lawton reflected the immense regard in which he was held and proved that he was one of the most accomplished net-minders of his era.

However, Marks, who had served with the RAF during the war, lost his Highbury place to George Swindin in January 1946 after failing to gain leave to play in an FA Cup tie.

Seven months later came the move to Blackburn, for whom he played magnificently for half a season before suffering a severe jaw injury in December. Thereafter a combination of fluctuating form and the fact that he lived and trained in his native West Country combined to bring about a transfer to Bristol City in August 1948.

Two months later Marks, by now 33, signed for Reading, whom he served nobly in the old Third Division South until 1953. There followed two years as a trainer-coach at Elm Park before he left the professional game, no doubt wondering what might have been had the war not coincided with his footballing pomp.

Marks, a delightfully modest fellow, spent the remainder of his working life as a local government officer in his native Wiltshire.

William George Marks: born Figheldean, near Salisbury, Wiltshire, 9 April 1915; played for Arsenal 1936-46, Blackburn Rovers 1946-48, Bristol City 1948, Reading 1948-53; died Salisbury, Wiltshire, 22 January 1998.

Robbie James

Robbie James gave his life to Welsh football. He played 47 times for his country, always displaying the passionate fervour demanded of every man who dons the red shirt, but arguably it was for his immense achievements at club level that he made the most vivid impression. James played an integral part in Swansea City's prodigious feat in sweeping from the Football League's basement division to its top flight in the space of four years.

Then, having earned his place among the elite, he did not flounder as some lower-League performers do following such a meteoric rise. Indeed, he excelled, not missing a game during the 1981/82 campaign in which the Swans finished sixth in the table, the most exalted position in their history. In addition, he was top scorer with 14 goals, no mean attainment in a side containing fellow Welsh luminary Leighton James and the prolific English marksman Bob Latchford.

Though it was clear from childhood that he was a talented footballer, Robbie James did not plunge straight into the professional game on leaving school, instead taking a job with an electrical firm. However, in March 1973, after attracting interest from both Cardiff City and Arsenal, he signed as an amateur for his local club, Swansea.

Under the shrewd guidance of manager Harry Gregg, the former Manchester United goalkeeper and survivor of the Munich air crash, the solidly-built James made such rapid progress that he was given his senior debut only two months later, aged only 16, on the day City slipped from the Third to the Fourth Division.

Thereafter he became a Swansea stalwart, enormously strong and combative, but also skilful and versatile enough to perform in either midfield or the front line.

The Swans' astonishing sequence of promotions, all during the managerial reign of John Toshack, began in 1977/78, the season in which James made his full international debut in a 7-0 victory over Malta at Wrexham. The rise continued in 1978/79 and 1980/81, but sadly the golden peak of 1981/82 was followed by relegation a year later.

At this point, having helped Swansea to three consecutive Welsh Cup triumphs, James opted to remain in the top grade by accepting a £160,000 transfer to Stoke City. Somehow he never did himself justice in the Potteries, but spent three more productive First Division campaigns with Queen's Park Rangers before dropping to the Second with Leicester City in 1987. At Filbert Street James became a right-back, helping in the development of a young defence before returning to Swansea as captain in January 1988. That spring proved eventful as he won his last Wales cap on his 31st birthday, then led his new charges to promotion from the Fourth Division.

James pocketed another Welsh Cup winner's medal in 1989, before serving Bradford City for two seasons and joining Cardiff City in 1992. Still as enthusiastic as ever at the age of 36, he took a prominent role in the Bluebirds' Division Three title triumph of 1992/93 and collected his fifth and final Welsh Cup gong. When his League career ended later that year, he had made 782 appearances, a total bettered by only a handful of others, and scored 133 goals.

James went on to serve non-League Merthyr Tydfil and Barry Town, and was player-manager of Llanelli when he collapsed and died during a match with Porthcawl. To the very last he played the game the only way he knew how, with every ounce of his being.

Robert Mark James: born Gorseinon, near Swansea, 23 March 1957; played for Swansea City 1973-83, Stoke City 1983-84, Queen's Park Rangers 1984-87, Leicester City 1987-88, Swansea City 1988-90, Bradford City 1990-92, Cardiff City 1992-93; capped 47 times for Wales 1978-88; died Llanelli, Glamorgan, 18 February 1998.

George Male

By common consent in the 1930s, George Male was the best right-back in England, some said the finest in the world; and to the majority of British football fans in an era before the expertise of overseas players had impinged on the national consciousness, it amounted to the same thing anyway.

The last surviving regular member of Arsenal's imperious pre-war team, which lifted four League titles and the FA Cup in the space of six seasons, he captained both club and country and was renowned for his sportsmanship and modesty, even in an era when such qualities were not in short supply.

Male's name will be linked forever to that of Eddie Hapgood, his full-back partner at Highbury and another man to skipper the Gunners and England. Like so many famous sporting pairs, they offered a sharp contrast both in character and the way they went about their business. Where Male was unassuming and calm, favouring a simple, solid, archetypally hard but fair style of play, the more ambitious Hapgood was a volatile extrovert, all elegant poise and smooth technique. They complemented each other ideally.

George Male was born in West Ham and represented the Hammers at schoolboy level before taking a job in insurance and playing his football for a local amateur team, Clapton of the Isthmian League. However, his potential was spotted by Arsenal and he signed amateur forms for the north Londoners in November 1929, turning professional six months later.

His progress was rapid and in December 1930 he made his senior debut, at left-half, in a swingeing 7-1 home victory over Blackpool. That season was to end with the Gunners winning the League championship for the first time in their history, and although Male made insufficient appearances to qualify for a medal, he was soon to make up for it with a vengeance.

First, though, would come disappointment when an injury-induced team reshuffle secured him a place at Wembley for the 1932 FA Cup final, only for Newcastle United to triumph thanks to a famously controversial goal.

Next came a crucial crossroads in the Male career. Hitherto the solidly-built Eastender had been a competent but hardly outstanding wing-half, a fact recognised by his manager, the inspirational but often intimidating Herbert Chapman. At the outset of the 1932/33 campaign, Arsenal had a problem at right-back and the great man summoned Male to his presence, announcing portentously: 'George, you are going to be a right-back.' Then, without awaiting a reply, he proceeded to work on the modest 22-year-old's self-esteem.

Many years later Male recalled: 'By the time I got out of that room, I wasn't merely convinced that I was a full-blown right-back, I knew without doubt that I was the best right-back in the country!' It was a typical example of Chapman's mesmeric power over his players, illustrating a key constituent in the benevolently despotic personality of one of the most successful soccer bosses the game has known. In this case, Chapman's wisdom in decreeing a change of position was evident immediately. Male settled into his new role as if born to it and within a few months had been called up for an international trial.

Come 1933/34, arguably the finest English club side of the first half of the 20th century was approaching its prime. That term Male didn't miss a match as Arsenal, employing the then-innovative 'stopper' defensive method and with bounteously gifted forwards such as Alex James and Cliff Bastin a joy to behold, won the first of three successive titles. In 1936, they lifted the FA Cup, with Male performing majestically in the 1-0 final victory over Sheffield United, and two years later took yet another championship.

On the international front, Male had received his first cap in 1934, one of seven Gunners involved in the so-called 'Battle of Highbury', in which England defeated World Cup holders Italy by three goals to two. The match was for the unofficial championship of the world because, at that time, England didn't deign to enter the tournament, instead allowing the foreigners to fight it out amongst themselves before challenging the winners. In the event it was a brutally physical affair and a supremely trying baptism for Male, but one from which he emerged with credit for his characteristic coolness under extreme provocation.

Thereafter he played a further 18 times for his country, including a spell as captain towards the end of the decade, and but for the Second World War, which began when Male was 29 and at his peak, it is likely that his caps total would have been considerably higher.

After the conflict, during which he had served with the RAF in Palestine, Male returned to first-team duty and although he managed only intermittent outings, having reached a grand old age in footballing terms, his eight games in 1947/48 made him the first man to figure in six title-winning campaigns. When he finished, in an 8-0 trouncing of Grimsby Town that May, he had represented the Gunners in 314 senior matches (without scoring a goal), in addition to 181 games for the club in wartime competition.

Reaching the end of his playing career did not signal Male's departure from Highbury, however. He became a coach, guiding first the juniors and then the reserves, a firm but kindly and avuncular figure who rejoiced in the affection of his young charges. After that he earned further respect as a shrewd talent-spotter – 1970s star Charlie George was his best-known discovery – and he went on to serve Arsenal in various administrative roles. He retired in 1975, living in Yorkshire, then joining his son in Canada.

The last of Chapman's magnificent side to stop playing, and the last to die, George Male was never the most feted of Gunners, but he was one of the worthiest.

Charles George Male: born West Ham, London, 8 May 1910; played for Arsenal 1929-48; capped 19 times for England 1934-39; died Canada,19 February 1998.

Jimmy Hagan

Jimmy Hagan was a most singular football man, quiet yet controversial, and one of the most unsung achievers of his era. As a player he exhibited ball skills which bordered on the magical yet he played only once for England in a full international. As a manager he knew startling success, most notably with the mighty Benfica of Portugal, but he upset many of his charges through his stern disciplinary approach and was less feted than numerous contemporaries with comparatively modest records.

North-easterner Hagan was born into a footballing family, his father Alf having played for Newcastle, Cardiff and Tranmere after the First World War, and from his early days both his love of the game and his fiercely independent character became evident. Indeed, he gave up the chance to attend his local grammar school because football was not played there, and despite living between the soccer strongholds of Newcastle and Sunderland he signed amateur forms with Liverpool, then Derby County, with whom he turned professional in 1935.

Hagan had won England honours at schoolboy level, excelling as a scheming inside-forward, so much was expected of him at the Baseball Ground. However, he could not agree with manager George Jobey and in November 1938 he was sold to Sheffield United for £2,500. At Bramall Lane he blossomed, his fluent distribution, magnetic control and shrewd positional play inspiring the Blades to clinch promotion to the top flight at the end of his first season. Then came the war, which devastated many soccer careers, but not Hagan's. So irresistible were his talents that he was picked for England in 16 wartime internationals, which did not qualify for full caps but emphasised his burgeoning stature as he performed brilliantly alongside stars such as Stanley Matthews, Tommy Lawton and Raich Carter.

After the conflict, during which he rose to the rank of major in the Army's Physical Training Corps, Hagan was unfortunate that the likes of Carter, Wilf Mannion and Len Shackleton provided white-hot competition for England inside-forward berths, but still it was surprising that he was limited to one outing, a goalless draw against Denmark in September 1948. Nevertheless he continued so majestically at club level that United were accused of being a one-man team, one photographer mocking up a picture of the Blades with 11 Jimmy Hagan heads, a stunt not of his doing but which rankled with some of his colleagues. Having collected a Second Division title medal with the club in 1953, as well as suffering demotion from the top flight in both 1949 and 1956, Hagan finished playing in 1958 to become manager of Peterborough United.

The Posh, a dominant power in the Midland League, had long deserved elevation to Football League ranks, and they made it under Hagan in 1960. The rookie boss led them to the Fourth Division title at their first attempt, as they notched a League record of 134 goals that still stands today. Creditable consolidation in the Third followed, but Hagan was sacked in October 1962 after a bitter dispute with players, a scenario which would be echoed later.

In April 1963 he took over at First Division West Bromwich Albion, declaring: 'I don't tolerate dodgers.' He adhered to old-style puritanical virtues which did not sit easily with a new breed of footballer, recently freed from the iniquitous strictures of the archaic maximum wage system, and turmoil was inevitable.

Soon the players, led by future England coach and Arsenal manager Don Howe, rebelled against what they claimed were boring training methods and a harsh, unapproachable attitude. It came to a head when ten of his squad refused to train without tracksuit bottoms on a freezing day and there was talk of a full-blown strike, though the situation was resolved. Meanwhile he was assembling an enterprising side which in 1965/66 finished sixth in the First Division and won the League Cup in a two-legged final against West Ham. However, after Albion lost the 1966/67 final to Third Division Queen's Park Rangers, the manager was dismissed.

One story, perhaps apocryphal, sums up his Hawthorns sojourn. It has Hagan driving away from the training ground when his foot slips from the brake pedal and his car plunges 80 feet down an embankment towards a canal. The players, torn by conflicting emotions, peer over the edge and find him relatively unscathed by the side of the water. They lift him into a hastily summoned ambulance, only for him to growl: 'You lot are puffing, you need extra training!'

There followed spells of working in a driving school and scouting for Manchester City before Hagan embarked on his greatest challenge. Benfica, one of the world's leading clubs, had hit a slump and wanted a tough English taskmaster and organiser to meld their artistic but frequently wayward talents into an effective unit. After being turned down by Sir Alf Ramsey, in March 1970 they astonished many observers by turning to Hagan. It seemed like a desperate measure; in fact, it was a stroke of inspiration. After provoking a minor revolution by his rigorous regime, he transformed the Eagles, leading them to title triumph in each of his three campaigns in Lisbon. Typically, he left following a dispute in 1973, going on to coach in Kuwait for two years before completing his career in Portugal. It is tempting to wonder what Jimmy Hagan might have achieved had he been placed in charge of one of the giants of the English game. Egos would have been dented, for sure, but on the evidence of his record elsewhere, the trophy cabinet would not have remained empty.

James Hagan: born Washington, County Durham, 21 January 1918; played for Derby County 1935-38, Sheffield United 1938-58; capped once by England 1948; managed Peterborough United 1958-62, West Bromwich Albion 1963-67, Benfica 1970-73, Sporting Lisbon 1976, Oporto 1976-77; died Sheffield, 26 February 1998.

Peter Sillett

Peter Sillett was one of those rare individuals, a Chelsea footballer with a League championship medal. The Blues have won the domestic game's highest honour only once, in 1954/55, and the tall, burly defender was a stalwart member of that mould-breaking side. Indeed, it was Sillett who struck the blow which determined the destination of the trophy, if not mathematically then certainly in the hearts and minds of the Stamford Bridge faithful. With only a handful of matches remaining, Chelsea were at home to their chief rivals, Wolverhampton Wanderers, needing victory to establish what seemed sure to be decisive ascendancy in the title race. Some 15 minutes from the end, with the scoresheet still blank, the hosts were awarded a penalty and, in front of more than 75,000 spellbound fans, right-back Sillett strode forward to take it. Outwardly calm but, as he revealed later, seething with apprehension, he hammered the ball low past England goalkeeper Bert Williams before being submerged by ecstatic team-mates. Chelsea, for so long the subject of music-hall derision, were champions elect.

A month later, Sillett was involved in another high-profile penalty incident which ended less happily. Having been called up for his international debut against France in Paris, he conceded the spot-kick which resulted in the only goal of the game. Apart from that one aberration, however, he played well enough in a side containing the likes of Stanley Matthews, Billy Wright and Duncan Edwards to retain his place for the remaining two matches of England's spring tour, against Spain and Portugal.

Thereafter, he slipped from the international reckoning, his movement a little too ponderous for that exalted level, though other aspects of his game were outstanding. Sillett was a cultured distributor of the ball, his positional play was astute and he was utterly imperturbable under fire, but it was as one of the most explosively powerful dead-ball kickers of his era that he earned most renown. Indeed, he was a menace anywhere within 40 yards of the opponents' goal and was the author of some of the most spectacular strikes ever seen at Stamford Bridge.

Sillett hailed from a footballing family. His father, Charlie, had captained their home-town club, Southampton, before being killed in the war, and his ebullient younger brother, John, was to join him at Chelsea, then win fame for guiding Coventry City to FA Cup victory in 1987. Sillett's own career began with the Saints in 1950. Then, after performing creditably in a poor team which was relegated from the old Second Division in 1952/53, the richly promising 20-year-old was transferred to Chelsea for £12,000.

Duly he cemented a berth in manager Ted Drake's enterprising side – colleagues included star centre-forward Roy Bentley and future England manager Ron Greenwood – and played his sterling part in the subsequent championship glory. The Blues did not build on their success of 1955, becoming increasingly unpredictable as the decade wore on and Sillett, an easy-going fellow adept at wicked deadpan humour, matured into elder statesman and skipper of the youthful combination known as Drake's Ducklings. Had it not been for the prodigious goal-scoring exploits of Jimmy Greaves, they might have been relegated in 1959/60 but they managed to retain their status until 1961/62, when new manager Tommy Docherty was unable to prevent demotion.

By this point Sillett's top-flight career had been effectively finished by a broken leg suffered in August 1961 and although he had recovered by season's end he was unable to oust gifted rookie Ken Shellito. There being no place for him in the Docherty set-up, and feeling that his leg was not strong enough to warrant accepting offers from other Football League clubs, he left Chelsea to embark on a lengthy non-League career, at first operating as a player-coach and later solely as a manager.

Among his employers were Guildford City, Ashford Town, Folkestone Town, Hastings United and Hastings Town and he became a well-loved fixture on the semi-professional scene. Between 1987 and 1990 he scouted for his brother at Coventry, but it is as a Stamford Bridge bulwark of the 1950s that Peter Sillett will be best remembered.

Richard Peter Sillett: born Southampton, Hampshire, 1 February 1933; played for Southampton 1950-53, Chelsea 1953-62; capped three times for England 1955; died Ashford, Kent, 13 March 1998.

Jimmy Scoular

Jimmy Scoular was a footballing volcano, and certainly not of the dormant variety. A fearsomely combative Scot from a flinty mining upbringing, he tackled like a runaway coal wagon and was prone to explosive eruptions of fury, yet he possessed precise passing skills which could change the course of a game.

It was said of him that he played sometimes as if he hated everyone on the field, demolishing opponents, bawling-out team-mates and confronting referees, but it wasn't true. He was a decent man with a tremendous sense of humour, and there was no hate in him. It was just that he was obsessed with the game and, more particularly, the winning of it.

There are those who reckon that, barring his abrasive temperament, the small but enormously muscular right-half would have won many more honours, but the counter-argument is that without that irrepressible fire he would have been but a pale shadow of 'Scoular the Scourge'.

As it was, he didn't do badly, picking up two League championship medals with Portsmouth, leading Newcastle United to FA Cup glory and earning nine international caps. Most importantly, perhaps, he was utterly honest, truly formidable as a foe but unshakeable as a friend.

It had always seemed likely that Scoular would follow his father, Alec – who played for Alloa Athletic, Stenhousemuir and Leith Athletic before the Second World War – into the professional game. However, the conflict diverted his energies and it was during his service as a submarine engineer on HMS *Dolphin* at Gosport, Hampshire, that he was spotted in Royal Navy football by Portsmouth, then a major soccer power.

He signed in 1945 and lost little time in winning a regular berth in the Fratton Park team, forming a vividly contrasting wing-half partnership with the placid, gentlemanly Englishman, Jimmy Dickinson. Together the two men provided the solid midfield platform on which was built Pompey's consecutive title triumphs of 1949 and 1950, an immense achievement in the face of stern opposition from the likes of Matt Busby's Manchester United and Stan Cullis' Wolves.

However, despite his inspirational play, Scoular frequently fell foul of the authorities, and his absence through suspension from the last two games of the 1949/50 campaign (following a sending-off, which was relatively uncommon in that era) provoked much controversy and personal criticism.

Come 1952/53, with the side struggling, Scoular was dropped briefly and asked to leave. Though he was restored almost at once, he was granted his wish in the summer, and while the ostensible reason for his £22,250 move to Newcastle United was that transfer request, the feeling persisted that his lurid image did not suit the Pompey management.

The south-coast club's loss proved to be the north-easterners' gain, as Scoular was installed as the Magpies' skipper, driving his colleagues relentlessly and setting a rousing personal example. Though League form was disappointing for a club with such lofty aspirations, there was compensation in the FA Cup final defeat of Manchester City in 1955.

That day at Wembley saw Scoular at his most irresistible, neutralising the much-vaunted threat of deep-lying centre-forward Don Revie through his ruthless marking and providing the springboard for victory with a stream of raking crossfield passes to left-winger Bobby Mitchell.

Man-of-the-match awards were not in vogue at the time, but had there been one it must have gone to the Geordies' motivator supreme. The City fans had barracked him, as did most opposition supporters, but he claimed such treatment merely spurred him to greater efforts, and so it seemed. As for Newcastle followers, they had abhorred him as a dirty so-and-so during his Portsmouth days, but now they described him as 'robust but fair', which might have been a tad euphemistic but, nevertheless, was pretty much the truth. Thereafter Scoular remained a cornerstone of United's team for the rest of the decade, not departing until he was 36 in January 1961, when he joined Fourth Division Bradford Park Avenue as player-manager for a nominal £1,500. Only four months later he tasted success, leading his new charges to promotion to the Third but sadly, after one season of apparent consolidation, they returned to the basement in 1963.

Scoular continued to play into his fortieth year, laying aside his boots in February 1964, three months before his Yorkshire sojourn terminated with the sack. His sterling efforts on slender resources had not gone unnoticed, however, and in June he was appointed as boss of Second Division Cardiff City.

A traumatic start at Ninian Park, involving an initial run of 12 games without a win, was followed by recovery to finish the season in mid-table, but consecutive narrow escapes from demotion followed before Scoular's energetic regeneration work bore fruit. As frequent winners of the Welsh Cup (seven times under Scoular), Cardiff were accustomed to qualification for the European Cup Winners' Cup, and in 1967/68 they reached the semi-finals, where they lost 4-3 on aggregate to SV Hamburg. That stands as the highlight of the Scoular reign, though he built an enterprising side which came close to promotion in 1970/71.

However, they fell away dramatically over the two subsequent terms, culminating in the manager's dismissal in November 1973. After that he scouted for Aston Villa and Wolves, managed Fourth Division Newport County for a year, then scouted again, now for Swansea City and Newcastle. Outside the game, he worked as a representative for a chemical firm and ran a guest house in Cardiff before retiring to live near the city.

In his final years Jimmy Scoular was severely incapacitated by illness, a poignant end to a vibrantly active life.

James Scoular: born Livingston Station, West Lothian, 11 January 1925; played for Portsmouth 1945-53, Newcastle United 1953-61, Bradford Park Avenue 1961-64; capped nine times by Scotland 1951-52; managed Bradford Park Avenue 1961-64, Cardiff City 1964-73, Newport County 1976-77; died Cardiff, 19 March 1998.

Justin Fashanu

For individuals a little different from the crowd, professional football can be a cruelly insular world, and while sensitivity does exist in the macho environment of dressing room, practice pitch and bar, often it is well advised to keep its head down. Justin Fashanu was very different: he was gay and he admitted it, a combination which, it seemed, many people within our national game could not cope.

The son of a Nigerian barrister, he had been abandoned as a baby, then dispatched to a Barnardo's home before being rescued by middle-class foster parents in Norfolk and growing up to be intelligent, articulate and a fellow of persuasive charm.

Tall, strong and blessed with delicate skills for a man of his size, he was a centre-forward who played for England Youth, then signed for Norwich City in 1978. He progressed quickly to the Canaries' senior side – then in the old First Division, the equivalent of today's Premiership – and represented his country 11 times at under-21 level.

But the incident which catapulted Fashanu to sporting fame occurred in February 1980 when, in a televised match against Liverpool, he scored an utterly sensational goal, a curling, rising drive from far outside the penalty box. From that moment he lived his life in the public spotlight and, six months later, he became the first black player to cost £1 million when Brian Clough bought him for Nottingham Forest. At the time, Fashanu was in a 'straight' relationship but he had not been in Nottingham for long when his outlook was transformed, first by Christianity, then by the city's gay scene to which he found himself drawn irresistibly. His form for Forest, then one of the leading clubs in the land, was bitterly disappointing and when Clough discovered his new signing's sexual leanings, he suspended him. Fashanu wasn't having that and turned up for training, only for his manager to have him escorted publicly from the premises by the police.

Clearly his future lay away from the City Ground and, after much heartache, in 1982 he joined Notts County, then also in the top division and managed by Howard Wilkinson. For a while at Meadow Lane his career got back on course, only for a knee wound to become poisoned, after which he was never quite as effective again.

Following a brief interlude with Brighton, and as gossip about his sexuality became common currency, Fashanu went to the United States, then Canada, where he hoped to continue his footballing life while running a gay bar. In 1989 he returned to England and after abortive attempts to resurrect his professional fortunes with several clubs, and feeling sickened by the prejudice he encountered constantly, he 'came out' in 1990. In fact, the decision only increased the pressure on Fashanu, who became the subject of ever more frequent and lurid publicity, and there were stories of a rift with his brother John, who had risen to eminence with Wimbledon and England.

Courageously, he refused to give up on football, joining Newcastle United fleetingly but without making a senior appearance, doing well in a stint with Torquay United, then serving Airdieonians and Hearts in Scotland. More recently he had been living and coaching in Maryland, USA, where he was being hunted by police last week after being charged with sexually assaulting a teenage boy. He was found dead in a lock-up garage in Shoreditch, east London, on Saturday. He had apparently hanged himself.

Justinus Soni Fashanu: born Hackney, London, 19 February 1961; played for Norwich City 1978-81, Nottingham Forest 1981-82, Southampton on loan 1982, Notts County 1982-85, Brighton and Hove Albion 1985, Manchester City 1989, West Ham United 1989, Leyton Orient 1990, Torquay United 1991-93, Airdrieonians 1993, Heart of Midlothian 1993; died London, 2 May 1998.

Gottfried Dienst

It was the most controversial goal in football history, yet Gottfried Dienst, the Swiss referee who allowed it to stand, admitted afterwards that he didn't know whether the ball went in or not. The scene was Wembley, the occasion the 1966 World Cup final between England and West Germany. Ten minutes into extra-time with the scores level at two-apiece, Alf Ramsey's men were on the attack. Nobby Stiles passed to Alan Ball on the right flank, and the dynamic little redhead cut the ball back to Geoff Hurst, who was about ten yards out from the near post. He collected the ball cleanly, then swivelled and hit a ferocious shot which cannoned against the crossbar and bounced to the ground before being headed clear by Wolfgang Weber. By then the England players, certain that the ball had crossed the line, embraced ecstatically while the dismayed Germans, equally adamant that it hadn't, protested vehemently to the referee. Dienst, a calm and dignified figure, consulted his Russian linesman – Tofik Bakhramov, who died in 1993 – and after an agony of waiting in which the stadium fell unnaturally quiet, he allowed the goal. England went on to win 4-2 when Hurst completed his hat-trick at the end, but it was that dramatic third goal which truly demoralised the weary Germans.

Should it have stood? Roger Hunt, who was closest to the incident, was unequivocal: 'I was about six yards out when the ball hit the turf and I turned instantly to celebrate. I believed at the time that it was over the line and I believe it now (1998). If there had been the slightest shred of doubt in my mind I would have followed up to make sure.'

But Dienst himself, when interviewed in 1989, was honest enough to admit: 'I still don't know if the shot by Hurst in the 100th minute was in or not. I have to say that I was standing in a poor position for that shot, exactly head-on instead of diagonal to the goal. I wouldn't have allowed the goal if linesman Bakhramov hadn't pointed to the middle with his flag.' Exhaustive television replays and countless photographs proved inconclusive in settling the argument, though British soccer historian Philip Evans wrote in 1990: 'We can now say that it probably was not a goal. But to establish that fact, it took a lot of people many hours of very hard work in cinema laboratories all over the world.'

Dienst never hid from the issue, revealing that strangers still asked him daily about the decision more than two decades later. 'I gladly respond,' he said.

Actually, of course, it was a goal. Just look in the record books . . .

Cris Freddi added: Ivan Ponting's obituary of Gottfried Dienst concentrated, not surprisingly, on the ball-over-the-line goal in the World Cup final – but there was much more to his career, including an uncannily similar incident five years earlier.

In the 1961 European Cup final, when Dienst was the referee, Benfica had just drawn level with the hot favourites Barcelona when a misplaced defensive header drifted back towards Barcelona's goalkeeper and captain Antonio Ramallets.

Apparently dazzled by the sun, he could only push the ball against his crossbar, whence it bounced along the goal line. Dienst awarded the goal, Barcelona lost the match and had to wait another 31 years to win the European Cup for the first time.

In 1965 Dienst achieved the unique feat of refereeing two European finals in the same year; the European Cup again and the Fairs Cup (later the UEFA Cup).

He also took charge of the 1968 European Championship final between Italy and Yugoslavia and refereed five matches in World Cup tournaments, including one of the semi-finals in 1962. Prominent though he was, the Germans of 1966 knew what they'd like to have done with him. One of their publications misspelt his name: Goodfried!

Gottfried Dienst: born 9 September 1919; died Basle, Switzerland, 1 June 1998.

Keith Newton

Keith Newton was a distinguished, if somewhat underrated component of one of England's finest international football teams. Indeed, there is no shortage of shrewd contemporary observers who would place the side which he graced as a stylish full-back, and which was eliminated so dramatically by West Germany from the 1970 World Cup, ahead of the more famous combination which had lifted the Jules Rimet trophy four years earlier.

In defensive mode, the tall, sparely-built Mancunian was a study in quiet efficiency, an expert tackler, effective in the air and adept at intelligent interceptions, but it was his capacity for attack which illustrated his quality most vividly. At his peak he was renowned as a raiding overlapper, virtually doubling as a winger at a time when those entertaining worthies were sadly out of fashion, and no one deployed him more effectively than England manager Sir Alf Ramsey.

Newton is best remembered for what might have been a decisive contribution on a fateful day in Leon, Mexico, in 1970, when England faced the Germans in a World Cup quarter-final. Galloping unstoppably down the right flank, he set up memorable goals for Alan Mullery and Martin Peters, putting his side into a seemingly unassailable position.

However, Gerd Muller and company fought back with astonishing resilience to score three times, thus dumping the holders out of the tournament. Though he was only 28 and playing for the reigning League champions, Everton, Newton was never to represent his country again. Instead he was supplanted by a succession of younger men as Ramsey planned for what proved to be a traumatic future, with England failing to qualify for the 1974 World Cup finals and the manager being sacked.

Keith Newton began his career with Blackburn Rovers, who had spotted him as a skilful but rather ungainly inside-forward in Manchester junior football. Soon after his arrival at Ewood Park he was converted into a centre-half, a role in which he excelled as he helped Rovers to win the FA Youth Cup in 1959. Clearly a professional future was beckoning for the talented youngster, but Blackburn already had a gifted rookie stopper in Mike England and when Newton made his senior debut in September 1960, in an old First Division encounter with Chelsea, it was at left-half. Thereafter he moved to left-back, where he established a regular place in 1961/62 before switching to the right flank in mid-decade and graduating to England's under-23 team in that position.

For several seasons Newton was an integral part of a vibrant team, in which Bryan Douglas, Ronnie Clayton and England were outstanding, and he was a major factor in an enterprising title challenge in 1963/64. But impetus was lost as the infinitely richer Manchester and Liverpool clubs gained in influence following the abolition of the maximum wage for footballers, and Rovers were relegated in 1966.

In the circumstances it seemed inevitable that the classy Newton would join a more fashionable club, especially as he had stepped up to full international status, winning the first of his 27 caps against West Germany at Wembley in the February before that demoralising demotion. However, despite frequent rumours of a transfer – notably to Nottingham Forest – he soldiered on in the Second Division until December 1969, when he was sold to high-riding Everton for £80,000.

In that he helped his new employers to lift that season's League championship, despite missing the title run-in through injury, it proved an admirable career move. Also, it did nothing to harm his England prospects, the higher profile helping to cement his place for the 1970 World Cup tournament.

But the anticipated lengthy spell at Goodison never materialised, due mainly to a difference of opinion with manager Harry Catterick over his style of play. Newton was a cool, cultured performer who preferred passing his way out of difficult situations rather than employing the time-honoured safety-first method of hoofing the ball upfield. While Catterick was by no means a slave to the long-ball game and put a high value on technique, he felt that the full-back dwelt too long in possession on occasions, and something of a rift developed.

Possibly as a result, Newton's form became patchy, he found himself in and out of the team at a time when he should have been in his prime, and he was freed to join Burnley in June 1972. The Clarets were delighted with what they saw as a windfall and Newton justified their reaction by shining as they clinched the Second Division championship at the end of his first Turf Moor campaign. He went on to complete six years of sterling service for the club before retiring in 1978, not long before his 37th birthday.

Thereafter Newton, an unassuming fellow whom team-mates revered for his patience and affability, sampled the non-League scene with Morecambe and Clitheroe, whom he managed briefly. After leaving the game he worked in the motor trade in Blackburn.

Keith Robert Newton: born Manchester, 23 June 1941; played for Blackburn Rovers 1958-69, Everton 1969-72, Burnley 1972-78; capped 27 times by England 1966-70; died Blackburn, Lancashire, 16 June 1998.

Jack Rowley

Amid the adulation and hyperbole directed at the precociously talented current generation of Manchester United footballers, several of whom have been campaigning rousingly for England in France this summer, it is easy to underestimate the stature of Old Trafford heroes from another age. Of those, few were more substantial than Jack Rowley.

Indeed, only Sir Bobby Charlton has scored more League goals for the Red Devils than the bluntly-spoken Black Countryman, whose prolific post-war prime made him a bulwark of Sir Matt Busby's first outstanding side and an early *eminence grise* of his second, the famous and ill-fated Babes.

On the international front, Rowley was unfortunate that his most effective years coincided with those of other fine centre-forwards, the likes of Tommy Lawton, Stanley Mortensen and Jackie Milburn, and that the war shortened his service by six seasons. However, his tally of six goals in as many outings for his country hints tellingly at a vast potential.

Rowley was born into a footballing family, his father having been a goalkeeper with Walsall and his younger brother, Arthur, destined to become the highest scorer in English League history, a record which still stands.

The older boy exhibited tremendous promise and signed for his home-town club, Wolverhampton Wanderers, on leaving school. Such was the fierce competition at Molineux, though, that he didn't make the grade, failing to play a senior game for Wolves before leaving for Bournemouth of the former Third Division South in February 1937.

Predictably given Rowley's determined nature, that was to prove but a momentary blip. So impressively did he perform for the south-coast club that within eight months he was sold to Manchester United for £3,000 and an ultimately illustrious career was under way.

In fact Rowley, a left-winger at that stage, made a tentative start at Old Trafford, asking to be dropped after his debut and spending a few weeks in the reserves before returning to help his new employers gain promotion to the top flight in 1938. In the following season he developed encouragingly in the old First Division, only for his impetus to be halted abruptly by war.

Rowley served in the Army's South Staffordshire regiment and took part in the D-Day landings in Normandy, but still found time to further his soccer ambitions. He helped to win trophies as a high-scoring guest performer with both Wolves (for whom he netted eight times in one game) and Spurs (one seven-goal show was his best effort for them) and others. In addition, he won one unofficial wartime cap for England.

On the resumption of peace, with Busby newly installed as United boss, soon Rowley was converted into a centre-forward and he flourished apace. Though shortish for a spearhead at 5ft 9ins, he was solidly built and exuded aggression, he was extremely quick and was dangerous in the air. But it was his powerful shooting with either foot, especially his favoured left, which won him renown and his nickname of 'The Gunner'. He was intelligent, too, and blessed with efficient ball control, but these facets of his play tended to be overlooked in favour of his more spectacular virtues.

Between 1946/47 and 1950/51 Rowley was a leading light as Busby's side finished as title runners-up in four campaigns out of five. Come 1951/52, when United finally clinched the championship, he was top scorer with 30 goals, then a club record. But his best-remembered individual display came in 1948, when he scored twice in the 4-2 FA Cup final victory over Blackpool. In what was feted at the time as the most entertaining showpiece Wembley had hosted, he equalised twice after the Seasiders had led 1-0 and 2-1, and linked brilliantly with his attacking partners.

The United forward line of that era – comprising Jimmy Delaney and Charlie Mitten on the wings, Johnny Morris and Stan Pearson as inside-forwards and Rowley in the centre – was a joy to behold and fit to stand comparison with any of the starry combinations which have worn the red shirt since.

Rowley won his first full England recognition in the same year as his Wembley triumph, scoring on his debut against Switzerland, and plundering four against Northern Ireland 11 months later. However, his international career never really took off, a circumstance which might have had something to do with selectorial distaste for his combative, eye-for-an-eye approach, and a personality which was either down-to-earth or abrasive, depending on interpretation.

Whatever, Rowley continued to do well for his club, and became something of a father figure to many of the Busby Babes who emerged in the first half of the 1950s. As he approached his mid-thirties and his own position in the team was becoming precarious, he showed admirable care and patience to the bright young things who would supplant him. Eventually, in 1955, after reverting to outside-left for the closing period of his Old Trafford tenure, Rowley left United having scored 208 League and FA Cup goals in 422 games.

Keen for a future in management, he was freed to join Plymouth Argyle as player-boss, but his passionate advocacy of attacking football could not prevent their relegation to the basement division in 1956. After passing the milestone of 200 League goals on the same afternoon as his brother achieved the same feat – Arthur beat Jack by 12 minutes – Rowley retired as a player in 1957. Thereafter he presided over an upturn in Argyle fortunes which culminated in the Third Division title in 1959.

A year later he left Home Park after the Pilgrims had struggled in Division Two and went on to revamp an ailing Oldham Athletic, only for disagreement with the board to result in his resignation three days after leading the Latics to promotion from the Fourth. There followed a stint as coach of Ajax in Amsterdam and spells in charge of Wrexham, Bradford Park Avenue and Oldham before he left professional soccer in 1969, rather disillusioned by what he saw as negative modern methods and scornful of some of the 'prima donnas' then making their living from the game. He maintained his connections with grass-roots football, however, which he saw as possessing more realistic values.

Rowley became a newsagent and sub-postmaster in Shaw, near Oldham, then worked for a mail-order firm before retiring in 1983.

John Frederick Rowley: born Wolverhampton, 7 October 1920; played for Bournemouth 1937, Manchester United 1937-55, Plymouth Argyle 1955-57; capped 6 times by England 1948-52; managed Plymouth Argyle 1955-60, Oldham Athletic 1960-63, Ajax of Amsterdam as coach 1963-64, Wrexham 1966-67, Bradford Park Avenue 1967-68, Oldham Athletic 1968-69; died Shaw, near Oldham, Lancashire, 27 June 1998.

Jackie Blanchflower

Jackie Blanchflower was not quite 25 and approaching his footballing prime. Already he had been showered with bouquets as one of Manchester United's vibrantly successful Busby Babes and was firmly established as a Northern Ireland international. With the Red Devils seemingly poised for limitless conquests, the future beckoned alluringly for the versatile younger brother of Danny, the famous captain of Tottenham Hotspur.

But tragedy intervened. When United's plane crashed at Munich on the way home from a European tie in Belgrade in February 1958, eight players and 15 other passengers lost their lives; Blanchflower lost his livelihood and, for many years, his peace of mind.

After the accident on the snowy German runway he received the last rites, but he survived. However the hitherto vigorous young athlete was a physical wreck – he suffered a fractured pelvis, a complete set of broken arms and legs, shattered ribs and severe kidney damage – and even when the bodily devastation began gradually to be repaired, the mental scars remained vivid.

For three traumatic years he was consumed with bitterness, railing against his reversal of fortune and did precisely nothing. Even after that, as he tried to reshape his future outside football, there were more blows in store and only much later in life did the eloquent Irishman regain contentment, earning renown as an entertaining raconteur and drolly hilarious after-dinner speaker.

Jackie Blanchflower left his native Belfast to follow Danny over the Irish Sea as a precociously talented 16-year-old in 1949, when he signed on at Old Trafford. Skilful, intelligent and industrious, though a little short of pace, he made rapid strides through United's junior teams and made his senior debut at right-half in 1951. But it was as an inside-forward that he attained a regular place in 1953/54, the season in which he won his first full international cap. Emerging as both a creator and scorer of goals, he netted 24 times over two campaigns and was rewarded with a championship medal in 1955/56. However, following an accomplished defensive stint for his country and with increasingly brisk competition for inside-forward berths – the likes of Dennis Viollet, Liam Whelan, John Doherty and the exciting young Bobby Charlton were all in contention – Blanchflower was converted into a centre-half during 1956/57.

Thereafter he vied for the number-five shirt with Mark Jones, an immensely tough stopper in the traditional mould who contrasted nicely with the more subtle Irishman. In this new role Blanchflower played in the 1957 FA Cup final against Aston Villa, but spent most of the match as an emergency goalkeeper after regular custodian Ray Wood was injured, substitutes not being allowed in those days.

As a magnificent all-round sportsman, he surprised no one by excelling between the Wembley posts but was unable to prevent the two goals which stopped United becoming the first club this century to complete the League and FA Cup double.

Come the ill-fated expedition to Belgrade, Jones was back in the side and Blanchflower travelled merely as a reserve, being declared fit to do so only at the last moment. Clearly, though, there was no doubt that he remained an integral part of Matt Busby's ambitious long-term plans.

At first, after Munich, there were hopes that he would recover well enough to resume his career and he remained on United's books until June 1959. But the injuries proved insuperable and the devastated Ulsterman faced a grim outlook.

Understandably enough he felt the world was against him as a succession of occupations, all in the Manchester area, brought frustration. He ran a sweetshop – and a supermarket opened around the corner; he did a stint with a bookmaker – and horse-racing was so hard hit by cruel winter weather that he lost the job; he took a pub – and two weeks later the breathalyser was introduced; then he became a printer only to be made redundant in 1976. After that he studied to become an accountant but that brought no change of luck as positions as finance officer for a youth association and as a company accountant ended in lay-off.

Happily a turning point was to arrive, courtesy of his wife, Jean. During the 1950s she had been a successful club vocalist with the Vic Lewis Big Band and three decades later she took to performing again. Blanchflower, who had been blessed with liberal quantities of self-deprecating charm, began introducing her to audiences before her shows and found that both he and the punters enjoyed his unrehearsed patter.

As a result husband and wife became a double act, from which public platform Jackie moved on to the after-dinner speaking circuit, rapidly finding himself in such demand that he had to relinquish another accountancy post.

Before an engagement not far from his Stalybridge, Cheshire, home in the mid-1990s he reflected: 'Life has been full of ups and downs, but without pathos there can be no comedy. The bitterness goes eventually and you start remembering the good times. I loved it at United. From this distance, even going through the accident was worth it for those years at Old Trafford.' He added softly: 'I feel happy and at ease now.' All who knew Jackie Blanchflower during his dark days in the wake of Munich will give thanks for that.

Only two weeks ago, though very ill, he was able to attend a testimonial match at United's headquarters for the Munich survivors; it was an emotional night.

John Blanchflower: born Belfast, 7 March 1933; played for Manchester United 1949-58; capped 12 times by Northern Ireland 1954-58; died Manchester, 2 September 1998.

Ray Bowden

Ray Bowden was paid perhaps the ultimate footballing compliment in March 1933 when the most successful manager the English game had then known asked him to replace a star performer in one of the greatest of all club sides.

The Arsenal boss Herbert Chapman was keen for the mild-mannered Cornishman, then plying his trade with Second Division Plymouth Argyle, to succeed the brilliant but ageing inside-forward David Jack in a Gunners team which was on the verge of lifting the championship and which would sweep all before it as the decade progressed. So keen, in fact, that when Bowden refused his first approach, he made another, and another, agreement finally being secured on Chapman's third visit to Devon.

Such apparent reluctance to embrace the big time might seem peculiar to observers of the cash carnival that football has become in the 1990s, but in an era when all players received a maximum wage, a transfer did not have the same financial implications that it has today. Eight pounds a week was still eight pounds a week, whether it emanated from the gleaming marble halls of Highbury or the more modest surroundings of Home Park.

Still, the manager's persistence paid off and Bowden, who cost £4,500 and was Chapman's last major signing before his premature death in 1934, immediately justified the great man's judgement by helping Arsenal to clinch that term's title, though he had arrived too late for a medal.

He made up for that in comprehensive manner, playing a significant role as his new club went on to complete a championship hat-trick over the next two campaigns. In addition, he took part in the 1936 FA Cup final triumph over Sheffield United, won six England caps and was selected twice for the Football League.

Bowden was a graceful ball-player whose slender, almost frail build belied a sinewy strength, although he would have made more than his 136 League and Cup appearances for the Gunners but for a nagging vulnerability to ankle injuries. His passing was smooth and thoughtful, making him a regular creator of goals for others as well as scoring 47 of his own in senior club competition.

He formed a productive right-wing partnership with the dashing Joe Hulme and became an able if often unobtrusive foil for the rest of a sumptuous forward line consisting of Ted Drake, Alex James and Cliff Bastin.

All his England honours were earned during his Arsenal sojourn, the highlight of his two-year international career being the so-called Battle of Highbury in 1934, when he helped to defeat the world champions, Italy. The game – in which he played alongside no fewer than six of his club colleagues, a record – earned its lurid tag when the visitors, apparently misconstruing the intent of a vigorous early challenge from the ultra-competitive Drake, resorted to brutal tactics.

Bowden, who had worked as a solicitor's clerk on leaving school, came to the notice of Plymouth Argyle after netting ten times in an amateur match for his native Looe. He joined the Pilgrims in 1926 and won a Division Three South title gong in 1929/30 before Chapman persuaded him that he had a glittering future in north London.

In 1937 George Allison, Chapman's successor, opted to reshuffle his side and Bowden was sold to Second Division Newcastle United for £5,000. The West Countryman enjoyed his time with the Tynesiders, for whom he scored a hat-trick against Swansea on the day before England declared war on Germany.

The last surviving major contributor to Arsenal's remarkable achievements in the 1930s saw his professional soccer career end with the outbreak of hostilities and later he returned to Plymouth, where he became a sports outfitter.

Edwin Raymond Bowden: born Looe, Cornwall, 13 September 1909; played for Plymouth Argyle 1926-33, Arsenal 1933-37, Newcastle United 1937-39; six England caps 1934-36; died Plymouth, Devon, 23 September 1998.

John Osborne

John Osborne was never likely to keep goal for England – the consistent excellence of Gordon Banks, then Peter Shilton and Ray Clemence saw to that – but there was a time in the late 1960s and early 1970s when he was one of the most accomplished non-international net-minders in the country.

His playing pomp was spent in the English top division with West Bromwich Albion, for whom he preserved a clean sheet in their single-goal FA Cup final victory over Everton in 1968. But the tall, rather spidery Osborne's athletic exploits between the posts accounted for only part of his appeal to fans of the Baggies. Equally important was his engaging, outgoing personality which ensured a warm rapport with paying customers at the Hawthorns, even when their side was struggling.

Osborne spent his formative years as an outfielder, winning England schoolboy honours as a wing-half and being converted into a keeper only in his late teens. His first professional club was Chesterfield – traditional nurturers of goalkeeping talent, including that of the incomparable Banks – and he compiled more than a century of appearances for the Spireites before joining Albion for £10,000 in January 1967.

Instantly installed as first choice, Osborne emerged as an agile shot-stopper, generally reliable claimer of crosses and courageous diver at feet, who was blessed with a shrewd positional sense and who radiated confidence. For several seasons under the enterprising management of Allan Ashman he was part of a compact, attractive team which held their own in the middle reaches of the old First Division and reached Wembley for a second time in 1970, when they lost the League Cup final to Manchester City.

Thereafter Osborne suffered injuries – he was dubbed 'the bionic goalkeeper' after a plastic joint was inserted into a finger – and he lost his place intermittently, even retiring briefly in 1972. After a few months he returned to the Hawthorns, but was unable to prevent Albion's relegation to the Second Division in 1973. After languishing for a term in Peter Latchford's shadow he recovered his berth and starred as a revived side, now guided by Johnny Giles, regained a place among the elite in 1976.

When Osborne left full-time football – aged 37 in 1978, after 312 senior outings for the Baggies – many believed he would pursue a career in the media, for which he had apparently paved the way by excelling on the TV show *Quiz Ball* in 1969/70 and then hosting his own local radio programme. Instead he opted to work in the promotions department of a local newspaper, later becoming commercial manager of Worcestershire County Cricket Club.

John Osborne: born Barlborough, Derbyshire, 1 December 1940; played for Chesterfield 1960-67, West Bromwich Albion 1967-72 and 1973-78, Walsall on loan 1973; died Evesham, Worcestershire, 7 November 1998.

Matt Gillies

Though comparisions to Matt Busby and Bill Shankly are unrealistic purely in terms of silverware accumulated, Matt Gillies was as seminally important to Leicester City during the 1960s as were his famous fellow Scots to Manchester United and Liverpool respectively.

Certainly both of them held Gillies in immense esteem and believed that he had deserved better than his single 1964 League Cup triumph with the unfashionable Foxes, so inspired was his work on resources which were meagre compared to the riches on tap at Old Trafford and Anfield.

Indeed, Gillies transformed Leicester from a club which had yo-yoed dizzily between the First and Second Divisions during the second half of the 1950s into one of the elite flight's more solid citizens. Apart from that one trophy success, between 1961 and 1967 there were four top-eight League finishes, the first European foray in the club's history, FA Cup final appearances in 1961 and 1963 and a second League Cup final outing in 1965. By the previous standards of the Filbert Street club, this was a rapturously impressive record.

In terms of personality, Gillies resembled the stately Busby more closely than the abrasively excitable Shankly. Gentlemanly, unassuming and a silver-tongued diplomat, he rejoiced in the respect of most players, possessing the priceless knack – from Leicester's viewpoint – of deflecting wage demands with pure charm, footballers tending to leave his office with smiles on their faces but with little extra in their pockets.

He was a shrewd judge of raw talent, too, a gift illustrated most vividly, during his pre-managerial coaching days with City, by his assessment of the rookie Frank McLintock. After an inconclusive trial, the club was about to reject the scrawny, Gorbals-raised teenager, but Gillies saw something in his young countryman that others had missed. McLintock stayed and matured into one of Leicester's most influential performers, going on eventually to star for Arsenal.

When occasion demanded, Gillies was a canny operator in the transfer market, his most vaunted transaction being the £7,000 acquisition of Gordon Banks, a youthful goalkeeper destined for greatness, from Chesterfield in 1959. There were other bargains, notably Scottish play-maker Davie Gibson and winger Mike Stringfellow, but he was not afraid to invest boldly, either, as he proved by paying Fulham a British record £150,000 fee for marksman Allan Clarke in 1968.

Indeed, Gillies was never less than decisive as he demonstrated repeatedly. For instance, in 1961 he astounded the soccer world by axing his prolific centre-forward, Ken Leek, for the FA Cup final meeting with mighty Spurs, opting instead to field the inexperienced Hugh McIlmoyle. Another example came six years later when his faith in the unproven Peter Shilton prompted him to sell the world's best goalkeeper, Banks, to Stoke City. Shilton went on to play more League games and make more appearances for England than anyone in the history of the game.

Finally, Gillies even left Leicester on a point of principle, resigning after the board had sacked his trusted coach, Bert Johnson, following a lean spell of results which was to culminate in relegation. Though Gillies spent his working life in football, that had not always been his intention. In his teens he was bent on a career in medicine but his studies were interrupted by war and he became a navigator in RAF Bomber Command. Meanwhile he had emerged as a promising half-back and served Motherwell as an amateur before signing for Bolton Wanderers in 1942. After the conflict he broke into the Trotters' senior side at right-half, then became a reliable centre-half and captain before losing out to younger men.

In January 1952 Gillies joined Leicester for £9,500 and was the regular stopper in the side that lifted the Second Division championship in 1954. His playing days drew to a close during the subsequent disappointing First Division campaign and in 1956, after contemplating a future in physiotherapy, he turned to coaching.

Then, when David Halliday vacated the boss' chair in November 1958, Gillies became caretaker manager, accepting the job permanently two months later. Working closely with Bert Johnson, he turned around the fortunes of the struggling First Division outfit, his success based on a formidably sound defence.

The team reached its peak in 1962/63 when, for a time, there was a genuine possibility of the hallowed League and FA Cup double, and it was a telling mark of Leicester's new-found stature that they were favourites to win the Wembley meeting with Manchester United. Around Easter they were pressing for the title but fell away on the last stretch, then lost the FA Cup final. The following season brought compensation with a two-legged League Cup final victory over Stoke, and City came close to retaining the trophy in 1964/65, being beaten by Chelsea in the final. After that Gillies' Foxes remained splendidly competitive until 1968/69, when a poor start to the season precipitated Johnson's dismissal and the manager's departure.

Towards the end of his Filbert Street tenure Gillies had become careworn and many observers were surprised when he took charge of Nottingham Forest, then struggling near the foot of the First Division. Though he remained at the City Ground for nearly four years, it proved an unhappy reign. The club seemed intent on selling its best players, the replacements proved inadequate and they were relegated in 1971/72. Come October 1972, with Forest doing poorly in the Second Division, Gillies resigned. It was a sadly anti-climactic ending to an accomplished career.

Matthew Muirhead Gillies: born Loganlea, West Lothian, 12 August 1921; played for Bolton Wanderers 1942-52, Leicester City 1952-56; managed Leicester City 1958-68, Nottingham Forest 1969-72; died Nottingham 24 December 1998.

Brian Lewis

Brian Lewis, one of the most versatile performers in English League football throughout the decade and a half from 1960, played an integral part in an extraordinary feat of giant-killing which astounded the sporting world. In February 1971 the effervescent utility man with the distinctive bow-legged gait was plying his trade on the right flank of humble Colchester United's attack when the Layer Road minnows played host to Don Revie's awesomely formidable Leeds United in the fifth round of the FA Cup.

Though they were destined to finish the season trophyless, Leeds were, by common consent, the finest team in the land. Meanwhile Colchester – dubbed 'Grandad's Army' due to the preponderance of veterans in their ranks – were confined to relative anonymity, about midway in the Fourth Division. So one-sided did the contest appear that even the ritual pre-match tub-thumping about Davids overcoming Goliaths appeared more spurious than usual.

Cue sensation, with Lewis at its heart. Early in proceedings he laid on a goal for former England centre-forward Ray Crawford, then he continued to beaver inspirationally as Crawford added a second, and capped his contribution by delivering a sumptuous lob from which Dave Simmons gave the underdogs a 3-0 advantage. The Elland Road aristocrats clawed back to 3-2 but no further; Lewis, Crawford and company had achieved a soccer miracle.

Not that Lewis needed a one-off glory-day to cement his stature in the game. That was already evident from a career which had taken in Crystal Palace, whom he had served in the League's lower reaches; Second Division Portsmouth, his dearest footballing love; Coventry City, for whom he was bought by Jimmy Hill and whom he helped to clinch the Second Division title in 1967; Luton Town (Third Division) and Oxford United (Second Division). Finally, after leaving Colchester, he returned to Pompey for an enterprising Indian summer.

During the course of his travels, Lewis occupied every outfield position, but was at his best as an attacking right-half who packed a savage shot, whose sweeping crossfield passes were a trademark, and who was wirily resilient in the tackle.

Something of a lovable scamp both on and off the pitch, he was feted by his supporters, especially at Portsmouth, for cheeky dribbles which lured opponents into rash tackles, thus securing free-kicks in menacing situations. Though his only taste of England's top flight was for one term in and out of the Coventry team, he appeared to have the requisite ability for that level and his failure to hold his own there perplexed many contemporaries.

In 1975 Lewis entered non-League circles with Hastings, then worked in the furniture trade while retaining his contact with the game as a successful youth coach near his home in Bournemouth. Passionate about his football – he named his only son after Duncan Edwards, the Manchester United prodigy who perished in the Munich air disaster – Lewis retained his enthusiasm until the end, and was laid to rest wearing the shirt of his beloved Pompey.

Brian Lewis: born Woking, Surrey, 26 January 1943; played for Crystal Palace 1960-63, Portsmouth 1963-67, Coventry City 1967-68, Luton Town 1968-70, Oxford United 1970, Colchester United 1970-72, Portsmouth again 1972-75; died Bournemouth, Dorset, 14 December 1998.

John McGrath

The lurid public persona of John McGrath – something between Desperate Dan and Attila the Hun, as perceived by the average English football fan during the 1960s and early 1970s – was viewed wryly by those who had monitored the progress of the burly Mancunian at his first professional club.

At Bury, whom he had joined in 1955 after failing to break through as an amateur with Bolton Wanderers, McGrath was seen primarily as a constructive centre-half for whom lofty ambitions were harboured. Indeed, there were those at Gigg Lane who saw in the personable son of a policeman a certain likeness to John Charles, the 'Gentle Giant' whose name was then a byword for polished central-defensive excellence. In the event, McGrath never proved remotely close to the majestic Welshman in terms of class, but he did enjoy a worthy and colourful career, much of which was spent in England's top division.

After becoming established at Bury, he left the Shakers three months before they claimed the Third Division championship in 1961, though he had played enough games to earn a medal. Evidence of his burgeoning status were his destination, Newcastle United, and his fee, £24,000 plus the services of the hugely respected veteran, Bobby Stokoe. However, despite winning England under-23 honours shortly after his move, McGrath took time to settle at St James' Park and the hopes of boss Charlie Mitten that the newcomer would be instrumental in saving the ailing Magpies from relegation were dashed.

It was not until the pragmatic Joe Harvey became the long-term replacement for the adventurous Mitten that the young defender began to flourish. Under Harvey his game was transformed, a new and often fearsomely abrasive approach belying his genial character, and he formed a formidable half-back line alongside Stan Anderson and Jim Iley which inspired Newcastle to the Second Division title in 1964/65.

Back among the elite, McGrath prospered for a season, but then found himself squeezed out by a combination of Ollie Burton, John McNamee and the richly promising Bobby Moncur. Accordingly in February 1968 he accepted a £30,000 transfer to Southampton, for whom he became the commanding cornerstone of one of the First Division's most rugged rearguards. So outstanding was his form at The Dell that he moved to the verge of full England recognition, although selection for the Football League in 1969 was the closest he came.

In 1973, McGrath took up coaching with Southampton, whom he left in 1979 to become manager of Port Vale. After a sticky start with a poor side, he led them to promotion from Division Four in 1983, only to be sacked later that year when the Burslem-based club floundered at the higher level. He encountered further travail at the helm of Chester before tasting success with Preston North End, whom he guided up to the Third Division in 1987 and to the promotion play-offs two years later.

However, he returned to the basement with Halifax Town, where cash was so short that, as he put it at one press briefing, there wasn't enough to feed the club cat. The upshot was that The Shay was deluged with catfood from animal-lovers all over England – and Halifax had no cat!

Though McGrath's wit did not save him from dismissal in November 1992, it served him admirably in his subsequent successful career as an after-dinner speaker and as a soccer pundit on local radio in Lancashire.

John Thomas McGrath: born Manchester, 23 August 1938; played for Bury 1955-61, Newcastle United 1961-68, Southampton 1968-74, Brighton on loan 1972; managed Port Vale 1979-83, Chester City 1984-85, Preston North End 1986-90, Halifax Town 1991-92; died Middleton, Manchester, 25 December 1998.

Dennis Viollet

There is a compelling case for citing the Busby Babes as the most joyously precocious collection of soccer talent ever drawn together under the banner of one English club. That Manchester United team, so savagely devastated by the Munich air disaster in 1958, boasted the likes of Duncan Edwards and Tommy Taylor, Roger Byrne and Eddie Colman, and there was a young fellow called Bobby Charlton who could play a bit, too. Yet one of the side's key performers was widely and peculiarly underrated, though not, it should be emphasised, by Matt Busby himself.

In terms of appearance, Dennis Viollet did not correspond with the popular image of a goal-scoring hero. Wan of countenance and slim to the point of scrawniness, he seemed pathetically equipped physically to mix it with strapping defenders. Yet the prolific Mancunian was a gem, both as a foil for the magnificent Taylor and as a marksman in his own right. Indeed, the fact is that no one – not Law, not Best, not Cantona – has netted more times than he in a single season for the Red Devils.

Viollet was blessed with instinctive ball control, searing acceleration and the vision to use these attributes to full advantage. Arguably he was at his most effective when working in tandem with Taylor, the bold Yorkshireman who lost his life on that slushy German runway. Big Tommy was majestic in the air while his less conspicuous but formidably lethal partner was a steel dart at ground level. During the mid-1950s, when the Babes were sweeping all before them, the duo struck up a seemingly telepathic understanding, creating space for each other by their imaginative movement and registering a river of goals that showed no signs of drying up.

Yet while Taylor was rewarded by frequent international recognition, the equally if contrastingly talented Viollet had to wait until two years after the crash before winning the first of only two England caps, a circumstance rendered all the more mysterious by the uninspired nature of some of his rivals.

However, nothing could detract from Viollet's derring-do on the club scene. After captaining Manchester schoolboys – and also playing regularly for his country at that stage – he joined Manchester United as an amateur in 1949, turning professional a year later and making his first-team debut in 1952/53.

Thereafter he held his own against white-hot competition as Busby's youthful revolution gathered exhilarating momentum and he won a regular place during 1953/54.

Settling brilliantly at inside-left and contributing at least 20 senior goals per season, Viollet went on to share in a succession of heady triumphs, notably the League championships of 1955/56 and 1956/57. As United blazed a trail into Europe, his pedigree shone through ever more vividly and his evident relish for continental opposition made his sojourn in the international wilderness increasingly perplexing.

Cruelly, the United idyll was halted at Munich, on the way home from a European Cup trip to Belgrade, when the club's plane crashed on its third attempt at take-off. Eight players and 15 other passengers died but Viollet, seated next to Charlton, was thrown clear and survived.

As the extent of the tragedy sunk in, it was feared that even those footballers who had escaped with their lives would never be the same again. Viollet had suffered head injuries and took no part in United's immediate future, missing their emotional progress to the FA Cup final. However, after a couple of League outings he was pronounced fit enough to play at Wembley, where he proved sadly unable to do himself justice in the defeat by Bolton Wanderers.

Fears that Viollet might be diminished as a performer in the long term were banished rapidly during 1958/59 when, converted to Taylor's old role as centre-forward, he excelled as the depleted Red Devils confounded most predictions by finishing as First Division runners-up. Come the following campaign his form was even more remarkable as he notched 32 goals in 36 matches, which remains a club record despite the wealth of expensive strikers employed at Old Trafford over the subsequent four decades. As a result the long-awaited England call arrived, though Viollet was to be granted only a paltry two games among the elite.

Still, it seemed certain that he would retain a vital part in Busby's team-rebuilding process for the foreseeable future, but the great manager decreed otherwise. Shocking both the player and every United fan, in came David Herd from Arsenal, plans were laid to capture Denis Law from Torino and Viollet – having scored 178 goals in 291 games and hardly a has-been at 28 – was sold to Stoke City for £25,000 in January 1962.

Happily that was not the end of the footballing world for the popular, easy-going Viollet. Lining up alongside the amazing Stanley Matthews, who was old enough to be his father, he helped the Potters take the Second Division title in his first full season and he remained productively at the Victoria Ground until 1967.

After that Viollet joined British soccer's mini-exodus to the USA, serving two summers with Baltimore Bays, before re-crossing the Atlantic for a brief stint with non-League Witton Albion in 1969. Later that year he joined Linfield as player-coach and did well in Ulster, pocketing an Irish Cup winner's medal for his pains in 1970.

There followed a coaching spell at Preston North End in 1970, an abortive flirtation with management at Crewe in 1971 – he was sacked after his side was knocked out of the FA Cup by non-League opposition – and a more fulfilling engagement in charge of football for Washington Diplomats between 1974 and 1977.

Viollet went on to achieve further coaching success in the States, settling in Jacksonville, Florida, his home at the time of his death.

Dennis Sydney Viollet: born Manchester, 30 September 1933; played for Manchester United 1949-62, Stoke City 1962-67, Baltimore Bays, USA 1967-68, non-League Witton Albion 1969, Linfield, Northern Ireland 1969-70; capped twice by England 1960-61; managed Crewe Alexandra 1971; died Jacksonville, Florida, 6 March 1999.

Sir Alf Ramsey

'England will win the World Cup.' He might as well have touted Charlie Drake for prime minister or Albert Steptoe for Mr Universe. Yet on 30 July 1966, after three and a half years of sticking stolidly to what had seemed like an increasingly improbable prediction, Alf Ramsey was vindicated. England were champions of the world and he, as the manager responsible, was assured of an unperishable place among the most gilded names in football history.

Habitually taciturn, often downright cold, towards almost everyone but his players, Ramsey was never widely popular, either inside the game or among the fans. Even after his finest hour, he was vilified for the stultifying effect his so-called 'wingless wonders' and all-round caution bequeathed, via countless inferior imitators, to the wider game.

Many criticised him for a mistrust of foreigners that bordered on xenophobia and for a lack of communication skills that was born, perhaps, of an ultimate professional's contempt for amateurs, whether well-meaning or not. Finally, he was damned for head-in-the-sand tactical naivety and refusal to move with the times, and that cost him his job. But none could dispute that England's 1966 glory, coupled with arguably even more astounding earlier achievements with Ipswich Town, qualified him as a truly great manager.

The Ramsey outlook had always been singular. As a youth blessed with considerable footballing ability, he might have been expected to dream of high attainment on the field; instead, the ambition of which he spoke was to emulate his father as a successful grocer.

In 1940 he joined the Army and served in the Duke of Cornwall's Light Infantry, but his sporting aptitude could not be ignored. He was already an amateur with Portsmouth when Southampton spotted him playing services football and took him to The Dell as a stocky, powerful and skilful centre-half cum centre-forward.

Converted by his manager Bill Dodgin into a right-back, Ramsey matured into a cool, stylish performer; a perceptive passer and shrewd tactician whose only perceptible weakness was lack of pace. By 1948 he had played for England but then, surprisingly, was ousted from both club and country teams by Bill Ellerington and the following year joined Tottenham Hotspur, valued at £21,000 in a player-exchange deal.

Now Ramsey found himself under the aegis of a fellow deep-thinker, the Spurs manager Arthur Rowe, who was in the process of putting together the north Londoners' famous push-and-run side. Though the expensive newcomer was not made captain, he was highly influential, and his calm, single-minded approach offered an ideal complement to his ebullient boss. Tottenham topped the Second Division in 1950, then lifted the League title in 1951. Meanwhile, Ramsey had become an England regular, taking part in the 1950 World Cup finals in Brazil – he played in the humiliating 1-0 defeat by the unfancied United States – and retained his place until an even more far-reaching national setback, the 6-3 drubbing by Hungary at Wembley in 1953.

Though his 32-cap England career was at an end, Ramsey remained a force at club level, going on to become Spurs skipper before losing his place and moving into management with the unfashionable Ipswich Town in 1955.

At Portman Road he found few resources, scant support and no tradition, yet on this apparently stony ground he sowed the seeds of a remarkable renaissance. Cobbling together a collection of other clubs' rejects and hitherto unregarded individuals already in situ, he led the East Anglians to the Third Division South championship in 1957, then stretched the bounds of credibility still further by taking the Second Division title in 1961.

That, the experts said, was that; in the top flight Ipswich would sink without trace; quite simply, they were not good enough. A year later the soccer establishment was reeling as 'Ramsey's Ragbag' were crowned League champions, leaving Tottenham Hotspur – winners of both League and FA Cup the previous season – to trail in their wake.

The success of the so-called Cinderellas was founded on hard work, rigid method and each player making the absolute most of what abilities he had.

No one typified the Town more than Jimmy Leadbetter, a seemingly frail 33-year-old winger who might have passed for 53. At Chelsea he had been an also-ran, but his new manager had seen possibilities in him, gave him an innovative deep-lying flank role and opponents were puzzled to deadly effect.

It was at this time that the public picture of Ramsey as a frosty, inscrutable personality began to take shape. The image was fed on stories such as one that had him seated alone in the stand, watching a youth match while the title celebrations were in full swing only yards away. When asked to join the revellers, he is said to have declined, replying: 'I'm working.'

When Walter Winterbottom stepped aside as England manager in January 1963, there could be little argument that the Ipswich boss was the ideal replacement. After considering Jimmy Adamson of Burnley, the Football Association duly appointed Ramsey to the national game's top job. He was the first man to be given full control over all aspects of team selection and preparation, and immediately made it plain he would brook no interference from officialdom or anyone else.

Thus the team selection committee was renamed and reduced to irrelevance as the senior international committee, a body towards which Ramsey could scarcely disguise his indifference, even his contempt. He told one member that their places on tours ought to go to extra players, though he conceded, no doubt acidly, that they had one saving grace – they could attend cocktail parties in his stead.

On the field, Ramsey's reign began with an emphatic reverse, 5-2 in France, but that did not stop him from asserting, at the time and repeatedly thereafter, that England could win the World Cup in 1966. Over the ensuing three and a half seasons his results, taken overall, were acceptable, though many of the performances lacked style.

Far from being 'wingless' at that time, Ramsey experimented with a succession of flankmen, using them even in the first three matches of the World Cup finals. In the early stages of the tournament, a lacklustre England were given little chance of ultimate triumph despite playing on home soil, and Ramsey came under increasing pressure, especially over his employment of the combative Nobby Stiles. Indeed, after one particularly bruising encounter with France he was urged by FIFA's disciplinary committee to drop Manchester United's tough nut. He responded, with an unswerving loyalty that was typical and mutual between him and his players, by declaring: 'If Stiles goes, so do I.'

Of course, both stayed, England improved enormously to beat the talented but unruly Argentinians in a stormy quarter-final, then they overcame the brilliant Portuguese in a showpiece semi, before defeating West Germany in highly dramatic circumstances to take the Jules Rimet Trophy.

Alf Ramsey's critics – and they were legion, inside and outside the press – had fallen flat on their faces. They had refused to believe his bold assertion, they had ridiculed him for the 'negativity' of his tactics, they had pilloried him for preferring the dependable workhorse

Geoff Hurst to the mercurial goal-scoring genius Jimmy Greaves and many had slammed him for his persistence with Stiles.

Now England had won the World Cup, Hurst had scored a hat-trick in the final, and Stiles was a hero following a disarming dance of celebration around Wembley which had enchanted the nation.

Ramsey's reaction to his second soccer 'miracle' was in keeping with the manner in which he had met his first. When the final whistle went, his colleagues alongside him on the Wembley bench went wild with joy, the trainer Harold Shepherdson leaping to his feet in exultation. Ramsey, still seated and utterly deadpan, merely grated: 'Sit down, Shepherdson!'

Though he was knighted and became Sir Alf in 1967, Ramsey was allowed little time to bathe in the glow of his achievement. Soon, as many club managers followed his lead by dispensing with entertaining wingers, his influence on an increasingly staid British game was denigrated long and loudly.

Nevertheless, come 1970 England – who had finished third in the 1968 European Nations Cup – were making a spirited bid to retain their world crown when, at the last-eight stage of the Mexico finals, Ramsey's fortunes took a downward turn from which they never recovered.

From being 2-0 up against West Germany (despite being deprived of top goalkeeper Gordon Banks by illness), they lost 3-2, and the manager was criticised hysterically for substituting the ageing Bobby Charlton when victory had seemed likely, to save him for future matches.

Now his ever-uneasy relationship with the media deteriorated still further, his state of mind seeming sometimes to border on paranoia.

Two years later England lost to the same opponents in the European quarter-final and Ramsey's policy – one in which perspiration appeared to be valued infinitely more highly than inspiration – was decried as naive and outdated. The final straw was failure to qualify for the 1974 World Cup finals. England needed victory over Poland at Wembley but could manage only a 1-1 draw. The steadily building cries for his head mounted to a crescendo and in May 1974 the man responsible for his country's finest footballing moment was sacked.

Poignantly, there was little overt sympathy for a figure who never enjoyed one iota of the public affection bestowed on the likes of, say, Matt Busby or Bill Shankly. Ramsey's apparent hauteur and disregard for the opinions of others – he never made the slightest concession to diplomacy – had upset countless people down the years, and now they were happy to see him go.

Those who knew him reasonably well reckoned that he was deeply hurt behind his mask, but outwardly he remained intransigent to the last. He simply didn't, or wouldn't, or couldn't recognise the necessity for change.

After 18 months out of the game, he joined the board of Birmingham City, then put in a creditable stint as caretaker manager between September 1977 and March 1978 before poor health precipitated his retirement. Thereafter he lived quietly near Ipswich, a flawed hero if ever there was one. But a hero, nevertheless.

Alfred Ernest Ramsey: born Dagenham, Essex, 22 January 1920; played for Portsmouth 1942 (as amateur), Southampton 1943 (as amateur) and 1944-49, Tottenham Hotspur 1949-55; capped 32 times for England 1948-53; managed Ipswich Town 1955-63, England 1963-74, Birmingham City (as caretaker) 1977-78; knighted 1967; died Ipswich, Suffolk, 28 April 1999.

Arthur Ellis

Bob Paisley was one of sport's quiet men, yet an incident involving one of his rare rages offers a telling illustration of how Arthur Ellis elevated soccer refereeing into an art form.

The man who would go on to become the most successful manager in English football with Liverpool was playing one of his last matches for the Anfield club when he was clattered by a Middlesbrough opponent. Paisley rounded on his tormentor, threatening darkly to part his hair if it happened again, and it is fair to speculate that violence was contemplated. Ellis, scenting trouble and anxious to defuse it, reacted instantly by whipping a comb from his pocket and offering it to the aggrieved north-easterner with the words: 'There you are Bob, do it now if you like.'

Everyone laughed, a potential crisis was averted and the game continued peacefully. It was brilliant refereeing and it epitomised Arthur Ellis, the stern but cheerful Yorkshireman who, in his 1950s prime, was the world's most famous whistleblower.

He had turned to officiating after realising as a youngster that he would not make the top grade as a player and by 22 he was a Yorkshire League referee. Displaying characteristic authority and a natural flair for interpreting the game's finer points, he progressed rapidly and was a Football League linesman within two years.

After moving into the middle, Ellis was soon noticed for his fairness and his man-management skills, and was rewarded with his first high-profile task in 1948 when he took charge of an FA Cup semi-final between Tottenham Hotspur and Blackpool.

Thereafter the credits piled up in quick succession. In 1950 he refereed West Germany's first international, against Switzerland in Stuttgart, and that same year took part in the World Cup finals in Brazil. He wielded the whistle in several games and then ran the line in what was effectively the final – the competition being run on a league basis – between Uruguay and Brazil. Then came the 1952 FA Cup final, in which Newcastle United defeated Arsenal, for which he was offered the choice of a medal or a £10 fee. Predictably for a fellow who gloried in football's tradition, he opted for the gong.

But it was for his composed handling of one of the most ill-tempered of all international contests that Ellis won deathless renown. That was the 1954 World Cup quarter-final clash between Brazil and Hungary, the so-called 'Battle of Berne', in which he dismissed Brazil's Nilton Santos and Joseph Bozsik, a Hungarian MP, for fighting. Later he issued another Magyar with his marching orders and a Brazilian was struck on the head by a bottle thrown from the Hungarian bench, allegedly by the great Ferenc Puskas.

Recently Ellis recalled: 'I thought it was going to be the greatest game I'd ever seen. I was on top of the world at the prospect. But it turned out to be a disgrace. In today's climate so many players would have been sent off that the game would have been abandoned. My only thought was that I was determined to finish it.'

So he did, and it was a major achievement which ensured that Ellis would preside over a succession of showpiece occasions. Thus he officiated at the first European Cup final, in which Real Madrid beat Reims in 1956, and the first European Nations final when the Soviet Union overcame Yugoslavia four years later in Paris. Compulsory retirement from refereeing followed at the age of 47 but Ellis, who had served in three World Cups and taken charge of more than 40 internationals, did not disappear from the limelight. Indeed, the celebrity of the former traveller for a Yorkshire brewery increased immensely as he enforced the rules in BBC Television's *It's A Knockout* for 18 years, effectively playing straight man to the ebullient Stuart Hall and Eddy Waring.

In addition, for many years he chaired the Pools Panel, which pronounces on matches postponed due to bad weather. Roger Hunt, who succeeded him in that role, spoke of Ellis as a zestful optimist who was wonderful to work with. 'As a referee he always had a smile on his face, but there was never any point in arguing with Arthur. He was strong and he had the total respect of the players.'

A revealing token of that regard came at the end of the 1952 FA Cup final, when he was invited to the post-match celebrations of both Newcastle and Arsenal. Arthur Ellis resolved his dilemma with typical decision: 'I didn't want to show any favouritism – so I went to both,' he grinned.

Arthur Ellis: born Halifax, Yorkshire, 8 July 1914; died 23 May 1999.

Laurie Scott

Laurie Scott played his football hard, but with a smile never far from his face. He was good at it, too, an unfashionably nimble right-back for Arsenal and England immediately after the Second World War, an era when all too many defenders relied on brawn rather than mobility.

Undoubtedly the affable Yorkshireman would have thrived in the modern era, when overlapping full-backs have become the norm. As it was he served club and country nobly, and would have enjoyed an even more illustrious career had he not lost a large portion of his prime to the conflict with Germany. Stocky and immensely strong, Scott was a natural athlete, excelling at all games as he grew up, but football was his primary concern. Thus he enlisted with Bradford City as a 14-year-old outside-right in 1931, but he was converted to a full-back before turning professional in 1935.

There followed two seasons of Second Division service with the Bantams before he made a momentous move, joining Arsenal, then the dominant force in the English game, in exchange for the utility player Ernie Tuckett.

However, this was no path to instant glory for the talented but still raw 19-year-old. First the majestic form of George Male and Eddie Hapgood, and then the war, meant that Scott would wait nearly nine years until his senior baptism as a Gunner.

This did not mean, though, that he was deprived of high-quality football in the intervening years. Indeed, he won two London Combination medals with Arsenal reserves, then he helped his new club to triumph in several wartime competitions.

Scott, who served as a physical training instructor in the RAF, was maturing into a fine all-round player. A crisp and combative tackler, he was quick to recover if a winger had the temerity to give him the slip, his distribution was sensibly safe and he was blessed with a shrewd positional sense. As a result he donned an England shirt for 16 unofficial internationals during the war, and it was no surprise that he retained his place when peace resumed. Though in his 30th year when he made his official debut in 1946, Scott performed splendidly on the world stage. He won 17 successive caps, most of them in a polished partnership with Middlesbrough's George Hardwick, before suffering a knee injury when facing Wales at Villa Park in 1948 which ended his England days.

Before and after that setback, he prospered at club level, helping the Gunners lift the League championship in 1947/48 and the FA Cup two years later, when they defeated Liverpool 2-0 at Wembley.

Sadly, though, by the turn of the decade Scott's knee was proving increasingly troublesome, leading to several lengthy lay-offs, and his top-flight tenure ended in October

1951 when he became player-manager of Crystal Palace, then struggling near the foot of the old Third Division South.

Despite working prodigiously, he was unable to transform the Glaziers' fortunes, and, after they narrowly missed having to apply for re-election to the Football League in 1954, he left the club.

Subsequently Scott made his living as a sales representative for a London-based hardware firm, but his love affair with the game was not over. He entered wholeheartedly into non-League football, bossing Hendon from 1954 to 1957 and then coaching Hitchin Town. Meanwhile he continued to play as a regular member of the Showbiz XI for some 20 years, lining up alongside the likes of Sean Connery and Tommy Steele to raise money for charity.

In 1984 Scott retired from his job, and he and his wife, Gerry, moved to the village of Hoylandswaine, near Barnsley. The couple, who lost their only child, Valerie, when she was ten, celebrated their diamond wedding anniversary in 1998.

Lawrence Scott: born Sheffield, 23 April 1917; played for Bradford City 1933-37, Arsenal 1937-51, Crystal Palace 1951-53; capped 17 times by England 1946-48; managed Crystal Palace 1951-54; died Barnsley, Yorkshire, 18 July 1999.

Frank Bowyer

Like a fellow Stoke City stalwart, Jimmy Greenhoff, in later years, Frank Bowyer was one of the finest footballers of his generation never to win an England cap.

Standing between the unassuming local boy and international recognition was the proliferation of exceptionally talented inside-forwards who were plying their trade after the war, such men as Raich Carter, Wilf Mannion and Len Shackleton.

At club level, though, Bowyer was a star in his own right, a craftsman who could create and score goals with equal facility. He was renowned for devastatingly accurate long-distance distribution, an explosively powerful shot and a certain grace of movement which delighted the eye. A one-club man throughout his League playing career, he served the Potters for more than two decades, making 436 senior appearances and netting 149 goals, three short of Freddie Steele's Stoke record.

The teenage Bowyer enlisted at the Victoria Ground in 1937, turning professional two years later. He was part of a sparkling crop of gifted youngsters whose impetus was jolted by the war, though he turned out for the club regularly in emergency competitions during the conflict. When peace resumed Stoke were a leading side, featuring the top player of the day, Stanley Matthews, and were beaten to the 1946/47 championship by Liverpool only on the season's final Saturday. However, Bowyer missed out on that, taking time to become re-established after his demob from the forces, and there were rumours about a possible transfer. They came to nothing, though, and after making his senior debut in a home defeat by Manchester United in February 1948, he claimed a regular place at inside-right in 1948/49.

That campaign was to be his most successful as he led the First Division scoring charts until the spring, finishing with 21 goals, only four behind the top flight's most prolific marksman, Willie Moir of Bolton Wanderers. Blossoming alongside such accomplished performers as centre-half Neil Franklin and defender cum half-back Frank Mountford, Bowyer moved to the verge of the England side, though never went closer than a Football Association tour of Canada in 1950.

He continued to excel for City but the side declined and was relegated in 1952/53. Thereafter he remained a key contributor until 1959/60, which he finished as Stoke's leading scorer and, although he was aged 38, there was widespread disappointment among Potters fans when he was not retained for another term.

Instead he accepted the player-managership of Macclesfield Town, then a non-League club, before leaving the game to become the caretaker of a secondary school in Newquay, Cornwall, also involving himself in local football.

Back in Stoke, Frank Bowyer is remembered as one of the most eminent of all City players, a reminder of long-gone days when the Potters were a genuine power in the land.

Francis Bowyer: born Chesterton, Staffordshire, 10 April 1922; played for Stoke City 1937-1960; died Newquay, Cornwall, 11 November 1999.

Bill Dodgin Snr

'Father of Football' was an affectionate label commonly bestowed on the late Sir Matt Busby, the benign patriarch of Manchester United. But to countless young players making their way in the professional game during nearly four decades after the war, albeit at a rather less exalted level than that graced by Old Trafford's famous Babes, the tag could have been coined for Bill Dodgin.

The diminutive north-easterner managed a succession of clubs, notably Southampton, Fulham and Bristol Rovers, and always displayed a particular talent for discovering and moulding raw talent. Indeed, among those whose early careers he presided over and nurtured at Craven Cottage were Johnny Haynes, who would go on to captain his country, and Bobby Robson, who one day would manage it.

Dodgin was a natural coach, given more to homespun philosophy and gruff common sense than fashionable jargon, but invariably he enjoyed the respect both of his peers and his youthful charges. He knew the game instinctively and he was adept at passing on its finer points, even well into his seventies, when he was still the sprightly chief scout for the Bristol club.

The sturdy son of a Gateshead miner, Dodgin began making his living from soccer in 1929 as a combative, skilful, £6-a-week wing-half with Huddersfield Town, then one of the leading powers in the English game.

Such was the brisk competition for places at Leeds Road, however, that he never settled and during the 1930s he plied his trade in the colours of Lincoln City, Charlton Athletic (whom he helped to rise from the Third to the First Division), Bristol Rovers and Clapton (now Leyton) Orient, before arriving at Southampton in 1939.

In his mid-thirties by the end of the war, Dodgin became a coach at The Dell, taking over as manager in 1946. Twice he led the Saints to the brink of promotion to the top flight, but after missing out by a single point in 1949, he accepted the reins of Fulham, who had just pipped his side for the Second Division championship.

Despite operating the successful youth policy which produced Haynes and Robson, Dodgin struggled to establish the Cottagers among the elite and when they were relegated in 1952 he was given one season to restore their fortunes. Having failed to do so, he was dismissed in October 1953.

A subsequent four-term sojourn with Brentford began with demotion to the Third Division South, where the Bees spent the next three seasons before Dodgin departed to take over team affairs for the Italian club, Sampdoria.

He returned to England with Southern League Yiewsley in 1959, after which he began a successful association with Bristol Rovers which was to last more than two decades. Living up to his reputation for unearthing promising youngsters, Dodgin spent eight years as chief scout at Eastville, then three as manager, before resuming his talent-spotting duties for 11 years until his retirement in 1983.

Rovers entertained royally during his trio of campaigns at the helm, narrowly missing elevation to the Second Division in 1970, never finishing outside the top six and playing the attractive attacking game that was central to their boss' beliefs.

The family atmosphere he fostered at the homely club was particularly appropriate during an FA Cup tie with Fulham in 1970 when the Londoners were managed by Dodgin's son, Bill Junior, who had previously enjoyed a successful playing career with Arsenal and Fulham. Rovers won that day, but the boy had his revenge on the father with two League victories that same term.

Dodgin took football seriously and played it hard, but always he retained a reassuring sense of proportion. One of his most frequently dispensed pieces of advice to an aspiring footballer was: 'Friends are better than money, son, and don't you forget it.' Nothing could have summed up Bill Dodgin more aptly.

William Dodgin: born Gateshead, County Durham, 17 April 1909; played for Huddersfield Town 1929-33, Lincoln City 1933-34, Charlton Athletic 1934-36, Bristol Rovers 1936-37, Clapton Orient (now Leyton Orient) 1937-39, Southampton 1939-45; managed Southampton 1946-49, Fulham 1949-53, Brentford 1953-57, Sampdoria (Italy) 1957-59, Yiewsley (non-League) 1959-61, Bristol Rovers 1969-72; chief scout Bristol Rovers 1961-69 and 1972-83; died Godalming, Surrey, 16 October 1999.

Johnny Byrne

One story about Johnny Byrne sums up the effervescent, bounteously gifted goal-scorer cum creator to perfection.

It was May 1964 and the eve of England's departure for Lisbon, where Alf Ramsey's men would face Portugal in a showpiece international to help celebrate the 50th anniversary of the host country's Football Association. Byrne, or 'Budgie' as he was dubbed for his non-stop nattering both on and off the field, was one of seven players who ventured into London's West End for a spot of socialising which resulted in the curfew imposed by the disciplinarian Ramsey being comprehensively shattered. Afterwards the culprits were left in no doubt by their scathingly caustic boss that if alternatives had been available at such short notice, then they could have packed their bags and gone home.

Unlike some of his fellow offenders – the illustrious likes of Bobby Moore, Bobby Charlton and Jimmy Greaves had joined him on the tiles – Byrne was not an established bulwark of the team and, as a comparative rookie in international terms, might have been apprehensive over the consequences of his escapade. Not quite. Budgie chuckled gleefully when the reproachful Ramsey had withdrawn, then responded to the rebuke in the most effective manner possible, by performing fabulously and scoring a hat-trick against Portugal, including a sublimely chipped late winner.

It seems likely that, had Byrne's dedication matched his talent, then he would have won far more than his 11 full caps. Indeed Ron Greenwood, who managed Budgie during his prime at West Ham, described his visionary, deep-lying predator as 'England's di Stefano'. Any such reference to the great Alfredo, majestic centrepiece of Real Madrid's incomparable side of the 1950s, represented glowing praise, especially from a man who did not dispense compliments lightly.

Though he began his career with Fourth Division Crystal Palace, it soon became clear that the teenage Byrne was a star in the making. He was a telling factor in the Glaziers' transformation from perennial post-war strugglers into a team which won promotion from the basement in the 1960/61 campaign, during which he contributed 30 goals.

That term Byrne became the first player from the League's bottom flight to win England under-23 honours, and he went on to become one of the few Third Division footballers to attain full international status. Clearly it was only a matter of time before he joined a top club and duly, in March 1962, he moved to West Ham United in exchange for £58,000 and Upton Park marksman Ron Brett, who was valued at £7,000.

At the time it was the biggest deal ever completed between British clubs, but if Byrne felt any consequent pressure, it didn't show. Soon he was the most eye-catching member of Greenwood's skilful, sweet-passing team and in 1964 he helped them lift the FA Cup, beating Preston North End 3-2 in one of Wembley's more memorable finals.

He was voted Hammer of the Year, too, no mean achievement in a side which included Moore, Geoff Hurst and the emerging Martin Peters, and it was a shame when a knee injury sustained when playing for England against Scotland ruled him out of his club's European Cup Winners' Cup triumph of 1965.

By then Johnny Byrne was a compelling entertainer at the peak of his powers. Blessed with superb technique, he was an imaginative distributor and crisp finisher who coped bravely with the heavy marking he attracted. His subtle twists and clever one-two passing interchanges unlocked many a defence, while his speciality was opening out play with sudden volleyed dispatches to his wingers, Peter Brabrook and John Sissons.

Certainly, playing alongside such a perceptive partner helped massively in the development of Hurst from a humdrum wing-half into a top-class striker and the man whose hat-trick would clinch the World Cup for England in 1966.

By then, though Byrne was only in his mid-twenties, his own international career was over, perhaps because Ramsey perceived him as too much of an individualist to be accommodated into his regimented team structure.

Considering that he contributed eight goals in his brief England tenure, the West Ham man could consider himself unfortunate to be discarded.

His chirpy demeanour, though, never changed and he was a renowned prankster. Once he pushed a fully-clothed Greaves, a non-swimmer, into the deep end of a hotel pool, then dived in to rescue him. Another time, in Sao Paulo during a match between Brazil and Argentina, he endeared himself to a volatile crowd by conducting their chants, then enraged them by holding up three fingers to indicate the score by which their team was losing. As a result, Byrne, a seething Ramsey and the rest of the England party had to run for their lives as they were showered with missiles.

Come 1967, only 27 but suffering weight problems, he was past his best and returned to Crystal Palace, then in Division Two, for £45,000. A £25,000 transfer to Fulham followed in 1968, but a switch to midfield failed to prolong his effectiveness and, with the Cottagers having plunged from First to Third Division since his arrival, Byrne joined Durban City in 1969.

He settled well in South Africa, going on to enjoy success as manager of Hellenic in Cape Town, and he won plaudits for courageously entering the black townships in search of soccer talent long before segregation was halted.

Later he became involved with South Africa's national side, taking an advisory role when the African Nations Cup was won in 1996, then managed Cape Town Spurs before returning to Hellenic, for whom he was chief scout at the time of his death. His three sons and son-in-law all successfully coached South African teams.

John Joseph Byrne: born West Horsley, Surrey, 13 May 1939; played for Crystal Palace 1956-62, West Ham United 1962-67, Crystal Palace again 1967-68, Fulham 1968-69, Durban City 1969-72; played 11 times for England 1961-64; died Cape Town, South Africa, 27 October 1999.

Ken Keyworth

A brave and brilliant strike by Ken Keyworth had Manchester United wobbling momentarily before clinching their first trophy since the Munich air disaster.

Leicester City were trailing by two goals with only ten minutes of the 1963 FA Cup final remaining when Keyworth launched himself horizontally to net with a glorious diving header. That ball met forehead only inches from a defender's flailing boot was typical of the scorer's style: he was fearless, well-nigh indestructible, and an important component of the unspectacular but feistily effective Leicester combination assembled by Matt Gillies in the early 1960s.

Sadly for Keyworth and his fellow Filberts, his heroics proved in vain on that sunlit Wembley afternoon, as United scored again to secure a 3-1 victory. It was a crushing disappointment as Leicester, with new England goalkeeper Gordon Banks between their posts, had been overwhelming favourites to lift the FA Cup, having finished the League campaign among the First Division's leading group while United had escaped only narrowly from relegation. There had been no Wembley joy for City and Keyworth two years earlier, either, when they had lost 2-0 to Tottenham Hotspur, who thus became the first club that century to complete the coveted League and FA Cup double.

On that occasion the rugged marksman had little chance to register a goal as City full-back Len Chalmers suffered an early and serious injury. No substitutes were permitted then, so Gillies had to reshuffle, pulling Keyworth back into midfield. That he performed competently there was hardly surprising, because he had been signed as a wing-half from his home-town club, Rotherham United, in May 1958.

Keyworth, who had failed to break through as a teenage amateur with Wolverhampton Wanderers, proved a bargain at £9,000 for Leicester, who converted him into a spearhead in 1959. Tall and muscular, he was formidably combative when the ball was in the air and capably efficient when it wasn't, a durable all-rounder renowned for his selflessness. Thereafter he thrived, scoring 77 goals in 215 appearances before he was freed to join Coventry City in December 1964.

Earlier that year Keyworth had garnered his sole club honour, helping Leicester take the fledgling League Cup by defeating Stoke City over two legs. Subsequently he became less mobile following a road accident and he made little impact either at Coventry or with Swindon, his final club.

On leaving the game, Keyworth returned to Rotherham to work as a steelworks quantity surveyor, then an office manager for a building firm.

Kenneth Keyworth: born Rotherham, Yorkshire, 24 February 1934; played for Rotherham United 1952-58; Leicester City 1958-64; Coventry City 1964-65; Swindon Town 1965; died Rotherham, 7 January 2000.

Bert Sproston

Bert Sproston was something of a rarity on the pre-war English soccer scene, an elegant defender who could pass the ball with both accuracy and perception.

True, he was quick, agile and unremittingly gritty like most of his fellow full-backs of that era, but there was a cultured dimension to the Sproston game which delighted the connoisseur. Indeed, so splendidly did the muscular, compact Cestrian perform at club level that he ousted Arsenal's George Male from the England team for two years, and that at a time when the Highbury man had been his country's captain.

Yet Sproston's career had got off to a faltering start when, as a promising teenager, he had joined Huddersfield Town on trial, only to be rejected. Undaunted, he joined his home-town club, the amateurs Sandbach Ramblers, who selected him at the expense of his brother. He performed so ably that he attracted the attention of Leeds United, for whom he signed in 1933.

Seven months later he made his First Division debut, became a first-team regular in 1934/35 and earned his England call-up as a 21-year-old in 1936. Sproston flourished on the international stage and when his reputation burgeoned, cash-strapped Leeds opted to capitalise by selling him to Tottenham Hotspur for the then-substantial fee of £9,500.

However, though continuing to play well, he could not settle in the south and moved back north in unusual circumstances. One Friday he travelled to Manchester with his club ready for the following day's match with City. That evening he joined the Blues, with another £9,500 changing hands, and on the Saturday he took the field against his former team-mates.

Sproston fitted in splendidly at Maine Road but his impetus was halted by the outbreak of war and he served with the Army in India. Though his prime was past when peace was made, he was not a spent force and in 1946/47 he helped Manchester City to win the Second Division title.

In 1950 he was released to join non-League Ashton United, then enlisted with Bolton Wanderers as a coach and trainer in 1951, soon adding physiotherapy to his responsibilities.

Sproston remained at Burnden Park for the next 31 years, contributing to the Trotters' FA Cup triumph of 1958, and the championships of Division Two (1978) and Division Three (1973). After his retirement from full-time activity he scouted for the club.

Bert Sproston: born Elworth, near Sandbach, Cheshire, 22 June 1915; played for Leeds United 1933-38; Tottenham Hotspur 1938; Manchester City 1938-50; capped 11 times for England 1936-38; died Bolton, Lancashire, 25 January 2000.

Sir Stanley Matthews

His sublime, magical skills graced the soccer fields of the world for a third of a century; his name will live as long as the game itself; truly, Stanley Matthews was a unique sporting phenomenon. The only football man to be knighted before the end of his playing days, he was an international institution in a way that no Briton before or since, no matter how brilliant his talent or widespread his fame, has come close to equalling. That he scaled such hitherto unknown heights without either playing for a glamorous club or being a long-term automatic selection for his country makes his achievements and historical stature all the more remarkable.

Yet the Matthews mystique, which inspired awe and affection even from opposing supporters, did not stem from his incandescent footballing ability alone. Throughout his career – which began in the depressed days of the early 1930s, continued through the Second World War and did not end until the Swinging '60s were halfway spent – he remained a self-effacing, undemonstrative figure, utterly dedicated to the work ethic, a footballing Everyman who but for his special gifts might have expected to earn his crust in office or factory.

Still more telling, though, was that amazing longevity. Throughout at least half his performing span, Matthews was ignoring ill-considered advice to 'call it a day' from critics who would pigeonhole thirtysomethings as automatically past it. Instead he simply refused to grow old, becoming the Peter Pan of sport as he played on at the top English club level until he was 50, fulfilling the fantasy of every middle-aged fan in the process.

But what, exactly, made the man a maestro? What was so different about this spare, stooping, almost frail-looking outside-right that could reduce strong, fit, high-quality opponents to helplessness, match after match, season after season, decade after decade?

In fact, his game comprised a spellbinding cocktail of finely-honed attributes. His control was magnetic, his vision all-encompassing, and it was said he could cross a ball to such perfection that his centre-forward was never required to head the side containing the lace! But, most effective of all, his deadliest manoeuvre, was a devilish ploy that earned for him the wholly inadequate tag of a 'one-trick magician'. The ball attached to his feet by means surely sorcerous, Matthews would shuffle towards a defender at little more than a brisk walk; as he closed on his hapless victim, 'The Wizard of Dribble' would sway beguilingly to his left, so far that it seemed he must either cut inside or fall flat on his face. Thus enticed, the full-back would spring, only to find himself tackling thin air, Matthews having changed direction at the last possible moment and flitted past him on the outside.

So scorching was the wingman's acceleration over ten yards that once he was past there was no hope of catching him. He did it so often that opponents knew what was coming but, such was the great man's balance, timing and dexterity, they could do nothing to stop it.

Indeed, so complete was his habitual mastery that foul means availed no better than fair. Though Matthews was the mildest of men, who never deigned to commit a misdemeanour, he was not above taking revenge on brutish hackers by humiliating them – outwitting them once, then turning back coolly to gull them again, most likely leaving them squirming on the seat of their pants.

Some detractors reckoned his wiles slowed the game down, yet in doing so it lured defenders out of position, thus creating space for his colleagues. Others made much of a negligible goal tally of 71 in almost 700 League games, a distinctly fatuous point in view of his exploits as a provider.

Born in the heart of the Potteries during the Great War, Stanley was the third of Jack and Ada Matthews' four sons. Jack, who made his living cutting hair and supplemented his earnings in the boxing ring – hence his sobriquet 'The Fighting Barber of Hanley' – was a veteran of some 350 contests, a pugilist skilled enough to grace the National Sporting Club. That competitive streak was inherited by young Stan, a fleet-footed child who once won his father – a fitness fanatic who enforced the same dedication in his sons – a sizeable bet in a local race.

But it was always soccer at which he showed outstanding aptitude, once scoring eight times in a school match while playing at centre-half, and after a brief spell as a bricklayer's apprentice, he joined Stoke City as a 15-year-old office-boy cum boot-cleaner. Word of his exceptional talent spread quickly to other clubs, but City beat off all-comers, allegedly employing 'minders' to see that he was not poached on his way to sign professional forms on his 17th birthday, and Matthews became a Potter in 1932.

That same year he made his senior debut, and a season later had helped Stoke win promotion to the First Division, a feat he was to repeat an incredible 30 years later. Before long he was cutting a swathe among the elite and in 1934, still only 19, Matthews had scored in his first game for England. However, his earliest full international forays were not an unqualified success and – bizarrely in view of what was to follow – one eminent contemporary scribe criticised him roundly for being slow and hesitant. Thereafter he was to find himself in and out of the England reckoning, playing in only 54 of the 119 internationals (excluding wartime matches) between 1934 and 1957, a statistic for which the selectors were pilloried constantly by outraged fans. To them he was to become little less than a soccer deity and they saw the post-war emergence of Tom Finney as a rival for his role as offering scant excuse for his omission.

Even more overt anger surfaced in Stoke in 1938 when a cash dispute, exacerbated by a simmering personality clash with manager Bob McGrory, boiled over into Matthews making a transfer request. Consternation reigned at the prospective departure of the city's favourite son, to such an extent that local businessmen claimed the unrest was affecting production. A protest meeting attended by 3,000 supporters, with 2,000 more waving banners outside the hall, underlined the scale of his celebrity and the local hero, warmed by such adulation, reached amicable settlement with the club.

Come the Second World War, Matthews joined the RAF as a fitness instructor, a role which allowed him freedom to link with the likes of Raich Carter and Tommy Lawton in an emergency England side and to give some of the most exhilarating performances of his career. Ironically those wartime matches, though most were against sterling opposition, were never granted cap status.

After the conflict, Matthews resumed his duties at the Victoria Ground, but remained at odds with McGrory and in 1947, the year in which he made the first of two appearances for Great Britain against the Rest of Europe, he broke his ties with his home town. Now aged 32, he was considered to be approaching the veteran stage but remained a compelling performer. Thus when he let it be known he really would move this time, but only to Blackpool where he owned a hotel, the Seasiders were happy to snap him up for a mere £11,500. It proved to be one of the biggest transfer bargains of all time.

Matthews relished the north-west, where he maintained a rigorous, almost religious training routine on the beach, stuck to a spartan diet which involved fasting one day a week, and adhered to a rather prim and proper lifestyle. Though the modest Midlander stressed unfailingly that he was surrounded by splendid team-mates – especially his great friend, the prolific marksman Stan Mortensen – Matthews was undeniably the leading light as Blackpool reached three FA Cup finals in six seasons.

The first, against Matt Busby's Manchester United in 1948, was billed as the 33-year-old's last realistic opportunity of pocketing the winner's medal he craved, but the Seasiders lost a breathtaking match 4-2. The next, three years later, was described as positively the final chance for a man aged 36. But instead of Matthews, the hero was Newcastle United's Jackie Milburn, as the Geordie fans rattled the Wembley rafters with a victorious rendition of The Blaydon Races.

By 1953 Matthews was 38; surely by now it was too late. Certainly it seemed so for the first 60 minutes of Blackpool's all-Lancashire clash with Bolton Wanderers, as Nat Lofthouse and company surged into a 3-1 lead and the much-vaunted Stan was reduced to a shadowy, almost anonymous presence.

But cometh the hour-mark, cometh the man. Suddenly the tangerine-shirted wizard reached for his wand and the script was transformed from anti-climax to fairytale. As an injury-stricken Bolton began to tire, Matthews seemed to sprout wings on his heels, dancing and weaving his way through their limp rearguard almost at will. He set up one goal with a tantalising cross, kept up the pressure until Mortensen restored parity with a free-kick, then set off on an unstoppable mazy run to create the winner for Bill Perry two minutes into stoppage time. The stadium, the country, the footballing world went wild with excitement; Matthews had his medal at last and was chaired off in triumph.

That might have been a fitting moment to hang up his boots, especially after several recent bouts of knee trouble, but Matthews decided, with impeccable judgement, that he still had more, much more, to give. So he carried on, won back his England place for the umpteenth time, put on some of his most dazzling international shows during the mid-1950s, and had many sound judges calling in vain for his inclusion in the 1958 World Cup squad. For good measure he was awarded the CBE in 1957.

By 1961, however, with young men pushing for recognition, his productive sojourn with the Seasiders ended, not with retirement but with an emotional return to Stoke City, who paid Blackpool £3,500 for the services of a 46-year-old. Many expected Matthews' second coming in the Potteries to be no more than a gimmick, a sentimental peep show, but how wrong they were.

When he re-signed, Stoke were near the foot of the Second Division, averaging gates of around 10,000 and fears of bankruptcy were rife. But Matthews gave new hope to the old place; crowds rocketed to 30,000-plus, relegation was avoided, top names such as Jimmy McIlroy and Dennis Viollet were persuaded that Stoke was the club to join.

Two years on fron his arrival, with Methuselah still performing miracles, they lifted the Second Division championship, and there are no prizes for guessing who scored the goal that clinched the crown, even if it was his first of the season. For his efforts, Matthews was made Footballer of the Year for the second time (he had won the inaugural award in 1948), but even that was not the final pinnacle.

In the New Year's honours list of 1965, he was created Sir Stanley for his services to football, and that February, aged 50 years and five days, he became, in a game against Fulham, the oldest man to play in the First Division. In April some of the world's greatest stars – Ferenc Puskas, Alfredo di Stefano, Lev Yashin – turned out in his testimonial match and only then did Matthews give up playing the game he loved.

Of course, Stoke should have retained him in some capacity, but there was inevitable jealousy and he moved on to a hard-working three-year stint as general manager of nearby Port Vale. That ended sadly when the club was expelled from the Football League for financial irregularities (they were re-elected immediately) and he stepped down, disillusioned by a turn of events beyond his control.

That coincided with divorce from his long-time wife Betty, the daughter of a former Stoke trainer, but soon he was married again, to Mila, whom he had met on worldwide coaching travels. For a time he lived in Malta (where briefly he managed a local side, Hibernian, during their European campaign) and then Canada, before returning once more to his beloved Potteries, where he has been honoured by an imposing statue.

Matthews continued playing kickabout football well into his seventies, his enthusiasm undimmed. He never sought the limelight – indeed, his shyness, which made him rather a loner, was often misinterpreted as aloofness – yet he lit up his chosen game like no one else. His value in today's transfer market would be incalculable, as would his worth as a soccer ambassador. His like, we can depend, will not be seen again.

Stanley Matthews: born Hanley, Staffordshire, 1 February 1915; played for Stoke City 1932-47 and 1961-65, Blackpool 1947-61; capped 54 times for England 1934-57; CBE 1957; knighted 1965; general manager Port Vale 1965-68; manager Hibernian of Malta 1969; died Newcastle-under-Lyme, Staffordshire, 23 February 2000.

Wilf Mannion

After one breathtaking performance for Great Britain in the 6-1 annihilation of the Rest of Europe at Hampden Park, Glasgow, in 1947, Wilf Mannion – hailed by the world's press as undisputed man of the match – described himself as 'just a useful cog in a well-oiled machine'.

What the diminutive, blond inside-forward omitted to mention, with becoming modesty, was that he was the component which made a crucial contribution to the smooth running of such assorted big wheels as Stanley Matthews and Tommy Lawton.

Mannion was invariably the creative fulcrum of any team for which he played. Weaving mazy patterns with his tiny, dancing feet, the stockily-built 5ft 5in Teessider possessed dexterity on the ball that dazzled the eye, exceptional balance and a body swerve that left befuddled opponents tackling thin air.

His mastery over the ball was remarkable, even in confined spaces and under heavy challenge, and with his clever, penetrative passing he conjured goal-scoring opportunities from the most unlikely of situations. That said, his critics maintained that rather too many of his dispatches were of the square, safe variety, which in their eyes placed him fractionally below the standard of his two magnificent contemporaries, Raich Carter and Peter Doherty.

However he, like they, was an accomplished maker as well as taker of goals, and in his 19-year professional career he contributed many sensational individual strikes. He was capable in the air, too, for such a small man, his timing tending to compensate for lack of inches.

For all but his final season, Mannion served his local club, Middlesbrough, but despite his distinctly cherubic, choirboyish looks he did not fit easily into the archetypal mould of faithful homegrown retainer. He resented the way in which top footballers were paid lowly wages while clubs cashed in heavily on the post-war soccer boom, and he had the courage not only to say so, but to do something about it. Indeed, in 1948 he spent six months out of the game without pay after refusing to re-sign for 'Boro, earning a living as a representative for a building firm across the Pennines in Oldham.

Humble Oldham Athletic saw this as a chance to secure the services of the England star for themselves, but were quoted the then-astronomical price of £25,000. Nevertheless they were so keen that they scraped together £15,000, including £2,000 from a public collection, before giving up their unlikely quest.

Eventually Mannion patched up his differences with Middlesbrough, and re-signed in time to play a crucial part in their successful campaign to avoid relegation from the First Division.

However, he was not through with controversy. In 1955, having joined Hull City, he was suspended by the Football League after he refused to divulge details of alleged illegal payments to players, an explosively sensitive matter he had raised in newspaper articles. In the event, by then aged 37, he left the League to play for a series of semi-professional clubs until, finally, he set aside his boots some seven years later.

The career Wilf Mannion could look back on, though periodically turbulent, was one of splendid achievement. After sparkling as a schooldays' prodigy, he turned professional with Middlesbrough in 1936, winning a regular place in 1937/38 and helping 'Boro to finish a mere six points behind the League champions, Arsenal. By the following season he was maturing into a top-class play-maker, only for his progress to be interrupted by the outbreak of the Second World War. At first he served in the Auxiliary Fire Service, then joined the Army, all the while continuing to play football and impressing sufficiently to be called up for his first wartime international, against Scotland in 1941.

A posting to the Middle East with the Green Howards cost him his place – Raich Carter stepped in – but on being demobbed in 1946, Mannion found himself winning his first full England cap alongside 'The Great Horatio', against Northern Ireland. Mannion responded with a hat-trick that day at Windsor Park, Belfast, going on to claim regular tenure of his country's number-ten shirt and cementing his international reputation with his famous performance for Great Britain in 1947, during which he scored twice.

With colleagues of the calibre of Matthews, Carter, Lawton, Tom Finney and others, he was part of a hugely enterprising set-up, but a gruesome shock was in store. In June 1950, at Belo Horizonte in Brazil, England were defeated 1-0 in a World Cup tie by the unconsidered USA. Of the aforementioned stars, only Finney lined up alongside Mannion that day, but that did nothing to offset a national sporting humiliation of staggering proportions. Mannion was omitted for the next game, though later he regained his inside-forward berth, only to suffer agony of a different sort, a fractured cheekbone against Scotland in 1951.

Soon after that he won the last of his 26 full caps, at the age of 33, but remained an influential member of a Middlesbrough side which was finding First Division life increasingly hard to sustain. After the club lost the battle to remain in the top flight in May 1954, Mannion retired, only to be lured back to the professional game by Second Division Hull City.

He made his debut for the Tigers on 27 December 1954, attracting a crowd of nearly 40,000, almost double that season's average at Boothferry Park. Sadly, at 36, he was able to make little difference to a struggling side and, amid the unpleasantness over his allegations in the press, he departed in the spring.

Mannion went on to sample management in the non-League ranks, but he was not cut out for administration and drifted out of football in middle age. Thereafter he experienced cruelly lean and harrowing times, being reduced to working on building sites and for the railway, doubtless reflecting that countless less talented individuals were making a fortune from the modern game.

If it was any consolation, Wilf Mannion was safe in the knowledge that it would be he, and not they, who would occupy the attention, and stimulate the imagination, of soccer historians in years to come.

Wilfred James Mannion: born South Bank, Yorkshire, 16 May 1918; played for Middlesbrough 1936-54, Hull City 1954-55; capped 26 times for England 1946-51; died Redcar, Cleveland, 14 April 2000.

Shay Brennan

He didn't bask in the idolatry heaped on George Best or enjoy the reverence inspired by Bobby Charlton, but no member of Manchester United's European Cup-winning side of 1968 was better loved by his fellow footballers than Shay Brennan.

Despite being born in Manchester, Brennan was of Republican stock and an archetypal easy-going Irishman, twinkling of eye, broad of grin, a disarming mixture of mischief and modesty. Without allowing it to interfere with his work, he was keen on a drink and relished a bet, and the manner in which he played down his own part in United's multiple triumphs defined his gentle, unassuming nature.

In fact, his role was immense and it began when the future Republic of Ireland skipper enlisted on the Old Trafford groundstaff in 1953, overjoyed at the prospect of cleaning the boots of his erstwhile heroes, the likes of Johnny Carey and Stan Pearson.

Though destined to mature into a high-quality right-back, Brennan began as a silkily skilful inside-forward, and it was in that role that he helped the Red Devils to retain the FA Youth Cup in 1955. However, a more dramatic contribution was imminent.

This was the era of Matt Busby's Babes, arguably still the most gloriously gifted collection of rookie footballers ever assembled by a British club, and the nation was stunned when eight of those young leviathans were killed, and two more were maimed, in the Munich air disaster of 1958.

However, one inevitable upshot of the tragedy was the opening of doors for other United boys and one of them was Brennan, who found himself pitchforked into his senior debut against Sheffield Wednesday in the FA Cup, the club's first game after the crash.

Despite filling the unfamiliar slot of outside-left for the first time in his professional life – 'I had as little idea about playing on the wing as the man in the moon', as he put it later – Brennan emerged as the unlikely hero, scoring twice on an emotion-charged night as the Red Devils completed a rousing 3-0 victory.

Thereafter, as Munich survivors Bobby Charlton and Dennis Viollet returned to action, he was unable to hold a regular place and despite netting in the 5-3 semi-final replay defeat of Fulham, he was not selected for the final at Wembley. His own date with destiny at the famous old stadium would be delayed for another ten years.

As Matt Busby set about the painstaking task of rebuilding Manchester United, Brennan's inexperience saw him slip out of contention for a season before he emerged as a wing-half during 1959/60. However, it was not until his conversion to right-back at the outset of the following campaign that he was to demonstrate his full worth. Now he stood out as a poised and unflappable defender, a master of canny positional play who was more likely to jockey his opponent away from the danger area than to dive in with a wild tackle. Then, when the time was right, Brennan would steal the ball from the unsuspecting attacker's foot before laying off a simple, sensible pass to one of his more creative colleagues.

Gradually, as newcomers such as Denis Law and Paddy Crerand were added, the reconstructed side grew into a headily entertaining unit which recorded its first triumph in 1963, lifting the FA Cup after a disappointing League campaign which had seen them flirt with relegation.

Unhappily for Brennan, he was denied Wembley glory again, suffering a springtime injury and then proving unable to oust club skipper Noel Cantwell in time for the big day.

In the subsequent half-decade, though, he made up for it comprehensively. Brennan pocketed League championship medals in 1964/65 and 1966/67, and in May 1968 finally enjoyed his moment in the Wembley spotlight when the Red Devils attained their version of the holy grail, beating Benfica of Portugal by four goals to one after extra time, thus becoming the first English winners of the European Cup.

In truth, whereas he had been unlucky in missing out on previous finals, this time around fortune smiled on Brennan, who had spent most of that season in the reserves while youngster Francis Burns had held sway. But come the second leg of the semi-final against Real Madrid, Busby opted for the older man's experience to counter the potent menace of the brilliant Francisco Gento. So splendidly did Brennan perform that he retained his berth for the most important match in the club's history.

In parallel to his success with United, he earned international recognition, and by what was then an unconventional route. Back in 1962 Brennan had reached the fringe of the England squad but then slipped back, and it seemed that his trophy cabinet would remain unadorned by caps. But in 1965 a new FIFA ruling enabled him to become the first English-born player to represent the Republic of Ireland, and he went on to make 19 appearances for the land of his ancestors, five of them as captain.

Back at club level, after 1968 the slowing thirtysomething remained on the fringe of the side for two more terms before moving to Ireland, where he became player-manager of Waterford. For a while he prospered at Kilcohan Park, leading his charges to two League titles, but then decided that the cares of management were not for him and became involved in a local courier business.

Shay Brennan died suddenly while playing golf, one of his great passions, leaving his countless friends to comfort themselves with the thought that the genial charmer couldn't have conceived of a more convivial way to go.

Seamus Anthony Brennan: born Manchester, 6 May 1937; played for Manchester United 1955-1970, Waterford 1970-74; capped 19 times for the Republic of Ireland 1965-70; managed Waterford 1970-74; died Tramore, County Waterford, Republic of Ireland, 9 June 2000.

Willie Maddren

Despite being dogged by cruel misfortune both on the pitch and off it, Willie Maddren was one of the most influential figures to have graced football on Teesside. He served Middlesbrough nobly, both as a player who shared in heady triumphs during the 1970s under the management of Jack Charlton and, a decade later, as a boss who toiled courageously through troubled times during which the future of his club was under dire threat.

At his performing peak the tall, affable north-easterner was one of the most talented central defenders in the land, as strong and resourceful as all stoppers must be, but distinguished further by the precision of his distribution and the intelligent manner in which he anticipated danger before snuffing it out, unfussily but with calm authority.

In most other eras, his all-round excellence might have yielded full international honours, but Maddren was competing for an England berth with the starry likes of Roy McFarland, Colin Todd, Dave Watson and Phil Thompson, and he was limited to five appearances at under-23 level before injury halted his still-flourishing career at the age of 26.

The ill luck which was to hound this charming, down-to-earth fellow began in his teens when he was playing for Port Clarence Juniors and broke his ankle two days before he was due for a trial with Leeds United. Don Revie's ultra-successful club did not monitor the youngster's recovery but Middlesbrough did and Maddren turned professional at Ayresome Park in 1968.

The following January he made his senior debut as a substitute, then demonstrated his commitment when selected as an attacker – he was versatile enough to fill virtually any outfield position – for his full senior debut in the final home game of that campaign. After ten minutes he left the pitch with a broken nose, returning to the action to score, though his heroics were unavailing as 'Boro lost to Bury.

Over subsequent seasons Maddren became established in the heart of the rearguard, eventually making nearly 350 appearances and forming a majestic partnership with big Stuart Boam. The two men complemented each other perfectly, Boam an archetypal commanding stopper and Maddren reading the game cannily at his side, covering and tidying up when the team was under pressure, prompting attacks with canny distribution when possession was regained.

His glory days were enjoyed under Charlton. In 1973/74, the World Cup winner's first term at the helm, 'Boro romped away with the Second Division championship and Maddren didn't miss a match as only 30 goals were conceded, the table was topped by a record 15 points and promotion was ensured with seven games still to play.

Thereafter he flourished over the next three terms as 'Boro became solidly established in the top flight, also reaching FA Cup and League Cup quarter-finals and winning the now-defunct Anglo-Scottish Cup in 1974/75, losing a League Cup semi-final in 1975/76 and contesting another League Cup quarter-final in 1976/77.

Then came sporting calamity when Maddren suffered a chronic knee injury in the autumn of 1977 and he never played again. However, he remained in the game, coaching with Hartlepool United before returning to Middlesbrough as coach and physiotherapist.

Come the spring of 1984, with 'Boro floundering towards the bottom of Division Two, boss Malcolm Allison was sacked and Charlton returned to help the cash-strapped club through its immediate crisis, assisted ably by Maddren. Relegation was avoided and that summer Maddren accepted the managerial reins.

He reckoned he would need three years to put the Ayresome Park outfit back on its feet but, with the club more than £1 million in debt – a huge amount at that juncture – he was not granted the time. After a season of travail in which demotion was narrowly avoided, the struggle continued into the following campaign and in February 1986 he was dismissed in favour of his recently appointed coach, Bruce Rioch.

Perhaps Maddren was not ruthless enough for the management rat-race, but he was popular with his charges and certainly had an eye for a promising footballer, as demonstrated by his acquisition of future stars such as Gary Pallister and Bernie Slaven. In particular, the signing of Pallister from non-League Billingham was a massive coup, as reputedly the giant centre-half cost no more than a set of strips and a few balls, yet eventually he was sold to Manchester United for £2.3 million.

Saddened but undaunted, Maddren left football and made a success of a sports outfitting business, but lying in wait for him was a catastrophe which put all so-called sporting 'tragedies' into stark perspective. In 1995 he was diagnosed as suffering from motor neurone disease, a degenerative condition which was to claim his life five years later.

However, he never bowed to his fate, instead campaigning ceaselessly and inspirationally with his wife, Hilary, to heighten public awareness of MND and together they were instrumental in raising some £200,000 for research.

William Dixon Maddren: born Haverton Hill, County Durham, 11 January 1951; played for Middlesbrough 1968-79; managed Middlesbrough 1984-86; died Stockton-on-Tees, 29 August 2000.

Geordie Armstrong

Though he was immeasurably too modest to contemplate such a notion himself, it can be stated without fear of credible contradiction that Geordie Armstrong was one of the finest footballers never to win a full cap for England.

Happily there was ample compensation at club level, the chunky little north-easterner earning deathless renown for his workaholic wing-play in 1970/71 as Arsenal became only the second side during the 20th century to lift the League and FA Cup double.

Yet while he was well-nigh indispensable to manager Bertie Mee's strategy during one of the most glorious campaigns in the Gunners' history, no single achievement should be allowed to obscure his monumental overall contribution to the Highbury cause, which was spread over some 26 years, taking in stints as both player and coach.

During the course of 16 seasons, Armstrong – whose given name of George was so aptly adapted to his affectionately and universally employed epithet – made 621 senior appearances for the north Londoners. That was considerably more than any previous wearer of the famous red-and-white shirt, and only two men – David O'Leary and (recently) Tony Adams – have since surpassed his record.

Fitness-wise, Geordie was a phenomenon. So perpetual was his motion, and so frequently did he materialise in every corner of the pitch, that harassed opponents could have been excused for surmising that his mother had given birth to triplets and that they all played for Arsenal.

Though he could feature on the right, his usual beat was up and down the left flank and grateful colleagues would joke that they didn't need a left-back when he was on the wing because he did the work of two men, one minute raiding exuberantly in attack, the next tackling wholeheartedly in defence. At the training ground, he was equally energetic, often staggering team-mates by demanding a game of tennis after a workout which had left everyone else dead on their feet.

But let no one run away with the idea that Armstrong was merely a workhorse. In fact, he was an all-round technician of vast accomplishment, an assured manipulator of a football blessed with blistering pace, a fierce shot and the priceless attribute of being able to deliver crosses accurately with either foot. He was never a prolific scorer, but such was his massive percentage of assists, that was scarcely relevant.

After being allowed to leave both Newcastle United and Grimsby Town as a teenage trialist, and commencing employment as an apprentice electrician, Armstrong joined Arsenal as a promising inside-forward in August 1961. The following year he was awarded three England youth caps and made his First Division debut for an Arsenal side which was undergoing a period of transition.

By early 1963 Armstrong had cemented a regular berth and quickly matured into a key supplier of chances to a high-scoring forward line which also included Joe Baker, Geoff Strong, George Eastham and Alan Skirton. The rearguard under Highbury boss

Billy Wright was not as reliable, though, and after making five appearances for England's under-23 team in mid-decade, the endlessly enthusiastic flankman had to wait until the reign of Bertie Mee to become part of a side in genuine contention for honours.

After enduring the disappointment of defeat in the League Cup finals of 1968 and 1969, Armstrong produced such magnificent form in 1969/70 that he was voted the Gunners' player of the year and celebrated with a European Fairs Cup winner's medal.

But even richer prizes awaited. The following term a supremely workmanlike and hard-nosed Arsenal combination outstripped Don Revie's much-fancied Leeds United to lift the League title and came from behind to conquer Bill Shankly's Liverpool in the FA Cup final. Armstrong's input was massive, his pinpoint centres providing fabulous fodder for marksmen John Radford and Ray Kennedy, his ceaseless industry creating space for marauding full-back Bob McNab and elegant midfielder George Graham.

In another era, surely, Geordie would have been rewarded with England recognition, but national manager Sir Alf Ramsey held little brief for wingers. Thus, while many lesser performers were honoured, his opportunity never came.

Undaunted, he soldiered on at Highbury, continuing to maintain his own lofty standards as the team lost the 1972 FA Cup final to Leeds and then began to disintegrate, rather unexpectedly, around him.

Sadly, after labouring mightily to help the Gunners through a mid-1970s slump, Armstrong experienced differences with new manager (and former team-mate) Terry Neill, prompting him to leave his beloved Highbury and join Leicester City for £15,000 as a more-than-useful thirtysomething in 1977. There followed one unfulfilling term at Filbert Street, which ended with the Foxes being relegated from the top flight, before he moved on to Fourth Division Stockport County in September 1978.

Finding himself in the basement for the first time in his career, Armstrong strove nobly in a poor side before retiring as a player, aged 35, in the summer of 1979. However, such was his undying love of the game that he determined to remain in it, completing coaching stints with Aston Villa, the Norwegian club Narvik, Fulham, non-League Enderby Town, Middlesbrough under first Malcolm Allison and then Jack Charlton, Queen's Park Rangers and another non-League outfit, Worcester City.

Having thus accumulated diverse experience, Armstrong took his expertise to Kuwait, where he enjoyed enormous success with the national side as well as transforming the fortunes of two leading clubs.

Unhappily, this was achieved against a background of political intrigue and chicanery which led to frustration, outrage and ultimately even fear for his family's safety before he returned to Arsenal in 1990, manager George Graham placing him in charge of the reserves. This was a task at which Armstrong excelled, communicating his unquenchable fervour, his staunch belief in the passing game and a burning hunger to succeed which might have stemmed from his hard-working origins in a ship-building community.

Until the last he brimmed with zest and remained seemingly super-fit for a man of 56, so much so that current Arsenal boss Arsene Wenger spoke recently of his remarkably unchanging attitude and condition. How poignant, then, that the brain haemorrhage which led to his death a few hours later should have occurred while he was supervising a training session at the club's training ground, London Colney in Hertfordshire.

Shrewd, loyal and honest, unshakeable in his commitment to his young charges and a devoted family man, Armstrong was an impeccable role model, both through his inspirational attainments as a player and his vast proficiency as a coach.

On a personal note, for ten years he had been helping me with writing projects and we had become friends. It so happened that on the day of his death I was due to referee a boys' football match, which delayed the delivery of this obituary. Somehow I think Geordie Armstrong would have approved.

George Armstrong: born Hebburn, County Durham, 9 August 1944; played for Arsenal 1961-1977, Leicester City 1977-78, Philadelphia Fury on loan 1978, Stockport County 1978-79; coached with Aston Villa, Narvik of Norway, Fulham, Enderby Town, Middlesbrough, Queen's Park Rangers, Worcester City, Kuwait national and club sides and Arsenal reserves; died Hemel Hempstead, Hertfordshire, 1 November 2000.

Len Shackleton

Len Shackleton was a footballing maverick, an entertainer blessed with a sublime talent but with not an ounce of propriety.

An habitually eccentric, occasionally outrageous showman whose extravagant skills were not always tailored to meet his team's needs, he lit up the post-war soccer boom, charming the fans who gloried in his impish mastery of the ball. But by both word and deed he continually exasperated, even affronted, the conformists of his day. Unfortunately for this most singular of inside-forwards, they were in the majority – and they ran the game.

The most famous example of Shackleton's often-contemptuous dissidence bears repetition, because it sums up his piercing, anarchic sense of humour so tellingly. His 1955 autobiography, aptly titled *Clown Prince of Soccer*, included one chapter headed 'The average director's knowledge of football'. All that followed was a blank page.

Out of character with all that was to follow, Yorkshireman 'Shack' made conventional progress through schoolboy football, his slick skills and gift for scoring goals attracting the inevitable posse of talent scouts from the big clubs. The upshot was a place on the Arsenal groundstaff in 1938, but he lasted only a year before being rejected as 'too frail' for the hurly-burly of professional soccer.

The disappointed teenager spent a year working for the London Paper Mills company before returning to his home town of Bradford in a job assembling aircraft radios. That was in 1940, by which time he had volunteered for all three services, each time unsuccessfully, as he was engaged in work essential to the war effort.

Meanwhile he resurrected his football career with Bradford Park Avenue, going on to score 160 goals during six seasons of wartime competition, as well as guesting for the other local club, Bradford City. Indeed, on Christmas Day 1940, the eager rookie turned out for Park Avenue in the morning and City in the afternoon.

Come 1945 and peacetime, Shackleton, having served in a coal-mine as a Bevin Boy, began making his living from soccer once more. But despite some splendidly artistic displays for Park Avenue he encountered terrace abuse for 'not getting stuck in' – chasing lost causes was never one of his virtues – and in 1946 he accepted a £13,000 transfer to Newcastle United, who recognised quality when they saw it.

Shackleton's debut as a Magpie could hardly have been more sensational. He netted six times in the 13-0 annihilation of Newport County, including a first-half hat-trick in 155 seconds, believed to be the quickest in the history of English professional football at the time. That year, too, he was called to his country's colours for an unofficial Victory international, but did not impress and lost his place.

At club level, he linked delightfully with fellow attackers Roy Bentley and Charlie Wayman, and he played an integral part in Newcastle's progress to the 1947 FA Cup semi-finals. The following term he remained on song, but disagreements ensued and in February 1948 Shackleton was sold to Sunderland for a British record-equalling £20,000.

With the Wearsiders he produced some of his most irresistible form, both as a scorer, and, more especially, as a creator of goals, and was rewarded by a first full England cap that September. However, though he could be as effective as any of his peers on his day Shack could be frustratingly inconsistent, too, and failed to hold his international place.

Of course, a major factor in his exclusion – even after England suffered humiliating defeats in his absence – was connected to his outspoken eccentricity. There were times when the national selectors paid lip service to Shackleton's undeniable class by pronouncing him 'too good for the rest of the team', implying the other players could not react to his speed of thought, but such statements were greeted sceptically by the supporters, who deserved better than such platitudes.

When, after a lengthy absence, Shack was recalled in 1954, he signed off in his fifth and final international with a beautiful, subtly dispatched goal against the world champions West Germany, an irony which seemed to encapsulate his England career.

However, it would be wrong to suggest that Len Shackleton was an easy man to accommodate in any team. His differences with the Welsh star Trevor Ford at Sunderland, for example, were well known. There was at least one occasion, during a friendly game in Holland, when he made a point at Ford's expense. The impudent play-maker dribbled through the entire opposition defence but then, instead of pushing the ball into the empty net, he passed back to Ford and snapped: 'Don't say I never give you a pass!'

Shackleton – a man of diverse interests who owned a barber's shop on Wearside, was qualified as a boxing referee and later became a sports journalist in the north-east – bowed out of the game, aged 35, after injuring an ankle against Arsenal at Roker Park in 1957.

Regrettably, he departed without a major medal to his name, though it would be inappropriate to view such an individualistic career in terms of conventional honours. Better to recall the impish ball-juggler in his element, shoulders hunched, arms flapping, slicing defences to ribbons by the magical feats he could perform with a football.

Leonard Francis Shackleton: born Bradford, Yorkshire, 3 May 1922; played for Bradford Park Avenue 1940-46, Newcastle United 1946-48, Sunderland 1948-57; capped five times for England 1948-54; died Grange-over-Sands, Cumbria, 28 November 2000.

Stan Cullis

If you kicked Stan Cullis in the heart, you'd only break your leg. So ran a typical testimony to one of the most successful bosses in British football history, a driven, endlessly dynamic disciplinarian who built Wolverhampton Wanderers into a thunderously potent post-war power. In fact, the words were delivered during his days as an abrasive but deceptively skilful centre-half, though they summed up his autocratic managerial style with a brisk succinctness that was entirely apt. And, while many men might have winced to have been described thus, Cullis would have taken it as a compliment.

In truth, the Cheshire-born martinet deserved rather more bouquets than his fearsome reputation allowed. Before he became Wolves' guiding light in 1948, the Black Countrymen had never won the League title and had not lifted the FA Cup for 40 years. Yet after a dozen seasons of the Cullis tenure, the championship pennant had fluttered over Molineux on three occasions and the coveted knockout trophy had been adorned twice by the club's gold-and-black ribbons.

In addition, Wolves had blazed the British trail into Europe, albeit in friendlies, paving the way for Manchester United, Liverpool et al in future campaigns and doing much to revive English prestige at a time when the national team had suffered a series of debilitating setbacks.

For all the glory that was to follow, the teenage Cullis' first brush with professional soccer ended in rejection. Bolton Wanderers deemed him 'too slow' and he was forced to lower his sights, signing instead for his home-town club, non-League Ellesmere Port, in 1932. A serious, conscientious youth, he turned his thoughts to journalism as a possible career and took evening classes in shorthand, Esperanto, French and book-keeping as an insurance against failure as a footballer.

In the event, he need not have worried. In February 1934, his father asked Wolves to give the boy a trial; they did so and they liked what they saw. Though standing only 5ft 10in, not tall for a centre-half, Cullis combined flinty aggression with far more natural talent than was then expected of a defender and, crucially, he was intelligent enough to blend his qualities to maximum effect. With an unlovely, crouching gait, which was to attract the nickname of 'Flipper', proving no barrier to constructive distribution, he was in the senior team by season's end.

A dominating personality who gelled productively with his similarly-inclined manager, Major Frank Buckley, Cullis proved a natural leader, and by the age of 19 the Bolton reject was captain of Wolves. Thereafter he consolidated rapidly, performing majestically as the Wanderers suffered the triple frustration of being championship runners-up in both 1938 and 1939, and losing the 1939 FA Cup final to the underdogs Portsmouth.

Rich personal consolation came in the form of an England call-up in 1937 and his rise to become his country's last skipper before the war. Sadly, Cullis was never to win another full cap, though during the years of conflict, in 20 unofficial international matches, he contributed some of the finest performances of his career. In most of them he joined Cliff Britton and Joe Mercer in what many pundits maintain was the best half-back line England has known, the trio linking also as guest players for Aldershot and for the Army.

On demob from his service as a physical training instructor, Cullis resumed as Wolves' stopper in 1945, still effective enough but without quite recapturing the form of his youth. He suffered from frequent concussion, thought to be caused by heading the ball, and an hour before the last match of 1946/47 he announced he was to retire at the end of the afternoon.

He believed he would be bowing out at the top as Wolves had only to win the home game to take the title, but, mortifyingly, they lost to Liverpool and the championship went to Anfield instead.

Cullis did not leave Molineux, however, becoming assistant to the manager Ted Vizard and then, a year later, assuming full control of team affairs. Now followed the most illustrious era in Wolves' history as the bald-headed, bleak-faced workaholic began to mould a truly formidable team. Blessed with utter confidence in his own ability, Cullis the perfectionist drove his players relentlessly, demanding that their dedication be as passionately all-consuming as his own.

The result was a robust, virile, ultra-fit combination dubbed 'kick-and-rush merchants' and 'cloggers' by detractors but which, at its peak, served up truly exhilarating fare. Wolves' long-ball tactics were simple but devastating, relying mainly on pace and power, although –

and this tended to be overlooked – high-quality footballers were needed to make the most of the system. Though Cullis announced that 'our players are not encouraged to parade their ability in an ostentatious fashion' he was well aware of his debt to thoroughbreds such as the wingers Johnny Hancocks and Jimmy Mullen, and his captain, the defender Billy Wright.

All three featured prominently as Cullis celebrated his first term at the helm with an FA Cup final victory over Leicester City and remained in situ in 1953/54 when, after several near-misses, Wolves landed that elusive first League championship. For the rest of the decade, the club vied for dominance with Matt Busby's Manchester United and it is a tribute to 'Mr Molineux' that when more titles arrived, in 1958 and 1959, he had assembled practically a whole new team.

Then there were those visionary forays into Europe. After rousing mid-1950s floodlit victories over the likes of Moscow Spartak, Honved of Hungary and Real Madrid, Cullis proclaimed his Wolves to be world club champions, and in those pioneering days before organised club competitions, it was a perfectly arguable case.

However, 1960 saw a watershed in the fortunes of both Wolves and Cullis. That year they won the FA Cup and missed a hat-trick of championships – as well as the League and Cup double, at the time not performed in the 20th century – by a single point. Thereafter, with Molineux's hitherto bountiful youth system stuttering and with rivals increasingly able to counter Cullis' tactics, a decline into mediocrity set in.

Yet, even in a climate where the average football manager's job security was tenuous in the extreme, it appeared inconceivable that the man who had transformed his club into a major force was in danger – but he was. Come September 1964, with Wolves at the wrong end of the First Division table and at a time when work-related stress was playing havoc with his health, Stan Cullis was sacked.

The decision provoked shock waves throughout the Black Country and beyond, and many Wolves fans remain angry to this day by what they see as outrageously shabby treatment. The man was nothing less than an institution and the general feeling was that if he could be dismissed, then no one – not even Matt Busby at Old Trafford – could be safe. True, there was an opposing view, that Cullis was a dinosaur who was incapable of embracing modern methods, but adherents to that were in a distinct minority.

After 15 months out of the game, during which he was not short of offers from England and abroad, Cullis took charge of Second Division Birmingham City, one of soccer's so-called sleeping giants. But although he improved their performances and attendances – as well as surprising fearful players with his good humour – he couldn't lead City to promotion. Rousing cup runs in 1967 and 1968 were not enough to quell supporters' unrest and in March 1970, as abuse towards him mounted, Cullis resigned rather than allow his health to be jeopardised for a second time. He went on to work for a travel agency and write for a Midlands sports newspaper before retiring to Malvern, Worcestershire. It was a low-key exit for one of the dominant figures of English football during the 20th century's middle years. Though reviled by some for his tyrannical leanings and vehement manner, he was respected massively for achievements which could not be gainsaid.

Stan Cullis meant as much to Wolves as did Busby to Manchester United, Bill Shankly to Liverpool or Bill Nicholson to Spurs. Praise could not come any higher than that.

Stanley Cullis: born Ellesmere Port, Cheshire, 25 October 1915; played for Wolverhampton Wanderers 1934-47; capped 12 times for England 1937-39; managed Wolverhampton Wanderers 1948-64, Birmingham City 1965-70; died Malvern, Worcestershire, 27 February 2001.

Colin Webster

Colin Webster was a Busby Babe, and proud of the fact until his dying day.

Though hardly sprinkled with stardust in the manner of more famous Manchester United team-mates of the 1950s – the likes of Duncan Edwards, Tommy Taylor and Bobby Charlton – the perkily scampish little Welshman served the Old Trafford cause with industrious distinction both before and after the Munich air crash.

A formidably robust attacker who filled all five forward positions for the Red Devils, Webster never quite cemented a regular first-team berth, but was a commendably reliable deputy who contributed 31 goals in his 79 senior outings.

On the international front, while standing in for the great John Charles, who was injured, Webster played an enthusiastic role in his country's greatest soccer achievement, that of stretching mighty Brazil in the quarter-final of the 1958 World Cup in Sweden.

As he mentioned once with a combination of typical modesty and wit: 'We lost by only one goal to nil and I remember one cross which parted my hair as I jumped for it. I was only a little 'un but Big John would have nodded that in, no trouble. Then where would Pele and company have been?'

Webster arrived at Old Trafford in 1952 after being released by his home-town club, Cardiff City, for whom he had played at reserve level while working part-time as a motor fitter.

Having scored around 75 goals per season for the Army during National Service, he went on to carve a productive niche among the emerging Babes, making his senior entrance as a deputy outside-right when Johnny Berry was unavailable in 1953. He was at his happiest and best at centre-forward, though, where the awesome eminence of Tommy Taylor ruled out further progress.

Nevertheless, Webster made enough appearances to earn a League title medal in 1955/56, and remained an integral part of the squad at the time of the air crash in February 1958, in which eight players died on the homeward journey from a European Cup tie in Belgrade.

Indeed, but for a bout of flu, Webster would have been on that fateful trip, a narrow escape which he reckoned had a profoundly unsettling effect on his outlook. Thereafter the 25-year-old, always a combative performer, found himself in trouble with referees rather more often and his concentration level plummeted.

For all that, he played an immense part in the devastated club's emotional progress to the 1958 FA Cup final, notably netting the late winner in a quarter-final replay against West Bromwich Albion, then lining up on the left flank for the Wembley defeat by Bolton Wanderers.

That summer came Webster's World Cup exploits, but in the autumn he bade farewell to Old Trafford as Matt Busby sought to build a new side in the wake of the Munich calamity.

Swansea Town (now City) paid £7,500 for the versatile Welshman, who enjoyed five productive campaigns at the Vetch Field in the old Second Division. Then came a less contented 15-month spell with Fourth Division Newport County, after which he served non-League clubs Worcester City, Merthyr Tydfil and Portmadoc.

Having bowed out of football he ran a scaffolding business in the Swansea area before spending nine years as a park ranger. Eventually he took early retirement after he slipped on wet leaves and broke his leg while looking after parrots. Since then he has lived on the outskirts of Swansea while retaining a keen interest in his beloved United and Liz, his wife of 33 years, hopes to have his ashes scattered at Old Trafford.

Colin Webster bore the lengthy illness which cost him his life with both dignity and a characteristic humour which would have been thoroughly tickled at the thought of taking his last breath on St David's Day.

Colin Webster: born Cardiff, 17 July 1932; played for Manchester United 1952-58, Swansea Town 1958-63, Newport County 1963-64; capped four times by Wales 1957-58; died Sketty, Swansea, 1 March 2001.

David Rocastle

As spring turned to summer in 1989, there were few young men who seemed more thrillingly and comprehensively qualified than David Rocastle to bestride the coming decade with their all-round excellence.

A few weeks on from his 22nd birthday, the multi-talented Londoner had just celebrated his dazzling part in lifting Arsenal's first championship crown for 18 years and, having made his England debut the previous autumn, he could look forward to an international future which oozed with limitless potential.

For George Graham's Arsenal and Bobby Robson's England, David Rocastle looked to be a priceless asset, a smoothly creative but resiliently tough midfielder cum winger and the sort of performer around whom serially successful sides might be built.

And yet somehow, although he went on to gain further honours and the immensity of his early achievements can never be forgotten, his career petered out in frustratingly anti-climactic fashion.

As the years wore on, Rocastle was plagued increasingly by injuries and, perhaps, suffered a consequent reduction in confidence. In addition, he was unfortunate enough to become part of several teams which performed with surprising inconsistency after his rather unexpected departure from Highbury when the soccer world appeared still to be at his dancing feet in August 1992.

Rocastle had been recruited by the Gunners after excelling for South London schoolboys, signing as an apprentice in August 1983 and turning professional on the last day of 1984. Thereafter his star rose rapidly and his senior debut followed at home to Newcastle United in September 1985.

In 1986 'Rocky' was voted the Gunners' player of the year after becoming a regular on the right of midfield and, having earned the first of 14 England under-21 caps, he covered himself in glory during the club's successful League Cup campaign.

His most memorable moment was contributing the late winner in the semi-final replay against bitter north London rivals Tottenham Hotspur at White Hart Lane. He excelled in the subsequent Wembley victory over Liverpool, too, and topped a campaign of unalloyed personal triumph by being named in his fellow professionals' team of the season. By this time Rocastle was a darling of the Highbury faithful, who revelled in his ability to weave his way past bewildered defenders with the ball seemingly glued to his bootlaces. His exquisitely balanced dribbling skills were supplemented by startling acceleration and a fierce shot, and he could pass a football with both crispness and accuracy.

There was a whiff of fire and brimstone about the Rocastle game, too, and if he could lose his temper on occasions, usually that necessary steely streak was harnessed to the good of manager George Graham's ever-improving team.

The most effective season of his life was 1988/89 when he didn't miss a game as the Gunners lifted the championship in the most dramatic of all title races, winning 2-0 at Anfield in the final game to snatch the prize from their hosts' grasp thanks to a late goal from Michael Thomas.

By then appearing regularly in the full England side, having made his entrance against Denmark in September 1988, Rocastle received yet another accolade, that of Barclays Young Eagle of the Year; he was honoured once more by selection in his peers' team of the year, and there appeared not a cloud on his horizon.

However, the 1989/90 term did not go according to plan. Arsenal's form slipped and with it, temporarily, went Rocastle's sureness of touch. Suddenly he seemed prone to releasing the ball at the wrong moment, his distribution became wayward and, come the spring, he fell prey to knee trouble and his club place was no longer a formality.

Rocastle was hugely disappointed not to be picked for the 1990 World Cup finals and during the domestic campaign of 1990/91 a broken toe caused him to miss more games than he played. However, he recovered in time to compile enough appearances to earn a second championship medal, as Graham's Gunners recorded another title triumph with a body of performances far more entertaining than the 'Boring Arsenal' brigade of snipers ever acknowledged. Buoyed by that, Rocastle returned to his best in 1991/92, his gifts glowing so incandescently in a new central midfield berth that he earned an international recall and seemed to have overcome an irritating mid-career falter, despite his failure to make Graham Taylor's England squad for that summer's European Championships.

Then, to the dismay of most Arsenal supporters, in August 1992 he joined Leeds United in a £2 million deal, the reigning champions thus seeming likely to benefit from his prime years.

Sadly, it wasn't to be. In fact, his international career – comprising seven wins and seven draws in his 14 senior outings – was over, and although Rocastle sparkled intermittently during his first term at Elland Road, Howard Wilkinson's team was struggling to live up to its mighty deeds of the previous season. Also, to make the newcomer's situation more testing, he suffered further injury problems and the veteran Gordon Strachan proved feistily disinclined to yield his place.

Accordingly in December 1993 Rocky switched to Manchester City in a transaction which saw David White travel in the opposite direction, but his career lost further impetus in an indifferent side at Maine Road, and eight months later he was on the move again, this time alighting at Chelsea. Still only 27, Rocastle flickered tantalisingly for several months under Glenn Hoddle, only for foot injuries to sideline him for most of 1995/96, after which he was never able to force himself back into the first team, by then managed by Ruud Gullit.

Though Rocastle offered generous guidance to youngsters in Chelsea's reserves, that was no suitable role for such an accomplished footballer in his prime. He was reduced to loan stints with Norwich City in 1996/97 and Hull City the following season.

Thereafter he played some football in Malaysia but David Rocastle was out of the mainstream of the professional game when he was diagnosed with non-Hodgkin's lymphoma, a form of cancer which attacks the immune system, in February this year. The so-called 'tragedies' of sport were placed into stark perspective by the death of the popular father-of-three at the age of 33.

David Carlyle Rocastle: born London, 2 May 1967; played for Arsenal 1984-92, Leeds United 1992-1993, Manchester City 1993-94, Chelsea 1994-98, Norwich City on loan 1997, Hull City on loan 1997-98; capped 14 times by England 1988-92; died 31 March 2001.

Alec Stock

Few football managers have achieved more with less than Alec Stock. Immensely ambitious despite eschewing a variety of opportunities to employ his gifts on a loftier plane, the dapper, disciplined, unfailingly courteous West Countryman emerged as a giant-killer supreme with Yeovil Town, led Queen's Park Rangers of the Third Division to fairytale Wembley glory, and guided unfashionable Fulham to the FA Cup final for the only time in their history.

Perhaps a tendency to worry persuaded him to avoid the merciless spotlight directed on the top echelons of the game, or maybe he preferred to build from his own foundations rather than inherit someone else's work, a situation which pertained more readily at a less exalted level. Whatever, it speaks eloquently for the talent and durability of Alec Stock that he entered League management as the country's youngest boss and left it as the oldest.

Born in a Somerset mining village, he attended a rugby-playing school but soccer was in his soul and, while nodding unconvincingly at a career in banking, he made up his mind to devote his life to the game if possible.

An enthusiastic and thoughtful inside-forward, Stock began as an amateur with Tottenham Hotspur in the mid-1930s, then switched briefly to Charlton Athletic before making a handful of League appearances, his only ones, for Queen's Park Rangers. Then the war intervened and he served in the Royal Armoured Corps, rising to the rank of major before being invalided out when he suffered injury in Normandy.

After the conflict, aged 29 and clearly not destined for the heights solely as a player, Stock accepted the post of player-boss-secretary-general dogsbody with Southern League Yeovil Town. Soon his capacity for military-style organisation began to bear fruit and in 1949 he masterminded one of the greatest shocks in sporting history when the humble Glovers knocked mighty Sunderland out of the FA Cup.

Before the game Stock made much of the slope at Huish – Yeovil's quaint ground which has since been replaced – exaggerating it so much in the press that when the Wearsiders arrived they expected a gradient like the side of a house, a delicious piece of psychology which appeared to work wonders.

Certainly, Sunderland – the brilliant Len Shackleton et al – never played to their potential, allowing Stock himself to put the Somerset side ahead with a fierce left-foot drive. Thereafter the illustrious visitors equalised, but Yeovil grabbed the winner in extra time, thus setting up a fifth-round clash with Manchester United. It mattered not at all that Stock's valiant band were humbled 8-0 by Matt Busby's team, as Yeovil banked a healthy sum and a deathless slice of soccer folklore had been created.

His reputation burnished by such derring-do, he was head-hunted by Leyton Orient in August 1949 and proceeded to transform the fortunes of that hitherto lowly club. In 1951/52 Orient embarked on a stirring FA Cup run, seeing off Everton and Birmingham City before bowing out to Arsenal, then came an FA Cup quarter-final appearance in 1954. Meanwhile the Londoners' League position improved gradually, culminating in Third Division South title triumph in 1956.

However, Stock was absent from Brisbane Road for 53 days of that eventful campaign, having been made assistant manager to Tom Whittaker of Arsenal. At that point his prospects appeared limitless, but he disliked not being the ultimate decision-maker, despite the obvious carrot of one day taking the Highbury reins. As it turned out, Whittaker died not long after Stock returned to Orient just in time to oversee the clinching of promotion, so had he hung on a little longer at the more glamorous club, his own future, and that of Arsenal – who were destined for a period in the comparative doldrums – might have been radically altered. There was another colourful interlude on the horizon. During 1956/57, having stabilised Orient in the Second Division, Stock accepted the management of AS Roma, lured by the opportunity to learn continental methods and, presumably, by a large amount of cash.

He excelled in Italy, lifting Roma to third place in the table, but the language barrier proved a problem and he was not impressed by the intrusion of business interests into football matters, so he opted for another return to Brisbane Road.

Stock needed a new challenge, though, and he left Orient in February 1959, spending six months out of the game before taking over at Third Division Queen's Park Rangers in August 1959. As was his wont, he encouraged an attractive, attacking mode of play, his new charges scoring 111 goals in 1961/62, though they conceded 73.

Then new chairman Jim Gregory provided money to spend and Stock proved his acumen in the transfer market, acquiring the likes of Les Allen from Spurs and Rodney Marsh from Fulham, while encouraging a new wave of talented youngsters.

The upshot in 1966/67 was an inspiring season in which Rangers romped to the Third Division title and won the first League Cup final to be played at Wembley, coming from two goals down to defeat First Division West Bromwich Albion in a fabulous match illuminated by a classic Marsh goal.

The upward trend continued the following term as Rangers secured promotion to the top flight for the first time, only for Stock to resign in the summer, citing poor health as the cause.

Having recovered, he became boss of Luton Town in December 1968, guiding the Hatters up to the Second Division in 1969/70, but then left in April 1972, giving as his reason that he did not enjoy the daily journey from his Epsom home.

Two months later he was back in the game with Second Division Fulham, a cash-strapped club with a swashbuckling tradition, which he enhanced by recruiting former England captain Bobby Moore to play alongside Alan Mullery. Often Stock's Cottagers entertained royally, and though they didn't rise above mid-table status, they notched a club first by reaching the FA Cup final in 1975, losing 2-0 to West Ham United. Still, it was a remarkable feat by the gentlemanly Stock and his sacking in December 1976 by an aggressive, financially oriented regime was mourned widely.

Subsequently he served briefly as a director and caretaker boss of Queen's Park Rangers, then became the League's oldest manager, at 61, when he took over at Fourth Division Bournemouth in January 1979. He stepped down in December 1980, continuing as the Cherries' general manager until October 1981 and as a director until 1986.

Alec Stock was an old-fashioned, impeccably mannered football man, adept at fashioning silk purses from sows' ears and invariably popular with his players. It was appropriate that Fulham, his former charges, should have clinched the First Division title on the day of his death, and how fitting it would be if his beloved Yeovil Town should attain League status in the coming weeks.

Alexander William Alfred Stock: born Peasedown St John, Somerset, 30 March 1917; played for Charlton Athletic 1936-38, Queen's Park Rangers 1938-39; player-manager of Yeovil Town 1946-49; managed Leyton Orient 1949-56, 1956-57 and 1958-59, Arsenal (assistant) 1956, AS Roma 1957, Queen's Park Rangers 1959-68, Luton Town 1968-72, Fulham 1972-76, Bournemouth 1979-80; died Wimborne Minster, Dorset, 16 April 2001.

Don Roper

English football was sprinkled liberally with extravagantly gifted entertainers in the years immediately following the Second World War but, with every respect to Don Roper, he was never numbered among that sumptuously talented elite.

Yet, over a decade of invariably steady, intermittently dashing and occasionally explosive service to Arsenal, the loyal, quietly spoken, Hampshire-born attacker picked up two championship medals while the stellar likes of fellow wingers Stanley Matthews and Tom Finney managed to accumulate none between them.

Such was his versatility that Roper occupied all five forward positions during his Highbury sojourn and, highlighting his doughtier qualities, he excelled as an emergency full-back in an ultimately unsuccessful but memorably glorious rearguard action after team-mate Walley Barnes was injured during the 1952 FA Cup final clash with Newcastle United.

The Tynesiders triumphed in the end, but one of the abiding images of that Wembley afternoon was the heroic struggle waged by makeshift defender Roper against the marauding Geordie hordes. However, he will be remembered chiefly for his stirring sorties down both right flank and left, his hard-running style garnished by the savage shot he packed in either foot and his ability to cross the ball accurately at speed.

The teenage Roper was helping the war effort as an aircraft fitter and playing his football as a centre-forward for a local amateur side, Bitterne Nomads, when he attracted the attention of Second Division Southampton in 1940. Soon he swapped the role of spearhead for that of outside-right and in 1943 he formed a productive partnership with Ted Bates, who was destined to become the club's longest-serving manager.

When League football resumed in 1946/47, Roper excelled in a rather ordinary side and he was targeted by a host of major clubs. Following a transfer saga which was lengthier than the norm in that pre-agent era, he joined Arsenal that summer, being valued at £17,000 in a transaction which saw George Curtis and Tom Rudkin move in the opposite direction.

After a season of uncharacteristic lethargy, the Gunners – guided by new boss Tom Whittaker – were desperate to improve and the introduction of Roper, along with Archie Macaulay, a Scottish international wing-half recruited from Brentford, proved hugely efficacious.

Indeed, Arsenal led the First Division table from start to finish, beating runners-up Manchester United to the title by a crushing seven-point margin, a success to which Roper contributed ten goals in his 40 appearances on the right flank.

Thus established, he consolidated in 1948/49, but after spending much of 1949/50 on the left wing and at centre-forward, he fell victim to his own versatility, failing to oust either Freddie Cox (outside-right) or Denis Compton (outside-left) from the side which defeated Liverpool in that term's FA Cup final.

Typically of the phlegmatic Roper, there were no histrionics and back he bounced to claim a regular berth, usually on the left, with his derring-do at Wembley in 1952 a vivid highlight.

Probably, though, he did not peak until 1952/53 when he missed only one League outing, and struck 14 goals, as the Gunners lifted another League crown. Roper was rewarded by selection for England 'B' in the March and for the Football League two months later, but for many Arsenal fans the campaign's most enduring memory was his five-goal show in a floodlit friendly with Hibernian in the autumn. That night Roper gave a sensational display of power-shooting which, reportedly, inched him to the edge of full international recognition. That honour, alas, was never to materialise.

Undaunted, he continued to labour nobly in the Arsenal cause until losing his place midway through 1955/56. The following term brought only a handful of outings at centre-forward before the industrious 34-year-old rejoined Southampton in January 1957, having compiled an admirable record of 95 goals in 319 League and FA Cup games as a Gunner.

Back at The Dell, Roper adjusted admirably to the rigours of Third Division football, netting 32 times in 85 senior appearances before retiring in 1959.

A natural all-round sportsman who had played one county cricket match for Hampshire in 1947, he remained active, serving non-League Weymouth before setting aside his boots altogether.

Later he worked in an engineering business, then retired to live in Southampton, but it is in north London where he remains most celebrated. A Matthews or a Finney he wasn't, but Don Roper held his own in England's top flight for some ten years, an achievement which marks him out as a footballer of immense quality.

Donald George Beaumont Roper: born Botley, Hampshire, 14 December 1922; played for Southampton 1940-47 and 1957-59, Arsenal 1947-57; died Southampton, 8 June 2001.

Ronnie Allen

There is a persuasive theory that footballing visionary Ronnie Allen was born too soon to enjoy the full fruits of his remarkable talent.

The slim, nimble Midlander, who scored freely for West Bromwich Albion throughout the 1950s but was selected for England with mortifying infrequency, was a thoughtful centre-forward who dared to be different in an era when any wearer of a number-nine shirt was expected to rely rather more on sheer power than subtlety.

Allen, who was the only man to score at Football League level in each of the 20 seasons which immediately followed the Second World War, was a free spirit who roamed at will, dropping deep to avoid his markers and confusing them by unpredictable absences from his front-line beat.

He was blessed with a delicate touch on the ball, was full of guile and possessed the speed to make the most of his wonderful deftness. A few far-sighted souls trumpeted him as the complete footballer, and surely he would have thrived in more enlightened times, but to many of the closed minds who ruled his country's archaic selection committee in the Allen heyday, he was a dangerous maverick and not to be trusted.

Accordingly, after playing his fifth game for England – in which he scored against the reigning world champions, West Germany, at Wembley in December 1954 – Allen was cast into the international wilderness at the age of 25. It was hardly a coincidence that the flamboyant Len Shackleton, an eccentric showman who disdained all attempts at regimenting his extravagant gifts, should be discarded for good on the same sad day.

As a schoolboy Allen, who did not take up soccer until he was 13 and majored in rugby even after that, had planned to be a chemist. But after his exceptional aptitude for the round-ball game became apparent he joined Port Vale of the Third Division South as an amateur in 1944 and thereafter made rapid progress.

He made his debut for the Burslem club as an outside-left that year, lining up in a wartime competition alongside brilliant Irish inside-forward Peter Doherty, who was playing as a guest. At that point Allen stood only 4ft 10ins tall and weighed 7st 12lbs, but as he gained in stature so did his game mature, and he turned professional in 1946.

Always versatile, he served Vale in all forward positions except the central one in which he was destined to excel, as well as turning out in both wing-half slots and at full-back. Duly the young man's exceptional prowess was noted by England's top clubs of the day and in March 1950 he signed for West Bromwich Albion in an £18,000 transaction which was completed just ahead of the transfer deadline.

The Baggies had not been back in the top flight for long and when they experienced a goal drought early in 1951/52, manager Jack Smith switched Allen from right wing to centre-forward with fabulous results. That term the newly-converted marksman scored 35 goals in League and FA Cup and at season's end he was rewarded with his first full cap.

Over subsequent campaigns Allen was encouraged by Albion's imaginative new boss, Vic Buckingham, to use his bountiful all-round ability to the full. Thus, instead of leading the front line in conventional spearhead fashion, he roamed elusively, confusing opponents with his pacy dribbling and cute distribution, and it is fair to say that he tasted success as a deep-lying centre-forward even before that revolutionary role was showcased so fabulously by the magnificent Hungarian, Nandor Hidegkuti.

With Allen hugely prolific, West Bromwich became one of the leading sides in the land, rivalling the likes of Wolverhampton Wanderers and Manchester United in the chase for top honours. Indeed, in 1953/54 they almost entered soccer folklore by becoming the first team during the 20th century to lift the League and FA Cup double, eventually finishing as title runners-up to Wolves but triumphing over Preston North End at Wembley.

Fittingly in view of his form all season, Allen was Albion's brightest star on their big day, scoring twice in their 3-2 victory and keeping a characteristically cool head at one moment of high drama. With the Midlanders trailing 2-1, they were awarded a penalty and their dapper number-nine strode up to take it. Twice a divot on the spot caused the ball to roll away and twice, in the midst of unbearable tension, he replaced it. Then he scuffed his shot and, as he later recalled: 'The ball seemed to take an hour to reach the net.' It got there, though, and Allen was the hero.

However, even though he topped the First Division goal chart in 1954/55, the England selectors remained unmoved. Allen himself was philosophical, continuing to supply Albion with goals – 231 of them in 457 senior outings – before joining Crystal Palace, aged 32, in May 1961.

Still he offered a potent threat, employing his vast experience to telling effect and helping the Selhurst Park club rise to Division Two in 1963/64.

Allen retired from playing as a 36-year-old in 1965 and in the following January he entered management with Wolverhampton Wanderers, then struggling in the Second Division.

The rookie boss proved an able coach and an astute judge of players, buying extrovert centre-forward Derek Dougan and wing-half Mike Bailey in the course of leading his new charges to promotion to the top flight in 1967.

Life among the elite proved difficult, though, and Allen was sacked in November 1968. Undeterred, he took his belief in free-flowing, flexible football to Spain, learning the language and leading Athletic Bilbao to glory in the Spanish Cup. After narrowly missing a League title – Bilbao were pipped by Atletico Madrid on goal average – he guided the fortunes of Sporting Lisbon, Walsall and, briefly, his beloved West Bromwich before accepting a lucrative assignment to run the Saudi Arabia national side.

Allen did well enough with the Saudis, then sojourned briefly in Greece with Panathinaikos before returning to the Hawthorns and leading the Baggies to the semi-finals of both major domestic cups in 1981/82.

There followed a stint as general manager and he remained a part-time coach with the club until 1996, even playing in one final game – a testimonial at Cheltenham – as a 66-year-old in 1995.

Allen, whose son Russell started with Albion before serving Tranmere Rovers and Mansfield Town in the 1970s, was one of the most influential figures in Hawthorns history. What a shame that he was offered so few opportunities to shine on a wider stage.

Ronald Allen: born Fenton, Staffordshire, 15 January 1929; played for Port Vale 1944-50, West Bromwich Albion 1950-61, Crystal Palace 1961-65; capped five times by England 1952-54; managed Wolverhampton Wanderers 1966-68, Athletic Bilbao 1969-71, Sporting Lisbon 1972-73, Walsall 1973, West Bromwich Albion 1977, Saudi Arabia national coach 1977-79, Panathinaikos 1980, West Bromwich Albion 1981-82 (general manager until 1983); died Great Wyrley, Staffordshire, 9 June 2001.

Billy Liddell

Anfield, the famous home of Liverpool FC, has been graced by a plethora of footballing heroes since the Second World War. Roger Hunt and Ian St John, Kevin Keegan and Kenny Dalglish, Ian Rush and John Barnes; it is difficult to imagine a more exalted collection. Yet not one of these luminaries, each worshipped rabidly in his prime by the fanatics who stood on the Kop, was more revered on Merseyside than Billy Liddell.

From 1945, when first-class soccer resumed its place on the roster of mass entertainment, until the onset of the Bill Shankly-inspired soccer revolution at Anfield in the early 1960s – a movement which transformed the club from chronic under-achievers into the dominant power in English football for a quarter of a century – popular perception had it that the durable, self-effacing, yet explosively exciting winger cum centre-forward *was* Liverpool.

Indeed, often the club was referred to as 'Liddellpool', and while the darkly handsome Scot's surname lent itself conveniently to such glib wordplay, it was a sentiment which contained more than a little truth. Yet, there was more to the Liddell phenomenon than purely footballing attributes. A chivalrous and loyal fellow who was not too proud to stud the boots of junior and infinitely less gifted colleagues when he was occasionally omitted from the side in the twilight of his playing days, Liddell was ever ready to help people who enjoyed fewer social advantages than himself, later becoming a youth worker, lay preacher and Justice of the Peace.

In fact, unlike many players, he was acutely aware that there was more to life than the game and, despite his sporting prowess, he remained a part-timer throughout his career, combining soccer with accountancy and eventually becoming assistant bursar at Liverpool University.

This clear appreciation of wider issues, together with his characteristic uprightness on and off the field, made him a symbol of principle and integrity, an almost saintlike figure in a distinctly unsaintlike city. If few of the fans who gloried in Liddell's every deed aspired to his Presbyterian rectitude – he was a teetotaller who refused even a sip of champagne at moments of celebration – it didn't stop them idolising him.

The oldest of a coalminer's six children, Liddell grew up on salt porridge, kail (Scotch broth in the parlance of Sassenachs) and plenty of bread, a diet that did nothing to arrest a sturdy physical development which stood him in good stead in the boyhood football games in which he both revelled and excelled.

He graduated through his own village side to the enchantingly named Lochgelly Violet, with whom he caught the eye of his countryman Matt Busby, then playing for Liverpool and who recommended him to the Anfield regime.

Liddell signed as an amateur in the summer of 1938, turning professional the following spring at a cost to the Reds of £3 per week. His early progress intimated that his new employers had made a wise investment, only for the war – in which he served as a navigator in the RAF – to slice six prime years from a burgeoning career.

However, his soccer talents were not entirely redundant during the years of conflict; in addition to some 150 appearances in emergency competitions for his own club there were guest outings for the likes of Chelsea, Dunfermline Athletic and Linfield of Northern Ireland, as well as wartime international games for Scotland.

When the Football League resumed business in 1946/47, Liddell was 24 years old and bursting with natural ability, pace and power. He was particularly dangerous when running at defenders and cutting inside from the left wing, and though he found the net only seven times that season he demonstrated the dashing style that was to make him one of the most prolific marksmen in the Merseysiders' history.

As he grew in experience his influence on the team mushroomed and he became renowned among defenders as one of the most fearsome and courageous opponents in the land. Tackling Billy Liddell was akin to tangling with a runaway tank and yet, so fair was his approach that he attracted no hint of rancour, becoming well-loved and respected throughout the game.

Sadly, as Liddell sparkled ever more incandescently, so Liverpool declined, first into dull mediocrity and then – and this might be difficult for fans who followed them only through their 1970s and 1980s pomp to comprehend – into a woefully poor team.

Apart from reaching the 1950 FA Cup final, which they lost 2-0 to Arsenal and in which Liddell was rendered largely ineffective (for once) by clam-like marking, there was precious little for Kopites to cheer. Then, in 1954, the unthinkable happened – Liverpool were relegated to the Second Division.

But instead of seeking the greener pastures which his talent deserved, Liddell buckled down to help the Reds recover. Frequently lining up at centre-forward instead of in his more customary left-flank berth, he notched more than a century of League goals in the next four seasons as Liverpool strove unavailingly to regain their place among the elite.

Anyone who doubts the faithful Scot's world-class standing during this period would do well to note that only two players were selected for Great Britain against the Rest of Europe in both 1947 and 1955. One was Stanley Matthews, whose incomparable gifts and astonishing longevity need no further tribute here, and the other was Billy Liddell.

As his pace waned with age, he lost that rousing ability to surge past opponents but compensated with a more thoughtful passing game from a deep-lying position. The devotion of the supporters never wavered and when he returned from one absence at the age of 37, against Bristol City in August 1959, he scored two spectacular goals. The acclaim was rapturous, and deservedly so.

By that time managerial and coaching offers had started to arrive, but Liddell's future in accountancy was well mapped out and, after staying to play a few times under Shankly, he retired in 1961.

Had he been born a few years later and reached his peak during the reign of his inspirational fellow Scot – or, come to that, during the tenures of Bob Paisley, Joe Fagan or Kenny Dalglish – then Billy Liddell's trophy cabinet would have been bulging with considerably more than a single title medal, an FA Cup loser's gong and 28 caps for Scotland. But as to the affection, even reverence, in which this most eminent of adoptive Merseysiders was held by his community and beyond, it could not have been any higher.

William Beveridge Liddell: born Townhill, Fife, 10 January 1922; played for Liverpool 1938-61; capped 28 times by Scotland 1947-56; died Liverpool, 3 July 2001.

Les Sealey

Les Sealey offered potent evidence to support the time-honoured footballing adage that all goalkeepers are crazy. An exuberantly eccentric Eastender who wore his heart not unadjacent to his gloves, he was renowned for his madcap rants at his own defenders, his irrepressibly gleeful celebrations and a seemingly total disregard for his own safety.

Although he wasn't in the front rank of British goalkeepers, never reaching international stature, the widely-loved Sealey was a hugely accomplished performer and in the early 1990s he played a crucial role in launching Manchester United on their current era of near-omnipotence.

Yet for all his derring-do as a Red Devil towards the end of his colourful career, arguably it was with Luton Town in the mid-1980s that he reached his peak, starring for the Hatters as they finished in the top half of the old First Division – the equivalent of the modern Premiership – for three seasons in succession.

Ferociously committed and sometimes courageous to the point of foolhardiness, Sealey was a born entertainer. A superbly acrobatic shot-stopper, he was prone to charge impetuously from his line, barging friend and foe alike out of his path as he homed in on the ball, brooking no argument as to who ruled his penalty box. Invariably he struck up a warm rapport with the fans behind his net, who warmed to his extrovert antics and unshakeable confidence, while cringing at his occasional recklessness.

Sealey began his career as an apprentice with Coventry City in 1976 and made his top-flight debut before his 20th birthday. In 1978/79 he was the Sky Blues' regular custodian, then shared the duties for several campaigns with Scottish international Jim Blyth before resuming sole sovereignty over the position in 1982/83.

The following August Sealey joined Luton Town in a £100,000 deal and excelled as the Hatters became firmly established among the elite. Understandably he was devastated when forced by injury to miss Luton's League Cup final triumph over Arsenal in 1988, and was inconsolable when his error – the unnecessary concession of a penalty – turned the tide against his team in the 1989 final, which was won by Nottingham Forest.

During the following term, at the age of 32, Sealey was loaned unexpectedly to Manchester United as cover for Scottish star Jim Leighton. Soon the newcomer found himself as a central figure in one of the great FA Cup final dramas as Alex Ferguson dropped the unfortunate Leighton after a poor performance in a 3-3 Wembley draw with Crystal Palace in May 1990. Sealey was called up for the replay, helped United to prevail with a typically gutsy display, and was rewarded with a one-year contract at Old Trafford. With Leighton alienated and out of favour, the Londoner saw a chance for glory and he seized it, emerging as United's first-choice goalkeeper in 1990/91, during which he appeared in two finals. First came the League Cup reverse against Sheffield Wednesday, which was remarkable for his furious refusal to be substituted after his knee was sliced to the bone in a collision. Soon after the final whistle he fainted and the limb was in danger, yet three weeks later he was between the posts in Rotterdam as United defeated mighty Barcelona to lift their first European trophy under Ferguson, the Cup Winners' Cup.

Now Sealey wanted a two-year contract which was not forthcoming, so he joined Aston Villa, but in January 1993 he returned to Manchester as deputy to Peter Schmeichel. Senior opportunities proved limited, but when the Dane was suspended during the following season, Sealey stepped up for the League Cup final against Villa. The Red Devils lost, though the 36-year-old stand-in could not be faulted and he was disappointed to be given a free transfer two months later.

Thereafter his incessant patter and ebullient spirits brought good cheer to the dressing rooms of Blackpool, Leyton Orient and West Ham United, for whom he made the last of his 550-plus senior appearances, as a substitute against Manchester United at Old Trafford on the final day of 1996/97.

Since then Sealey has served West Ham as a goalkeeping coach, a job he left this summer, but he retained his links with Upton Park through his two teenage sons, Joe and George, who are goalkeeping trainees with the club. He was watching them in action on the day before he died. Also there is an older connection to the Hammers. Sealey's uncle, Alan Sealey, was the two-goal hero of United's victory over TSV Munich in 1965. Sadly he, too, died prematurely, in 1996.

Leslie Jesse Sealey: born Bethnal Green, London, 29 September 1957; played for Coventry City 1976-83 and 1992 on loan, Luton Town 1983-90; Plymouth Argyle on loan 1984; Manchester United 1989-91 and 1993-94; Aston Villa 1991-93; Birmingham City on loan 1992; Blackpool 1994; West Ham United 1994-96 and 1996-97; Leyton Orient 1996; died 19 August 2001.

Bertie Mee

He never claimed to be a football expert, and some of his closest colleagues compared him to Captain Mainwaring of *Dad's Army*, but during his reign as Arsenal manager Bertie Mee scaled one towering soccer peak of which most of the game's household names could merely dream.

In 1971 he became only the second boss of the 20th century to guide his club to the coveted League and FA Cup double, thus following in the exalted footsteps of his friend, Bill Nicholson of Tottenham Hotspur, ten years earlier.

A delegator supreme who relied heavily and openly on the excellence of coaches such as Dave Sexton and Don Howe, Mee was a stern disciplinarian and a magnificent motivator whose inner steel was concealed to slight acquaintances beneath an unassuming demeanour. In fact, no hint of slackness was tolerated as he pursued his frequently stated purpose of stopping mediocrity being perpetuated, his punctiliousness straying towards pomposity at times, but always he retained the respect of the football men around him.

Mee's double achievement was all the more remarkable in that he transformed the under-achieving Gunners after being promoted from the role of club physiotherapist, a route taken by a previous Highbury boss, Tom Whittaker, but nevertheless an extremely unusual one.

Though he had been a professional footballer before the Second World War, his left-wing exploits for Derby County reserves and Mansfield Town had been overwhelmingly inconsequential. Mee went on to guest for Southampton and appear for the Army Wanderers side in the Middle East during the conflict – in which he served as a sergeant in the Royal Army Medical Corps – but the injury which caused his retirement as a player at the age of 27 was not greeted with widespread consternation.

For a dozen years from 1948 Mee worked as a rehabilitation officer for disabled servicemen and then, having become a specialist in football injuries and organised treatment courses for the Football Association, he replaced Billy Milne as Arsenal's physiotherapist and trainer in 1960.

In this role he flourished, proving a fearsomely hard but impeccably fair taskmaster to sidelined players who knew they could never take the slightest liberty with the dapper, rather fussy, ultra-efficient newcomer.

One of his charges, Alan Skirton, credits Mee with reviving his career after he had been hospitalised with tuberculosis, but adds that no one ever relished the physio's ministrations because he was so rigorous: 'After being treated by Bertie you were fitter than the lads who hadn't been injured!'

However, for all his success in that position it was a major shock when Mee was handed the massive task of replacing Billy Wright as manager of a club in turmoil in 1966. Though the former England captain had not been an unmitigated flop, and had instigated a youth system which would bear impressive fruit in the future, he had failed to lift the Gunners above mid-table, and that was not good enough.

Mee, who accepted the job for an initial trial period before making the arrangement permanent in March 1967, began shrewdly by choosing Dave Sexton as his coach. Then, having a clear image of the side he wanted, he wheeled and dealed on the transfer market, bringing in the likes of defender Bob McNab from Huddersfield and forward George Graham from Chelsea, and nurturing talented youngsters such as strikers Charlie George and Ray Kennedy.

For the players, it was a stimulating but challenging time. Mee knew he had the rudiments of a successful side but was aware, also, that in certain cases there was a lack of the dedication and pride indispensable to big-time winners. Thus he delivered a metaphorical boot up the backside of those who needed it, while employing more subtle psychology where he deemed it suitable. He established stringent ground rules; standards were set and maintained; prima-donnas were out and workaholics were in; preparation was meticulous; swearing, which he abhorred, was frowned upon and consequently decreased.

Sometimes individuals railed against the stern Mee regime, but they honoured him for his stark honesty, which was illustrated vividly one day when Sexton had missed his train to work. Faced with the necessity of coaching them himself, he spent 20 uncomfortable minutes on the pitch before admitting openly that he was out of his depth. The footballers spent the rest of the session pounding out laps, which they hated, but at least they knew where they were with this ostensibly shy little man with a will of iron.

The loss of Sexton to Chelsea in 1967 was a blow but he was replaced successfully by Don Howe and gradually Arsenal inched towards mightiness once more.

There were crushing disappointments along the way, notably League Cup final defeats against Leeds United in 1968 and, even more demoralisingly, at the hands of humble Swindon Town in 1969.

But a year later a Gunners side skippered by the inspirational Frank McLintock lifted the club's first major trophy for 17 years when they beat Anderlecht of Belgium over two legs in the European Fairs Cup final. Mee, a studious avoider of personal publicity, seemed almost embarrassed by the praise that triumph attracted, but even more elaborate bouquets were on the way.

In 1970/71 his superbly organised and ultra-functional but deceptively talented side confounded those who declared that Don Revie's brilliant Leeds United were unassailable, and pipped the Yorkshiremen to the League title by a single point after an attritional springtime during which they had ground out one narrow victory after another.

Appropriately enough, the prize was claimed with a 1-0 win at White Hart Lane, the home of north London rivals Tottenham Hotspur. Then, five days later, Arsenal came from behind at Wembley to defeat Liverpool 2-1 in the FA Cup final, thanks to a spectacular injury-time winner from Charlie George. McLintock was chaired aloft brandishing the famous bauble and, contrary to all expectations at the start of the season, the Gunners had won the double.

To put that in perspective, it must be understood that, in that era, the double was an elusive, almost hallowed target which had been reached only once in the 20th century and then by a team of universally acknowledged magnificence. Many great sides had tilted at that particular windmill and failed, and it provoked a certain chagrin in many quarters that Mee's combination – perceived as worthy but dull by numerous pundits and rival fans – had pulled it off.

Having done so, it seemed that Arsenal had laid the foundations for a lengthy spell at the summit of the domestic game, but somehow it never happened. Although they reached Wembley again in 1972, they lost a dour final to Leeds and after finishing as First Division runners-up to Liverpool in 1973 they declined alarmingly in the League.

Perhaps, despite putting on a brave public face, Mee was stung by criticism that his team was boring and therefore was induced to break it up more rapidly than was necessary. Arguably the key error was dispensing with the ageing but fierily determined McLintock, who proved he was not a spent force by excelling for several years in the top flight with Queen's Park Rangers, and also the sales of Graham and Kennedy seemed perplexing.

The upshot was that the Gunners spent two seasons flirting with relegation before Mee, hurt by the growing barrage of brickbats and no longer enjoying his work, resigned to give way to Terry Neill in 1976.

It was no manner for a man who had graced the game so nobly to depart it, and duly, after a short sabbatical, he returned as assistant manager of Watford in 1977. Taking charge of scouting and youth policy, he was of inestimable help to the Hornets' young manager, future England boss Graham Taylor, and later he served as general manager before retiring in 1986 to become a director until 1991.

But it is as Arsenal's first double-winner – Arsene Wenger repeated the feat in 1997/98 – that Bertie Mee secured his place in football folklore.

Bertram Mee: born Bulwell, Nottinghamshire, 25 December 1918; played for Derby County 1937-39, Mansfield Town 1939; managed Arsenal 1966-76; died London, 21 October 2001.

Reg Matthews

Reg Matthews was the world's costliest goalkeeper, the first Third Division custodian to play for England, and the most-capped individual while operating in the Football League basement, all at the age of 22.

Yet ironically, although he went on to taste top-flight action with Chelsea and earn immense popularity with Derby County during the course of an accomplished career which stretched from 1950 to 1968, he would never return to the international stage after leaving his then-lowly home-town club, Coventry City.

Matthews' feat in accumulating five England caps while performing in comparative obscurity was all the more remarkable in that he faced opposition from a plethora of outstanding established keepers, the likes of Tottenham Hotspur's Ted Ditchburn and Ray Wood of Manchester United, as well as a posse of gifted up-and-comers including Alan Hodgkinson (Sheffield United), Eddie Hopkinson (Bolton Wanderers), Colin McDonald (Burnley) and Ron Springett (Sheffield Wednesday).

A six-footer whose markedly round shoulders belied a lithe athleticism, Matthews was renowned for his spectacular goal-line acrobatics and his fierce, sometimes excitable determination to boss his own penalty area. Unnervingly courageous when diving at opponents' feet, occasionally he would cannon into unwary team-mates as he charged single-mindedly to claim the ball.

In general, though, his presence was massively and consistently reassuring to any beleaguered defence, and he played in front of a few of those.

After majoring in rugby at school, Matthews took his place in a soccer trial match only because someone else failed to turn up, and so evident was his natural ability that he was drafted straight into Coventry City's nursery side, Modern Machine Tools FC.

After consolidating impressively at junior levels, he was called up for his senior debut, a Division Three (South) encounter at Southend, in March 1953. For a while, however, he was thwarted in his bid for a regular berth by Peter Taylor, who would go on to become famous for his management partnership with Brian Clough at Derby County and Nottingham Forest, and it was not until 1954/55 that Matthews became a bastion of the Bantams' rearguard.

Thereafter he performed so brilliantly in a moderate side that soon he was a transfer target for First Division clubs, but their early overtures were resisted by Coventry and Matthews alike.

Initially, at least, it seemed that playing beneath his station was not interfering with his international propects. In 1955 he represented England under-23s, England 'B' and the Football League, and in April of the following year he was awarded his first full cap against Scotland at Hampden Park.

There followed four more opportunities in swift succession, against Brazil, Sweden, West Germany and Northern Ireland, and when he was replaced by Ditchburn in November 1956, few believed that the young Midlander – who had acquitted himself capably enough over the five matches and never finished on the losing side – would never be called to the colours again. Perhaps ambition to regain the England jersey played a part in Matthews' record-breaking £22,500 move to Chelsea later that month, a transaction which caused widespread consternation in Coventry where he had become a folk hero.

However, he found it difficult to settle in London, instead commuting from Coventry to Stamford Bridge, where he never quite lived up to expectations. In fairness, it can't have been easy to build an understanding with his defence when circumstances dictated that he did not always train with them, especially as the back-line in question was distinctly ponderous and inclined to be caught square.

Come the spring of 1960 Matthews suffered an ankle injury which allowed a hugely talented rookie, Peter Bonetti, to demonstrate his class and soon the older man was marginalised, eventually switching to Derby County in a £6,500 deal in October 1961.

Reunited with Harry Storer, the manager who had given him his chance at Coventry, Matthews thrived once more, setting a club appearance record for a goalkeeper, which was destined to be outstripped later by Colin Boulton. During several campaigns his excellence was integral to the Rams retaining their Second Division status, and he maintained a splendid standard all the way to retirement in 1968.

Thereafter Matthews became player-boss of non-League Rugby Town before leaving the game to work for many years in the paint shop of the tractor company, Massey Ferguson, in Coventry.

Reginald Derrick Matthews: born Coventry 20 December 1932; played for Coventry City 1950-56, Chelsea 1956-61, Derby County 1961-68; capped five times by England 1956; died October 2001.

Charlie Mitten

Few observers of Charlie Mitten in his swashbuckling pomp, entertaining exuberantly on the left flank of Matt Busby's first great Manchester United side immediately after the Second World War, would deny that he was the finest of all uncapped English wingers.

That he was the sole member of that lovely team's celebrated 'Famous Five' forward line never to play in a full international owed something to the circumstance that he peaked in an era rich in flankmen, but rather more, conceivably, to a rebel streak which tended to upset people in football's high places.

The irreverent Rangoon-born Englishman's outlaw leanings were defined by his controversial defection from the domestic game to play in Colombia in 1950, a decision which proved as reckless career-wise as it was bold.

Charlie Mitten was the most flamboyant of United's breathtakingly gifted attack, his dash and daring, speed and trickery, making him a crowd-pleaser sublime who meshed magnificently with his four cohorts.

While making due allowance for distance lending a rosy glow of enchantment, Busby's scintillating 1940s quintet can be deemed exceptional. There was veteran Scot Jimmy Delaney, a match-winner on the right wing; the feisty, multi-talented Johnny Morris at inside-right; free-scoring Jack 'Gunner' Rowley led the line; at inside-left was the silkily subtle, stealthily incisive Stan Pearson; and patrolling the left flank was the dressing-room joker-in-chief, the irrepressible Mitten.

How the Old Trafford faithful loved 'Cheeky Charlie'. They never knew what he was going to do next, but there was a fair bet it would be exciting, and frequently it would climax in a goal.

He loved to run at defenders and there wasn't a full-back in the game that he couldn't master on his day. He could destroy them with outright pace, or he could bamboozle them with wizardry and then, having created the necessary space, he would employ his fabulous left foot to wreak the maximum havoc.

Mitten was a magnificent crosser, and marksmen Rowley and Pearson feasted on his pinpoint service, while he was a sharp-shooter himself, netting 50 times in 142 senior outings, a splendid return for a wingman and one massaged significantly by his prowess from dead-ball situations, particularly penalty kicks.

In addition, Mitten was blessed with a shrewd football brain and integrated so smoothly with his team-mates that he could find them with his unerring dispatches as if by radar, seemingly sure where each man would be in any given situation.

Yet for all his accomplishments, he never landed a title medal, United finishing second, second, second and fourth in his four seasons in the side. Still, there was spectacular consolation in 1948 when the FA Cup was lifted by the Red Devils, who played some of the most inspirational football ever seen at Wembley in their 4-2 defeat of Blackpool. That day the Seasiders' two famous Stanleys, Matthews and Mortensen, were overshadowed comprehensively by United's sublime passing interchanges, with Mitten and company dazzling even by their own lofty standards.

As the second half of the century dawned, with Old Trafford's twinkle-eyed charmer in incandescent form, it must have seemed to outsiders that club and player were made for each other, but the relationship was doomed to a bitterly controversial end.

However, viewing the situation objectively, it would be a harsh judge who blamed Charlie Mitten for the split. At a time when clubs were filling their coffers during the post-war football boom, top players earned £8 per week during the season and a mere £6 in the summer. Suddenly, against a backdrop of constant muttering about a possible strike by unhappy professionals, he was offered the staggering signing-on fee of £10,000 to join a leading Colombian club, Santa Fe of Bogota.

Mitten had never dreamed of such a crock of gold. Indeed, he could have spent 25 years with United and never received anything like it. The Colombians were ready to give him enough to buy a row of houses, with a huge weekly wage on top.

Not surprisingly, he accepted, but then his luck ran out. At the moment he left Old Trafford, Colombia was outside FIFA and any player based there was considered an outlaw. But then, after he and his family had spent one season in Bogota, the South Americans were re-admitted by the sport's governing body – but only on condition that the so-called rebels were sent home.

So Mitten was greeted as a criminal by the English soccer establishment, and that included Manchester United. He was suspended for six months, fined £250 and sold to Fulham, where he went on to spend four productive years before becoming player-boss of Mansfield Town. Thus he emerged from the nightmare chastened but intact, though The Bogota Bandit (the title of Richard Adamson's excellent 1996 biography) was left to reflect on a further infuriating 'if only'.

In the early 1950s Real Madrid were assembling what many believe still to be the finest club side of all time, and they wanted to sign three of the Colombian mercenaries. They acquired the majestic Alfredo di Stefano and his fellow Argentinian Hector Rial, but were frustrated in their quest for Charlie Mitten because his family was homesick for England.

Had he headed for Spain he might have become one of the world's soccer immortals. As Alfredo the great reflected later: 'Ah, Charlee Meeten, numero uno. If we have heem we never need Francisco Gento. Gento he queeck, but Meeten, he more clever.'

As a manager, Mitten exhibited enough flair and promise with Mansfield to land the Newcastle United job in June 1958, and at St James' Park he lived up to his colourful reputation. True to his creed for entertainment, he assembled an attractive side, notably the fine inside trio of Ivor Allchurch, Len White and George Eastham, but could not achieve a consistent blend and after the Magpies were relegated to the Second Division in 1961, he was sacked in the autumn.

Unbowed, and as gloriously irreverent as ever, he went on to become player-manager of non-League Altrincham, then took charge of Manchester's White City greyhound stadium in the 1960s, and later ran a sports promotion business in the city before retiring.

Charles Mitten: born Rangoon, Burma, 17 January 1921; played for Manchester United 1936-50, Santa Fe of Bogota 1950-51, Fulham 1952-56, Mansfield Town 1956-58; managed Mansfield Town 1956-58, Newcastle United 1958-61; died Stockport, Cheshire, 2 January 2002.

Jeff Astle

Jeff Astle was a monarch of Midlands football, more specifically the 'King of the Hawthorns', who reigned imperiously as West Bromwich Albion's marksman-in-chief during one of the most productive decades in the Baggies' history.

True, England fans might view the strapping centre-forward in a less regal perspective, due to his horrible miss against Brazil during the 1970 World Cup finals in Mexico, but it would be monstrously mean if that aberration should stand as the principal epitaph to such a bountiful and accomplished career.

Astle was an archetypal muscular spearhead, awesomely commanding in the air, a ferociously powerful shooter and, while not exactly renowned for delicacy when the ball was at his feet, he could link neatly and effectively with his fellow attackers.

Unfailingly courageous, he soaked up untold punishment from defenders frustrated by his commendable knack of shielding the ball, and as well as scoring prolifically himself, he laid on plenty of goals for other Albion predators such as Tony Brown and John Kaye.

A Nottinghamshire boy, Astle gravitated to Notts County from junior football, turning professional at Meadow Lane in 1959. By then, he had already received priceless instruction in the art of centre-forward play from arguably the finest of all England number-nines, Tommy Lawton, who had managed County for a brief spell.

From the great man, acknowledged as the most brilliant header of a football the game has seen, Astle had learned to time his leaps so that he seemed to hang in the air, an ability he put to promising use when making his Third Division breakthrough in 1961/62.

During the following term he struck up a potent partnership with Tony Hateley, but after the Magpies were relegated in 1963/64 he accepted a £25,000 transfer to top-flight West Bromwich Albion.

At the Hawthorns Astle prospered apace, netting twice on his home debut against local arch-rivals Wolverhampton Wanderers and eventually contributing 171 goals in 353 senior outings for the Baggies.

Along the way he notched six hat-tricks, including two in three days against soon-to-be-crowned European champions Manchester United, and then West Ham United, in the spring of 1968. In addition Astle starred in a succession of rousing knockout campaigns, featuring in four major cup finals in as many years. In 1966 he hit the target in the first leg of the League Cup final against West Ham, a 2-1 defeat which was turned into a 5-3 aggregate triumph in the second leg at the Hawthorns.

A year later, after scoring in every previous round, he was in the side which sought to retain the trophy in the first League Cup final staged at Wembley, only for Albion to squander a two-goal lead and lose to Third Division Queen's Park Rangers.

There was ample consolation in 1968, though, when Astle grabbed an extra-time winner to defeat favourites Everton in the FA Cup final, bludgeoning home a savage left-footer after his original shot had been blocked. This time he achieved his ambition of striking in every round, and was duly elected Midlands Footballer of the Year.

Now moving into his pomp, Astle produced irresistible form in 1969/70, topping the First Division scoring charts with 25 goals, earning the first of his five full England caps and opening the scoring in yet another League Cup final, only to see his side overhauled by Manchester City. That goal, though, made him the first man to register at Wembley in both major domestic finals.

In two games each for England 'B' and the Football League he managed a total of eight goals, but failed to get on the scoresheet at full international level and it was his misfortune to squander his clearest opportunity in the highest-profile contest of his life.

That was near the end of a World Cup encounter with mighty Brazil in Guadalajara after rising from the bench to replace Francis Lee. With the South Americans clearly troubled by Astle's aerial prowess, they were struggling to protect their 1-0 lead when the ball fell to the Midlander some ten yards out. Sadly, with only goalkeeper Felix to beat, he pulled his shot narrowly wide and England lost.

In terms of the tournament it was not decisive, as Sir Alf Ramsey's men went on to face West Germany in the quarter-finals, but it was a moment which, sadly, defined Astle's international experience. Back on the club scene he suffered knee problems and Albion struggled, being relegated in 1972/73, and he made only a handful of Second Division appearances before leaving the professional game at the age of 32.

Later he served non-League clubs Dunstable Town, Weymouth, Atherstone Town and Hillingdon Borough before putting aside his boots in 1977 to concentrate on his successful industrial cleaning business, based in Burton-on-Trent.

During the 1990s, Astle was returned to public attention by comedian and Baggies fan Frank Skinner, who recruited him as the resident crooner on his and partner David Baddiel's irreverent *Fantasy Football* TV show, and subsequently the former footballer ran his own Jeff Astle Roadshow. But it is as a hero of the Hawthorns, where he rarely missed a match until he became ill some two years ago, that Jeff Astle will be recalled most vividly.

Jeffrey Astle: born Eastwood, Nottinghamshire, 13 May 1942; played for Notts County 1959-64, West Bromwich Albion 1964-74; capped five times by England 1969-70; died Burton-on-Trent, Staffordshire, 19 January 2002.

Duggie Reid

Duggie 'Thunderboots' Reid was a spectacularly explosive force in the days when Portsmouth ruled English football.

As his nickname implies, the tall, muscular Scot packed a shot of devastating velocity and his goals were integral to Pompey's back-to-back League championship triumphs of 1948/49 and 1949/50. Such was Reid's power that once he hammered the ball through the net and into the crowd when scoring from the penalty spot at home to Manchester City, and further vivid testimony to his fearsome prowess was offered by Wolves and England goalkeeper Bert Williams.

When asked by a reporter just how hard the Portsmouth marksman could propel a football, the rueful custodian simply lifted his jersey to reveal a large and livid bruise, in the midst of which the imprint of the ball's panels could be clearly discerned.

Not that Reid relied entirely on brawn to notch his 134 League and FA Cup goals, including seven hat-tricks, in his 300-plus Pompey appearances. Though gangling of gait, he was a skilful operator, a precise and intelligent passer who created plenty of scoring opportunities for his fellow forwards.

Having moved south from his native Ayrshire to take a job as an apprentice plumber in Manchester as a 15-year-old, Reid excelled in local amateur soccer before joining Stockport County, turning professional in 1936. In his first season he played a minor part in lifting the Third Division North title, then featured at wing-half as the Edgeley Park club was relegated the following term. His progress was interrupted by the war, during which he served in the Army, and in 1946 he was transferred to top-flight Portsmouth for £7,000. At first the Fratton Park fans were sceptical of the seemingly ungainly 28-year-old, but he convinced them of his worth in the most emphatic fashion, by finishing as the club's top scorer with 29 strikes in his first campaign.

Thereafter Reid became a south-coast folk hero as he developed impressively along with the rest of manager Bob Jackson's exhilarating side. The accent was on team spirit rather than star individuals, though wingers Peter Harris and Jack Froggatt were justly feted, along with schemer Len Phillips and the majestic half-back line of Jimmy Scoular, Reg Flewin and Jimmy Dickinson.

Reid was joint leading scorer with Harris as the championship was claimed with five points to spare in 1948/49 and he was prolific again in 1949/50, when his last-day hat-trick in a 5-1 home victory over Aston Villa was instrumental in Pompey retaining the title on goal average (the precursor of goal difference), edging out Wolves.

Thereafter Portsmouth slipped from their lofty pedestal as the team began to age, but still they held their own in the top division for the remainder of Reid's Fratton Park tenure, the last years of which were spent at centre-half. The conversion had taken place in the spring of 1953, when he was 35, and he continued performing to a high standard until leaving the club to become player-boss of non-League Tonbridge in 1956.

Reid had always been fascinated by tactics – he moved salt and pepper pots around many a train restaurant table-top to illustrate his ideas to team-mates during long journeys – but management did not suit him and in 1958 he returned to Pompey as a groundsman.

Though never a keen gardener previously, he discovered a flair for the work and transformed the hitherto poor Fratton Park surface into one of the finest in the land, moving no less an authority than England skipper Bobby Moore to remark: 'If you can't play at Portsmouth, then you can't play anywhere.' Reid, a kindly, modest man who spoke little but whose few words tended to be meaningful, looked after his beloved pitch for two decades until his retirement in 1978.

For many years, also, he ran a hostel for the club's young footballers in Southsea, and he encouraged the soccer development of his son, David, who played for Pompey juniors, then Leatherhead and England at amateur level.

Few men have ever become part of the very fabric of a football club more comprehensively than did Duggie Reid at Portsmouth.

John Douglas Jamieson Reid: born West Kilbride, Ayrshire, 3 October 1917; played for Stockport County 1936-46, Portsmouth 1946-56; died Park Gate, Hampshire, 8 February 2002.

Walter Winterbottom

Walter Winterbottom was the first and longest-serving manager of the England football team – and also the least powerful. Unlike his successors, from Alf Ramsey through to Sven-Goran Eriksson, he had to submit his chosen sides for ratification by a selection committee. Thus hamstrung, Winterbottom – an eloquent, affable intellectual – was burdened with huge public responsibility without true authority to discharge it, so he could never justly be judged on results alone.

However, despite being answerable to often meddlesome if mostly well-meaning amateurs at the Football Association, and although he failed to take England beyond the quarter-final stage in four successive World Cup tournaments, the dedicated, enthusiastic Lancastrian made a worthy fist of an unenviable task.

When evaluating Winterbottom's record between 1946 and 1962 – 139 matches played, of which 78 were won, 33 drawn and only 28 lost – it should be remembered that not only was he national team boss, but also managed England's amateur side and served as the FA's director of coaching. In the last-mentioned role he had to travel thousands of miles, giving lectures, supervising courses, liaising with managers, schoolteachers, referees, youth leaders and local authorities, as well as drafting coaching manuals.

Those close to Winterbottom maintain that it was in this less public, unglamorous part of his brief – establishing a national coaching framework where none had existed – that he was most happy and fulfilled. Of course, it will not be for those labours, but for his efforts in charge of Stanley Matthews and Tom Finney, Bobby Charlton and Jimmy Greaves, that he will take his place in soccer history.

Born in Oldham in the year before the First World War, Winterbottom was educated at his local grammar school, then went to college at Chester, where he developed an abiding love of football theory that was to shape his working life. Thereafter he taught for three years in his home town, and played centre-half for amateur teams such as Royston and Mossley before being spotted by the famous Manchester United scout Louis Rocca and turning professional at Old Trafford.

Two years later Winterbottom made his senior debut for the Red Devils and, enjoying spells at both centre- and wing-half, was hailed as one of the major discoveries of season 1936/37. Tall, strong and well-built, he was not an ostentatious performer but passed well and possessed an acute positional sense. Though United struggled unavailingly against relegation to the Second Division, Winterbottom's star shone brightly and much was expected of him. However, frustration was lying in wait, a spinal injury suffered in 1937 ending his playing career after only 25 League matches.

Though he was left with a slight stoop, there followed a partial recovery which allowed him to guest for Chelsea and lead representative sides during the war, in which he served as the RAF's head of physical education and rose to the rank of wing commander.

After the conflict, Winterbottom might have resumed full-time teaching, but he had impressed highly-placed soccer administrators with an array of attributes: a deep knowledge of the game and visionary tactical approach were underpinned by sharp intelligence, unimpeachable integrity and, not least, a delightful, unassuming charm which made him at home in any company.

At the time the FA were laying plans to develop the game on a grand and organised scale and they also wanted someone to 'take charge' of the national side. Thus Walter Winterbottom became England's first director of coaching and team manager.

At the top level in that era, he was able to call on some fabulously talented individuals – the likes of Matthews, Finney, Tommy Lawton, Raich Carter, Wilf Mannion – and the new supremo tended to let them have their heads, suggesting but rarely insisting, and all the while working closely in harness with skipper Billy Wright. Such a stellar combination should have been capable of conquering the most accomplished opposition but – not helped by selectorial foibles, which included the periodic axing of the future Sir Stan, among a bewildering succession of team changes – a stable side was not achieved.

There were plenty of rousing victories but, at a time when the English soccer establishment appeared to believe in their nation's divine right to rule the world, there were fearful debacles, too.

One of the biggest came in 1950 when England, having condescended for the first time to enter the World Cup, were knocked out in the first stage of the finals in Brazil, losing to the unfancied United States along the way. But if that was embarrassing, what followed in 1953 was positively humiliating: England suffered their first reverse on home soil against opposition from beyond these islands, being thrashed 6-3 by the brilliant, innovative Hungarians, a result which put firmly into perspective this country's oft-repeated boast that it gave football to the world.

In those days, of course, turnips were merely vegetables which bore no perceived relationship to the head of the England manager and Winterbottom suffered no such hysterical crucifixion as did Graham Taylor some 40 years later in the pages of a national tabloid. But he did receive severe criticism, much of which was unfair as he recognised the need for new thinking. Sadly, all too often his hands were tied by blinkered traditional influences at the FA.

Nevertheless he achieved plenty. An England youth team was launched in 1947 and an under-23 side in 1954, the year in which he led the seniors to the last eight of the World Cup tournament in Switzerland, where they bowed out to Uruguay.

Four years on, with expectations unrealistically high, Winterbottom's England flopped in Sweden, but that setback should be viewed in the context of the Manchester United air disaster earlier in 1958, which had claimed the lives of three of his key men – Roger Byrne, Tommy Taylor and the incomparable young leviathan, Duncan Edwards.

Significantly, despite the disappointments, Winterbottom retained the respect and, in many cases, the affection of his players. Though he was distinctly donnish, perhaps too academic to get the best from some of his charges, and lacked the hard-nosed pragmatism of, say, a Ramsey, he was ready to roll up his sleeves in the common cause, even cooking for the squad during part of one tour.

Kind and sincere, he was intensely loyal to his footballers, ever ready to deflect in his own direction verbal barbs aimed at them. Arguably he was a little too nice at times, perhaps offering a gently-delivered and rather complicated tactical discourse when a touch of fire-and-brimstone oratory might have served better, but that was the nature of the man.

There were, of course, many times when he got it right, never more so than in 1960/61 when his team – captained by Johnny Haynes and including Greaves and Charlton – enjoyed a sequence of six straight victories, conceding eight goals and scoring no fewer than 40.

What a pity that was not a World Cup season. When the premier tournament came round once more in 1962, the side had slipped from their pinnacle of excellence and progressed no further than the quarter-finals in Chile. Not for the first time Winterbottom battled bravely in the fate of administrative incompetence – for example, there was no doctor in the England party and centre-half Peter Swan fell so ill that he nearly died.

Perhaps feeling he had achieved all he could expect to, Winterbottom retired from his gruelling combination of roles at the end of that year, making way for Alf Ramsey, who was to lead his country to World Cup glory in 1966.

It had been widely expected that after relinquishing the England management Winterbottom would replace his mentor, Sir Stanley Rous, as FA Secretary. But the job went instead to Denis Follows and Winterbottom joined the Central Council of Physical Recreation, where he made full use of his gift for organisation, and later served on the Sports Council.

In 1978 he was knighted for his services to British sport, an honour greeted warmly throughout the world of football. It was a tribute that was thoroughly deserved. Walter Winterbottom was a gentleman who had graced his beloved game, long and enterprisingly, as enthusiastic student, learned professor and impeccable ambassador.

Walter Winterbottom: born Oldham, Lancashire, 31 March, 1913; played for Manchester United 1934-37; England's manager and director of coaching 1946-62; OBE 1962; CBE 1972; general secretary, Central Council of Physical Recreation 1963-72; director, Sports Council 1965-78; knighted 1978; died Guildford, Surrey, 16 February 2002.

Ray Wood

Ray Wood kept goal for Manchester United's Busby Babes, by common consent the most scintillating collection of youthful footballing talent ever assembled in these islands, collecting two League title medals in the process. Yet it is for his central role in an FA Cup final melodrama for which the amiable north-easterner, a survivor of the Munich air disaster, is enshrined in the game's folklore.

Having already been crowned as champions when they faced Aston Villa at Wembley in 1957, United were white-hot favourites to become the first club in the 20th century to lift the coveted League and FA Cup double. With a line-up which included such stellar individuals as England stalwarts Duncan Edwards, Tommy Taylor and Roger Byrne, and with young Bobby Charlton an increasingly irresistible addition to that sumptuous roster, there seemed little likelihood of an upset.

But some six minutes into the action Wood suffered a fractured cheekbone in a collision with Villa's rumbustious Irish winger Peter McParland and, in those days before substitutes were allowed, the contest was transformed.

United were forced to reshuffle, putting centre-half Jackie Blanchflower in goal, and though he performed nobly, he was unable to prevent the two strikes – by a cruel irony, both plundered by McParland – which sealed victory for the Midlanders.

The fateful incident caused passionate controversy because Wood had the ball under control in his arms when McParland charged at him. It seemed certain that the attacker would veer clear at the last moment, but instead he continued to advance and clattered into the Manchester man. Wood was knocked unconscious, then left the action before returning as a passenger on the wing, only resuming his place between the posts – and risking further injury – when the Red Devils pulled back a goal in the dying minutes.

Even in an era when goalkeepers did not receive the rigorous protection from physical contact that they do today, the failure of referee Frank Coultas to punish McParland confounded most neutral observers, though Matt Busby accepted the outcome with characteristic grace.

Ray Wood had started his career with another United, Newcastle, whom he served as an amateur before joining Darlington of the Third Division North in 1949. He impressed instantly with the Quakers and within three months had secured a dream £5,000 transfer to Old Trafford. Although bought primarily for the long term, an injury crisis necessitated an immediate first-team entrance – against Newcastle.

Thereafter, while completing an apprenticeship as an electrical fitter, Wood buckled down to learn more about his trade from the club's two senior keepers, Jack Crompton and Reg Allen, as well as demonstrating rare all-round ability by playing three games at centre-forward for United's 'A' team. This unexpected interlude, during which he netted six times, dumbfounded most of his new team-mates, but not old pals from the north-east, who recalled his productive earlier days as a professional printer, dashing for cash at weekends in the pit villages.

For all that versatility, though, his future was to be in goal and in 1953/54, with Allen ill and Crompton past his best, Wood claimed a regular berth. Such was his progress that by the spring he was in line for the England squad for that summer's World Cup finals in Switzerland, only for a broken wrist to wreck his opportunity.

Now, though, Wood's star was firmly on the rise and he made his full England debut in a 2-0 victory over Northern Ireland in Belfast in October 1954. Though he failed to make the international jersey his own, he continued to excel at club level, pocketing successive championship medals in 1955/56 and 1956/57, and turning in a series of memorable displays as the Red Devils blazed Britain's trail into European competition.

Wood was a fabulously athletic shot-stopper, quick off his line at need and unfailingly courageous, though perhaps a slight inconsistency at dealing with crosses prevented his attaining the very front rank. Duly in December 1957 his Old Trafford prospects were dimmed when Busby paid Doncaster Rovers £23,500 to make Harry Gregg the world's costliest goalkeeper.

Nevertheless, Wood remained in the senior squad and travelled as a reserve to Belgrade for a European Cup quarter-final encounter with Red Star in February 1958. On the way home United's plane stopped to refuel at a snowy Munich and, while attempting to take off for a third time, it crashed into a building. The accident claimed 23 lives, including those of eight players, but Wood was spared, regaining consciousness with a wheel on top of him.

He suffered leg, hip and head injuries from which he recovered quickly, but he could not win back his place from Gregg and joined Second Division Huddersfield Town, then bossed by Bill Shankly, in December 1958. Still only 27, Ray served the Terriers expertly, remaining at Leeds Road until 1965, after which he saw out his playing career with Bradford City and Barnsley.

However, Wood was not finished with football. Having qualified as a coach in 1962 and enjoyed successful close-season spells in Canada and Zambia, he became a soccer globetrotter. He ran Los Angeles Wolves, served the Irish FA in Dublin and then, between 1969 and 1972, revitalised the previously downhearted Cypriot national team. Next came club stints in Cyprus, Greece and Kuwait, then four years at international and club level in Kenya and another four in the United Arab Emirates.

Later Wood ran a sportswear business in Bexhill, then took charge of a suit department for a store in Hastings for nine years before retirement in the mid-1990s. Since then he has played plenty of golf and quietly relished being the answer to a frequently posed quiz question: which keeper started and finished an FA Cup final between the posts and didn't let in a goal, yet went home with a loser's medal?

Raymond Ernest Wood: born Hebburn, County Durham, 11 June 1931; played for Newcastle United (amateur) 1948-49, Darlington 1949, Manchester United 1949-58, Huddersfield Town 1958-65, Bradford City 1965-66, Barnsley 1966-68; capped three times by England 1954-56; died Bexhill, Sussex, 7 July 2002.

Ian Hutchinson

Ian Hutchinson was the warrior centre-forward who spearheaded one of the finest of all Chelsea teams to FA Cup glory in 1970. Brave almost beyond belief and ferociously aggressive, he paid a daunting penalty for his courage, being invalided out of the game following a grisly catalogue of injuries when he should have been in his prime. When the rangy six-footer was rampaging through top-quality defences like a human battering ram he had seemed indestructible. But, of course, he wasn't.

Though he was never feted as an outright star in the manner of fellow Blues Peter Osgood, Charlie Cooke and Alan Hudson, Hutchinson was hailed as a talisman by those illustrious comrades. Such was his willingness to scrap for every ball, he offered the ultimate 'get-out' for team-mates under pressure.

Hudson, for example, described him as a midfielder's dream, a selfless performer who could turn bad passes into good ones, though arguably it was Osgood who benefited most from his close friend's abrasive style. Hutchinson was the first of Osgood's co-strikers to take on the role of target-man, thus creating space and time for his infinitely more artistic partner to prosper.

Yet for all his ox-like strength and his evident relish in crashing through tackles which would floor most men, it would be unjust to dismiss Hutchinson as a mere clodhopper. Though he could look ungainly, even clumsy, there were moments when he would reveal a delightfully delicate touch on the ball.

In addition he offered formidable pace, he was majestic in the air – like all outstanding headers, such was the precision of his timing that he created the optical illusion of seeming to hang in space while waiting for a cross to arrive – and he packed a fierce shot in either foot.

Then there was the Hutchinson speciality, a prodigiously long throw, which was once measured at some 112 feet and which, due to its power and remarkable variety of trajectory, was as valuable an attacking weapon as any corner-kick. Indeed, he employed it to devastating effect in the 1970 FA Cup final replay against Leeds United at Old Trafford when, deep into extra time, he launched a raking projectile which Jack Charlton could only deflect into the path of the charging David Webb, who bundled home the winning goal.

In the first meeting with Leeds at Wembley a few days earlier, Hutchinson had made another typical and crucial contribution to the Chelsea cause. With only four minutes remaining of a game which had been substantially dominated by the Yorkshiremen, the Blues' dreadnought had headed a dramatic equaliser, valiantly disregarding Charlton's flailing boot to hurl himself at a near-post cross.

Surprisingly, for all his exceptional attributes, Derby-born Hutchinson did not enter professional football straight from school, instead playing for non-Leaguers Burton Albion and Cambridge United before being signed by Chelsea for £5,000 in July 1968, shortly before his 20th birthday.

Two months later manager Dave Sexton, duly impressed by the progress of the muscular newcomer, gave him his senior baptism and he enjoyed a fruitful springtime run during which he scored six goals in 11 outings.

That earned him a regular berth throughout most of the 1969/70 campaign, in which Chelsea finished third in the title race and lifted the FA Cup, and he plundered 22 goals in 35 senior starts. Alas, never again would he make as many appearances in one season or be anything like as prolific.

Come 1970/71, during which Hutchinson was capped by England in under-23 encounters with Wales and Scotland, his fitness record began to deteriorate, some would say inevitably in view of his high-risk style. For instance, when his nose was smashed in a fiery clash with a Nottingham Forest defender, he broke his arm in attempting to retaliate.

Thereafter he suffered two broken legs and needed two major knee operations, but he fought his misfortunes with the same indomitable fortitude which characterised his football. Indeed, such was his inspirational determination in the face of adversity that at one point Sexton was moved to draw an unfavourable comparison with the attitude of Osgood, whom he transfer-listed temporarily for not equalling the Hutchinson spirit.

However, despite a series of gritty comebacks – including a memorable two-goal performance against Norwich City at Stamford Bridge in December 1972 – there was to be no long-term salvation for the Midlander's career and in 1976, at the crushingly premature age of 27, he was forced to depart the big time, having scored 58 goals in 144 games and created countless others for his colleagues.

Chelsea were left to weep for what might have been, as a fully-fit Hutchinson would have been a long-term asset of colossal value. Socially, too, he left a yawning gap as he was a celebrated bon viveur who lived life to the full alongside the likes of Osgood, Hudson and other team-mates, notably Tommy Baldwin.

All that remained of his playing days was a brief and harrowing stint with non-League Dartford, during which he took the field in immense pain.

There followed a spell as Chelsea's commercial manager in the late 1970s and in more recent years he worked in corporate hospitality for several clubs.

Ian Hutchinson: born Derby, 4 August 1948; played for Chelsea 1968-76; died London, 19 September 2002.

Arthur Rowley

He was never feted as a star and he was outshone comprehensively by his brother Jack of Manchester United and England fame; but the fact remains that no one in the history of English League football has popped the ball into the net more times than Arthur Rowley.

In a playing career which spanned four clubs, 19 years and 619 matches spread over all four divisions, Rowley plundered 434 goals, and it is a mark of his staggering pre-eminence that the next most prolific marksman is pre-war icon Bill 'Dixie' Dean, who accumulated 379. True, the burly Black Countryman spent only three seasons in the top flight, and his style of play boasted all the finesse of a runaway steamroller, but neither his employers nor their supporters were heard to complain about lack of artistic merit.

Fearsomely combative in the air, a dreadnought at ground level and possessed of a savage left-foot shot, Rowley was a single-minded goal machine whose final haul surely would have been even more bountiful had his teenage years not coincided with the Second World War.

Hailing from a footballing family – his father was a goalkeeper with Walsall – he made his first impact five days after his 15th birthday when he appeared alongside his brother as a guest for Manchester United in unofficial wartime competition.

In 1942 he signed amateur forms for his home-town club, Wolverhampton Wanderers, but he failed to become established at Molineux and switched to West Bromwich Albion, with whom he turned professional in 1944.

Rowley achieved little of note at the Hawthorns, where often he was used on the left wing, rather curiously in view of his lack of pace, but his career gained dramatic impetus when he moved to Fulham in exchange for flankman Ernie Shepherd in December 1948.

Now deployed at centre-forward, he was a revelation, scoring 19 goals in 22 appearances on the way to a Second Division championship medal. However, he performed unimpressively in his first term among the elite and accepted a £12,000 transfer back to the lower level with Leicester City.

At Filbert Street Rowley was shifted to inside-left, blossoming luxuriantly and achieving remarkable consistency. His tallies over the next nine League campaigns never dipped below 20, while there were several in the high 30s, with a personal best of 44 goals in 42 outings, including four hat-tricks, in 1956/57.

In that season, as in 1953/54, he spearheaded Leicester to the Second Division crown and both times he went on to prove his worth in the higher echelon, recording healthy totals for a team which was struggling to cope with their own elevation. Certainly Leicester benefited from Rowley's prime years, which featured his only major representative honours. There was one appearance for England 'B' against Switzerland in March 1956 – he scored once in a 4-1 victory – and another for the Football League against the Irish League the following October when he failed, for once, to hit the target. With the dynamic likes of Bolton Wanderers' Nat Lofthouse and Tommy Taylor of Manchester United on the scene, there was little scope for Rowley to forge an international career.

In June 1958, in his 33rd year, it seemed likely that his playing days were winding down when a £7,000 deal made him player-boss of lowly Shrewsbury Town, but he confounded expectations of an early demise by continuing to score freely.

He proved capable at management, too, succeeding spectacularly in his dual roles during his first term at Gay Meadow, transforming a previously lacklustre side and leading them to promotion from the newly-formed Fourth Division, netting 38 goals in the process.

In 1959/60 Rowley's Shrews narrowly missed rising to the Second Division, and in 1960/61 they claimed the scalp of Everton in the first League Cup competition before bowing out 4-3 on aggregate to Rotherham United in the semi-final.

Though he became increasingly bulky and ponderous of movement, Rowley remained an important influence on the pitch, using himself as a central defender at times and continuing to play until laying aside his boots in 1965, his 40th year.

After spending most of the 1960s in mid-table, Shrewsbury finished among the Third Division leaders in 1968 and he was rewarded with the boss' chair at Sheffield United, newly relegated from the First Division.

The Blades attained a top-half place in 1968/69 but Rowley, who was renowned for a defensive managerial approach ironically at odds with all those years spent as an attacker, could not get on with general manager John Harris and he was sacked at season's end.

In 1970 he took over the reins of Southend United, plotting their first-ever promotion from the League's basement in 1972, but he was dismissed after they went down again four years later.

Thereafter Rowley, a quiet fellow and not a natural mixer, left the game, going on to become a district manager for Vernons Pools before retiring to the Shrewsbury area.

George Arthur Rowley: born Wolverhampton, 21 April 1926; played for West Bromwich Albion 1944-48, Fulham 1948-50, Leicester City 1950-58, Shrewsbury Town 1958-65; managed Shrewsbury Town 1958-68, Sheffield United 1968-69, Southend United 1970-76; died Shrewsbury, 18 December 2002.

Albert Stubbins

Albert Stubbins was a goal-scoring idol, revered in two of the most passionate hotbeds of soccer in the world, his niche in English folklore underlined by his presence on the sleeve of one of the best-selling pop music albums of all time.

The flame-haired north-easterner, loved on both Tyneside and Merseyside for his unfailingly equable approach to the game almost as much as for his prolific exploits with Newcastle United and Liverpool, was chosen by the Beatles as one of 63 famous faces to adorn the artwork of their ground-breaking *Sgt Pepper's Lonely Hearts Club Band* in 1967.

Wearing a characteristic broad grin, he is wedged cosily among the likes of Marlene Dietrich, Lewis Carroll and Karl Marx, and it is a tribute to his stature in popular culture that he doesn't seem the slightest bit out of place.

As a Newcastle player, Stubbins accumulated more goals than anyone else in English football during emergency competitions staged during the Second World War, then he helped Liverpool to become the first League champions in the wake of the conflict, yet he never earned a full cap for England, being overshadowed by the stellar likes of Tommy Lawton and Jackie Milburn.

A ball-playing centre-forward, endowed with subtle skills, searing pace and a scorching shot in both of his size-11 boots – though he was quite tall, the immensity of his feet was rather incongruous in such a slender fellow – Stubbins was not merely a taker, but also a maker of goals. He led his forward line intelligently, constantly seeking to bring colleagues into play with his perceptive passing, and for all his dead-eyed menace it was clear that he enjoyed his work, his nickname of 'The Smiling Assassin' being singularly apt.

Born in Wallsend, a particularly productive seedbed of star footballers, he might have been lost to the game when his family moved to the United States during his infancy, but after living in New York and Detroit the Stubbinses returned to England when the boy was 12.

Soon his vast potential became obvious and he joined Sunderland as an amateur, but only on the understanding that should Newcastle, whom he supported from the Gallowgate terraces, make an approach then he could switch clubs. Duly the Magpies' interest materialised and he turned professional at St James' Park in April 1937.

Stubbins made his senior debut for Second Division United while still a teenager in 1938 and quickly he became established in the first team, but it was his ill fortune to find himself on the threshold of a richly promising career just as war broke out.

Throughout the hostilities, he remained on Tyneside doing essential work as a shipyard draughtsman, but arguably his prime contribution towards lifting the communal gloom was as a footballer. Over the next six years he scored 245 times in 199 appearances for Newcastle, including four consecutive hat-tricks during a purple patch in 1941.

When peace was declared, the 26-year-old, who had represented his country in unofficial wartime internationals, reviewed his options and decided that he needed to play in the First Division to make the most of his potential. Accordingly he asked for a transfer, which was granted, and it is a mark of his prowess that only two top-flight clubs failed to register an interest in acquiring Newcastle's goal-grabbing phenomenon.

In the end it came down to a straight contest between Liverpool and Everton, and he tossed up to decide which Merseyside institution to meet first. The coin came down in favour of the Reds, who quickly clinched a £12,500 deal – then not far behind the British record – by promising to secure Stubbins a regular column in the *Liverpool Echo*, something on which he was extremely keen, having learned shorthand in his teens as preparation for employment in later life.

The Anfield newcomer was an instant success, netting with a brilliant individual effort in a victorious debut at Bolton and going on to total 24 League strikes in his first campaign, including the winner against Wolves at Molineux which clinched the 1946/47 title for Liverpool.

The following term Stubbins was equally effective, one four-goal demolition of Huddersfield being especially spectacular, but the summer of 1948 brought discord when the club rejected his request to live and train on Tyneside, where his heart would always remain. Initially he refused to re-sign, but although he relented after two months and spent another five seasons at Anfield, he was never quite the same force again, falling prey to serial injuries.

However, Stubbins played a major part in the Reds' progress to the FA Cup final in 1950, in which they lost 2-0 to Arsenal and might have prevailed had he not been narrowly off target with several attempts to score. That same year, though by then in his thirties, he demonstrated eloquently that he was far from finished, netting five times in the Football League's annihilation of the Irish League.

Tellingly, throughout his twilight years as a player, Stubbins remained wildly popular with the fans even when team performances were disappointing, and it was as much a tribute to his enduringly warm and gentlemanly persona as to his footballing ability that this should be so.

After leaving Liverpool in 1953, he served non-League Ashington before putting aside his boots a year later, then made a brief return to the game as coach of the United States in 1960.

By then he was making his living as a journalist, working for the *Shields County News* and then the *People*, as well as sampling local radio prior to his retirement in 1984.

Thereafter Albert Stubbins, an engagingly modest and humorous man, lived in his beloved north-east, following the football scene closely and relishing occasional references to his Beatles link.

Perhaps it is appropriate, then, to leave the final word to Paul McCartney, who on the release of *Sgt Pepper* in 1967, sent Stubbins a copy of the record accompanied by the message: 'Well done, Albert, for all those glorious years of football. Long may you bob and weave.'

Albert Stubbins: born Wallsend, Northumberland, 17 July 1919; played for Newcastle United 1937-46, Liverpool 1946-53; died Cullercoats, Northumberland, 28 December 2002.

Billy Morris

Welsh international Billy Morris was the last surviving member of the fine Burnley side which lost the FA Cup final to Charlton Athletic in 1947, but garnered rich consolation a few weeks later by gaining promotion to English football's top flight.

Thereafter the quicksilver little inside-forward, who spent his entire playing career at Turf Moor, flourished among the elite for half a decade, helping the Clarets to finish third, behind champions Arsenal and Manchester United, in 1947/48.

Morris brought to his work a lively intelligence, delicious ball control and a sharp sense of anticipation which enabled him to turn many a marginal scoring opportunity into a goal. He created countless openings for his team-mates, too, typically ghosting past a posse of hulking opponents before delivering a decisive pass.

The great misfortune of Morris' professional career was that it had barely begun when it was halted for six years of what should have been his prime by the Second World War.

Having been scouted by a bevy of League clubs, he had been recruited by Burnley from Llandudno Town in January 1939 and was pitchforked immediately into Second Division action. He thrived on the grander stage, but all too soon he was enlisting with the Royal Welsh Fusiliers, serving as a sergeant in India and Burma, where he was shot in the neck while fighting the Japanese. Luckily it was only a flesh wound and Morris, who guested for Wrexham during the conflict, was fit and raring to go when peace resumed.

His contribution to the Clarets' memorable 1946/47 campaign was immense, including goals against Aston Villa and Middlesbrough during the FA Cup run, and two rousing displays as champions-elect Liverpool were overcome after a replay in the semi-final.

At Wembley in the final, he had an early chance to give Burnley the lead, but it went begging and Charlton prevailed with the only goal of the game, scored by Chris Duffy near the end of extra-time. That year Morris won the first of five full caps for Wales, against Northern Ireland in Belfast, and he remained in the international reckoning until 1952, when he faced the Rest of the United Kingdom. Having helped Burnley to reach the First Division, Morris was hugely influential in their subsequent consolidation at that level and made his most prolific contribution, with 19 senior goals, in 1951/52, his last complete season.

He retired from League football in 1952, then went on to coach youngsters at Turf Moor, playing an important part in the development of some of those who would lift the championship in 1960. At the end of that momentous term Morris entered management with Wrexham, newly relegated to the Fourth Division, but after a season in which the Welsh club continued to struggle in the League, though reaching the quarter-finals of the newly-launched League Cup, he was replaced by Ken Barnes.

That was a major disappointment to Morris, who believed he had the foundations of a decent side, which included 18-year-old centre-forward Wyn Davies, who would go on to become a stalwart of the Welsh international team for many years.

After leaving football to run a guest house in Llandudno, Morris was tempted back to the Wrexham job in March 1965, though more disillusion lay in wait and he was dismissed in the following October following a poor start to the new campaign.

In later years Morris, a softly-spoken and modest individual, worked for a steamship company and ran a village shop in Llysfaen, near Colwyn Bay.

William Morris: born Llandulas, near Colwyn Bay, Denbighshire, 30 July 1918; played for Burnley 1939-53; capped five times by Wales 1947-52; died St Asaph, Clwyd, 31 December 2002.

Peter Harris

The durable, diamond-bright brilliance of right-winger Peter Harris offered persuasive contradiction to glib descriptions of the Portsmouth side which lifted back-to-back Football League championships midway through the 20th century as 'the team without a star'.

Though denied more than fleeting moments in the international limelight by the incomparable talents of Stanley Matthews and Tom Finney, the placid, modest Harris was a massive achiever for his only club.

A cursory examination of his statistics reveals him to be Pompey's record scorer, having netted 208 times in more than 500 senior outings during a 15-year career. Those are remarkable figures for any flankman, but they barely begin to do justice to his overall impact in a beautifully co-ordinated team which was damned all too frequently by faint praise.

Harris was a monument to flair, loyalty and dedication, but what commanded the attention most insistently was his searing pace. He was particularly devastating in sudden bursts of acceleration, a natural gift but one which he honed meticulously by his prodigious application to training.

After seeming to dawdle harmlessly near the touchline, Harris would erupt explosively, his characteristic high-velocity scurry capable of embarrassing the classiest of opponents. Indeed, few men were better equipped to combat speed merchants than the celebrated Manchester United and England left-back Roger Byrne, who lost his life in the Munich air disaster of 1958, but even he was the subject of serial chasings by the Fratton Park flyer.

Of course, Harris would not have flourished so productively by sprinting power alone. He possessed immense guile, as evidenced by the subtle feints and dummies with which he tormented defenders, his ball control was immaculate, and he was a reliable purveyor of tantalising crosses. Crucially, too, he was a fine finisher, packing a shot both powerful and accurate.

Born a short bus ride from the Portsmouth headquarters, Harris trained as a carpenter and played his early football for local club Gosport Borough before being signed by colourful Fratton Park boss Jack Tinn towards the end of the Second World War.

The slim teenager, who favoured long, baggy shorts in the style of his hero, the great Arsenal schemer Alex James, got off to an impressive start in unofficial wartime competition, then made his senior debut in a 3-1 home victory over Blackburn Rovers in August 1946. During the following campaign he established a regular place under the quietly inspirational leadership of new manager Bob Jackson, then emerged as a key component of the Pompey combination which romped away with the 1948/49 title, outstripping runners-up Manchester United by an emphatic five-point margin.

Harris' 17 goals made him joint leading scorer with Duggie 'Thunderboots' Reid, the pair being supplied with ammunition by fellow members of an underrated team whose plentiful ability was buttressed by extraordinary degrees of comradeship and co-ordination. Outstanding among them were wing-halves Jimmy Scoular and Jimmy Dickinson, left-winger Jack Froggatt, inside-forward Len Phillips, and Reg Flewin, centre-half and a skipper of imposing authority.

At one point in the spring Portsmouth had a genuine chance of becoming the first club in the 20th century to lift the League and FA Cup double. Harris had set their Wembley sights with a hat-trick in the 7-0 third-round thrashing of Stockport County, but after reaching the semi-finals they fell rather tamely to Leicester City, then toiling in the lower reaches of the Second Division.

Pundits who trumpeted the causes of more fashionable clubs from London and the North predicted that Pompey would falter in 1949/50, but they confounded the doubters by retaining their First Division crown, this time pipping Wolverhampton Wanderers by two-fifths of a goal (at that time a difficult goal-average system was used to split teams on equal points, rather than goal-difference).

Thereafter Portsmouth remained an effective side for several seasons, though they became more unpredictable and gradually the title-winning line-up was dismantled as the 1950s progressed. Harris, however, remained on prime form throughout that decade and, had he not shared nationality with Matthews and Finney, surely must have received more than his two international caps.

Sadly, both his England appearances coincided with dreadful team displays. At Goodison Park in 1949, England were defeated for the first time on home soil by a foreign country when they bowed 2-0 to the Republic of Ireland, and in Budapest in 1954, given the task of avenging the previous year's Wembley humiliation by 'The Magnificent Magyars', they were annihilated 7-1 by Hungary.

On the domestic scene, Harris enjoyed his most fruitful scoring term in 1952/53, striking 23 goals, and in 1958/59 he became the first winger to net five times in a top-division game when he dominated the 5-2 triumph over Aston Villa.

By then, though, Portsmouth had deteriorated horribly and at season's end they were nine points adrift of their nearest rivals, being relegated for the first time since the war. However, 33-year-old Harris featured only briefly in the Second Division, succumbing to tuberculosis in November 1959 and never playing again.

On recovery after six months in a sanatorium, he turned down several offers to remain in the game and managed a restaurant complex in Hayling Island, as well as enagaging in local charity work.

Peter Philip Harris: born Southsea, Hampshire, 19 December 1925; played for Portsmouth 1944-59; capped twice by England 1949-54; died Hayling Island, Hampshire, 2 January 2003.

Len Duquemin

No one who spent time with Len Duquemin was surprised to discover that the squarely-built centre-forward in Tottenham Hotspur's first League championship-winning team had worked in a monastery before stepping into the hectic world of professional football at White Hart Lane.

The Guernsey-born marksman, a ceaselessly competitive study in perpetual motion on the pitch, was a quiet, gentle, engagingly unassuming fellow away from the action, and somehow it was not difficult to imagine him moving tranquilly among the monks as he tended their garden during the German occupation of the Channel Islands in the Second World War. Indeed, of his two nicknames, 'Reliable Len' and 'The Duke', the first fitted his character far more neatly, offering due recognition of his unobtrusive but incalculably valuable service to one of the outstanding sides of the era, while the second was no more than a glib abbreviation of his surname.

Duquemin scored 134 goals in 308 senior games for his solitary Football League club, and despite his lack of extravagant natural ability, he was considered a key man by both manager and team-mates as he helped to lift the Second Division title in 1949/50, then the First Division crown in the following campaign.

Arthur Rowe's team won renown for their flowing push-and-run style, which involved slick interchanges of short, accurate passes as they swept from one end of the pitch to the other. It was a fresh, swashbuckling approach which lit up the post-war soccer scene and won lavish plaudits for the ball-playing likes of inside-forwards Eddie Baily and Les Bennett, wing-half and skipper Ronnie Burgess, wingers Les Medley and Sonny Walters, and a full-back named Alf Ramsey, who one day would lead England to World Cup glory.

But there was a need, too, for players who would run ceaselessly when they were not in possession, providing extra passing options for their artistic colleagues; they didn't always get the ball and rarely took the eye, but without them the system would have foundered. One such was wing-half Billy Nicholson, destined to become the most successful manager in Spurs history, and another was Duquemin, whose honest sweat was an important lubricant to the smooth running of Rowe's captivating machine.

After being recommended to the club by a Guernsey-based fan, Reliable Len joined Tottenham as an amateur in January 1946, turning professional nine months later. Quick, strong and immensely effective in the air though standing an inch under six feet, he netted on his senior debut, a 5-1 win at home to Sheffield Wednesday in August 1947, and thereafter retained a regular place. At that point Spurs were a tolerably enterprising but unexceptional second-flight outfit, but they were transformed when Rowe replaced Joe Hulme as manager in 1949, sweeping to their divisional championship in his first season at the helm with the help of 16 Duquemin goals.

The Channel Islander supplied 14 more on the title trail in 1950/51, including the sole strike of a tense springtime encounter with Wednesday at the Lane which clinched the domestic game's top prize. In 1951/52 he continued to prosper as Tottenham exchanged places with the previous year's runners-up, Manchester United, and enjoyed his most prolific personal season in 1952/53, when he registered 24 goals in League and FA Cup.

Duquemin never made it to an FA Cup final at Wembley, though he went close in both 1948 and 1953, each time scoring in a semi-final only to be beaten by Blackpool.

He never made the international reckoning, either, being kept at bay by such top-quality operators as Tommy Lawton, Stan Mortensen and Nat Lofthouse, though he had the satisfaction of riding out mid-1950s rumours that Bolton's Lofthouse was about to replace him at club level.

In fact, when competition did arrive at Tottenham in the shape of York City's David Dunmore in February 1954, he resisted it doggedly, and it was not until 1956, when he was past 30, that finally he was supplanted as first-choice number-nine by future England spearhead Bobby Smith.

By then Spurs had declined into mid-table mediocrity, Rowe had departed due to ill health and Duquemin was one of the few survivors of the revered title-winning combination.

He played his last senior game in March 1957 but remained at the club until 1958, when he entered non-League circles with Bedford Town, then served Hastings United and Romford. Later he ran a newsagent's shop in Northumberland Park, not far from White Hart Lane, before becoming a pub landlord at the Haunch of Venison in Cheshunt, Hertfordshire, until his retirement.

Leonard Stanley Duquemin: born Cobo, Guernsey, 17 July 1924; played for Tottenham Hotspur 1946-58; married, one son; died London, 20 April 2003.

Trevor Ford

Trevor Ford was a colourful, fearsomely physical centre-forward who led the Welsh attack for a decade soon after the Second World War. One of the fieriest spearheads in football history, he provoked fervently strong feelings both for him and against, and he thrived on the notoriety generated by his crash-bang-wallop methods.

An amiable, wryly humorous fellow off the pitch, Ford reckoned that his personality was transformed when he ran out to play. Though maintaining that he was scrupulously fair, never setting out to injure an opponent, he once declared: 'I was like an animal.'

It was a disarmingly frank verdict delivered without a trace of regret, and when lurid descriptions of his style were brought to his attention – 'a half-crazed Welsh dragon' and 'the dirtiest so-and-so in the business' were two of the milder offerings – he was not abashed. By his own lights, he was merely doing his job and doing it well – he netted freely for a succession of clubs, notably Aston Villa and Sunderland, and set a new scoring record for his country – all within the rules of what he referred to proudly as a man's game.

After all, in Ford's day it was acceptable for centre-forwards to charge goalkeepers, and he could point to an unblemished disciplinary record, with not a solitary caution or dismissal during a professional career which spanned nearly 20 years. In today's climate, it is fair to say that he would have to amend his approach drastically or be outlawed.

Ford, a blast furnace worker in his teens, was a promising but diminutive left-back when he enlisted with his local club, Swansea Town (now City) as an amateur in 1942, turning professional two years later.

During war service as a physical training instructor in the Royal Artillery, he gained height and weight and, although the Welsh youngster was still no giant at 5ft 10ins, a sergeant major felt encouraged to switch him to centre-forward. Immediately it became clear that he had found his niche, and on returning to Swansea he scored 41 goals in the 1945/46 wartime regional competition, which led to a call-up for the Wales team to face Northern Ireland in an unofficial Victory international.

At that point, with the Swans struggling in the Second Division, it was clear that the muscular swashbuckler could better himself elsewhere and, after almost signing for Chelsea, he was transferred to top-flight Aston Villa in exchange for inside-forward Tommy Dodds plus a cheque for £9,500.

Ford did well enough at Villa Park, netting 60 goals in 120 League appearances, and even his sternest critics were forced to admit that his game consisted of considerably more than brute force. True, his raw bravery, tireless industry and aerial dynamism riveted the eye, but also he was imbued with assured control and an accurate shot in either foot, and he was particularly effective when pulling markers out of position by roaming to the wings.

However, Villa's bid to become championship contenders petered out tamely and in October 1950 Ford was head-hunted by Sunderland, then known as the Bank of England club because of their colossal spending, who shattered the British transfer record to sign him for £30,000.

The Welshman exploded on to the Roker Park scene with a spectacular hat-trick on his home debut against Sheffield Wednesday, charging Owls keeper Dave McIntosh over the line for one of the goals and further fuelling his abrasive image by breaking an upright with one savage effort.

But although Ford continued to score freely for the Wearsiders, registering 67 times in 108 First Division outings, he could not lift them out of mid-table and, with scapegoats being sought, much was made of his clash of styles with his infinitely more inventive team-mate, Len Shackleton. For his part, Ford claimed that Shackleton wouldn't give him the ball when and where he wanted it, while the anarchically inclined Englishman accused the Welshman of lacking the positional sense to make the most of his subtle deliveries.

During one friendly encounter with a Dutch side, Shackleton made his point with typical waspishness. After dribbling past several defenders and rounding the keeper, he stopped on the goal-line, then rolled the ball to the feet of the nearby Ford, with the withering comment: 'Here, don't say I never give you a pass!' In December 1953, disappointed that the expensively assembled Sunderland combination had failed to realise its full potential, 30-year-old Ford joined Cardiff City in another £30,000 transaction, and his goals helped them to finish tenth in the First Division at season's end.

Thereafter, though, the Bluebirds struggled and Ford hit controversial new heights with his book *I Lead The Attack*, in which he revealed that under-the-table payments had been made during his Sunderland tenure. When he refused to name names he was banned by the English game's authorities and announced his retirement in November 1956, making a lucrative comeback three months later with the Dutch club PSV Eindhoven.

For three years Ford prospered in Holland, spearheading PSV to domestic success before the suspension was lifted in 1960 and he returned to Wales, finishing his career with brief stints at Newport County and non-League Romford.

On the international front, his 38 appearances had yielded 23 goals, a magnificent tally subsequently equalled by Ivor Allchurch, then eventually bettered by Ian Rush, who had played in many more matches than Ford when he annexed the record.

After leaving the game, Ford worked in the motor trade before retiring to live close to Swansea's Vetch Field, where he had set out on the road which was to earn him an unperishable niche in Welsh folklore.

Trevor Ford: born Swansea, Glamorgan, 1 October 1923; played for Swansea Town 1942-47, Aston Villa 1947-50, Sunderland 1950-53, Cardiff City 1953-56, PSV Eindhoven 1957-60, Newport County 1960-61; capped 38 times by Wales (1947-57); died Swansea, 29 May 2003.

Ray Harford

The twin peaks of Ray Harford's career offered compelling testimony to his stature as one of the most accomplished English football coaches of the last two decades.

In 1988 he managed unfashionable Luton Town to the sole major prize in their history when they overturned Arsenal in an enthralling League Cup final at Wembley; and in 1995 he played a colossally influential role, as Kenny Dalglish's number-two, in enabling Blackburn Rovers to pip Manchester United to the Premiership title.

For all that, Harford was never a glamorous figure, being noted for his uneasiness with the media and a taciturn public demeanour. In private he was warm, engaging and forthright, but the stern image – heightened by one club chairman, who remarked that he did not smile at the fans enough – could not be shaken off.

Essentially Harford was a gifted organiser who excelled repeatedly when working with meagre resources. He was a devoted student of the game, always questing for technical improvement, and whenever possible his teams played neat, attractive football, though he was practical enough to employ less pretty long-ball methods at need.

A Yorkshireman by birth, Harford grew up in the Elephant and Castle area of London, emerging as a promising central defender and turning professional with Second Division Charlton Athletic in 1964.

However, he failed to make his mark at that level and, despite occasional whispers of a transfer to the big time, the hardy six-footer joined Exeter City in January 1966, experiencing relegation to the Fourth Division with the Grecians that term, then spending the remainder of his playing career in the Football League's lower reaches.

There was a 170-match spell with Lincoln City – performing alongside Graham Taylor, a future England boss who would one day employ Harford briefly to coach his country's under-21 side – followed by stints at Mansfield Town, Port Vale and Colchester United, whom he helped to win promotion from the basement flight in 1973/74.

When knee problems signalled a premature end to his playing days in 1976, Harford was appointed youth coach at Layer Road, where he remained for five years before accepting a similar post at Fulham in 1981.

In his first season the Cottagers were promoted to the Second Division, after which he became assistant boss to Malcolm Macdonald, and was instrumental in producing the fluent play which almost secured an immediate rise to the top flight.

Deservedly Harford was awarded his first full managerial job when Macdonald left in 1984, but financial restraints and the consequent sale of key players such as midfielder Ray Houghton limited his scope drastically, and he resigned after Fulham were relegated in the spring of 1986.

With his reputation as a fine coach intact, Harford had no difficulty in graduating immediately to employment on a higher plane, becoming assistant to John Moore, the boss of Luton Town, then a decent side in the old First Division (the equivalent of the modern Premiership).

After helping the Hatters to finish a highly creditable seventh in 1986/87, he took over from Moore the following summer and embarked on the most successful season the club had ever known. Harford's team retained their top-half League status, lost an FA Cup semi-final to Wimbledon (the eventual winners), but best of all they lifted the League Cup, producing two late goals to defeat mighty Arsenal 3-2 in a rousing final.

Even in that moment of triumph Harford sat stone-faced on the Wembley bench while bedlam broke out around him, and he was lampooned unkindly for his apparent coldness. In truth, as he revealed later, he was extremely emotional and, after spotting his family in the stands, was fighting to hold back the tears.

In 1988/89 Luton reached the League Cup final again, this time losing to Brian Clough's Nottingham Forest, but their League form deteriorated and when they struggled again during the following campaign he was sacked, controversially, in January 1990.

Harford continued to be in demand, though, becoming assistant manager of top-flight Wimbledon that February, then succeeding Bobby Gould as boss in June before presiding over a seventh-place finish – a mere three points adrift of Manchester United – in 1990/91.

History repeated itself that autumn when he resigned following the sale of an important player, this time Keith Curle, and swiftly he was enlisted by Kenny Dalglish to become his right-hand man in the revival of Blackburn Rovers, which was about to be funded by wealthy industrialist Jack Walker.

With Dalglish the figurehead and Harford a crucial power behind the throne, Rovers earned promotion to the new Premier League via the play-offs that term, then consolidated spectacularly by finishing fourth and second among the elite in the next two seasons.

Finally, in 1994/95, fielding a splendid side starring Alan Shearer and including the likes of Chris Sutton, Colin Hendry and Tim Sherwood, Blackburn became League champions for the first time in 81 years.

Most of the public accolades went to Dalglish, but insiders recognised the enormity of Harford's contribution and, though they were stunned by the Scot's decision to move 'upstairs' as director of football, they applauded the appointment of the erstwhile assistant to the top job.

Harford had accepted the challenge despite vowing that never again would he occupy a manager's chair, and subsequent events could be said to have borne out his apprehension.

In 1995/96 injury-ravaged Rovers were found sadly wanting in the Champions League and were a shadow of their former selves in domestic competition. Then, after the sale of Shearer to Newcastle United was followed by a chronic start to 1996/97, the Ewood Park boss fell on his sword in the autumn.

Dalglish had proved too hard an act to follow, yet arguably Harford had been victim to the club's new wave of supporters, attracted by the recent dazzling renaissance. Ironically he retained the backing of the board and the players, and he had real money at his disposal for the first time in his life, but when the fans started calling for his head, he had to go.

Still in love with the game, Harford went on to manage West Bromwich Albion and Queen's Park Rangers in the First Division, resigning from the first because he was attracted to a move back to London, and the second after disagreements with his board.

Millwall persuaded him out of semi-retirement in 1999 and benefited hugely from his coaching expertise, which helped to secure Second Division title glory in 2001. He served under several bosses and was still employed by the Lions when cancer claimed his life.

Raymond Thomas Harford: born Halifax, Yorkshire, 1 June 1945; played for Charlton Athletic 1964-66, Exeter City 1966-67, Lincoln City 1967-71, Mansfield Town 1971, Port Vale 1971-73, Colchester United 1973-76; managed Fulham 1984-86, Luton Town 1987-90, Wimbledon 1990-91, Blackburn Rovers 1995-97, West Bromwich Albion 1997, Queen's Park Rangers 1997-98; died London, 9 August 2003.

John Aston Snr

Many more illustrious names than John Aston Snr's intertwine the history of Manchester United, but few men have made a more varied and lengthy contribution to the Red Devils' cause, or been more steeped in their tradition, than the selfless, straightforward, quietly efficient Mancunian.

An archetypal one-club man, Aston once declared: 'After my family, United have been the number-one love of my life,' and certainly that devotion was strikingly apparent during 35 years at Old Trafford, first as a footballer of international class, then as a briskly motivational coach, and finally as a shrewd talent-spotter.

An integral part of Matt Busby's buoyantly exhilarating post-war side, usually operating at full-back but also filling in effectively at centre-forward, Aston helped to lift the FA Cup in 1948 and the League championship four years later, and earned a place in the England team for the 1950 World Cup finals.

Eventually he introduced his son, also John, to Old Trafford, then watched with quiet pride as the rookie winger shone brighter than any of his starry colleagues on the balmy Wembley night in 1968 when United became the first English club to win the European Cup.

Beyond that, Aston the elder occupied a unique position as the only man alive at the turn of the century to have played on all four grounds which have been home to United and its predecessor club, Newton Heath Lancashire and Yorkshire Railway FC.

As a boy he turned out at North Road and Bank Street; Old Trafford was his base throughout his career, and the fourth was Manchester City's Maine Road, used by United after their own headquarters had been devastated by Hitler's bombs.

Aston was 15 when he enlisted with the Red Devils as an amateur in 1937, not turning professional until after serving in the Middle East as a Royal Marine Commando during the Second World War. At the time he was an inside-forward and that was the berth in which he made his League debut at home to Chelsea in September 1946. For his next appearance, ten days later, he was switched to wing-half and then completed his transformation from attacker to defender by settling as skipper John Carey's regular full-back partner during the second half of the season.

The conversion was a typically inspirational touch by his manager, Busby, who was seeking a left-back endowed with strength, stamina, pace and skill. There was no shortage of candidates who boasted the first three attributes but the fourth, which Aston possessed in abundance, made him an exceptionally effective addition to the rearguard.

As team-mate Johnny Morris put it: 'John was so good with the ball that it was like having an inside-forward at full-back. A lot of our opponents simply didn't know what to make of it.'

Undoubtedly it worked as United emerged as the most entertaining team in the land, though they suffered the mortification of finishing as First Division runners-up in the first three campaigns after the war.

In that era, though, the FA Cup was of massive, even overriding importance, so the serial League disappointments were mitigated enormously by a breathtaking Wembley triumph against Blackpool in 1948.

That day John's direct opponent was the nation's darling, Stanley Matthews, whom most neutrals were willing to claim a winner's medal in what they believed, misguidedly as it transpired, to be the twilight of his career. But although 'The Wizard of Dribble' contributed enterprisingly as the Seasiders shaded the first half, Aston's incisive tackling and perceptive interceptions nullified the future knight in the second period as United surged to an uplifting 4-2 victory.

A consistent sequence of such composed, accomplished performances earned him a full international call-up that autumn and soon he had cemented his England slot for the next two years, occasionally on his favoured right side but more frequently on the left.

The highlight of this spell should have been the country's first foray into the World Cup finals, in Brazil in 1950, but instead Aston found himself part of the most excruciatingly embarrassing of all England anti-climaxes when they lost 1-0 to rank outsiders, the United States. The Mancunian was blameless, the team's luck was outrageously bad and the result was a travesty, but years later he would still grimace as he recalled the woeful occasion.

Still he continued to thrive for United, but soon afterwards his invaluable adaptability was to cost him dearly. When the club's spearhead, Jack Rowley, was injured midway through 1950/51, Aston was switched to centre-forward and so devastating was his form – he plundered 15 goals in 22 games – that he retained the job, with Rowley moving to the left flank when he regained fitness.

However, the upshot was the loss of his England place because national boss Walter Winterbottom, himself a United old boy, insisted that a current left-back be selected.

The uncomplaining Aston never played for his country again, even after resuming full-back duties and helping the Red Devils to win the League title in 1951/52. Though he was in his thirties by then, his form remained impressive and it came as a hammer blow when, after nearly 300 appearances – a figure which would have been much higher but for the war – his career was ended prematurely by tuberculosis in 1954.

Aston's Old Trafford involvement was far from over, however. He took up coaching and played a part in the development of the Busby Babes, the likes of Duncan Edwards and Bobby Charlton, before knee problems presaged a switch to become chief scout in 1970. It was a role he relished but he lost it in 1972, proving that there was little sentimentality in football when he departed in the backroom clearout which accompanied the dismissal of manager Frank O'Farrell.

Severely disheartened by that grisly exit, though never losing his affection for United, he picked up the threads of his soccer career only briefly, scouting for Luton Town and Birmingham City before leaving the game to work in the family pet foods business alongside his son.

John Aston retired in 1986, continuing to live in his long-time home in Audenshaw, Manchester, then suffering a protracted illness which began during the 1990s.

John Aston: born Prestwich, Manchester, 3 September 1921; played for Manchester United 1938-54; capped 17 times for England 1948-50; died Manchester, 31 July 2003.

Trevor Smith

Trevor Smith was the fearsomely rugged defensive cornerstone of the most successful side in Birmingham City history.

A granite buttress of a centre-half, he was an emerging force as the Blues won the Second Division title in 1954/55, then finished sixth in the top flight and reached the FA Cup final a year later.

At that point he was being touted freely as the likely long-term successor to Billy Wright at the core of England's rearguard, but although he remained a colossal influence at St Andrew's for more than a decade, playing in two finals of the Inter Cities Fairs Cup (the forerunner of the modern UEFA Cup) in 1960 and 1961 and starring as City lifted the League Cup in 1963, he didn't realise fully the vast potential he had demonstrated at the outset of his career.

Smith was tall, tough and fearless, a relentless competitor who was majestic in aerial combat and tackled like a speeding juggernaut, but whereas he was lithe and bouncy in his teens and early twenties, as he grew increasingly muscular with maturity, so he became a tad cumbersome and sometimes struggled to cope with nippy, clever opponents.

A Black Country boy who played schools football alongside Duncan Edwards, the Manchester United prodigy destined to lose his life in the Munich air disaster of 1958, Smith signed amateur forms for Second Division Birmingham City in 1951 and enjoyed an early taste of glory in helping the Blues to win the European Youth Cup a year later.

Developing rapidly, he claimed a first-team berth in 1953/54 and despite the distraction of National Service with the Army during the middle of the decade, he became a fixture in a notably parsimonious defence which included Gil Merrick in goal, full-backs Jeff Hall and Ken Green, and wing-halves Len Boyd and Roy Warhurst.

During the promotion campaign, and the subsequent top-six finish among the elite, Smith took the eye not only with his uncompromising physical presence, but also with admirable all-round technique.

The 1956 Wembley showdown might have proved a showcase for his skills, but Birmingham were undone that day by Manchester City, for whom deep-lying centre-forward Don Revie proved too elusive for Smith to dominate, and the northerners ran out comfortable 3-1 winners.

Still, though the Blues declined first to mid-table and then to regular strugglers against relegation over the next eight years, the promising young stopper distinguished himself at England under-23 level and when Billy Wright finally ended his illustrious international tenure in 1959, to Smith fell the first chance to replace him.

On his full England debut against Wales at Ninian Park, Cardiff, he was stretched by the subtle movement of Graham Moore but performed competently enough in a 1-1 draw and was given a second chance 11 days later against Sweden at Wembley.

This time Smith was exposed cruelly by the pace and invention of Agne Simonsson as the visitors triumphed 3-2, and he was never offered another opportunity at the top level.

He continued to excel for his club, though, and was the defensive rallying point throughout a series of Fairs Cup campaigns, which included defeats in successive two-legged finals by Barcelona and AS Roma respectively.

After such sterling service, which included a spell as skipper, and so many disappointments in finals, it was fitting that Smith remained a key man when Birmingham collected their first – and still, in 2003, their only – front-line trophy since joining the Football League in 1892.

Indeed, he was an inspirational figure in both legs of their League Cup victory over local rivals Aston Villa in 1963, especially in the goalless second game at Villa Park when his tight marking of the combative Bobby Thomson was a crucial factor in the Blues maintaining their 3-1 advantage from the opening encounter.

When Smith joined Third Division Walsall in an £18,000 deal in October 1964, he was the last remnant of the outstanding class of '56, and past his peak after playing 430 senior games for City. Sadly he made only a handful of outings for the Saddlers before arthritis forced him to retire prematurely, shortly before his 30th birthday in 1966.

After leaving football he became landlord of a pub in Tamworth, then managed wine stores in Birmingham's Bull Ring shopping centre and at Dagenham in Essex.

Trevor Smith: born Brierley Hill, Staffordshire, 13 April 1936; played for Birmingham City 1951-64, Walsall 1964-66; capped twice by England 1959; died Essex, 9 August 2003.

Joe Baker

Joe Baker was a swashbuckling cavalier of a footballer and, that extreme rarity, an English international with a broad Scottish accent.

A free-scoring centre-forward, notably as a teenager with Edinburgh-based Hibernian and later with Arsenal, he was the first man to win a full England cap while playing for a club outside the Football League, typically finding the net on his international debut in a 2-1 victory over Northern Ireland at Wembley in November 1959.

Baker's policy was to entertain, and he stuck to it exuberantly throughout an 18-year career which took in six clubs in three countries. Thrustful, pacy and extremely clever, he was blessed with the ability to control a ball instantly, at virtually any speed or angle it might reach him; he was a delightfully slick passer and, crucially, he was a pitiless finisher, with his head and with either foot.

Unyieldingly combative and inclined to be fiery in the heat of the action, he was unfailingly courageous, too, ever ready to accept possession no matter how tightly he was marked. But what endeared him most surely to supporters on both sides of the border was the irrepressible glee which he felt – and which he communicated vividly through his customary impudent demeanour – at being paid well for playing the game he loved.

Off the field he was equally engaging, a mischievous fellow who inspired spontaneous affection in practically everyone he met, and in some way it was appropriate that such a gregarious man should die among friends, suffering a suspected heart attack during a charity golf match.

Born in Liverpool of Scottish parents, Baker was an infant when the family moved to Motherwell, where he was raised, demonstrating precocious football talent which earned honours with Scotland Schoolboys.

In 1955 he spent a month on trial with Chelsea but was not signed, gravitating instead to Hibernian via junior clubs Coltness United and Armadale Thistle. Soon it became clear that he would make the grade in the Scottish top division and by 1957/58 he was a regular in the Easter Road side, scoring for fun.

That season Baker featured in the Scottish Cup final defeat by Clyde, after which his strike rate became prodigious, the highlight being a club record 42 goals in 33 appearances during 1959/60, the term in which he added to his England under-23 honours with a full call-up to replace Middlesbrough's Brian Clough.

By 1960/61, during which he scored nine times (and missed a penalty) in the 15-1 cup annihilation of non-League Peebles Rovers, Baker's name was being flashed around the football world, and even though he lost his England place to Bobby Smith of Tottenham Hotspur, it became clear, with all due respect to Hibernian, that his long-term future lay away from Easter Road.

It was a time when some of Britain's top performers were succumbing to the lure of Italian lira and in May '61 Baker joined Torino in a £70,000 deal, linking up with his countryman Denis Law.

Alas, though he played pretty well for his new employers, his Turin sojourn was to prove traumatic and almost fatal. He began by scoring twice in his first home match, but then was sent off for retaliation and was punished by a heavy fine, which he resented. It was the first of a succession of scrapes which placed him under intense public scrutiny, and the homesick 21-year-old came to loathe the press harassment to which he was not accustomed. As a result he and Law spent much of their time in their apartment, bored rigid but reluctant to venture out, hardly the ideal state of mind for a professional athlete.

Still Baker was prominent in a promising start to the season by Torino, making light of ultra-defensive Italian tactics, and his winning goal in the local derby triumph over Juventus was rapturously received. But then he crashed his new Alfa Romeo sports car, suffering such hideous injuries that he needed life-saving surgery and spent 42 days on a drip. Though he recovered to play again by season's end, he was unhappy with the club regime – he had once resorted to a hunger strike in protest at a lengthy team stay in an isolated hotel – and was desperate for a return to home shores.

In August 1962 salvation materialised in the shape of Arsenal, whose manager Billy Wright signed him for a club record fee of £70,000, and after announcing his arrival with a brilliant debut goal against Leyton Orient at Brisbane Road, he became a Highbury hero.

Baker linked beautifully with inside-forwards George Eastham and Geoff Strong, and for three and a half seasons he scored prolifically, accumulating a century of goals in 156 games for the Gunners, and for sheer excitement Arsenal fans were not to see his like until the arrival of Ian Wright nearly 30 years later.

However, the defence was not quite as efficient, and the team never finished above seventh in the First Division during Baker's sojourn in north London, though life around the colourful spearhead was rarely dull.

For instance, there was a tumultuous 1964 FA Cup encounter with Liverpool in which Baker exchanged blows with Ron Yeats, a serious business which ended with both men being sent off, but the sight of Arsenal's 5ft 8in marksman squaring up to Liverpool's colossal stopper was unavoidably comical. Incidentally, the pair were reconciled over a drink later that afternoon, and laughed about their clash for years afterwards.

Meanwhile Baker's form was good enough to earn a fleeting England recall in January 1966, but a month later the under-pressure Arsenal manager decided that a fresh approach was needed and the striker was sold to Nottingham Forest for £65,000.

Still only 25 and in his prime, he flourished at the City Ground, narrowly missing selection for that summer's World Cup finals in England, but excelling as Forest finished as League runners-up to Manchester United in 1966/67.

Once more he was adored by the fans, most of whom opposed his £30,000 sale to Sunderland in June 1969, but although he demonstrated at Roker Park that he was far from finished, he could not prevent relegation to the Second Division at the end of his first Wearside campaign.

Having entered his thirties, in January 1971 Baker accepted a £12,000 transfer back to his first club, Hibernian, then went on to score heavily for Raith Rovers, one of the better sides in the Scottish Second Division, before appearing in his last senior game in October 1974.

He remained addicted to football and served two spells as boss of Albion Rovers during the 1980s, also working as a publican and in the building trade before suffering health problems in the 1990s.

But the generous Baker, whose older brother Gerry was also a fine centre-forward – playing for St Mirren, Manchester City, Hibernian, Ipswich Town, Coventry City and Brentford – remained active in charity events, a popular figure to the last.

Joseph Henry Baker: born Liverpool, 17 July 1940; played for Hibernian 1956-61, Torino of Italy 1961-62, Arsenal 1962-66, Nottingham Forest 1966-69, Sunderland 1969-71, Hibernian again 1971-72; Raith Rovers 1972-74; capped 8 times by England 1959-66; managed Albion Rovers 1981-82 and 1984-85; died Wishaw, Lanarkshire, 6 October 2003.

Ted Bates

As Matt Busby was the man who made Manchester United, and Bill Shankly laid the foundations for the modern Liverpool, so Ted Bates was the Father of the Saints.

For two thirds of a century he served Southampton Football Club, first as a player, then coach, manager, chief executive, director and president, and while he never came remotely close to emulating the glorious deeds of the eminent Scottish pair, even they did not wield more comprehensive influence over their grand Old Trafford and Anfield empires than did Bates in the homely surroundings of The Dell.

An uncomplicated, shrewd, endlessly enthusiastic fellow, he thrived in an era when clubs and their fans possessed a degree of patience and retained a sense of perspective which 21st-century bosses can only envy.

His principal achievements were to preside over Southampton's rise from the obscurity of the old Third Division South in the mid-1950s to the English game's top flight during the next decade, and later to take a mammoth role as the club developed into the established Premiership force it is today.

Bates' management style was based on working around the clock, utter integrity and a level-headed character which eschewed undue euphoria in victory and despair in defeat.

He was a hands-on, tracksuited boss, a natural motivator without being a martinet, and when he picked a player he would believe in him, offering protracted opportunities even during periods of indifferent form. Unfailingly positive, he concentrated on improving his charges' strengths rather than dwelling on their weaknesses, and he preached a gospel of fast-moving, attacking football.

Bates was born into a sporting family, his grandfather Willie having been an England international at cricket and rugby, and his father Billy having played cricket for Yorkshire and Glamorgan and football for Leeds United and Bolton Wanderers.

As a teenager growing up in Norfolk he played for his local side, non-League Thetford Town, before joining Norwich City in 1936. However, he did not break into the first team at Carrow Road and soon after his manager, Tom Parker, had moved to fellow Second Division club Southampton, Bates also opted for a fresh start at The Dell, signing on his 19th birthday in May 1937.

A dynamic inside-forward, he made his senior debut during the following season, impressing particularly with his aerial prowess, but soon his impetus was halted by the outbreak of the Second World War.

While serving in the Army he turned out for the Saints in unofficial competitions and when peace resumed he formed an effective dual spearhead with the prolific Charlie Wayman. His goals – 64 of them in 202 League outings – were immensely valuable, and so was the versatility which enabled him to play in every position, once even taking over in goal when regular custodian Hugh Kelly was injured.

As he moved into his thirties Bates could not imagine a future outside the game, and in October 1952 he began combining his first-team duties with coaching the reserves. The end of that season brought relegation to the Third Division South and Bates retired from playing to help manager George Roughton with the onerous task of regenerating a club at a low ebb.

In September 1955 he took over as manager, inheriting a £60,000 overdraft, an intimidating sum at the time, but the challenge was not beyond him.

The Saints' new boss proved adept at nurturing young talent such as centre-forward Derek Reeves and future England winger Terry Paine, while operating within a tight budget to pick up bargains in the transfer market, the likes of Scottish marksman George O'Brien, who cost a mere £10,000 from Leeds United before scoring more than 150 goals for Southampton.

A combination of financial prudence and painstaking team-building culminated in 1959/60 with the lifting of the Third Division championship. That term Bates' team offered breathlessly exhilarating entertainment, with their 46 League games producing 181 goals, of which they scored 106. In that context, though the 75 concessions were more than for any other side in the top ten, the fans were not complaining.

During the first half of the 1960s, Southampton consolidated in the Second Division and reached an FA Cup semi-final, which they lost narrowly to Manchester United in 1963.

Three years on, with Paine still starring and young striker Martin Chivers excelling, the Saints finished as runners-up to Manchester City and gained promotion to the top grade for the first time in their history.

At first survival was not easy, despite the acquisition of free-scoring Ron Davies from Norwich City, but Bates continued to operate cannily – for instance, he sold Chivers to Tottenham Hotspur for a big fee, knowing that he had a ready-made replacement in brilliant rookie Mick Channon – and in 1968/69 they ascended to seventh place in the First Division. There followed qualification for the European Fairs Cup in 1969/70 and its successor, the UEFA Cup, in 1971/72, and although achievement in those competitions was modest, Southampton's very presence in them represented enormous progress given their hitherto humble record.

However, the Saints were struggling by the time Bates, then the Football League's longest-serving boss, was appointed chief executive in December 1973, handing over team affairs to his heir apparent, Lawrie McMenemy, and they were relegated at season's end. While the new man prospered at the helm, Bates retained a key role as tactical consultant, contributing hugely to the club's finest hour, the triumph over Manchester United in the 1976 FA Cup final. After scouting United extensively, he advised the strategy of denying possession to their key men, wingers Steve Coppell and Gordon Hill, and turning their defenders with early passes, a ploy which resulted in Bobby Stokes' winning goal.

In 1978, as the Saints regained their top-flight status, Bates joined the board, remaining in that role until becoming club president during the 1990s, a position which he held until his death.

In 2001 he was awarded the MBE, and later that year he continued to fulfil an integral part in Southampton's affairs as they relocated from his beloved Dell to their new St Mary's stadium. After Bates' 66 years of faithful service, there was a case for naming it Saint Ted's.

Edric Thornton Bates: born Thetford, Norfolk, 3 May 1918; played for Southampton 1937-53; managed Southampton 1955-73; MBE 2001; died Chandler's Ford, Hampshire, 26 November 2003.

Gil Reece

In the spring of 1963, 20-year-old Gil Reece was earning his living as a plumber while reflecting ruefully on a glorious football career that might have been. A little more than two years later he was playing on the left wing for Wales against England at Ninian Park, Cardiff, winning the first of 29 full caps spread over a decade on the international stage.

For Reece the future had beckoned alluringly after he had represented his country at schoolboy level, then began an apprenticeship with home-town club Cardiff City, only for the script to go disappointingly awry.

He failed to break into the senior ranks with the Bluebirds and was loaned to non-League Ton Pentre before joining Pembroke Borough as a part-timer.

Reece's reversal of fortune arrived in the form of Newport County manager Billy Lucas, who spotted the feisty, goal-scoring flankman and recruited him back into the professional ranks in June 1963.

Thus afforded a second chance, he impressed mightily for the Somerton Park side, scoring nine times in 32 League outings, and was rewarded with a £10,000 transfer to top-flight Sheffield United in April 1965.

Reece shone immediately in the higher grade, slotting effectively into an attack spearheaded by Mick Jones – who would go on to star for Don Revie's Leeds United – and also featuring the flamboyant Alan Birchenall.

In 1965/66 the Blades, managed by shrewd Glaswegian John Harris, finished ninth in the First Division and Reece proved himself ready for an even more exalted level as he strode into the international arena that autumn.

The following term his impetus was jolted by a broken leg, but he recovered to hit the best form of his life in 1967/68, finishing as United's top scorer with 13 League goals. Unfortunately the side was breaking up, with Harris accepting hefty fees for both Jones and Birchenall, and the Blades were relegated to the Second Division.

It was a shame that Reece, who was versatile enough to fill any attacking position, should experience demotion while in his personal prime. Fast, clever and tough, he was elusive for markers to pin down, difficult to knock off the ball, packed a venomous shot and was magnificent in the air for a relatively small man.

Over the next three seasons he remained a Bramall Lane mainstay, and excelled alongside gifted schemer Tony Currie and fellow forwards Alan Woodward and Billy Dearden as promotion was secured in the runners-up spot behind Leicester City in 1970/71. As that memorable campaign approached its climax, Reece hit a purple patch, contributing five goals in four matches as the Blades inched clear of their rivals. United fans still wax lyrical about his brace in the victory over Birmingham City, one a sweet shot at the end of a mazy dribble and the other a flying header, and it was ironic that his victims during this sequence included Cardiff City, who were also in contention for a First Division berth.

United flourished back among the elite, even leading the table for a rarefied interlude during the autumn, but by then Reece's part was becoming peripheral and in the summer of 1972 – having made more than 200 League appearances and notched 58 goals for the Yorkshiremen – he was dispatched to Cardiff, along with defender Dave Powell, in exchange for striker Alan Warboys.

Back at Ninian Park, he proved a grittily resilient presence in a struggling side which dropped out of the Second Division in 1974/75, but bounced straight back a season later as runners-up to Hereford United. In addition, he played key roles in two Welsh Cup triumphs – netting a hat-trick against Bangor City in the 1973 final and scoring in the 1974 win over Stourbridge – and he continued to feature for Wales until May 1975, when he bade farewell in a 1-0 defeat by Northern Ireland in Belfast.

After ending his senior career with a brief stint at Swansea City, Reece served non-League Barry Town, then ran a plumbing and heating business with his brother before becoming a hotelier in Cardiff.

A fiercely independent character, Reece could be spikily stubborn at times, such as when he walked out on the Welsh team in 1970 after being dropped to the substitutes' bench for a match against England, but he remained an enduringly popular figure among peers at both club and international level.

Gilbert Ivor Reece: born Cardiff, 2 July 1942; played for Newport County 1963-65, Sheffield United 1965-72, Cardiff City 1972-76, Swansea City 1976; capped 29 times by Wales 1965-75; died Cardiff, 20 December 2003.

Bob Stokoe

Bob Stokoe was a gritty, hard-grafting football manager, renowned throughout the game for honesty and competitiveness rather than high achievement, but on a damp afternoon at Wembley in May 1973, he enshrined himself in English sporting folklore with a victory celebration of pure, unbridled, memorably sustained glee.

His spiritedly combative side, Sunderland of the Second Division, had just beaten the white-hot favourites Leeds United, a team dripping with star quality, to win the FA Cup, a triumph rendered all the sweeter by the circumstance that Don Revie, whom he had long despised, was bossing the Yorkshiremen.

At the final whistle Stokoe, with beige raincoat covering red tracksuit and trademark pork-pie hat perched on balding head, leapt from the bench and hit the pitch running. Like some ancient spidery sprinter, he accelerated in the direction of the goal his men had been defending heroically against a late Leeds bombardment.

As his stride lengthened, so his grin broadened and finally his arms spread wide to engulf Jim Montgomery – the goalkeeper who had denied United an equaliser with a stupendous double save – in a gigantic bear-hug which proclaimed more eloquently than any words: 'Thanks for giving me the most beautiful moment of my career.'

Nearby, offering a memorably stark contrast, stood Revie, grey with shock and stress, momentarily unable to come to terms with the scale of such an overwhelming reverse.

However, if that pinnacle of Wembley glory defined Stokoe's place in soccer history, it was untypical of his overall managerial experience, which encompassed six clubs, most of them unglamorous, whom he served in a total of 12 spells.

Unusually among football folk of the north-east, Stokoe was held in affection by fans of both Newcastle United and Sunderland, having spent the cream of his playing days on Tyneside. After graduating from the Magpies' junior ranks, he made his senior entrance as a centre-forward on Christmas Day 1950, scoring in a derby defeat by Middlesbrough, but it was not until his conversion to wing-half, then centre-half, that he secured a regular berth.

Tall and flinty but not heavily built, Stokoe was a waspish tackler, formidable in the air and a sensible passer, and at the end of his debut season he was selected as 12th man – there were no substitutes then – for Newcastle's FA Cup final win over Blackpool.

Thereafter he took several years to become established, missing out on another FA Cup final appearance in 1952 but featuring prominently in central defence as the Magpies defeated Manchester City to lift the trophy again in 1955.

That day he did plenty to negate City's much-vaunted deep-lying centre-forward Don Revie in a foretaste of their 1973 confrontation, and for the next half-decade he became the principal bulwark of Newcastle's rearguard, also demonstrating impressive leadership qualities in a lengthy stint as club captain.

Throughout most of that period the team vacillated between mid-table and the lower reaches of the old First Division – the equivalent of the modern Premiership – and after a creditable eighth-place finish in 1959/60, they were relegated in 1960/61.

However, instead of suffering the drop that spring, the 30-year-old Stokoe was toasting promotion, having bade farewell to Newcastle in the February to join Bury, whom he helped to clinch that term's Third Division title.

Having arrived at Gigg Lane as a makeweight in the deal which saw the Shakers' stopper John McGrath switch to the Magpies, Stokoe became the inspirational skipper of his new team and he didn't finish on the losing side during the remainder of the campaign.

Always a leader on the field, it was no surprise when he moved into management as Bury's player-boss in December 1961, a taxing assignment as the team was mired near the foot of the Second Division. He led his new charges clear of demotion, but not before falling out with his old adversary Revie, who was managing fellow strugglers Leeds by then, and whom Stokoe would later allege attempted to bribe him to lose a vital relegation clash.

The new Bury boss was famous for his integrity and would have scorned any such approach, as evidenced by a superb personal performance in the match, which was drawn and helped both sides to climb out of trouble. In 1962/63 he led the Shakers to the semi-final of the new League Cup competition, losing 4-3 on aggregate to Birmingham City over two legs, and to eighth place in the Second Division, but then economic considerations enforced the sale of talented youngsters and the side toiled accordingly.

Despite that, Stokoe, who retired as a player in May 1964, had forged a reputation as an enterprising young manager and in August 1965 he took over the reins of Charlton Athletic, a bigger club but one facing similar travail in the same division. Once more he was forced to sell key players, Mike Bailey to Wolves and Billy Bonds to West Ham United, and after two disappointing finishes he was sacked in September 1967.

A month later he was appointed by Rochdale, a poor club rooted near the bottom of the Fourth Division, and he revitalised them before being tempted back into the second flight with Carlisle United in October 1968.

At Brunton Park Stokoe's admirable combination of dedicated professionalism and efficient organisation, together with a knack of bringing on unknown rookies, proved successful and the Cumbrians reached the 1969/70 League Cup semi-finals.

They were still on the crest of a wave in December 1970 when Stokoe was offered his first opportunity of top-level management, with Blackpool, and he could not turn it down.

However, his taste of the top division was only brief as the Seasiders were relegated at the end of that season, and winning the Anglo-Italian tournament at the start of 1971/72 was scant consolation for a subsequent sixth-place League finish.

In December 1972, lured by what he saw as more attractive long-term possibilities in his native north-east, he moved into the boss' seat at Sunderland and soon began lifting the veil of mediocrity which had descended over the once-great Wearside institution.

The Rokerites were fourth from bottom of the Second Division as they set off on the FA Cup trail, but Stokoe transformed their fortunes in spectacular fashion.

Eliciting scintillating contributions from the likes of defender Dave Watson and attackers Dennis Tueart and Billy Hughes, he led them up the League table to sixth place, past FA Cup favourites Manchester City in the fifth round and on to stun mighty Arsenal in the semi-final.

Stokoe's passion, and the unashamed tears he shed on reaching Wembley, captivated the nation's imagination, while in Sunderland he was granted icon status. His success meant so much to the town, with ships being painted in the team colours, productivity mushrooming in the factories and the community gripped by general euphoria in the run-up to the showdown with Leeds.

Stokoe prepared his men brilliantly, having them relaxed but ready to fight like demons, and he waged a psychological war on Revie which would have done credit to mind-games expert Sir Alex Ferguson in later years. Where Revie was tense and careworn, Stokoe was expansive and full of fun, emphasising that Sunderland were enjoying themselves while Leeds had everything to lose, and so it proved. On the big day the Wearsiders won through a solitary Ian Porterfield goal and goalkeeper Montgomery performed near-miracles between the posts to deny Trevor Cherry and Peter Lorimer as the pressure mounted. Afterwards, having mocked Revie roundly over the failure of his so-called lucky suit, Stokoe led his party back to Sunderland, where they were greeted by more than half a million ecstatic fans celebrating the first FA Cup triumph by a Second Division side in 40 years.

The next term they beat Vasas of Budapest in the European Cup Winners' Cup before falling to Sporting Lisbon, and though promotion to the top flight was delayed by the enforced sale of top players – a recurring theme in the Stokoe career – it was attained in 1976 when Sunderland went up as champions. Now the future beckoned alluringly, but a distressingly rapid decline was in prospect.

Stokoe was suffering ill health as his team made a disastrous start to life back in the premier grade and he resigned in the autumn, a decision he was to bitterly regret in later years. Subsequently he made managerial returns to Bury, Blackpool and Rochdale, with whom he finished at the bottom of the Fourth Division in 1979/80, before experiencing more joy with Carlisle whom he guided out of the Third Division in 1982.

Stokoe, who received a long-service medal from the Football League in 1984 and proved the regard in which he was held by being invited back by so many former employers, retired in August 1985, but then resumed control only to resign in 1986 after United had been relegated.

In 1987 there was a fleeting comeback at Sunderland as caretaker boss, followed by a consultancy role until 1989 and a succession of coaching stints, but it is for his gloriously uplifting achievement of 1973 that he will always be revered.

Robert Stokoe: born Mickley, County Durham, 21 September 1930; played for Newcastle United 1947-61, Bury 1961-64; managed Bury 1961-65, Charlton Athletic 1965-67, Rochdale 1967-68, Carlisle United 1968-70, Blackpool 1970-72, Sunderland 1972-76, Bury 1977-78, Blackpool 1978-79, Rochdale 1979-80, Carlisle United 1980-85 and 1985-86, Sunderland (caretaker) 1987; died Hartlepool, County Durham, 1 February 2004.

Henry Cockburn

There wasn't very much of Henry Cockburn but it was difficult to remain unaware of his presence on a football pitch. If he wasn't tackling like a miniature tank, or sprinting at full tilt in pursuit of ball or opponent, then probably he was issuing instructions at the top of his voice. Indeed, so perpetual was Cockburn's motion, and so passionate was his fervour during his prime in the decade following the Second World War, that the Manchester United and England wing-half created the irresistible impression that he was engaged in all three activities at once, physically impossible though that would have been.

The diminutive Lancastrian, who stood a mere 5ft 5in in his stockinged feet, operated in a defensive midfield role in the first of Matt Busby's three outstanding teams, the one which purveyed the most exhilarating football in the land as the game offered much-needed entertainment in the era of post-conflict austerity.

In many ways Cockburn was similar to Nobby Stiles, the tigerishly abrasive destroyer who played a key role as United piled up the honours throughout the 1960s and who was integral to England's World Cup triumph of '66.

Admittedly tactics were different in the Cockburn heyday, so usually he occupied a more advanced position than Stiles, who thrived in a withdrawn position alongside stopper centre-half Bill Foulkes, but the two pocket battleships had plenty in common.

Eager, bright-eyed bundles of energy and enthusiasm, they were both combative and constructive, their boundless spirit, honesty and endeavour making up generously for their lack of inches. The pair of them were pacy, doggedly tenacious and unfailingly brave in the tackle, but also – and this was crucial to their success – they were instinctive readers of the game who were blessed with far more pure skill than many critics maintained.

Cockburn, a natural all-round sportsman who also excelled at cricket, made his first footballing impact as a teenager with Goslings, a local feeder to Manchester United, the Old Trafford club enlisting him as an amateur in September 1943.

While continuing with his work as a mill-fitter, he impressed the Reds' coaching staff enough to earn a professional contract a year later and he made his first United appearance as a nippy, elusive forward during unofficial wartime competition, in which he had guested also for Accrington Stanley.

By 1945 Cockburn had been converted into a left-half, despite being right-footed, and he was awarded his senior debut in an FA Cup meeting with his former Accrington team-mates in January '46. Making light of ferocious competition for places, he made such prodigious progress that he was chosen along with eight other new caps – including Billy Wright of Wolves, Preston North End's Tom Finney and Frank Swift of Manchester City – to play for England in September 1946 after only seven First Division outings.

That afternoon at Windsor Park, Belfast, Cockburn shone as the first post-war successor to the majestic Joe Mercer, contributing massively to a 7-2 triumph over Northern Ireland and looking utterly at home on the international stage.

He retained his berth for the next two games, which yielded victories over Wales and the Republic of Ireland, slotting in effectively alongside Wright and the stylish Neil Franklin, and it seemed that England had a settled half-back line for the foreseeable future. However, Cockburn was ousted by Harry Johnston of Blackpool, and although he extended his cap total to 13 over the next five years, he never cemented the regular place which most United fans reckoned to be his just deserts.

Back on the club scene, though, the Cockburn career flourished royally. He was a crucial component of the side which finished as League title runners-up in each of the first three post-war campaigns, won the FA Cup by defeating Blackpool – Stanley Matthews et al – by four goals to two in a titanic Wembley clash in 1948, then finally claimed the championship crown in 1951/52.

Cockburn meshed splendidly with John Aston, being swift to cover when the adventurous left-back embarked on his characteristic forays into opposition territory, and with left-winger Charlie Mitten, who benefited constantly from the wing-half's crisp and canny distribution. Indeed, reminiscing during the late 1990s about Busby's breathtaking post-war creation, Mitten declared: 'It was fabulous to play in front of Henry. When he got the ball I always knew that I would be the next to touch it. He was totally reliable, both as a player and as a comrade.' The manager agreed, frequently praising Cockburn's slick one-touch passing technique and lauding the little man for responding to a cherished Busby maxim with which he drilled his players religiously: the ball is round, so keep it rolling!

Unusually for one so short, Cockburn was magnificent aerially, too, being capable of leaping above much taller opponents from a standing start, thanks to a combination of exceptional athleticism and well-nigh perfect timing.

Such was his fitness and consistency that the advent of his thirties seemed unlikely to signal the closure of his Old Trafford sojourn, but an accident in a friendly encounter with Kilmarnock in the autumn of 1953, staged to mark the installation of floodlights at Rugby

Park, altered that perception. As Cockburn climbed high to meet a ball, he was dazzled by the Killies' new lights and clashed heads with his marker. He was led away with a smashed jaw, a young phenomenon by the name of Duncan Edwards trotted on to take his place, and the number-six shirt was never again his automatic preserve.

Still hardly a gnarled veteran at the age of 30, Cockburn was not content with life in United's reserves and in October 1954 he accepted a transfer to Second Division Bury, where he linked up once more with former Red Devil Stan Pearson, the deliciously gifted inside-forward behind whom he had performed so superbly for so long.

At Gigg Lane he added 39 League and FA Cup appearances to the 275 he had accumulated at Old Trafford, then switched to Peterborough United, at the time plying their trade in the Midland League, in the summer of 1956.

Cockburn adored playing football so much that he was eager to continue, even at lesser levels, later assisting Corby Town and Sankeys of Wellington before being attracted back to the Football League by another former United chum, Oldham Athletic manager Jack Rowley, as a trainer at Boundary Park in February 1961.

Three years later he signed for Huddersfield Town as assistant trainer, eventually working under yet another ex-Old Trafford colleague, Ian Greaves, as senior coach before bowing out of the professional game in 1975.

Cockburn was ideally suited to his role at Leeds Road, being especially adept at working with rookies, as he had proved in the twilight of his Manchester United days when his help to the emerging Busby Babes had been invaluable.

Indeed, he played an important and selfless part in the development of that remarkable wave of fresh talent, making light of the inevitable circumstance that the precocious newcomers would soon be depriving him of employment.

It was tragically ironic that when he was working part-time on a Peterborough newspaper in 1958, one of his duties was to write the posters which told of the Munich air disaster in which so many of his proteges had perished.

Henry Cockburn: born Ashton-under-Lyne, Lancashire, 14 September 1923; played for Manchester United 1943-54, Bury 1954-56; capped 13 times by England 1946-51; died Mossley, Lancashire, 2 February 2004.

John Charles

The finest all-round footballer to come out of Wales is an accolade often accorded to John Charles and yet, while well intended and as meaningful as any comparison across the ages can ever be, it remains a chronic understatement.

With all due respect to a nation which has produced some remarkable performers – from Billy Meredith, whose international career began in the 19th century and continued until 1920, through to Ryan Giggs, currently enjoying pop icon status – there is a plausible body of opinion which elevates 'The Gentle Giant' to a yet more exalted plane. It places him, with no hint of equivocation, among the greatest players the world has ever seen.

What made Charles special was his mastery of virtually every aspect of the game, his awesomely muscular physique and commanding presence matched by a nimbleness and delicacy of touch which seemed at odds with that massive frame.

What caused him to be underestimated at times, when fans and pundits alike assembled lists of soccer 'immortals', was that the bulk of his mighty prime was passed in the service of Juventus between 1957 and 1962, an era when stirring deeds on foreign fields attracted far less attention than would be the case today.

The sad fact is that this amiable colossus, who was equally at home in the heart of defence or as a goal-plundering spearhead, and whose only perceptible flaw was a lack of ruthlessness, spent just one season in the English top flight. That was 1956/57, when he netted 38 times in 40 League outings for Leeds United, thus making himself an irresistible proposition to the lire-laden Italians.

Born and raised in the Welsh valleys where rugby was a way of life, Charles was always devoted to the round-ball code. However, on leaving school as a 15-year-old in 1946, he was on the brink of accepting a factory job when a trainer at his local professional club, Swansea Town (now City), persuaded him to join the Vetch Field groundstaff.

Thus the skilful youngster, then slender and showing little sign of growing into the man-mountain who would thunder across the world's football fields in years to come, found himself weeding terraces, cleaning boots and, when time permitted, playing football.

As Charles filled out, and his soccer development kept pace with his physical advancement, his vast potential became increasingly apparent, yet the Swans allowed their uncut gem to slip away. The young leviathan was playing in a public park when he was spotted by a Leeds scout, and he headed north to Elland Road in 1947.

After turning professional in January 1949, Charles made meteoric progress under the stern but shrewd tutelage of United's manager, Major Frank Buckley, who insisted that all his charges should labour prodigiously to hone their all-round game. Within three months the Welsh teenager was promoted to the senior side, then ensconced midway in the old Second Division, and he excelled at centre-half, a position he made his own in 1949/50, during which he didn't miss a match.

By now Charles' burgeoning prowess was receiving widespread attention and that spring, still only 18, he became the youngest full international in his country's history when he was picked to face Northern Ireland at Wrexham.

Though he didn't become a Wales regular until 1953, during the decade's early years he emerged as an ever-more dominant force at the heart of the Leeds rearguard as United strove unavailingly to attain First Division status.

However, the comprehensive nature of the Charles talents became apparent only after his deployment at centre-forward, a periodic arrangement which became gradually more frequent and then permanent with the emergence of Jack Charlton as a ruggedly capable stopper.

In 1952/53 'Big John' played the first third of the campaign at centre-half, then switched to centre-forward and notched 26 goals in the 28 matches that remained. The following term he netted 42 times – the League's next highest scorer managed 30 – and subsequent occasional stints at centre-half served only to emphasise what the Leeds attack was missing.

But while he was a towering influence at the back, it was difficult for any manager to forego Charles the marksman. There were days when he seemed utterly unstoppable, majestic in the air and a dreadnought on the deck, capable of both subtlety and imagination with the ball at his feet, liable to unlock the most clamlike of defences with a sudden surge of destructive acceleration climaxed by a pulverising shot with either foot.

Had he been born with the 'devil' to complement all that power and expertise, then there can be no doubt that he would have been hailed universally as the world's most complete player. But, as he remarked when still a rookie: 'If I have to knock them down to play well, then I don't want to play the game at all.'

For all that engaging placidity, though, he could look after himself, having a natural tendency to enter challenges with his arms outstretched, his immense physical presence thus rendering him a difficult man to dispossess.

In 1955/56 Charles finally inspired Leeds to promotion, then hit the top flight like an irresistible force of nature, outgunning all his First Division rivals to end the season with 38 goals, the most compelling statistic behind his club's creditable sixth-place finish.

Distressingly for his legion of devoted fans at Elland Road, their hero's derring-do had made him a prime target for many of Europe's leading clubs, who had been seduced by his strike-rate of a goal every two games, a ratio rendered all the more impressive because roughly half of his appearances had been as a defender.

The interest came to a head in April 1957 when a fabulous display while captaining his country against Northern Ireland captivated Umberto Agnelli of the giant Fiat corporation, who also happened to be president of Juventus, then a slumbering behemoth of Italian football.

A record offer of £65,000 was made for his services and the cash-strapped Yorkshire club accepted with alacrity but, even at a time when Football League players were at the mercy of the iniquitous maximum wage system, the home-loving Charles went through weeks of heart-searching before opting for a future in Turin.

Despite the life of luxury that beckoned – his pay increased from £20 per week to an estimated £300 plus fabulous fringe benefits – it was a brave decision, as few British footballers to that point had managed to thrive overseas.

After an uncertain period of acclimatisation, it was a trend he reversed to spectacular effect. In his first season in a notoriously defensive league, Charles scored 28 times and helped his new employers to lift the championship, being voted player of the year for his pains. As a result he became the darling of fans and press alike, receiving film-star treatment every time he ventured outside either of his two capacious villas, one in Turin and the other on the Italian Riviera.

Part of his appeal in his adoptive land was the vivid contrast of his modest, easy-going nature to the passionate Latin temperament. He was a magnificently built, handsome fellow blessed with boundless athletic talent, yet he refused to throw his weight around either on or off the pitch. Thus he became 'Il Buon Gigante' ('The Gentle Giant') and a national idol.

Ever sociable, Charles lived life to the full, investing in a restaurant and making both a film and a record with a team-mate, the Argentinian star Omar Sivori, and life, it seemed, could get no better.

Come the World Cup of 1958 he was the focal point of the finest Wales team there has ever been, featuring the likes of inside-forward Ivor Allchurch, flying winger Cliff Jones, goalkeeper Jack Kelsey and his own younger brother, Mel, who played at centre-half.

Against most predictions they reached the quarter-finals, only for Charles to miss the clash with Brazil through injury. Pele and company triumphed 1-0 and went on to win the competition, leaving Wales to ponder on what might have been had their most inspirational contributor been fit.

Back in Italy Charles helped Juventus to two more League titles and two domestic cup victories before the dolce vita began to go sour. Absences from home caused by the Italians' penchant for lengthy sojourns in training camps produced domestic strain, he grew weary of spurious reports of his night life, he ran into business problems and was worried about his children's education. As his homesickness grew, there were rumours of a move to either Manchester United or Arsenal but in 1962 he returned to Leeds, his departure sadly acrimonious, for a fee of £53,000.

Now 30, Charles was no longer the player who had left Elland Road five years earlier and although his homecoming provoked untold joy among his former admirers, the move was not a success. After starring for one of the world's leading clubs, he found it hard to settle to the grind of the English Second Division and played only a handful of games before joining Roma for £65,000.

Poignantly, though, his former dash had disappeared and Charles failed to win a regular place, transferring instead to Second Division Cardiff City, where he joined brother Mel, for a knockdown £25,000 in August 1963.

By now he was considerably slower and more ponderous, but still some of the old magic remained and the large crowd attracted by his debut was rewarded with a freak 75-yard goal from a free-kick. Once more alternating between defence and attack, Charles spent three years at Ninian Park before entering non-League ranks as player-boss of Hereford United.

Though suffering from increasing weight problems, he overcame them by pure ability, scoring more than a century of goals before his retirement in his fortieth year and helping to lay the foundations for the club's later successful application to join the Football League.

Thereafter a figure of such vast repute and experience might have been expected to land a prestigious role, but Charles was never one for theory or tactics, preferring to rely on his instinct, and he was confined to a spell as manager of Merthyr Tydfil and a stint of coaching youngsters for Swansea before leaving the game in 1976 to run a pub in Leeds.

Later there was a consultative job in Canada but that did not last and Charles, who was awarded the CBE in 2001, returned to Yorkshire to live near Bradford with his second wife. Thereafter he was beset by health problems, including cancer and Alzheimer's disease, and in January 2004 he needed emergency heart surgery when he fell ill during a promotional tour of Milan. Complications set in and part of his right foot was amputated before he was flown home earlier this month.

In his declining years John Charles – who was voted Wales' all-time sporting hero in 2003, coinciding with the publication of an autobiography – remained a genial, engaging character, perhaps rather bewildered to be no longer part of the game he had once bestrode so regally. But those who remember the big man in his prime still bear eloquent witness to his pedigree – and it was of the very highest.

William John Charles: born Cwm-du, Glamorgan, 27 December 1931; played for Leeds United 1947-57, Juventus 1957-62, Leeds United 1962, Roma 1962-63, Cardiff City 1963-66; managed Hereford United 1966-71, Merthyr Tydfil 1971 (both non-League); capped 38 times by Wales 1950-65; CBE 2001; died Wakefield, West Yorkshire, 21 February 2004.

George Hardwick

George Hardwick was the last man to captain the England football team on his international debut.

In normal circumstances, players work up gradually to such lofty elevation by serving time in their country's ranks, but Hardwick made his entrance in 1946, when pre-war skippers such as Eddie Hapgood and Stan Cullis were no longer in contention, and the selectors had no hesitation in entrusting the responsibility to the charismatic 26-year-old Yorkshireman.

A natural leader who had tossed the coin for every team he represented, the handsome Hardwick cut a dashing figure, his matinee-idol looks set off by a Ronald Colman-style moustache, a strikingly individual touch in an era when facial hair was a distinct novelty on the football fields of England. Not that earthy denizens of the terraces at Ayresome Park, where he forged his reputation, would have been remotely impressed by 'Gentleman George's' shaving arrangements had he not proved equally as immaculate in the role of Middlesbrough's left-back.

In fact, he was a delightfully stylish performer, crisp of tackle, cultured of distribution, intelligent in his reading of the game, and invariably composed no matter how chaotic the action which swirled around him.

Hardwick hailed from a footballing family – his grandfather, Frank, having played for long-defunct Middlesbrough Ironopolis in the 1890s – and he grew up with the ambition of joining his local club. Thus, when starring at a junior level with South Bank East End, he had no difficulty in resisting the blandishments of both Arsenal and Glasgow Rangers, instead enlisting with Middlesbrough as a 15-year-old amateur in 1935, then turning professional two years later. Soon he was elevated to 'Boro's First Division team but he made an inauspicious beginning, scoring an own goal in the opening minutes of his debut at home to Bolton Wanderers in December 1937.

Still his class was evident, and although he had slipped out of the senior side by the spring, Hardwick remained one of the brightest prospects in the League.

However, his gathering momentum was halted by the outbreak of war, during which he served as a sergeant in RAF Bomber Command and suffered leg injuries in a raid on his base on the Isle of Sheppey.

He recovered in time to guest for Chelsea, for whom he appeared in two Football League South Cup finals, losing the first in 1944 but collecting a winner's medal the following season, and he wore an England shirt in 17 unofficial wartime outings.

After the conflict Hardwick went back to Middlesbrough, where he became part of an attractive side which featured the brilliant inside-forward Wilf Mannion and which, despite occasional flirtations with relegation, usually occupied a comfortable mid-table position.

Internationally, too, he flourished, earning his first cap when he captained England in their 7-2 victory over Northern Ireland at Windsor Park, Belfast, in September 1946. Thereafter, forging an effective full-back partnership with Arsenal's Laurie Scott, a former RAF colleague, Hardwick retained his place for 13 consecutive games, all of them as skipper, before being injured against Scotland in April 1948.

He didn't regain fitness in time for the meeting with Italy that May, which allowed Frank Swift of Manchester City to become the first goalkeeper to captain England during the 20th century, and he never re-entered the international arena, losing his left-back berth in the long term to Manchester United's John Aston.

By then Hardwick, who also made three appearances for the Football League, had been honoured further as captain of Great Britain in their 6-1 mauling of The Rest of Europe at Hampden Park, Glasgow, in 1947.

Come 1950 he remained one of the best-known players in the land, so it was a surprise when he left top-flight Middlesbrough that November to become player-boss of Oldham Athletic, who were struggling in the lower reaches of the Third Division North.

To secure the services of the eminent 30-year-old, who had turned down a coaching offer from Everton in order to try his hand at management, the Latics had spent £15,000 they could ill afford, but the investment paid rapid dividends as Hardwick led them to their divisional championship in 1952/53.

Unfortunately it left them with no cash to consolidate in the higher echelon and, though Hardwick continued to contribute influentially both on and off the field, they were demoted at the end of the following campaign.

After another disappointing season in 1955/56, Hardwick departed Boundary Park to work with the USA Army team in Germany, then he coached PSV Eindhoven in Holland and completed a brief stint as director of coaching for the Dutch Football Association.

In 1961 he returned to Middlesbrough, where he coached for two years before taking charge of Sunderland in November 1964. The Rokerites were toiling to avoid the drop from the First Division at the time, but Hardwick saved them, drawing inspirational performances from the likes of centre-half Charlie Hurley and inside-forward Johnny Crossan.

His reward, after improving the side during his mere 169 days in the job, was the sack from a board of directors who, rather unrealistically, expected better than a 15th-place finish.

That was the end of Hardwick's Football League days, though there followed an unsuccessful spell at the helm of Northern Premier League club Gateshead before he left the game to become chairman of a steel construction company in 1970.

Hardwick was granted the freedom of the Borough of Redcar and Cleveland in 2001.

George Francis Moutrey Hardwick: born Saltburn, Yorkshire, 2 February 1920; played for Middlesbrough 1935-50; Oldham Athletic 1950-56; capped 13 times by England 1946-48; managed Oldham Athletic 1950-56, PSV Eindhoven of Holland 1957-59, Sunderland 1964-65; died Teesside, 19 April 2004.

Eddie Hopkinson

Even in an era before goalkeepers tended routinely to be giants, Eddie Hopkinson was one of the shortest among Football League net-minders, but lack of stature did not prevent the thickset north-easterner from becoming England's finest for a spell during the late 1950s.

While still in his early twenties, the 5ft 9in Hopkinson collected 14 caps for his country and excelled as Bolton Wanderers beat Manchester United in the 1958 FA Cup final. After that, although he slipped from the international reckoning, he maintained a resilient, ultra-competitive presence between the club's posts for another decade, making nearly 600 senior appearances, more than any other Trotter before or since.

Born in County Durham, he moved to Royton, Lancashire, with his family as a boy, and showed early promise as a wing-half for his school team. One day the team's goalkeeper failed to show up for training, Hopkinson was pressed into duty as an emergency custodian and he displayed such natural ability in his new role that within two years he had signed amateur forms with Oldham Athletic.

That was in June 1951 and during the following season, still only 16, he made three appearances for the Latics in the former Third Division South, conceding a total of ten goals but revealing immense potential.

Now he faced a choice: take a part-time job outside the game while continuing with Oldham, or seek his fortune at a higher level. Hopkinson opted to raise his eyes, enlisting with First Division Bolton as an amateur in August 1952 and turning professional three months later. Thereafter he settled down at Burnden Park to hone his craft, but after finishing his National Service with the RAF in February 1956, still he languished in a lengthy queue of goalkeeping hopefuls and might have been excused for rueing his decision to gamble on a future in the game.

Suddenly, however, his fortunes were transformed, as the long-serving Stan Hanson retired and Ken Grieves, his Australian replacement, remained on cricketing duty for Lancashire as the 1956/57 football season commenced.

Thus Hopkinson was brought in for his Bolton debut in a local derby with Blackpool, and impressed so comprehensively that he achieved the rare distinction of being ever-present throughout his first top-flight campaign.

The meteoric rise was emphasised by his call-up to the England under-23 squad within six weeks of making his club entrance, and then confirmed when he was awarded his first full cap in a 4-0 victory over Wales at Ninian Park, Cardiff, in October 1957.

It was a time of opportunity for young goalkeepers, with the England selectors unable to decide on a regular number-one, and now Hopkinson vied for the berth with Alan Hodgkinson of Sheffield United and Colin McDonald of Burnley, who unseated the Bolton man for the 1958 World Cup finals in Sweden.

However, McDonald's career was ended by a broken leg and Hopkinson was recalled, only to lose his place in 1959 to Ron Springett of Sheffield Wednesday, who became England's first regular custodian since Gil Merrick back in mid-decade.

Considering the subsequent rise of the brilliant Gordon Banks, it was unsurprising that Hopkinson never played for England again, though he featured twice for the Football League and at club level he continued to thrive.

At Wembley in May 1958 he was a key figure as Bolton overcame Manchester United, who had reached the FA Cup final despite losing the majority of their first team, dead and injured, in the Munich air disaster only three months earlier.

Riding on a wave of emotional nationwide support that bordered on hysteria, the Red Devils represented a uniquely taxing barrier, but Bolton coped coolly and professionally with the pressure, with Hopkinson making several tremendous saves.

Over the next two seasons, as the Wanderers finished fourth and sixth in the elite division, the keeper remained in magnificent form behind one of the League's most fearsomely physical rearguards, in which full-backs Roy Hartle and Tommy Banks, and stopper John Higgins were prominent.

Hopkinson was elastically agile and unfailingly brave, nothing loth to plunge head-first amid the flailing feet of marauding attackers, and his daring style was complemented by a priceless positional sense which compensated amply for lack of height and reach.

A speciality was in dealing with one-on-one situations; as a forward bore down on him, he would stand up until the last feasible moment, then spread himself as the shot was released or his opponent attempted to dribble around him, and it was rare that he was bested in such confrontations.

Crucially, too, he was almost metronomically consistent, colossally determined, and spikily ready to stand up for himself, never being short of a spirited rebuke to forwards whom he felt might have exceeded the limits of fair play.

In the early 1960s, when the abolition of the footballers' maximum wage agreement signalled a massive redemption in the power of small-town clubs, Bolton's star began to wane and in 1963/64 they were relegated to the Second Division.

Hopkinson remained loyal, though, and his standard of performance did not drop at the lower level. With the likes of Francis Lee and Freddie Hill shining, the Trotters almost returned to the top grade at the first attempt, finishing third in 1964/65, but thereafter they fell away to struggle towards decade's end.

Throughout this anti-climactic process, Hopkinson continued to repel all attempts by younger men to supplant him until injury forced him to yield to Alan Boswell and retire as a player, aged 34, in November 1969.

After that he coached the club's reserves and youngsters until 1974, when he began a stint as assistant manager of Stockport County. There followed a return to Burnden Park as a goalkeeping coach in 1979, then he left the game to become a representative for a chemical company.

Still Hopkinson, whose son Paul kept goal for Stockport during the mid-1970s, retained close connections with Bolton Wanderers, becoming an inaugural member of the club's hall of fame and working as a corporate hospitality host on matchdays.

Edward Hopkinson: born Wheatley Hill, County Durham, 29 October 1935; played for Oldham Athletic 1951-52; Bolton Wanderers 1952-69; died Royton, Lancashire, 25 April 2004.

Dennis Wilshaw

Dennis Wilshaw was a dynamic, free-scoring inside-forward who netted 25 times as Wolverhampton Wanderers lifted the Football League championship in 1954, then entered the record books as the first Englishman to notch a hat-trick against Scotland.

Yet even an impressive tally of ten goals in a dozen appearances for his country failed to secure a regular international place for the prolific Midlander. Would that England's current manager, Sven-Goran Eriksson, could be so choosy as to discard such a proven marksman in the run-up to Euro 2004.

Wilshaw was strong, resilient and direct, an awkward customer for any opponent to control, and thus was perfectly suited to Stan Cullis' formidable all-action Wolves side which provided the main opposition for Matt Busby's more refined, sweet-passing Manchester United of the mid-1950s.

He was capable of sudden bursts of searing acceleration which equipped him ideally to exploit gaps in opposition defences opened by the pinpoint deliveries of schemer Peter Broadbent and wingers Johnny Hancocks and Jimmy Mullen. His shooting was explosively powerful, especially with his left foot, and he was combative in the air, forming a potent dual spearhead with centre-forward Roy Swinbourne.

Together they terrorised not only First Division defences but also the more cultured rearguards of continental powers such as Spartak Moscow and Honved, the crack Hungarian side, during a crucial period of dawning enlightenment for the domestic game.

United are credited handsomely, and rightly so, as pioneering British football's expansion overseas by becoming England's first entrants into the European Cup in 1956, but a little earlier the Black Countrymen were also immensely influential in blazing the fresh trail as they embarked on a series of enthralling friendlies, mostly against teams from the Eastern bloc.

The intelligent Wilshaw, who particularly relished the challenge of new horizons, made his first impact as a footballer at Hanley High School, where he was a contemporary of future West Bromwich Albion and England centre-forward Ronnie Allen, but it was for his prolific work with Packmoor Boys' Club in the North Staffordshire League that he riveted the attention of Wolves' scouts.

Shortly after plundering ten goals in one match he was enlisted as an amateur by the Molineux club in September 1943, being elevated to the first team for a wartime league match only seven days later.

While training to be a teacher, he agreed professional terms with Wolves in March 1944 and, with the club being well endowed with forwards, he was loaned to Walsall of the Third Division South in May 1946.

Wilshaw flourished at Fellows Park, establishing a productive frontline partnership with future Arsenal star Doug Lishman, eventually doing so well that he was recalled to Molineux in September 1948 as an understudy for centre-forward Jesse Pye.

Competition for senior places was intense, but when the versatile Wilshaw was given his top-flight debut at outside-left in March 1949, he responded with a hat-trick against Newcastle United, then underlined his burgeoning status with a brace in each of his next two outings, both as leader of the line.

Though still nominally a Wolves reserve – he was overlooked for that term's FA Cup final triumph over Leicester City – he was called up by England 'B' in the May, and scored twice against Finland in Helsingfor. Gradually it became impossible for Wilshaw's club boss, Cullis, to ignore his claims for a regular berth, which he finally secured in 1952/53; then he enjoyed his most productive campaign in 1953/54 as the hard-running Wolves pipped West Bromwich Albion and Huddersfield Town – how the balance of power has shifted – for the title.

By then he had earned his first full cap, against Wales at Ninian Park, Cardiff, in October 1953, a milestone which he celebrated in typical manner, netting twice in a 4-1 victory. There followed a trip to the 1954 World Cup finals in Switzerland, where he made two appearances, registering against the host nation but drawing a blank as England were knocked out by Uruguay in the quarter-finals.

Wilshaw's most glorious international achievement, though, was reserved for a memorable encounter with Scotland at Wembley in April 1955 when he netted four times in a 7-2 annihilation of the old enemy, linking brilliantly with Bolton's Nat Lofthouse and Don Revie of Manchester City.

But, at a time when the England line-up was in a state of constant flux, Wilshaw never managed to become a fixture and he collected his last cap, as a 30-year-old, against Northern Ireland at Windsor Park, Belfast, in October 1956.

Back at club level, he remained a force with Wolves, who had been superseded by Manchester United's Busby Babes as the country's dominant force, until he joined his home-town club, Second Division Stoke City, a £10,000 fee changing hands in December 1957.

At Molineux Wilshaw had maintained an enviable strike rate of better than one goal for every two games – his precise record was 112 hits in 219 senior outings – and he was not far off equalling it at the Victoria Ground where he totalled 49 in 108.

His peak for the Potters came in 1958/59, when he knocked in 15 as the side finished just outside the promotion places. Thereafter, as Stoke declined towards the lower reaches of the Second Division and Wilshaw approached his middle thirties, he became less of a force but had no immediate plans for retirement until he suffered a broken leg in an FA Cup clash with Newcastle United in February 1961.

He never played League football again, opting instead to pursue a successful teaching career which included the headship of a school in Stoke and a leading role in the Service and Community Studies department at Crewe and Alsager College of Education.

Dennis James Wilshaw: born Stoke-on-Trent, Staffordshire, 11 March 1926; played for Wolverhampton Wanderers 1943-57, Walsall on loan 1946-48, Stoke City 1957-61; capped 12 times by England 1953-56; died Stoke-on-Trent, 10 May 2004.

Ron Ashman

For the better part of two decades immediately following the Second World War, the name of Ron Ashman was synonymous with that of Norwich City. First as the Canaries' long-serving wing-half and captain, then as their manager, the imposing, rather stately East Anglian was one of the most influential figures in Carrow Road history.

Ashman was the Norwich skipper when the Third Division side beat mighty Manchester United and Tottenham Hotspur on the way to an FA Cup semi-final in 1959; he led them to promotion to the Second Division a year later, and he held aloft the League Cup in 1962 when City defeated Rochdale in the final of that fledgling competition.

Though his management honours were limited to guiding Scunthorpe United out of the Football League basement in 1972, he was renowned throughout the game for his loyalty and integrity, and he is remembered as the man who awarded a senior debut to Kevin Keegan when the future England captain and team boss was a diminutive teenager at Scunthorpe's Old Show Ground.

Ashman was a bakery worker playing his football for the Eastern Counties Air Training Corps when he was recruited by Norwich, but then he became a Bevin Boy, being called up to serve in a Nottinghamshire coal mine to help the war effort.

City permitted him to combine his pit duties with turning out for Peterborough United, a non-League club at the time, then he spent 18 months in the RAF before accepting professional terms at Carrow Road as a promising centre-forward in January 1946.

He was still a spearhead when he made his League entrance at home to Aldershot in October 1947, but soon he was converted into a defensive wing-half by City's imaginative manager, Norman Low, and he became a key presence, both competitive and constructive, in the side which narrowly missed promotion from the old Third Division South in several successive seasons during the early 1950s. Though the Canaries grew inconsistent as the decade wore on, Ashman remained a dependable bulwark, and his leadership was a crucial factor in the cup and league glory that was in store as he approached the veteran stage.

On the FA Cup trail in 1959, Ashman shone alongside the likes of stopper Barry Butler and striker Terry Allcock as Matt Busby's United were humbled 3-0, then Cardiff City, Spurs and Sheffield United were overcome before the Canaries bowed out to Luton Town, after a replay, in the last four.

The promotion which followed, as runners-up to Southampton in the Third Division title race of 1959/60, offered ample compensation, and Ashman remained active as City consolidated in the second flight with fourth place in 1960/61, then finally garnered silverware in the shape of the League Cup in 1962. In December of that year, he became acting manager of the club, and took the job on a full-time basis a year later. By then he had finished playing after 662 senior appearances for Norwich, a club record at the time and since exceeded only by goalkeeper Kevin Keelan, whom Ashman had signed. In addition, courtesy largely of penalty kicks, he had contributed more than half a century of goals.

Though he was both liked and respected, Ashman – a cultured fellow with strong religious convictions – did not find occupation of the boss' chair easy at first, perhaps being a trifle too nice in his dealings with some of his former team-mates, who might have taken advantage of his gentle nature.

Still, he pulled off a magnificent coup in signing Ron Davies from Luton Town – the Welshman served the Carrow Road cause nobly before going on to become one of the top marksmen in Britain with Southampton – and Norwich rallied to finish sixth in the Second Division in 1964/65.

However, they could climb no higher than mid-table in the subsequent campaign, and Ashman paid a harsh price, losing his job in May 1966, just a month after being devastated by the death of his close friend and ally, Butler, in a car crash.

He returned to football as manager of Scunthorpe in October 1967, only for United to be relegated as bottom club in Division Three at the end of his first season.

Ashman took his new charges to the fifth round of the FA Cup in 1970, then they rose to the Third Division two years later, but finished last in 1972/73.

There followed a brief stint in charge of Grimsby Town before he returned to the Old Show Ground for another five years, spent mostly in the wrong half of the Fourth Division. In 1981 he left football to run the transport side of a travel agency in Scunthorpe, but retained a keen interest in the game until his death.

Ronald George Ashman: born Whittlesey, Cambridgeshire, 19 May 1926; played for Norwich City 1944-63; managed Norwich City 1962-66, Scunthorpe United 1967-73, Grimsby Town 1973-75, Scunthorpe United 1976-81; died Scunthorpe, Lincolnshire, 21 June 2004.

Brian Clough

No one man is bigger than the game of football, the saying goes; yet there were times when Brian Clough seemed larger than life itself. A precociously brilliant goal-scorer who became an inspirational if arrogantly idiosyncratic manager, he was a phenomenon who transcended sporting boundaries.

Often Clough was dubbed the best boss England never had and, certainly during his peak in the 1970s and early 1980s, he was the people's choice. He could be overbearing and rude, pompous and conceited – he even christened himself 'Old Big 'Ead' – and his name was a byword for controversy. But most fans were willing to forgive the vast ego, indeed were charmed by it; they loved him for his steadfast refusal to bow the knee before authority and for his abrasive, often outrageous outspokenness on virtually any issue.

Then, of course, there was the little matter of his success, and the attractive manner in which his teams played the game. He specialised in taking unfashionable clubs and unconsidered players by the metaphorical scruff of the neck (actually, in the case of certain individuals it wasn't so metaphorical) and inspiring them to undreamed-of heights. Clough transformed Derby County, then Nottingham Forest, from comparative nonentities into League champions before, incredibly, leading the latter to two European Cup triumphs. Yet throughout the pomp of his headline-hogging, ceaselessly stormy career, soccer's most celebrated maverick so alarmed and alienated those he delighted in calling 'the grey men in grey suits' at the Football Association, the very people in whose gift was the post of England manager, that he had little realistic chance of landing the job which he craved so passionately.

Brian Clough was born on a Middlesbrough council estate in 1935, the sixth of nine children and the only one to fail the 11-plus examination. The whole family was football crazy and every Christmas each of the six boys received a pair of boots. The young Brian, a bright and forthright boy despite his examination setback, flourished in the close-knit, loving environment and on leaving school became a clerk at the local works of ICI.

He displayed a rare talent for soccer, excelling as a marksman in local teams before joining Middlesbrough as an amateur in November 1951. Six months later he turned professional and continued his success at junior level. Two years of National Service preceded Clough's senior début in 1955, after which be grew rapidly into Second Division 'Boro's prime asset. In 1956/57, his first term as a regular, he scored 38 times in 41 League outings, after which his seasonal returns were 40, 43, 39 and 34.

Strong, fearless and fast, and very selfish where scoring chances were concerned, the crew-cut spearhead became an idol on Teesside. However, not everyone at his club shared the public's affection for Brian Clough. Ever brash and opinionated, and prone to bossiness, he became frustrated with what he saw as Middlesbrough's lack of ambition, even making a transfer request (which was refused) after only nine appearances in the first team. He was particularly critical of the side's admittedly rather porous defence, being wont to declare that no matter how many goals he scored, his colleagues seemed to concede more.

Perhaps in part due to his prickly persona, Clough was never given an extended chance to show what he could do at international level. Such was his weight of goals for 'Boro that he was called up for the Football League against the Irish League in Belfast in September 1959 and responded by scoring five times.

After that the Football Association selection committee could hardly omit him from the full England side and duly awarded him two caps later that year. But he failed to score on either occasion and thereafter was consigned to the wilderness. It did not escape his notice, and he did not fail to stress, that players of inferior ability had been given far greater opportunity.

Clough, who had married local girl Barbara Glasgow in 1959, continued to score freely at club level but became increasingly keen to leave Middlesbrough. He got his wish in July 1961 when a £42,000 deal took him to Sunderland, who were also in the Second Division but were perceived as a better bet to reach the top flight. Clough reacted positively to the more disciplined Roker Park regime and maintained his fine strike rate for his new employers, who nevertheless missed out on promotion by a single point in his first season.

Come Boxing Day 1962 and Sunderland's 27-year-old star had contributed 28 goals in 28 senior games that term to date. But that afternoon, in a slushy Roker quagmire, he collided sickeningly with Bury goalkeeper Chris Harker. Lying in the mud, Clough could barely move his right leg; the worst was feared and, ultimately, was realised. He had torn the cruciate ligament, an injury from which Paul Gascoigne was to recover in 1991 but which three decades earlier invariably signalled career's end.

Yet despite the gloomy prognosis, Clough worked long and ferociously to repair the knee. He was out of action for 18 months, and when he was recalled by newly-promoted Sunderland in September 1964 it seemed that some sort of miracle had taken place.

Alas, the comeback was to end in tears. After three games, the only appearances he was ever to make in the First Division, it was obvious that the joint could not withstand the pressure. The bitterly frustrated Clough was forced to retire, leaving behind him the astonishing record of 267 goals in 296 senior matches. Later, in his autobiography, *Clough*

(1994), he described himself as the finest goal-scorer in the country and one of the best the game has ever seen. The assessment was characteristically immodest but well supported by the facts. Now Clough, unqualified for anything else, had little choice but to remain in football. Sunderland boss George Hardwick put him in charge of the youth team and he discovered a liking for coaching and aptitude for motivation that was destined to make him a household name. That job ended in dismissal when Hardwick got the sack but the next step up the ladder was not long in coming.

In October 1965, Clough became a football manager, albeit with humble Hartlepools United (now Hartlepool United), and the die was cast. His first decision was his most important, ensuring that Peter Taylor, a former colleague and confidant from his Middlesbrough days, was appointed as his assistant. The two men, destined to tread a glorious path together before their unhappy estrangement 18 years hence, complemented each other perfectly and enjoyed a seemingly telepathic understanding: Clough blessed with charisma, a flair for publicity and a gift for psychology which allowed him to extract the best from the most unlikely of individuals, Taylor the talent-finder supreme who possessed a deep, instinctive knowledge of the game.

The task which faced them at Hartlepools was immense. Run-down United were viewed widely as the League's worst club but Clough set to work with almost evangelical zeal, touring the area to raise cash by inspired oratory. He set out to transform the ground, the team and the image, giving the club and its fans pride and confidence. It seemed he would do anything to put Hartlepools in the headlines, even being known to drive the team coach, and one Christmas he went without his own wages so the players could be paid. Results improved dramatically, and when he and Taylor departed for Derby County in June 1967 they left behind them a revamped club destined for promotion in the coming season.

At Derby, the job was on a grander scale and expectations were higher, but Clough proved more than equal to the challenge. He signed the ageing but still magnificent wing-half Dave Mackay from Tottenham Hotspur and brought in other excellent if little-known players, including future England centre-half Roy McFarland, and County won the Second Division title in 1968/69. More shrewd signings followed, the likes of defender Colin Todd and schemer Archie Gemmill, and in 1971/72 the Rams won the League championship for the first time in their history. When that was capped by a rousing European Cup campaign which saw Derby beat Benfica before losing controversially to Juventus in the semi-final, it seemed that Clough and Taylor were on the verge of something special.

Yet behind the scenes all was not well. There had been a succession of acrimonious disputes between Clough and the directors, many of whom resented the enormous say he demanded in all aspects of club affairs. He fell out with the chairman, Sam Longson, who earlier had treated him like a son, and his increasing media commitments – he became the most acerbic and watchable of television pundits – exacerbated boardroom irritation.

Accordingly, outsiders but not insiders were stunned in October 1973 when Clough and Taylor announced they were leaving because of the board's attitude. The decision caused uproar, underlining the messiah-like stature of the 38-year-old Teessider. In an echo of the situation when Stanley Matthews left Stoke City just after the Second World War, fans held protest meetings to get Clough restored. Even the Derby players threatened to strike and Clough helped to orchestrate their efforts.

In the end Mackay was installed as his replacement and gradually the affair blew over, leaving Clough to regret his resignation at leisure. As he reflected later, had he and Taylor remained at the Baseball Ground, there was no limit to what Derby might have achieved.

Faced with the need to work, Clough and Taylor now made a move which amazed many – they took over the reins of Third Division Brighton. Crowds doubled at the Goldstone Ground but there were inevitable doubts about his long-term intentions – few observers credited that he would be content to operate at so low a level for long – and so it proved. After just over half a season of appalling results, he departed, minus Taylor this time, to succeed Don Revie at Leeds.

Clough, who turned down a lucrative offer to run Iran's team during his seaside sojourn, always maintained that he had not used Brighton as a convenience, but the fact remained that the most fascinating events during his reign there concerned not football but politics.

A lifelong Socialist whom many believed would have made an ideal sports minister, he campaigned vigorously for Derby North Labour MP Philip Whitehead at the February 1974 election, helping him to retain the seat, and it was predicted that one day he would become a candidate himself. But though he was ready to march with protesting miners and laboured enthusiastically under the red flag, his future did not lie in politics.

Probably wisely, he stuck to what he knew best, although wisdom was hardly the word to associate with his ill-fated interlude at Leeds. It lasted a mere 44 days and that, in retrospect, is hardly surprising given his personality and approach to the job.

Clough had always been anti-Revie and anti-Leeds, calling them dirty and cynical and declaring that they had won their prizes by cheating. This hardly endeared him to the players at Elland Road, and when he repeated his views at his first team talk he was met by a wall of animosity which he never dismantled. Results proved abysmal, and after a mere six matches he left by mutual consent with the board, taking with him a massive pay-off which gave him financial security for life.

Despite that supremely ill-judged episode, Clough's self-belief remained intact, and in January 1975 he accepted charge of Nottingham Forest, at that time a sleepy, well-nigh comatose outfit lodged in the lower reaches of the Second Division. Soon he had signed two of his most trusted players from his previous clubs, John McGovern and John O'Hare, and the revival was under way. In truth, it was slow at first, and it wasn't until he was reunited with Peter Taylor, who arrived to assist in July 1976, that lift-off really took place. Together they recruited some unlikely characters and rehabilitated under-achievers already on the staff. Most notable of these was John Robertson, a slow, overweight, under-motivated midfielder who was soon to become one of the most bewitching wingers in the world.

The fruits of this revolution were staggering. In 1976/77 Forest were promoted, although at that point their progress might have been arrested had Clough's application for the England job been accepted. However, he was considered too controversial by the FA, who put him in control of the youth team and gave the top post to Ron Greenwood.

About the only fans not outraged by this decision were those of Forest, who now watched their side buck the odds to become League champions of 1977/78 and lift the League Cup for good measure. To put this feat into context, it took place in a period of dominance by a vintage Liverpool side, so there was no question of stealing the title in a weak year. To make it even sweeter, in December Forest completed a sequence of 42 League games undefeated, a top-flight record which stood until outstripped by Arsenal in recent weeks.

Incredibly, even greater days lay ahead. After making Birmingham's gifted forward Trevor Francis Britain's first £1m footballer, Clough set off on the trail of the European

Cup and confounded most pundits by winning it, a perfect cross from the revitalised Robertson and a lunging header from Francis being enough to defeat Swedish side Malmo in the final. Forest retained the League Cup, too, to complete a momentous season.

In 1979/80 Clough and Co continued to defy the big battalions. They kept hold of the European Cup, beating Hamburg in the final through a combination of a Robertson goal and shrewd, if rather more defensive tactics than Forest usually employed.

In the wake of so much glory, it was inevitable, perhaps, that the remainder of Clough's career should be something of an anti-climax. During the early 1980s he spent heavily on players who did not come up to expectation, the likes of Justin Fashanu and Ian Wallace, and Forest slipped from their eminent perch. Not that he allowed them to slide far, at least not until the very end. Throughout the 1980s and into the 1990s they played a clean, positive passing game that was easy on the eye but less successful than of yore. There were no more titles or European trophies, and no FA Cup – the nearest they got was defeat by Spurs in the final in 1991 – though they did win the League Cup twice more, in 1989 and 1990.

One of Clough's delights during this period was the development under his aegis of his son, Nigel, into a skilful forward who was to play for England. But there was abiding sadness, too, about his split with Taylor, who had resigned in May 1982, apparently having had enough of the business. However, he resurfaced as boss of Derby later that year and signed Robertson from Forest without consulting his former partner. Clough never forgave him and the pair barely spoke again. Taylor died in 1990, leaving Clough to rue the sorry ending of a sublime collaboration.

Indeed, it's fair to speculate that, without Taylor, Clough may not have achieved anything like as much as he did. Taylor it was with the golden knack of unearthing gems from unlikely sources, and Clough relied heavily on his judgement.

As the years passed, the Forest boss appeared ever more eccentric, an impression heightened by his cuffing of two fans who had invaded the City Ground pitch after a cup victory in February 1989, an outburst for which he was fined £5,000 by the FA. He became renowned, too, for his method of greeting other managers – a peck on the cheek – and stories began to circulate that he was drinking too much. These were given credence in the early 1990s by his bloated, blotchy appearance, though he admitted little more than a semblance of a problem in his book. Subsequently there were occasions when he appeared a poignant parody of his former self, and his years of indulgence culminated in a liver transplant in January 2003.

Sadly for such a remarkable figure, Clough – who had been offered the part-time task of managing Wales in 1988 but was blocked from taking it by his club – was to retire on a low note after Forest were relegated from the Premier League in 1992/93. He had made mistakes, principally the sale of several key players and the failure to replace them, and it seems he realised them too late.

However, he had given the game so much that was good and uplifting, startling and downright amusing, that the charismatic name of Brian Clough was proof even against such an anti-climactic ending.

Brian Howard Clough: born Middlesbrough, Yorkshire, 21 March 1935; played for Middlesbrough 1952-61, Sunderland 1961-64; capped twice for England 1959; managed Hartlepools United 1965-67, Derby County 1967-73, Brighton and Hove Albion 1973-74, Leeds United 1974, Nottingham Forest 1975-93; died Derby, 20 September 2004.

Bill Nicholson

Despite the avalanche of glib superlatives with which sporting heroes tend to be engulfed, genuine and universally acknowledged greatness remains as properly rare in football as in any other sphere of life. But there can be no doubt that Bill Nicholson attained it with Tottenham Hotspur in 1960/61.

He was the architect of a team as exhilarating, as balanced, as downright beautiful as any British combination in living memory, a glorious fusion of silk and dynamite which became the first in the 20th century to win the coveted League and FA Cup double.

Yet in scaling that lofty pinnacle relatively early in his managerial career, the gruff, deep-thinking, inscrutable Yorkshireman had condemned himself to perpetual frustration in his never-ending quest for soccer perfection.

The names of the class of '61, which read like a sacred litany to Spurs fans of that era, bear repetition here: Brown; Baker, Henry; Blanchflower, Norman, Mackay; Jones, White, Smith, Allen and Dyson. By no means all of them were 'great' players; indeed, of the 11, only wing-halves Danny Blanchflower and Dave Mackay, winger Cliff Jones and inside-forward John White merit anything approaching such an accolade.

But Nicholson's achievement lay in blending disparate talents into a magnificent whole. An impeccable judge of character and ability, he bought brilliantly, got the best out of players already at his disposal and coached imaginatively. The chemistry was right and the rest followed, often sublimely.

The glitter and gloss of White Hart Lane were far removed from Nicholson's beginnings, between the wars in Scarborough, as the second youngest of a hansom cab driver's nine children. Growing up during the Depression, he became so used to austerity that it was to remain integral to his way of life even when he was earning the wages of a top manager.

Indeed, while his star players would inhabit lavish homes in the north London commuter belt, Nicholson didn't move from a modest end-of-terrace house close to Tottenham's ground, though that was due only partly to his simple tastes and lack of ostentation. The most pressing reason was his utter dedication to his work, which was so near that he could – and usually did – burn the midnight oil disposing of routine matters neglected during the day's tracksuit toil.

On leaving school, Nicholson took a job as a laundry boy and played his football for Scarborough Working Men's Club. In 1936 he was spotted by Spurs and moved south to gather experience with their nursery club, Northfleet, before turning professional in 1938. He made impressive strides, being awarded a Second Division debut at left-back that same year, only for his encouraging progress to be halted brutally by the war.

During the hostilities he served in the Durham Light Infantry, being stationed mainly in England – first as an infantry instructor, then a physical training instructor – and found time for guest appearances with Middlesbrough, Sunderland, Newcastle United and Darlington among others.

When normality was restored at the war's end, Nicholson switched to centre-half before a permanent move to right-half, a role in which he excelled until the end of his playing days. He was an unspectacular performer, sturdy, industrious and efficient, his play as unadorned by fripperies as his lifestyle. Playing alongside his flamboyant skipper, Ronnie Burgess, and in front of the enterprising Alf Ramsey, Nicholson acted as an endlessly consistent linkman, becoming a crucial component in the mould-breaking push-and-run side assembled by manager Arthur Rowe.

In 1949/50 he pocketed a Second Division title medal, then went one better the next term as Spurs became League champions for the first time in their history. Unaccustomed personal glory followed in May 1951 when, at the age of 32, Nicholson was called up for his sole full England cap. He celebrated in untypically dramatic manner by scoring with his first kick, a powerful shot from long range, a mere 19 seconds into the action against Portugal at Goodison Park. The lack of further international recognition could be ascribed to a combination of injuries, advancing age and the excellence of Billy Wright.

Come 1954 Nicholson, whose honesty was a byword, told Rowe it was time to replace him in the team, and he accepted an invitation to join the club's coaching staff. By then he had demonstrated considerable aptitude for passing on his knowledge of the game, gaining his FA coaching badge at the first attempt and working with the Cambridge University team.

In 1957 he became assistant to manager Jimmy Anderson, who had replaced the far-from-well Rowe, and a year later helped England boss Walter Winterbottom prepare his side for the World Cup finals in Sweden.

But even that was merely a prelude to the most important moment of his career, his appointment as Tottenham manager in October 1958. The reign got under way with an astonishing 10-4 home victory over Everton, but Bill Nicholson's head was not for turning. He realised there was much work to be done on a flawed team and suffered early setbacks as Spurs flirted with relegation that season, eventually scraping to safety by an uncomfortably narrow margin.

Before long, though, he got it right, extracting the absolute best from Blanchflower – as romantic and loquacious as Nicholson was dour and taciturn – and the rest as he pieced together that most lovely of sides. A stern realist, he was ever a grudging dispenser of praise, and it grated on some observers that even in the hour of his most memorable triumph, when defeat of Leicester City at Wembley in 1961 secured football's most famous double, he appeared unable to relax and enjoy the moment.

Instead he bemoaned the fact that, in a disappointing match marred by injury to Leicester's Len Chalmers, his Spurs had not shown the world how well they could really play.

That summer he strengthened his side by the acquisition of Jimmy Greaves from AC Milan and in 1961/62 Tottenham retained the FA Cup, beating Burnley 3-1 in the final; reached the semi-final of the European Cup before losing narrowly and controversially to Benfica, and finished third in that term's title race. In 1962/63 they were First Division runners-up and, more momentously still, became the first British club to lift a European trophy, the Cup Winners' Cup.

Yet that milestone 5-1 annihilation of Atletico Madrid in Rotterdam proved to be a valedictory triumph for Nicholson's wonderful team. It broke up, as even the best teams must – though the horrific loss of White to a bolt of lightning in 1964 could hardly have been foreseen – and the manager set about rebuilding.

He did so ably, maintaining the Tottenham tradition for attractive football and backing his judgement with a series of big-money signings; but alas, having scaled Olympian heights with his first creation, the only way was down.

True, with victories in the FA Cup (1967), the League Cup (1971 and 1973) and the UEFA Cup (1972) Spurs were hardly on short rations compared with most other clubs, but Nicholson never again presided over a championship triumph and his teams resembled mere mortals compared with what had gone before.

Inevitably, in view of his perfectionist's outlook, he became increasingly dissatisfied, a situation which defeat in the 1974 UEFA Cup final did nothing to relieve. Still, few people imagined that the sprightly 55-year-old was on the verge of quitting the job with which he had become synonymous, yet in September 1974, after a run of dismal results, he did just that.

In truth, Bill Nicholson was reacting not merely to current circumstances at White Hart Lane, but to what he considered were disturbing trends in football. He despised the onset of functional modern modes of play, was out of tune with the new, precocious breed of player, was disenchanted at the creeping commercialisation of his beloved game – much later, his condemnation of the avaricious Premiership age was savagely trenchant – and sickened by widespread hooliganism.

Though the board and the players tried to get him to change his mind, in the end Nicholson's departure was handled clumsily. Upset that he couldn't choose his successor – he wanted Blanchflower, the club chose Terry Neill – he took a brief rest (during which he was awarded an OBE) before spending a year as an adviser to West Ham United.

Happily for both Spurs and 'Bill Nick', he was back at White Hart Lane in 1975, having been requested to return as a consultant by new boss Keith Burkinshaw. He continued to fill that role under successive managers until 1991, when he became club president.

During a life dedicated well-nigh totally to football, Nicholson had been fortunate to enjoy the support of a loyal wife, Grace (or 'Darkie' as she preferred to be called), who assumed the major responsibility for bringing up their two daughters. Though his habitually stern exterior gave little away, close associates maintained that it masked deep emotions, which were never more apparent than when he weighed up the cost to private life of his work-enforced absences.

Such matters, though, are between a man and his family. As far as the public domain is concerned, Bill Nicholson was a marvellous manager, one of the greatest of them all.

William Edward Nicholson: born Scarborough, Yorkshire, 26 January 1919; played for Tottenham Hotspur 1936-55; capped once for England 1951; manager, Tottenham Hotspur 1958-74; managerial consultant with West Ham United 1975-76; OBE 1975; managerial consultant with Tottenham Hotspur 1976-91; president, Tottenham Hotspur 1991-2004; died Potters Bar, Hertfordshire, 23 October 2004.

Keith Weller

Keith Weller was blessed with all the natural talent necessary to become a top footballer with either Tottenham Hotspur or Chelsea. Both offered the bright, dynamic Londoner enticing opportunities early in his career, but he failed to sparkle quite persuasively enough among the forbidding firmaments of stars at White Hart Lane and Stamford Bridge.

Instead, eventually, he accepted a move to the less rarefied, altogether homelier surroundings of Filbert Street, where he matured during the 1970s into one of the most revered figures in Leicester City's history, perhaps deserving more than the four caps he was awarded by England caretaker manager Joe Mercer.

Weller was an attacking midfielder endowed bountifully with flair and dash, frequently deployed on the right wing but arguably more effective in a central role. Admirably direct and determined, he possessed the skill and pace to leave defenders floundering in his wake, often his stamina appeared limitless, and he packed an explosive shot which yielded some memorably spectacular goals.

Also in the Weller mix was a slightly temperamental bent. He was emphatically his own man and once, utterly frustrated by perceived shortcomings at the club, he refused to return to the pitch for the second half of Leicester's home encounter with Ipswich Town in December 1974, for which rash act he was fined and temporarily transfer-listed.

His verve and his independence apart, Weller ensured an unperishable entry in City's folklore in one of his last matches for them, an FA Cup tie against Norwich City. Aghast at the conditions which had caused the postponement of most of the football programme that icy day in January 1979, he donned a pair of fetching white tights under his shorts, then ignored the inevitable ribaldry from the terraces and scored in his team's 3-0 victory.

Weller, who was on Arsenal's books as a schoolboy, turned professional with Tottenham in January 1964 and impressed White Hart Lane boss Bill Nicholson with his exuberant ability. Whenever called to the colours as a deputy for League and FA Cup double-winning heroes Cliff Jones or Terry Dyson, the rookie acquitted himself splendidly. On one summer tour of Mexico he was particularly prominent, astounding team-mates and opponents alike by his boundless energy in the baking heat, but sadly Nicholson, untypically, was not there to see it.

Eventually, demoralised at not being able to pin down a regular place, he agreed to join Millwall of the old Second Division for £20,000 in June 1967, even though the Spurs manager, sensing the 21-year-old's potential, had been reluctant to sell.

Sure enough, he flourished at The Den, where he linked sweetly with former Tottenham team-mate Derek Possee, who played as an out-and-out striker with Weller in a slightly deeper role. Emerging as a key component of Benny Fenton's enterprising team, he regained career impetus, earned selection for an FA tour of New Zealand and the Far East – during which he scored 11 goals in as many matches – and secured a £100,000 switch to the FA Cup holders, Chelsea, in May 1970.

Now Weller found himself in an attractive and fashionable side replete with household names – the likes of Peter Osgood, Charlie Cooke and Alan Hudson – but he was not overawed.

Operating on the right flank, he had netted a dozen times by Christmas – including a sumptuous volley against Newcastle United – and although his form fell away towards the end of the season, he topped the Blues' scoring charts with 14 strikes in all competitions.

More importantly, he had played a major part in Chelsea lifting the European Cup Winners' Cup, missing only one game during the glorious progress to a replayed final, in which the mighty Real Madrid were vanquished in Athens.

Still, though manager Dave Sexton had a cornucopia of riches from which to choose, it seemed a pity to Weller's admirers that he was not given an extended chance in central midfield, where his influence might have been even more pervasive.

As it was, he was plagued by illness and injury at the outset of the following campaign, then the arrival of Chris Garland and Steve Kember shunted him down the pecking order, and in September 1971 he was transferred to Leicester City, newly promoted to the top flight, for another £100,000 fee.

At last Weller was in his element as a crucially important component of Jimmy Bloomfield's team, one which entertained wonderfully even if it suffered from a maddening tendency to under-achieve. With a lovely attack in which Weller was joined by Jon Sammels, Frank Worthington, Alan Birchenall and Len Glover, City were rarely dull, but they flattered to deceive, suggesting on several occasions that they might qualify for Europe, only to fall short in the end.

Weller highlights included a magnificent hat-trick to beat Liverpool after falling two goals behind in a League clash in August 1972; a run to the 1974 FA Cup semi-finals, in which they lost to Liverpool, and a stunning strike against Luton on that same cup trail, which fans voted to be City's greatest ever goal.

During his eight years at Filbert Street, City never finished higher than seventh in the First Division, but there was some consolation on the international front when he was called up by the genial Mercer, ever a man with an eye for an entertainer, for four games in the space of 11 days in May 1974. One of them, against Northern Ireland at Wembley, he graced with a rare headed goal, which was enough to secure victory, but he never caught the fancy of new England boss Don Revie and never represented his country again.

Towards the end of the decade, Weller began to suffer serial knee trouble, and he was not at his best in 1977/78 when Leicester, after Frank McLintock had replaced Bloomfield as manager, were relegated as the bottom club.

He contributed gamely under Jock Wallace in the difficult rebuilding term of 1978/79, stretching his Foxes record to 43 goals in 297 senior appearances, before crossing the Atlantic to join New England Tea Men, with whom he had already put in a loan stint.

There followed a spell playing for Fort Lauderdale Strikers before he became a sought-after coach, serving Fort Lauderdale Sun, South Florida Sun, Houston Dynamo, Dallas Sidekicks, San Diego Sockers, Tacoma Stars and Sacramento Knights. He settled in Seattle, where he also drove an outside-broadcast rig for a television station and ran a coffee shop.

Keith Weller died at his home following a lengthy battle with a rare form of cancer. In 2002 Leicester fans raised £40,000 to pay for therapy and at the end of the 2003/04 football season Alan Birchenall, who described his former City comrade as one of the five best Leicester players of all time, raised £27,500 for research into the disease with a sponsored run.

Keith Weller: born Islington, north London, 11 June 1946; played for Tottenham Hotspur 1964-67, Millwall 1967-70, Chelsea 1970-71, Leicester City 1971-79; capped four times by England 1974; died Seattle, USA, 12 November 2004.

Emlyn Hughes

Emlyn Hughes was a study in footballing fervour. One of the principal bulwarks of Liverpool's domestic and European glory in the 1970s, he made his initial impact as a youthful midfield dreadnought who rampaged among his opponents like some demonically frisky rhinoceros released suddenly from captivity.

Later, having added composure, polish and a measure of subtlety to his game, he matured into a majestically effective defender, and an inspirational captain of the Merseyside Reds and of England.

The ebullient, endlessly ambitious Hughes exuded an insatiable will to win that was almost frightening in its intensity, personifying the sporting gospel as preached by his mentor and first Anfield manager Bill Shankly.

Yet for all that unbridled enthusiasm there was a time, in his mid-teens, when the second of Great Britain and Wales rugby league international Fred Hughes' three sons appeared to have no future in professional football. He joined his home-town club Barrow, then in the old Fourth Division, but got no further than the youth team and took a job as a mechanic in a local garage.

However, help was at hand in the form of an old friend of his father, Ron Suart, the boss of First Division Blackpool, who invited Hughes for a trial at Bloomfield Road. Such was the youngster's boundless energy and determination that soon he was rewarded by a part-time contract, which was upgraded to professional terms when he was 17 in 1964.

At first he struggled in a midfield berth and it appeared that he might be destined for a role in the family Tarmacadam business, but when offered an opportunity at left-back in one of the junior sides, he began to thrive.

On the last day of the 1965/66 season, still aged only 18, he made his senior debut in a local derby at Blackburn, attracting the ire of Rovers fans with a passionately committed display – one of their men, George Jones, was sent off after a clash with the fiery newcomer – and, more significantly, riveting the attention of Liverpool manager Bill Shankly, who was watching from the stand.

So captivated was Shankly by Hughes' performance that he lodged an immediate £25,000 offer to sign him. The advance was rejected summarily, but after the rookie confirmed his promise by striking up a formidable full-back partnership for the Seasiders with England veteran Jimmy Armfield in the first half of the subsequent campaign, Liverpool secured their quarry in February 1967. Even though the price had rocketed to £65,000, the irrepressible Shankly could not contain his glee, describing his acquisition as one of the major signings of all time and predicting correctly that he would captain England.

Hughes' arrival marked the beginning of the end of an Anfield era. Shankly was making his first tentative moves towards dismantling his wonderful side of the mid-1960s and the bubbly Barrow boy became the first new recruit to gain a regular place.

Certainly he wasted no time in making an impact on Merseyside, being deployed in midfield in his first game at home to Stoke City and utterly dominating the Potters' gifted schemer George Eastham.

A few matches later, having been switched temporarily to left-back as deputy for the injured Gerry Byrne, Hughes earned a nickname that would stick for the rest of his life. From the day he felled Newcastle United forward Albert Bennett with an impetuous rugby-style tackle – there was nothing malicious in the challenge, he was merely desperate to be noticed – he was branded 'Crazy Horse', a label that tied in perfectly with his galloping gait and overwhelming zest.

Not that such eccentric behaviour was necessary to draw attention to a dynamic performer who made gigantic strides in 1967/68, replacing Willie Stevenson at left-half and attracting an offer from Leeds United which included rising Scottish star Peter Lorimer in part-exchange.

Shankly rebuffed the approach emphatically, having identified the young leviathan as an indispensable cornerstone of the new Anfield order. Hughes' strength and stamina were prodigious, and even if he committed himself to rash tackles at times, and if his savagely powerful shooting was unpredictable, his potential was awesome.

Though no trophies were garnered around the turn of the decade, Liverpool remained a major force, never far from the League table's summit, and with new talents such as goalkeeper Ray Clemence, winger Steve Heighway and strikers John Toshack and Kevin Keegan being added to stalwarts such as Hughes, defender Tommy Smith and flankman Ian Callaghan, they gathered unstoppable impetus in the early 1970s.

Hughes, whose progress was reflected by the first of his 62 England caps, playing at left-back against Holland in 1969, had his first close encounter with club glory when the

Reds lost the 1971 FA Cup final to Arsenal, an experience which left him mortified. Soon enough, though, he was pocketing winners' medals, starting with a pair in 1972/73 when Shankly's team lifted the League title and the UEFA Cup.

In 1973/74 Hughes, having replaced Smith as captain and formed an enterprising central defensive liaison with Phil Thompson, led Liverpool to FA Cup glory against Newcastle United. By this time his playing style was calmer, more reliant on anticipation than in his buccaneering days of old, and he was all the more impressive for it, his value further enhanced by the ability to turn out at full-back when needed.

Ahead of him was a half-decade of fabulous achievement, skippering the side, now guided by Bob Paisley, to another UEFA Cup and League double in 1976, to two European Cup triumphs – against Borussia Moenchengladbach in Rome in 1977 and over FC Bruges at Wembley a year later – and he pocketed further title gongs in '77 and '79.

For good measure, he was voted Footballer of the Year in 1977, a year which would have reach even more rarefied heights had not Manchester United beaten Liverpool unexpectedly in the FA Cup final.

The taste of an isolated defeat that afternoon offered a telling illustration of Hughes' rage to win. Ever one to wear his heart on his sleeve, he replaced his characteristic all-embracing grin with a look of such sheer desolation that in the immediate aftermath, when he bumped into Conservative party leader Margaret Thatcher, she was startled by the depth of his emotion. On inquiring how he felt, she was informed: 'To tell the truth, love, I'm absolutely knackered.'

In 1978/79 he suffered serial knee problems which limited him to 16 appearances on that term's title trail and in the following August, shortly before his 32nd birthday and having made 665 appearances for the Reds, he joined First Division rivals Wolverhampton Wanderers for £90,000.

Though past his barnstorming best, Hughes had become a canny operator and had lost none of his drive, so it surprised no one in 1979/80 when he captained the Molineux club to League Cup final triumph over Nottingham Forest and to a sixth-place finish in the top flight.

It was during his Wolves tenure that he earned his final England caps, closing an illustrious international career in which he skippered his country 23 times and served under four bosses: Sir Alf Ramsey, Joe Mercer, Don Revie, who outraged him by axing him as a full-back before restoring him eventually as a central defender, and Ron Greenwood.

Having received an OBE in 1980 for services to football, he left to become player-manager of Second Division Rotherham United in July 1981, and enjoyed an invigorating first season in charge, steering the Merry Millers to within four points of promotion.

But he could not maintain the momentum and, with United embroiled in a relegation battle they were doomed to lose, he departed in the spring of 1983. Later he played briefly for Hull City and Swansea City before retiring in that November.

After leaving the game Hughes carved a niche as a TV celebrity on shows such as *A Question Of Sport* and *Sporting Triangles*, though his career in that medium did not progress in the leaps and bounds that had seemed likely. A hugely successful after-dinner speaker and a generous worker for charity, also he sat on Hull City's board for a short stint at the end of the 1980s, and he emerged as an outspoken guest columnist in tabloid newspapers, upsetting many people with his trenchant opinions.

For all the inspirational motivational skills he displayed during his pomp with Liverpool and England, Hughes alienated some colleagues who resented his immense belief in his own worth. Indeed the flinty, down-to-earth Tommy Smith, a Liverpool team-mate through so many memorable campaigns, made no secret of his dislike, though always he stressed that Hughes' status as a magnificent player was beyond doubt.

Still, nothing could besmirch the body of work assembled over nearly 20 years of top-level football. Emlyn Hughes ranks as one of Liverpool's finest – and that's mighty high.

Emlyn Walter Hughes: born Barrow-in-Furness, Lancashire, 28 August 1947; played for Blackpool 1964-67, Liverpool 1967-1979, Wolverhampton Wanderers 1979-81, Rotherham United 1981-83, Hull City 1983, Swansea City 1983; capped 62 times by England 1969-80; OBE 1980; managed Rotherham United 1981-83; died Sheffield, 9 November 2004.

Bill Brown

Characteristically calm and unfussy yet breathtakingly acrobatic at need, Bill Brown was the last line of defence in 1961 when Tottenham Hotspur became the first club in the 20th century to lift the coveted League and FA Cup double, and two years later the first Britons to sample European footballing glory.

He excelled between the posts for Scotland, too, becoming their most capped custodian until his record of 28 appearances was surpassed by Alan Rough in 1979, yet Brown did not conform to the popular notion of what a goalkeeper should look like.

Though he stood half an inch over six feet, his frame was spare, stringy and seemingly insubstantial, in vivid contrast to the imposingly muscular individuals employed by most clubs to mind their nets.

Every line of the Brown figure was angular, an impression emphasised by his aquiline features, though if some contemporary observers referred to him half-slightingly as willowy, there was no doubting his wiry resilience when it came to physical challenges with hulking centre-forwards.

All that mattered to White Hart Lane boss Bill Nicholson was that Brown was perfectly suited to Spurs' defensive needs. Though his collection of crosses could be erratic occasionally and he was no commander of his penalty box in the manner of, say, Manchester United's Harry Gregg, that scarcely mattered with the giant centre-half Maurice Norman stationed in front of him, invariably heading balls to safety while leaving the keeper to patrol his line.

In all other respects, Brown was impeccable. Elastically agile, but not a show-off, he was a brilliant shot-stopper endowed with remarkably sharp reflexes, he possessed a perceptive positional sense which made much of his work seem misleadingly easy, and his ability to maintain concentration was exceptional.

This last quality was crucial in a free-flowing, attack-minded team accustomed to dominating games, so that he might spend lengthy periods in virtual isolation. It was reassuring for the Tottenham supporters to see their goalkeeper half-crouching in an attitude of extreme involvement even though most of the action was unfolding at the opposite end of the pitch. In his own mind, it appeared, Brown kicked every ball and made every tackle, and sometimes he left the arena looking shattered after contests in which he had been a virtual onlooker.

With the ball in his hands, he was an asset, too, being an accurate kicker and launcher of attacks, adept at finding play-makers Danny Blanchflower and John White with pinpoint dispatches from hand or foot.

Another of Brown's prime assets was composure, particularly when the stakes were highest. He was never known to falter in a big match, turning in immaculate displays in the victorious FA Cup finals of 1961, against Leicester City, and 1962, when Burnley were the opponents, on both occasions making a mockery of supposed aerial weakness.

But it was during the triumphant European Cup Winners' Cup campaign of 1962/63 that the Scot attained his zenith, especially in the quarter-final first-leg defeat by Slovan in Bratislava. Sporting a plaster across his nose after receiving a heavy blow, he defied the Czechs with a series of splendid saves, limiting their lead to two goals and paving the way for second-leg victory.

Next came two fine semi-final performances against OFK Belgrade but, fittingly, his climactic effort was reserved for the final clash with Atletico Madrid in Rotterdam. By the interval Tottenham were 2-0 up and seemingly in control, but then the Spaniards struck back with a penalty and for 15 minutes they pounded the north Londoners' rearguard. Some of his fellow defenders reeled in the face of the onslaught, but Brown stood firm, coping heroically until the crisis had passed and three more Spurs strikes secured the trophy, the fourth and last major prize of his White Hart Lane tenure.

In 1964/65 the 33-year-old's position was threatened by the arrival of a precociously gifted young Ulsterman named Pat Jennings. After the pair had vied with one another over two seasons, inevitably the older man was judged surplus to requirements, winding down his playing days in 1966/67 with Second Division strugglers Northampton Town, then featuring briefly for Toronto Falcons before leaving the game.

As a youngster, Brown had been an exceptional all-round footballer, talented enough to earn a trial for Scotland Schoolboys as a left-winger. But it was as a goalkeeper that he thrived, first with local sides Arbroath Cliffburn and Carnoustie Panmure, then with Scottish League club Dundee, for whom he made his senior debut in 1949/50, having already received international honours at schoolboy and youth level.

The following term he was on the fringe of the team as the improving Dens Park outfit finished third in the top division; he was a regular as they won the Scottish League Cup in 1951/52, beating Rangers 3-2 in a tense final at Hampden Park, and as the decade wore on he graduated to the Scottish League and Scotland 'B'.

Brown won his first full cap in June 1958, replacing the more experienced Tommy Younger against France in what was to prove his country's last match in the World Cup tournament in Sweden. Despite performing superbly, he could not prevent a 2-1 defeat and the Scots returned home after the opening phase.

However, he had demonstrated his potential on the grandest stage, and soon he became a transfer target among leading English clubs. Tottenham's Bill Nicholson, wary of the competition after watching his quarry impress for Scotland against England at Wembley, swiftly agreed a £16,500 fee with Dundee and took a night train north to be sure of clinching the signing in the 1959 close-season.

Now Brown faced a formidable task as the long-term replacement for veteran Spurs favourite Ted Ditchburn, whose goalkeeping style was rather more spectacular, and the critical White Hart Lane fans took some time to warm to the newcomer.

But eventually he bedded in successfully, seeing off the challenge of the workmanlike but less consistent John Hollowbread, and when Tottenham recorded their majestic double triumph in 1960/61, Brown was absent for only one match.

He established himself in the international arena, too, adding 24 more appearances to the four caps garnered at Dundee, before bowing out in 1965 with the reputation as

Scotland's best goalkeeper since the war. Arguably, despite his advancing years, his tenure between his country's posts should have been considerably longer, as none of the plethora of immediate replacements appeared to be his equal.

Later, while playing in Toronto, Brown grew to love Canada and he settled there, working for a property developer, then joining the Ontario government's land department in 1975 before retiring to live in the province in 1995.

Back in north London, he is remembered by his surviving former team-mates as an endearingly modest individual who smoked incessantly and never put on weight despite indulging a voracious appetite. As for Spurs fans with clear memories of the most glorious interlude in their club's history, while not placing Bill Brown on the same rarefied pedestal as his fabulous Irish successor at White Hart Lane, they recall a top-notch performer, a man worth his place in any team.

William Dallas Fyfe Brown: born Arbroath, Angus, 8 October 1931; played for Dundee 1949-59, Tottenham Hotspur 1959-66, Northampton Town 1966-67, Toronto Falcons 1967; capped 28 times by Scotland 1958-65; died Simcoe, Ontario, 30 November 2004.

Eddie Spicer

Footballing full-back Eddie Spicer was one of the doughtiest and most reliable of Liverpool defenders during the middle years of the 20th century, but he was never one of the luckiest. Despite excelling on the title run-in of 1946/47, the squarely built Merseysider narrowly missed out on a medal as the Reds lifted the first post-war League championship, then he finished on the losing side against Arsenal in the 1950 FA Cup final.

Finally, and most demoralisingly of all, he was invalided out of the game by a broken leg when he was still at the peak of his powers in 1953, a particularly cruel blow to a dedicated performer who had recovered nobly from a similar career-threatening accident some 30 months earlier. Spicer emerged as an outstanding player in his early teens, being capped by England at schoolboy level, joining his home-town club as an amateur in 1937, then turning professional at Anfield in 1939.

But his career had no chance to gather momentum before war broke out and he joined the Royal Marines, in whose service he earned decoration for bravery during the conflict.

When peace resumed Spicer, still in his early twenties, lost little time in making his senior breakthrough with Liverpool, being called up for an FA Cup encounter with Bolton Wanderers in 1946.

He was a left-half at that point, the position he filled when League competition restarted the following August. However, for most of that ultimately triumphant campaign, manager George Kay preferred Bob Paisley in the number-six shirt, and Spicer's contribution was intermittent until the closing sequence of games, in which he performed persuasively. Unfortunately, his appearances totalled only ten, four short of the number needed to secure a medal.

Surprisingly, the next two seasons proved anti-climactic and he was unable to secure a regular first-team place until 1949/50, when he moved to his preferred slot of left-back, with Welsh international Ray Lambert switching to the right to accommodate him.

Now Spicer consolidated as Liverpool – for whom the multi-talented Scottish winger cum centre-forward Billy Liddell shone brilliantly and consistently – enjoyed a storming autumn and early winter, going unbeaten for their first 19 games and raising hopes of another title challenge.

Such optimism was scuppered by a dismal springtime slump, but there was consolation in a rousing run to Wembley, which included a passionately acclaimed semi-final victory over local rivals Everton, only for the FA Cup to be presented to a Liverpudlian who was plying his trade down south, Arsenal captain Joe Mercer.

Despite the disappointment of 2-0 defeat in the showpiece, Spicer had enhanced his reputation considerably, and he burnished it further as an ever-present in 1950/51 as Liverpool finished ninth in the League table. By now he was thoroughly at home in the English top flight, a tenacious marker and a stern tackler, ready to use his formidable strength at need but never inclined to gratuitous violence, as were certain defenders of his era.

Crucially, too, if he was beaten by a winger, invariably he was quick to recover with a secondary challenge. When his team was under pressure there was no more valiant occupant of the last ditch, and though he was happiest on the left flank of defence, he was accomplished with both feet and was not embarrassed when shifted to the right.

Sadly, having established an impetus which might have led to international recognition, Spicer suffered a broken leg on a short tour of Sweden in the summer of 1951 and was side-lined for the whole of the subsequent season.

With characteristic fortitude he fought back to gain the right-back berth for 1952/53, and proved a much-needed bulwark in a Liverpool side which was slowly disintegrating.

Demotion was narrowly avoided that term and though the Reds, now bossed by Don Welsh, were nosediving towards inevitable relegation in 1953/54, Spicer continued to play with poise and spirit until he shattered his leg in a sickening three-man collision at Old Trafford shortly before Christmas.

Manchester United centre-forward Tommy Taylor and Liverpool's debutant goalkeeper Dave Underwood were relatively unscathed by the impact, but Spicer was injured so seriously that he never played again.

The pain of his enforced retirement at the age of 31, after 168 appearances for his only club, was mitigated somewhat by a testimonial match between a combined Liverpool and Everton side and a Lancashire XI, which attracted more than 41,000 supporters to Anfield and raised £4,500 for the popular defender. Later Eddie Spicer became a football correspondent with the *Liverpool Daily Post* and ran a pub near Ruthin, in North Wales.

Edwin Spicer: born Liverpool 20 September 1922; played for Liverpool 1939-53; died Rhyl, Denbighshire, 25 December 2004.

Jackie Henderson

Scottish international footballer Jackie Henderson was a one-man forward line. The swashbuckling, pacy raider, feted by admiring contemporaries as quick enough to catch pigeons in his 1950s heyday, occupied every attacking position in a 13-year top-flight career during which he excelled with Portsmouth, failed to settle with Wolves, then served Arsenal impressively before falling prey to injury at Fulham.

Everything Henderson did was carried out at high velocity, and most aspects of his work were of impeccable quality. His running was hard and direct, he packed an explosive shot in either foot, and he was adept at crossing at speed, all of which made him a fearsome proposition for opposing defenders, though occasionally his hurry to control an awkwardly bouncing ball would let him down.

Frequently he featured on the wing, mostly the left, but he was a dashing centre-forward at heart, and was far more combative than most flankmen of his day, many of whom withered at the merest scowl from a hulking full-back. Not so the muscular Henderson, who relished a physical contest, be it in the air or on the ground, and raw courage earned him many a goal.

Unusually for a sports-mad young Glaswegian, he didn't play football at school, but tasted his first action with a church team near his home in Bishopbriggs. Soon he graduated to Kirkintilloch Boys' Club, where his potential was spotted by a Portsmouth scout in 1948. Later that year he enlisted as an amateur at Fratton Park, turning professional in January 1949 with a club on the threshold of the most glorious interlude in its history. That season and the next, Pompey won the League title with a beautifully balanced team renowned more for comradeship and co-ordination than for star individuals, and it is a telling tribute to the raw 19-year-old's progress that he was entrusted with spearheading such an eminent attack for most of the 1951/52 campaign.

After making his debut against Sunderland in the autumn, Henderson featured regularly, totalling eight goals in 27 appearances as Portsmouth finished fourth in the old First Division table. His vigour and verve complemented the more measured skills of inside-forward Len Phillips, he linked neatly with flying winger Peter Harris and he provided an industrious, ever-willing target for the perceptive dispatches of wing-halves Jimmy Scoular and Jimmy Dickinson.

There followed two down-table terms, but Henderson continued to flourish, demonstrating his adaptability by appearing frequently on the left wing and at inside-forward, then returning to centre-forward to shine alongside local boy Johnny Gordon as Pompey rose to third in 1954/55.

By then he was a full international – his case advanced by the fervent advocacy of his countryman, Scoular – and having impressed while winning his first cap as an outside-right against Sweden in 1953, he consolidated with further enterprising displays at centre-forward and on the left flank.

Back on the club scene, Pompey slid inexorably towards the foot of the First Division as the decade wore on and in March 1958, having netted 70 goals in 217 League outings for the Fratton Park club, he joined the new champions elect, Wolverhampton Wanderers, in a £16,000 deal.

Given his direct, all-action style, Henderson seemed a natural for Stan Cullis' aggressive, strong, long-passing side, but he didn't fit in at Molineux, being unable to unseat steady performers such as Jimmy Murray and Norman Deeley, and, only seven months later, he was transferred to Arsenal for £20,000.

Never mind that he had enabled Wolves to turn a quick profit, it seemed that Highbury boss George Swindin had pulled off a considerable coup in capturing a 26-year-old Scottish international in his prime, and it was expected that the newcomer would bring a fresh, incisive dimension to an Arsenal team in the throes of transition.

Henderson could hardly have started life as a Gunner more auspiciously, netting on debut with two flashing headers in a rousing 4-3 home victory over West Bromwich Albion, and he continued to spark through the remainder of the 1958/59 season, contributing a dozen strikes to Arsenal's creditable third-place finish.

He did so well, in fact, that he earned a fleeting recall to his country's colours late in 1958, which was no small achievement at a time when Scotland's attacking ranks were dripping with sumptuous talent, the likes of Denis Law, John White, Ian St John and any number of others, a stark and poignant contrast with the dearth of quality available to the national coach in the early years of the 21st century.

But that Arsenal team never quite gelled, receding into mid-table over the next two terms, and arguably Henderson became a victim of his own versatility, his consistency dipping as Swindin experimented with numerous forward options. Despite having impressed in a deep-lying creative role as well as in his customary front-line berths, the 30-year-old was released to join Fulham, perennial top-flight strugglers, for £14,000 in January1962.

Though past his pomp, he acquitted himself manfully for the Craven Cottage club, helping them to steer clear of relegation in two successive seasons, only for a broken leg suffered at Blackburn in March 1963 to signal an effective end to his senior career.

Henderson managed a handful of games during the following term, but his trademark pace had declined, understandably, and in the summer of 1964 he entered the non-League ranks with Poole Town.

Not that the still-enthusiastic veteran was looking for an easy billet. In 1964/65 he was vastly influential as he helped his new club gain promotion to the Southern League Premier Division, then in 1967 he began four years of sterling service with Dorchester Town of the Western League, not ending his playing days until 1971 when he was nearing 40.

Henderson, an amiable fellow and a lively dressing-room spirit, had remained passionate about the game and had been keen to put something back at the lower level, an objective he achieved comprehensively and for which he deserved immense credit.

Later he spent 30 years as a storeman for a builders' merchant in the Poole area, and was a regular attender of Pompey reunions until the onset of his final illness.

John Gillespie Henderson: born Bishopbriggs, Glasgow, 17 January 1932; played for Portsmouth 1951-58, Wolverhampton Wanderers 1958, Arsenal 1958-62, Fulham 1962-64; capped seven times for Scotland 1953-58; died Poole, Dorset, 26 January 2005.

Ron Burgess

In the case of Ron Burgess, mining's loss was football's immeasurable gain.

People who knew him as a boy joked that, with his boundless vitality, immense strength and readiness to toil until he dropped, he might singlehandedly have emptied the South Wales coalfield in which he grew up expecting to spend his working life.

Instead he hewed out a glorious niche as one of the most influential performers in the history of Tottenham Hotspur, emerging as a titanic presence at the heart of the team which took English club football by storm midway through the 20th century.

Burgess was both skipper and midfield inspiration as the north Londoners topped the Second Division table in 1949/50, then lifted the League championship a year later, and if one man embodied the ethos of visionary manager Arthur Rowe's exhilarating combination, it was the genial, prematurely balding Welshman.

His perpetual motion and irrepressible enthusiasm, melding potently with the wily passing game of inside-forward Eddie Baily, facilitated the side's fluid push-and-run style, which highlighted Rowe's credentials as one of the game's most progressive thinkers.

Not that Burgess was merely a workhorse, his characteristic dynamism and resilience being gilded by comprehensive all-round ability; his ball control was neat, his distribution assured, he was positionally astute, formidable in the air and quick over the ground.

He excelled, too, at international level, missing only two appearances for his country in eight post-war seasons, winning most of his 32 caps as captain. In addition he was the first Welshman to represent the Football League and he played for Great Britain against the Rest of Europe in 1947.

Burgess learned the game on rough pitches next to Rhondda Valley slagheaps, shining initially as a prolific centre-forward. Soon he attracted the attention of Cardiff City, whom he joined as an amateur in his mid-teens, but the Bluebirds' interest cooled and he took a mining job while playing for local side Cwm Villa.

Now a future in the pits appeared inevitable, but after plundering 59 goals in one season he was spotted by Tottenham, who recruited him, again on amateur terms, in 1936.

Initially it seemed likely that Burgess' reprieve from the coalface was only temporary as he failed to make the grade at White Hart Lane, and he was on his way home to South Wales when he stopped off to watch his Spurs contemporaries in a junior game. They were a man short, he stepped in at right-half and performed so impressively that he was offered a place at the club's Northfleet nursery in Kent.

In the new role he progressed rapidly, turning professional in 1938 at the age of 21 and making his senior debut in a Division Two fixture at Norwich in February 1939, only for his momentum to be shattered by the outbreak of war.

During the conflict Burgess served as a physical training instructor in the RAF, but found there was plenty of time for football, turning out for both Tottenham and Wales in unofficial competition as well as guesting for Huddersfield Town, Millwall, Nottingham Forest, Notts County and Reading.

When peace resumed he settled as Tottenham's regular left-half and it was a tribute to his insatiable drive that he emerged as leader of a team which included two men marked out for massive achievements in management – Alf Ramsey was destined to guide England to World Cup triumph in 1966, five years after Bill Nicholson had presided over Spurs becoming the first club that century to lift the League and FA Cup double.

At first Burgess' swashbuckling determination to surge forward, sometimes heedless of defensive duties, was perceived as a weakness, but after Rowe became boss in 1949 the skipper tempered his adventure with a dash of caution, and became even more effective. Indeed, years later the shrewd Nicholson would describe him as the best midfielder the club had ever known, thus outranking the illustrious likes of Danny Blanchflower, Dave Mackay, Glenn Hoddle and Paul Gascoigne.

The back-to-back successes of promotion and League title were followed by a near miss as Tottenham finished as runners-up to Manchester United in 1951/52, then came two more seasons of top-flight action before Burgess, having entered his 38th year, joined Second Division Swansea Town in 1954.

A year later he became player-manager at the Vetch Field, laying aside his boots in 1956 but consolidating the Swans' mid-table position until a slump in 1957/58 preceded departure and a fresh coaching challenge with lowly Watford.

In March 1959 Burgess ascended to the managerial seat at Vicarage Road, leading the Hornets to promotion from Division Four and on a thrilling run to the fifth round of the FA Cup in 1959/60. The following term brought more success, with Watford finishing fourth in the higher echelon, but after differences with popular marksman Cliff Holton had cost him the backing of many supporters, the club endured two disappointing terms and he was sacked in May 1963.

Some close observers believed that the amiable Burgess was not ruthless enough for the job, being loth to make crucial decisions affecting players' livelihoods, and their predictions that he would not return to the League scene proved correct.

However, he was not finished with the business of gathering silverware, taking over at non-League Hendon and guiding them to FA Amateur Cup glory against Whitby Town at Wembley in 1965.

That Burgess still hankered after the big time was evident, though, in his application to manage Wales in 1964. He was rejected in favour of Dave Bowen, though he took charge of the team briefly when the Northampton Town boss was unavailable because of club commitments.

Later Burgess was a trainer at Fulham under former Spurs colleague Vic Buckingham, then manager of Bedford Town, and a scout for Luton Town. Also there was a brief stint in charge of a Soccer Hall of Fame in the West End of London before work as a stock controller for a stationery firm in Wealdstone and as a warehouseman in Harrow.

William Arthur Ronald Burgess: born Cwm, Monmouthshire, South Wales, 9 April 1917; played for Tottenham Hotspur 1938-54, Swansea Town 1954-56; capped 32 times by Wales 1946-54; managed Swansea Town 1955-58, Watford 1959-63; died Swansea, 14 February 2005.

Bill McGarry

Bill McGarry was a spiky, formidably aggressive, yet admirably intelligent wing-half who surprised none of his contemporaries in English football when he forged an ogre-like reputation as a manager.

However, lurid tales of the fearsome discipline he dispensed after laying aside his boots should not obscure the fact that the brusque, occasionally truculent Trentsider was an immensely accomplished player, who won four caps for England and was a key man in Huddersfield Town's extraordinarily stable defence and midfield in the early to middle 1950s. As a boss, his principal achievement was in reviving Wolverhampton Wanderers, one of the most powerful clubs in the land for a decade and a half immediately after the Second World War but which had slumped alarmingly by the late 1960s.

McGarry led them to a European final in 1972 and to League Cup triumph at Wembley two years later, cementing the widespread respect he had accumulated during some 30 years, to that point, in the professional game.

As a fiercely determined teenager, McGarry shone for an amateur side, Northwood Mission, at Hanley in the heart of the Potteries, before beginning his League career with Port Vale of the Third Division South in June 1945. Soon he became a central figure at the Recreation Ground, which preceded Vale Park as the club's headquarters, and earned a £12,000 transfer to First Division Huddersfield in March 1951.

All McGarry's grit was needed in his first full season at Leeds Road, which ended in relegation to the Second Division, but he emerged as a leading light under new manager Andy Beattie as the Terriers bounced back into the top flight at the first attempt, finishing as runners-up to Sheffield United.

That season, remarkably, seven of Huddersfield's players were ever-present in the side, including the entire defence and both wing-halves. Thus for years afterwards the names of goalkeeper Jack Wheeler, full-backs Ron Staniforth and Laurie Kelly, and the half-back line of McGarry, Don McEvoy and Len Quested rolled off the tongues of Town supporters like some sacred litany.

The most eye-catching member of this redoubtable sextet was McGarry, who reached new personal heights as Beattie's hard-edged combination exceeded the expectations of most neutral observers in 1953/54, their initial campaign back among the elite, by finishing in a hugely creditable third place, six points adrift of title-winning Wolves and only two behind runners-up West Bromwich Albion.

The stockily built McGarry was a veritable dreadnought in midfield, crunching of tackle and ultra-dependable, but also capable of imaginative distribution, which often tended to be overlooked when his attributes were assessed.

Fittingly he was rewarded for his progress by an England call-up, first in a 'B' international in May 1954, then in the senior side during that summer's World Cup finals in Switzerland. On his debut against the home nation he set up a goal for Dennis Wilshaw in a 2-0 victory, then retained his right-half berth for the quarter-final against Uruguay, which ended in a 4-2 defeat.

McGarry's sojourn on the world stage was to last for only two more matches, ending in 1955, his path being blocked by the emergence of two younger wing-halves, Ronnie Clayton and the prodigiously talented Duncan Edwards.

Still, the Huddersfield man was only 28 and continued to excel on the domestic scene, despite his club suffering relegation in 1956. Thereafter he spent five more years toiling nobly in the Second Division – including a three-year spell under Bill Shankly, who was destined for untold glory with Liverpool – before becoming player-manager of Third Division Bournemouth in March 1961.

Having played 363 games and scored 25 goals for the Yorkshire club, and earned renown for his dynamism, McGarry was billed as a potential miracle-worker at Dean Court and he almost obliged in his first full term, in which the Cherries missed promotion by a single place.

In July 1963 he took over as boss of fellow Third Division club Watford and, bizarrely, spent much of his first season trying to buy himself, as he was still registered as a player with Bournemouth.

At Vicarage Road he lost no time in revealing the abrasive management style for which he would become famous, as Oliver Phillips wrote in his excellent *Centenary History of Watford FC:* 'Perhaps half-a-dozen players were in dispute over their terms and they were given appointments at five-minute intervals. Less than an hour later, McGarry announced that all would be re-signing. He then lined up the professional staff and walked down the line, staring into the eyes of each individual and giving curt, not always pleasant summaries of their careers. When he came to Charlie Livesey, McGarry goaded the striker, jeering at his descent from "boy wonder" to his request to try out at wing-half in the reserves the previous season. "You used to be a star, Charlie," said McGarry.'

Soon the new boss proved the efficacy of his approach, drawing from Livesey a succession of exceptional performances as the Hornets went agonisingly close to promotion, missing out by two points. He had grabbed the club by the scruff of its metaphorical neck, overrode the board when he deemed it necessary, instilled much-needed pride and made several shrewd signings but still it wasn't quite enough, and he was mightily frustrated.

That summer he sold the best young goalkeeper in the country, Pat Jennings, and there was an air of anti-climax about the place as Watford made a poor start to the new season. But Second Division Ipswich Town recognised McGarry's promise and in October 1964 he moved to Portman Road, where he instituted a typically tough regime.

Engendering rather more respect than affection among many of his new charges, he improved the players' strength and stamina, and cleared out a few veteran survivors of Alf

Ramsey's 1961/62 championship-winning campaign, replacing them cheaply but cannily. A further stroke of inspiration was to buy back centre-forward Ray Crawford, still revered by Ipswich fans for his magnificent performances under Ramsey, and duly the Second Division title was garnered in 1967/68.

The East Anglians laboured during their early months back in the top flight, but McGarry did not stay to lead them to safety, opting instead that November to accept the challenge of restoring the faded fortunes of once-mighty Wolves, who were struggling towards the foot of the First Division.

Painstakingly, and with a strong hand, he rebuilt and transformed that ailing team, which rose to fourth place in the table in 1970/71, then reached the UEFA Cup final the following season, there to be beaten 3-2 on aggregate by Tottenham Hotspur.

At this point McGarry's Wolves were an entertaining bunch, featuring the likes of strikers Derek Dougan and John Richards, winger Dave Wagstaffe, midfielder Mike Bailey and a doughty defence. He kept the majority of the side together for the next two campaigns, reaching a League Cup semi-final in 1972/73, then finally lifting a trophy, the League Cup, with victory over Manchester City in 1973/74. Thereafter, surprisingly, impetus drained away gradually until Wolves were relegated in 1976, after which McGarry resigned.

Still brimming with self-belief despite the setback, he embarked on a 15-month stint coaching the Saudi Arabian national team before taking the managerial seat at bottom-of-the-table Newcastle United in November 1977. He could hardly have been expected to avoid demotion from the top grade, and he didn't, but when major team rebuilding work failed to achieve promotion over the next two terms, he was sacked in August 1980.

After that, McGarry became even more of a wanderer, scouting for Brighton in 1980, coaching Power Dynamo of Zambia in 1981, then taking over that country's national side in 1983 before a coaching interlude in South Africa.

In 1985 an ill-fated return to Wolves, by then wallowing in the Third Division, lasted a mere 61 days, after which he resigned, heavily disillusioned.

Still, though, he loved the game, guiding African side Bophuthatswana in the mid-1990s and settling in South Africa, where he died.

William Harry McGarry: born Stoke-on-Trent, 10 June 1927; played for Port Vale 1945-51, Huddersfield Town 1951-61, Bournemouth 1961-63; capped four times by England 1954-55; managed Bournemouth 1961-63, Watford 1963-64, Ipswich Town 1964-68, Wolverhampton Wanderers 1968-76, Saudi Arabia national team (coach) 1976-77, Newcastle United 1977-80, Wolverhampton Wanderers again 1985; died South Africa, 15 March 2005.

Bedford Jezzard

First as a free-scoring, fearsomely pacy centre-forward and then as a strong-willed, quietly inspirational team boss, Bedford Jezzard was one of the most influential figures in the history of Fulham FC.

During his playing pomp as a high-velocity spearhead in the 1950s, he was a scourge of Second Division defenders and was rewarded with two England caps. Then, having been invalided out of the game by a grievous ankle injury in his late twenties, he moved into the manager's seat at Craven Cottage, guiding the homely west London club into the top flight of English football by decade's end.

In both roles the engagingly unassuming 'Beddy' was immensely popular, and there was no shortage of shrewd observers who believed he had the potential for vast achievement in management. However, that will always remain an untested theory, because he left the game in jarring circumstances as a 37-year-old in 1964, deeply perplexed and feeling betrayed by the Fulham board's agreement to sell star wing-half Alan Mullery without consultation with the man who picked the team.

A practical individual, he didn't relish the seemingly futile task of toiling to improve a club at which financial resources were likely to remain slender. The pub trade beckoned and he heeded its call.

Jezzard grew up in Croxley Green, Hertfordshire, and after excelling as a footballer with the local boys' club he joined Watford as an amateur during the early 1940s, making several appearances for the Hornets' first team in emergency wartime competition.

Towards the end of the conflict he served some 18 months in India with the Essex Regiment, then returned to Croxley Green after demobilisation to become assistant secretary of the Old Merchant Taylors Sports Club.

Having continued to thrive in local football, Jezzard was taken to Craven Cottage by Fulham stalwart Joe Bacuzzi and signed on as an amateur. He was an instant success, being elevated to the senior side and turning professional after only three outings for the reserves. In his first term, playing at inside-left with gleeful exuberance, he helped his new employers win the old Second Division championship.

There followed three seasons of struggle among the elite, operating in a variety of forward positions as Fulham strove desperately to survive against wealthier and more powerful opponents. Though he didn't score heavily during this period, Jezzard acquitted himself manfully but couldn't prevent the Cottagers' relegation as bottom club in 1951/52.

Unwelcome though demotion was, it proved a watershed in the muscular marksman's development. Back in the second grade, he could barely stop scoring, plundering 123 goals over the course of four campaigns – including five at home to Hull on one prodigiously productive afternoon in October 1955 – and setting a new club aggregate record which would stand until surpassed by Johnny Haynes in the late 1960s.

Jezzard was not a subtle operator – indeed, his ball control left much to be desired – and although he was one of the fastest central attackers of his era, such was his physical constitution he was prone to put on weight during any enforced absences from training, so much so that he was nicknamed 'Pud'.

But he was sturdy, direct and unfailingly courageous, invariably revelling in conditions that becalmed daintier talents, charging through glutinous quagmires like a runaway plough. He carried a fulminating shot in either foot, he was fierce and agile in aerial combat, and his capacity for hard graft was endless.

Crucially, too, in his most bountiful years Jezzard was at the centre of a beautifully balanced inside trio, completed by the artistic schemer Haynes and the slightly more prosaic but still gifted Bobby Robson. The three meshed splendidly and Fulham duly prospered, usually finishing above the halfway mark of the Second Division.

As a result of his club exploits, Jezzard was called up for his first full cap in May 1954, though it was a chastening experience for England, who plunged to the worst defeat in their history, 7-1 to Hungary in Budapest. In fairness, it was a daunting match in which to make an international debut, with Walter Winterbottom's side seeking revenge for the 6-3 humbling they had received from 'The Magnificent Magyars' six months earlier at Wembley, only to touch a new nadir.

Jezzard, who also made three appearances each for England 'B' and the Football League, fared rather better in his second and last full outing in his country's colours, when he was involved in setting up all three goals – two for Dennis Wilshaw and one for Tom Finney – in the 3-0 home victory over Northern Ireland in November 1955.

Come the summer of 1956 he remained in the selectors' thoughts, being taken on a Football Association tour of South Africa, but that ended in footballing calamity when he suffered a severe ankle injury, after which he was never to play again.

It was a crushing blow to a performer in his prime, but Jezzard remained positive and, keen to remain in the game, he accepted the post of youth coach at Craven Cottage in August 1957.

To no one's surprise, he proved a natural in the role and, nine months later, his promotion to replace Dugald Livingstone as Fulham boss, with long-serving Craven Cottage administrator Frank Osborne as general manager, was a popular choice.

Jezzard inherited a talented side, but one full of colourful and disparate characters, many of whom were his friends and former team-mates. Some pundits wondered whether his old chums would take liberties, but although they called him Beddy rather than Boss, he handled them brilliantly, continuing to foster the warm camaraderie that was a hallmark of the club.

Thus in Jezzard's first term at the helm, he guided Fulham to promotion to the First Division. They finished only two points behind champions Sheffield Wednesday with an enterprising team featuring the likes of the majestic Haynes, full-back Jim Langley, former England centre-forward turned defender Roy Bentley, bearded inside-forward Jimmy Hill (the future players' union shop steward, successful manager and broadcaster), winger Trevor 'Tosh' Chamberlain and new Scottish international flankman Graham Leggat. There was a mammoth contribution, too, from teenage full-back George Cohen, who would help Alf Ramsey's England to lift the World Cup in 1966, and rookie wing-half Alan Mullery, destined for greater things with Tottenham Hotspur and England, was blooded to telling effect in the spring.

Jezzard's part in the development of this inexperienced pair, while guiding his team to the top level, deserves huge praise. Though he was no fire-and-brimstone motivator, he did not lack passion, and he analysed the game logically and calmly, always making the most of the limited funds at his disposal.

Now, though, came the even harder task of consolidating in the First Division, and in 1959/60 he confounded numerous prophets of doom by leading Fulham to a vastly creditable tenth place in the table.

The four subsequent seasons proved more difficult, with a series of (successful) relegation battles mitigated by a run to the semi-finals of the FA Cup in 1962; a brave and exhilarating campaign was ended in a replay by high-riding Burnley.

All the while Jezzard's easy-going but firm style of man-management continued to earn the respect and affection of his footballers, but with the early-1960s abolition of the players' maximum wage having made life more difficult for medium-sized clubs like Fulham, his job was increasingly demanding.

Eventually, when the cash-strapped board sanctioned the £72,500 sale of the ever-improving Mullery to Spurs in March 1964 without securing the manager's agreement, Jezzard decided that his long-term future lay outside the game.

Still he did not leave immediately, as many men might have, but remained at the Cottage until the end of that year, continuing to do his best for a struggling side and even taking on the duties of general manager from the retiring Osborne for a month or so before departing in December.

After leaving football, Jezzard ran his family pub in Stamford Brook, near Hammersmith, for many years.

Bedford Alfred George Jezzard: born Clerkenwell, London, 19 October 1927; played for Fulham 1948-56; capped twice by England 1954-55; managed Fulham 1958-64; died 21 May 2005.

Tommy Walker

Tommy Walker was an oft-underrated gem during Newcastle United's most recent golden era, the first half of the 1950s, when he featured prominently in two successive FA Cup triumphs.

Though the majority of the Magpies' headlines were garnered by the likes of dashing Tyneside idol Jackie Milburn, Chilean goal-getter George Robledo and extravagantly gifted Scottish flankman Bobby Mitchell, the modest Walker, too, made a telling contribution to an exhilaratingly entertaining team.

A one-time professional sprinter who won handicap races at Powderhall, Edinburgh, he was a direct and penetrative winger whose exceptional pace and selfless industry created countless scoring opportunities for his starry colleagues. Indeed, so searing was his acceleration that pre-match advice from one manager, George Martin, tended to be limited to the pithy instruction: 'Show 'em your backside, Tommy.'

The wiry Walker, dark-haired and gaunt-faced, was at his lung-bursting peak as Newcastle, his local club, defeated Blackpool 2-0 at Wembley in 1951, then returned a year later for a more fortuitous 1-0 victory over Arsenal, who had been reduced to ten men by injury to Walley Barnes.

Against national institution Stanley Matthews and his fellow Seasiders, Walker had been particularly compelling, helping to create one of the most spectacular goals ever witnessed at the famous old stadium. Carrying the ball out of his own half, he motored past two would-be markers before finding tiny schemer Ernie Taylor, whose impudent backheel was hammered into the Blackpool net by Milburn from 25 yards.

Walker was spotted as a schoolboy centre-half in the late 1930s, being recruited by the Magpies from Netherton Juniors in 1941 and impressing in unofficial wartime competition, including a guest stint with West Ham United. By the end of the conflict he had been converted into a winger versatile enough to patrol either touchline and, having returned to St James' Park, he made his senior debut for Second Division Newcastle at home to Coventry City in September 1946.

It was not easy breaking into a side pushing for promotion to the top flight and the newcomer managed only a handful of appearances that season; then his second term – at the end of which United did reach the First Division, as runners-up to Birmingham City – was curtailed by a broken arm suffered in training.

However, in 1948/49 he blossomed as the Geordies surprised many observers by cutting a swathe through the ranks of the elite, topping the table shortly before Christmas and finishing the campaign in a hugely creditable fourth place.

The side was buttressed by doughty defenders such as centre-half Frank Brennan and right-back Bobby Cowell, with whom Walker struck up a productive understanding, and driven by dynamic half-backs Joe Harvey and Charlie Crowe. But the essential appeal of an unforgettable team was a swashbuckling forward line whose names tripped delightedly off the tongues of United fans: Walker, Taylor, Milburn, Robledo and Mitchell.

A key element in their success was the vivid contrast between the hard-running Walker on one flank and the beguilingly intricate Mitchell on the other, though the former's input was not solely related to speed. He was a crisp and powerful striker of the ball, too, and quite a few of his 38 goals in 204 senior outings for the club came from shots propelled from long distance.

Though the Newcastle side of the mid-20th century tends, reasonably enough, to be revered for its FA Cup exploits (in 1955, after Walker had departed, United lifted the trophy for the third time in five years), their League achievements were not negligible, with First Division placings of 5th in 1949/50 and fourth in 1950/51, both high enough to have qualified for European competition in current times.

After that, however, they slipped into mid-table and in February 1954, the 31-year-old Walker was sold by boss Stan Seymour to Second Division Oldham Athletic for £2,500.

He excelled immediately at the lower level, and while he was unable to prevent the Latics slipping into the Third Division North that spring, he became a favourite at Boundary Park. Thus many supporters were aggrieved when he was transferred to Chesterfield for £1,250 in February 1957, having been released by new boss Ted Goodier as part of his team-reconstruction process.

Soon, though, there were second thoughts and the Tynesider returned to Oldham in the following summer, remaining popular there until his retirement in April 1959 to become a newsagent in Middleton, Manchester.

Walker, who later served as a Methodist lay preacher, died in a nursing home after a short illness. He was one of only two survivors of Newcastle's 1951 FA Cup-winning combination, Charlie Crowe being the one member of the team to outlive him.

Thomas Jackson Walker: born Cramlington, Northumberland, 14 November 1923; played for Newcastle United 1941-54, Oldham Athletic 1954-57 and 1957-59, Chesterfield 1957; died Manchester, 13 June 2005.

Noel Cantwell

Noel Cantwell was a cultured footballer, an eloquent, deep-thinking charmer who enjoyed an accomplished 15-year playing career, mostly as a full-back, with the Uniteds of West Ham and Manchester, and captained the Republic of Ireland.

Later he became a bold and imaginative team boss, but ultimately his achievements in management proved a trifle anti-climactic, certainly in view of the enormous expectations his early work had generated, and that begged some nagging questions.

Most pertinently, why didn't Cantwell succeed Sir Matt Busby as guiding light of the Old Trafford club in the late 1960s, as many close observers of the Manchester scene both expected and advocated?

Also, might such an appointment have averted United's demoralising decline of the early 1970s, during which the glorious empire built up by the inspirational Scot stumbled into a lengthy period of painful mediocrity?

The two men, both pillars of integrity and natural leaders, liked and respected each other, they shared an all-consuming love of the game and both cherished a compelling vision of how it should be played.

However, though each of them espoused a fluid, attacking style of play, there was a fundamental chasm between their preferred methods of obtaining it and, probably, that is what precluded Cantwell's succession.

In general terms, the Busby creed encompassed off-the-cuff adventure, whereby a collection of richly talented individuals tore opponents apart through instinctive brilliance, untrammelled by detailed instructions. Meanwhile Cantwell hailed from a more theoretical school, believing passionately in the benefits of careful coaching.

This divide caused confusion from the outset in an otherwise harmonious relationship. Soon after his arrival at Old Trafford, Cantwell told friends that he was dumbfounded by Busby's pre-match talks, which apparently involved little more than wishing the players all the best and telling them to enjoy themselves.

The newcomer had been looking forward to receiving detailed tactical insights from the great man, and was dismayed to discover Busby's credo that if he had to tell his footballers how to play, then he wouldn't have signed them in the first place.

Indeed, later Cantwell was to describe the Busby approach as 'so simple it was frightening', so it was hardly surprising that Sir Matt overlooked the Irishman when recommending to United's board the man to carry on his life's work.

Cantwell made his first footballing impact as a teenager with his home-town club, Cork Athletic, before being recruited to the West Ham cause in 1952 by their manager Ted Fenton, a charismatic Cockney who fired the teenager's imagination.

Meteoric progress rocketed him from the Hammers 'A' team to their Second Division side during his first season at Upton Park and soon he formed an enterprising full-back partnership with John Bond. Neither of them conformed to the old-fashioned image of static, brutally physical defenders, instead becoming involved in build-up play and relishing overlapping runs into attack. Cantwell, in particular, was a versatile performer who could switch to centre-half or centre-forward at need, and he emerged as one of West Ham's key men during the remainder of the decade, skippering the side to the Second Division title in 1957/58, then proving a bulwark as they consolidated in the top flight.

It was during this period that Cantwell became enchanted by coaching, joining the renowned West Ham 'academy' of soccer thinkers, a group which included the likes of Malcolm Allison and Bond (two Manchester City managers of the future), and Frank O'Farrell and Dave Sexton (both destined to boss United).

After training they would adjourn to a cafe near Upton Park to spend countless hours talking football, moving sugar bowls and salt cellars across the table-top to make their tactical points. Meanwhile, too, Cantwell had become an integral part of the Republic of Ireland set-up, making his debut as a centre-half in 1953, then becoming a fixture at left-back and taking over the captaincy in 1957.

In November 1960 Cantwell joined Manchester United, having become Britain's most expensive full-back when he was transferred for £29,500, and charged with the task of providing much-needed stability as Busby strove to rebuild his team, which had been savagely depleted by the Munich air disaster of 1958.

Thanks to a combination of strong character and ample ability, he grew into a hugely influential figure at his new club, which he captained to FA Cup triumph against Leicester City in 1963. That sunny afternoon at Wembley, when Cantwell horrified officials by hurling the famous silver bauble skywards in glee (he caught it safely), United reached the turning point in their reconstruction, putting five years of unrewarded toil behind them and moving once more into the front rank of English footballing powers.

Thereafter the articulate Irishman, who earned widespread plaudits for his efforts as chairman of the Professional Footballers' Association, was a regular throughout most of 1963/64, during which the Red Devils finished as championship runners-up to Liverpool.

But with his movement becoming distinctly ponderous in his early thirties, he was out of the side during the title-winning campaign that followed, bouncing back to offer cover for full-backs Shay Brennan and Tony Dunne and centre-half Bill Foulkes in 1965/66, then receding once more to the periphery and missing out on another championship triumph in 1966/67.

At that point, however, it spoke volumes for his stature at Old Trafford that, although Denis Law skippered the team, Cantwell remained club captain, fuelling speculation that he was being groomed as the club's next boss.

In fact, a move into management was imminent, but instead of assuming United's reins he took over from Jimmy Hill at newly-promoted Coventry City, guiding them resourcefully clear of relegation during their first term in the top division as well as completing a brief part-time stint in charge of the Republic of Ireland. Over the next four years he impressed at Coventry, leading the Sky Blues to sixth place in 1969/70, thus qualifying for the European Fairs Cup (now the UEFA Cup) and bowing out honourably at the hands of mighty Bayern Munich.

There were more relegation scraps but, crucially for City's long-term good, Cantwell launched a successful youth policy, only to be ousted by an impatient chairman in 1972. Thereafter, surprisingly, the only other English club he managed was Peterborough United, in two spells sandwiched by successful coaching appointments in the United States.

During his first sojourn at London Road, he took over a team struggling at the foot of the Fourth Division and led them to promotion as champions some 18 months later in 1974. A decade later, he brought shrewdness and authority to the task of maintaining the Posh in a respectable mid-table berth in the basement flight. Subsequently the sociable Cantwell thrived as the landlord of a Peterborough pub, then returned to football as a scout for the Football Association.

Noel Cantwell: born Cork, Republic of Ireland, 28 December 1932; played for West Ham United 1952-60, Manchester United 1960-67; capped 36 times by Republic of Ireland 1953-67; managed Coventry City 1967-72, Republic of Ireland 1967-68, New England Tea Men 1972 and 1978-82, Peterborough United 1972-77 and 1986-88; died Peterborough, 7 September 2005.

Johnny Haynes

Johnny Haynes elevated the act of passing a football into an art form, and as a result he became Britain's first £100-a-week player in an era when that represented riches almost beyond comprehension.

Yet despite his stature as one of the most sumptuously gifted midfield generals of the 20th century, he spent two trophyless decades and virtually his entire career with unfashionable Fulham, a telling reflection of the sport's commercial transformation since his heyday in the 1950s and 1960s.

An imposing England captain whose international days were curtailed prematurely by injuries suffered in a car crash, Haynes was a charismatic perfectionist whose deliciously imaginative distribution teased defenders to distraction. He was particularly adept at spearing long, penetrative passes through miniscule gaps in opposing rearguards, the weight and angle of these devilish dispatches invariably wrong-footing would-be interceptors, while his short-ball game could be equally devastating.

However, some critics accused the majestic Haynes of overawing lesser talents on his own side, and displays of melodramatic admonition were not unknown. Certainly if a Fulham colleague failed to read his visionary intentions – which happened quite a lot, especially when the Cottagers were mired in the old Second Division – then the maestro might be spotted in attitudes of exaggerated disdain, hands on hips and oozing perplexity.

In fairness, perhaps he was castigating himself for not meeting his own ultra-demanding standards, but that was not an explanation which convinced his many northern detractors, who saw Haynes as a pampered golden boy of the detested south. This view, undoubtedly rooted in jealousy as he was a popular figure with fellow footballers everywhere he went, was massaged by his emergence as 'The Brylcreem Boy' at a time when sportsmen's involvement in advertising was in its infancy.

The son of a Post Office engineer, Haynes was born not many miles from Tottenham Hotspur and grew up supporting nearby Arsenal, yet he opted to enlist with Fulham as a 15-year-old amateur in 1950, believing it would be easier to become established at comparatively humble Craven Cottage than at White Hart Lane or Highbury.

He was small for his age, measuring only 5ft tall on joining the club – once a month he stood with his back to the office safe so that his growth could be marked on the door – but even at that stage it was evident that his ability was immense.

Haynes burst into the wider public consciousness that spring, scintillating for England Schoolboys as they hammered their Scottish counterparts by eight goals to two in a match which, unusually for that time, was televised live.

Despite his extreme youth, there were calls for the diminutive wunderkind to be plunged straight into first-team action, but Fulham handled his development cannily, loaning him out to local non-League sides, including Wimbledon, before calling him up for his senior debut at the age of 18 in the home clash with Southampton on Boxing Day 1952.

Almost immediately Haynes became a fixture in a swashbucklingly entertaining but frustratingly inconsistent Fulham side which maintained mid-table respectability in the Second Division throughout the mid-1950s, the club earning an enviable reputation for its friendly atmosphere but being a ready target for music-hall jibes about under-achievement.

The classy young play-maker, who also contributed his share of goals, was supported ably by the likes of future England boss Bobby Robson, then an inside-forward, prolific marksman Bedford Jezzard, journeyman winger Trevor 'Tosh' Chamberlain and industrious midfielder Jimmy Hill, who would earn renown in 1961 as the leading light of the players' successful battle to outlaw the iniquitous maximum wage, a campaign from which Haynes was the most prominent early beneficiary. Later the free-thinking Hill went on to succeed as a manager with Coventry and as a ubiquitous television broadcaster.

As Haynes began to peak towards the end of the decade, so the status of Fulham, now chaired by comedian Tommy Trinder, improved correspondingly. In 1957/58 they finished fifth in the table and reached the FA Cup semi-finals, where they lost to Manchester United – admittedly still reeling from the depredations of the recent Munich air disaster – only after two pulsating contests.

Next, strengthened by the arrival of dashing Scottish flankman Graham Leggat from Aberdeen, the following term Fulham won promotion to the top flight as runners-up to Sheffield Wednesday, then consolidated briefly among the elite before sliding to the unwelcome status of perennial strugglers against relegation.

Their fortunes were linked inexorably to those of Haynes, who had made his full international entrance while still a teenager, against Northern Ireland in 1954, and since become a star at that level.

An ever-present in the England side which failed narrowly to reach the 1958 World Cup quarter-finals in Sweden, he scored a hat-trick against the USSR later that year and in 1960 he succeeded Ronnie Clayton as captain of his country, an honour he would retain for 22 consecutive games.

Now he became the creative fulcrum of a free-scoring attack which featured goal-poacher supreme Jimmy Greaves and spearhead Bobby Smith, with Bobby Charlton and Bryan Douglas on the wings. During one undefeated six-game period of 1960/61, Walter Winterbottom's exhilarating side totalled 40 goals while conceding only eight, the highlight being the 9-3 annihilation of Scotland, to which the skipper contributed two strikes. That afternoon in the Wembley sunshine marked the pinnacle of Haynes' achievement as he was chaired off amid scenes of ecstatic triumph worthy of any cup final, feted royally for an inspirational display which appeared to cement his eminence for the foreseeable future. Soon his status was underlined by a massive bid for his services from Internazionale of Milan but Fulham, now free of maximum-wage strictures, announced their mould-breaking pay award and spurned the offer.

Still only 26, Haynes appeared to be on the threshold of unlimited achievement, but gradually the script began to go awry. During the 1962 World Cup finals in Chile he made little impact against well-organised defences, particularly those of Hungary and Brazil, who marked him tightly and stifled his effectiveness.

Then, in the following August, he was seriously injured in a road accident at Blackpool and barely played for the remainder of that season. He recovered fitness but found himself surplus to the requirements of new England boss Alf Ramsey, who studiously ignored a concerted 'Bring Back Johnny' campaign. Thus Haynes never added to his 56 caps, losing the captaincy to Bobby Moore and his schemer's role to Bobby Charlton, and missed out on World Cup glory in 1966.

Back on the club scene he remained in demand, however, and Tottenham Hotspur bid a then-record £90,000 to sign him in 1964 after their subtly magnificent Scottish schemer John White met his death through a bolt of lightning on a golf course.

Though the move to Bill Nicholson's wealthy Spurs, one of the top sides in the land, would have offered a likelihood of garnering some medals in the twilight of his career, instead he remained as the biggest fish in the comparatively tiny Fulham pool, where there were never sufficient funds to radically improve the team and promising performers such as Alan Mullery had to be sold to balance the books.

Duly Haynes found himself immersed in successive demotion dogfights and after several narrow escapes he returned to the Second Division as Fulham finished bottom in 1967/68, then plummeted unthinkably into the Third a season later as manager Bill Dodgin junior failed to arrest their headlong slide.

Accordingly one of the first superstars of modern times, a man who could transform a game with a fleeting moment of artistry, completed his final English term in the lower reaches of the Football League.

In 1970, having scored 157 times in 657 senior appearances for the Cottagers, 35-year-old Haynes joined the South African club, Durban City, for whom he played one season and, ironically, earned his first and only honour in club football by helping them to become champions.

An intelligent fellow, and demonstrably a loyal one, he never aspired to football management, maybe seeking to avoid the almost inevitable trauma such work entails, though he did tide his beloved Fulham over one crisis, spending 18 days as player-boss following the sacking of Bobby Robson in 1968.

After laying aside his boots in 1970, he left the game he had graced so nobly, and with his wife Avril ran a dry-cleaning business in Edinburgh.

John Norman Haynes: born Kentish Town, London, 17 October 1934; played for Fulham 1950-70; Durban City 1970; capped 56 times for England 1954-62; died Edinburgh, 18 October 2005.

George Swindin

As one of the most composed and reliable goalkeepers of his era, George Swindin helped Arsenal to lift three League championships and the FA Cup, and that despite losing six years of his prime to the Second World War.

But when he returned to Highbury as manager, a favourite son entrusted with the task of leading the becalmed north Londoners out of a period of dismal mediocrity, the blunt, undemonstrative Yorkshireman failed to meet the challenge, and he left the club in tears.

At that point, Swindin – an often painfully honest, immensely dedicated individual who upset certain of his charges with his acerbic, some would say tactless, manner – was sorely disillusioned, but it would be poignantly unjust if his managerial travail was allowed to obscure his consistent high achievement as guardian of the Gunners' net in nearly 300 senior games.

That he never played for his country was due principally to being a contemporary of Frank Swift, one of the most majestic of all custodians, though twice during 1947/48 he occupied the England bench as first reserve, and arguably was unfortunate to fall behind the likes of Bert Williams, Gil Merrick and Ted Ditchburn in the struggle to succeed the Manchester City hero.

Swindin was not tall for a keeper and, unlike the extrovert Swift, there was not the merest hint of flamboyance about his game. But he was fearless and agile, a safe handler and intelligent anticipator of crosses, the type who radiated an aura of security which instilled confidence in his defenders.

As a boy he rose through the local footballing ranks of Rotherham YMCA and New Stubbin Colliery, then served Rotherham United as an amateur before turning professional with Bradford City. He made his Second Division debut as a 20-year-old in a 3-0 home victory over Port Vale on Boxing Day 1934, and although he never became an automatic choice for the Bantams, his potential attracted a £4,000 bid from Arsenal, which was accepted in April 1936.

During the 1930s the Gunners side built by Herbert Chapman, then taken on by George Allison, was the dominant footballing power in the land and some youngsters who joined the multiple trophy-winners were daunted by the challenge. Certainly Swindin seemed hesitant at first, maybe lacking self-belief at that early stage, but his essential strength of character stood him in admirable stead and he prevailed.

A career-ending injury to the splendid Frank Moss had created a vacancy between the Arsenal posts and, after tasting senior action during 1936/37, Swindin gradually rose above fellow hopefuls Alex Wilson and Frank Boulton to become the club's long-term net-minder.

Having languished behind his rivals for much of 1937/38, he produced a succession of commanding performances in the spring as a memorable team including free-scoring marksmen Ted Drake and Cliff Bastin, defensive bulwarks George Male and Eddie Hapgood and fearsomely combative wing-half Wilf Copping pipped Wolverhampton Wanderers to lift the League title.

Swindin's momentum was jolted by the Second World War, during which he served as an Army PT instructor in Germany, but after the conflict he became firmly established as first choice at Highbury, excelling as an ever-present during the 1947/48 championship triumph, conceding only 32 goals, a League record at the time.

Two years later he was characteristically solid as Arsenal beat Liverpool in the FA Cup final, then suffered injury and shared goalkeeping duties with Ted Platt in 1950/51 before returning to his dominant best in 1951/52. That term climaxed with a valiant Wembley rearguard action in which he was prominent as the north Londoners, reduced to ten men for most of the match following a serious injury to full-back Walley Barnes, lost the FA Cup final to Newcastle United.

By now, though, there was a rising new goalkeeping star in the Highbury camp, and while the ageing Swindin enjoyed just enough outings to secure a medal as Arsenal took the title again in 1952/53, future custody of the team's net would be in the safe hands of brilliant young Welshman Jack Kelsey.

Duly the veteran bowed out during the next term – sadly he conceded seven goals in his final appearance, against Sunderland at Roker Park – and in February 1954 he was freed to join non-League Peterborough United as player-manager.

Swindin took to his new responsibilities with alacrity, leading the Posh to three Midland League championships in the space of four seasons as they built impetus which culminated in admission to the Football League in 1960.

By then, however, Swindin was back at Highbury, having turned down offers from several other clubs in favour of becoming Arsenal boss in the summer of 1958.

He took over a mundane side for which the road to resurrection looked long and hard, but he wrought wholesale changes in his playing staff – including the recruitment of dynamic Scottish wing-half Tommy Docherty – and by February the Gunners were topping the First Division table.

Though they had slipped to third place by season's end, still there were grounds for heady optimism, but there followed three years of frustrating ordinariness leading to his resignation and replacement by former Wolves and England hero Billy Wright in 1962.

Swindin had been unlucky with serial injuries to key players, notably the expensive Mel Charles, which laid him open to charges of constant team-changing, and his side suffered hugely by comparison to the great Tottenham Hotspur combination of that era. Clearly, having to watch the local antagonists lift the League and FA Cup double in 1960/61 did not engender patience among Highbury regulars.

Also Swindin was panned savagely for perceived mistakes such as the failure to sign Denis Law from Huddersfield Town and the sale of free-scoring David Herd to Manchester United. On the credit side he did enlist the gifted play-maker George Eastham from Newcastle, after a lengthy saga during which Eastham emerged as a successful freedom fighter for footballers' rights, but that was not to prove enough.

He had worked prodigiously in the Arsenal cause, and he cared passionately – his sorrow on the day of his departure was deeply moving – but when he could not procure success for employers who craved it urgently, the upshot was inevitable.

There followed a few months in charge of Norwich City before he accepted a more tempting offer from fellow Second Division club Cardiff City, newly demoted from the top flight, in October 1962. His 18-month sojourn at Ninian Park proved a turbulent one, with seemingly endless comings and goings by players, more chronic luck with injuries and several disagreements with the board, such as one over the signing of the fading maestro John Charles from Roma against his advice.

However, he blooded a crop of promising youngsters and, immediately after his sacking in April 1964 – having guided the Bluebirds clear of relegation – Cardiff won the Welsh Cup, enabling them to enter European competition for the first time.

Swindin was bitterly disappointed by his treatment, but he remained in love with football, going on to manage non-League clubs Kettering Town and Corby Town. Also he ran a garage business and general store in Corby, later moving to Spain before returning to live in Northamptonshire.

George Hedley Swindin: born Campsall, near Doncaster, Yorkshire, 4 December 1914; played for Bradford City 1933-36, Arsenal 1936-54; managed Arsenal 1958-62, Norwich City 1952, Cardiff City 1962-64; died Kettering, Northamptonshire, 26 October 2005.

Ted Ditchburn

For a generation and beyond, Ted Ditchburn was the yardstick by which all Tottenham Hotspur goalkeepers were judged. Even now, more than half a century on from his pomp, there are shrewd monitors of the White Hart Lane scene who maintain unswervingly that he remains the most accomplished custodian in the history of a club whose net-minders have included the revered Irishman Pat Jennings and 2005 England incumbent Paul Robinson. Though never flamboyant in the style of his extrovert contemporary, the Manchester City veteran Frank Swift, Ditchburn was tall and imposing, muscular and utterly fearless, his very presence engendering a feeling of security among defenders and supporters alike.

For more than a decade after the war, he reigned majestically between the Tottenham posts, making a colossal contribution to Tottenham's lifting of the Second and First Division championships in successive campaigns, 1949/50 and 1950/51.

Although called up six times by his country, he never made a major impact on the international stage, being overshadowed by the popular Swift and, more surprisingly, by the likes of Wolverhampton Wanderers' Bert Williams and Gil Merrick of Birmingham City. Somehow he never seemed quite so bold or confident for England, for whom he earned his first cap in 1948 and bowed out eight years later.

The son of a professional boxer, Ditchburn followed his father into the ring and during the mid-1930s he raised money for an early pair of football boots through a series of bouts at Rochester Casino. At that point there were influential voices in the local fight fraternity urging him to make a career out of pugilism, but his heart was set on soccer and, after working in a paper mill, he joined the Tottenham groundstaff in 1937.

After toiling single-mindedly to hone his craft during a stint on loan at non-League Northfleet, he returned to White Hart Lane to sign professional forms in 1939, only for his encouraging momentum to be jolted by the outbreak of war.

Service in the RAF afforded plenty of opportunities for football, however, and the big Kentishman represented Spurs in the Football League South, an emergency competition which ran during the conflict and which he helped them to win in 1943/44.

In addition he guested for Aberdeen, Birmingham City and Dartford, and also excelled consistently for the RAF team, being rewarded by selection for two unofficial wartime internationals, against Scotland and Wales, in both of which he performed superbly. However, just as he was becoming established at that level he was posted to the Far East, and others prospered in his absence.

When peace resumed, though, there was no questioning his pre-eminence back at Tottenham, where he made his senior debut in a Second Division encounter with Birmingham in August 1946. Once in the team, as a succession of reserve keepers discovered to their frustration, Ditchburn was damnably difficult to dislodge. He missed only two League games over the next seven seasons, including an unbroken spell of appearances between April 1948 and March 1954. Until eventually overhauled by Jennings, and then Steve Perryman, he held the club record for senior outings (453), an achievement rendered doubly remarkable by the fact that the war had cost him seven years of action.

Ditchburn's longevity owed plenty to superlative athleticism and strength, towards which he strove constantly and with an almost obsessive attention to detail. He was renowned for daring plunges at the feet of lone marauders; indeed, no goalkeeper of his era was more adept at winning one-on-one confrontations with attackers. This knack was due in part to sharp reflexes and a raw courage which verged on foolhardiness, but also was a result of a rigorous training routine which he devised, in which he dived, saved, threw the ball out, then dived again, continuing the sequence over and over again until he was exhausted.

Generally assured when plucking crosses from the air and a fierce concentrator whom it was difficult to drag out of position, he was fiery and aggressive, too, ready and willing to withstand fearsome physical challenges from the bustling spearheads of the day.

His kicking was a slight weakness, but there was ample compensation in his close understanding with full-back Alf Ramsey – the diffident future knight destined to lead England to World Cup glory in 1966 – which involved the goalkeeper launching swift attacks with instant throw-outs. When the thoughtful Ramsey spoke of this then-rare manoeuvre as a tactical advance, the irreverent Ditchburn would grin and maintain that he'd started doing it merely because his kicks were so poor.

Whatever its origin, the strategy was perfect for the fluid push-and-run style with which Spurs won their two consecutive titles – of Second and First Division – under enterprising manager Arthur Rowe. There was no other silverware, but there were several near-misses, with Tottenham finishing as championship runners-up in 1952 and 1957 and suffering two FA Cup semi-final defeats, both to Stanley Matthews' Blackpool, in 1948 and 1953.

Throughout that prolonged quest for honours, Ditchburn was a tower of rock-like stability, though arguably his most memorable display came in less rarefied circumstances, during a Second Division defeat at Newcastle in January 1947. Three days after suffering concussion and severe bruising to his hip, he stood defiant as shots rained in on his goal, no sooner making one stupendous save than another was necessary. In the end he was beaten only once, by Len Shackleton, and at the final whistle some 62,000 Geordies treated the limping hero to one of the most moving ovations ever accorded to a visitor at St James' Park.

Ditchburn's unbending attitude on the pitch was underpinned by a forthright character, which occasionally upset those who were shy of home-truths, but many of his team-mates had cause to be grateful for his willingness to confront authority, and often he was asked to state the players' case in discussions with management.

By the late 1950s, with the team lacking consistency and Ditchburn in his advanced thirties, he began to lose his place periodically, sharing first-team duties with Ron Reynolds, but he was never heard to complain, always buckling down to fight for the goalkeeping jersey that had been his private preserve for so long.

When his top-flight tenure was ended by a broken finger sustained at Chelsea in August 1958, he was the last member of the 1951 championship side still playing, and his place in White Hart Lane folklore was inviolate.

In the following spring he moved to non-League Romford, where he spent six years, including a spell as player-boss, before leaving in April 1965. By now in his middle forties, Ditchburn still yearned to play and he turned out for Brentwood Town while building up a successful sports' outfitters business, and also becoming involved in an office equipment venture. During his retirement he lived at Wickham Market in Suffolk.

Edwin George Ditchburn: born Gillingham, Kent, 24 October 1921; played for Tottenham Hotspur 1937-59; won six caps for England 1948-56; died 26 December 2005.

Ron Greenwood

'I wanted to see pleasure on the pitch and pleasure on the terraces . . . football is a battle of wits or nothing at all.' The words are those of Ron Greenwood and they sum up, with characteristic simplicity, the sporting creed of one of the most imaginative, idealistic and downright decent men to have made their living as a manager in English soccer since the war.

True, he lacked the ruthlessness of more feted contemporaries with whom his success-rate in terms of winning trophies did not compare. But his West Ham United team of the mid-1960s had their own moments of heady triumph and, crucially, were invariably easy on the eye even in defeat. Later, when he guided the fortunes of the England national side, Greenwood remained faithful to his belief that footballers must set out to create rather than to destroy. It must be admitted, however, that results were largely disappointing in view of the outstanding players – the likes of Kevin Keegan, Trevor Brooking, Glenn Hoddle and Bryan Robson – he had at his disposal.

The son of a painter and decorator, Greenwood was born in the Lancashire village of Worsthorne, becoming an adoptive Londoner at the age of ten when his family moved south. After school he became a signwriter, often working at Wembley stadium, where he was to experience joyous fulfilment in the years ahead.

After impressing as a schoolboy footballer, he joined Chelsea as a teenage centre-half, making his debut in 1940 in the wartime league. There followed intermittent appearances during the conflict, sandwiched between service with the RAF mobile radio unit in France.

However, on the resumption of peace he could not win a regular place at Stamford Bridge and, with his wife and young daughter having evacuated to Yorkshire during the bombing of London, he was happy to sign for Bradford Park Avenue.

Greenwood, who cost the Second Division club £3,500, became skipper and starred in a rousing FA Cup victory over League champions-elect Arsenal in 1948. A year later he returned to the capital but remained in the second flight, a £9,000 fee taking him to Brentford, with whom he reached his playing peak.

A cool, constructive defender and a natural leader of men, the thoughtful Lancastrian became skipper at Griffin Park, too, and in 1952 won an England 'B' cap against Holland in Amsterdam. It was to be the only time he represented his country as a player, though his yen for the international scene was destined to he gratified in a different way. Greenwood's splendid form for the Bees precipitated a £16,000 move back to Chelsea in October 1952, and in 1954/55 he helped the Pensioners lift the League championship, playing for half the season and qualifying for a medal before switching to Fulham in the February.

By now he was 33 and captivated by coaching. He had fallen under the spell of England chief Walter Winterbottom and already he had instructed several teams, including Oxford University and Walthamstow Avenue. Both men were profoundly influenced by the magnificent Hungarian side of that era, being enchanted by their deceptively simple short-passing game, and before long Greenwood would be working under his mentor.

As he was past his best as a footballer, it seemed that Greenwood's next natural step would be into management. There was a suggestion that he might take over at Fulham but that came to nothing and in 1956 he became boss of non-League Eastbourne United, as well as assuming responsibility for the England youth side.

A return to the soccer mainstream was only a matter of time, and it came in December 1957 as coach of Arsenal, a job he was to combine with the supervision of the England under-23 team. Greenwood proved a stimulating influence on a Gunners side undergoing radical reconstruction and he was considered for the manager's chair when Jack Crayston left in 1958. However, he was judged too inexperienced and the job went to George Swindin, a man who held a less scientific soccer philosophy than the young coach. Gradually it became apparent that the two could not work together and in April 1961 Greenwood accepted an invitation to manage First Division rivals West Ham United.

Now began the most productive phase of his career. Immediately he felt rapport with this most wholesome of clubs, which had a close-knit family atmosphere, a comforting bedrock of east London support and a playing staff oozing with potential, much of which had yet to be realised. It was the perfect setting for a man of Greenwood's ability and outlook, and he set about moulding the Hammers into a formidable, if somewhat inconsistent force. That entailed a little shrewd dealing on the transfer market but, more importantly, making the most of the talent already at his disposal.

He did so to sensational effect, converting Geoff Hurst from stodgy wing-half to prolific goal-scorer, moving Bobby Moore from wing-half to central defence and bringing the best out of the young and versatile Martin Peters. Those three, plus creative centre-forward Johnny Byrne, formed the basis of the side which won the FA Cup in 1964 (Peters was missing from that particular triumph) and the European Cup Winners' Cup in 1965. Then there was the little matter of the trio's conclusive contribution to England's World Cup victory in 1966, in which their perfection of Greenwood's refined near-post cross ploy proved so devastating.

The FA Cup win over Preston North End was exhilarating enough, but it was the European conquest of Munich 1860 which thrilled their manager the most. That night at Wembley his Hammers were irresistible, sophisticated, mature, expressing themselves expansively against top-class continental opposition.

Thereafter, though Greenwood's creation remained attractive, there was less to cheer. There were runs to the Cup Winners' Cup semi-final and the League Cup final in 1966, but lean years followed and many fans were upset by the sale of Peters to Spurs – a deal which saw an ageing Jimmy Greaves join West Ham. There was some erosion of the old West Ham ethos, too, with Greenwood suspending Moore, Greaves and two others for nightclubbing on the eve of a cup defeat. Sadly, his relationship with the England skipper was to be strained for the rest of their association.

However, Greenwood remained in charge until the spring of 1974 when, relegation having been avoided only narrowly, he moved 'upstairs' to become general manager, allowing his protege John Lyall to take over team affairs and bring further success to Upton Park.

For three and a half years Greenwood occupied his executive role, becoming increasingly glum at his non-involvement in day-to-day football, when he was rescued by the controversial resignation of England manager Don Revie. The former Leeds man had left his country in dire straits, facing almost certain elimination from the World Cup, and the Football Association needed a caretaker at short notice. Greenwood, with his pedigree, was ideal and he did so well during a trial three-match period – including a stirring win over Italy – that he was given the job on a permanent basis.

When 1978 World Cup qualification became mathematically impossible, Greenwood faced up to the challenge of the 1980 European Championships, for which England were among the favourites. But an injury to star forward Trevor Francis upset team balance and they disappointed hugely in a desperately dull tournament, failing to win any of their three matches.

Greenwood was criticised roundly for not building his team around the exquisitely gifted schemer Glenn Hoddle, but the manager had doubts about the Tottenham man's overall contribution and refused to be browbeaten by public opinion.

Accordingly, he embarked on the qualifying campaign for the 1982 World Cup without the popular play-maker and when results went awry he encountered an avalanche of criticism. So unprepared was he for such hysteria that, after a particularly miserable defeat in Switzerland, he decided to resign. However, in a moving testimony to the respect and warmth in which he was held by his players, they persuaded him to change his mind on the homeward journey.

There followed the finest England performance of Greenwood's reign, a victory in Hungary, and eventually a place in the final tournament was secured. However, despite not losing a match, England were eliminated at the quarter-final stage following frustrating draws with Spain and West Germany.

By then aged 60, Greenwood elected to stand down, having done an honourable and competent job without ever capturing the imagination of the public. Part of that problem stemmed from his getting the job ahead of the 'people's choice', Brian Clough, a circumstance that was dredged up repeatedly in moments of adversity.

Overall, though, Greenwood had been a strong and positive influence on English football throughout his days as a coach and manager. An impeccable sportsman, he deplored the greed and hostility, the cynicism and win-at-all-costs attitude which had become increasingly pervasive. He was a deep thinker and skilled communicator who painted pictures with words on the training ground, believing simplicity was beauty and building his teams from that standpoint. He was no shouter of odds, no conventional hard man, treating players as adults and expecting them to impose their own self-discipline. Yet there was steel in his make-up, too, as Moore and company found when they flouted his authority.

Ron Greenwood was a noble servant to football: with more men like him, the game would be much the richer.

Ronald Greenwood: born Worsthorne, Lancashire, 11 November 1921; played for Chelsea 1940-45, Bradford Park Avenue 1945-49, Brentford 1949-52, Chelsea 1952-55, Fulham 1955, Walthamstow Avenue (non-League) 1955-57; managed Eastbourne United (non-League) 1957, Arsenal (assistant) 1958-61, West Ham United 1961-74 (general manager 1974-77), England 1977-82; CBE 1981; died Sudbury, Suffolk, 8 February 2006.

Charlie Wayman

Charlie Wayman was an ebullient, bouncily inventive, prodigiously prolific centre-forward, a pint-sized predator who topped the scoring charts for a succession of major football clubs in the decade immediately after the Second World War.

Many knowledgeable observers of the contemporary scene deemed the affable north-easterner a world-class finisher, and it was an outrage to them that he didn't win a single England cap.

The most obvious explanation for the omission was that Wayman was in competition for his country's number-nine shirt with the stellar likes of Tommy Lawton, Nat Lofthouse and Roy Bentley. A more contentious theory was that he couldn't find favour with members of the selection committee with which team coach Walter Winterbottom was required to work – a group often derided by professionals for its collective lack of knowledge about the game – because they believed that, at 5ft 6in, he was too short for the international arena.

Such a stance was risible, as anyone would testify who had witnessed the quicksilver left-footer making buffoons out of towering defenders and rattling in the goals, 255 of them in 382 League appearances, season after season for Newcastle United, Southampton, Preston North End, Middlesbrough and, at the tag end of his career, humble Darlington. Intelligent team-mates did not play the ball to Wayman in the air. They would deliver it to his feet, or into space behind his markers, a territory of uncertainty in which he was lethal.

Endowed with exquisite mastery over a moving ball, he loved to demonstrate a trademark trick, which involved flicking the leather over the head of a bemused opponent, nipping round the other side and catching it on his instep before clouting an invariably ferocious shot towards goal. It wasn't that he was flamboyant – in fact, for all his pugnacious manner on the pitch he was an engagingly unassuming individual – but it was a crowd-pleasing manoeuvre that the brave, elusive little marksman simply couldn't resist.

Like most of his schoolfriends, Wayman started his working life in the local coalfield, but after excelling in the Chilton Colliery football team, then moving up to non-League Spennymoor United, he asked Newcastle United for a trial, which earned him a contract in 1941.

During the war he served as an able seaman in the Royal Navy before returning to essential work in the mines, but still found time to further his football development, scoring 35 goals in 71 games for the Magpies in unofficial emergency competitions as well as guesting briefly for Portsmouth.

When peace resumed, Wayman was Second Division Newcastle's first-choice inside-left, making his senior entrance in a home FA Cup encounter with Barnsley in January 1946, then becoming leader of the attack in the following autumn.

His first game at centre-forward, against Newport County at St James' Park, was to prove eventful. After missing a penalty in the first minute, he netted four times, then contributed significantly to a double hat-trick for debutant Len Shackleton as the hapless visitors were thrashed 13-0, a Football League record. That season the 24-year-old scored 34 goals in 46 outings as the spearhead of an extravagantly entertaining forward line which also contained star inside-forwards Shackleton and Roy Bentley, and high-quality wingers Jackie Milburn and Tommy Pearson.

But the term was soured, not only by United's narrow failure to gain promotion but also by what appeared to Wayman to be a mild disagreement with trainer Norman Smith on the eve of an FA Cup semi-final against Charlton Athletic. However, the club took a dim view of perceived insubordination, the leading scorer was controversially dropped for the match and the Magpies were drubbed 4-0.

It was a time of turbulence at the club, when other players were threatening strike action over a housing dispute, so Wayman might have been a victim of circumstance. Whatever the truth, which never came out publicly, his relationship with his employers never recovered and in October 1947 he was sold to Southampton, also of Division Two, for a club record fee of £10,000.

It was a transfer which upset many supporters, but which facilitated the subsequent relocation of Milburn from outside-right to centre-forward, a position in which he blossomed luxuriantly as the Magpies lifted the FA Cup three times in the early 1950s.

On the south coast, where he had been promised 'a strawberries-and-cream lifestyle', a vivid contrast to his gritty north-eastern upbringing, Wayman was seen as the catalyst for the future success of a rapidly improving side which included full-back Alf Ramsey, destined to lead England to World Cup ecstasy in 1966, and dynamic inside-forward Ted Bates. Almost instantly he became a folk hero at The Dell, his reputation massaged by a five-goal spree at home to Leicester City in October 1948, but there was serial frustration in three successive near-misses in the promotion race.

Having seen the Saints pipped by goal average (the absurdly complicated precursor to goal difference) in 1949/50, and with his family not settling contentedly despite the ample supplies of soft fruit, Wayman hankered for a move back to the north. Thus in September 1950 he was transferred to Preston North End in exchange for £10,000 and fellow striker Eddy Brown, and quickly became established as a Deepdale favourite.

Meshing fluently with the brilliant Tom Finney, practically a one-man forward line in himself, Wayman delivered an avalanche of goals, 27 in 34 matches, as the Lilywhites romped to the Second Division title in his first season on Ribbleside.

Thereafter he continued to provide a fearsome cutting edge as Preston consolidated their place among the elite by finishing seventh in 1951/52, then ending 1952/53 as championship runners-up to Arsenal, Wayman again suffering goal-average agony.

There was yet another close encounter with glory at the climax of the 1953/54 campaign when North End were beaten in the FA Cup final by West Bromwich Albion. Wayman had found the net in every round on the way to Wembley, and did so again beneath the twin towers, albeit from a position which looked suspiciously offside when he latched on to a raking through-pass from Tommy Docherty to give his side a 2-1 advantage. However, the Baggies proved resilient, fighting back to triumph 3-2.

Not surprisingly, there was uproar in the town during the following autumn when Wayman, the top scorer in each of his four terms at Deepdale and with six goals in his six games to date in the latest campaign, was dispatched to Middlesbrough for £8,000.

Manager Frank Hill's rationale was that, at 33, the centre-forward's best days were behind him, but he continued to hit the target regularly on Teesside, his goals hugely instrumental in the Second Division club attaining two years of mid-table safety.

In December 1956, having slowed appreciably, Wayman accepted his final move, to Darlington of the Third Division North, whom he served conscientiously – he had always been dedicated to physical fitness – until a knee injury prompted his departure from the professional game in April 1958.

Later he coached briefly at non-League Evenwood Town, and worked as a representative for Scottish and Newcastle Breweries before retiring to live in his native north-east. Wayman, whose younger brother Frank played fleetingly for Chester and Darlington, was a warm and lively character, beloved of supporters for his ear-to-ear grin as well as his goals.

Charles Wayman: born Bishop Auckland, County Durham, 16 May 1922; played for Newcastle United 1941-47, Southampton 1947-50, Preston North End 1950-54, Middlesbrough 1954-56, Darlington 1956-58; died County Durham, 26 February 2006.

Ferenc Bene

Who were the stars of the 1966 World Cup, the tournament which bathed English football in perpetual glory and from which Pele, the peerless Brazilian, limped piteously, having been hounded with systematic brutality by unscrupulous opponents?

Certainly there were the host nation's golden Bobbys, Charlton and Moore; the stately young West German, Franz Beckenbauer; and the pulsatingly athletic 'Black Panther', otherwise known as Eusebio of Portugal. All wondrous entertainers, all rewarded with icon status the planet over, but others scintillated, too, during those three memorable weeks in July, notably two swashbuckling but vividly contrasting Hungarians who illuminated arguably the most attractive team on show.

The more charismatic of the pair was Florian Albert, the elegant, deep-lying centre-forward who could dictate the rhythm of any game with his vision and subtlety, but who was also prone to periods of moody lassitude on the fringe of the action.

More rooted in the practical business of striving to win every contest he graced was the thrillingly penetrative Ferenc Bene, who operated mainly on the right attacking flank of that lovely free-flowing side, which also included the sharp-shooting Janos Farkas and the perceptive midfielder Istvan Nagy.

Bene offered a compelling mixture of thrustful pace and nimble balance, deft skills and sensible composure in front of goal. Where Albert, three years his senior, tended towards the languidly artistic, Bene was ceaselessly dynamic, a dasher brimming with vitality, and they complemented each other beautifully.

For his principal club, Ujpest Dozsa, the younger man was deployed regularly as a central striker, but was forced to the wing for his country by the presence of Albert.

Having made a startling impact as a teenager with the powerful Budapest side, with whom he would embark eventually on a succession of rousing European campaigns, Bene was first called to his country's colours at the age of 17, to face Yugoslavia in October 1962.

But it was not until 1964 that he catapulted to widespread international attention, helping the Magyars to take the bronze medal at the European Championships in Spain, then leading them to gold at the Tokyo Olympics, top-scoring with 12 goals, including one in the 2-1 victory over Czechoslovakia in the final.

Thus it was as a footballer of burgeoning status that the 21-year-old Bene arrived in England to contest the Jules Rimet Trophy in 1966, and he did not disappoint, finding the net in all of Hungary's four games.

After firing an equaliser and looking generally menacing in the opening defeat by Portugal, he shone in what many discerning judges declared to be the match of the tournament, a stirring 3-1 triumph over the holders, Brazil.

Only three minutes into the action at Goodison Park, Bene dribbled at speed past several challenges before gulling the goalkeeper, Gylmar, with a clever near-post finish. The reigning champions equalised, but midway through the second period Albert and Bene combined in a slickly inventive manoeuvre to create a spectacular goal for Farkas.

Now the Hungarians were rampant, truly reminiscent of their predecessors, the gloriously fluid 'Magnificent Magyars' of the 1950s, who had twice humiliated England and changed the perception of all thinking men of the way that football might be played.

Bene was fouled in the box, Kalman Meszoly converted from the spot, and the Goodison crowd rose in unison to this enchanting side, installing them as their favourites should England fall by the wayside.

The Ujpest Dozsa marksman sparkled, and scored again, as Bulgaria were beaten in the final group match, and also he netted in the quarter-final against the USSR. But the Soviet battalions proved too tough for the skilful but less abrasive Hungarians, who yielded 2-1.

Bene's country was never so strong again, but he continued to excel at club level, taking a prominent role as Ujpest piled up the domestic prizes. Altogether he pocketed medals for eight League championships and three national cup triumphs, headed the league's scoring charts five times and totalled 341 strikes in 487 competitive outings for the Lilac-and-Whites.

His international days continued until 1979, when he earned his 76th and final cap for Hungary, for whom he had notched 36 goals.

By then the balding attacker, who had been voted his homeland's footballer of the year in 1969 and is in the all-time top ten for both appearances and goals in the NB1 (first division), was beginning to wind down his playing days with more modest clubs. Later he coached his beloved Dozsa and helped with the preparation of Hungary's under-21 team.

Ferenc Bene: born Hungary 17 December 1944; played for Kaposzvar, Ujpest Dozsa 1961-78, Volan 1978-79 and 1983-84, Sepsi of Finland 1981-82, Soroksari 1984, Kecskemeti 1985; capped 76 times by Hungary 1962-79; died Budapest, Hungary, 27 February 2005.

Roy Clarke

For a decade in the middle of the 20th century, Roy Clarke offered everything that might be expected of a winger in the top flight of English football. Manchester City's wiry Welsh international flier was a dashing entertainer, both pacy and tricky; he packed a venomous left-foot shot and he refused to be intimidated by the violent attentions of hulking defenders whose delight it was to deposit slim flankmen such as he over the touchline and into the (mostly) cloth-capped crowd.

Clarke, who turned in a brightly inventive Wembley display against polished England right-back Jeff Hall as the Mancunians beat Birmingham City in the 1956 FA Cup final, also excelled for his country throughout the first half of the 1950s, until he was supplanted by Cliff Jones, a world-class performer ten years his junior.

A natural all-round sportsman, Clarke excelled at swimming and rugby as a boy, though the oval-ball code lost some of its attraction when his front teeth were kicked out at the age of 11. He experienced an early taste of international competition with the Welsh schools baseball team, but it was at football that he shone most persistently.

After leaving school he worked in coal mines during the war, but found time to play for the Newport amateur side Albion Rovers, then was spotted by Cardiff City, who signed him in December 1942.

Clarke's game developed rapidly at Ninian Park and he played for Wales against Northern Ireland in an unofficial Victory international in 1946, then starred as the Bluebirds romped to the Third Division South title in the first post-conflict League campaign.

By then his penetrative talent was being sought by several leading clubs, and in April 1947 the shy 21-year-old was sold to Manchester City for £12,000. Soon he claimed the unusual, probably unique, distinction of playing in three different divisions of the Football League in consecutive games.

After his farewell outing for Cardiff, Clarke lined up for the Maine Road club in their final match of a Second Division season in which they had already secured promotion as champions; thus his next appearance was in the First Division at the outset of 1947/48.

From the day of his Manchester City debut – in which he had made a notable contribution to the 5-1 drubbing of his home-town club, Newport County, and in which spearhead George Smith had plundered all five goals – there was little doubt that Clarke would make his mark in the top tier.

By the time he made his full international entrance against England at Villa Park in November 1948, he was a regular member of the City attack, having emerged as an elusive raider with a devastating body-swerve, his distinctive head-down running style proving no bar to the dispatch of accurate crosses and fulminating shots.

In 1949/50 City suffered the trauma of relegation, but they bounced back at the first attempt, then spent several terms in the wrong half of the table before stabilising in mid-decade, when they reached two consecutive FA Cup finals.

Clarke was outstanding on the Wembley trail in 1955, scoring the only goal of the semi-final against Sunderland with a spectacular diving header on a Villa Park quagmire, only to be shattered by a knee injury in the dying moments which was destined to sideline him for the final.

As he contemplated his likely absence on the gala day, he shed tears in the after-match bath, and though subsequently he looked likely to make a timely recovery, he received another knock on the damaged joint and missed the Wembley defeat by Newcastle United.

Happily for Clarke and City, there was rich redemption in store as the much-improved Blues – they finished fourth in the elite division in 1955/56 – reached the next final, where they faced Birmingham.

Resplendent in vivid new maroon-and-white striped shirts, rendered necessary by a colour-clash with their opponents, they made an ideal start, with Clarke playing an integral role in a slickly worked goal after three minutes. Centre-forward Don Revie slid the ball to the Welshman on the left flank, then the deep-lying schemer ran forward to take a precise return before deftly setting up Joe Hayes to net from close range.

Soon Birmingham equalised, but in the second half, with Clarke tormenting the normally dominant Jeff Hall – destined to lose his life to polio while still in his playing prime – Manchester City seized control. Dynamic skipper Roy Paul and the creative Ken

Barnes were in masterful form, and the northerners prevailed 3-1, thanks to further goals from Jack Dyson and the bubbly Bobby Johnstone.

In fact, for all the fluent football on display, the match is remembered mainly because the Manchester goalkeeper, the former German paratrooper Bert Trautmann, played on after breaking his neck, though the extent of the injury was not known for several days.

By now Clarke had reached his thirties and had won the last of his 22 caps for Wales – he scored in his final international, a 1-1 draw with Northern Ireland at Ninian Park in April 1956 – but he completed another two terms in the top flight before accepting a move to Third Division Stockport County in September 1958.

After one season at Edgeley Park, which ended in demotion and during which he sampled coaching, he spent a brief spell as manager of non-League Northwich Victoria before establishing a local sportswear business.

But Roy Clarke was far from finished with Manchester City. In 1960 he returned to Maine Road to run the development office for six years, then he and his wife Kath took over the management of the Blues' new social club. The personable couple ran it for more than 20 years with enormous success, and their venture was widely acclaimed, being used as a model for similar clubs around the country.

The Clarkes booked such famous performers as Frankie Vaughan, Ken Dodd and the Drifters, but Roy was nothing loth to get his hands dirty with menial tasks, being ready to sort out the plumbing or use a hammer and nails in an emergency.

An affable character, he was a leading light in the Manchester City Former Players Association, and after his retirement he conducted supporters' tours of Maine Road, proving an eloquent ambassador for the club to which he had given most of his life.

Royston James Clarke: born Crindau, Newport, Monmouthshire, 1 June 1925; played for Cardiff City 1942-47, Manchester City 1947-58, Stockport County 1958-59; capped 22 times by Wales 1948-56; died Sale, Cheshire, 13 March 2006.

Nobby Lawton

West Ham United were captained by the illustrious Bobby Moore, while Preston North End were led out by the rather less renowned Nobby Lawton, but when the two clubs staged one of the most exhilarating of all Wembley FA Cup finals in 1964, the unassuming Lancastrian was anything but upstaged by the recently appointed England skipper.

Indeed, though Preston of the Second Division were pipped by a stoppage-time goal as the top-flight Hammers prevailed 3-2, many neutral observers made Lawton the man of a hugely entertaining rollercoaster of a contest in which his plucky side had twice led.

A stylish, cultured wing-half, Lawton had been characteristically composed as the action had raged around him, taking the eye with his intelligent, imaginative distribution and quietly authoritative leadership. Like Moore, he was no ranter, but he inspired loyalty and affection from the men in his charge. Thus he became one of the most prominent figures in Preston's modern history, yet there had been a time in the late 1950s when Lawton might have been destined for eminence with Manchester United, the club with whom he shared a birthplace of Newton Heath.

After excelling as a teenager with Lancashire Schoolboys he signed amateur forms with the Red Devils in 1956, training on two evenings a week while working for a coal merchant.

His early progress at Old Trafford as a creative inside-forward or wing-half – a midfielder in modern parlance – was encouraging, and he played a prominent part in United's FA Youth Cup triumph of 1957, scoring in the first leg of the 8-2 aggregate victory over West Ham in the final.

In the wake of the Munich air crash of February 1958, which claimed the lives of eight United players and left two others maimed so that they never played again, cultured young talent such as Lawton's was at a premium. Accordingly, on the following Good Friday the tall, rather slender 18-year-old gave up his job with the coal company and became a professional footballer.

However, within days his fledgling career, and possibly even his life, were in jeopardy. After playing for the reserves while suffering from heavy flu he succumbed to double pneumonia, lost the use of his legs and was out of action for many months.

Some employers would have let him go, but United manager Matt Busby – himself still recuperating from life-threatening injuries suffered at Munich – retained faith, and that positive attitude proved the turning point on Lawton's tortuous road to recovery.

With the club's post-Munich reconstruction still in full swing, it remained a time of rare opportunity and duly he made his first-team debut as an inside-forward at Luton in April 1960. By the middle of 1961/62 he had gained a regular berth, forming a promising left-wing partnership with Bobby Charlton, and after scoring a Boxing Day hat-trick in the 6-3 home drubbing of Nottingham Forest, his prospects appeared buoyant.

Lawton was ever-present in United's run to the semi-finals of the FA Cup, where they were well beaten by Tottenham Hotspur, but somehow his confidence was never quite on a par with his abundant ability and soon, in the face of inevitably brisk competition for midfield places – the arrival of Paddy Crerand from Celtic was the final straw – he slipped out of Busby's plans. Devastated by such rejection at the age of 23, he determined to rebuild his career elsewhere and in March 1963 he accepted a transfer to Preston North End.

At Deepdale he found the space to develop his game that had not been afforded him in the more demanding situation at Old Trafford, at last feeling he could relax and concentrate on playing rather than striving constantly to prove himself.

Quickly he matured into an influential figure, being made skipper for the 1963/64 campaign which ended with North End missing out narrowly on promotion to the top division, then losing at Wembley. It was a crushing double disappointment, but now, at least, he was established at the heart of a team which appeared to be going places.

As it turned out, the side did not improve under manager Jimmy Milne, relapsing into mid-table, and although Lawton continued to flourish personally despite being hampered by serial knee problems, he never quite fulfilled all that early potential.

He remained as captain at Deepdale until the pace of Second Division football became too much for his painful joints and in September 1967 he moved down a grade, joining Brighton and Hove Albion.

On his own admission, Lawton skippered the Seagulls virtually on one leg for three years before finishing his career with a season and a half at Fourth Division Lincoln City, playing alongside future England boss Graham Taylor.

After retiring as a player in 1972 he was not tempted to remain in the game, despite having earned plaudits as an eloquent committee member of the Professional Footballers' Association. Some thought he was ideal sports administrator material, but instead he took sales jobs with several companies. In 1977 he returned to his roots in

Newton Heath, Manchester, to work for an export packaging firm of which he became sales director.

Norbert Lawton: born Newton Heath, Manchester, 25 March 1940; played for Manchester United 1956-63, Preston North End 1963-67, Brighton and Hove Albion 1967-71, Lincoln City 1971-72; died Manchester, 22 April 2006.

Brian Labone

To characterise a professional footballer as noble, and to reflect on his sensitive side, might seem incongruous when set against the greed, cynicism and rampant self-aggrandisement which go hand in hand with the modern game. But in the case of Brian Labone, whose name has been synonymous with that of Everton for nearly half a century, such treatment seems singularly apt.

An archetypal one-club man, dubbed 'the last of the great Corinthians' by former Goodison Park manager Harry Catterick – a fearsome fellow not noted for dispensing fulsome praise – Labone was a colossally influential figure as the Toffees won the League championship in 1963 and 1970 and the FA Cup in 1966, the last-mentioned pair of successes under his captaincy. Tall and naturally commanding, he operated at centre-half, a position traditionally associated with flint-hearted bruisers prone to crunching physical excess, but Labone was cut from a contrasting, altogether more stately cloth.

He played the game as he lived his life, with dignity, composure and integrity, and during his 15-year career he picked up a mere two bookings in more than 530 games for the Merseysiders, a total of appearances exceeded by only two other Evertonians, the goalkeepers Neville Southall and Ted Sagar.

Yet there was a myth about Labone, perpetuated by his calm, almost tranquil character and his polished, unflappable style of play. The contention among some critics was that he was devoid of 'devil', that he was simply too easy-going for a role which demanded a more ruthless approach, that both he and Everton would have achieved more if he had been tougher.

However, that was a theory flawed seriously on two counts. Firstly, 'Labby' had to be true to his own nature, which precluded random violence or unnecessary harshness. Secondly, although he played the game with impeccable fairness, he was a hard footballer, imbued with every ounce of steel needed to survive and prosper at the top club level for almost a decade and a half, and to earn 26 caps for his country.

Had he been anything approaching a soft touch then he would never have progressed beyond the junior football in which he excelled during his education at Liverpool Collegiate School in the early 1950s.

In fact, though he was always enthusiastic about sport, the thoughtful, intelligent youngster might never have signed on at Everton anyway, even after joining the club as an amateur in 1955. He was sorely tempted to go to university – emphatically not an option for a would-be professional footballer in that era – and deliberated coolly before accepting the offer of professional terms at Goodison as a 17-year-old in 1957, spurning local rivals Liverpool in the process.

Having taken that momentous decision, Labone made meteoric progress, first riveting the attention of hard-boiled Everton insiders with his masterful shackling of the rumbustious centre-forward Dave Hickson – a lovely fellow off the pitch but famously combative on it – in a public trial game.

Indeed, so impressive was the callow newcomer that he leapfrogged the Toffees' three junior teams to claim a place in the reserves. Seven months later he made his first-team entrance following an injury to Tommy E Jones, but it was not until his next senior outing, at home to Tottenham Hotspur in April 1957, that he discovered the cruel reality of top-flight football when he was subjected to an embarrassing runaround by Bobby Smith, another from the raging-bull school of spearheads. Now the rookie proved he was made of the right stuff, returning to the 'stiffs' to hone his craft, then earning a regular place in the First Division line-up in 1959/60 and winning England under-23 recognition in 1961.

Slim and rather more elegant than most stoppers, but formidably powerful in the air, Labone was fearless in his tackles and an astute anticipator of the unfolding action, enabling him to specialise in timely interceptions. On the ball he was accomplished and often constructive when using his right foot, invariably employing his left only for emergency clearances.

His game had developed serenely under the management of John Carey, but it was when that benevolent Irishman was replaced in the summer of 1961 by the abrasive Catterick that Labone, and Everton, truly began to prosper.

In 1962/63, with a team in which star forwards Alex 'The Golden Vision' Young and Roy Vernon tended to monopolise the headlines, the Toffees lifted the League title, and Labone's part as the rearguard's principal bulwark was recognised with a first full England call-up in October, to face Northern Ireland in Belfast. Astonishingly in view of his club's historical eminence, he was the first Everton player to be capped by England at senior level since the war.

At that point, though, he was unable to inch ahead of Sheffield Wednesday's Peter Swan and Maurice Norman of Tottenham Hotspur to claim a regular international berth. Still he continued to advance his case, being made Everton skipper in 1964/65, succeeding Tony Kay who, along with Swan, was banned from football and imprisoned for his part in a bribes scandal which had recently rocked the game.

Come 1965/66 Labone remained in imperious form but now was headed by Jack Charlton in the pecking order of England centre-halves. However, during the run-up to the 1966 World Cup finals which would climax with Alf Ramsey's men triumphing so gloriously on home soil, the Everton captain stunned the football establishment by asking not to be considered for the tournament, so that he was free to go ahead with his planned summer wedding to a former Miss Liverpool, Pat Lynam.

He had already postponed the marriage once because of football, and later explained that he hadn't expected to be in contention for a World Cup place: 'I had fixed the date, made all the arrangements, issued all the invitations. What could I do?'

Happily for Labone, soon his controversial announcement was overshadowed by Everton's breathtaking victory in that season's FA Cup final, fighting back from two goals down to defeat Sheffield Wednesday, and as he brandished the coveted bauble aloft in the Wembley sunshine all seemed well with his world.

But another shock declaration was in the offing. In September 1967, notionally in his prime at 27 and leading one of the best teams in the land, he revealed that he was no longer enjoying his football, having lost both form and confidence, and planned imminent retirement, either when his contract expired 18 months hence or earlier if the club could find a suitable replacement.

It seemed that the modest Merseyside, a strong-willed but sensitive individual, was feeling the pressure of his high-profile job in a soccer-mad city and preferred a future in the family central-heating business. However, having bared his soul, he felt his mind clear and his anxiety lift. Now he produced arguably the finest football of his life; he replaced the ageing Charlton as England's first-choice number-five and he was happy to reverse his decision to depart prematurely.

In 1969/70 Labone was majestic as an exhilaratingly entertaining Everton side, featuring the beautifully balanced midfield trio of Alan Ball, Colin Harvey and Howard Kendall, romped away with the League crown, and that summer he recovered from injury in time to perform smoothly for his country in the World Cup finals in Mexico.

A successful defence of the Jules Rimet Trophy appeared possible when England seized a two-goal advantage over West Germany in the quarter-final in Leon, only for Franz Beckenbauer and company to complete a devastating comeback to prevail 3-2.

That proved to be Labone's final international appearance and, now in his thirties and increasingly prone to injuries, there was little left of his club career, either, and he laid aside his boots in 1972.

Subsequently he enjoyed a successful sojourn in insurance and served for many years on the Littlewoods 'spot the ball' panel. Meanwhile his love affair with Everton never abated. In recent years he worked for the club as a match-day host, a convivial role to which this courteous, patient, gently amusing man was ideally suited, and he enjoyed mixing with the fans right up until the time of his sudden death.

Brian Leslie Labone: born Liverpool, 23 January 1940; played for Everton 1957-72; capped 26 times by England 1962-70; died Liverpool, 24 April 2006.

Les Olive

There was never the faintest hint of stardust about Les Olive, yet for three decades he was a vastly influential figure behind the throne of Manchester United, one of the world's most glamorous sporting institutions.

When United's plane crashed at Munich in February 1958, costing the lives of 23 people including eight players and leaving team manager Matt Busby hovering perilously close to death, into the temporary footballing breach stepped assistant boss Jimmy Murphy.

Rightly the emotional Welshman, who kept the Reds' flag flying and led them to Wembley for that season's FA Cup final, was rewarded for his heroic efforts with a unique niche in the annals of both the club and the wider game.

Less highlighted, however, was the administrative void created by the loss of club secretary Walter Crickmer on that slushy German runway, and he had no such battle-hardened deputy as Murphy to step into his shoes.

Instead there was 29-year-old Olive, who had once harboured hopes of a glorious playing career with United but who more recently had been concentrating on his work in the Old Trafford office, carrying the title of assistant secretary since 1955.

To him fell the arduous and harrowing task of ensuring the smooth day-to-day running of United at a time when the club, the city and the country were gripped by the immediate tragedy and the still-unfolding tale of woe as the most famous of the Red Devils, the grievously injured Duncan Edwards, was added to the list of fatalities.

Olive responded in a manner which was to become his hallmark – by toiling unobtrusively but with prodigious dedication, radiating composure and compassion while paying meticulous attention to detail.

Together with his wife, Betty, he broke the calamitous news to many of the families of the victims, he helped to organise funerals, and he supervised the arrival and laying out of coffins containing the dead footballers in the club gymnasium.

Having acquitted himself so admirably in the aftermath of the disaster, Olive was confirmed as secretary during the following summer. It was a post he filled with unfussy efficiency and undeviating devotion to duty until his retirement in 1988, by which time he had witnessed the departure of six team managers and the arrival of the current boss Alex Ferguson. Yet for all his colossal input into United's behind-the-scenes business over 30 years, shunning the spotlight but utterly integral to the Red Devils' success, he could point to a footballing achievement which was also, in its way, remarkable.

Having joined the club as a 14-year-old office-boy cum would-be player straight from school in 1942, Olive made more marked progress behind his desk than on the pitch, and when he left the RAF in 1948 he was faced with a tantalising dilemma. Should he opt for a career in administration or take a chance on making the grade as a footballer under Matt Busby, one of the most progressive managers in the country?

Many young men in such an enviable position might have tilted at the windmill of soccer stardom, but the sensible Salfordian took the infinitely more secure option.

However, he did enjoy his moments in the big time after all, as he recalled in 1997: 'After the war United were playing their first-team home games at Maine Road (Manchester City's headquarters) because Old Trafford had been bombed. That meant both clubs' reserves played at our ground and it was my job to open the turnstiles, pay the referees and so on. When we went back to Old Trafford in 1949 the consequent return of the senior administrative staff left me with a lighter burden, which gave me time for training.

'Before long I was playing in the 'A' and 'B' (junior) sides, occasionally for the reserves, occupying every position except outside-left, with my favoured slots being full-back or centre-half.'

Still he had not the remotest ambition of a senior call-up, but it arrived when injury and illness laid low three goalkeepers, Reg Allen, Ray Wood and Jack Crompton, and Olive was picked between the posts for the First Division visit to Newcastle in April 1953.

'I must have been a bit nervous but my overriding consideration was not to let the side down. I had come through the ranks with Dennis Viollet (destined to become a leading goal-scorer), who was also making his debut, and I think we helped each other remain calm.' In the event Olive performed competently enough in a 2-1 victory to retain his place for one more match, which was drawn, before he returned to 'A' team duty at left-back. Typically level-headed, he understood that he had been helping out in an emergency, did not mind standing aside and, eschewing all thought of turning professional, resumed his office routine.

After Munich, Olive grew rapidly into an increasingly demanding job, earning a reputation for loyalty, integrity and uncompromising principles as the club mushroomed in both stature and complexity. He was renowned, in particular, for his scrupulously fair dealings with the fans, whose cause he championed tirelessly.

When he retired in 1988, United were not about to relinquish all that accumulated experience and encyclopaedic knowledge of their affairs, and soon he joined the club's board, taking on special responsibility for the reserves and junior teams, travelling with them all over the country until he was prevented by deteriorating health.

That genuine interest in the lesser lights reflected a passion for grass-roots football which was evident in his work for the Manchester Football Association from 1959 until shortly before his death. That he should have taken on such a burden in his retirement was laudable; that he should have carried it for so many years while making Manchester United tick was little short of astonishing.

Away from football he was an elder and treasurer at the Salford Central United Reformed Church, a contented family man and a modest, quiet raconteur with an engagingly dry sense of humour.

As Sir Alex Ferguson put it on hearing of Les Olive's death after 64 years of service to his club: 'I can't think of a more decent man.'

Robert Leslie Olive: born Salford, Lancashire, 27 April 1928; served Manchester United as player 1953, assistant secretary 1955-58, club secretary 1958-88, director 1988-2006; died Salford, 20 May 2006.

Ferenc Puskas

Precisely where Ferenc Puskas stands in the pantheon of all-time great footballers is a matter for passionate and pleasurable debate. Suffice it to say that there can be no doubting the flamboyant Hungarian's right to his own personal pedestal alongside those of Pele and Maradona, di Stefano and Cruyff, and perhaps just a handful of others in the history of the world game.

Puskas was remarkable in so many ways, scoring more senior international goals than anyone else before his total was surpassed by Ali Daei of Iran, and enjoying a uniquely dramatic career of two glittering and vividly contrasting halves.

First he was the charismatic focal point of 'The Magnificent Magyars', who twice humiliated England and, with their breathtakingly imaginative tactics, practically reinvented football in the 1950s, thus bringing untold pride and joy to their strife-torn homeland.

Then, aged 31 and with his belly bulging, he commenced a celestial sojourn with star-spangled Real Madrid, who epitomised all that was glamorous and successful at club level.

Beyond that, he was a swashbuckling character, a vibrantly humorous fellow who captivated all sections of society with his blend of swaggering, earthy charm and audacious impudence in his frequent dealings with military and sporting authority.

Ferenc Puskas grew up as a hardy, scuffling street kid in Kispest, a small community on the outskirts of Budapest. His was a poor family which, he liked to recall, could afford only one pair of shoes for himself and his brother so they took one each. Ferenc put his on his right foot and didn't dare kick with it for fear of damage, thus explaining the development of the most famously potent of all left feet.

Even at that stage it was evident that 'Ocsi' (kid brother), as he was known affectionately all his life, possessed extraordinary ability and he graduated rapidly through the ranks of the local club, where his father coached. Small but strong and prodigiously skilful, he progressed meteorically, making his league debut for Kispest at 16 and becoming a full international as an 18-year-old against Austria in August 1945.

Hungarian football had been virtually unaffected by the Second World War, continuing even during fierce fighting when German-occupied Budapest was besieged and then 'liberated' by the Russians.

Further dark days lay ahead for Hungary, but for a time, though poverty was widespread, there was sufficient semblance of normality for the nation's soccer in general, and Puskas in particular, to flower luxuriantly.

Visionary national coach Gusztav Sebes assembled a group of exceptional players known as 'The Golden Squad' and revolutionised tactics by employing a deep-lying centre-forward, which led eventually to the universally adopted 4-2-4 formation. The new system depended on fluid interchanging of positions and sweetly accurate passing. It produced football which flowed freely, it was both lavishly entertaining and immensely effective, and the sharpshooting Puskas was at its heart.

In 1949 it was decided that Hungary's team would benefit from improved understanding and esprit de corps if all the top players were brought together in two clubs under the auspices of the Army. Kispest FC was chosen as the principal star vehicle and – renamed Honved and captained by Puskas – it lifted five domestic championships between 1949 and 1955, the great man netting 50 goals in one campaign and topping the scoring charts in several more.

What set him apart? Certainly not prowess with head or right foot, both of which were negligible. But his left foot was an instrument of wondrous precision, by turns brutally powerful – many of his hundreds of goals were crashed home from outside the box – and silkily smooth.

With it he was the absolute master of the ball, his control instant, his placement of both pass and shot virtually unerring, and he was phenomenally strong, almost impossible to dispossess. Crucially, too, Puskas was blessed with the acute intelligence, intense concentration and magical spontaneity to make the most of his physical gifts. He was an instinctive tactician, able to adapt in a flash to the ever-changing picture around him, and a natural leader.

Thus he was perfectly equipped to flourish on the international stage and he did so with a vengeance, excelling alongside the world-class likes of wing-half Jozsef Bozsik, scheming centre-forward Nandor Hidegkuti, fellow marksman Sandor Kocsis and goalkeeper Gyula Grosics.

Between 1950 and 1956 Hungary dominated world football, winning Olympic gold in 1952 and conceding defeat only once. Unfortunately that was in the 1954 World Cup final, when they lost 3-2 to West Germany, perhaps falling prey to complacency after leading by two early goals, one of them struck by a not fully-fit Puskas.

But it is not for that sadly anti-climactic performance that the incomparable Magyars are primarily remembered. Their indelible mark on sporting history was made at Wembley in November 1953 when they took on England, who had given the game to the world and had never been beaten on their own soil by foreign opposition.

Hungary won 6-3, but it was the manner of the victory as much as the margin which made it so emphatic. The visitors humbled their hosts, utterly outclassed them, with breathtakingly beautiful football which was summed up by one moment of sheer sorcery from Puskas.

As Zoltan Czibor's dispatch came in from the right, the Hungarian skipper was lurking on the near corner of the six-yard box but was marked by England captain Billy Wright, who lunged forward to clear. But he kicked air as, in one sumptuous movement, Puskas had dragged the ball back with the sole of his boot, then pivoted on the spot before thundering a savage drive into the net over the shoulder of startled goalkeeper Gil Merrick.

It remains one of the most famous of all goals and after the match its scorer was promoted by his Army masters, duly entering folklore as 'The Galloping Major'.

As if that lesson was not enough to ensure that the notoriously arrogant and complacent English soccer hierarchy realised that times had changed, Hungary

George Best: on a pedestal of his own.

Jack Kelsey: a presence that bordered on omnipotence.

Danny Blanchflower: innovative, eloquent, inspirational.

Billy Wright: football's first international centurion.

Raich Carter: 'The Great Horatio.'

Johnny Carey: an unflappable thoroughbred.

Bob Paisley: told Liverpool he would do his best…

Tommy Lawton: straddled his era like a titan.

Sir Alf Ramsey: made his critics eat their words.

Sir Stanley Matthews: the Peter Pan of football.

Wilf Mannion: creative maestro with a rebel streak.

Len Shackleton: impish charmer without an ounce of propriety.

Stan Cullis: dynamic, tyrannical, a born winner.

Billy Liddell: chivalrous, humble and an Anfield icon.

John Charles: one of the best the world has seen.

Brian Clough: most fans forgave his vast ego.

Bill Nicholson: created a team of breathtaking beauty.

Ferenc Puskas: achieved greatness twice over.

Johnny Haynes (left): a charismatic perfectionist.

(Left)
Alan Ball: youngest
and fieriest of
England's champions.

(Right)
Sir Bobby Robson:
rose above an army of
petty tormentors.

Malcolm Allison:
brought more light
than darkness to the
English game.

Ronnie Clayton: a monument to integrity and sportsmanship.

Nat Lofthouse: Bolton's mighty but humb[...] talisman.

Gary Speed: colossally influential and widely cherished.

Alfie Biggs: 'The Baron', local hero and m[...] about town.

delivered an even more comprehensive tutorial in Budapest six months later in the form of a 7-1 drubbing. Back in England, those with eyes to see marvelled at the new order and adjusted their sights accordingly, while, inevitably, others in positions of power buried their heads in the sand.

During this period of Hungarian ascendancy, Puskas and company, who were nominally members of the Army, enjoyed a privileged existence at home against a harrowing backdrop of increasing public hardship as discontent against the repressive Stalinist regime simmered dangerously.

These paper soldiers, who were used shamelessly as propaganda tools to promote the government's socialist ideal, were allowed to train full time, they were rewarded lavishly with under-the-counter goods and the authorities looked the other way when they used football trips overseas to smuggle luxuries into the country.

Puskas, who described himself as non-political, made the most of his position as national hero and, despite the fact that his constant manipulation of favours for friends and family became common knowledge, he was admired, even honoured, as a generous and loveable rascal, both by those in high office and the bulk of his suffering compatriots.

Not surprisingly, that virtual untouchability faltered after the World Cup defeat, for which he was unfairly blamed by many, and even another long unbeaten run was not enough to recover it.

However, graver concerns were looming. Political unrest culminated with the October Uprising of 1956 and Soviet tanks moved in to crush the revolt. At the time the Honved team, cocooned from everyday life and barely aware of the situation on the streets, were on a foreign tour. When the immediate crisis was resolved they were ordered home but some, including Puskas, refused to go, perhaps fearing the personal consequences under new rulers, maybe yearning for a more prosperous future abroad.

As a result, he was banned from playing for 18 months and, for an ever-more-portly thirtysomething, career prospects did not appear bright. However, serial European champions Real Madrid were confident of his quality and in 1958 they recruited him to play alongside the fabulous Argentinian, Alfredo di Stefano.

At first Puskas was ridiculed as a tubby has-been, but he worked assiduously to regain fitness and soon he was scoring freely. At first, there was tension with the great Alfredo, who was used to ruling the Real roost, but the newcomer defused the situation with typically astute psychology.

Come the last game of his first Spanish season, the two men were tying as the League's top scorer, for which there was a much-coveted individual trophy. Towards the end, Puskas had the goal at his mercy but instead of claiming the prize for himself, he passed to di Stefano, who duly netted. Thereafter the animosity evaporated and the pair scaled lofty peaks together as Real Madrid cemented their reputation as the finest club side of all time. This was symbolised rivetingly in 1960 when they claimed their fifth consecutive European Cup triumph – at that point no other side had ever won the competition – by defeating Eintracht Frankfurt 7-3 at Hampden Park, Glasgow. Puskas scored four times and di Stefano three, and the game is now revered as the most luscious feast of soccer entertainment ever put before the public. Still, though, Puskas was not finished. Starting in 1960/61, he pocketed five consecutive Spanish title medals, he was the league's premier marksman on four occasions, he plundered a hat-trick as Real lost the 1962 European Cup final to Benfica, and he picked up another loser's medal two years later when the Spaniards were defeated by Internazionale of Milan.

In addition, though he never played for Hungary after 1956, he earned four caps for his adopted country, culminating in an appearance in the 1962 World Cup finals. When eventually he bowed out of the Bernabeu Stadium in 1967, he was 40 years old.

Thereafter, football remained his life. First he coached in Spain and Canada before accepting the reins of the Greek club, Panathinaikos. Against all expectations he inspired them to reach the final of the European Cup in 1971, losing 2-0 to mighty Ajax of Amsterdam, Johan Cruyff et al, only after a gallant struggle.

Two Greek championships followed, then Puskas embarked on a coaching odyssey which took him to Chile, Saudi Arabia, back to Spain and Greece, then Egypt, Paraguay and Australia, improving teams wherever he went.

In 1991, arguably the most famous of all Hungarians returned home to spend his declining years in Budapest, putting in a spell as caretaker coach of the national team in 1992 before accepting a role in youth development.

Though the influence of this colossally colourful character transcends mere statistics, a few are apposite here. In club football he scored 358 goals in 349 games for Kispest/Honved, 324 in 372 for Real Madrid; for Hungary there were 83 strikes in 84 matches (some sources say 84 in 85), a total which transcends even Pele's magnificent return for Brazil.

He spent two decades straddling the game's giddiest pinnacles, achieving greatness twice over. Few men have had a more profound influence on their chosen sport than Ferenc Puskas.

Ferenc Puskas Biro: born Kispest, Hungary, 2 April 1927; played for Kispest/Honved 1943-56, Real Madrid 1958-67; capped 84 times by Hungary 1945-56, four times by Spain 1962; died Budapest, Hungary, 17 November 2006.

Joe Walton

Joe Walton, one of the classiest uncapped defenders in British football during his 1950s pomp with Preston North End, became the most expensive full-back in the domestic game when Preston North End paid £12,000 to sign him from Manchester United in March 1948.

Yet Old Trafford boss Matt Busby, the man who agreed to sell the diminutive, wavy-haired Mancunian to one of his chief Lancastrian rivals, did his utmost to dissuade the richly promising 22-year-old to remain with the Red Devils.

Even as he drove his player to Deepdale to finalise the transfer, the young manager, still in the early stages of transforming United from dismal under-achievers into one of the world's premier sporting institutions, offered to turn the car around and call off the move.

But the ambitious Walton, the target of several other major clubs, was tired of life in the shadow of Johnny Carey and John Aston, the two polished internationals who graced the flanks of Busby's rearguard, and remained adamant that he wanted to leave.

So he did, and after making only tentative progress for several seasons, he matured into a thoroughbred performer who chalked up 435 senior appearances in nearly 13 years as a Lilywhite, a period during which Preston, inspired by the enduringly magnificent Tom Finney, went agonisingly close to lifting both League championship and FA Cup.

Having excelled for both Manchester and Lancashire Schoolboys, Walton enlisted with United as a 14-year-old in 1940, then was loaned out to a local feeder club, Goslings, for further development before turning professional in October 1943.

During the remainder of the war he became a regular for the Reds in the emergency Football League North competition and was selected three times to represent the Football Association.

The conflict over, the 20-year-old made his senior debut against his future employers, Preston, in an FA Cup encounter in January 1946 and continued to gather impetus so impressively that within eight months he was called up by England to face Scotland in the unofficial international staged at Maine Road, Manchester, to raise money for the Bolton Wanderers disaster fund (33 people had died due to overcrowding at a Burnden Park cup tie that March).

No cap was awarded but the slim, skilful Walton made his mark, positioning himself intelligently, tackling cleanly and exhibiting cool assurance with the ball at his feet.

But back at club level, where Busby was in the process of constructing the first of his three dazzlingly fluent sides, there was a problem. Though Walton could operate with equal facility as a right- or left-back, he was confronted not only by the almost metronomic splendour of Carey and Aston, but also by another enterprising rookie, Billy Redman.

Hence, after enjoying only 23 first-team outings in nearly two peacetime terms, he felt his prospects at Old Trafford were limited and succumbed to Preston's blandishments.

Some contemporary observers believed Walton had made a mistake in leaving such an upwardly mobile big-city club, but his initial success at Deepdale suggested that he had made a wise decision. Within a month of the switch he had played for the Football League against the League of Ireland, gained a regular berth in North End's defence, and netted two springtime penalties, though these would turn out to be his last goals for a decade.

However, in 1948/49, with Finney injured for much of the campaign and the influential Scottish wing-half Bill Shankly having retired from playing to embark on a management career which would climax with his messianic revival of Liverpool, Preston were transformed from a confident top-six outfit into a pallid combination which could not avoid relegation to the Second Division.

That season and the next Walton retained his place at left-back but his form grew variable. Thus when the Lilywhites, now fortified by the addition of abrasive midfielder Tommy Docherty and free-scoring marksman Charlie Wayman, rose from the second flight as champions in 1950/51, the full-back slots were usually filled by Willie Cunningham and Billy Scott, and although Walton played enough games to earn a medal, he was almost transferred to Grimsby Town, only for the transaction to fall through at the last moment.

There was talk of an exchange deal with Blackburn Rovers, too, which would have seen England left-back Bill Eckersley move in the opposite direction, but that also failed to materialise and gradually the former Manchester United man returned to prominence.

Though he made only a minor contribution as Preston were deprived of the 1952/53 League title on goal average – the method used to separate clubs on the same number of points before the less complicated device of goal difference was introduced – he regained the number-three shirt from Scott in 1953/54, and struck up a convincing partnership with Cunningham.

That season he played a key role as the Lilywhites, invariably inspired by Footballer of the Year Finney, reached the FA Cup final at Wembley, where they were beaten 3-2 by West Bromwich Albion after leading 2-1.

Now, barring brief absences through injury, the left-back berth became Walton's personal property for the remainder of a decade during which the team experienced contrasting fortunes.

In 1955/56 they finished only one point above demoted Huddersfield Town, then in 1956/57, under the guidance of new manager Cliff Britton and with Finney, Docherty and the prolific Tommy Thompson in superb form, they rose to third in the table.

A year later, with Walton a model of reliability and the team reaching its compelling peak, Preston went one better, finishing as runners-up behind Wolverhampton Wanderers. But thereafter, with Docherty departing and Finney retiring, they fell away and in 1960/61 were relegated as the bottom club.

By then Walton himself had been supplanted by a younger man, Irishman John O'Neill, and that February, aged 36, he was sold to lowly Accrington Stanley for £1,590, the fee being paid in four instalments.

However, although impecunious Stanley were already experiencing hard times, that was nothing to what was in store for the Lancastrian strugglers. After Walton had helped them to finish 18th in the Fourth Division at the end of his first campaign, they plunged to the foot of the table during 1961/62, a season which was to end, prematurely and (in sporting terms) catastrophically for them in March, with the penniless club resigning ignominiously from the Football League because it could not meet its financial commitments. There would be no return until August 2006. It was a poignant way for Walton's professional career to close, but he still loved the game and served non-League Horwich RMI, near Bolton, as a player-coach. Later he ran a newsagent's shop in Fulwood, Preston, then worked as a progress chaser for an electrics firm in the town.

Back at Deepdale he was missed not only for his footballing ability, but also his modesty, his engaging bonhomie and his piano-playing. When Joe Walton left North End, the players' sing-songs were never quite the same again.

Joseph Walton: born Manchester, 5 June 1925; played for Manchester United 1940-48, Preston North End 1948-61, Accrington Stanley 1961-62; died Preston, Lancashire, 31 December 2006.

Don Weston

When progressive young manager Don Revie guided Leeds United into the top tier of English football as champions of the old Second Division in the spring of 1964, Don Weston was one of his most potent attacking weapons.

The foundation of the Yorkshiremen's success was a formidably flinty rearguard featuring the likes of Jack Charlton, Norman Hunter and Paul Reaney, while the most influential individuals were the tiny but inspirational Scottish schemer Bobby Collins and his rising midfield henchmen Billy Bremner and Johnny Giles. But it was the wing-heeled Weston, frequently damned by historians' faint praise as a mere journeyman front-runner, who supplied much of the crucial cutting edge.

As Collins put it: 'Don had a turn of foot like nobody's business' and during that memorable season, as Revie proceeded with his painstaking construction of a team destined to bestride the national game by decade's end, the north Midlander employed it to such devastating effect that he finished joint top-scorer, on 13 goals, with left-winger Albert Johanneson.

Usually operating at centre-forward or inside-right, the shortish, wiry Weston relished dropping deep, where he was difficult for his designated marker to locate; then he would sprint at wrong-footed defenders, frequently climaxing his dash with a powerful shot.

He compensated for lack of extravagant natural talent through fitness and dedication to his craft, and though later he would be revealed to lack the necessary class to thrive among the First Division elite, he had done enough to fashion a niche in Elland Road history.

When Weston had arrived at Leeds in December 1962 as part of the 'Revie Revolution', he was enlisting with the club for the second time. After appearing for East Derbyshire Schoolboys, then working briefly as a coalminer near his home-town of Mansfield, he served United as a 16-year-old amateur, but refused to sign as a professional for personal reasons.

There followed National Service at an army camp near Rhyl, in North Wales, and it was while excelling in military competition that he was spotted by the local Football League club, Wrexham. After enlisting at the Racecourse Ground on amateur terms, Weston was so keen to impress that he went AWOL to play in one game, being confined to barracks for two weeks for his pains.

Undeterred, the intrepid escaper bounced back from his porridge to earn a professional contract with the lowly Third Division club, for whom he netted 21 goals in 42 appearances during 1958/59 and the first half of the following campaign, before joining Birmingham City for £15,000 in January 1960. However, he failed to settle with the top-flight strugglers and 11 months later he stepped down a division, moving to Rotherham United in a £10,000 deal.

At Millmoor Weston flourished immediately, his goals helping United to reach the two-legged final of the League Cup in 1960/61, and after a 2-0 first-leg home victory over Aston Villa the Merry Millers seemed set to lift the trophy in its inaugural season. But although Weston went close to netting three times in the second game, Villa prevailed 3-0 on the night, 3-2 on aggregate. Thereafter the pacy marksman continued to perform creditably for Rotherham, enough to persuade Revie to pay £18,000 for his services in December 1962. Having been bought to fill a gap left by departed hero John Charles – the great Welshman's brief return to Elland Road from Italy had not proved a success – Weston might have been on a hiding to nothing, but he slotted in smoothly in central attack alongside fellow recent purchase Jim Storrie, his cause enhanced immeasurably by a debut hat-trick at home to Stoke City.

He missed only seven games in the Second Division title campaign which followed, but although Revie kept faith with him at first as Leeds made a rousing return to the First in 1964/65 – they were pipped to the League crown by Manchester United on goal average and lost the FA Cup final to Liverpool in extra time – he receded to the fringe of the team following the purchase of England centre-forward Alan Peacock.

In October 1965, with his 30th birthday approaching, Weston moved to Huddersfield Town but featured only intermittently for the Second Division promotion hopefuls before rejoining Wrexham, by now in Division Four, in December 1966.

Weston departed the Racecourse for the second time in 1968 following differences with new boss Alvan Williams, then served Chester fleetingly before finishing his playing days with non-League Altrincham and Bethesda Athletic. Later he returned to Mansfield, where he ran a car dealership.

Donald Patrick Weston: born New Houghton, Nottinghamshire, 6 March 1936; played for Wrexham 1958-60, Birmingham City 1960, Rotherham United 1960-62, Leeds United 1962-65, Huddersfield Town 1965-66, Wrexham 1966-68, Chester 1968; died Mansfield, 20 January 2007.

Jock Dodds

Jock Dodds was a defender's worst nightmare, a fearsome goal-scoring phenomenon brimming with brio, and with the physical presence of a rampaging bull. Though hardly a giant in terms of height, the rumbustious Scot was broad of beam and vastly muscular. He was unnervingly pacy, too, and, whether the football was on the ground or in the air, his aim tended to be true.

Between 1934 and 1950, Dodds plundered some 450 goals in around 500 games for Sheffield United, Blackpool, Shamrock Rovers, Everton, Lincoln City, Manchester United, Fulham and West Ham United, serving the last-mentioned trio as a wartime guest. It represents a remarkable strike rate, even though many of his appearances were made in emergency competitions during the conflict. Some of those matches, in which he netted six, seven, even eight times, were against weakened opposition, but his bountiful peacetime tally was more than prolific enough to remove any doubt about his exceptional prowess as a marksman.

Ephraim 'Jock' Dodds, only two when he lost his father, crossed the border from Grangemouth to live in Durham when his mother remarried, and he thrived in junior football, representing the county and turning professional with Huddersfield Town in 1932. He failed to break through with the Terriers, then one of England's top teams, but his potential had been noted by Second Division Sheffield United, who signed him on a free transfer in May 1934.

Though still in his teens, the burly, dashing Dodds was pitched into the senior side during the following autumn and commenced hitting the net, 114 times in his 178 League outings over nearly five seasons at Bramall Lane, all of which he finished as the club's leading scorer. During that time the Blades twice missed promotion by narrow margins, in 1935/36 and 1937/38, on the latter occasion losing out to Manchester United on goal average, the crazily complicated means of splitting clubs with the same number of points before goal difference was introduced.

But the highlight of Dodds' Sheffield sojourn was helping to reach the 1936 FA Cup final – until his death, he was believed to be the oldest surviving Wembley finalist – and then making a valiant attempt to win it. In a thrillingly tense encounter, United lost 1-0 to mighty Arsenal, the English game's dominant force throughout the decade, though the Scot went agonisingly close to levelling the scores. Shortly after Ted Drake had registered for the Gunners, Dodds hit the crossbar with a looping 18-yard header, later maintaining that he would have scored but for a push in the back by the Londoners' combative wing-half, Wilf 'Iron Man' Copping.

In 1938/39 the Blades finally earned a place in the top flight as runners-up to Blackburn Rovers, though Dodds, who had asked for a move to Lancashire for family reasons, had been transferred to Blackpool two months before the season's end. The Seasiders had invested £10,000 in the spearhead to help them avoid relegation from the top flight and duly he obliged, his ten strikes in a dozen games proving the decisive factor in their escape.

Dodds started the next campaign in similarly productive mode, netting three times as Blackpool topped the table after three matches, but then war broke out and the First Division programme was abandoned. Now he joined the RAF, stationed in the town as a physical training instructor, and when he wasn't putting air crews through their paces on the promenade, he was racking up the goals in prodigious quantities as the Seasiders triumphed in a succession of emergency competitions.

Among Dodds' most eye-catching feats were banging in eight in a 1941 cup meeting with Stockport County, and seven in a 15-3 annihilation of Tranmere Rovers a year later. In that one-sided Bloomfield Road encounter, he notched a hat-trick in two and a half minutes, the fastest ever known in major English football to that point. That mark was equalled, at least, by Jimmy Scarth of Gillingham in 1952 (sources differ as to the precise timing) and beaten by James Hayter of Bournemouth, who shaved ten seconds off the record against Wrexham in February 2004.

Though never called up for an official cap, a surprising omission surely due to his prime coinciding with the conflict, Dodds made nine appearances for Scotland in wartime internationals and did not disappoint. He netted nine times, including a hat-trick in a 5-4 victory over England at Hampden Park, Glasgow, in April 1942, when future Liverpool manager Bill Shankly hit the winner.

Come 1946, having contributed more than 200 goals to the Blackpool cause, Dodds – always an independent-minded character – found himself in dispute with the Seasiders and made a handful of appearances for the Dublin club, Shamrock Rovers.

Blackpool retained his registration, however, and in November 1946 they sold him for £8,250 to Everton, who were in urgent need of a centre-forward, having lost Dixie Dean to retirement and Tommy Lawton to Chelsea. Though the Toffeemen were enduring a period of relative mundanity, Dodds acquitted himself honourably with 36 strikes in 55 top-tier outings before enlisting with Second Division strugglers Lincoln City for a club-record £6,000 in October 1948.

Though at the veteran stage of his career, he continued to score heavily but couldn't prevent relegation. Still, he remained fit and soldiered on impressively in the Third Division North during 1949/50, but his playing days were to end in unexpectedly controversial fashion. At that time Colombia was setting up an outlaw league outside the umbrella of Federation Internationale de Football Association (FIFA), and were looking to enlist star players from all over the world. Their quest found fertile ground in England, where footballers' incomes were capped by the iniquitous maximum wage system enforced by the clubs.

Dodds, who had been considered by the Colombians but then rejected on the grounds of his age, became a recruiting agent instead and, as a result, was banned by the Football League in July 1950 for bringing the game into disrepute. Justice was done when he was cleared by the Football Association soon afterwards, and there were opportunities to enter management with both Port Vale and Stoke City.

However, Dodds decided that his future lay in business in Blackpool, and the game lost one of its most colourful practitioners.

Ephraim Dodds: born Grangemouth, Stirlingshire, 7 September 1915; played for Sheffield United 1934-39, Blackpool 1939-46, Shamrock Rovers 1946, Everton 1946-48, Lincoln City 1948-50; died Blackpool, Lancashire, 23 February 2007.

John Ritchie

John Ritchie was the big, bold, swashbuckling spearhead of the most successful football team in the history of Stoke City.

He scored goals in copious quantities and, in his second spell at the club during the first half of the 1970s, led a multi-talented forward line with fluency and courage, spiced with an occasional dash of engaging panache.

Ritchie linked deliciously with his silkily subtle front-running partner, Jimmy Greenhoff, as the Potters lifted their first (and still only) major honour, the League Cup, in 1972. In addition, they sampled European competition for the first time, reached two successive FA Cup semi-finals, and when Ritchie's career was halted by a shattered leg in the autumn of 1974, they were on the brink of a genuine challenge for the League championship.

So there was no doubting the gravity of his input to Tony Waddington's upliftingly entertaining team, yet the imposingly upright, darkly handsome marksman managed to play the game with a smile on his face, too. Usually it was of the wry variety.

For instance, there was the priceless moment when, stung by Southampton rival Peter Osgood's jibe that he could score only by means of his trademark aerial prowess, Ritchie stopped, knelt and nudged the ball over the Saints' unoccupied goal-line with his head.

That afternoon at Stoke's old Victoria Ground in March 1974, 'Reggie' – his team-mates had no idea how he acquired the nickname, but it stuck – completed a fine hat-trick in a comprehensive victory over the chastened Osgood and company, as if to emphasise his point still further. Then there was the yarn that as he rose to meet a corner at the Vic's Boothen End, he winked at the fans on the terraces before burying the ball in the opposition's net. That one was surely apocryphal, but it captured the buccaneering essence of a local hero gifted enough to represent the Football League, and who fell only marginally short of international quality.

Though Ritchie was a large man, he did not lumber in the manner of many strapping centre-forwards, and he didn't dither. Rather he was quick in both thought and action, he was prodigiously industrious and he possessed far more skill at manipulating a football than often he was credited with, as he illustrated graphically at home to Coventry City in March 1973. Receiving the ball with his back to goal, he flicked it into the air, swivelled adroitly and volleyed into the net from the edge of the penalty box. As the Sky Blues' general manager Joe Mercer put it, with a characteristic rueful grin: 'A goal like that shouldn't happen to a dog.'

Ritchie was an enthusiastic subscriber to the team ethic, yet was affected nevertheless by the traditional striker's malaise of temporary gloom virtually every time he left the pitch without scoring. Invariably, though, his dry humour re-asserted itself rapidly, especially when he was sharing a dressing room with his good chum Greenhoff.

Ritchie was 20 when Stoke boss Waddington recruited him from non-League Kettering Town in June 1962, having not seen him play but being happy to accept the enthusiastic recommendation of a trusted talent scout.

He made his senior entrance in April 1963 as the Potters, enhanced by the timeless magic of 48-year-old Stanley Matthews, clinched the championship of the Second Division and with it a place in the top tier of English football.

But it was in the subsequent term that he came of footballing age, claiming a regular berth and bagging 30 senior goals as City preserved their new status among the elite and reached the final of the League Cup, in which they were narrowly defeated over two legs by Leicester City.

Ritchie meshed beautifully with more experienced attackers such as Dennis Viollet, Jimmy McIlroy and Peter Dobing, and continued to prosper throughout the decade's middle years as Stoke consolidated.

As his goal tally mounted to 110 in 64 outings in the League alone, he became an idol of the supporters, many of whom were outraged in November 1966 when he was transferred to fellow First Division side Sheffield Wednesday for £70,000.

Often Ritchie had excelled against the Owls in the past, netting four times in one encounter and three in another, and now he proceeded to perform creditably for the Hillsborough club, combining neatly with the enterprising Johnny Fantham. However, although he contributed an invaluable 18 hits to Wednesday's successful relegation fight in 1967/68 – the season in which he scored twice for the Football League in the 7-2 drubbing of the League of Ireland – he fell prey to niggling injuries and his strike rate declined. His record in Sheffield was respectable, but he had continued to live in the Potteries and there was an impression that he never quite settled at his new club. Thus it came as little surprise in July 1969 when he rejoined Stoke for £25,000.

Clearly Waddington, who cheerfully admitted his mistake in allowing Ritchie to leave in the first place, could hardly believe his luck. He had secured a reliable goal-scorer, who was in his prime at 28 and whose heart was in Stoke, while pocketing a profit of £45,000.

Now public expectation was immense and Ritchie met it admirably, forming the focal point of an attack in which Greenhoff, Dobing, the clever veteran George Eastham and Terry Conroy all shone.

Spring 1971 brought their first major joint achievement when the Potters reached the FA Cup semi-finals for the first time in nearly three-quarters of a century. Their opponents at Hillsborough were Arsenal, destined to lift the League and FA Cup double that term but whom Stoke led 2-0, the second goal poached smartly by Ritchie. However, the Gunners fought back to parity through a late penalty, then triumphed in the replay.

A season later City suffered the same fate, losing the semi-final to Arsenal after two contests, but by then they had finally claimed some silverware, beating far more fashionable Chelsea 2-1 at Wembley in a pulsating League Cup final.

In 1972/73, with Ritchie now partnered in attack by England World Cup winner Geoff Hurst while Greenhoff dropped a little deeper, Stoke embarked on their first European campaign, only to bow out lamely to the German club Kaiserslautern after winning the first leg of their UEFA Cup meeting. For Ritchie, who had netted in that victory, defeat was compounded by being sent off in the second match for retaliation to a violent foul, almost immediately after joining the action from the substitutes' bench.

Boosted by the arrival of the sublimely gifted midfield general Alan Hudson during 1973/74, the Potters rose from their customary mid-table status to finish fifth in the First Division, a feat repeated in 1974/75 when they were only four points behind the champions, Derby County.

By then, however, Ritchie's tenure at domestic football's top table was over. At Ipswich in September an awkward collision with future England defender Kevin Beattie left City's centre-forward with a double leg-fracture from which he never recovered sufficiently to lead the Stoke attack again.

Thus in spring 1975, as he approached his 34th birthday, Ritchie left the Victoria Ground as the club's record scorer, with more than 170 first-team goals to his credit. There followed a brief spell with non-League Stafford Rangers, and later he ran a pottery business in Stoke.

John Ritchie died after a lengthy illness, seven years to the day after the demise of the legendary figure who had lined up alongside him when he had made his debut for his beloved Potters, the incomparable Stanley Matthews.

John Henry Ritchie: born Kettering, Northamptonshire, 12 July 1941; played for Stoke City 1962-66 and 1969-74, Sheffield Wednesday 1966-69; died Stoke-on-Trent, 23 February 2007.

Brian Miller

If the spirit of Turf Moor ever assumed human form, it might appear as a strapping claret-and-blue dreadnought, dispensing inspiration and good cheer in the broad, earthy tones of north-east Lancashire, and answering to the name of Brian Miller.

Miller was the personification of Burnley Football Club throughout the second half of the 20th century, first as a muscular, unselfish, relentlessly consistent wing-half in the team from the middle-sized cotton town which snatched the League title from under the noses of the big-city brigade in 1959/60, then later as a coach, manager and chief scout.

Already firmly entrenched in Clarets folklore through doughty exploits on the pitch, Miller cemented his place still further in 1986/87 during his second spell as boss, guiding the impecunious club to safety on the last afternoon of the season when they appeared on the brink of slipping out of the Football League, of which they were founder members.

It was a day of unrestrained emotion, and the big-hearted Miller was at its centre, offering an enduring image as he rallied his ragged troops courageously to transform what might have been the Clarets' darkest hour into an occasion of tumultuous relief.

Born in Hapton on the western outskirts of the town, the young Miller excelled for nearby Blackburn Schoolboys, but it was Burnley whom he joined as a 15-year-old in 1952 after being spotted in a local cup final by a Turf Moor director. At first he doubled as an office worker at the club before signing professional forms in February 1954.

Two years later he made his senior debut at Stamford Bridge as a deputy for the injured Les Shannon in a drawn FA Cup replay against Chelsea, the second instalment of a five-match marathon in the era before penalty shoot-outs.

Over the next three campaigns Miller, who was equally effective as a central defender or a left-half, became an increasingly useful member of the senior pool, earning the approbation of shrewd judges by his close marking of John Charles in one of the majestic Welshman's last appearances for Leeds United before his transfer to Juventus in the spring of 1957.

Despite brisk half-back competition from the likes of Shannon, Jimmy Adamson, Bobby Seith and Tommy Cummings, Miller became fully established in 1959/60, and didn't miss a game as Burnley pipped Stan Cullis' ever-menacing Wolves to the League crown. Uncompromisingly solid at the back and a formidable force when he rampaged forward in support of his attack, the yeoman six-footer complemented ideally the silkier contributions of Adamson and Irish midfield maestro Jimmy McIlroy as the glittering prize was claimed. His comrades ribbed him for being 'all left foot', but that didn't limit his effectiveness, and his aerial power offered an added bonus to a grittily competitive combination.

Team spirit was crucial to a side in which only McIlroy might truly be termed a star, and Miller exemplified the pervading good humour fostered by manager Harry Potts.

An earlier boss, Alan Brown, had encouraged his young players to follow a trade in case they didn't make the football grade, and Miller had been a fitter with the National Coal Board, which afforded him two mornings off each week to train with Burnley. He relished arriving in the dressing room covered in oil and grime, then hanging up his dirty overalls next to his team-mates' natty suits or casuals and berating them good-naturedly for not being proper working men.

Such was Miller's progress during the championship term that he garnered three England under-23 caps during the subsequent summer, then was called up for his only full cap, out of position at right-half, in a 3-1 defeat by Austria in Vienna in May 1961.

During the following season he was picked twice for the Football League but couldn't overcome the reliability of Wolves' Ron Flowers to claim a regular berth for his country.

At club level, though, he continued to shine in 1961/62, as Burnley sought to emulate Tottenham Hotspur, who a year earlier had become the first club to lift the League and FA Cup double that century. In the end they missed out agonisingly on both fronts, finishing as First Division runners-up to unfancied Ipswich Town and bowing to Spurs in the FA Cup final.

As the 1960s wore on Miller remained a Turf Moor stalwart, helping to achieve third-place League standings in 1962/63 and 1965/66 and being the only man to feature in all 12 of Burnley's European matches. But a few days after scoring in both legs of their Fairs Cup quarter-final with Eintracht Frankfurt in April 1967 – they lost 3-2 on aggregate – the 30-year-old twisted his knee horribly at Villa Park and never made another senior appearance.

Manager Potts was not ready to dispense with his services, however, and Miller joined the Burmley coaching staff, first working with the reserves before stepping up to first-team duties. After contributing to Second Division title success in 1972/73, he replaced Potts at the helm in 1979, but couldn't reverse the slide of an ailing team, which was relegated at season's end, plummeting to the third level of the professional game for the first time in their history.

He rebuilt both quickly and astutely, though, and an enterprising side featuring veteran Martin Dobson and youngsters Trevor Steven and Micky Phelan took the Third Division title in 1981/82. But rapid disillusionment was in store as the Clarets struggled during the next term in the higher tier and Miller was sacked on the morning of his 46th birthday, poignantly only a few hours before his erstwhile charges pulled off a remarkable 4-1 League Cup quarter-final triumph over Spurs at White Hart Lane.

Still staunchly loyal to the Turf Moor cause, after Burnley had sunk to the basement division he resumed as manager in July 1986, but was hamstrung by lack of both players and cash so it was hardly surprising that the Clarets nosedived towards calamity in the fateful spring of 1987.

That year the rules had been altered so that the bottom team was relegated automatically from the League and as Miller's men faced their final match, at home to Orient, they had to win while results elsewhere had to go their way. In the event, with sporting media from all over the world sensing the imminent demise of an institution which had been ever-present in the League since its formation in 1888, Miller steered the Clarets to victory and Lincoln City were demoted in their place.

Capitalising on that memorable high, he led them to Wembley in 1987/88, and although they were defeated by Wolves in the final of the Sherpa Van Trophy in front of more than 80,000 fans, the day amounted to a celebration of their very existence.

In January 1989 Miller was replaced as manager by Frank Casper for the second time, but he remained in Burnley's employ as chief scout, a post he held until his retirement in 1996.

Brian Miller gave most of his working life to the club, and his family was closely involved, too. In January 1983, shortly before being dismissed, he gave a debut in defence to his son, David, who rose from the bench to replace Derek Scott, a long-serving full-back and also the manager's son-in-law. Since then Scott's two sons, Chris and Paul, have also represented the Clarets, while their grandfather, his passion for Burnley undimmed, looked on approvingly.

Brian George Miller: born Hapton, Burnley, Lancashire, 19 January 1937; played for Burnley 1954-67; capped once by England 1961; managed Burnley 1979-83 and 1986-89; died Burnley, 7 April 2007.

Bobby Cram

If Bobby Cram's ability to manipulate a football had matched the speed and endurance of his running, he would have been the best right-back in the world. Those might not have been the precise words employed in the dressing-room banter directed at the stalwart West Bromwich Albion defender by less athletic team-mates during his 1960s prime, but they convey the intended message.

Frequently his comrades were embarrassed on cross-country training runs by the prowess of the amiable, blond north-easterner, who would leave them trailing hopelessly in his wake and be on his second cup of tea when eventually they made it back to base.

Accordingly, two decades later, his former Albion contemporaries nodded knowingly when Cram's nephew Steve, 'The Jarrow Arrow', emerged as a record-breaking world champion middle-distance runner.

Though late in his career he experienced unexpected glory as captain of lowly Colchester United – notably when the Essex club from the basement division humbled mighty Leeds United in the FA Cup – Cram enjoyed his personal zenith with the top-flight Baggies when they won the League Cup in 1966. Performing with characteristic honesty and enthusiasm, he helped to beat West Ham United 5-3 on aggregate in the competition's last final to be contested on a home-and-away basis.

A season later Albion shone once more in the League Cup, reaching the first final to be played at Wembley but falling victim to a rousing comeback by Third Division Queen's Park Rangers who, inspired by the flamboyant Rodney Marsh, overturned a two-goal half-time deficit to lift the trophy. Though Cram was only 27 at the time, it proved to be his last appearance for the club.

Unearthed by the Baggies' enterprising north-east regional scouting operation which had already recruited Bobby Robson to the Hawthorns, Cram enlisted as a 15-year-old amateur in September 1955, turning professional in January 1957.

In the closing years of the decade Albion were a force to be reckoned with, finishing regularly in the top five of the elite division, and their established right-back was the stylish England international Don Howe. Early opportunities for the muscular young newcomer were limited, therefore, although he was granted his senior entrance while still in his teens, in a goalless draw at Bolton in October 1959 alongside fellow defensive debutants Jock Wallace, the goalkeeper, and left-back Graham Williams.

Despite an efficient display at Burnden Park, Cram was dropped when Howe returned from England duty and figured only intermittently over the next three campaigns.

Then manager Archie Macaulay opted for a bold experiment. In the autumn of 1962, needing a right-half (or midfielder, in modern parlance) and impressed by the youngster's pace, energy and stamina, he handed him the number-four shirt.

Cram rose gamely to the challenge, surging endlessly from box to box, tackling with all his heart and generally making up what he lacked in sophisticated skills by unlimited commitment and supreme professionalism.

However, it was not his natural role. He lost his place to Doug Fraser during 1963/64, and it was not until Howe departed for Arsenal at the end of that term that Cram, restored to his original berth, truly flourished. Now he took the eye as an overlapping attacker of prodigious athleticism, an accurate crosser and a dead-ball expert who could strike with formidable power. In this latter mode, in September 1964, he became only the second full-back to score a hat-trick in the top flight – Aston Villa's Stan Lynn was the first – when he lashed in two penalties and a goal from open play in a 5-3 home win over Stoke City. Arguably, though, he missed the most important spot-kick of that season, in the 2-1 FA Cup loss to Liverpool at the Hawthorns. In fact, there was an element of natural justice about his blunder as the Merseysiders' Ron Yeats had been duped by a phantom whistler in the crowd into picking up the ball in his own penalty area.

After experiencing the joy and despair of League Cup final victory and defeat in successive terms, Cram surprised many observers in the summer of 1967 by joining non-League Bromsgrove Rovers, then moving on to Vancouver Royals, the side coached by his one-time Albion colleague Robson. He had fallen under the spell of Canada during an Albion close-season tour and eventually he would settle there permanently.

Having entered his thirties, however, Cram returned temporarily to the English game with Fourth Division Colchester and excelled as their on-field leader, cutting an inspirational figure as they brought Don Revie's Leeds to their knees on an unforgettable afternoon at Layer Road in February 1971.

With a side dubbed 'Grandad's Army' because it was packed with veterans, they overcame the Elland Road giants 3-2, and it was Cram who marshalled the heroic rearguard action as Peter Lorimer, Allan Clarke and company laid siege to Colchester's goal in the vain quest for a late equaliser.

At the outset of the following campaign the skipper was hoisted on the shoulders of his team-mates to celebrate triumph in the final of the Watney Cup, a curtain-raiser to the new season. Ironically, the scene of that gleeful elevation was the Hawthorns, where Colchester beat West Bromwich Albion in a penalty shoot-out after a 4-4 draw.

Cram retired from League football at the end of 1971/72, later returning to Vancouver, where he set up a successful coaching school.

Today Colchester play Sunderland, the League club nearest his birthplace of Hetton-le-Hole, in a match which might secure promotion for the Black Cats, and he had planned to fly from Canada to watch it.

Robert Cram: born Hetton-le-Hole, County Durham, 19 November 1939; played for West Bromwich Albion 1955-67, Vancouver Royals, Vancouver All Stars, Colchester United 1970-72; died Vancouver, British Columbia, April 2007.

Alan Ball

Rarely has any footballer personified a rage to win more vividly, or been more comprehensively consumed with self-belief, than Alan Ball, the youngest and fieriest of England's 1966 World Cup champions.

The dynamism and precocity of the flame-haired Lancastrian was matched by phenomenal athleticism, fanatical dedication and, above all, fabulous natural talent.

In a club career which lasted more than two decades, Ball shone like a beacon as an impish upstart with Blackpool, was inspirational in his breathtaking early pomp with Everton, further demonstrated his mettle as he battled to overcome unexpected difficulties with Arsenal, then attained satisfying and vastly influential maturity at Southampton.

But it was for his country, at the tender age of 21, that the diminutive midfielder with the high-pitched voice made his most indelible mark. On a blazing hot afternoon at Wembley in July 1966, he ran his West German opponents into the ground as England lifted the ultimate prize in football.

As manager Alf Ramsey, a fellow famously reticent with praise, told him afterwards: 'Young man, you will never play a better game of football in your life than you did today.' For all the player's subsequent success, it proved a sage judgement.

Alan Ball's lifetime obsession with football, his must-win attitude, and his strident ambition bloomed while watching his father, Alan senior, perform as a modestly gifted part-timer with Southport, Oldham Athletic and Rochdale in the late 1940s and early 1950s.

The boy grew up in dressing-rooms, the pungent smell of liniment in his nostrils, and when it became clear that he possessed special ability, his father – a publican, then later a joiner – hot-housed him zealously. There was an hour's ball practice every night whatever the weather, he was encouraged to strain every sinew in boxing and athletics, and to hone his fitness further he was urged to run the five miles to and from school, and to sprint between houses on his newspaper rounds.

Though Ball was the smallest lad in most gatherings, invariably he was the toughest and the best footballer, and it was no surprise when he was offered an opening with Wolverhampton Wanderers, then a mighty power in the land, when he was 14.

However, after impressing for one of the Molineux club's junior sides, he was rejected as too tiny, and less committed individuals might have despaired. The Balls, however, were made of sterner stuff and the son sampled senior football at non-League Ashton United, managed by the father, when he was only 15, then had an amateur stint with Bolton Wanderers. Again he was snubbed on size grounds – this time with the advice that he'd have a better chance as a jockey, a jibe that hurt his pride grievously – but he continued to contact other major clubs and he was offered a trial by Blackpool.

Years later Ball wrote in his autobiography, *Playing Extra Time*, that he approached that challenge as if he were playing for his life. His effort paid off and he was taken on to the Bloomfield Road groundstaff in 1961.

Now, enjoined by his father to work harder than ever, he responded with characteristic single-mindedness, putting in countless hours of extra training and earning a professional contract, aged 17, in 1962.

His lust for recognition given an outlet at last, Ball prospered at this new, rarefied level, quickly demonstrating that reputations meant nothing to him. When he found himself in a practice game alongside Stanley Matthews, one of the most celebrated players of all time, he was anything but overawed, at one point castigating the great man for not running to collect a pass, then warning the future knight that he was out to take his right-wing berth.

Matthews was outraged at such flagrant cheek, but manager Ron Suart liked the rookie's spirit and soon, when the veteran was injured in August 1962, Ball was given his senior debut against Liverpool at Anfield, and excelled. There followed a return to the reserves to continue learning, but early in 1963/64 he was recalled to senior duty, never to be dropped again.

Almost instantly, with Matthews having departed to Stoke, Ball became Blackpool's star. Operating nominally at inside-right but roaming ungovernably at will, he was a study in perpetual motion, fearless in the tackle, imaginative in his passing and deadly in front of goal. Dripping with passion and relentlessly outspoken, he was an abrasive motivator, endlessly goading and cajoling team-mates and snarling at opponents, his forthright approach bringing the best out of some colleagues but alienating others.

Inevitably his hot temper earned him sendings-off and suspensions, but they were accepted as a necessary adjunct of his all-round brilliance, and his star continued to ascend.

In November 1964 he won the first of eight England under-23 caps and, with Blackpool never threatening to climb out of the bottom half of the First Division, a move to a bigger club became increasingly inevitable.

No one appreciated that more keenly than Don Revie, the ruthless, driven boss of Leeds United, who coveted Ball to complete a formidable midfield trio with Billy Bremner and Johnny Giles.

To that end, in mid-decade Revie set up a clandestine meeting with his transfer target on Saddleworth Moor, urging him to escalate a contract dispute already launched at Bloomfield Road, thus encouraging his employers to sell. Until that happened, Revie would look after Ball financially, and a number of cash payments were made, later becoming the subject of an FA charge for disrepute for which Ball was fined £3,000.

In the event, in August 1966 the Blackpool man signed for Everton for £110,000, then a record fee for a deal between two British clubs, by which time his value had been enhanced immeasurably by his magnificent showing in the World Cup finals.

With typical bravado, Ball had always maintained that he would make his full England debut before he was 20, and he succeeded with three days to spare, facing Yugoslavia in May 1965. Thereafter he was in and out of the side as Ramsey tried various permutations, and although he featured in the opening match of the 1966 tournament, against Uruguay, he was on the sidelines for the next two games as the manager toyed with orthodox wingers.

But he was recalled for the quarter-final against Argentina, helped to defeat Portugal in the semi, then dazzled against the Germans in the final. Starting wide on the right, where his direct opponent was the classy and experienced Karl-Heinz Schnellinger, he harried the blond defender to distraction, and so potent was Ball's cocktail of energy and invention – he created England's controversial third goal for Geoff Hurst – that many observers made him man of the match, Hurst's unforgettable hat-trick notwithstanding.

Thus expectations were colossal when he clocked in at Goodison Park to start the following season, and he didn't disappoint. After scoring the winner in his opening game, against Fulham, then contributing a brace to a rousing victory over Liverpool in his first Merseyside derby, he overcame initial antipathy in the Toffees' dressing room to his brash style to become the catalyst who transformed a good team into a superb one.

Alongside Howard Kendall and Colin Harvey, he was part of a wonderful midfield unit, his game a mixture of delicate skill and rampant fervour. Ball was uncannily precise in executing quickfire one-two passing movements, he was equally adept at raking crossfield dispatches, he was an instinctive and prolific poacher of goals, and he was remarkably consistent as he scampered and strutted in his trademark white boots.

Now Everton were equipped to chase major prizes and in 1968 Ball was mortified when they dominated the FA Cup final against West Bromwich Albion, only to lose to an extra-time strike by Jeff Astle. After receiving his loser's medal, he hurled it to the ground in disgust, though later he was grateful it had been retrieved for him.

The side continued to improve, though, and in 1969/70 got their just deserts when they romped away with the League title. It did not seem fanciful that they might be embarking on a period of domestic supremacy, but the following term they slumped mysteriously and soon autocratic manager Harry Catterick began tinkering unsuccessfully with the team.

Ball, who was made captain in the forlorn hope that the responsibility might curb his occasional temperamental excesses, became frustrated, his goals drying up and confrontations with colleagues ensuing.

Still, he had no wish to leave Everton and in December 1971 the 26-year-old was shocked to learn that the club had accepted a £220,000 bid from Arsenal, Catterick explaining unconvincingly that he could not spurn the chance to double his money on a player who had given five years' top service, even though he was still in his prime. While Ball was still debating the switch, Manchester United attempted to sign him, but the Gunners swiftly closed the deal.

Arsenal and Alan Ball should have been made for each other, but there followed five years of intense frustration, the union between the great club and one of the world's leading midfielders failing to yield a single trophy. Indeed, there were even a couple of seasons, 1974/75 and 1975/76, when the hitherto unthinkable spectre of relegation loomed frighteningly large; a losing appearance in the 1972 FA Cup final and runners-up spot in the 1973 title race offered scant consolation.

Ball arrived with the Gunners having gone inexplicably stale following their League and FA Cup double of 1971 and at first he was resented by some of his new colleagues as a prime cause behind the break-up of that successful team. In addition, he loathed the Arsenal long-ball tactic which bypassed him in midfield and his fierce demands for a change of tactics was a further cause for strife.

He prevailed and soon he was directing a slick, short-passing game, but when the slide gathered force he became restless and disillusioned, even after being made skipper. In 1974 he suffered a broken leg, then a fractured ankle, and later there was a row with boss Bertie Mee when the club wouldn't back his appeal over a dismissal.

During 1975, too, the World Cup hero of '66 – who had also shone as England had reached the quarter-finals of the 1970 tournament, then gone on to lead his country six times under his old acquaintance Don Revie – was axed unexpectedly after collecting 72 caps. He was only 30, felt he still had plenty to offer, and believed that it was his irreverent attitude to Revie's fussy regime rather than sound footballing reasons which cost him the job of which he was so proud.

As footballing tensions mounted, there were off-field problems, too, as he drank and gambled unwisely, such living beyond his means bringing temporary financial inconvenience. Finally, late in 1976 he clashed with new Arsenal manager Terry Neill, whom he had never liked, and was sold to Second Division Southampton for £60,000.

Soon it became obvious that the Saints had secured a rare bargain as Ball, having gelled instantly with boss Lawrie McMenemy, played beautifully alongside thoroughbreds such as Mick Channon and Peter Osgood and made a masterful contribution to the buoyant promotion campaign of 1977/78.

Back in the top grade, he continued to thrive, helping Southampton to consolidate their status and to reach the 1979 League Cup final, which was lost to Nottingham Forest.

Then in July 1980, after brief service to Philadelphia Fury and Vancouver Whitecaps, Ball made one of the biggest mistakes of his life by returning to his first club, Blackpool, as player-boss of the struggling Third Division outfit. The former hero was greeted rapturously, but the team was dismal, he became bogged down in boardroom politics and was sacked after seven months with the Seasiders hurtling towards the basement division.

He could still run and run, though, and went back to The Dell for a terrific Indian summer in the top flight, linking fruitfully with Kevin Keegan and not leaving until autumn 1982, when he was in his 38th year. There remained brief spells with Eastern Athletic in Hong Kong and Bristol Rovers before Ball accepted that his legs had finally 'gone', and he turned again to management.

The record books offer eloquent evidence that Ball the boss was nowhere near the equal of Ball the footballer, but no one could accuse him of not trying his heart out. Perhaps his biggest faults were impatience and frustration with charges who could not meet the rigorous standards he had set in his own playing days. Arguably he was more of a natural coach than a manager, often impressing with his work on the training pitch but suffering in boardrooms for his chronic lack of diplomacy.

After taking over Second Division Portsmouth in May 1984, he led them to promotion in 1987 only to suffer relegation a year later as the club ran into dire financial trouble. They struggled back in the second flight and he was sacked within four months of the arrival of new owner Jim Gregory, whose business methods he despised. A brief but happy stay at Colchester United, helping Jock Wallace save their League status in 1988/89, was followed by a traumatic 15-month stint with Stoke City, with whom he plunged to Division Three in 1989/90 before being dismissed amidst bitter boardroom turmoil during the following term.

After that he vowed to finish with the game and took a pub near Ascot, but was lured back to enjoy a fulfilling, if precarious spell with Third Division Exeter City, twice narrowly avoiding demotion to the Fourth before heeding the siren call of Southampton and the Premiership in January 1994.

Taking charge of a club of which he had happy memories, and being assisted by former boss McMenemy, held many attractions, and back at The Dell he enjoyed the zenith of his management career.

Making the most of the delectable but sometimes wayward talent of Matthew Le Tissier, Ball saved the Saints from relegation in his first spring, then led them to tenth in the table in 1994/95, and professed bitterness when the club did not seem keen to retain his services when old friend Francis Lee asked him to take over at Manchester City for 1995/96.

He accepted but it proved a disastrous decision. City were deeply in debt, and he inherited a plethora of average players on high wages. His previous experiences seemed unlikely to qualify him for success in such a situation and so it proved, with City going down that season and, inevitably, Ball losing his job.

Still in love with the game, he was tempted back to manage cash-strapped Portsmouth again, and moved mountains to steer them clear of dropping out of the First Division in 1998, only to be sacked by new owner Milan Mandaric when the team was struggling once more in December 1999. That was Ball's last post, and early in the new millennium his energies were consumed in supporting daughter Mandy's successful fight against cancer, and wife Lesley's losing battle with the same disease.

Alan James Ball: born Farnworth, Lancashire, 12 May 1945; played for Blackpool 1962-66, Everton 1966-71, Arsenal 1971-76, Southampton 1976-80, Blackpool again 1980-81, Southampton again 1981-82, Bristol Rovers 1983; capped 72 times by England 1965-75; managed Blackpool 1980-81, Portsmouth 1984-89, Stoke City 1989-91, Exeter City 1991-94, Southampton 1994-95, Manchester City 1995-96, Portsmouth again 1998-99; died Warsash, Hampshire, 25 April 2007.

Warren Bradley

It was a storyline which the scriptwriters for Roy of the Rovers, the enduringly popular comic-strip which riveted readers' attention with rousing yarns of footballing derring-do for several decades in the second half of the 20th century, surely would have rejected as too far-fetched.

In February 1958 Warren Bradley was a wholehearted and bold but hardly remarkable amateur outside-right in his middle twenties. A mere 15 months later he was a key member of the prolific Manchester United forward line which had propelled the Red Devils to within touching distance of the League championship and he had scored for England on his full international debut.

Yet the irony was that Bradley had never intended to make his living from football; to him it was a game to play for fun on a Saturday afternoon. Unlike most lads with his talent for sport, what fuelled his boyhood dreams was a passionate ambition to teach; and so he did, eventually excelling in a trio of challenging inner-city headships.

Alas, the catalyst for the diminutive flankman's meteoric progress as a footballer was one of the most tragic events in the history of the game. When United's plane crashed at Munich on the way home from a European Cup tie in Belgrade, eight top players lost their lives and two more were maimed so that they could never take the field again.

Jimmy Murphy, the inspirational Welshman who kept the Old Trafford flag flying while grievously injured manager Matt Busby fought successfully for his life, sent out an SOS for emergency recruits and Bradley was one of three amateur internationals with Bishop Auckland to answer the call.

Initially it was envisaged that he, Derek Lewin and Bob Hardisty would bolster United's reserves, but such was the positive impact of the industrious winger that in November 1958, when he made his senior entrance, he signed a part-time professional contract and took the First Division – the equivalent of the modern Premiership – by storm.

In their first full campaign after the disaster, United might have been expected to struggle, but a free-flowing attack consisting of Bradley, Albert Quixall, Dennis Viollet, Bobby Charlton and Albert Scanlon plundered 82 of the side's 103 League goals as they finished as title runners-up to Wolverhampton Wanderers.

Bradley was a revelation. Sturdy and tough, pacy and irrepressibly determined, he was ever willing to chase back and harass opposing defenders in the feisty manner of his illustrious predecessor in the United number-seven shirt, Johnny Berry, one of those invalided out of football by wounds received at Munich.

He packed a rasping shot, too, which flashed past goalkeepers a dozen times in his 24 appearances that season, and if he wasn't endowed with the flair and pure skill of Berry, there was no doubting the immense value of his contribution.

Indeed, so eye-catching was his form that the England amateur – he garnered 11 caps at that level as well as two FA Amateur Cup winner's medals during his three-year tenure with the Bishops – was rewarded with a call-up by his country's professional team in May 1959.

In truth this elevation startled some observers, who questioned his class, but he confounded them by introducing himself to the full international arena with a goal in a 2-2 draw with Italy at Wembley, then netted again against the United States three weeks later in Los Angeles on his third and final outing. This strike was greeted with enormous relief as it equalised an early goal by the hosts which had raised the spectre of a second humiliation at the hands of the humble (in footballing terms) USA. The first had come in the form of a shock defeat during the 1950 World Cup tournament; this time, though, the final tally was 8-1 to England.

Thereafter Bradley never played for England again, and although he performed creditably for United during 1959/60, the irresistible rise of the young Johnny Giles was dimming his first-team prospects. Soon it became apparent that he was not part of Matt

Busby's long-term reconstruction plan and, following a knee problem which limited his effectiveness and demanded an operation, he was sold to Second Division Bury for £2,500 in March 1962.

Now his football career petered out with a brief stint at Gigg Lane followed by enthusiastic service to non-League Northwich Victoria, Macclesfield Town and Bangor City. But Bradley was not dismayed. As he said in 2005: 'Even when I signed schoolboy terms for Bolton Wanderers as a 14-year-old, I never saw myself spending too long at Burnden Park, although I enjoyed myself there in the junior teams for quite a few years. All I really wanted was to be a headmaster.'

After Hyde Grammar School, there followed a degree in geography at Durham University, National Service as an officer in the RAF and a first teaching job at the Great Stone secondary modern school at Stretford, Busby having persuaded him to take a job in Manchester while commencing his Old Trafford sojourn.

Then came a few years of living a double life, teaching by day, training for United on two evenings a week, all the while playing top-level matches. Eventually the conflicting demands of work and football dictated a full-time move into education, and he relished it.

In 1968 Bradley became a head teacher, presiding over the conversion of a large secondary modern into a comprehensive school. In his next job he oversaw the change from single-sex to co-ed, and then he was responsible for the successful amalgamation of three schools in Bolton – one grammar and two secondary moderns – into a 2,000-pupil comprehensive.

He trained as a school inspector in 1988 and set up his own educational management consultancy, contracting work from the newly-formed OFSTED until retirement in his sixties. However, throughout his distinguished teaching career, Bradley – a meticulously courteous, gently humorous man – never stopped loving football, and served as treasurer of the Manchester United Former Players Association from its inception more than 20 years ago, also putting in a stint as chairman.

Warren Bradley: born Hyde, Cheshire, 20 June 1933; played for Manchester United 1958-62, Bury 1962-63; capped three times by England 1959; died Manchester, 6 June 2007.

Derek Dougan

For a footballer to shave his head in the 21st century is almost de rigueur; but when Derek Dougan shed his dark locks in 1961, it marked out the lean, lanky Ulsterman with the hawkish good looks of a screen cowboy as something of a maverick.

The flamboyant, outspoken, periodically combustible Dougan was, indeed, both a formidable non-conformist and an enigma. Charming and intelligent, not averse to riding the waves of adulation he attracted, he was one of the most colourful and controversial characters in professional sport.

However, none of that should obscure the fact that, during his late-career pomp with Wolverhampton Wanderers, when he finally achieved balance between showmanship and his immense natural talent, Dougan was also an exceedingly fine centre-forward.

Earlier he was an inveterate, rather wild rover, serving six clubs and his country, tending to thrill managers and fans alike with his spikily effective individualism. At others, though, he might infuriate them with a volatility which, on his bad days, could be spiced unattractively with a dash of arrogance.

Happily, when he settled at Molineux in 1967 it was as if a lifelong quest to discover his true niche was at an end. Over the next eight and a bit seasons he scored 123 goals in 323 games, in the process becoming one of the most revered and enduring heroes in Wolves' history.

Alexander Derek Dougan was born to a Protestant family in a bleak area of east Belfast where unemployment, poverty and religious bigotry were rife, the eldest of a shipyard boilermaker's six sons. He learned his football in rough pick-up games on the back streets, then progressed to more formal contests through boys' clubs, excelling sufficiently to win schoolboy international caps as a centre-half.

Away from the game, although a bright boy, he couldn't wait to leave school in order to earn money, and there followed jobs in a toy factory and as an apprentice electrician. All along, however, in his heart was the desire for a football career, which began when he signed for Distillery at the age of 15. Having switched from defence to attack, he helped the west Belfast club to beat his childhood favourites, Glentoran, in the Irish Cup final, and won amateur international recognition.

Such was Dougan's progress that English clubs were bound to take note and duly, in August 1957, he was transferred to Portsmouth, then struggling in the League's top flight, for £4,000. Two months later, still only 19, he made his senior debut at Old Trafford and shone in a startling 3-0 victory over reigning champions Manchester United.

But he was raw and homesick, proving unable to settle at Fratton Park. Feeling suppressed and misunderstood, he railed against authority, criticised the training regime and clashed frequently with manager Freddie Cox, which landed him with a reputation as a rebel which he never wholly shook off. Still, he continued to develop promisingly as a player, and was rewarded with his first full cap for Northern Ireland against Czechoslovakia in the 1958 World Cup finals in Sweden.

The following season Pompey were relegated but Dougan wasn't, having been transferred to fellow First Division side Blackburn Rovers for £11,000 in March. By now the gangling spearhead was emerging as an increasingly dangerous marksman, but he remained feistily difficult to manage and his Ewood Park sojourn proved to be tempestuous.

Soon he was lauded by the fans, who nicknamed him 'Cheyenne' for his resemblance to the TV western actor Clint Walker and relished both his goals and his unorthodox character. However, he became involved in more disagreements, again finding fault with training methods, then showed distressing immaturity and lack of professionalism when he was on the verge of what might have been his greatest triumph to date.

Shortly after scoring the two goals against Sheffield Wednesday which secured Blackburn's place in the 1960 FA Cup final against Wolves, Dougan strained a muscle. Then, having posted a transfer request on the morning of the game – a provocative act which was to create immense hostility among Rovers fans – he declared himself fit for the Wembley showpiece, apparently believing that his team-mates would be able to carry him.

In fact, he was limping badly a few minutes into the game and, with no substitutes allowed in those days, his side was reduced to ten fit men. Soon that was nine when Dave Whelan – destined to become a millionaire and preside over the rise from obscurity of Wigan Athletic – suffered a broken leg, and Blackburn were crushed 3-0 in a dismal contest.

Later he admitted he had been at fault, but at the time, despite amassing a commendable 34 strikes in 76 starts for the club, his popularity waned.

Inevitably he moved again, this time in July 1961 to Aston Villa, where the manager, Joe Mercer, was initially delighted with his £15,000 capture, whom he reckoned was a better player than his predecessor, the England centre-forward Gerry Hitchens, recently sold to Internazionale of Milan for £85,000.

Ever the extrovert, Dougan prepared for his latest challenge by shaving his head, maintaining it was not a gimmick but to make him 'feel fresh'. His new supporters found it difficult to judge him in that first term because he missed much of it following a car crash; but at the start of the subsequent campaign Mercer, perturbed by the Irishman's relentlessly independent outlook, told him if he wanted to be different to try scoring goals more consistently. Dougan responded with two brilliant efforts to beat the formidable Spurs, but still there was trouble ahead. Villa struggled, Mercer's health deteriorated and he upset his stormy petrel of a centre-forward by leaving him out of the 1963 League Cup final, which was lost to Birmingham City.

Thus it was no surprise when Dougan departed that summer, but his destination raised plenty of eyebrows. In fact, his £21,000 switch to Third Division Peterborough United was a sensation, and it was felt widely that his decision to drop two flights might signal the end of his days at the top level. However, although he slipped temporarily out of the Irish team, he flourished with ambitious Posh. They saw him as a talisman who suited their brash, go-ahead image, and he got on well with manager Gordon Clark.

Dougan scored plenty of goals for Peterborough but one in particular, the shock winner against Arsenal in an FA Cup tie in January 1965, whetted his appetite for a return to the big time, which he achieved at season's end with a £25,000 transfer to Leicester City.

The advent of such a luminous personality generated record ticket sales at Filbert Street, where he made a superb transition back to the First Division, netting freely and regaining his international berth. Playing the best football of his life to date, he brought panache, industry and authority to his role, and Foxes fans were dismayed when the charismatic 29-year-old joined Second Division Wolves for £50,000 in March 1967.

On arrival at Molineux Dougan declared that his stay in the lower flight would last only 11 games, and so it proved. He netted a hat-trick on debut against Hull City and fired six more as his new employers secured promotion.

Thus began easily the most settled and fulfilling phase of a hitherto tumultuous career, during which Dougan became the first Irishman to exceed 200 goals in England – he totalled 222 in 546 League appearances. In his maturity, he was a comprehensively fine leader of the attack: powerful but also subtle in his aerial work, adept at protecting the ball with his back to goal, deceptively quick with his loping stride, unselfish for such a natural individualist and unfailingly brave. Such was his form at the outset of 1969/70 that Arsenal tried to sign him, but were firmly rebuffed by the Black Countrymen, who had no intention of parting with their swashbuckling hero.

He excelled alongside a succession of frontline partners – Alun Evans, Hugh Curran, Peter Knowles, John Richards – and took a major role as Wolves beat Manchester City in the 1974 League Cup final. He battled valiantly, too, in the two-legged UEFA Cup final defeat by Spurs in 1972, and if there persisted a few disciplinary wrangles – he served one lengthy ban for swearing at a linesman – that seemed a small price to pay.

Off the field, too, Dougan's profile continued to burgeon. He became a vociferous campaigning chairman of the Professional Footballers' Association, pushing hard for freedom of contract, which was achieved in 1978. He was deeply involved in charity work, hosted a local radio programme, penned several books and in 1970 served on ITV's provocative World Cup panel – alongside Malcolm Allison, Paddy Crerand and Bob McNab – after which screen punditry was never the same again.

His collection of Northern Ireland caps stretched to 43 and was not concluded until he was 35 in 1973, two years before he played his last professional game, for Wolves.

Later he managed non-League Kettering Town and worked as a Yorkshire TV presenter before returning to Molineux as chief executive in August 1982, fronting a consortium to rescue the now-ailing club. Before that season there was speculation that debt-ridden Wolves would go out of business but the financial cavalry, led by Dougan, averted disaster some three minutes ahead of the Official Receiver's deadline. The club's fortunes continued to fluctuate, however, and he departed midway through the 1984/85 term which would end with relegation to the Third Division, going on to work in marketing.

In June 2006 Dougan – always passionate about politics, particularly the problems which afflicted his homeland – appeared on the BBC's *Question Time* as a representative of the United Kingdom Independence Party.

But it is for his incandescent impact on the football world that Derek Dougan will be remembered most vividly. His career encompassed rarefied heights and unaccountable troughs, but it was never boring.

Alexander Derek Dougan: born Belfast 20 January 1938; played for Distillery 1955-57, Portsmouth 1957-59, Blackburn Rovers 1959-61, Aston Villa 1961-63, Peterborough United 1963-65, Leicester City 1965-1967, Wolverhampton Wanderers 1967-75; capped 43 times for Northern Ireland 1958-73; chief executive Wolverhampton Wanderers 1982-85; died Wolverhampton, 24 June 2007.

Danny Bergara

English football plays host to Jose Mourinho and Arsene Wenger, Rafael Benitez and Sven-Goran Eriksson; but long before foreign managers were commonplace in the domestic game, Danny Bergara was blazing the trail for the luminaries who would follow.

The achievements of the effervescent little Uruguayan peaked with a six-year stint at Stockport County, during which he transformed the serially under-achieving Hatters, leading them to promotion from the bottom tier of the Football League and on four uproarious, if ultimately unsuccessful, excursions to Wembley.

Sadly and controversially, his Edgeley Park adventure ended with the sack following a bitter fall-out with his chairman, and although an industrial tribunal ruled in 1996 that he was unfairly dismissed, his career never regained full impetus.

That was a shame, because Bergara had proved himself an imaginative and enlightened coach who was adept at coaxing the best from his players, often through subtle psychology, and who believed passionately in the improvement of individual technique.

To the fans, meanwhile, he became a cult hero. They loved the invigorating style of his team and relished both his infectious enthusiasm and the homespun wisdom which peppered his programme notes.

Farmer's son Bergara, one of seven children, excelled as a young footballer, joining Racing Club at the age of 14 and making his debut in the Uruguayan First Division a year later. A skilful and prolific inside-forward, he played for his country at under-18 level and attracted the attention of the Spanish club, Real Mallorca, who signed him for £5,000 as a 20-year-old in 1962.

He thrived in his new surroundings, helping to win the Second Division championship in 1965 and finishing as the club's top scorer three times before a £25,000 transfer took him to Sevilla in January 1967. On the mainland Bergara continued to flourish, picking up another Second Division title medal and top-scoring three times, but following an £8,000 move to Tenerife his playing days were ended by a calf injury.

Having met and married an English travel guide during his Spanish sojourn, he moved to England in 1973, initially intending to work in the travel business but eventually accepting a job as youth coach with Luton Town following a failed attempt to revive his playing fortunes at Kenilworth Road.

He proved a natural in his new role, inspiring youngsters such as future England international Ricky Hill with his emphasis on skill, and when Luton boss Harry Haslam moved to Sheffield United in 1978 he took Bergara with him. At Bramall Lane the Uruguayan became assistant manager and chief coach, and his work attracted the notice of the Football Association, who enlisted him to coach the England under-18 and under-20 sides in 1980 and 1981.

However, after Haslam left United, Bergara returned to a youth role, then lost his job in 1981 following another managerial change. There followed a succession of short-lived coaching stints, including a spell in charge of the Brunei national team, a brief sojourn at Middlesbrough which ended when the receivers were called in, and a fleeting return to Sheffield United.

But it was not until 1988 that he achieved his ambition of managing a club, when he accepted the reins of Fourth Division Rochdale.

At Spotland he did well with few resources and in March 1989 the new owner of fellow basement club Stockport County offered him the formidable task of reviving the Hatters' woeful fortunes. Bergara set about the challenge with pride and gusto, leading Stockport to the divisional play-offs in 1989/90, where they lost, and to their first promotion in 24 years as runners-up to Darlington in 1990/91.

The success which followed was more than most long-suffering Edgeley Park regulars could credit. Over the next three seasons they reached Wembley four times, and although every expedition resulted in defeat, nevertheless it represented a gloriously glamorous renaissance for a shoestring club accustomed to dismal subsistence in the shadows of Manchester giants United and City.

The quartet of reverses, all by a single goal, were at the hands of Peterborough United and Burnley in the Third Division play-offs of 1992 and 1994, and Stoke City and Port Vale in the Autoglass Cup finals of 1992 and 1993.

It was a sequence which would have withered the morale of many men, but Bergara, who had inspired exceptional performances from mostly ordinary footballers and enabled the club to profit considerably from his transfer-market dealings, remained buoyant.

But then in 1995 came the rift with his chairman, Brendan Elwood, and he was sacked, leaving behind him the bones of a team which his successor, Dave Jones, would lead into the second tier of English football in 1997.

Thereafter, despite the tribunal ruling in his favour, Bergara struggled to fulfil himself. He worked fleetingly for Rotherham United, Doncaster Rovers and Grantham, and there were scouting assignments for the likes of Tottenham Hotspur and Sunderland, but the long-term berth he craved did not present itself.

Before leaving Spain he had been warned by Vic Buckingham, the Englishman then in charge of Sevilla, that British football would be too insular for a Uruguayan to flourish, no matter how bright his ideas or how hard he worked. Poignantly, in later years, he came to believe that he had, indeed, been the victim of some early prejudice, and that following his dismissal a false and cliched impression of 'a Latin temperament' had made potential employers unjustly uneasy.

But he did leave a mark, and a positive one. Just ask the grateful fans who rattled the Wembley rafters, four times in two years, with their rousing rendition of 'Danny Bergara's Blue-and-White Army'.

Daniel Alberto Bergara: born Montevideo, Uruguay, July 1942; played for Racing Club 1956-62, Real Mallorca 1962-67, Sevilla 1967-72, Tenerife 1972; managed Rochdale 1988-89, Stockport County 1989-95, Rotherham United 1996-97; died Sheffield, 25 July 2007.

Norman Deeley

Norman Deeley was a tiny ball of high-octane energy and verve that never lost its bounce during his medal-rich prime with Wolverhampton Wanderers at the end of the 1950s.

An irrepressibly dynamic goal-scoring winger versatile enough to thrive on either flank, he excelled as part of the second thunderously powerful combination moulded by the formidable disciplinarian Stan Cullis, helping to lift two consecutive League titles and the FA Cup, and earning England recognition along the way.

There was never very much of the effervescent Midlander. When he made his entrance on to the international stage at schoolboy level during 1947/48 he stood a mere 4ft 4ins and was said to be the smallest ever to play for the team. Indeed, he was to grow only a foot taller in adulthood, but he compensated amply in skill, determination and bravery for what he lacked in physical stature.

Deeley might have joined West Bromwich Albion as a teenager, encouraged by his Throstles-supporting father, but the boy had his heart set on Wolves and he got his way, enlisting at Molineux as an amateur straight from school in 1948 at the outset of the successful Cullis managerial era.

Nothing daunted at being surrounded by comparative giants, the diminutive newcomer played for the reserves at 16 and assisted in the capture of three successive Central League (reserve) championships, earning his first professional contract in December 1950.

At that point he was a right-half – that's a midfielder in today's terms – and it was in that role that he made his senior debut in a 2-1 home victory over Arsenal in August 1951. There followed sporadic first-team opportunities, some of them at inside-forward, as he completed his National Service in the Army, and he remained a fringe player as Wolves won the first League crown in their history in 1953/54. Deeley scored his first goal for the club in a pulsating 4-4 draw with West Bromwich in the FA Charity Shield the following August, but it was difficult to imagine such a small man forging a regular centre-field berth in the fearsomely muscular, hard-running unit Cullis had created.

However, the canny Molineux boss was loth to dispense with such a talented and punchy performer and towards the end of 1956/57 he gave him an extended run on the left wing, where Deeley began to hint at realising his full potential. Thereafter he shone on a summer tour of South Africa, which set him up to star throughout the title-winning campaign of 1957/58 as a right-flank replacement for the equally minute local hero Johnny Hancocks, who had reached the veteran stage.

During that triumphant term, which saw Cullis' men finish five points clear of second-placed Preston North End, Deeley missed only one game and contributed 23 goals, including a rampant spell of 13 in 15 outings during the autumn. It was a remarkable total for a winger and he finished second only to centre-forward Jimmy Murray in Wolves' scoring chart, but he was no mere converter of chances.

With his non-stop movement and incisive football brain, Deeley meshed fluently with his fellow forwards and was integral to Wolves' characteristic quickfire build-up play. He was particularly compelling in tandem with his closest friend, the silkily skilled inside-right Peter Broadbent, and linked beautifully, too, with the hugely underrated Murray, the industrious inside-left Bobby Mason and the experienced left winger Jimmy Mullen.

In 1958/59, at the end of which the vastly influential Wolves and England centre-half Billy Wright retired, Deeley and his fellow attackers remained equally potent as the Black Countrymen retained their championship, finishing six points ahead of runners-up Manchester United, who were still in the early stages of rebuilding after the ravages of the Munich air disaster. At this point he was rewarded for his achievements in Wolves' famous gold-and-black with a full international call-up, being selected for England's springtime tour of South America, but made scant impact in defeats by Brazil and Peru and was summarily discarded by coach Walter Winterbottom.

At club level, though, he remained as effective as ever and in 1959/60 Wolves went agonisingly near to what would have been their greatest glory – becoming the first club in the 20th century to win the League and FA Cup double. Having completed their First Division programme they topped the table, with Deeley having netted 14 times, but then came the mortification of being overhauled by Burnley, who played their last match two days later. However, there was consolation in store against Blackburn Rovers in the FA Cup final, in which Deeley was to prove the central figure, notching two second-half goals in a comfortable 3-0 victory. In fact, he went close to a Wembley hat-trick as he was poised for a tap-in to open the scoring shortly before the interval, only for Rovers' Mick McGrath to slide in ahead of him for an own goal.

Less happily, with the score at 1-0 he was involved in a collision with Dave Whelan in which the Blackburn full-back – destined eventually to make a fortune in business and preside over Wigan Athletic's remarkable rise to the Premiership – suffered a broken leg. In those days before substitutes were permitted, the injury rendered the final an uneven contest and infuriated Blackburn fans, who reckoned Deeley should have been dismissed for the challenge. However, the Wolves winger always maintained stoutly that the clash had been an accident, a view with which most neutral observers agreed.

In 1960/61, which was to prove his last full campaign at Molineux, Deeley remained on sprightly form as the team finished third in the table and compiled a century of League goals for the fourth successive season, but his star was beginning to decline as he approached his thirties and in February 1962, with Cullis seeking to rebuild his fading force, the little flankman was freed to join Leyton Orient.

At Brisbane Road, under the sage and enterprising guidance of manager Johnny Carey, Deeley enjoyed a brief, initially satisfying Indian summer, assisting Orient's rise to the First Division at the climax of that term. Thereafter he missed only a handful of games as the hopelessly outclassed Londoners proved incapable of holding their own among the elite, then he left the League after half a season of toil back in the Second.

Later he served a succession of non-League clubs, including Worcester City, Bromsgrove Rovers and Darlaston Town, before retiring from the game in 1974. In subsequent years Deeley, a founder member of the Wolves Former Players' Association, managed the Caldmore Community Agency in Walsall, and worked as a steward at Walsall FC's VIP lounge.

Norman Victor Deeley: born Wednesbury, Staffordshire, 30 November 1933; played for Wolverhampton Wanderers 1948-62, Leyton Orient 1962-64; capped twice by England 1959; died Wednesbury, 7 September 2007.

Ian Porterfield

With a single swing of his unfavoured right foot, Ian Porterfield, an elegantly skilful but hitherto scantly feted Scottish midfielder with Second Division Sunderland, plunged a nation's football-lovers into transports of rapture not witnessed since England had won the World Cup nearly seven years earlier.

In planting the ball into the net of all-powerful Leeds United a little more than half an hour into the 1973 FA Cup final, a blow from which Don Revie's sumptuously talented but unremittingly hard-faced team never recovered on that momentous Wembley afternoon, Porterfield had demonstrated that the flame of romance, the possibility of undiluted fantasy, still flickered at the heart of a national game beleaguered, seemingly as ever, by its critics.

Bobby Stokoe's Wearsiders clung on to win 1-0, producing arguably the most seismic shock ever to engulf the famous old stadium, and the name of the scorer was inscribed indelibly in sporting folklore.

Inevitably that goal came to define Porterfield, yet it should not be allowed to obscure his myriad subsequent achievements as a manager, which included stints in charge of five national teams, the latest of which earned him descriptions as a miracle worker.

Indeed, the ecstatic fans of Armenia might argue that his feat in inspiring the smallest of the former Soviet republics to victory over Poland and a draw with Portugal in the current round of European Championship qualifiers was at least on a par with that spellbinding Wembley strike.

Porterfield set his sights on a career in professional football as a teenager, but his early attempts as a trialist at Leeds, Heart of Midlothian and Glasgow Rangers failed to secure a berth. However, he broke through at Raith Rovers, helping the Kirkcaldy club to reach the Scottish First Division in 1966/67.

A lanky left-footer who compensated for a slight lack of pace by his assured manipulation of the ball, he began to attract suitors from south of the border and in December 1967 he joined Sunderland for £38,000, plus a further £5,000 when he had made 20 appearances.

Deployed in midfield to replace his vastly gifted but frequently wayward countryman Jim Baxter, whose own transition from Scottish to English football was not a success, Porterfield thrived, efficiently but unobtrusively, impressing particularly with his fluent and imaginative passing.

The Rokerites were relegated to the second flight in 1970, but Porterfield continued to do well and his intelligent promptings were one of the main planks for supporters' optimism that a return to the elite tier was imminent.

But first came that incandescent Wembley moment: Billy Hughes took a corner from the left, Dave Watson distracted the Leeds defence, and the loose ball cannoned from Vic Halom's knee to the lurking Porterfield, who controlled it instantly on a thigh before half-turning to smash a savage right-foot volley high into the net from eight yards.

At the final whistle an hour or so later, the virtually universal explosion of glee – Leeds fans were the exceptions, of course – was due partly to a natural English tendency to champion any underdog, partly to Leeds' widespread unpopularity despite their undoubted excellence, and partly because nowhere needed such an uplifting tonic more desperately than depressed, unemployment-riddled Wearside. It was particularly exhilarating for Sunderland fans after watching their players spend most of the previous winter levering themselves edgily clear of demotion to the Third Division.

Thereafter, as Stokoe's improving side developed into genuine promotion contenders, Porterfield began to display the best form of his career and was on the verge of a full international call-up, but a crushing setback was at hand. Only 24 hours after starring in a 4-1 hammering of Portsmouth in December 1974 he almost lost his life in a car accident, escaping with a fractured skull and broken jaw. He recovered rapidly, however, and by season's end was appearing for the reserves wearing a rugby skull-cap for protection.

By the autumn of 1975 the Scottish play-maker was back in the senior side, making 22 appearances in the campaign which would climax in Sunderland's elevation to the top flight as Second Division champions.

But as he moved into his thirties his effectiveness began to fall away and, his international possibilities having passed him by, he was loaned briefly to Reading in November 1976. The following summer, with little chance of re-establishing himself at Roker Park, Porterfield accepted a £20,000 transfer to Third Division Sheffield Wednesday, of whom he became captain before laying aside his boots to enter management with another club from the same tier, Rotherham United, in December 1979.

At Millmoor Porterfield revealed a talent for leadership, and guided the Merry Millers to the Third Division crown in 1981. That earned him the reins of Sheffield United, a bigger club with more potential but which had slumped to the Fourth Division.

At Bramall Lane he presided over an immediate recovery, the Blades finishing his first term as champions of the basement tier, and in 1984 he took them up to the Second. At most clubs that would have been satisfactory, but with less than expected cash available for new players the impetus slowed and he was sacked in January 1986.

Porterfield's next stop on the managerial merry-go-round was a surprising one, at Aberdeen, where in November 1986 he was chosen to replace Alex Ferguson, who had just departed to take over at Manchester United.

Many Dons supporters, accustomed to silverware under Ferguson, had expected a bigger name and were disappointed by Porterfield's arrival. In the event they were not won over by his record, the highlight of which was a penalty shoot-out defeat by Rangers in the League Cup final of 1987/88.

After leaving Pittodrie that spring, the Scot put in an unmemorable spell in charge of Third Division Reading, but he was gaining a reputation as an enterprising coach and in June 1991 he took up his highest-profile appointment to date, succeeding Bobby Campbell at Chelsea.

Immediately he estranged many of the Stamford Bridge faithful by selling much-loved marksman Gordon Durie to Tottenham Hotspur, but there were hints of better times ahead as he stabilised the side in mid-table and led them to the semi-final of the League Cup in his first season.

But in his second term a series of lacklustre displays, culminating in a 12-match winless sequence, earned him the sack in February, and with it the dubious distinction of becoming the first Premier League boss to be dismissed.

Still mad about the game, and still rated highly in many quarters for his tactical shrewdness and ability to improve young players, Porterfield next accepted the challenge of rebuilding the Zambia national team after it had been decimated by an air crash which claimed the lives of 18 players. So successful was he that the Zambians came within a goal of qualifying for the 1994 World Cup finals, and he was acclaimed a national hero.

Thereafter he embarked on a coaching odyssey which embraced Saudi Arabian club football, Zimbabwe's national side, a stint as Colin Todd's assistant manager at Bolton Wanderers, non-League Worthing and the national teams of Oman and Trinidad & Tobago. In 2003 he took the reins of Busan l'Park of South Korea, leading them to success in their FA Cup and the K-League first-half title, before returning to the international arena with Armenia in 2006.

Expectations were not high in a troubled nation striving to recover from the depredations of genocide, natural disaster and mass migration, but he inspired his new charges to punch above their weight, culminating in their magnificent showings against Poland and Portugal this year.

At an open training session packed with fans who had arrived to marvel at the likes of Portuguese stars Cristiano Ronaldo and Deco, Porterfield received a spontaneous ovation as he strode on to the pitch. At that point he was already engaged in a grim and ultimately losing battle with cancer, insisting on attending to his team despite the remorseless advance of the disease. As his wife, Glenda, remarked so movingly, he had said that he wanted to die in harness, and his wish was granted.

John 'Ian' Porterfield: born Dunfermline, Fife, 11 February 1946; played for Raith Rovers 1964-67, Sunderland 1967-77, Reading on loan 1976, Sheffield Wednesday 1977-79; managed Rotherham United 1979-81, Sheffield United 1981-86, Aberdeen 1986-88, Reading 1989-91, Chelsea 1991-93, Zambia 1993-94, Zimbabwe, Oman, Trinidad and Tobago, Busan l'Park of South Korea 2003-06, Armenia 2006-07; died Surrey, 11 September 2007.

Bill Perry

Bill Perry scored the goal which unleashed the most joyous communal celebration British football had ever known. True, it was trumped by the Geoff Hurst hat-trick which won the World Cup for England 13 years later, but on a sunlit May afternoon in 1953 the Blackpool winger's injury-time strike, which secured an FA Cup winner's medal for national sporting treasure Stanley Matthews in his third final, was in a category of glory entirely of its own. When the veteran Matthews had been denied at Wembley in 1948 and again in 1951, there was a collective tear in the nation's eye. Now, a month before the conquering of Everest and the crowning of the Queen prompted a double eruption of unrestrained euphoria, the future Sir Stan, the 38-year-old Peter Pan of sport, was back at the famous old stadium for what was surely his last chance at claiming that coveted gong.

With little more than 20 minutes of the contest remaining and Blackpool trailing 3-1 to Bolton Wanderers, another crushing disappointment was in the offing. Cue a dramatic comeback to upstage anything the game's most venerable competition had ever witnessed.

With Matthews running amok – admittedly against a tiring side reduced to nine fit men in an era when substitutes were not permitted – and Stanley Mortensen completing the only hat-trick in Cup final history, the Seasiders surged back to 3-3 shortly before the end of normal time. Then Matthews danced past two weary Wanderers and crossed from the right to Bill Perry, who emblazoned his name indelibly into the annals of sport by shooting low into the net from 12 yards.

Yet momentous as it was for the 22-year-old South African to be the instrument of triumph in what would be known forever as 'the Matthews Final', it was inevitable that it would overshadow everything else he achieved throughout a lengthy career. In fact Perry, who spent more than a decade at Bloomfield Road when Blackpool were one of the most glamorous sides in the land, deserved rather better than that. In his pomp he was a searingly pacy, formidably muscular goal-scoring flankman, skilled enough to earn three England caps – he was elegible because his father was a Londoner – and widely deemed unlucky to be discarded after playing his part in two victories and a draw, netting twice in the process.

Perry's rise to prominence was remarkable after he had concentrated on rugby union until he was 14, only switching codes when he moved to a soccer-playing school in his native Johannesburg. Though he was naturally right-footed, the only vacancy in the school team was on the left wing, so he honed his left-foot technique in the time-honoured fashion of the age, by kicking a tennis ball against a wall for countless hours.

It paid off and when he left school at 16 he was recruited by the prestigious Johannesburg Rangers, for whom he performed so impressively that in 1948 he was offered the chance to join Charlton Athletic, then firmly established in the English top flight.

Perry declined that invitation, feeling unready to take such a mammoth step to an alien hemisphere. But a year later when the call came from Blackpool, one of the most fashionable names in football, offering the opportunity of playing in tandem with the incomparable Matthews, he could not resist. After a brief trial, he accepted a one-year contract with the understanding that the price of his return ticket to South Africa would be covered if he failed. Never did he look like needing it.

Within three months of his recruitment, the 19-year-old Perry made his senior debut in a 2-1 victory against Manchester United at Old Trafford, earning the frank admiration of Johnny Carey, his direct opponent and one of the most respected defenders in Europe.

Though dismayed initially by the vivid contrast between the dank Lancashire weather and the sunny climes of home, he overcame a bout of homesickness and claimed a regular left-wing berth for virtually the remainder of the decade, still the most successful years the Seasiders have ever known.

Linking fluently with multi-talented attackers such as Matthews on the opposite wing, the spearhead Mortensen and inside-forwards Ernie Taylor, Allan Brown and Jackie Mudie, the South African dasher became an integral part of an exhilaratingly entertaining unit. He offered an ideal balance to his revered counterpart on the right, specialising in direct, high-speed sprints to the opposition byline, in contrast with Matthews' far more intricate sorcery.

In 1950/51 Perry and company reached the FA Cup final, in which they lost 2-0 to Newcastle United, and finished third in the First Division, the equivalent of today's Premiership. Two years later came their timeless Wembley masterpiece against Bolton, then they enjoyed a rousing run of top-half League finishes throughout the 1950s, except in 1954/55.

In that term, unaccountably, essentially the same group of players flirted perplexingly with relegation, and one of the principal reasons they escaped was a Perry hat-trick in an astonishing 6-1 away win over high-riding Manchester City in the spring.

The first South African to pocket an FA Cup winner's medal remained in dazzling form when manager Joe Smith's tightly knit side hit their stride again in 1955/56, plundering a personal-best seasonal tally of 20 goals, including two hat-tricks in the space of a week, as the Seasiders came second in the title race to Manchester United. It was Blackpool's highest ever finish, albeit 11 points adrift of the exceptional Busby Babes.

Perry was rewarded for his consistent excellence with a first full international call-up against Northern Ireland at Wembley in November 1955, when he set up a goal for Dennis Wilshaw of Wolverhampton Wanderers in a 3-0 victory. Later that month he scored twice, shot against a post and made a goal for Bristol City's John Atyeo as England beat Spain 4-1, again at Wembley, and figured in a 1-1 draw with Scotland at Hampden Park the following April.

Though he had linked promisingly with his inside partner, the brilliant Fulham play-maker Johnny Haynes, he was replaced after his three consecutive appearances by Sheffield United's Colin Grainger and was never picked again.

As he moved into his thirties during 1960/61, Perry encountered knee problems which were to signal the beginning of the end of his tenure in the top tier. Duly he became a fringe member of a declining side and in June 1962, having scored 129 times in 437 senior outings for the Seasiders, he was transferred to Fourth Division Southport for £3,500.

At Haig Avenue he featured for one season, then dropped into English non-League ranks and enjoyed a fleeting stint with the Australian club South Coast United.

Later he returned to Blackpool, making a success of a printing business, outliving all but wing-half Cyril Robinson of his 1953 FA Cup comrades and modestly accepting a celebrity that never diminished. More than half a century on from his Wembley winner he remained, to coin the Babycham catchphrase of the era, the genuine champagne Perry.

William Perry: born Johannesburg, South Africa, 10 September 1930; played for Blackpool 1949-62; Southport 1962-63; capped three times by England 1955-56; died Blackpool, 27 September 2007.

Nils Liedholm

Nils Liedholm gave rare meaning to the over-used description of football as 'the beautiful game'.

A deeply thoughtful Swede who passed his playing pomp in Italy with AC Milan, he was one of the most elegant, imaginative and productive midfield generals of his generation, and it was no surprise that he matured into a perceptive, immensely successful coach in the adopted land he had come to embrace.

Liedholm scaled a whole range of footballing mountaintops. On the field he was a key contributor as Sweden won Olympic gold in London in 1948, he captained his country to the final of the World Cup a decade later and he glittered as Milan lifted four Italian League titles during the 1950s. From the dugout he guided AC to the same Serie A crown in 1979 and he repeated the feat with Roma in 1983, only to taste penalty shoot-out despair at the hands of Liverpool in the 1984 European Cup final.

His speciality was passing the ball, intelligently and with remarkable accuracy, over long distances and short, and there is a story that it was two years before he first misplaced a dispatch in front of his home supporters. Their reaction to this stunning occurrence, the tale goes on, was a five-minute standing ovation to indicate their recognition that they had witnessed a mere blip in the maestro's customary excellence.

Tall, lithe and smoothly skilful, the 20-year-old Liedholm began to emerge as an exceptional talent with one of his local clubs, IK Sleipner, during the war, and in 1946 he was transferred to the far more eminent IFK Norrkoping, whom he helped to lift two Swedish League championships.

By 1948 he had risen to international status and although he was unable to command a berth in his specialist position of inside-forward in the Olympic side, he excelled as a wandering left-winger and added considerable lustre to the Swedes' gold-winning combination which overcame Yugoslavia 3-1 in the Wembley final.

A year later his club manager, Lajos Czeizler, moved to AC Milan and made the signing of Liedholm and his prodigiously prolific goal-scoring team-mate, Gunnar Nordahl, an early priority.

At the San Siro, the pair teamed up with their countryman and fellow Olympic medallist Gunnar Gren, and the illustrious trio, affectionately dubbed 'Gre-No-Li' by their Italian admirers, proved central to the renaissance of a club which had spent decades in the doldrums.

Now AC Milan entered a golden age, winning the Scudetto (the League title) in 1951, 1955, 1957 and 1959. They became a major force in the newly launched European Cup, too, and Liedholm performed majestically in the second leg of the 1958 semi-final against Manchester United.

Admittedly, Matt Busby's side had been devastated by the recent Munich air disaster which claimed the lives of eight footballers and left two others so incapacitated that they would never play again, but somehow they had managed to prevail 2-1 in the first leg on their home turf. In Italy, though, a patchwork United were swept aside by a team inspired by the majestic Swedish play-maker, who netted once himself and set up two goals for Uruguayan sharpshooter Juan Schiaffino in a 4-0 victory.

Liedholm was equally potent in the Brussels final against the holders, the incomparable Real Madrid, orchestrating play and inspiring Milan to look the stronger unit as 90 minutes were completed with the score at 2-2. When Francisco Gento poached the winner for the Spaniards in added time, the Swedish schemer and his comrades could claim to be grievously unlucky.

A further demonstration of Liedholm's consummate class followed later that year when he led his country to the World Cup final in his homeland.

Faced in the Rasunda Stadium, Solna, by a Brazil side containing the sensationally gifted 17-year-old Pele, he laid down a marker of his own only four minutes into the action when he climaxed an enchanting dribble past two defenders with an emphatic finish to give Sweden a shock lead. The South Americans recovered to win 5-2, with the prodigy who is still recognised as the greatest player of all time netting twice, but the Scandinavians' 35-year-old skipper emerged with vast credit.

His immaculate distribution, particularly with his left foot, illuminated the gala occasion, and his lifelong dedication to physical fitness enabled him to hold his own among mainly much younger men.

Liedholm was an astute strategist, too, and there was little doubt that after his retirement as a player in 1961, having scored 81 times in 359 appearances for Milan, he would take up coaching. So he did, starting by working with the club's youngsters, proving a natural at passing on his expertise, and moving up to first-team duties in 1963.

There followed an extensive, varied and accomplished coaching career, the highlights of which included helping Verona and Varese to earn promotion.

The peaks, however, were taking his beloved Milan to the 1979 Scudetto, then doing the same for Roma four years later. When in Rome there were also Italian Cup victories in 1980, 1981 and 1984, and that agonising European Cup final defeat by Liverpool – in which the Merseysiders' eccentric goalkeeper Bruce Grobbelaar bemused Roma's penalty-takers with a bizarre wobbly-legs routine between kicks – at Roma's own headquarters, the Olympic Stadium.

In all there were three stints with Milan and four with Roma before 'The Baron', so tagged by his footballing peers after he married a member of the Italian nobility, retired in his mid-seventies in 1997.

After that there was never any question of Liedholm leaving Italy, which he loved and where he ran a family vineyard business with his son. He remained a revered figure until his death, which was greeted on the AC Milan website with the headline: 'Heaven makes room for Nils Liedholm.'

Nils Liedholm: born Valdemarsvik, Sweden, 8 October 1922; played for IK Sleipner 1942-46, IFK Norrkoping 1946-49, AC Milan 1949-61; capped 23 times by Sweden 1946-58; coached AC Milan 1963-66, Verona 1966-68, Monza 1968-69, Varese 1969-71, Fiorentina 1971-73, Roma 1973-77, AC Milan 1977-79, Roma 1979-84, AC Milan 1984-87, Roma 1987-89, Verona 1992, Roma 1997; died Cuccaro Monferrato, Italy, 5 November 2007.

John Doherty

Was John Doherty a victim of cruel footballing fate, or was he one of the luckiest men alive? Both views carry credible currency when evaluating the frustratingly truncated career of the former Busby Babe, an extravagantly talented member of the precocious Manchester United generation which fired the imagination of the sporting world in the 1950s.

As Matt Busby launched his exhilarating youth-based revolution at Old Trafford, Doherty grew up alongside the likes of Duncan Edwards, Bobby Charlton and Dennis Viollet, and there was no shortage of shrewd contemporary judges who deemed the locally-born inside-forward to be blessed with potential that was not out of place even in that exalted company.

He was exquisitely skilful with both feet, he packed an explosive shot to rival that of the prodigy Charlton, he passed like a dream, he worked ceaselessly and, crucially, he possessed the acute soccer brain to make the most of his other attributes.

However, he was cursed by chronic knee problems, and this is where the lot which befell John Doherty can be seen in contrasting lights. On one hand, his injuries caused him to be invalided out of the game when still in his early twenties, which came as a devastating blow to one of the most gifted young players in the land.

On the other, had he remained fit it's virtually certain that he would not have left the club to join Leicester City; and equally likely, therefore, that he would have been a passenger on the aeroplane which crashed at Munich in February 1958, killing eight of his erstwhile United team-mates and disabling two more so that they never played again.

Doherty had enlisted at Old Trafford in 1950, having shone for Manchester and Lancashire Schoolboys, and he made rapid progress, first working as an office boy cum apprentice footballer, then signing professional forms on his 17th birthday in March 1952, and making his senior debut only nine months later.

Though Busby's unprecedentedly extensive squad was bursting with enough high-quality players for two teams at that time, the rookie retained his place for a handful of games and also excelled as United reached the semi-finals of the inaugural FA Youth Cup.

But then he suffered his first major injury in the second leg against Bradford on the day before he was due to begin his National Service, which had to be deferred.

United recruited Irishman Liam Whelan, who was destined to die at Munich, as a replacement in time for the final triumph against Wolverhampton Wanderers, while Doherty began a slow rehabilitation before entering the RAF, from which he was eventually discharged as unfit for duty. Now his dreams of a professional career appeared to be in tatters, but he surprised the club medics by making a recovery of sorts and was re-introduced to First Division action, tentatively at first, in the autumn of 1955.

By now Manchester United were a thrilling side and they finished the season as runaway champions, with Doherty playing more than a third of the games in the face of white-hot competition for the inside-right berth, and qualifying for a title medal on merit.

But then, with his long-term prospects seemingly revitalised, he fell prey to further knee complications and was supplanted once more by the richly gifted Whelan.

There followed further harrowing but only partially successful efforts to regain fitness, as well as a difference of opinion with the manager over team selection, the two factors culminating in a £6,500 transfer to newly promoted Leicester City in October 1957.

Doherty got off to a bright start at Filbert Street, where he linked effectively with another former Red Devil, Johnny Morris, but within two months he was sidelined once more, and was in hospital for his umpteenth knee operation when he learned of the Munich tragedy. Already devastated by the loss of many close friends, soon Doherty received another crushing blow when informed that he would never play again at Football League level.

He reacted with resilience, accepting the player-management of Southern League Rugby Town, then in the autumn of 1958 received an offer which might have transformed his working life.

Jimmy Murphy, Matt Busby's inspirational lieutenant at Old Trafford, was courted by Arsenal to become their new boss and told Doherty that, if he accepted, he wanted his former United charge, whom he respected for his impeccable judgement of players, to become his own number-two at Highbury.

In the end, however, Murphy's loyalty to Busby moved him to reject the overtures from north London and Doherty remained in non-League circles, later serving Altrincham, Bangor City and Hyde United.

Thereafter the intelligent, acerbically witty Mancunian accrued wide experience in the world of finance during the 1960s and 1970s, served Burnley as chief scout for part of the 1980s, then went on to succeed in insurance and sports promotion.

In addition he was a founder member and long-serving chairman of the Association of Former Manchester United Players, which raises large sums for charity, and he was the moving force behind the club's belated testimonial match for victims of the Munich calamity, staged in 1998.

Ironically Doherty had grown up as a Manchester City supporter, yet he came to love United more passionately than anything except his family, and he earned renown as an outspoken sage in all matters relating to the club, showcasing his pithy, articulate and unsentimental views in a book, *The Insider's Guide To Manchester United*, published in 2005.

To return to the question in the first sentence of this obituary: John Doherty was not bitter about his ruined career, often describing himself as one of the luckiest men to walk the earth. As he put it to me as we finished work on the above-mentioned volume: 'I grew up making my living by playing a game, then I went on to a gloriously happy family life, while lots of my mates were dead before their time. What's to complain about?'

John Peter Doherty: born Manchester, 12 March 1935; played for Manchester United 1950-57; Leicester City 1957-58; died Heald Green, Greater Manchester, 13 November 2007.

Joe Shaw

If an unwary historian, researching the life and times of the footballer Joe Shaw, were to scan the record books, he or she might conclude that the stalwart Sheffield United stopper, whose total of some 700 senior outings for the Blades is a club record, was a giant of a man.

In fairness, it would be an understandable assumption. In the 1950s and early '60s, when Shaw was the trusty bulwark at the core of the United rearguard, a typical centre-half would be of behemoth proportions, relying mainly on brawn to police the vulnerable area immediately in front of his goal.

But if that same seeker after enlightenment were to look beyond the dry statistics, and chatted instead to one or two of the long-serving Shaw's Bramall Lane comrades, a serious misconception would be avoided.

In fact, Joe Shaw stood a mere 5ft 8ins in his football socks, no more than average height for any Englishman of his generation and notably diminutive for a professional central defender.

However, in the case of the intelligent, ultra-competitive north-easterner, it didn't matter, at least in terms of the efficiency with which he mopped up attacks for his regular employers. Where it might have made a difference was in the eyes of the widely ridiculed Football Association selection committee, which used to pick England teams in the days before Alf Ramsey rendered that anachronism redundant by insisting that he, as manager, would certainly make up his own mind about who should wear the three lions on their chests. Perhaps Shaw would have struggled to amass an extensive collection of international appearances due to the longevity of Billy Wright, but surely had he been several inches taller he would have escaped the complimentary but unwanted tag of the best uncapped English defender of his day.

An exceptional natural athlete as a boy, the teenaged Shaw played for Durham at county level but did not graduate straight into the professional game from school, instead working as a coalminer and playing his football for fun with Upton Colliery, near Doncaster.

Soon, though, he was spotted by Sheffield United, for whom he played briefly as a 16-year-old in unofficial wartime competition in 1944, then started earning his living with the Blades a year later.

He made his senior entrance as an inside-forward at home to Liverpool in August 1948, but switched almost immediately to left-half. However, United were a poor side that term and they were relegated from the top flight as bottom club.

Clearly, though, Shaw was a key buttress on which to build the club's future and in 1949/50 he made the number-six shirt his own as United finished level on points with local rivals Sheffield Wednesday, but suffered the excruciating fate of missing out on promotion by 0.008 of a goal, as dictated by the archaic goal-average system.

There followed a mid-table interlude of team reconstruction during which the Blades were described slightingly as 'brilliant inside-forward Jimmy Hagan and ten others', but that did less than justice to Shaw, who had forced himself to the fringe of international recognition and toured Australia with the FA in the summer of 1952.

His first tangible honour arrived at the end of the following season, which United finished as Division Two champions, and he was prominent in their narrow escape from instant demotion from the top tier in 1953/54, but it was in 1954/55 that he reached the turning point of his career.

After crushing defeats in their first two games of the new campaign, manager Reg Freeman shifted Shaw to centre-half and made him captain, and before long it became clear that the former pitman had found his true niche.

Though he was dwarfed by many of his immediate opponents, Shaw compensated amply by his canny positional sense and shrewd reading of the unfolding action, which enabled him to make timely interceptions, snuffing out attacks before his goal was threatened. Also he was quick over short distances, and agile enough to recover in a trice if a striker momentarily gave him the slip. Crucially, too, he was not over-ambitious with his passing, invariably preferring the safe, short option, whereas during his wing-half days he had needed a wider range of distribution, which was not his forte.

As one long-time observer of the Bramall Lane scene put it: 'Joe made his new job look as easy as shelling peas. He was brainier than most of the centre-forwards he faced and he outwitted them, made a lot of them look slow and stupid.'

In the April of that term Shaw was picked as England's one reserve for the side to face Scotland at Wembley, but when right-half Len Phillips pulled out with injury, he was replaced not by the Sheffield United man – now viewed as a specialist centre-half – but by Chelsea's Ken Armstrong. It seemed inconceivable at the time, but that was the nearest Shaw was ever to come to winning a full cap.

After that international setback, there followed a period of uncertainty at club level. Following United's patchy start to 1955/56, new manager Joe Mercer announced that he wanted a more physical presence at the heart of defence, but his drafting in of big Howard Johnson failed to achieve an improvement and, with Shaw on the sidelines, the Blades were relegated in the spring.

Early in the next campaign Mercer recruited the ageing Malcolm Barrass from Bolton Wanderers and it was only after the newcomer had struggled that the patient Shaw was recalled. Soon he was excelling as never before, Mercer apologised for ever doubting him, and he emerged as the trusty marshal of what became the most settled and revered rearguard in United's history.

To this day, Blades fans of a certain age recite the names lovingly: Alan Hodgkinson in goal, full-backs Cec Coldwell and Graham Shaw (no relation), wing-halves Brian Richardson and Gerry Summers, with Joe Shaw as the calm, unobtrusively competent pivot and organiser-in-chief.

Due to the centre-half's lack of inches, the splendid Hodgkinson covered more ground than most custodians, becoming a 'sweeper-keeper' before the phrase was in vogue. The understanding between all members of the unit was marked, a benefit heightened by the circumstance that they were nearly all local lads who enjoyed a close camaraderie both on and off the pitch.

For the next few campaigns, a United side based on this solid foundation remained in the higher reaches of the Second Division, and in 1959 Shaw's immense input was recognised by two appearances for the Football League.

However, promotion did not arrive until 1960/61 when the Blades, now bossed by John Harris, also reached the semi-finals of the FA Cup, only losing to Leicester City after three games – this was long before the introduction of penalty shoot-outs.

Some outsiders believed they were not equipped for the top flight, but their critics were confounded as they finished fifth among the elite in 1961/62, with their 33-year-old stopper performing majestically.

Thereafter Shaw remained a bastion of a side invigorated by the introduction of talented youngsters such as Len Badger and Mick Jones, enjoying a second stint as skipper, and scoring an astonishing goal – he didn't get many – at Highbury in March 1964, when an optimistic punt from his own half caught the wind and sailed into the Arsenal net.

It wasn't until February 1966, in his 38th year, that he took a step back, dropping into the reserves, where he helped emerging rookies with characteristic generosity.

Thereafter Shaw, a quiet and unassuming individual, coached briefly at Bramall Lane before sampling management, first with York City, who had to apply for re-election to the Fourth Division following his six months in charge.

Then, after a spell as Fulham's chief scout, he spent three years with Third Division Chesterfield, whom he almost led to promotion in his first term before two seasons of mid-table mediocrity preceded dismissal following a poor start to 1976/77. It seemed an inappropriately anti-climactic way for such a staunch football man to exit the game he had served so nobly.

Joseph Shaw: born Murton, County Durham, 23 June 1928; played for Sheffield United 1945-66; managed York City 1967-68, Chesterfield 1973-76; died Sheffield, 18 November 2007.

Graham Paddon

Graham Paddon was a feelgood footballer. He brought to the game a cocktail of flair, zest and determination which, combined with his characteristically sunny outlook, endeared him to the supporters of Norwich City and West Ham United during his 1970s heyday.

With his flowing blond locks and constant darting movement between penalty boxes, it was impossible to miss the chunky little Mancunian on the pitch. Even more compelling was what he could do with his left foot, whether piercing a defence with one telling dispatch or thumping in a spectacular goal from long range.

He wasn't quite of international class, though he made one appearance for England at under-23 level as a permitted over-age player in March 1976, but he was the type of skilful, effervescent entertainer without whom the domestic scene would have been so much the poorer.

Paddon served his apprenticeship with Coventry City, where he progressed impressively as a teenage midfielder under the expansive coaching regime of Noel Cantwell and made his top-flight debut for the Sky Blues as a substitute at home to Queen's Park Rangers in February 1969.

There were plenty of Highfield Road regulars who predicted as bright a future for Paddon as for his fellow rookie play-maker Dennis Mortimer, who went on to shine for both Coventry and Aston Villa, and those admirers were surprised when Cantwell sold him to Second Division Norwich City for £25,000 in October 1969.

He settled quickly at Carrow Road, thriving as a key constituent of the enterprising team being melded by the flinty taskmaster Ron Saunders. Operating mainly on the left of midfield, he was principally a prompter but he chipped in with crucial goals, too, especially in 1971/72, when the Canaries clinched their divisional title and rose to the elite tier. Four of his eight League strikes that term came in tense 1-1 draws and he demonstrated calm expertise from the penalty spot.

A season later Paddon performed brilliantly during Norwich's exhilarating surge to the final of the League Cup, notably in the last-eight encounter with Arsenal at Highbury, where he cracked a splendid hat-trick. Ranged against top-quality opponents such as Frank McLintock, Charlie George and John Radford, Paddon bloomed luxuriantly, then he was outstanding in the two-legged semi-final triumph over Chelsea. He strove nobly in the Wembley final against Tottenham Hotspur, too, but could not prevent the north Londoners prevailing by the only goal of the game.

With his own star firmly in the ascendancy but with City destined for relegation that term under new boss John Bond, Paddon joined fellow First Division club West Ham United in December 1973, valued at £170,000 in a deal which saw prolific marksman Ted MacDougall move in the opposite direction.

At Upton Park he dovetailed productively in centre-field with the vigorous Billy Bonds and the extravagantly creative Trevor Brooking. Paddon, who was also renowned for his chaos-inducing long throws, reflected aspects of both his high-profile comrades in his own footballing make-up, combining high energy and a willingness to dig into tackles with subtly perceptive distribution which equipped him ideally to mesh with the acute Brooking.

His high point as a Hammer came in 1975, when he played a prominent role in the FA Cup final victory against a Second Division Fulham side containing the ageing but still potent former England luminaries, Bobby Moore and Alan Mullery. West Ham won 2-0, with their second goal being poached by Alan Taylor after Fulham custodian Peter Mellor had spilled a Paddon drive. That qualified Ron Greenwood's fluent combination for the European Cup Winners' Cup, in which they exceeded some expectations by reaching the final. Once more Paddon was integral to their success, netting unforgettably with a 30-yard piledriver in the 2-1 semi-final defeat by Eintracht Frankfurt in Germany and excelling in the 3-1 home success which produced a 4-3 aggregate triumph.

The final against Anderlecht proved enthralling, too, with the Hammers taking an early lead before being disrupted by an injury to Frank Lampard Snr and conceding a controversial penalty on the way to a 4-2 reverse.

Paddon, now in his middle twenties, appeared to be at the peak of his powers and it surprised many supporters when he was sold back to Norwich – by now back in the First Division – for £110,000 in November 1976.

After an early setback, a broken leg suffered in a collision with Sunderland's Jim Holton in only his third outing after the transfer, Paddon flourished as skipper of the Canaries, forming an effective midfield partnership with Mick McGuire and going on to total 340 senior appearances during his two East Anglian sojourns.

However, as he entered his thirties he could do nothing to prevent City's demotion in 1980/81, only a few months after Bond had moved to Manchester City and been replaced as Carrow Road manager by his affable assistant, Ken Brown.

During 1981/82 Paddon, who had sampled USA soccer with a summer stint for Tampa Bay Rowdies in 1978, spent a brief spell on loan with Third Division Millwall before finishing his playing days in Hong Kong.

In 1985 he became a youth coach at Portsmouth under Alan Ball, and in 1989 the England World Cup winner recruited him again, taking him to Stoke City, where he became assistant manager at a time of travail for the Potters, who soon slumped to the Third Division. Come 1991 he was back with Pompey as assistant to manager Jim Smith, leaving when Smith was sacked in 1995. There followed scouting duties for Derby County, Liverpool and Leicester City, and another coaching post, in Brunei between 2003 and 2005.

Graham Charles Paddon: born Manchester, 24 August 1950; played for Coventry City 1968-69, Norwich City 1969-73 and 1976-81, West Ham United 1973-76, Tampa Bay Rowdies, USA 1978, Millwall on loan 1981; died Scratby, Norfolk, 19 November 2007.

Les Shannon

There was something about Les Shannon which fired the emotions of football fans.

As a feistily competitive yet subtly creative inside-forward cum wing-half with top-flight Burnley in the 1950s, he stirred his legion of admirers on the Turf Moor terraces to chant for his selection by England. It was a loud and passionate campaign which failed only narrowly.

Then, two decades on, as a successful coach in the northern Greek port of Salonika, he inspired a rash of posters which proclaimed 'Shannon is our god', and even moved two sets of local amateur players to name their teams after him.

The sandy-haired Merseysider was discovered by his home-town club Everton, scoring heavily as a teenaged centre-forward in junior football. However, although he was tough, skilful and endlessly industrious, soon he was rejected as too short at 5ft 7in, and he gravitated from Goodison Park to Anfield, joining Liverpool as an amateur in 1943.

A year later he turned professional and made an instant impact, scoring after two minutes of his Reds first-team debut against Everton in the Liverpool Senior Cup of 1945.

However, so brisk was the competition for places that Shannon was passed over when the League resumed business after the war and he did not make his First Division entrance until April 1948, when he deputised for crowd idol Albert Stubbins at home to Manchester City.

His window of opportunity opened a little wider at the outset of the following term, when Stubbins was in dispute with the club, but a settled sequence of ten games produced only one goal and Shannon returned to the reserves.

At that level he sparkled, attracting a £6,000 bid from Burnley, which was accepted in November 1949, but even then his career was slow to take off. Clarets boss Frank Hill tried him first on the right wing and then on the left but he didn't shine, and it wasn't until the late autumn of 1951, when he was deployed as a foraging inside-forward, that he began to realise his immense potential.

Certainly in 1952/53, Burnley saw the best of Les Shannon. Filling the deep-lying role recently vacated by the veteran Billy Morris, he proved an influential midfield partner for the more extravagantly gifted Irish youngster Jimmy McIlroy, and he contributed 15 League goals as an increasingly fluent side finished sixth in the First Division table. Though never a clogger, Shannon was ready to battle for every loose ball, and when he had seized possession, he had the craft to make the most of it, dispatching a steady supply of accurate passes to spearhead Bill Holden, wingers Jackie Chew and Billy Elliot, and the scintillating McIlroy.

Arguably he reached his zenith after switching to left-half, replacing the popular Reg Attwell in October 1954, though two of his outings for England 'B' (in 1952 and 1954) were as a forward and only one (in 1956) in the more defensive position.

So consistent did he become that headlines such as 'Cap now for Shannon' appeared in the local press, and the Turf Moor faithful echoed the demand with unrestrained enthusiasm.

That elusive recognition never arrived, however, and he slipped back into reserve football in 1958 as he entered his thirties and new boss Harry Potts began to reshape the Burnley side, introducing younger men ahead of the Clarets' remarkable League championship triumph of 1959/60.

In August 1959, having retired as a player, Shannon took up coaching with Everton, and soon he guided a team to the FA Youth Cup final. His talent for passing on his knowledge was duly noted, and in 1962 new Arsenal boss Billy Wright took him to Highbury, where he rose quickly to become assistant manager.

A cursory glance at the Gunners' record during the four seasons of Wright and Shannon's stewardship indicates a lack of trophies, but fails to recognise the enormous progress in nurturing the next generation of Arsenal stars. Under the strict but benevolent eye of Shannon, the likes of George Armstrong, John Radford, Peter Storey and others developed superbly, and ultimately they became bastions of the side which won the League and FA Cup double under Bertie Mee in 1971.

Along with Wright, the Liverpudlian was disappointed to be shown the Highbury door in 1966, but he was not out of work for long, accepting the considerable challenge of reviving the fortunes of Bury, an ailing and impecunious Second Division club. Forced to operate on a shoestring, he failed to prevent relegation at the end of his first campaign and he was sacked, only to be reinstated two months later following major boardroom changes. Shannon's second season at Gigg Lane brought instant redemption as his mainly youthful side earned promotion as runners-up to Oxford United, but the necessity of selling key players to survive contributed heavily to another demotion in 1969.

Still his reputation as an enterprising coach remained intact and he was re-employed immediately, taking the reins of Second Division Blackpool and, after a slow start, he guided them into the top division at the first attempt. Promotion was clinched as runners-up to champions Huddersfield Town in the penultimate game of the season.

However, Shannon's Seasiders proved out of their depth in the higher grade, and after a frantic autumn reshuffle of players had proved fruitless, he was dismissed with the campaign only 14 games old.

His next port of call was a distant one, Salonika in Greece, where he took over at the hitherto unsung club PAOK. Quiet, but with an aura which demanded respect, he made a seismic impact, guiding his new charges to the giddiest heights in their history. They won the Greek Cup in 1972 and 1974, and in 1973 they were runners-up in the championship race and quarter-finalists in the European Cup Winners' Cup, bowing out only to mighty AC Milan. As a result Shannon was practically canonised by the supporters, who were outraged when he was ousted following boardroom upheaval in 1974. Undaunted, he moved on to a smaller club, Iraklis, which he inspired to lift their first and only major trophy to date, the Greek Cup in 1976.

There followed a spell with Olympiakos in Athens during which he propped up a poor side, six months of coaching with Panachaiki, two stints with OFI in Crete, a fleeting interlude back in England as an adviser with Port Vale and a two-year stay with Brann in Norway before he returned permanently to his homeland in 1984.

In 1986 he started work as youth coach with Luton Town, later moving up to become chief scout and not retiring until the age of 75 in 2001. During that fulfilling sojourn at Kenilworth Road, he acted as consultant to the Channel 4 television series *The Manageress*, starring Cherie Lunghi and screened in 1989 and 1990. The programme-makers were desperate for an authentic footballing voice; they could scarcely have made a wiser choice than Les Shannon.

Leslie Shannon: born Liverpool, 12 March 1926; played for Liverpool 1943-49, Burnley 1949-59; managed Bury 1966-69, Blackpool 1969-70, PAOK 1971-74, Iraklis 1974-76, Olympiakos 1976-77, OFI 1977-79 and 1982-84, Brann 1980-82; died Leighton Buzzard, Bedfordshire, 2 December 2007.

Jimmy Langley

Jimmy Langley was that rare being in professional football during the middle years of the last century, a flamboyant full-back renowned for his impeccable sportsmanship.

Not for him the grim, frowning, overtly physical approach which characterised many of his contemporaries. The ebullient Londoner was a hugely accomplished performer who took his work seriously enough to earn three England caps, but still he conveyed the engaging impression of playing the game for fun.

Even in the heat of the most frenetic action, an ear-to-ear grin was prone to crease his homely features, and during his pomp with Fulham for eight years from 1957, he was invariably at the heart of dressing-room banter with the numerous Craven Cottage characters of that era. Reportedly most of the verbal cut-and-thrust between Langley and the incorrigible likes of winger Trevor 'Tosh' Chamberlain and club chairman Tommy Trinder, the famous comedian, tended to be good-hearted, but it was never less than wickedly irreverent.

On the field, unlike less expansive flank defenders, Langley was ever-ready to try something enterprisingly different. He was adept at sliding tackles which seemed to go on forever and spectacular bicycle-kick clearances which required astonishingly acrobatic contortions to complete. Indeed, his left foot was always liable to appear unexpectedly adjacent to his right ear, as his younger full-back partner George Cohen – destined to become a World Cup winner with England in 1966 – recalled affectionately a few days after his former comrade's death.

Occasionally Langley caused palpitations among team-mates and supporters alike by outrageously delicate manipulation of the ball when besieged by opposition forwards inside his own penalty box, and his swashbuckling left-flank attacking forays, rendered all the more eye-catching by his distinctive bandy-legged gait, sometimes left gaps which colleagues had to race to fill.

Still, he was quick and skilful enough to be caught out only rarely and there were few wingers who could give him a chasing, although Chelsea's Peter Brabrook did cause him more problems than most. Even then 'Gentleman Jim' tended not to resort to violence, although he could never have flourished for so long in a top-flight rearguard if he couldn't produce steel at need. In fact, he was no soft touch, and feisty opponents such as

Blackpool's Arthur Kaye could easily find themselves propelled beyond the touchline at high velocity by a trademark Langley slide.

A beautifully crisp striker of the ball with his favoured left foot, he was an expert penalty-taker, becoming only the second full-back in Football League history to reach half a century of goals – Stan Lynn of Aston Villa and Birmingham City was the first. Then there were his throw-ins, almost as long as corner-kicks, testimony to his wiry strength and capable of creating havoc among unwary defences.

Yet for all his ultimate longevity – he left the professional game after playing some 650 matches in 15 seasons – Langley had been a slow starter. As a teenager he played at non-League level for Yiewsley, Hounslow Town, Uxbridge and Hayes before joining Brentford, then in the League's top division, as an amateur in 1946.

However, he was rejected as being too small by Griffin Park boss Harry Curtis, and returned to the lower level, first with Ruislip and then, after demob from National Service with the Army in 1948, Guildford City.

His League breakthrough finally arrived when he joined Second Division Leeds United as a left-winger in the summer of 1952, but despite scoring on his debut in a 2-2 home draw with Bury, he failed to carve a niche at Elland Road and switched to Brighton of the Third Division South in July 1953.

At the Goldstone Ground he was converted successfully into a left-back, and soon shone so insistently that he won representative honours, three outings for England 'B' and selection for the Football League against the Irish League in October 1956.

After twice tasting the disappointment of narrowly missing promotion with the Seagulls, whom he captained for two years, the 28-year-old accepted a career-changing £12,000 move to Fulham, then in the second tier, in February 1957.

He settled quickly in west London, relishing the atmosphere in an attractive side marshalled by the masterful midfield general Johnny Haynes and containing diverse personalities such as the forthright and industrious Jimmy Hill, the versatile veteran Roy Bentley, the colourful Chamberlain and the exceedingly promising Cohen.

Duly in 1957/58 he excelled as never before, featuring prominently as Fulham reached the semi-finals of the FA Cup, where they were eliminated by a patched-up Manchester United – still reeling after the recent Munich air disaster, which had claimed the lives of eight players – only after a replay.

In the first game he created a goal for Arthur Stevens with a typically thrilling dash and cross, only to be off the pitch with injury when United squared the contest at 2-2. He reappeared for the second encounter, but could not prevent a 5-3 triumph for the Red Devils.

However, he had done enough to impress England manager Walter Winterbottom, who was in need of a left-back following the death of Roger Byrne at Munich, and called up Langley for his full international debut against Scotland at Hampden Park that April.

He gave a creditable account of himself in a swingeing 4-0 victory, but then missed a penalty as England beat Portugal 2-1 at Wembley before suffering in a 5-0 reverse against Yugoslavia in Belgrade, where his immediate opponent, Aleksandar Petakovic, bagged a second-half hat-trick. After that he was dropped, never to be selected again; his international tenure had ended after 22 days, which was particularly frustrating as the World Cup tournament in Sweden was only weeks away.

Nothing daunted, he maintained a lofty standard with Fulham in 1958/59 as the team, now managed by Bedford Jezzard and strengthened by the arrival of goalscoring flankman

Graham Leggat, finished as runners-up in the Second Division, thus securing elevation to the top tier.

Thereafter, despite the occasional brush with relegation, Langley helped Fulham consolidate in the First Division over the next half-decade, during which highlights included his goal in the 1962 FA Cup semi-final replay defeat by Burnley and selection for the London side which lost to Barcelona in the final of the Inter-Cities Fairs Cup (now the UEFA Cup).

Despite celebrating his 36th birthday in 1964/65, Langley remained in jaunty form and many fans were surprised when he was released that summer by new boss Vic Buckingham, who was seeking to construct a younger team.

Not long before his exit, though, there was a tribute from an unexpected source. Stoke City's recently knighted Sir Stanley Matthews, who had just turned 50, planned one last League appearance and scanned the Potters' remaining fixtures for a suitable finale. The great outside-right wanted as his marker a man he could trust not to dish out brutal treatment, and who was not himself in the first flush of youth. He chose Langley, and bowed out in honourable combat with the Fulham number-three, whose day was spoiled only slightly by Stoke's 3-1 victory. In July the still-sprightly left-back joined Third Division Queen's Park Rangers in a £5,000 deal, but he was not looking for an easy billet to wind down his career. Thus he was an ever-present as Alec Stock's men finished third in the table in 1965/66 and missed only a handful of games as they climaxed the following campaign by lifting the title and beating West Bromwich Albion of the top division in the first League Cup final played at Wembley. That was a pulsating encounter in which QPR, inspired by a scintillating goal by Rodney Marsh, clawed their way back from a 2-0 interval deficit to win 3-2.

Langley, now 38, had showed no sign of flagging against much younger opponents, but he was freed at season's end. Still as effervescent as ever, he was not ready to set aside his boots, and soon he became player-boss of non-League Hillingdon Borough, whom he led to the FA Trophy final in 1971. His team lost 3-2 to Telford after leading 2-0, but the irrepressible 42-year-old consoled himself by reflecting that he might have been the oldest man to appear in a recognised final at Wembley.

In August 1971 he started a coaching stint with Crystal Palace before returning to Hillingdon as club administrator in 1972, filling that role for the next 13 years.

Later Langley was the genial steward of West Drayton British Legion club, worked in the motor industry and continued to indulge his passion for collecting cigarette cards, of which he had more than a thousand sets. His favourites, of course, were those depicting the game to which he devoted virtually his whole life.

Ernest James Langley: born Kilburn, London, 7 February 1929; played for Leeds United 1952-53, Brighton and Hove Albion 1953-57, Fulham 1957-65, Queen's Park Rangers 1965-67; capped three times by England 1958; died West Drayton, Greater London, 9 December 2007.

Jimmy O'Neill

Jimmy O'Neill was the sort of goalkeeper football fans love to watch. Whether plunging acrobatically to repel shots on his line or springing skywards to pluck crosses from the heads of rampaging centre-forwards, the slim, almost willowy Republic of Ireland international was a natural crowd-pleaser.

He was no giant, standing two inches short of 6ft, but he was blessed with long, almost spidery arms, and when he was at the top of his form, his grasp appeared practically prehensile as he snatched high-velocity missiles from the air with consummate, near-infallible ease.

Like every net-minder ever born, he dropped the occasional clanger, and once in a while his confidence appeared to wilt. But few followers of Everton in the 1950s or Stoke City in the early 1960s – when the Potters' 'Old Crocks', an inspired amalgam of veterans illuminated by the incomparable Stanley Matthews – rose to the top flight as Second Division champions, had cause to complain about the cheerful Dubliner's contribution.

O'Neill, the son of the accomplished professional golfer Moses O'Neill, was adept at all ball games as a youngster, but exhibited most exceptional promise as a goalkeeper, first with local club Buffin United, then in his country's schoolboy side.

It was while excelling in a youth international at Brentford that he was spotted by Everton, with whom he turned professional in May 1949. At the time Goodison Park offered a tempting but potentially daunting prospect for any rookie keeper, as the Toffees were searching for a long-term replacement for the revered oldster Ted Sagar, who was finally approaching the end of his magnificent career. There was no shortage of candidates, with the likes of George Burnett, Harry Leyland and Albert Dunlop all in the frame, but it was O'Neill who picked up the gauntlet most convincingly.

He made his senior debut at Middlesbrough as an 18-year-old in August 1950, and despite being beaten four times in a crushing defeat, he was retained for a run of ten games in which he revealed immense raw talent, though clearly he was not quite ready to become the last line of defence in what was, frankly, a poor side.

Thus the 40-year-old Sagar was recalled, but could do nothing to prevent relegation to the Second Division, where O'Neill received another extended opportunity in 1951/52. Now more experienced, he made the most of it and was rarely absent when Cliff Britton's improving team secured promotion back to the top flight as runners-up to champions Leicester City – on goal average, the absurdly hard-to-calculate precursor of goal difference – in the spring of 1954.

By then he had begun to make an impact at international level, too, though he took little pleasure in remembering his first full outing for the Republic, against Spain in Madrid in June 1952. Ireland were hammered 6-0 and were two down before the debutant touched the ball, other than to pick it out of the net. He wasn't to blame, though, finding himself horribly exposed by a porous defence, and he was picked for the next match, going on to win 17 caps before being ousted finally at the end of the decade.

Back on the domestic front, for two seasons he helped Everton to consolidate as a worthy but uninspiring mid-table member of the top tier before he was supplanted as first-choice goalkeeper by the locally-born Dunlop, a colourful scallywag whom O'Neill considered to be an inferior performer.

Thereafter the Irishman's chances to impress at Goodison were limited to occasional outings as Dunlop's deputy, and it was ironic that one of his finest displays came in a home annihilation by Arsenal in 1958. That autumn day he was blameless for all six Gunners goals and single-handedly saved the Toffees from further humiliation with a succession of sensational saves.

Clearly it was an unsatisfactory situation for the still-ambitious O'Neill, who clashed with new manager Johnny Carey over what he perceived as unfair treatment, and hoped for a transfer to Liverpool, which was rumoured but never materialised.

Instead in July 1960, Tony Waddington, the new manager of Second Division Stoke City, offered £5,000 to sign the unsettled 28-year-old custodian, and Everton accepted. At first O'Neill, who had made more than 200 appearances for the Goodison club, was reluctant to switch to the Victoria Ground because he didn't want to move house, but he was persuaded by the shrewd Stoke boss.

Waddington had a vision of reviving the hitherto mediocre Potters, using mainly footballers of proven quality who were seen by less canny observers as being past their best.

O'Neill was his first capture and before long he added a string of ageing diamonds who hadn't lost their lustre, the likes of Jackie Mudie from Blackpool, Manchester United's Dennis Viollet, Jimmy McIlroy of Burnley, Eddie Clamp and Eddie Stuart from Wolves and, crucially, Blackpool's former Stoke idol Stanley Matthews, who wasn't far off 50 but had still been dancing down the right touchline at Bloomfield Road like a frisky young colt.

The upshot was promotion as table-toppers in 1962/63, with O'Neill playing in all 42 League games, proving a stabilising influence on the men in front of him and performing superbly in some of the key encounters such as the narrow springtime victories over their nearest rivals, Chelsea and Sunderland.

At the start of the following campaign, O'Neill was still short of his 32nd birthday, no age for a goalkeeper, and had realistic expectations of a lengthy Indian summer back in the top grade.

However, Waddington had other ideas, replacing him first with the much younger Bobby Irvine and then with Scottish international Lawrie Leslie. Believing passionately that he was a better goalkeeper than either of them, O'Neill became unsettled and declared himself unwilling to accept third-team football.

Accordingly, in March 1964 he joined Fourth Division Darlington, remaining at Feethams for a year, then completing his senior career with Port Vale, with whom he suffered demotion to the basement division in 1964/65.

After leaving the Football League, in which he had played more than 400 games for his four clubs, O'Neill put in a brief spell with Cork Celtic in his homeland before laying aside his gloves in 1968 to run a taxi business in Ormskirk, Lancashire.

James Anthony O'Neill: born Dublin, 13 October 1931; played for Everton 1949-60, Stoke City 1960-64, Darlington 1964-65, Port Vale 1965-66; capped 17 times by the Republic of Ireland 1952-59; died 15 December 2007.

Tommy Harmer

'Harmer the Charmer' was the evocative nickname, and it summed up the spindly little Eastender's footballing persona admirably as he captivated Tottenham Hotspur fans of the late 1950s with artistic sleight-of-foot and an almost brazen audacity which belied his rather anxious off-the-pitch demeanour.

Tommy Harmer was the archetypal ball-juggling inside-forward, and had he enjoyed his pomp in the first half of the 20th century he would have been hailed as a national treasure. As it was he was born too late to be a soccer superstar, the game having changed to place increased emphasis on steelier, more muscular attributes than he possessed, but there remained few more subtly beguiling manipulators of a football anywhere in England.

Even discounting his devilish skills, Tottenham's 'Tom Thumb' was unmissable on the field of play, with his jerkily inelegant mode of running, his voluminous shorts and his mop of thick black hair crowning a head which appeared fractionally too big for his puny, pipe-cleaner of a frame.

When Harmer's creative muse was with him, though, all notions of awkwardness dissolved. The nervy individual who maintained a tense ritual of smoking half a cigarette before every game, with the rest saved for the interval, was transformed into a bold enchanter of devastatingly assured touch, a dribbler and passer sublime who was adept at escaping from the tightest of corners.

When Harmer dispatched the ball, every manner of trajectory was his to command, his repertoire containing back-spin, swerve and one or two impudent incantations of his own invention. Yet for all that technical mastery, he was never a self-aggrandising trickster better suited to circus ring than football field; rather he was an instinctive improviser whose subtle wiles were employed faithfully in his team's cause.

Growing up as the son of a French polisher in London's East End, Harmer honed his remarkable natural abilities in traditional manner, kicking a tennis ball around the streets near his home at every opportunity. It was a method of self-improvement to which he was wedded, to such an extent that invariably he carried a small ball in his pocket even after turning professional.

His talent first became apparent when he played for London Fields School, though at that stage he was deemed too frail for representative honours. Undeterred, he remained in love with the game and moved on to a team of naval cadets, with whom he was excelling when spotted by a Tottenham Hotspur scout during the war.

After joining the White Hart Lane club as a 17-year-old amateur in 1945, he was farmed out to non-League Finchley to gain experience, and to grow physically. A beef-steak-and-milk diet failed conspicuously to flesh out that gaunt outline, but he continued to develop as a player and signed professional forms for Spurs in August 1948.

For a footballer of his delicate type, it was not the most propitious time to be seeking a senior breakthrough at that particular club. Under the guidance of new boss Arthur Rowe, Tottenham were developing an exhilarating push-and-run style which would earn them the championship of the Second and First Divisions in consecutive seasons, 1949/50 and 1950/51. The deep-thinking manager understood Harmer's exceptional quality, but he believed that the diminutive play-maker interrupted the rapid flow of his successful system. Accordingly it was not until September 1951, at the age of 23, that Harmer made his first-team debut, at home to Bolton Wanderers, when he made up for lost time by delighting supporters with a dazzling virtuoso performance in a 2-1 victory.

However, that did not cement his position and for nearly five years he was reduced to a peripheral role on the fringe of the side, enormously frustrating for a performer in his middle twenties who should have been nearing his peak. Maddeningly, too, when he was picked he did not always show himself to best advantage, sometimes being brushed aside and rendered ineffective by more vigorous adversaries.

So disenchanted did he become that he asked for a transfer, but the only firm offer came from Cardiff City, who were located too far from London for the home-loving Harmer, who thus had no choice but to bide his time.

His moment arrived in mid-decade following the departure of veteran midfield general Eddie Baily and Rowe's retirement through ill health. New boss Jimmy Anderson rated Harmer highly and employed him alongside the recently acquired wing-half Danny Blanchflower, the pair of them melding magnificently to become one of the most creative centre-field pairings in English football.

With the eloquent Irishman prompting intelligently and inspirationally at his shoulder, Harmer switched play constantly like some gawky but increasingly self-assured signalman on rush-hour traffic duty.

Largely as a result of this happy liaison, Spurs were transformed from the lower-to-mid-table mediocrities they had become into championship challengers in 1956/57. That term Harmer played in every match, and answered the criticism that he was a lightweight luxury by scoring 17 League goals, including ten penalties, as the side finished as title runners-up to Manchester United's Busby Babes.

He continued to thrive as Tottenham took third place in the next campaign, and even though he had entered his thirties by the time another new manager, Bill Nicholson, embarked on radical team reconstruction in October 1958, it did not seem fanciful to suppose that Harmer might play a central part in the fresh era. Indeed, he gave the display of a lifetime in Nicholson's first game in charge, an astonishing 10-4 triumph over Everton in which, some contemporary observers maintain, he set up nine goals and scored the other one. That may be stretching the facts a tad, but he had laid down a compelling marker and could not be blamed for contemplating the prospect of a stimulating Indian summer at White Hart Lane.

However, his prospects dimmed when the gloriously gifted John White was signed from Falkirk in October 1959. At first they were used as twin inside-forwards, then they were employed in tandem on the right flank (with Harmer on the wing), but the balance wasn't quite correct and, by decade's end, the older man was out of the team for good.

In October 1960 the 32-year-old Charmer was sold for £6,000 to Watford of the Third Division, and it was poignant in the extreme that such a beautifully skilful operator should miss out on the greatest achievement in Tottenham's history. That season, with thoroughbred newcomers such as Dave Mackay, Cliff Jones and White joining the evergreen Blanchflower, Spurs were incandescently brilliant as they became the first team in the 20th century to win the League and FA Cup double.

Blanchflower, in particular, regretted Harmer's exit and sang his praises lavishly, dubbing him 'the beloved outcast' as he left for Vicarage Road, where his intricate touches were largely wasted among the inevitable crudities of the lower grade.

He had been courted by bigger clubs in the Midlands and the North, but he remained loth to stray far from London, to which he returned in September 1962 to enlist with Second Division Chelsea. Tommy Docherty's precocious young bloods benefited only briefly from the 34-year-old's experience, but although he made a mere handful of appearances for the Pensioners, he did contribute the goal which kept their promotion hopes alive with a win at Sunderland's Roker Park.

After rising to the top flight with Chelsea that spring, Harmer played three more times for his new employers, notably engineering the two goals which beat Tottenham at White Hart Lane in February 1964.

Thereafter the still-skinny veteran coached at Stamford Bridge before leaving the game in 1967, later working as a bank messenger in the West End of London.

To aficionados of pure skill, it remained anathema that Harmer's sole international honour was an appearance for England's 'B' side against Holland in 1952; to his loyal supporters that lack of recognition signified a disgraceful triumph of functionalism over flair.

Thomas Charles Harmer: born Hackney, London, 2 February 1928; played for Tottenham Hotspur 1948-60, Watford 1960-62, Chelsea 1962-64; died Edmonton, London, 25 December 2007.

Billy Elliott

In the far-off football world that was the 1950s, massed banks of cloth-capped fans roared passionate imprecations at burly, snarling full-backs to terrify the living daylights out of diminutive, dainty wingers. Admittedly that's a vast generalisation employing three shameless stereotypes, but it serves to conjure an image which is not devoid of truth.

But not in the case of Billy Elliott.

When that feisty little flankman went on the warpath – which he did every time he ran on to the pitch, albeit in a scrupulously sporting spirit and utterly devoid of malice – it tended to be opposition defenders who were counting their bruises when the final whistle was blown.

Elliott won five England caps and at club level patrolled the touchline for Bradford Park Avenue, Burnley and Sunderland in the decade and a half following the Second World War. He was revered by supporters at his every port of call.

Perhaps not surprisingly for such a combative operator, he was also adept in defence or midfield, being capable of performing competently in the top domestic flight both at left-back and left-half, as he did frequently for the Wearsiders towards the end of his playing days.

Elliott in action was a study in high-velocity pugnacity laced with deceptively subtle skills. His attacking speciality was racing beyond his marker to reach the byline, then driving a low cross into the penalty area, often through a tangled forest of legs, for conversion by lurking marksmen.

But it was his notion of 'defending from the front' for which he was renowned. When any opponent in his vicinity was in possession, the 5ft 7in Yorkshireman would be snapping at his ankles to win the ball, and he was never deterred by either the threat or the reality of physical aggression.

On Christmas Day 1951, when Burnley were facing Lancashire rivals Preston North End at Turf Moor, his personal battle with the formidable Lilywhites' full-back Willie Cunningham became so intense that the Preston captain, the gentlemanly Tom Finney, switched Cunningham to the other side of the pitch to prevent matters getting out of hand.

How ironic, then, that when Elliott was sent off for the only time in his career, against Manchester City at Maine Road in March 1952, the referee gave 'a look of intent' as the singularly quaint reason for dismissal.

What was to become a lifetime in football commenced when Elliott signed amateur forms with Bradford Park Avenue as a 14-year-old in 1939, turning professional three years later. During the war he guested for Huddersfield Town, but it was with his home-town club that he became an established Second Division performer in the late 1940s, sometimes as a left-half but usually on the left wing, the position from which he scored the goal which dumped Arsenal out of the FA Cup at Highbury in January 1948.

But after Bradford's relegation in 1950 it became obvious that the classy Elliott needed to step up. Duly, in September 1951, he was sold to First Division Burnley for £23,000, then a record fee for the Lancashire club, with another winger, Terry Lyons, moving in the opposite direction as part of the deal.

At Turf Moor Elliott fared so well that his first campaign as a Claret was capped by an England call-up for a summer tour of Europe. He made his international entrance in a 1-1 draw against Italy at the Stadio Communale in Florence, and a week later he relished his role in a famously physical 3-2 victory over Austria which saw Bolton Wanderers' courageous centre-forward Nat Lofthouse attain the lasting sobriquet of 'The Lion of Vienna'.

Now Elliott was in the form of his life, and arguably 1952/53 was his finest season as he helped Burnley finish sixth in the First Division and won three more England caps, netting three goals in the process. The first was a late equaliser in a pulsating 2-2 draw with Northern Ireland at Windsor Park, Belfast, the others coming in a 5-0 drubbing of Belgium at Wembley.

However, although he also made four appearances for the Football League, thereafter he slipped out of the international reckoning during a period in which most wingers were eclipsed by the incomparable pairing of Tom Finney and Stanley Matthews.

Back on the club front, though, Elliott continued to be in brisk demand and in June 1953 a £26,000 transaction took him to Sunderland, then known as 'The Bank of England club' for their lavish spending.

In his first outing for the home side at Roker Park he made the best possible initial impression, scoring in the 7-1 annihilation of Arsenal, but despite fielding the stellar likes of Welsh stars Trevor Ford and Ray Daniel, clever Irish winger Billy Bingham and the brilliant but unorthodox England play-maker Len Shackleton, Sunderland found success elusive.

There was a fourth-place finish in 1954/55 and FA Cup semi-final defeats in 1955 and 1956, but otherwise there was mediocrity and worse, culminating in the club's first ever relegation, amid allegations of financial irregularities, to the second tier in 1958.

Despite that travail, Elliott endeared himself to the Wearside fans by his endless enthusiasm and determination, and often he combined effectively with his friend Shackleton, a former comrade from his Bradford days. Perhaps they gelled because they were such stark footballing opposites, 'Shack' brilliant when he was in the mood but notoriously mercurial, Elliott splendidly consistent. Indeed, he was Sunderland's only ever-present during their dismal demotion season, which he began at left-half and finished at left-back.

Having reached his middle thirties, he left the Football League in 1959 to join Wisbech Town of the Southern League, then took up coaching and directed operations for the Libyan national team from 1961 to 1963. There followed a scouting stint for Sheffield Wednesday before further coaching appointments, with the United States Forces team in Germany from 1964 to 1966, then Daring FC of Brussels until 1968, when he returned to Sunderland as trainer-coach.

Back at Roker, Elliott played a significant part in the development of the side which stunned the sporting world by defeating Don Revie's mighty but not universally popular Leeds United in the 1973 FA Cup final under manager Bobby Stokoe. Shortly before that, in November 1972, he had served a brief spell as caretaker boss, during which he switched Dave Watson from centre-forward to centre-half, the position in which the strapping Midlander became the club's most capped England player.

Shortly after that triumph Elliott moved to Norway, where he spent four years as coach of Brann Bergen, then in December 1978 he made a second Roker return as caretaker manager, and was considered unlucky not to be offered the job on a permanent basis after taking them to within a point of promotion to the elite division at the end of that term. The fans petitioned to keep him, but after Ken Knighton was appointed instead, Elliott took over as manager of cash-strapped Darlington of the Fourth Division. There was one successful application for re-election to the League – this was before the era of automatic

272

ejection for the bottom clubs – and a perilous brush with bankruptcy, but he made the most of a parlous situation before departing in June 1983.

Wherever he roamed during his 44 years in the game, Billy Elliott was a bonny battler who never gave less than value for money.

William Henry Elliott, footballer and manager; born Bradford, Yorkshire, 20 March 1925; played for Bradford Park Avenue 1939-51, Burnley 1951-53, Sunderland 1953-59; capped five times by England 1952; managed Sunderland as caretaker 1972 and 1978-79, Darlington 1979-83; died Sunderland, Tyne and Wear, 21 January 2008.

Len Boyd

Len Boyd was the staunch and steely skipper of the most successful Birmingham City side in the club's 132-year history. Under his uplifting leadership the Blues won the Second Division championship in 1955, then a year later came sixth in the top flight – their highest ever League finish – and reached the FA Cup final.

As a footballer the tall, long-striding Londoner was a fiendishly industrious wing-half, passably skilful on the ball as might be expected of a former inside-forward, and courageously combative, too, capable of dishing out physical punishment implacably and taking it without a whimper. Indeed, he once played four games with what turned out later to be a hairline fracture of the leg. Yet for all his intrepid, sometimes frenetic efforts in the midfield trenches, there was an aura of composure about him, and perhaps the most abiding image of captain Boyd is of his majestic bearing as he ploughed forward in support of his attack like some stately galleon in full sail, waving imperiously to direct the men ahead of him, the very heartbeat of his team.

Despite playing in the same West Ham schools team as Ken Green, destined to become a comrade at Birmingham in the 1950s, Boyd was a late starter in the professional game. It was not until he had served Ilford as an amateur that he was spotted playing for the Royal Navy in Malta as a 22-year-old in 1945, a Plymouth Argyle fan being sufficiently impressed to pass on his details to the Devon club.

A successful trial followed and Boyd enlisted at Home Park that December, but his progress as a Pilgrim was not rapid. For two years he was seen as a promising but not exceptional inside-forward, but when he was switched to right-half by soon-to-depart manager Jack Tresadern it became clear that he had located his true niche.

Suddenly he looked a more poised and confident performer, even in a side struggling perennially to avoid relegation from the Second Division under new boss Jimmy Rae, and it was inevitable that he attracted attention from bigger clubs.

Accordingly in January 1949 Boyd became the first Plymouth player to be sold for a five-figure fee, joining Birmingham for £17,500. Understandably the Argyle supporters had been incensed at the mere suggestion that one of their favourites might be allowed to depart, so the transfer negotiations were kept secret until the deal could be revealed as a fait accompli. Unfortunately for the newcomer at St Andrew's, City's hold on their tenure in the elite division was as tenuous as Plymouth's at their level, and when the 1949/50 campaign ended he found himself back in the second tier.

However, under the enterprising management of Bob Brocklebank – who had made Boyd his first signing on taking the reins at Birmingham – there was a marked improvement. Some proven players were signed, the youth system was revamped and a steady renaissance began.

In 1950/51 the Blues finished fourth in the table and reached the semi-finals of the FA Cup, where they lost to Blackpool only after a replay. Boyd, who was emerging as a natural leader, grew rapidly in influence, excelling as the side narrowly missed promotion in 1951/52, being pipped for promotion only on goal average (the absurdly complicated forerunner of goal difference) by Cardiff City.

His burgeoning stature was recognised by an appearance for England 'B' against Holland, and that season he was also selected for an FA representative XI, but he never received the full cap which most St Andrew's regulars reckoned was his due.

Brocklebank was replaced as Birmingham team boss by Arthur Turner in October 1954, and the new man led the Blues to the Second Division crown in his first term, this time goal average working in City's favour as they finished highest in a three-way tie on points with Luton Town and Rotherham United.

Now there were critics who protested that the Midlanders lacked sufficient class to flourish in the higher grade, but they were to be comprehensively confounded.

A solid combination built around the formidably flinty half-back line of Boyd, young centre-half Trevor Smith and feisty left-half Roy Warhurst, and featuring England goalkeeper Gil Merrick and talented full-back Jeff Hall – who would lose his life to polio before the decade was out – finished sixth in the table, only four points adrift of runners-up Blackpool.

Better still in an era when no club would have dreamed of treating the FA Cup with contempt by fielding a weakened team, they embarked on a glorious knockout campaign which took them all the way to Wembley without once playing on their home turf.

The inspirational Boyd featured mightily in all six ties, which included a memorable local derby victory at West Bromwich Albion, a stirring 3-1 triumph over Arsenal at Highbury at the quarter-final stage and a satisfying 3-0 drubbing of Sunderland at Hillsborough in the semi.

Alas for the Blues, the final against Manchester City produced a dismal anti-climax. In a game best remembered for the fact that Manchester's German goalkeeper Bert Trautmann played on after breaking his neck – he didn't discover the full extent of his injury until several days later – Birmingham never performed close to their full potential, losing 3-1.

In fairness, they had been weakened by the absence through injury of Warhurst, which had prompted Boyd's move from right to left-half, with young John Newman coming in as a replacement. Also Boyd himself was not fully fit, amazing team-mates by the manner in which he defied severe back pain, taking the field with heavy strapping.

By now the captain was in his 33rd year and after only one more appearance – in a 1-0 away victory against Dinamo Zagreb in the newly launched Inter-Cities Fairs Cup (later the UEFA Cup) – he opted for retirement from the professional game, going on to make his living first as a publican in Birmingham, then subsequently as a traffic warden.

He didn't give up on football altogether, however, moving into non-League circles to serve Hinckley Athletic briefly as a player, then coaching and scouting for Redditch United between 1960 and 1965.

For all his leadership virtues, Boyd was essentially a quiet and unassuming man, and he never entered football management as many observers had expected a character of such impressive gravitas and presence to do.

Leonard Arthur Miller Boyd, footballer; born Plaistow, London, 11 November 1923; played for Plymouth Argyle 1945-49, Birmingham City 1949-56; died Melton Mowbray, Leicestershire, 14 February 2008.

Brian Harris

Both as a versatile, high-quality footballer and an irrepressible character bubbling with vitality and wicked humour, Brian Harris became woven into the fabric of Everton as that great sporting institution rose from its mid-1950s doldrums to scale the English game's loftiest pinnacles during the next decade.

So comprehensive were his professional abilities that in the course of a 12-year first-team tenure at Goodison Park in which he majored as an endlessly industrious wing-half and played more than 350 games, Harris filled most outfield positions. Yet for many Toffees fans the defining image of the loyal, locally-born all-rounder involved a policeman's helmet perched jauntily above a grin as wide as the Mersey.

It happened during the 1966 FA Cup final after an over-exuberant supporter celebrated Everton's equaliser against Sheffield Wednesday by dashing uninvited across the sacred Wembley turf. The forces of law and order set off in hot pursuit and the sprinting interloper was felled by a flying rugby tackle, in the execution of which the detaining officer lost his headgear. Unable to resist such an opportunity for a laugh, even with the fate of the famous old trophy still in the balance, Harris picked up the helmet and tried it for size before it was restored to its rightful owner.

None of which is to suggest that the former England youth international was anything but deadly serious about his business. Recruited from amateur side Port Sunlight as a wiry 18-year-old winger for a mere £10 signing-on fee in January 1954, halfway through the season which would end in Everton gaining promotion back to the top flight, he worked diligently and made his senior entrance on the right flank at Burnley in August 1955.

For three years he progressed tolerably successfully, contributing a smattering of goals while drifting in and out of a team which never rose above mid-table, but it was not until Johnny Carey replaced Ian Buchan as manager in 1958 that Harris was switched to wing-half, the role in which he was to realise his full potential.

Operating on the left of midfield with a primarily defensive responsibility, his briskness in the tackle, admirable aerial combativeness for a fellow who stood only 5ft 8in and a willingness to run until he dropped were ideal for the job, but his constructive input was valuable, too. Although his attacking skills tended to be underrated, in fact he was a crisp and accurate passer adept at delivering early dispatches to his forwards which frequently caught opponents unawares. Despite the idealistic Carey having laid the foundations of Everton's long-term renaissance, he was sacked in 1961 and replaced by the more pragmatic, fearsomely ruthless Harry Catterick, who was to guide the Toffees to serial glory and under whom Harris continued initially to thrive.

But just as a team containing thoroughbreds such as fiery right-half Jimmy Gabriel, cultured young stopper Brian Labone and multi-talented attackers Alex Young and Roy Vernon started to emerge as genuine contenders for the top honours, Harris was replaced by the admittedly classier Tony Kay, signed in December 1962 from Sheffield Wednesday for £55,000, then a record fee for a British half-back.

Thus as Everton roared on to become League champions in the spring, the discarded 27-year-old, who had made enough appearances to qualify for a title medal, was left to rue his reversal of fortune, and some close observers of the Goodison scene believed he would demand a transfer.

However, he remained faithful, continuing to play his part as a utility man, deputising for injured comrades at both wing-half and full-back, until in 1964 he was restored as a regular in sensational and shocking circumstances. Kay, a thoroughbred performer in his prime, was banned and jailed for his part in a bribery scandal which rocked the sporting world; he would never make another professional appearance.

Catterick might have responded by seeking another star recruit, but for two terms he persisted with the tried and tested Harris, who responded nobly, helping Everton to finish fourth in the 1964/65 championship race. They slumped to a mid-table finish the next term but there was exhilarating compensation in their FA Cup campaign, in which Harris was ever-present. It culminated in a Wembley encounter with Sheffield Wednesday which produced not only the pantomime sequence in which he revelled, but also one of the most memorable comebacks in the competition's history.

When the Owls seized a two-goal advantage shortly after half-time, the Merseysiders seemed doomed to disappointment, but a brace of strikes in five minutes from inexperienced marksman Mike Trebilcock – the first following a clever chip into the penalty box by Harris – transformed the situation. Cue the gleeful invasion, and not long afterwards the Everton revival was completed when England winger Derek Temple coolly dispatched the winning goal ten minutes from time.

Thereafter Harris, by now in his thirties, lost his place in a reshuffle following the summer arrival of England World Cup winner Alan Ball, and after a handful of autumn outings as a deputy, he joined Second Division strugglers Cardiff City in a £10,000 deal.

He left behind him at Goodison memories not only of a stalwart, ultra-consistent performer, a players' player never lauded lavishly by press and public but valued enormously within the game, but also of a natural comedian whose predilection for banter and practical jokes had been of immeasurable worth in maintaining dressing-room morale.

Brian Harris stories proliferated for years after his departure, few more lovingly recounted than the one about his unscheduled impersonation of an archetypal upper-class English drunk, live on Australian television during a summer tour. It seems the show's eminent host was less than impressed and he had the irreverent Merseyside mimic – whom, it should be stressed, was scrupulously sober – ejected unceremoniously from the studio, much to the hilarity of his team-mates.

Unlike some players who step down a division to see out their days in a comfortable billet, Harris gave full value for money at Ninian Park, his experience and authority contributing hugely to the Bluebirds' improvement over the five seasons he spent with them. The glorious highlight of that service was the inspiration he provided during all nine games of City's rousing progress to the semi-finals of the European Cup Winners' Cup in 1967/68.

In July 1971 Harris switched to Fourth Division Newport County as player-coach, not laying aside his boots until he was approaching his 40th year, his longevity a testament to his lifelong dedication to physical fitness. There was also a stint as manager at Somerton Park between January 1974 and March 1975, before he resigned following a disgreement with the board. After that he returned to Cardiff as assistant manager under Richie Morgan from December 1978 to 1980, then coached briefly with Ipswich Town. Later he settled in Chepstow, managing the town's non-League club for a time, and there were spells working for the Post Office and as a publican.

Entirely appropriately, Brian Harris's funeral will take place at St Luke's Church, located at the corner of his beloved Goodison Park.

Brian Harris, footballer; born Bebington, Merseyside, 16 May 1935; played for Everton 1954-66, Cardiff City 1966-71, Newport County 1971-74; managed Newport County 1974-75; died Chepstow, Gwent, 17 February 2008.

Derek Dooley

Professional football has thrown up few more inspirational tales of triumph over adversity than that of Derek Dooley.

After being dismissed in his teens as a crude, ungainly ugly duckling of a centre-forward, the rumbustious redhead emerged in his early twenties as a prodigiously prolific goal-scorer with Sheffield Wednesday.

But just as he was being tipped freely for England honours, his career was halted horrifically by the amputation of his right leg following an accidental collision with a goalkeeper in 1953.

It was a calamitous blow, yet the resilient Dooley recovered to become Wednesday's manager, only to be sacked by the club he had worshipped all his life.

Even then he did not give up on the game, eventually crossing the city to join the Owls' bitter local rivals, Sheffield United, with whom he rose to become managing director, chief executive and chairman.

The dynamism and desire which earned Dooley his unique niche in Sheffield soccer folklore – no one else has been revered to the same degree by both Wednesday and United fans – was evident from childhood in the steelworker's son who learned his football on the streets and on the unforgiving surface of the local recreation ground, where grass was hard to spot among the flattened ash and sharp cinders.

He always yearned to play for Wednesday, and even after leaving school at 14 to work in a hearing-aid factory, despite having passed his 11-plus examination, he did not abandon his dream. Instead Dooley clawed his way up through the ranks of junior teams, excelling for Sheffield YMCA before joining Lincoln City as an amateur in his mid teens. Most of his outings as an Imp were made for the reserves, but he caught the eye of an Owls scout and was recruited by the Hillsborough club, turning professional in 1947, not long after his 17th birthday.

Soon he was netting regularly for Wednesday's minor sides but when offered senior opportunities, one in the Second Division in 1949/50 and another in the top flight a season later, he performed unremarkably, even disappointingly. Though he was quick, bullishly strong and utterly fearless when fighting for the ball, the 6ft 3in spearhead appeared cumbersome and poorly balanced when a degree of finesse was required, lacking even rudimentary ball control.

But the picture changed dramatically in October 1951 when, with his team languishing dangerously low in the Second Division table, manager Eric Taylor called up Dooley to face Barnsley at Hillsborough. The raw but eager 21-year-old responded with a double strike which beat the Tykes, then set off on a phenomenal goal rampage which carried the hitherto hesitant Owls to the divisional championship.

After a mere dozen appearances he had registered 24 times, including five in the annihilation of Notts County and four against Everton, and by season's end his tally was a barely believable 46 goals in 30 games. Fans who previously had denigrated his clumsiness now hailed the savagery of his right-foot finishing, his fearsome aerial prowess and a willingness to strike from any angle which yielded several seemingly impossible goals.

Though arguments continued to rage about the perceived rashness of the young warrior whose untempered aggression risked injury where more polished performers would hold back, his tigerish chasing of apparently lost causes was applauded, and the strains of 'Dooley, Dooley's There' echoed around the Hillsborough terraces to the tune of the Guy Mitchell hit of the day 'Truly, Truly Fair'.

Still there were doubts about how the ungainly barnstormer would fare among the elite, and when he was goalless as Wednesday struggled through their opening Division One fixtures of 1952/53, the 'I told you so' brigade were out in force.

But boss Taylor remained loyal, alleging a vendetta against his prodigy by opponents, rival fans and even referees, and soon his faith was justified as Dooley's touch returned with a vengeance, with 16 goals against the cream of the League's defences between September and February. But just as talk of an international call-up became increasingly insistent, disaster struck during Sheffield Wednesday's clash with Preston North End at Deepdale on Valentine's Day. As he chased a through-pass from Albert Quixall, Dooley bounced off goalkeeper George Thompson and fell in a heap.

A broken right shinbone was diagnosed, a serious setback but hardly one of career-threatening proportions until a small cut at the back of his calf became infected. Within two days gangrene set in, the leg was amputated to save his life, and an artificial limb was fitted to the six-inch stump.

Thus chronically handicapped, having been married for only six months, with no house, no trade and only meagre formal education, many men would have fallen prey to self-pity. But not Dooley. Having bought a semi-detached house with the proceeds of his benefit game, the first to be played under Hillsborough's new floodlights, he voiced his desire to retain his association with the club for whom he had notched 63 goals in as many games, 'even if they use me as the corner flag.'

Thus he scouted for the Owls at weekends while spending two years reporting for the *Daily Mirror*, then manned a switchboard at a bakery owned by a Wednesday director – rising from telephonist to assistant sales manager in the process – before returning to Hillsborough, first as youth team coach and then, in 1962, taking charge of the club's new lottery. In that role he played a major part in the redevelopment of the ground into one of the best in the country until, with the team labouring near the wrong end of the Second Division and desperately in need of fresh impetus, he was appointed as manager in January 1971. Starting with a tremendous fund of goodwill, and blessed with a bluff charisma, he seemed ideal saviour material and his side topped the table early in 1972/73. But that promise was not maintained, results declined and, with gates having plummeted and with his playing resources undermined by a mystery virus, he was sacked without warning on Christmas Eve 1973.

Embittered by what he deemed brutal treatment, the erstwhile hero of Hillsborough vowed never to return to the ground for a Wednesday match, and it was to be many years before the hurt had mellowed sufficiently for him to reverse that decision. (Happily, when eventually he relented for a Sheffield derby in 1992, his standing ovation from both sets of supporters would always remain one of his most treasured memories.)

After leaving Wednesday he worked as a representative for a boot manufacturer before his career path took the most unexpected of turns when Sheffield United offered him the post of commercial manager in 1974. At first he was dumbfounded by the notion of serving 'the old enemy', but he accepted the challenge and went on to become a highly successful administrator at Bramall Lane.

Dooley graduated to serve as director, then managing director and chief executive before retiring from day-to-day involvement in 1996, or so he thought. Three years later, aged 69 in 1999, he was made chairman of the Blades, who were £4 million in debt and toiling near the foot of the First Division.

He was instrumental in the appointment of Neil Warnock as manager and presided over a stirring revival, which included appearances in the semi-finals of both major domestic cup competitions and the play-off finals in 2003.

Still in store was a valedictory triumph in 2006, when United secured promotion to the Premiership as runners-up to Reading. Immediately afterwards he stepped down as chairman to become a life vice-president of the club.

Back in 2003 Dooley, already a Freeman of his home city, received an MBE for his services to football, and fans on both sides of the Sheffield divide were gratified but hardly surprised. To them he had long been regarded as little short of royalty.

Derek Dooley, footballer, manager and administrator; born Sheffield, 13 December 1929; played for Lincoln City 1946, Sheffield Wednesday 1947-52; managed Sheffield Wednesday 1971-73; died Sheffield, 5 March 2008.

Reg Flewin

Though the image of Portsmouth footballers cavorting around Wembley brandishing the FA Cup remains fresh in the memory following last month's Wembley triumph over Cardiff City, it is difficult in this commercial age of the game's domination by a handful of big-city giants to picture a time when Fratton Park was home to the side that was, unequivocally, the finest in the land.

Yet so it was for two successive seasons in the middle of the 20th century when Pompey were champions of England, a temporary stranglehold on the premier domestic prize for which the south-coast club's central defender and captain, Reg Flewin, could claim immense credit. Not that he was prone to do so. Flewin was an unassuming fellow, an appropriate leader indeed for a collection of players renowned – and sometimes underestimated – as 'the team without a star'.

A tall, commanding figure, uncompromisingly physical when the occasion demanded but capable also of unexpected delicacy with the ball at his feet, he operated as a stopper between two vividly contrasting wing-halves.

To his right was the fire and brimstone of the volatile Scot Jimmy Scoular, to his left the style and composure of England regular Jimmy Dickinson; together the trio made up one of the most balanced and effective half-back lines to be seen in British football since the war.

Flewin could count himself unfortunate not to join his club comrades in the full international ranks, but when he was in his late-1940s prime the silkily skilful Neil Franklin of Stoke City held sway with the England selectors, and the Pompey man's representative honours were limited to appearances in two unofficial wartime encounters with Wales, then berths on FA tours to Canada and Australia.

As a schoolboy, the Portsmouth-born Flewin divided his enthusiasm between football and boxing, and he showed immense promise in the ring, training under the demanding eye of the redoubtable Stoker Reynolds, a professional welterweight revered in local fight circles. But it was at the team game that he excelled, and after representing Portsmouth Boys he joined Ryde Sports, an Isle of Wight club used as a nursery by Portsmouth, for whom he left a job with the Danish Bacon Company to sign professional forms on his 17th birthday in November 1937.

At the time Pompey were struggling in the lower reaches of the old First Division – the equivalent of today's Premier League – and with regular stopper Tom Rowe reaching

the veteran stage, there were high hopes that the promising youngster would prove a long-term replacement. Duly he made his senior debut in a 2-1 victory over Grimsby Town at Fratton Park in April 1939, but remained on the Wembley sidelines as unfancied Portsmouth upset the formbook by beating Wolverhampton Wanderers in that season's FA Cup final.

Still, Flewin was poised for imminent promotion, only for his immediate ambitions to be frustrated by the outbreak of the Second World War, during which he served with the Royal Marines. However, he turned out regularly for Portsmouth in various regional competitions during the conflict – he also found time to win several boxing championships – and when peace resumed the 26-year-old was confirmed as the team's regular centre-half, soon also taking on the role of skipper.

Immediately Flewin emerged as the principal defensive bulwark of the side, his canny reading of the unfolding action, his steadiness under fire and, particularly, his aerial prowess – with his long neck he cut a distinctive figure as he soared into combat with opposing attackers – combining to make him a favourite of the Fratton Park faithful.

In 1946/47 Pompey consolidated by finishing in 12th place in the top tier, but it was not until Jack Tinn was replaced as manager by Bob Jackson at season's end that the pieces of an exceptional unit began to fall into place.

There was an improvement to eighth place in the following term, but it was not until 1948/49 that Portsmouth really hit their stride, coasting away from Matt Busby's Manchester United to become League champions by five points – a swingeing margin in the days of only two points for a win. Goal-scoring wingmen Peter Harris and Jack Froggatt shared the bulk of the bouquets with Scoular and Dickinson, but Flewin's calm authority was appreciated in high places, too, notably by club president Viscount Montgomery of Alamein, who wrote to the captain in rousing terms halfway through that triumphant campaign.

Some critics caught on the hop by Portsmouth's success, most of them based in London and the North, played down the achievement, hinting that it had been a fluke and predicting a return to the status quo of big-club supremacy in 1949/50. They were confounded, however, as Jackson's superlatively well organised combination took the title again, this time on goal average – the aburdly complicated forerunner of goal difference – ahead of Wolves. This time around Flewin played fewer games, principally because of an appendix operation in the autumn, but still he remained a key influence. However, that would change over the next two seasons when he fell prey to injuries and Froggatt switched from the left flank to take his place in the centre of defence.

During this unsettled period he rejected an approach from local rivals Southampton to become their manager, but after making the last of his 167 League and FA Cup appearances for his home-town club, as a 32-year-old in early 1953, he stepped up his interest in coaching, first taking charge of the Fratton Park youth scheme, then becoming assistant to Eddie Lever, Jackson's successor as boss.

Flewin remained Portsmouth's number-two until October 1960 and then, finding himself baffled by some decisions of yet another new manager, Freddie Cox, he accepted the reins of Fourth Division Stockport County. There followed three years of toil at Edgeley Park, enlivened by a run to the fourth round of the FA Cup in 1961, before he returned south to take over at Third Division Bournemouth in September 1963.

He led the Cherries to a fourth-place finish in his first term at Dean Court, narrowly missing promotion to the second tier, but he resigned due to eye problems in 1965.

Later there was brief service with non-League Hastings before he entered into partnership in a holiday camp venture on the Isle of Wight.

Reginald Flewin, footballer and football club manager; born Portsmouth 28 November 1920; played for Portsmouth 1938-53; managed Stockport County 1960-63, Bournemouth 1963-65; died Shanklin, Isle of Wight, 25 May 2008.

Derek Tapscott

Welsh football has produced bigger and brighter stars, more extravagantly talented performers, more celebrated folk heroes than Derek Tapscott. But no one tried harder for his country, or for Arsenal, or for Cardiff City, than the industrious marksman who top-scored in two successive seasons for the Gunners in the mid-1950's and then shone for the Bluebirds as they soared exhilaratingly into the top tier of the domestic game at decade's end.

Tapscott was an effervescent study in perpetual motion who never knew when he was beaten, a ball of energy whose speed and persistence hustled habitually composed opponents into uncharacteristic clangers on which he preyed voraciously throughout a 13-year professional career.

One enduring sadness was that a dip in form and confidence following a knee operation in 1957 cost him a place in Wales' squad for the World Cup finals in Sweden the following year, so he missed out on the glorious march into the last eight of the tournament.

The fifth of 16 children born to a coalman and his wife, Tapscott recalled with affection in his 2004 autobiography (*Tappy*, published by Vertical Editions) that he hailed from 'probably the biggest family in Barry, maybe in South Wales.' Their home was a three-bedroom corner terraced house so space was at a premium and he shared a bed with three brothers, but didn't consider the living conditions to be cramped as he had never known anything different.

After leaving school at 14 to become a butcher's delivery boy, Tapscott took a succession of jobs, working as a radio repairman's assistant, an apprentice bricklayer and a council odd-job man, all the while impressing as a junior footballer. In 1949 he signed for Barry Town of the Welsh League as an amateur, then as a part-time professional in February 1953 after completing his National Service in the Army.

Now his dashing displays began to attract a wider audience and in the following October, when he was 21, he was recruited by Arsenal, the reigning Football League champions, for £2,750. The step from homely Jenner Park to the marble-halled grandeur of Highbury was a mammoth one, but the sparky Welshman was not fazed, weighing in with 13 goals in his first 15 games for the Gunners' reserves. His reward, only six months after leaving Barry, was a senior debut at home to Liverpool, playing up front alongside the ageing but still potent England icon Tommy Lawton.

Tapscott responded to his unexpectedly early elevation by scoring twice in a 3-0 victory, then two days later, in best comic-strip-hero fashion, he was called up for his first full international cap, to face Austria a month hence. Thus assured as to his quality, he added another two goals in his next Arsenal match, against Portsmouth, and finished the League season with five strikes in as many outings.

In Vienna, playing in tandem with the formidably physical Trevor Ford, Tapscott buzzed in typical energetic style, infuriating the Austrians with a full-blooded shoulder-charge on their goalkeeper, a tactic which was legal at the time but which was frowned on in continental circles. Wales lost 2-0 but the newcomer had laid down a marker for a productive future.

Back at Arsenal, where manager Tom Whittaker was coping with a team in transition from the post-war combination which had collected two League titles and the FA Cup, he contributed a creditable 13 goals in 1954/55, lining up either on the right wing or in his favoured inside-right berth, but the rough edges on his game became evident. His pace, directness and fearlessness were admirable, but at times he was a tad too frenetic for his own good and it wasn't until he began reading the game more maturely, knowing when to charge forward and when to hold off, discovering how to capitalise on rebounds from the opposing goalkeeper, that he found the best of himself.

By 1955/56, the penny had dropped, and Tapscott entered his pomp, netting 21 times in League and FA Cup as the Gunners improved to fifth place in the old First Division table, adding a further 27 – better than any Arsenal man since Ronnie Rooke ten seasons earlier – in 1956/57 as another fifth spot was claimed.

At this point the 25-year-old had collected a dozen Wales caps and his horizon seemed cloudless, but his prospects darkened ominously during the run-up to 1957/58 when he damaged a knee. A subsequent cartilage operation sidelined him for the first 11 games of the new campaign and, in retrospect, it seems clear that he was never quite the same buoyant force again. Still, he returned to sporadic action, netting in the Gunners' 5-4 home defeat by Manchester United in February 1958 – five days before the Old Trafford club was devastated by the Munich air disaster, which claimed the lives of eight players – but that was the last goal Tapscott would ever score for the north Londoners.

That September, perhaps still smarting from missing his country's rousing World Cup adventure in the summer, he reluctantly accepted a £10,000 transfer to Second Division Cardiff City.

Having struck 68 times in 132 League and FA Cup outings for Arsenal, Tapscott faced high expectations at the less rarefied level, and he did not disappoint, forming an effective right-wing partnership with former Highbury chum Brian Walsh, helping to win the Welsh Cup in his first term at Ninian Park and earning a brief international recall.

Even better was in store in 1959/60 when he topped City's scoring chart with 20 goals and linked productively with the emerging Graham Moore as the Welsh club achieved promotion to the First Division, finishing a point behind champions Aston Villa.

He excelled among the elite, too, contributing 21 hits during 1960/61, including winners against Arsenal (very sweet) and Tottenham Hotspur, who were about to become the first club that century to lift the League and FA Cup double.

That season the Bluebirds were safe in 15th position, but in 1961/62, with Tapscott in and out of the side through injuries, they were relegated. Thereafter, as he slowed appreciably as a result of age and accumulated knocks, his form was variable but there was to be one more highlight.

Another Welsh Cup triumph (Tapscott missed the final) qualified Cardiff for the European Cup Winners' Cup in 1964/65, and the veteran striker plundered the goal which proved decisive in eliminating the holders, Sporting Lisbon. The Bluebirds went out in the next round, the quarter-final, to Real Zaragoza, but their first excursion into continental competition had proved memorable.

That summer Tapscott, who had been running a lottery for the club in his spare time, was released, having scored 85 times in 212 senior appearances. He finished his League days playing part of one season for Fourth Division Newport County, then served non-League clubs Cinderford Town, Haverfordwest and Carmarthen Town before laying aside his boots in 1970.

Later he worked as a representative for sportswear companies, retiring in 1997.

Derek Robert Tapscott, footballer; born Barry, Glamorgan, 30 June 1932; played for Arsenal 1953-58, Cardiff City 1958-65, Newport County 1965-66; capped 14 times by Wales 1954-59; died Cardiff, 12 June 2008.

Tommy Johnston

When 17-year-old Tommy Johnston's left arm was mutilated so badly in a coalmining accident that amputation was contemplated, his hitherto buoyant hopes of earning at least part of his living as a professional footballer appeared to be extinguished. But the hardy Scot kept the limb, and with it his dreams of glory, which duly came true.

A decade later, in 1954, he scored the two goals for unfashionable Norwich City of the old Third Division South which dumped mighty Arsenal out of the FA Cup, and he went on to become such a prolific marksman and folk hero with Leyton Orient that when he died the east London club decided to rename one of their Brisbane Road stands in his honour.

By then, in a 1999 poll of supporters, he had already been named the greatest player in Orient's history, and he was widely deemed grievously unlucky never to have won a Scotland cap.

Though Johnston always played with a bandaged left wrist because the misshapen joint had withered as a legacy of his near-calamity at the pit, his approach to the game owed nothing to fearfulness.

Broad of beam and craggy of countenance, standing nearly six feet tall and blessed with a wide forehead which might have been created with the propelling of a football in mind, Johnston was a rumbustious, combative dreadnought of a centre-forward, majestic in the air and the type no defender relished marking.

After rising through the ranks of junior clubs Gilmerton Drumbirds and Loanhead Mayflower, then Peebles Rovers of the East of Scotland League, Johnston made his big-time debut with Kilmarnock in 1949, rapidly demonstrating his potential by notching 20 goals in 26 senior outings for the Scottish B Division club. But there followed a personality clash with the Killies' boss, Malky MacDonald, and the disillusioned 23-year-old was given a free transfer.

Once again the pit beckoned, but in the spring of 1951, seeking his fortune south of the border like so many of his Caledonian contemporaries, he joined lowly Darlington. There followed brief service at Feethams, and a fleeting stint for Oldham Athletic, before he was recruited by Norwich in June 1952 for the princely sum of £500.

Johnston thrived at Carrow Road, averaging approximately one goal every two games during his 28 months at the club, including the brace of trademark headers which scuppered the Gunners on an icy East Anglian afternoon.

However, with the Canaries mired in mid-table, in October 1954 he accepted a £3,000 switch to fellow basement club Newport County, with whom he proved even more prolific, netting 46 times in 63 League outings. Thus it was no surprise in February 1956 when a fee of £5,500 plus Canadian marksman Mike Burgess took him to Leyton Orient, whom he helped to clinch that term's Third Division South title.

Johnston was in his element at the higher level, breaking Orient's scoring record in each of the next two Second Division campaigns, his 35 in 1957/58 still a club best, as is his feat of hitting the target in ten successive games.

However, by the time that season was over he had moved on again, joining Blackburn Rovers for £15,000 in the March, his immediate contribution helping the Ewood Park side to clinch promotion to the top flight and leaving the marauding Scot as the Football League's highest scorer with 43 strikes.

Johnston flourished among the elite, too, netting 14 times in 25 outings, including a hat-trick against Newcastle United. But by then he was approaching the veteran stage and in February 1959, his value now halved to £7,500, he returned to Brisbane Road, where he continued to terrorise defences and proved hugely influential in the east Londoners' climb clear of relegation from the second tier.

By the time he joined his last League club, Gillingham, for £3,000 in September 1961, Johnston had become Orient's all-time record scorer with 123 goals. There followed only one term at Priestfield before he retired having hit the net 290 times in 464 senior outings.

Later he became player-coach with non-League Folkestone Town before moving to Poulton-le-Fylde, Lancashire, where he ran a betting shop. In 1972 Johnston, whose affable character away from the game contrasted vividly with his fearsome mien on the pitch, emigrated with his family to Australia, where he coached and worked for a company which manufactured corrugated products. In 2004 he was the subject of a book, *The Happy Wanderer*, by Neilson Kaufman and Alan Ravenhill.

Thomas Bourhill Johnston, footballer; born Loanhead, Midlothian, 18 August 1927; played for Kilmarnock 1949-51, Darlington 1951-52, Oldham Athletic 1952, Norwich City 1952-54, Newport County 1954-56, Leyton Orient 1956-58 and 1959-61, Blackburn Rovers 1958-59, Gillingham 1961-62; died Dapto, New South Wales, Australia, 2 September 2008.

Bill Shorthouse

Ask most modern football fans to name the defender who was unluckiest never to win an England cap and the chances are they will speak of Steve Bruce, the staunchly courageous stopper at the heart of Sir Alex Ferguson's first successful Manchester United team. But pose the same question to those who followed the game during the middle years of the last century and, likely as not, they will mention Bill Shorthouse. The stalwart Black Countryman played at centre-half, and in both full-back positions, for what is by common consent the finest Wolverhampton Wanderers side in the club's 129-year history.

Shorthouse was vastly if often unobtrusively influential as Wolves, under the iron guidance of manager Stan Cullis, won the FA Cup in 1949 followed by the League championship five years later. However, veteran denizens of Molineux maintain that those twin peaks only begin to reflect the full glory of an exceptional team. They argue that an even more memorable achievement was blazing a trail for British clubs in Europe by embarking on a series of floodlit encounters which pitted them against many of the continent's top performers.

In the mid-1950s, even before Manchester United became the first English entrants in the European Champions Cup, Wolves took on and beat Moscow Spartak, Honved of Budapest and Moscow Dynamo in games which were billed as friendlies but played with the keenest of competitive edges.

The 3-2 home triumph over Honved in December 1954 was particularly significant as included in the visitors' line-up was Ferenc Puskas – then vying with Stanley Matthews for the title of the world's best-known footballer – and five other members of the 'Magnificent Magyars', who had only recently humbled England 6-3 at Wembley and 7-1 at the Nep Stadium.

On that misty Molineux evening during which Wolves prevailed after falling two goals behind, left-back Shorthouse was pitted directly against the pacy winger Laszlo Budai, and after being stretched in several early attacks, he subjugated his illustrious opponent comprehensively, employing the full array of redoubtable qualities which had earned him renown in the domestic game.

There were no frills about Shorthouse. Rather he stood out as a hard man in a hard side, tackling like a runaway steamroller, positioning himself shrewdly, and passing simply and sensibly to team-mates blessed with skills more creative than his own. He wasn't particularly big, but he was remarkably strong and his comrades were invariably desperate to be on his side in the often volcanically contested training clashes in the old car park behind Molineux. Above all he was phenomenally dependable, which was reflected by the extraordinary record of never being dropped – his only absences being through injury or illness – from the moment he earned a regular place during 1947/48 until he bowed out in his mid-thirties in 1956/57.

Staffordshire-born Shorthouse joined Wolves as an amateur in 1941, then served in the Army during the war, suffering a serious wound during the D-Day landings at Normandy.

Having recovered, he returned to work at Molineux and flourished under the physically rigorous training regime which manager Cullis reckoned made Wolves the fittest side in the land.

After an initial outing at left-back, he settled at centre-half in the autumn of 1947 and played in every tie as the men in the famous gold-and-black strip lifted the FA Cup in 1949, beating Leicester City 3-1 in the Wembley final.

During the following term Shorthouse was outstanding as Wolves were pipped to the League title only on goal average – the absurdly confusing precursor to today's goal difference as the means of separating teams on equal points – by Portsmouth, and thereafter he maintained his lofty standards during periodic shifts to either defensive flank.

He was back in the middle, and missing only two games, as Wolves were finally crowned champions for the first time in 1953/54, but soon switched to left-back to accommodate skipper Billy Wright's move from wing-half to centre-half for the subsequent campaign.

Now he was part of a granite rearguard comprising goalkeeper Bert Williams, full-backs Eddie Stuart and Shorthouse himself, wing-halves Bill Slater and Ron Flowers, with Wright as the classy pivot. It was a formidable unit which formed a solid base for a dashing forward line featuring the likes of wingers Johnny Hancocks, Jimmy Mullen and Les Smith, inside-forwards Peter Broadbent and Dennis Wilshaw, and spearhead Roy Swinbourne.

Nicknamed 'The Baron' for the imperious manner in which he presided over his area of the pitch, Shorthouse was appealingly unassuming away from the action and a dedicated professional who neither smoked nor drank.

When he gave way to youth in the form of Gerry Harris in the autumn of 1956 he began coaching young players for Wolves, later working with the youth teams of England,

Birmingham City (under Stan Cullis, who had been sacked controversially by Wolves), and Aston Villa, whom he guided to FA Youth Cup triumph in 1980.

In 1988 he helped to found the Wolverhampton Wanderers Former Players Association, of which he remained an active member until shortly before his final illness.

Bill Shorthouse never played for his country, but many a footballing friend and foe will maintain stoutly that he was the equal of plenty who did.

William Henry Shorthouse, footballer and football coach; born Bradley, Staffordshire, 27 May 1922; played for Wolverhampton Wanderers 1946-57; died Wolverhampton, Staffordshire, 6 September 2008.

Jimmy Sirrel

Like Sir Matt Busby and Bill Shankly before him, Jimmy Sirrel was a performer of soccer miracles, albeit in a more modest arena than his illustrious fellow Scots.

Whereas Busby and Shankly each took over clubs in the doldrums, transforming Manchester United and Liverpool respectively into sporting leviathans whose fame penetrated most corners of the planet, the ebullient, passionate, sometimes wickedly acerbic little Glaswegian lifted unfashionable Notts County from the basement division of the English professional game to its top flight, a feat all the more astounding because it was achieved on such a niggardly budget.

Yet while Sirrel was invariably short of cash as he strove ceaselessly to guide the Magpies ever higher up the Football League ladder, he never lacked confidence in his own ability. That much he demonstrated eloquently on his first day at Meadow Lane in September 1969, when he declared with characteristic brio: 'Ask any kid what he knows about Notts County and he'll tell you they're the oldest football team in the world. By the time I've finished, he'll know a lot more.'

That he was to prove as good as his word came as no surprise to those who knew him best. As his long-time friend Sir Alex Ferguson put it: 'I'd be confident in Jimmy Sirrel managing any team I supported, and that would be the general opinion from all the managers in the game.'

Having commenced his career with Renfrew Juniors while working as a coppersmith's apprentice, Sirrel spent the war in the Royal Navy, working in shipyards in Cairo and Mombasa, before signing for Celtic as a diminutive but clever and industrious inside-forward on the last day of 1945.

Ankle injuries and a sciatic nerve condition limited his progress at Parkhead, but such had been his promise that many fans were upset when he was freed to join Bradford Park Avenue of the English second flight in May 1949.

His impact in Yorkshire was minimal and fitness problems which reduced his pace continued to plague him through stints with Brighton and Hove Albion and Aldershot, both of the Third Division South, in the first half of the 1950s.

In mid-decade, aged 34, Sirrel became a trainer and coach with the Hampshire club, work to which his sharp, inventive mind and lively personality fitted him admirably, and it was no surprise when he moved into management with Fourth Division Brentford in 1967.

It proved a tough first assignment at Griffin Park, with the club heavily in debt, but he put in prodigiously long hours and within two years had re-invigorated the team and dramatically reduced the overdraft.

In November 1969, though, he left freshly buoyant Brentford to join Notts County, the club with the longest history of all but now ailing, having sunk so low that in recent seasons they had only narrowly avoided the indignity of having to apply for re-election to the Football League, of which they had been proud founder members in the previous century.

Supported by progressive new chairman Jack Dunnett, a local Labour MP, Sirrel rebuilt the team around the sumptuously gifted Scottish play-maker Don Masson. That season he stabilised the club and in 1970/71, having brought former County marksman Tony Hateley back to Meadow Lane, he inspired the Magpies to a runaway Fourth Division title triumph, completing an unbeaten home record in the process.

Sirrel's mission continued to gather momentum with County promoted from the Third Division as runners-up to Bolton Wanderers in 1972/73, then came two terms of consolidation in the Second before he shocked the Meadow Lane faithful by accepting the job of reviving top-tier whipping boys Sheffield United.

The Blades were at the foot of the First Division when the charismatic Scot took over in October 1975, but the rot at Bramall Lane was too entrenched for a speedy renaissance and they were relegated as bottom club. There followed a mid-table finish in 1976/77, but with United struggling at the outset of the subsequent campaign, Sirrel was sacked.

After only two weeks out of work, he returned to Notts County in October 1977, just in time to arrest a slide towards demotion to the Third Division. Two more seasons of reconstruction followed – which included the re-signing of Masson, who had been on his travels to Queen's Park Rangers and Derby County – before Sirrel experienced arguably his finest hour.

In 1980/81, aided by the coaching expertise of the younger Howard Wilkinson – destined to manage Leeds United to the League title, then become the Football Association's technical director and England's caretaker boss – Sirrel led the Magpies to second place in the Second Division (behind West Ham), ensuring a place among the elite for the first time since 1926.

At a time when Brian Clough was the talk of the football world for his staggering attainments across the Trent with Nottingham Forest, the older club's rise offered at least a slice of the local bragging rights to long-downtrodden County fans.

Against many expectations Sirrel's side, bolstered by several new signings including the gifted Nigerian winger John Chiedozie, held their own in the First Division, finishing the season in a highly respectable 15th place.

Now aged 60, Sirrel moved 'upstairs' to become general manager, with first Wilkinson, then Larry Lloyd and eventually Richie Barker becoming team boss, but the Magpies were relegated in 1984 and again in 1985, at which point Sirrel, by now also a director of the club, resumed the reins. Thereafter he kept County in the top half of the Third Division for two more seasons before retiring in 1987.

Since then he has remained part of the fabric of the club, having a stand named after him in 1993, and in 2007 his portrait was commissioned to hang at the entrance of Meadow Lane. As he had promised nearly four decades ago, the world knew considerably more about Notts County by the time Jimmy Sirrel had finished.

James Sirrel, footballer and football club manager; born Glasgow, 2 February 1922; played for Celtic 1945-49, Bradford Park Avenue 1949-51, Brighton and Hove Albion 1951-54, Aldershot 1954-57, managed Brentford 1967-69, Notts County 1969-75, 1977-82 and 1985-87, Sheffield United 1975-77; died Nottingham, 25 September 2008.

Jimmy Murray

Some footballers sail through entire careers on a tide of exaggerated praise, their names dripping with stardust carelessly dispensed. Others, somehow not cast naturally in the heroic mould, suffer by comparison, their reputations shining less lustrously even though their worth is immense. Jimmy Murray, the excellent, free-scoring, quietly unassuming Wolverhampton Wanderers centre-forward of the late 1950s and early 1960s, falls emphatically into the second category.

Murray never received a full England cap – the nearest he got were an outing for the Football League and two appearances for the under-23s – but his record of 166 goals in 299 games for the Molineux club suggests he was distinctly unfortunate not to be granted at least a fleeting opportunity at the top level.

Reaching his zenith in the second half of Wolves' golden era under the stern martinet Stan Cullis, Murray contributed bountifully as the Black Countrymen lifted the League crown in 1957/58 and 1958/59, then missed out by a single point on achieving a rare championship hat-trick in 1959/60, when they were pipped by Burnley on the competition's final day. Murray was the leading marksman as Wolves racked up a century of strikes in each of those three top-flight campaigns, and he was vastly influential, too, as Cullis's dynamic, hard-driving side beat Blackburn Rovers 3-0 in the 1960 FA Cup final on a sunlit Wembley afternoon, thus claiming rich consolation for their title-race frustration.

Rather surprisingly in a team renowned for its steely athleticism and predilection for long-ball tactics, the spearhead of the attack was no archetypal hulking bustler. Indeed, although he could hold his own physically in the heat of the action – Cullis would never have employed him, otherwise – Murray was not even a particularly muscular specimen, being slender of build and standing only 5ft 9in.

What he brought to the Molineux mix was skill, mobility, intelligence and that most precious of all qualities for any centre-forward, a poacher's instinct for arriving in front of goal at the optimum moment to propel the ball between the posts. Murray was a notably shrewd reader of the play and the way he anticipated the intentions of team-mates and opponents alike seemed almost uncanny at times. For such a prolific front-man, he was unselfish, too, frequently making clever decoy runs off the ball to allow the likes of inside-forwards Peter Broadbent and Bobby Mason and wingers Jimmy Mullen and Norman Deeley to capitalise on the space thus created.

Like the sumptuously gifted play-maker Broadbent, Murray hailed from the mining village of Elvington in Kent, between Canterbury and Dover, and while many of his young friends gravitated to the coal industry his father, who managed the local pit canteen, refused to let his son work underground. As it happened, that possibility was swept aside when the 16-year-old was spotted by Wolves talent scout George Poyser while playing for non-League Canterbury City. He enlisted at Molineux as a junior in 1951, turning professional in November 1953, during the season which ended in Wolves winning the League title for the first time in their history.

The callow newcomer was offered no part in that campaign, but when established sharpshooter Roy Swinbourne suffered a grievous knee injury in November 1955, Murray was called up for a high-prestige floodlit friendly against Moscow Dynamo at Molineux. Though only just turned 20, that night he revealed both verve and composure, creating one of the goals for Mullen in a 2-1 victory and signalling that he was ready for permanent promotion. Thereafter the level-headed and unfailingly loyal Murray was rarely out of the side for the next six years, peaking in the glorious trophy-laden terms but still carrying a potent threat into the new decade. However, as Wolves began to decline he became less sure of his place and in November 1963, still in his prime at 28, he was sold to Second Division Manchester City for £27,000.

Now operating under Poyser, his former mentor, Murray made a sensational start to his Maine Road tenure, netting 13 times in his first eight games – including two successive hat-tricks – and striking up a formidable partnership with ex-England man Derek Kevan.

Though his subsequent effectiveness was limited by injuries, and a new link with former Glasgow Rangers star Ralph Brand didn't quite gel, he helped City, by then managed by Joe Mercer, to rise to the top tier as Second Division champions in 1966.

Having entered his thirties, Murray lingered only briefly back among the elite, moving to Third Division Walsall in May 1967. After two seasons of sprightly contribution at Fellows Park he left the Football League to join Telford United, helping them to two FA Trophy finals, losing in 1970 but triumphing a year later. After laying aside his boots, Murray ran his own greengrocery in Tamworth, and later entered the car-hire business.

James Robert Murray, footballer; born Elvington, Kent, 11 October 1935; played for Wolverhampton Wanderers 1953-63, Manchester City 1963-67, Walsall 1967-69; died Lichfield, Staffordshire, 27 September 2008.

George Edwards

When graduates Steve Heighway and Brian Hall took the field for Liverpool's all-conquering team of the 1970s, the comedians on the Kop – and there has never been any shortage of them – thought it was hilarious. Thus Heighway was dubbed 'Big Bamber' and the diminutive Hall became 'Little Bamber', droll references to one Bamber Gascoigne, the host of the contemporary television quiz show, *University Challenge*.

The point, made with affection, was that highly educated footballers were seen as extreme rarities, but in fact they were by no means unknown, as evidenced by the varied attainments of Welsh international winger George Edwards several decades earlier.

While forging his niche in the game, Edwards obtained a degree in geography. Then, when his playing days were done, he went on to a wide-ranging career in the oil industry, as well as earning plaudits as a journalist and broadcaster, becoming a magistrate in Cardiff and serving as an active member of the Sports Council of Wales.

For all the breadth of his achievements, however, it is as his country's outside-left in 12 of its first 13 internationals after the Second World War, and for his accomplished stints with Birmingham City and Cardiff City, that Edwards will be most widely recalled.

He was a chunky, energetic, all-action type of performer, ready to chase back and hustle opponents in an era when plenty of his fellow flankmen were content to idle languidly near the touchline until presented with the ball by more industrious team-mates.

His most eye-catching attribute was his ability to deliver accurate crosses with his much-favoured left foot, either tempting floaters for marauding centre-forwards such as his craggy countryman Trevor Ford, with whom he linked at Cardiff towards the end of his career in the mid-1950s, or fizzing low dispatches which caused havoc in crowded penalty boxes.

Though he was principally a creator rather than a regular scorer of goals, Edwards packed a powerful shot and chipped in with his share of strikes, being blessed with the gratifying knack of breaking the deadlock in tight encounters.

He exuded, too, a certain ebullience which unsettled some defenders but occasionally nettled others, such as Manchester United's Bill Foulkes one grey afternoon at Cardiff's Ninian Park in November 1953. Though the visitors were in dominant mode, running out 6-1 winners, Edwards remained perky enough to toy with the redoubtably rugged Foulkes, teasing him with what the right-back considered to be unduly showy footwork.

Usually the big Lancastrian was proof against such provocation by comparitively diminutive flankmen, tending to counter it forcefully but legally. But on this occasion a red mist descended and he launched an untypically ill-judged challenge which deposited the Welshman over the perimeter fence and into the crowd, giving a whole new meaning to the phrase 'flying winger'.

Today such a tackle would provoke instant dismissal of the perpetrator, but Foulkes escaped with a booking, the only one of his career, and a sharp rebuke from his manager, Matt Busby.

As for the plucky if slightly foolhardy Edwards, he dusted himself down and played on, earning the last laugh when the teams met again later in the season, shining against his rival in Cardiff's surprise 3-2 victory at Old Trafford.

The Welshman had taken his first significant steps on the road to footballing eminence some 15 years earlier in 1938 when he had joined Second Division Swansea Town as an 18-year-old amateur while studying at the local university.

Before the war there was time for only a couple of senior outings for the Swans and a Welsh amateur international call-up against England, then he joined the RAF, serving on the technical side throughout the conflict. During this period he guested for Coventry City, initially as an inside-left before being converted to a wingman by manager Harry Storer, whom he followed to Birmingham City and turned professional in 1944.

Edwards flourished at St Andrew's, helping to win the Football League South, an emergency wartime competition, in 1945/46 while working for his degree at Birmingham University.

So impressive was his form that he represented Wales in unofficial end-of-war Victory matches, then made his full international debut in a 3-1 triumph over Scotland at Wrexham in October 1946, thereafter remaining Wales' first choice until November 1949, accumulating a dozen caps and contributing two goals in the process.

Meanwhile in 1947/48 he had proved a major influence as Birmingham ascended to the top flight as Second Division champions, finishing three points clear of Newcastle United, then in the following December he had returned to the second flight via a £12,500 transfer to Cardiff City.

At Ninian Park he replaced Roy Clarke, who had departed to Manchester City and who, coincidentally, was the man who had usurped his berth in the Wales team.

In 1951/52 Edwards remained at the peak of his powers, proving integral to the Bluebirds' promotion to the top division as runners-up to Sheffield Wednesday, ironically squeezing out his former club, Birmingham, on goal average, the perplexingly complicated predecessor to goal difference as a means of splitting teams on equal points.

Over the next three campaigns leading up to his retirement from the game, aged 34 in 1955, he strove to help Cardiff consolidate their place among the elite, at the same time making enterprising provision for his future by entering the oil retail industry.

At various times, too, the versatile Edwards also wrote a column for the now defunct Sunday newspaper *Wales Empire News*, and reported on Cardiff matches for BBC radio and television.

He went on to serve the Ninian Park club as a director in two spells, from 1957 to 1976 and 1981 to 1986. For many years, too, he was a magistrate in Cardiff and maintained his sporting profile through his work for the Sports Council of Wales and the Football Association of Wales.

George Edwards continued to follow the game with characteristic enthusiam until shortly before his death, attending an encounter between his former clubs, Cardiff and Birmingham, in September 2008.

George Edwards, footballer; born Treherbert, Glamorgan, 2 December 1920; played for Swansea Town 1938-39, Birmingham City 1946-48, Cardiff City 1948-55; capped 12 times by Wales 1946-49; died Cardiff, 21 October 2008.

Ray Deakin

When Burnley Football Club faced its darkest hour – poised on the brink of elimination from the Football League of which it had been a founder member 99 years earlier, and even contemplating the ugly possibility of long-term oblivion – stoutheart skipper Ray Deakin stood firm.

In their traumatic spring of 1987, the Clarets needed to beat Orient in the last game of the season to retain a chance of avoiding the sporting calamity of automatic relegation from the old Fourth Division into the GM Vauxhall Conference.

As Deakin led out his players at their Turf Moor headquarters to take on the promotion-chasing Londoners, he was confronted by a capacity crowd of more than 15,000 supporters, most of them wearing the colours of the troubled Lancashire club. The prevalent mood was one of black dread verging on utter despair, laced only faintly with the hope that their team – not a very good one, it was admitted – might somehow escape the big drop. Lesser men might have quailed at the responsibility and the scale of the task before him, but Deakin surveyed his slender resources, issued a steely call to arms and proceeded to deliver a man-of-the-match display which did much to inspire an unlikely 2-1 victory. Thanks also to events elsewhere, it was Lincoln City and not Burnley who became the first club, following a recent change in the rules, to suffer automatic demotion for finishing bottom of the Football League.

That day Deakin, operating as a doughty central defender although arguably he was more effective at left-back, made a series of crucial clearances before either side had scored, and he continued to hold firm as Orient poured forward and the Clarets clung on to their slim advantage during the unbearably tense closing minutes.

In truth the stocky, blond Merseysider was no cultured performer; rather he was a tough and canny pragmatist whose game was to win the ball with an emphatic tackle, then usually to launch a long-distance dispatch in the direction of his forwards. Thus he earned the affectionate nickname 'Whooshy' from Burnley fans, who anticipated his regular punts downfield with a prolonged cry of 'Whooooosh' as he prepared to release the ball.

Deakin had commenced his football life hoping to forge a productive future with home-town club Everton, whom he joined as an apprentice in 1975. But despite signing as a professional on his 17th birthday two years later, the England schoolboy international failed to make a senior breakthrough at Goodison Park and was freed to join Fourth Division Port Vale in August 1981.

Displaying admirable composure, the young left-back netted three penalties in his first five outings, but he couldn't keep his place. Still, he didn't lose heart, instead raising his eyes to find a billet with Bolton Wanderers of the Second Division. Soon he earned a first-team berth and kept it even though Bolton were relegated at the end of his first term at Burnden Park. Come 1984/85, with Jimmy Phillips having emerged as a highly promising left-back, Deakin became a central defender, which was the role in which he excelled initially for Burnley after his free transfer to Turf Moor at the end of that campaign.

With the Clarets in the basement tier for the first time in their illustrious history, new manager Martin Buchan saw Deakin as a key signing. However, although the player thrived, the boss departed in disillusionment within 110 days of his arrival and Burnley struggled in their new and inhospitable environment.

Although they stabilised enough to earn uneasy mid-table security at the end of that term, they struggled abysmally in 1986/87, culminating in that dramatic last-day assignation with Orient and the ever-present skipper's colossal contribution.

New manager Brian Miller set about rebuilding the side with Deakin as his defensive bulwark, and in 1987/88 the gritty Liverpudlian, by now switched successfully to left-back, was in the vanguard as Burnley attained a creditable tenth-place finish in the league table. In addition, there was the bonus of becoming the first Clarets captain for 26 years to lead out his men at Wembley, and although they were beaten 2-0 by Wolves in the final of the Sherpa Van Trophy, there was much pride and reason for considerable optimism among the Turf Moor faithful.

Sadly, soon afterwards Deakin fell prey to injury, and although he returned to consistent form by the turn of the decade, he was released, aged 31, at the end of season 1990/91 after making his last and 271st appearance for Burnley in a Division Four play-off semi-final against Torquay United.

Thereafter he left the game to run a business in the area, while retaining a lively interest in the club whose long-term prospects he had done so much to preserve.

Raymond John Deakin, footballer; born Liverpool, 19 June 1959; played for Port Vale 1981-82, Bolton Wanderers 1982-85, Burnley 1985-91; died 24 December 2008.

Bert 'Sailor' Brown

With his rolling gait and muscularly stocky build, he reminded his team-mates so irresistibly of the cartoon character Popeye that they nicknamed him 'Sailor'. But Bert Brown was never a figure of fun; rather he was an enchantingly gifted inside-forward who might have scaled the giddiest heights of the game had his career impetus not been shattered by the outbreak of the Second World War.

Brown was 23 and already making an impressive impact with Charlton Athletic, then one of the leading clubs in the English top flight, when the global conflict began in 1939 and professional sport was properly relegated to the periphery of life for the next six years.

As it was he served his country as an RAF sergeant, his footballing pinnacles being limited to half a dozen appearances for England alongside the likes of Stanley Matthews and Tommy Lawton in unofficial wartime internationals for which caps were not awarded, and representing the Addicks with intermittent brilliance in the 1946 FA Cup final.

It had been evident early in Brown's life that he was blessed with exceptional talent. At the age of ten he was excelling in a Yarmouth Boys team consisting mostly of teenagers, and after shining for his local Eastern Counties League club, Gorleston, while working as an apprentice sewing machine mechanic, he signed for Charlton, then in the Third Division South, in August 1934.

By the time he made his senior debut in a 2-0 victory over Birmingham City at The Valley in January 1938, the south-east London side had risen to the premier tier and were among the title challengers. Brown was not overawed by the rise in standard, contributing 24 goals in 60 senior games before Hitler invaded Poland, but it was as a creator of goal-scoring chances for his colleagues that he earned the most lavish bouquets.

'Sailor' was a subtle and supremely deft manipulator of a football, adept at dispatching inch-perfect through-passes to fellow attackers such as George Tadman and Don Welsh, and soon he was on the verge of international recognition.

When he did don the England shirt, though, it was in a non-ranking friendly in South Africa in 1939, and he was still in contention six years later, when he scored in a 3-2 victory over Scotland.

Throughout the war Brown remained an active footballer, captaining the RAF team, guesting for a host of clubs including Newcastle United, West Ham United, Millwall, York City, Leicester City, Manchester City, Wolves and East Fife, and continuing to serve Charlton.

He played in Wembley finals in four successive years – for Charlton in the League Cup South in 1943 and 1944, for Millwall in the same competition in 1945, and in Charlton's 4-1 defeat by Derby County in the first post-war FA Cup final in 1946.

Brown almost emerged as the Addicks' hero of the latter contest when, deep in the second half and before a goal had been scored, he dribbled past five defenders only to give the ball away with an uncharacteristically inaccurate pass instead of sending in skipper Welsh for what surely would have been the winner. As it was the game went to extra time and a Derby team which included the magnificent duo of Raich Carter and Peter Doherty prevailed with plenty to spare.

Shortly afterwards Brown had a sharp difference of opinion with Charlton manager Jimmy Seed and was transferred to Second Division Nottingham Forest for £6,750. In October 1947 he moved on again, returning to the top grade with Aston Villa, who paid £10,000 for his services, only to lose them for good when the 32-year-old suffered a severely broken jaw in an encounter with Portsmouth a year later.

Brown never featured at the top level again, but enjoyed serial success as player-boss of his old club, Gorleston, garnering several trophies and masterminding their progress to the first round proper of the FA Cup in 1951/52, when they bowed to Leyton Orient only after two replays.

He retired from the game in 1956, then ran a sportswear shop, worked as a bookmaker and a timber merchant, and for a time scouted for Arsenal. 'Sailor' Brown, a chirpy, charming individual who became Charlton's oldest surviving former player, lived for most of his life in Gorleston, later moving to Scotland to be near his daughter Julie.

Robert Albert John Brown, footballer; born Great Yarmouth, Norfolk, 7 November 1915; played for Charlton Athletic 1934-46, Nottingham Forest 1946-47, Aston Villa 1947-49; died Forres, Morayshire, 27 December 2008.

Ian Greaves

Ian Greaves was a redoubtable football man with a character to match.

As a solid and constructive full-back, he was accomplished enough in his mid-1950s prime to earn a League title medal on merit with Manchester United, and that in the days of white-hot competition before Matt Busby's wondrous young side was decimated by the

Munich air disaster in which eight players died. Yet Greaves was to carve an even more memorable niche as an implacably straight-talking, unfailingly enterprising manager, building fine teams for Huddersfield Town and Bolton Wanderers, and guiding both into the English game's top flight as Second Division champions. In addition, he became the most celebrated boss in the history of Mansfield Town, and also put in spells in charge of Oxford United and Wolverhampton Wanderers.

As a teenager the tall, athletic Greaves seemed certain to become a professional sportsman, although initially it wasn't clear whether it would be as a footballer or a cricketer. He excelled at the summer game for Crompton in the Central Lancashire League, but he leaned towards soccer, even when he was rejected after a trial by his local club, Oldham Athletic.

There followed a fleeting stint with non-League Buxton United, during which he impressed Old Trafford scouts and enlisted with the Red Devils in May 1953. His progress through the ranks of Busby's innovative youth system was rapid and he made his senior entrance at right-back at Wolverhampton in October 1954, standing in for the rugged Bill Foulkes, who was away making his sole appearance for England.

The Greaves rise gathered pace in February 1956 when, with Foulkes labouring with National Service commitments and carrying a niggling injury, the 23-year-old Lancastrian was recalled for a home encounter with Burnley.

So competently did he perform, tackling crisply and passing perceptively, that he retained his place for the rest of that title-winning term, playing just enough games to earn a medal.

However, Foulkes was a formidably determined competitor and thereafter he regained his berth, thus relegating Greaves back to the reserves until he was recalled to the colours in the most tragic of circumstances, in the wake of the air crash in February 1958.

Now operating at left-back – with United's preferred men in that role, Roger Byrne and Geoff Bent, both having perished on a slushy German runway – he proved a reliable operator as the stricken, under-staffed club defied logic by reaching the FA Cup final. They lost 2-0 to Bolton Wanderers, but Greaves let no one down, turning in a characteristically steady display.

He was admirably consistent in 1958/59, too, when Busby's still-depleted side astonished most pundits by finishing as runners-up to Wolves in the title race, but then knee injuries slowed him down and he slipped from contention.

In December 1960 he left Old Trafford for Lincoln City but was never again able to fulfil himself as a player, briefly serving Oldham and non-League Altrincham before turning to coaching with Huddersfield Town in 1964.

Four years later he replaced Tom Johnston as manager of the Terriers and, while nurturing richly promising youngsters such as the lavishly gifted, flamboyant centre-forward Frank Worthington and the high-quality defender Trevor Cherry, he led them to the Second Division crown in 1969/70.

Continuing to major on youth, while operating a stern regime in which supreme fitness and rigorous discipline were paramount, Greaves preserved Huddersfield's top-flight status in 1970/71, but not being wealthy and with insufficient strength in depth to survive for long, they were relegated as bottom club in 1971/72.

Inevitably Worthington and Cherry departed, their replacements were of lesser calibre and the downward trend continued with immediate demotion to the third tier a year later. Not unexpectedly, amid boardroom upheaval, Greaves resigned in June 1974, coaching briefly with Plymouth Argyle before being appointed assistant manager of Second Division Bolton Wanderers in August.

Within two months boss Jimmy Armfield had moved on to Leeds United and Greaves inherited the top job at Burnden Park. He made a tentative start, shuffling his pack of players extensively, but soon found he could place his faith in talented and determined youngsters such as future England international midfielder Peter Reid, centre-half Sam Allardyce and striker Neil Whatmore.

That term Bolton consolidated in mid-table before pushing on to miss promotion only narrowly in the next two campaigns before clinching it in top spot in 1977/78. Greaves' team – which had also reached the League Cup semi-finals of 1977, losing to Everton – was efficient and well-organised rather than expansive, but he had added entertainers such as Scottish midfielder Willie Morgan and Worthington, his former Huddersfield charge, and they appeared reasonably well equipped to compete in the First Division.

However, he experienced the same travail as at Huddersfield, enduring poor luck with injuries to key men such as Reid, and Bolton remained among the elite for only one season before being relegated in the spring of 1980.

Greaves was not present for the last rites, having been sacked in the January with his side rooted to the foot of the table, a crushing reversal of fortune for a man who had been mooted as a serious possibility to become manager of Manchester United when Tommy Docherty had departed in 1977.

He remained resilient, though, spending much of 1980 as assistant boss of Hereford United before taking over at Oxford United in December, rescuing them from likely demotion to Division Four, then leaving them in a much-improved state by the time he accepted the reins of top-flight strugglers Wolves in February 1982.

Despite a spirited attempt, he was unable to prevent their relegation and in August he was dismissed by a new Molineux regime headed by Derek Dougan, remaining out of the game until January 1983, when he embarked on what proved to be an upliftingly successful Football League management swansong with homely, unfashionable Mansfield Town. Combining an enlightened youth policy with judicious excursions into the transfer market, he improved the squad until he secured promotion from the Fourth Division in 1986, then led the Stags to triumph in the Freight Rover Trophy a season later, beating Bristol City on penalties in the Wembley final. He resigned in February 1989, declaring that six years was long enough at one club, and later coached at Bury, then managed briefly at non-League Emley before scouting for several clubs in the north-west.

Greaves was a shrewd psychologist – he took his Mansfield players down a local coal mine to show them how lucky they were to play football for a living – and a tough taskmaster, but also he inspired unswerving loyalty among those who recognised his essential fairness.

Unashamedly he was a man of the old school, who once summed up his approach to footballers thus: 'You can pat 'em on the back, you can kick 'em up the arse, you can speak softly or you can scream and shout, you can threaten 'em or you can ignore 'em. But one thing you can do that really counts is leave 'em out of the team.'

Ian Denzil Greaves, footballer and manager; born Oldham, Lancashire, 26 May 1932; played for Manchester United 1953-60, Lincoln City 1960-61, Oldham Athletic 1961-63; managed Huddersfield Town 1968-74, Bolton Wanderers 1974-80, Oxford United 1980-82, Wolverhampton Wanderers 1982, Mansfield Town 1983-89; died Ainsworth, Lancashire, 2 January 2009.

Tommy Casey

Nobody tried harder on a football pitch than Tommy Casey, and his prodigious effort took him to centre-stage on some of the game's grandest occasions.

The effervescent Ulsterman ran out for Northern Ireland to face France – goal machine Juste Fontaine et al – in the quarter-finals of the 1958 World Cup in Sweden, and his sweat lubricated the Newcastle United machine as the Magpies beat Manchester City at Wembley to lift the FA Cup in 1955, still their most recent major domestic trophy.

Casey wasn't the most subtle of operators, and he wasn't always first choice for club or country, but when he was picked the tenacious wing-half, whose tackles called to mind a speeding bulldozer and who routinely worked himself to a standstill in his team's cause, rarely failed to make his presence felt.

Yet all that ferocious on-the-field activity belied the essential good nature of the former trainee bricklayer from County Down who had been brought up in the gritty environs of Belfast's Shankill Road. He revelled in the cut and thrust of dressing-room banter, and his infectious humour made him a popular figure throughout his extensive travels during more than a quarter of a century in the sport.

Casey's professional journey began at Second Division Leeds United, who recruited him from Bangor, an Irish amateur club, in May 1949, but he made scant progress at Elland Road and moved down a tier with Bournemouth after only one season in England.

Over two campaigns at Dean Court, Casey became acclimatised to the English game, impressing Newcastle United scout and former St James' Park idol Bill McCracken sufficiently to earn a £7,000 transfer to Tyneside in August 1952.

Now Casey moved into his energetic prime, although during his six years in the top flight with the mid-table Magpies he was never guaranteed his place in the first team, having to contest the left-half berth with local boy Charlie Crowe.

Perversely the highlight of his Newcastle sojourn came in 1954/55, a season in which Crowe had held the upper hand. The Geordie suffered injury problems and the Irishman played in six FA Cup games, including the final in which United triumphed 3-1 after making a flying start through Jackie Milburn's first-minute headed goal.

That term, too, Casey made his international breakthrough, earning the first of his dozen caps in a 3-2 defeat by Wales in Belfast, standing in for the sidelined Bertie Peacock.

Northern Ireland boss Peter Doherty thought the world of Casey, loving his unbridled enthusiasm as a midfield ball-winner, but also valued his versatility, which made him an ideal squad man. Thus, occasionally, the wirily resilent wing-half was deployed in a more creative role and sometimes even as an all-out attacker.

He featured in three World Cup qualifiers, contributing a goal to the 3-0 home win over Portugal, and although he was out of the team as the finals started in the summer of 1958, he was called up at centre-forward to face West Germany in the final pool game in Malmo.

Casey bustled effectively in a 2-2 draw which earned the Irishmen a play-off meeting with Czechoslovakia, for which he was replaced by Jackie Scott and which ended in a heroic 2-1 victory thanks to two goals by Peter McParland.

But he was back in the side – which featured the stellar likes of skipper and fellow wing-half Danny Blanchflower, brilliant inside-forward Jimmy McIlroy and Harry Gregg, voted the best goalkeeper in the tournament – for the last-eight encounter with France at Norrkoping.

Operating at inside-right – second striker in modern parlance – and making light of a gashed shin which carried four stitches, Casey gave a characteristic high-octane performance. But the Irish, most of whom were playing their second game in three days, looked tired as a team and subsided to a 4-0 defeat, two of which were registered by the prolific Fontaine.

On returning from Sweden, 28-year-old Casey joined First Division Portsmouth in an £8,500 deal and retained his Northern Ireland place for their next game, at home to England. Proudly wearing the number-nine shirt, he scored in a 3-3 draw but slipped out of the international reckoning after one more outing.

Life at Fratton Park proved a struggle, with Pompey doomed to demotion from the top tier, but Casey left just ahead of the drop in March 1959, a £6,000 fee taking him to Second Division Bristol City, where he was reunited with Doherty, his Northern Ireland mentor.

Though the Robins, too, proved less than buoyant, sinking to the Third Division in 1960, Casey earned both respect and affection at Ashton Gate, where he remained until 1963, stretching his total of senior appearances beyond 400.

There followed a spell as player-boss of non-League Gloucester City, a succession of coaching jobs including stints at Everton and Coventry City, and two management posts, with Distillery in Belfast and then Grimsby Town.

At Blundell Park, where cash was in short supply, he steered the Mariners clear of relegation to the basement division in successive seasons and launched a successful youth policy, but was sacked in November 1976 with his team destined for demotion in the spring. Later Casey worked as a fishmonger in the Bristol area, still as effervescent as ever and relishing the craic with his customers.

Thomas Casey, footballer and manager; born Comber, County Down, Northern Ireland, 11 March 1930; played for Leeds United 1949-50, Bournemouth 1950-52, Newcastle United 1952-58, Portsmouth 1958-59, Bristol City 1959-63; managed Distillery 1967-68, Grimsby Town 1975-76; capped 12 times for Northern Ireland 1955-58; died Nailsea, North Somerset, 11 January 2009.

Johnny Dixon

The enduring image of Johnny Dixon is as the beaming skipper of Aston Villa, perched jauntily on the broad shoulders of team-mates Peter Aldis and Stan Lynn while brandishing aloft the FA Cup at Wembley in 1957.

The veteran inside-forward had just played one of the games of his life, proving colossally influential as the Midlanders had upset the formbook by overturning First Division champions Manchester United, thus denying Matt Busby's exhilarating young side the achievement of becoming the first in the 20th century to win the League and Cup double.

Not only had Dixon set up both Villa goals in the 2-1 victory for Peter McParland, but also he had lived up to his reputation as an inspirational leader, lifting his comrade's spirits after the Irish winger was barracked by enraged United fans following a controversial incident in the sixth minute on which, arguably, the outcome of the contest was to turn.

McParland had hurtled recklessly into the Red Devils' goalkeeper, Ray Wood, who suffered a fractured cheekbone. As substitutes were not permitted in those days, the stricken custodian spent most of the match as a passenger on the wing, centre-half Jackie Blanchflower taking over between the posts.

The Villa man, a rumbustious performer but an honest one and certainly not malicious, might have been distracted by the inevitable vitriol from the terraces, and was himself dazed by the impact. But Dixon acted decisively, putting an arm around McParland, stressing that the collision had been an accident, that it was all part of the game – and the upshot could hardly have been more positive for their team.

Yet central though that occasion was to the Dixon career, it should not be allowed to obscure the comprehensive extent of his attainments at Villa Park, which extended for nearly a quarter of a century from the moment in the summer of 1944 when he was recruited as an amateur from non-League Spennymoor United.

After 18 months of impressive displays in unofficial wartime competition, he accepted professional terms in January 1946 and seven months later, aged 22, he made his senior debut at home to Middlesbrough on the opening day of the first post-conflict League campaign. He scored his first goal in his third top-flight game, at Derby a week later, breaking his nose in the process but brushing aside suggestions that he might leave the action, thus confirming manager Alex Massie in his opinion that his acquisition was as courageous as he was skilful, industrious and determined.

It wasn't until mid 1948/49 that Dixon cemented his berth in a strong Villa side which usually finished in the top half of the First Division. He revealed himself to be a dynamic, direct performer endowed with seemingly limitless stamina, comfortable in possession of the ball but invariably eschewing unnecessary elaboration in favour of doing the simple thing well. In addition, he was combative in the air, passed imaginatively, could double as a winger and was a reliable finisher, witness his ultimate total of 144 goals in 430 Villa appearances. Dixon entered his prime at the outset of the 1950s, forging a productive inside-forward partnership with fellow north-easterner Tommy Thompson, finishing as the club's top scorer in four out of the decade's first six seasons.

He was at his most prolific in 1951/52, when he was ever-present, netting 28 times in 43 League and FA Cup outings, giving rise to demands from the Midlands press that he be picked for England. Sadly, he was never to be awarded the cap he coveted, suffering an injury shortly after being called up by national boss Walter Winterbottom for one training squad and never getting another chance.

Dixon, a calm, courteous individual, was too modest to voice his own disappointment, but new Villa manager Eric Houghton had no such inhibitions, later declaring: 'Of course Johnny Dixon should have played for England. Plenty of worse players did!'

Further proof of the shrewd Houghton's regard was evident in his appointment of Dixon as captain, a role for which he was naturally suited. A dedicated professional, a teetotaller and non-smoker, he set an impeccable personal example, especially to the club's youngsters, but also to senior colleagues, not least in the seething cauldron of emotion that was Wembley throughout most of the 1957 final.

That day he shone as a player, too, delivering a perfect cross for McParland to register the first goal with a high-velocity header midway through the second half, then nodding against the angle of post and bar six minutes later, enabling the rampant Ulsterman to grab the second with a thunderous volley.

Years later, Dixon recalled: 'With about ten minutes to go, I realised suddenly we were going to win. For 13 years I had been at Villa Park without winning a thing. Now the Queen was going to be handing me the FA Cup. I nearly burst into tears on the spot.'

In fact, he was a tad premature in his reflections as United's Tommy Taylor set up a tense finale with a goal seven minutes from the end, but Villa held out to claim the famous old trophy for the first time since 1920.

Though by then in his 34th year, Dixon continued to offer sterling service, but began to fall prey to nagging fitness problems and he was sidelined for part of the demoralising 1958/59 campaign which culminated in relegation from the top tier.

Still, he remained potent enough after switching to right-half to earn the Terrace Trophy as the supporters' player of the year, and there was considerable disappointment when injuries limited him to only four senior appearances as Villa became Second Division champions at the first attempt.

Come 1960/61, his last campaign, he scored in his only game, a 4-1 home win over Sheffield Wednesday, attaining a painful symmetry by playing on with a broken nose, as he had so early in his career. Afterwards Joe Mercer, by then the Villa manager, ventured the thought that his resources would be so much the richer if Johnny Dixon was at the beginning of his playing days rather than the end. There were no dissenting voices.

Dixon remained at Villa Park for six more years, coaching the youngsters, before becoming an ironmonger in the Midlands until his retirement in 1985.

Still he remained astonishingly fit for his age, playing for the Villa Old Stars team deep into his sixties, and protesting vehemently whenever his manager summoned him from the action to take a breather on the bench.

John Thomas Dixon, footballer; born Hebburn, County Durham, 10 December 1923; played for Aston Villa 1944-61; died Tamworth, Staffordshire, 20 January 2009.

Vic Crowe

Welsh international Vic Crowe was a fearless footballer, an enterprising coach and a steady manager, serving Aston Villa staunchly in all three roles for a total of 17 seasons.

As a player he was a flintily resolute but by no means crude wing-half, equally ready to battle in the last ditch or to split an opposing defence with a perceptive though-pass, both of which he did routinely throughout much of the 1950s and the early 1960s.

As a boss he presided over a gradual Villa renaissance from a wilderness period at the dawn of the 1970s, only to be sacked for his pains by chairman Doug Ellis after a disappointing campaign in 1973/74.

Crowe hailed from the South Wales coal-mining community of Abercynon, but grew up in Handsworth, Birmingham, where his family moved when he was two. Football was in his blood, his father playing to part-time professional standard, and soon it became clear that the boy had both the talent and the inclination to make his own way in the game.

As a teenage amateur he turned out for a West Bromwich Albion nursery side, Erdington Albion, but he failed to break through at the Hawthorns. There followed trials with Stirling Albion while on National Service with the Army, but it was with Villa that he became a professional as a 20-year-old in June 1952.

He made his top-flight debut in October 1954 and when Danny Blanchflower departed to Tottenham Hotspur two months later, Crowe nailed down a regular place in Eric Houghton's hard-working side, his cause aided by his ability to operate on either midfield flank.

That term he shone as the Midlanders finished sixth in the League table, only five points adrift of the champions, Chelsea, and he was steadfast during tougher times in 1955/56, when they escaped relegation only by goal average, the precursor to goal difference for separating clubs with equal points. But then, with the Welshman nearing his peak, came an interlude of dire frustration. In 1956/57 knee trouble limited him to a single appearance, which meant he missed the FA Cup final victory over Manchester United, which would have been the high point of his career.

However, although it was a sore setback which irked him until his retirement and beyond, Crowe was a resilient character and a better player than his Wembley replacement, Stan Crowther. Duly he returned to full fitness by the middle of the following term, regaining his former consistency to such effect that he was selected in the Wales squad for the World Cup finals in the summer of 1958.

The exemplary form of Cardiff City's Derek Sullivan and skipper Dave Bowen of Arsenal on the way to the quarter-finals in Sweden denied Crowe his international entrance, but only until the following November, when he helped his country draw 2-2 with England, appropriately at Villa Park, where he coped impressively with the explosive threat of his direct opponent, the young Bobby Charlton. Back at club level, though, he faced travail, with Aston Villa, now managed by Joe Mercer, being demoted to the Second Division in the spring of 1959, shortly after losing an FA Cup semi-final to Nottingham Forest.

Crowe was mortified by the reverses, but he was made of stern stuff and maintained a high level of personal performance. He was a quiet individual, not as gregarious as many of his colleagues, but he was respected for his integrity and consumed by an overwhelming drive to win every time he took to the pitch, qualities which convinced Mercer he was the man to captain Villa to promotion at the first attempt.

So it proved, the Welshman missing only one game as the Midlanders, buoyed by star forwards Gerry Hitchens and Peter McParland, finished 1959/60 as Second Division champions, the only sour note for Crowe being another FA Cup semi-final defeat, this time at the hands of Wolverhampton Wanderers.

His progress was underlined during the following autumn when he skippered Wales for the first time, against Scotland at Ninian Park, Cardiff, with his team-mates much amused that he was the only man in the dressing room who didn't speak with a Welsh accent.

For Villa he completed his busiest campaign, playing 55 times as his team consolidated the newly-regained top-tier status with a mid-table finish and won the League Cup in its inaugural season, coming from two down to beat Rotherham United 3-2 in the two-legged final.

Two years later they made it to the final again, but this time they were bested, gallingly, by local rivals Birmingham City, who triumphed 3-1 on aggregate.

By then Crowe was in his thirties and had won the last of his 16 caps, but was still performing well enough to be voted player of the year by the supporters. However, after one more term of solid endeavour, and having made more than 350 appearances for Villa, he accepted a £4,000 transfer to Third Division Peterborough United.

At London Road he flourished anew, captaining the Posh to the last eight of the FA Cup in his first season, a run which included a remarkable victory over Arsenal, and to the semi-finals of the League Cup a year later, overturning Newcastle United and Burnley in the process. In 1967, aged 35, Crowe became player-coach of Atlanta Chiefs under former Villa team-mate Phil Woosnam and played a prominent role in winning the North American Soccer League championship of 1968.

The following year he returned to Villa Park, initially to coach the reserves, but in January 1970 he succeeded the sacked Tommy Docherty as manager of a dispirited side at the foot of the Second Division. By then he was unable to avoid relegation, but he launched a rebuilding programme which began to bear fruit in his first full season at the helm. Villa missed promotion narrowly, but enchanted their long-suffering fans by beating Manchester United over two legs in a League Cup semi-final, before losing to Tottenham Hotspur in the Wembley final through two late goals.

Some called him dour, but Crowe earned respect as an intelligent coach and in 1971/72 he launched an exhilarating charge to the Third Division crown, getting the best from the likes of gifted midfielder Bruce Rioch, flying winger Willie Anderson, rugged spearhead Andy Lochhead and long-serving full-back Charlie Aitken.

There followed a commendable third place in their first term back in the Second Division, but after an unexpected slump to 14th in 1973/74 Crowe was dismissed. It was a harsh exit for a man who had laid the substantial foundations for a team that would rise to the top division and lift the League Cup under new boss Ron Saunders only a season later. Still Crowe was not done with football, returning to the United States to coach Portland Timbers, taking them to the Soccer Bowl final in 1975, where they lost to Tampa Bay Rowdies. He remained in charge for the 1976 competition, and put in another stint with the Oregon club in the early 1980s before lending his experience to several English non-League clubs as an advisor. Vic Crowe's death was announced only 24 hours after that of Johnny Dixon, another long-serving Aston Villa stalwart in the 1950s.

Victor Herbert Crowe, footballer and manager; born Abercynon, Glamorgan, 31 January 1932; played for Aston Villa 1952-64, Peterborough United 1964-67; Atlanta Chiefs 1967-69; capped 16 times by Wales 1958-62; managed Aston Villa 1970-74, Portland Timbers 1975-76; died Sutton Coldfield, Birmingham, 21 January 2009.

Paul Birch

Lothar Matthaus was in his majestic prime when he arrived at Villa Park with Internazionale of Milan for a UEFA Cup encounter in October 1990. But anyone hoping to witness the dynamic German midfielder, one of the most lauded and decorated footballers the game has ever known, at his devastating best was in for a sorry letdown – and the man to blame was Paul Birch.

That night the chunky little Midlander marked Matthaus so tightly, and with such fierce resolve, that the eminent visitor was little more than an anonymous bystander as the mighty Italian side slumped to a remarkable 2-0 defeat.

The unhappy footnote, from Villa's viewpoint, that Inter recovered to win the tie in the second leg did nothing to diminish Birch's mammoth achievement, which highlighted his immense if often unobtrusive contribution to the club over eight seasons of unstinting effort.

Often operating on the right flank, but equally effective when buzzing hyperactively at the heart of midfield, he made his senior entrance in claret and blue in unexpected circumstances, being called on as a substitute for striker Gary Shaw 12 minutes from the end of the European Super Cup clash at home to Barcelona in January 1983.

The 20-year-old helped to close out a 3-0 victory – 3-1 on aggregate – and made his domestic top-flight debut during the following season, laying claim to a fairly regular berth in 1984/85.

Birch became renowned for his ceaseless industry and passionate commitment, but also he was deceptively deft with the ball at his feet and specialised in sudden high-velocity shots from long range.

In 1985/86 he slaved with characteristic zeal as Graham Turner's men reached the semi-finals of the League Cup, where they lost to Oxford United, the eventual winners. But Villa were a team in decline from the gilded peaks of early in the decade – when they had lifted the League title and the European Cup in successive campaigns – and in 1986/87 they were relegated.

Birch remained irrepressible, though, proving hugely influential as future England manager Graham Taylor guided Villa back to the top tier at the first attempt, as runners-up to Millwall.

However, niggling injuries and the sprightly presence of Tony Daley limited his contribution as Taylor's combination struggled at first to adjust to the loftier standard, then rose spectacularly to finish runners-up to champions Liverpool in 1989/90.

There remained that memorable subduing of Matthaus before Taylor departed, then Birch found himself surplus to the plans of new boss Jozef Venglos and was sold to Second Division Wolverhampton Wanderers for £400,000 in February 1991.

At Molineux he proved a solid citizen in what was usually a disappointingly mediocre mid-table outfit, until he was loaned to Preston North End in the spring of 1996 in time to play a telling part in the clinching of the Third Division championship.

Having entered his mid-thirties, Birch was released by Wolves in the summer of 1996 and went on to brief but efficient spells with Doncaster Rovers and Exeter City, both members of the basement division, before leaving the full-time professional game with more than 450 senior appearances to his credit.

There followed two terms with non-League Halesowen Town, where he endeared himself to team-mates and fans alike with his undying enthusiasm and down-to-earth approach, and a stint as a postman before he accepted coaching roles, first with Forest Green Rovers, then with Birmingham City.

Paul Birch died from cancer at the age of 46.

Paul Birch, footballer; born West Bromwich, 20 November 1962; played for Aston Villa 1980-91, Wolverhampton Wanderers 1991-96, Preston North End on loan 1995, Doncaster Rovers 1996-97, Exeter City 1997-98; died Sutton Coldfield, Birmingham, 2 February 2009.

Joe Haverty

There was an impudent twinkle about the football of tiny Irish winger Joe Haverty which was sorely needed during a distinctly lacklustre interlude in Arsenal's history.

Occasionally the 5ft 3½in Dubliner, who wore the Gunners' number-11 shirt on and off throughout the second half of the 1950s and into the following decade, overdid his trademark trickery, thus losing the ball and with it the team's attacking impetus.

When that happened there would be catcalls from the terraces, but such was his charm, as both performer and personality, that frequently he redeemed himself with a sudden enchanting manoeuvre, and once more he was the laughing left-wing leprechaun who could dribble his way into all but the hardest of hearts.

Haverty was recruited by Arsenal as an 18-year-old in the summer of 1954 from St Patrick's Athletic, one of his home city's leading clubs, and Highbury boss Tom

Whittaker was so impressed by his potential that he pitched him into top-flight action that August.

Quickly it became evident that although the newcomer was a remarkably skilful manipulator of a football, he was not ready for a regular berth at a time when the Gunners were going through a difficult period of transition following the break-up of their 1952/53 title-winning combination.

Thus it was not until 1956/57 that Haverty was granted a settled sequence in the First Division, by which time he had made an explosive entry on to the world stage, netting with a rasping volley in a 4-1 triumph over Holland in Rotterdam.

That debut strike was followed by another on his third outing in emerald green, though the prolific strike rate would not be maintained over the next decade of intermittent service to his country, as he finished with only three goals in his 32 games.

Still, Haverty's form earned him a place in the London side which contested the first Inter-Cities Fairs Cup, the forerunner to the modern UEFA Cup, and he scored against Lausanne Sports in the semi-final, though he was not picked for the 1958 final against Barcelona. Back at domestic level, a combination of managerial experiments and recurring back problems limited his input until 1959/60, when he enjoyed the most productive season of his life, missing only a handful of games and contributing eight League goals.

He set up plenty, too, for the likes of fellow attackers David Herd, Jimmy Bloomfield and Vic Groves, continuing to please the crowd with his pace, guile and knack of crossing accurately, but Arsenal, now bossed by George Swindin, were mired discontentedly in mid-table mediocrity.

Perhaps understandably in view of his size, 'Little Joe' – so nicknamed after a character in the television western series *Bonanza* – was not keen to mix it physically with muscular defenders and he had a distinctive manner of hopping from their path, a habit marked one yuletide by the arrival at Highbury of a Christmas card addressed to Haverty and picturing a spectacularly agile kangaroo. To his credit, he laughed louder at the joke than anyone else, a reflection of his engagingly easy-going nature.

However, such personal popularity couldn't preserve his place as an increasingly desperate Swindin sought a more consistent player to patrol the left touchline, and in August 1961, still aged only 25, Haverty was sold to top-tier rivals Blackburn Rovers for £17,500.

He never settled at Ewood Park, and in September 1962 he returned to London with Third Division Millwall, with whom he flourished for two years, prompting Celtic to offer him a month's trial.

Rejected by the Bhoys after only one appearance, he enlisted with Bristol Rovers in December 1964, but made little impact for the Pirates and re-crossed the Irish Sea to join Shelbourne in Dublin, where he was playing when his international days ended in December 1966. There followed stints with Chicago Spurs, Kansas City Spurs and Shamrock Rovers before he laid aside his boots as a 34-year-old in 1970.

Later Haverty, who was inaugurated into the Football Association of Ireland's Hall of Fame in 2000, revived his link with Arsenal by scouting for the club.

Joseph Haverty, footballer; born Dublin, 17 February 1936; played for Arsenal 1954-61, Blackburn Rovers 1961-62, Millwall 1962-64, Celtic 1964, Bristol Rovers 1964-65, Shelbourne 1965-67, Chicago/Kansas City Spurs 1967-68, Shamrock Rovers 1969-70; capped 32 times by the Republic of Ireland 1956-66; died London, 7 February 2009.

Reg Davies

Reg Davies was a slip of a lad nursing two golden gifts as he grew up in wartime South Wales.

He was such a sweetly talented soprano that his parents envisaged for him a professional future on the world's most gilded stages, and indeed he toured the length and breadth of the land with a hugely popular choir.

But all the while the pallid, slender, almost frail-looking teenager was marching to the beat of a different drum. His dream was to play football at the highest level open to him, and he made it come true, most notably in the black-and-white stripes of Newcastle United and, though not as often as he would have liked, in the blood red of Wales.

Davies was a subtly inventive inside-forward, a schemer and a scorer both, in modern parlance an attacking midfielder. He possessed not a vestige of brawn but was endowed with an exceptionally astute football brain and sudden, searing acceleration over short distances which rendered him a menace both in centre-field and anywhere in the vicinity of opponents' penalty boxes.

His was not an obtrusive presence, but he had a priceless instinct for drifting into a telling position, and once there he had the ability to capitalise instantly, either with a penetrative pass or a waspish finish. All the enjoyment that such skills engendered surely would have been denied to the fans of his four Football League clubs and his country had he elected to build on his early musical success.

So sought-after was the Davies voice that he was invited to join the immensely successful Arturo Steffani's Silver Songsters, which also offered a place to Ronnie Ronalde, who went on to earn international fame as a singer, yodeller and melodic whistler.

Davies' father, in particular, believed his son should make his way in showbusiness, but the game proved too strong an attraction and after shining with non-League Cwm Athletic near Swansea, he signed amateur forms for Southampton in the mid-1940s.

His momentum was interrupted by National Service in the Army Medical Corps, but when he was demobbed in 1949 he turned professional with Southend United, then one of the better teams in the Third Division South.

After two seasons of shining at Roots Hall, Davies was snapped up by top-flight Newcastle, who bought him in April 1951, a month short of his 22nd birthday, for £9,000, which included £1,000 to be paid only if he attained full international stature. As it turned out the Shrimpers had to wait a mere 18 months before banking the full fee.

Davies made a scoring debut for the Magpies in a 3-1 home victory over Wolverhampton Wanderers in October 1951, but it wasn't until 1952/53 – when he made his entrance for Wales in a 2-1 defeat by Scotland at Ninian Park, Cardiff – that he achieved a major impact on Tyneside.

By then he had experienced the frustration of being 12th man – there were no playing substitutes in those days – as Newcastle won the FA Cup at Wembley for the second year in succession, luckily beating Arsenal through a late goal by George Robledo. Though he was delighted for his team-mates, he was a tad miffed on his own behalf, because just before the Chilean had headed into the net, manager Stan Seymour had promised him a start in the seemingly inevitable replay.

Davies was denied Wembley glory again in 1955, when he was picked to face Manchester City but went down with tonsillitis, looking on in discomfort as goals from Jackie Milburn, Bobby Mitchell and George Hannah secured the famous old trophy.

Although he played more games than he missed during most of his eight-year sojourn at St James' Park, and collected 50 goals in his 170 appearances, the Welshman – who could operate either on the right or the left, or even on the wing – rarely commanded an automatic berth, being faced by distinctly warm competition from the likes of Hannah, Ivor Broadis and latterly the young and beautifully skilful George Eastham.

Still, he contributed worthily to the cause of the Magpies, who were usually to be found in mid-table, before departing to join Swansea Town of the Second Division in October 1958 as a makeweight in the deal which took the brilliant Ivor Allchurch to the north-east.

By then Davies' international career was over, much to his chagrin as he believed he should have been part of the squad which reached the quarter-finals of the World Cup in Sweden in 1958.

His sixth and final outing for Wales was against England in Cardiff in October 1957, when he was pitted in direct opposition to Manchester United's youthful leviathan, Duncan Edwards.

Before the match manager Jimmy Murphy gave his team talk, running the rule over the tasks facing each player except Davies. As they headed for the pitch, the perplexed inside-forward apprehended Murphy, who worked with Edwards on a day-to-day basis as assistant boss at Old Trafford and fully understood the muscular Englishman's prodigious qualities. The willowy Davies piped up: 'Jimmy, what about me? What do I do if Duncan Edwards comes through with the ball?' Murphy's reply was succinct: 'Reg son, just get out of his f****** way. I wouldn't want you to get hurt.'

After the game, which England won 4-0, Edwards and Davies swapped shirts, and the Welshman's prize became a valuable asset after the United man perished in the Munich air disaster a few months later. However, Davies refused to cash in on it, eventually donating it to the United museum, declaring: 'That's where it truly belongs.'

Back at club level, he spent three seasons at the Vetch Field, featuring in a narrow escape from relegation in 1962, before making a £4,000 switch to Third Division Carlisle United that summer. His first term at Brunton Park ended in demotion, but he was prominent as the Cumbrians bounced back at the first attempt in 1963/64.

After that, aged 35, Davies left the League, spending a season with Merthyr Tydfil and enjoying a spell as player-manager of King's Lynn.

In 1971 he emigrated to Perth, working as player-coach with Bayswater United and Ascot, guiding them both to major trophies. He appeared for Western Australia against New Zealand when he was 47, and played on at a high standard into his 50th year.

Thereafter he remained a very fit man, living near the Indian Ocean and relishing his regular jogging sessions on the beach. Reg Davies never toured the world with Ronnie Ronalde, but he found his own place in the sun, and he relished it.

Ellis Reginald Davies, footballer; born Cymmer, near Swansea, 27 May 1929; played for Southend United 1949-51, Newcastle United 1951-58, Swansea Town 1958-62, Carlisle United 1962-64; capped 6 times by Wales 1952-57; died Perth, Australia, 9 February 2009.

Harry Parkes

Harry Parkes' prowess as one of the best of all English uncapped full-backs did not represent anything like his full value to his only professional club, Aston Villa, in the decade following the Second World War.

He was the dressing room's resident comedian, an irrepressible joker who could be relied upon to lift morale no matter how dire the circumstances. His propensity for clowning fostered a lively rapport, too, with the fans, with whom he was in the habit of exchanging quips before or after a match or even, very occasionally, over the touchline fence while the action was still unfolding.

Parkes, who was voted Villa's most popular player of the 1940s in a retrospective poll of supporters in 2000, began his working life as an apprentice toolmaker with GEC, the electronics and engineering company in Witton, Birmingham, not far from Villa Park.

Spotted while playing for local amateurs Boldmere St Michael's, he joined Villa as a 19-year-old amateur in April 1939, turning professional four months later, shortly before the outbreak of the Second World War.

During the conflict he guested for West Bromwich Albion and Northampton Town, and helped Villa to beat Blackpool in the final of the Football League North Cup in 1944, which wasn't classed as a senior competition because of the ad hoc nature of the wartime game. Still, it was an honour much prized by Parkes, who was never to collect a full-blown medal. At that point of his career, the sturdy Midlander was a utility performer, making his senior debut for Villa as a right-half in a 1946 FA Cup tie at Coventry, and occupying every outfield position except outside-left before settling at right-back in mid-1948/49, though still he swapped roles as the team's needs dictated.

Possibly such extreme versatility cost Parkes his international chance, with the England selection committee which held sway at that time invariably opting for specialists, though he was in the running for a cap in 1946, only to be thwarted by an arm injury.

Serving under three managers, Alex Massie, George Martin and Eric Houghton, Parkes helped First Division Villa to plough a steady mid-table furrow in most seasons, the peaks being sixth-place in 1947/48, 1951/52 and 1954/55, the trough being 15th in 1950/51, when relegation was averted by only five points.

Through it all Parkes offered a vein of near-metronomic reliability, proving a taxing and tenacious opponent even for world-class wingers such as Stanley Matthews of Blackpool, Tom Finney of Preston North End, and Liverpool's Billy Liddell, a particularly tough and dynamic performer whom many defenders dreaded to face but against whom the Villa man invariably shone.

Parkes was quick and strong, he never shirked a physical challenge, and also he was ahead of his time in that he enjoyed an occasional foray into opposition territory, probably a legacy of earlier experiences as an attacker. It was an adventurous approach rarely employed by full-backs in the middle years of the 20th century and it endeared him further to his legions of admirers on the terraces.

Probably Parkes peaked in the late 1940s, but he played some of his most attractive football in the first half of the 1950s, joining in smoothly with passing movements along the right flank involving the thoroughbred likes of wing-half Danny Blanchflower, the thoughtful Irishman who would lead Tottenham Hotspur to the League and FA Cup double in 1961, and clever inside-forward Tommy Thompson.

Parkes, who had several spells as Villa captain, was 35 when he retired in the summer of 1955 to continue developing his sports goods business, supplying his former employers with boots from his shop in Corporation Street, which became a celebrated haunt for local footballers, professionals and amateurs alike.

In 1968, at a time of turbulence in the Villa boardroom, he became a club director under new chairman Doug Ellis, though the two men experienced differences of opinion which led to Parkes' departure in the early 1970s. Later he served as a director of neighbours Birmingham City, but it is as a trusty bulwark of the Aston Villa rearguard, and an unfailing source of good cheer, that he will be remembered most vividly.

Henry Arthur Parkes, footballer; born Birmingham, 4 January 1920; played for Aston Villa 1939-55; died Solihull, West Midlands, 4 March 2009.

Eddie Lowe

England debutant Eddie Lowe was 21 years old with the ball at his feet and the massed ranks of the French defence ranged in front of him. The tall, lean Midlander swayed gently but persuasively and his opponents lurched with him, buying his subtle dummy and thus allowing him to deliver an exquisite through-pass with his favoured left foot into the path of his sublimely talented team-mate Raich Carter. 'The Great Horatio', needing no second invitation, strode on majestically to score his country's third and final goal, to which France offered no reply.

That afternoon at Highbury in May 1947 it seemed that in Midlander Lowe, who linked so fluently with fellow half-backs Billy Wright and Neil Franklin, a new international star had been born. But although he continued to excel in the short term for his club, Aston Villa, then went on to become a Fulham stalwart, making more than 500 appearances over 13 seasons of faithful and often inspirational service at Craven Cottage, he played just two more games for England and was never given another chance.

Why? There was a rumour that he had upset an influential member of the Football Association's selection committee, who had a vested interest in a rival club, by not agreeing to a certain transfer, but that could never be proved. As it was Lowe, an unassuming, studiously correct, thoroughly decent individual who rejoiced in universal respect throughout the English game, just got on with his career, giving impeccable value for money every time he walked on to a pitch.

Most of the time he played as a deep-lying left-half, in modern parlance a defensive midfielder who could also slot in alongside the centre-half at need. Although he was no greyhound, his distinctive loping stride carried him around the field with deceptive pace, and while fairness was his byword, he was unremittingly hard in the tackle. As a man-marker he was fiercely tenacious, too, proving adhesively effective in direct opposition to some of the most inventive schemers of the day.

In addition, he was powerful in the air, he was invariably composed and, as the French discovered to their chagrin, he could pass like a dream. For all that, often he was conservative with his distribution, preferring to break up attacks and feed his own creative inside-forwards which, when he was lining up with an artist like Johnny Haynes of Fulham, was a policy as eminently sensible as it was characteristically selfless.

As a teenager Lowe found employment at a tube-works in Birmingham, then moved to London to become an engineer during the war. While in the capital he guested for Millwall as an amateur, also representing Finchley and Walthamstow Avenue briefly, before returning to the Midlands, where he was discovered by Villa playing for his works side in a cup final.

After turning professional in September 1945 Lowe, who served as a Bevin Boy in Black Country coal mines towards the end of the conflict, soon broke into the first team, helping his new employers to finish runners-up in the Football League South, an emergency wartime competition, and became a regular when normal service was resumed.

So impressive was his form as Villa maintained a healthy presence in the top half of the First Division that he earned that England call-up against France, then took part in a 1-0 defeat in Switzerland and a 10-0 annihilation of Portugal in Lisbon – playing behind the sumptuous forward line of Stan Matthews, Stan Mortensen, Tommy Lawton, Wilf Mannion and Tom Finney – all in the space of three weeks.

However, he was overlooked when England returned to action in the autumn, and then suffered a couple of niggling injuries, while competition for Villa places hotted up as manager Alex Massie strove to combat a slight downturn in results. Thus in May 1950 Lowe, along with his younger brother Reg, a left-back whose career was to be ended prematurely by a broken leg, was transferred to fellow top-flight club Fulham, Eddie's fee being reported as £10,000, Reg's as £3,000.

At Craven Cottage, Lowe the senior became a pillar of strength with instant effect, but it was a poor side he had joined and though relegation was avoided narrowly in his first campaign, Fulham went down as bottom club in 1951/52.

He proved to be a shrewd acquisition, though, emerging as a key component of an attractive remoulded combination in which the jewel was the enchantingly gifted young inside-forward Haynes. As the decade progressed Fulham entertained royally, aided by a free-flowing attack containing the likes of inside-forwards Bobby Robson and Jimmy Hill, winger Charlie Mitten and spearhead Bedford Jezzard, but it was not until the arrival of Duggie Livingstone as boss in 1956 that a genuine belief in the possibility of promotion began to grow.

Now in came high-quality additions such as full-backs Jimmy Langley and future World Cup hero George Cohen, and ex-England centre-forward Roy Bentley, who was converted successfully into a half-back alongside the consistently efficient Lowe. Duly in 1957/58 Fulham finished fifth in the Second Division and reached the semi-finals of the FA Cup, bowing out only after a replay to a Manchester United team recently ravaged by the Munich air disaster, although Lowe missed that knockout sequence through injury.

A season later, however, he was back exuding authority as Fulham, with Jezzard newly installed as manager, finished runners-up to Sheffield Wednesday, thus reclaiming a place among the elite. Thereafter Lowe maintained a steady presence as Fulham consolidated with a commendable tenth-place finish in 1959/60, then embarked on a trio of successful battles against relegation leavened by another run to the last four of the FA Cup in 1961/62. By the spring of 1963, Lowe was approaching his 38th birthday yet looking back on a term in which he had finished fourth in the Footballer of the Year poll, the coveted statuette having gone to an even more gnarled campaigner, Stanley Matthews.

Now the Fulham veteran, who had been linked in the press with a move to high-riding Tottenham Hotspur only 18 months earlier, was at a crossroads, and instead of attempting to soldier on in the top tier he accepted an offer to become player-boss of Third Division Notts County, bowing out of Craven Cottage having played more times for the club than anyone except the icon Haynes.

Sadly, the move didn't work out. Heavily criticised for his early sale of thrusting young marksman Tony Hateley to Aston Villa, and the subsequent poor form of the replacement, Terry Bly, Lowe never truly recovered. County, who were not financially well endowed, were demoted as bottom club that term, then he sold another popular striker, Jeff Astle, to West Bromwich Albion during the subsequent mediocre season in the basement division. By then in his 40th year and thus incapable of making a meaningful impact on the field, he was sacked in the spring of 1965.

Still devoted to the game, Lowe scouted briefly for Plymouth Argyle while qualifying as an accountant, before earning his livelihood as a purchasing manager for a boiler-making company in Nottingham, where he lived for the rest of his life.

Edward Lowe, footballer and manager; born Halesowen, 11 July 1925; played for Aston Villa 1945-50, Fulham 1950-63, Notts County 1963-64; capped three times by England 1947; managed Notts County 1963-65; died Nottingham, 9 March 2009.

Hugh Kelly

Hugh Kelly was skipper of the finest Blackpool side in the club's 113-year Football League history, an exhilaratingly dashing combination which finished as runners-up to champions Manchester United in 1955/56 and contained as its jewel the wondrous Stanley Matthews, at that time the most famous player in the world.

Not that fame was any sort of spur for the engagingly modest Kelly, an unflinchingly steely defensive wing-half who, if he was performing today, would be termed a holding midfielder in front of the back four.

For all his sustained and integral contribution to the Seasiders' cause – between his debut in 1946 and his exit from Bloomfield Road a decade and a half later he made 470 senior appearances – the Scottish international one-club man was essentially unobtrusive. His way was to win the vast majority of his tackles through a combination of excellent timing and iron resolve, then to distribute the ball unfussily, and usually with the utmost accuracy, to more extravagantly gifted colleagues. It was an admirable approach, but one which meant he featured only rarely when the newspapermen composed their headlines.

How poignant, then, that such a selflessly loyal and persevering servant should miss out through injury on the most glorious of all Blackpool achievements, the lifting of the FA Cup in 1953 when the two Stanleys, Matthews and Mortensen, sparkled so incandescently in the Wembley sunshine.

Kelly, who played his early football for the Perth-based juniors Jeanfield Swifts, was recruited by Blackpool as a 19-year-old in the spring of 1943, the only cash which changed hands being the customary £10 signing-on fee.

Towards the end of the war he guested for East Fife before making his first-team entrance for the Seasiders in an FA Cup replay defeat by Middlesbrough in February 1946.

There followed a handful of outings as League competition resumed in the subsequent season, but it was not until midway through 1947/48, when George Farrow was sold to Sheffield United, that he gained a regular berth, captain Harry Johnston switching to right-half with Kelly slotting in on his favoured left side.

He finished that term at Wembley, part of a valiant team which twice took the lead in the FA Cup final against Manchester United before being swept aside by Matt Busby's first outstanding creation in a breathtakingly entertaining contest, and in 1951 he experienced another disappointment on what was then the gala day of the domestic game, as Blackpool were beaten by a Jackie Milburn-inspired Newcastle United.

All the while, though, Kelly had been consolidating his presence in a team which matured into one of the most powerful in the English top flight and in April 1952 he was rewarded by his sole full international call-up, putting in a characteristically efficient shift as the USA were routed 6-0 at Hampden Park.

He was denied further caps by a clutch of polished operators, the likes of John Cumming of Hearts, Dundee's Doug Cowie and Tommy Docherty of Preston North End, a circumstance which nettled his legion of admirers at Bloomfield Road, who were hardly mollified by his selection for two 'B' internationals during 1952/53.

That term Kelly struck a particularly rich vein of form, proving particularly effective in tense victories over Arsenal and Tottenham Hotspur in the quarter- and semi-finals of the FA Cup, only to suffer an ankle injury in Blackpool's penultimate League game, against Liverpool. Thus as hat-trick man Mortensen and the inspirational Matthews enchanted the sporting world by leading a remarkable comeback from two goals down to overcome Bolton Wanderers in the final, poor Kelly could only look on ruefully from the stand, though he accepted his fate with typical good humour.

There was a brief blip in his enduring love affair with Blackpool when he requested a transfer after he was dropped following another injury during 1953/54, but he bounced back from that to be awarded the captaincy when Johnston retired at the end of the next campaign.

He proved to be a canny and immensely respected leader as the Seasiders rose to hitherto unscaled League heights in 1955/56, and although they finished 11 points adrift of Busby's precocious pre-Munich champions, they fully merited their second place.

That proved to be the peak of Kelly's career. Having celebrated his 33rd birthday in the summer of 1956 he became vulnerable to the challenge of younger men, but although injuries and the persuasive form of Ewan Fenton saw him ousted for much of the following term, still the resilient Scot was far from done.

Once more he returned, missing only a handful of matches as Blackpool retained their status among the top half of the elite in both 1957/58 and 1958/59, emerging as a reliable penalty-taker to boot. It was not until 1960, by which time he was nearer 40 than 30, that finally he stepped aside, becoming an invaluable *eminence grise* to the reserves before leaving Bloomfield Road to become player-boss of non-League Ashton United in the summer of 1961.

Kelly excelled in his new post, his enthusiastic charges winning a couple of coveted prizes, while his shrewdness, dignity and quiet authority moved some observers to speculate that he might have a management future at Football League level.

However, after a spell on Blackpool's coaching staff, he elected to concentrate on his business interests in the town, running a café and making ice-cream, and thus he departed the game he had served so splendidly for so long.

Hugh Thomas Kelly, footballer; born Valleyfield, Fifeshire, 23 July 1923; played for Blackpool 1944-61; capped once by Scotland 1952; died Blackpool, Lancashire, 28 March 2009.

John Elsworthy

John Elsworthy was a colossal cornerstone of the Ipswich Town side which featured in one of the most romantic of all footballing success stories.

The lanky Welsh wing-half was a dynamic midfield driving force as the hitherto unfashionable Suffolk club ascended from the lower reaches of the Football League to its very pinnacle under the inspirational guidance of Alf Ramsey, who was destined to lead England to World Cup glory only four years later in 1966.

When the men from Portman Road lifted the First Division title – the equivalent of the Premier League crown today – it was hailed as a sporting miracle, and its essence was personified by the largely unsung Elsworthy.

In a patchwork team, stitched together expertly but frugally by the shrewdly imaginative Ramsey, he was a bastion of strength and reliability, but also a key creative influence.

He held a unique record, being the only man to collect a championship medal at the League's every level, and he was unswervingly loyal, too, serving only the Town during a professional career which encompassed nearly 450 games.

Gifted at most sports, the teenage Elsworthy chose football over cricket and rugby, spurning a chance to join Glamorgan County Cricket Club, enlisting instead with Newport County as an amateur. Spotted by Ipswich while excelling for the Somerton Park outfit at youth level, he signed on at Portman Road in May 1949.

There followed two years as a part-timer while he completed his National Service in the RAF and it was not until the 1952/53 campaign that Elsworthy, then an inside-left, secured a regular first-team berth, contributing 18 goals in senior competition for the perennial strugglers in the Third Division South.

In 1953/54 he tasted professional triumph for the first time as Ipswich topped the table, but he barely figured during the next season as they were relegated from the Second Division.

However, the defining watershed of his career was approaching. For 1955/56, Ramsey replaced Scott Duncan as Portman Road boss and Elsworthy moved back to left-half, a position in which he spent more time facing the play and in which he proved immeasurably more comfortable.

Under new management the Town narrowly missed promotion at the first attempt, but clinched it in style as champions in 1956/57, with the composed Elsworthy proving ever more integral to their industrious yet entertaining style.

By now he was reaching his peak, and during an FA Cup encounter with Manchester United in January 1958, only 12 days before Matt Busby's wondrous 'Babes' were to be decimated by the Munich air disaster in which eight players died, he gave the finest performance of his life.

In an Old Trafford quagmire likened by one observer to 'black porridge', Elsworthy tackled tirelessly and tailored his passes cannily to the atrocious conditions, even drawing a favourable comparison in several newspapers with United's young titan Duncan Edwards, who was playing in his last FA Cup tie before his tragic end.

By common consent Edwards was one of England's greatest ever players, so those journalistic parallels with Elsworthy might be a tad fanciful, but clearly he shone on that murky Manchester afternoon, although he was unable to prevent a 2-0 defeat.

Not surprisingly he was drafted into Wales' preliminary squad for that summer's World Cup finals in Sweden, but he failed to make the cut when the party was reduced from 21 to 19 to save money and, sadly, was never awarded a full cap.

But consolation on the club front was to be immense. As Ramsey continued to develop his side – in which prolific twin strikers Ray Crawford and Ted Phillips, and spindly little play-making winger Jimmy Leadbetter were outstanding – Ipswich first consolidated in the second tier, then topped it in 1960/61.

If this provoked surprise in many quarters, it was nothing to the seismic shock which rippled through the football world in the spring of 1962 when the Town overhauled much-fancied Burnley and the mighty Tottenham Hotspur – whom they beat home and away – to become Football League champions.

Ramsey's so-called 'miracle on a shoestring' owed plenty to every member of his team, but no one did more than the indefatigable Elsworthy, who was absent for only one game, and who toiled and prompted constantly. It was a remarkable achievement for a player who had been troubled periodically by injuries, including one potentially life-threatening instant when a cut leg led to a blood clot and hospitalisation.

'Big John' – so dubbed both for his physical stature and his enormous input to the team effort – played his part in the Town's first (and still only) European Cup adventure, scoring in the 10-0 home annihilation of Maltese champions Floriana, and showing up splendidly when the star-strewn Italians AC Milan were beaten 2-1 at Portman Road.

But harrowingly for Ipswich, an era was about to end. Alf Ramsey left to become England coach and the Town declined under his successor, Jackie Milburn, suffering demotion in 1964. By now at the veteran stage, and failing to respond to the hectoring style of the next manager, Bill McGarry, Elsworthy retired in 1965, having captained Ipswich on his last three appearances.

Now he left the game, running a grocery business and then a post office, both in Ipswich. But he remained close to the Town for the rest of his life, becoming honorary president of the supporters' club and rarely missing a game.

John Elsworthy, footballer; born Nantyderry, Monmouthshire, 26 July 1931; played for Ipswich Town 1949-65; died Ipswich, Suffolk, 3 May 2009.

Tommy Cummings

How fitting it was that towards the twilight of a football career in which he had shone steadily for more than a decade as one of the most stylish and reliable defenders in the English top flight without capturing any of the game's most coveted honours, Tommy Cummings of Burnley finally received his just deserts.

Though the veteran Wearsider wasn't always certain of his place during the tumultuous 1959/60 campaign in which the team from the middle-sized Lancashire cotton town outstripped much-fancied Wolves and the rest of the big-city battalions to become worthy League champions, he played in more than half the games that term and he was there at the climax, when the glittering prize was claimed with a nerve-shredding last-day victory at Manchester City.

Cummings was a thoroughbred performer, an invariably calm, assured centre-half whose exceptional fleetness of foot was matched by a quickness of thought which enabled him to interpret the action as it unfolded, typically snuffing out opposition attacks before they could threaten the Burnley goal.

He was particularly impressive when faced by speed merchants such as Jackie Milburn of Newcastle United or Blackpool's Stan Mortensen, but he was prepared for a physical battle, too, bravely taking the knocks from the likes of Bolton Wanderers dreadnought Nat Lofthouse and Trevor Ford, Sunderland's renowned tough nut.

The son of a miner, Cummings left school to work in a shipyard on the Wear while playing his football for local clubs Hylton Colliery Welfare and Stanley United. Trials with Blackpool and Tottenham Hotspur came to nothing but he enlisted with Burnley as a part-timer in October 1947 while continuing with an apprenticeship as a mining engineer.

His working days were arduous and long, his shifts underground being followed by rigorous sessions on the training pitch, but Cummings persevered and was rewarded by a senior breakthrough midway through 1948/49 when the Clarets' stalwart stopper Alan Brown departed for Notts County.

Thereafter he matured so rapidly in Frank Hill's well organised side which usually finished in the top half of the First Division that soon he was on the fringe of international recognition, travelling as reserve when England faced Northern Ireland in Belfast in October 1950. Later that month he played for the Football League against the Irish League at Blackpool, but the only caps he was to earn was a trio for the 'B' team during mid-decade, his path to the top honour being blocked by the doughty likes of Portsmouth's Jack Froggatt, Harry Johnston of Blackpool and, finally, Wolves and England skipper Billy Wright.

At club level Cummings, who could occupy either full-back berth at need, remained a paragon of defensive consistency, missing only a handful of matches throughout the first half of the 1950s, although ironically it is for a rare attacking adventure that many fans recall him most vividly.

Near the end of a taut encounter with Newcastle on a snowy Turf Moor afternoon in January 1952, he dispossessed Magpies marksman Jackie Milburn deep in Burnley territory, then surged past a succession of tackles before netting with a searing edge-of-the-box left-footer to win the match.

Cummings was a delightfully modest individual and, asked at the time why he had embarked on such an uncharacteristic sortie, he offered the dry reply: 'I looked up and I had nobody to pass to.' But he was a colourful and imaginative raconteur, too, and in later years his comrades maintained that the number of tackles he had evaded during his majestic progress grew with each telling – what had started as four became six or seven or even more!

What is not in dispute is that his goal was one of only three in his 15 years and 479 senior outings for the Clarets, for whom only a handful of men have played more often.

The hitherto serene momentum of Cummings' career, which included taking over from Harold Mather as skipper in 1951, was rudely jolted in August 1956 when he suffered a knee injury which kept him on the sidelines for almost two seasons and it was feared that his playing days were prematurely done.

But he fought back single-mindedly to regain his place in a side which was now even more purposeful and more impeccably drilled under new boss Harry Potts. In 1958/59, Cummings missed only three games as the Clarets finished in a creditable seventh place in the League table, but it was in 1959/60 that they experienced their ultimate glory.

The obvious stars of Burnley's champions were the dazzling Irish play-maker Jimmy McIlroy, cultured wing-half and captain Jimmy Adamson and dashing England winger John Connelly. But every member of Potts' unpretentious, tightly-knit squad contributed nobly, including the ageing Cummings, who started the campaign at left-back, lost his place to the emerging Alex Elder but then recovered in the spring to perform magnificently alongside young Brian Miller, who was switched from central stopper to defensive wing-half to accommodate him. True, he was helped by a clash between Bobby Seith and autocratic Turf Moor chairman Bob Lord which resulted in the Scot being axed, but Cummings made the most of his opportunity.

Indeed, having regained his berth and pocketed a title medal at the age of 31, he exhibited all of his former sure-footed solidity. In 1960/61 he helped Burnley to come fourth in the League and to reach the semi-finals of both the FA Cup and the newly launched League Cup.

Then in 1961/62 he was absent on only four occasions as the Clarets went agonisingly close to lifting the League and FA Cup double, finishing as First Division runners-up behind Alf Ramsey's surprise packet, Ipswich Town, and losing the FA Cup final 3-1 to Tottenham Hotspur.

By then approaching 34, Cummings played only twice more for Burnley, losing his place to the much younger John Talbut, then accepting an offer to become player-boss of Mansfield Town in March 1963. Unlike his auspicious team-mate McIlroy, whose simultaneous and hugely controversial transfer to Stoke City outraged fans who maintained he was still in his creative prime, the defender slipped away almost unnoticed.

However, he made an immediate impact at Field Mill, consolidating on the excellent groundwork of his predecessor, Raich Carter, by leading the Stags to fourth place in the Fourth Division, and thus to promotion that spring.

Now Cummings continued only briefly as a player, but he took naturally to management, almost guiding Mansfield to the second flight in 1964/65, missing out only on goal average, the absurdly complicated precursor to goal difference as a means of separating clubs on equal points.

There followed one poor season and one improved one at the Mill, after which he had established his reputation sufficiently to take on the reins of Aston Villa in July 1967.

This was not the powerful Villa of modern times, though, the Midlanders having just descended to the Second Division and being short of cash to revive their ailing team. Cummings brought in several new men, including top-scorer Brian Godfrey from Preston North End, but they proved insufficient for a transformation and after one term of dire mediocrity was followed by a rotten start to 1968/69, the Wearsider was sacked in November with his charges at the wrong end of the table.

Later, briefly, he bossed non-League Great Harwood and scouted for Burnley and Sunderland, but he went on to make his living outside the game, running a succession of pubs in the Burnley area. Later still there was a popular return to Turf Moor as a match-day host, where his lively recollections of that sensational goal some half a century earlier continued to rivet the punters.

Thomas Smith Cummings, footballer and football club manager; born Castletown, Sunderland, 12 September 1928; played for Burnley 1947-63, Mansfield Town 1963; managed Mansfield Town 1963-67, Aston Villa 1967-68; died Queensgate, Burnley, 12 July 2009.

Sir Bobby Robson

With his rumpled features and crooked smile he could look crushed and weary, but when Sir Bobby Robson began holding forth on his beloved game, those rheumy eyes would sparkle and his overwhelming enthusiasm would captivate all but the most cynical of listeners.

Almost always, despite the endearing malapropisms with which his conversation was scattered, his homespun philosophy would offer an oasis of wholesome sanity in the self-obsessed world of modern top-flight football, re-stating basic values at a time when such wisdom was desperately needed.

Robson was the doyen of the British game, a national institution whose public image had been comprehensively rehabilitated since the days of his unfair and frequently hysterical media maulings during his reign as England boss in the 1980s.

In fact, he was an immensely able, unswervingly honourable manager who never deserved the tabloid-fed calumny which descended on his head. His international record bears favourable comparison with all but one of his predecessors – Sir Alf Ramsey, whose side lifted the World Cup in 1966 – and the avalanche of criticism, both professional and personal, was as insulting as it was unjust.

Eventually and belatedly, when his marathon career could be placed in historical perspective, and particularly following his emotional stint in charge of his childhood favourites Newcastle United, his public stock rose tremendously. Significantly, he had never lacked the respect of his footballing peers – and they knew best.

Their approbation, and the chance to guide his country's fortunes, sprang from his achievements at club level with unfashionable Ipswich Town, for whom Robson had operated on a comparative shoestring to create delightful sides which could hold their own, and sometimes more, against the finest in the land. Once ensconced on the international front, he never brought home a trophy and his teams failed in two European Championships, but Robson's England endured horribly unlucky elimination from successive World Cup tournaments and had their moments of triumph along the way.

In addition, it should not be forgotten that the personable north-easterner had been a good-class wing-half cum inside-forward who won a score of caps at a time when there was no shortage of high-quality performers in both positions.

Robson hailed from the little mining community of Sacriston in County Durham, the fourth of five sons of a father who missed only one shift at the coalface in 51 years. Having noted the bleakness of that life at first hand, young Bobby was determined to avoid the pit and did so at first by becoming an apprentice electrician at his neighbourhood colliery.

Of course, Robson's ultimate salvation was football. He was a natural all-round sportsman, excelling at all ball games, but soccer was both his obsession – later he would describe it as his drug – and what he did best. After starring at schoolboy level, he was given trials by Middlesbrough and Southampton, both of whom rejected him. Nothing daunted, the 15-year-old inside-forward continued to impress and two years later a posse of clubs was hunting his signature.

Robson chose Fulham, enlisting with the Londoners in May 1950 and making his First Division debut within a year. He revelled in the friendly atmosphere fostered by chairman Tommy Trinder and shone in an enterprising line-up which also included Johnny Haynes. Despite experiencing the trauma of relegation in 1952, Robson made steady personal progress, a confident but level-headed young fellow who brought both skill and industry to his twin role of creating and scoring goals.

Inevitably he attracted attention from the top grade and in March 1956 he joined West Bromwich Albion, a successful club at the time, for a then-hefty £25,000. Robson blossomed at the Hawthorns in an attractive combination which never had the depth of talent to lift a major prize but which could entertain royally.

When England recognition arrived in November 1957, Robson responded with two debut goals in a 4-0 rout of France, suggesting that a lengthy international stint was in prospect. But selection policy was markedly inconsistent in those days, the team being picked by committee, and soon he was discarded. It was to be two years before he regained his place, by which time he had been converted into a wing-half, and he settled into one of the finest England sides of the post-war era.

During 1960/61 Walter Winterbottom's team enjoyed a glorious undefeated sequence, winning seven games and drawing one, scoring 44 goals in the process. Sadly they peaked too soon for the 1962 World Cup, just before which the 29-year-old Albion skipper was dropped, never to play for his country again. However, international football had not seen the last of Bobby Robson.

West Bromwich, though, had. During his Midlands sojourn he had supplemented what was then a paltry income for a married man with two (later three) sons by coaching schoolboys. But with the lifting of football's iniquitous maximum wage restrictions in 1961, the way was clear for clubs to reward their players more handsomely. Some did, Albion didn't and Robson demanded a transfer, returning to Fulham for £20,000 in August 1962.

Back at Craven Cottage he flourished in a mainly defensive role, bringing class to an indifferent side's annual struggle to avoid demotion from the First Division. Meanwhile, having been encouraged by Winterbottom to develop his coaching, Robson assisted Oxford University, and when he retired as a player in 1967 he set his sights on management.

After rejecting offers to coach Arsenal and to become player-boss of Southend United, he took charge of Vancouver Royals. An unhappy impecunious interlude followed during which he shared duties with the great Hungarian hero, Ferenc Puskas, with whom he found it difficult to work. The upshot was another return to Fulham in January 1968 to take over what had become an ailing club.

Robson was unable to prevent relegation and, despite major reorganisation of his staff, the Cottagers performed poorly in Division Two and the rookie manager strove, at times, to exercise authority over former colleagues. Following a row with a director, the influential businessman Sir Eric Miller, Robson was sacked in November and found himself on the dole.

However, his luck was about to turn. After scouting briefly for Chelsea, he became boss of Ipswich Town in January 1969, thus beginning one of the most fruitful and fulfilling periods of his life. Not that it was all plain sailing at Portman Road. Despite establishing an immediate rapport with the generous-spirited Cobbold family, who owned the club, Robson began by presiding over several disappointing seasons at the wrong end of the First Division. He had inherited a weak side and there were confrontations with players, including one bout of fisticuffs, as he settled in.

When a vocal minority of Ipswich fans demanded his sacking, Robson feared the worst. Instead, the board persevered with their man, even apologising for the supporters' ire and, gradually, the tide turned. Despite not having the cash to compete on equal terms with rich clubs, he assembled a first-rate team, built around the likes of Mick Mills, Kevin Beattie and Allan Hunter. In 1973 they finished fourth in the table, equalling the feat in 1974, then improving to third in 1975. Thereafter they became a genuine power, finishing out of the top six only once in a decade and missing the title only narrowly on several occasions.

The most heartbreaking of these was in 1980/81 when, most observers agreed, Robson had created the best side in England. They had surged into a commanding position in the League but then, straitened by injuries, won only one of their last five games to allow Aston Villa to take the prize. At this time, with inspiration furnished by Dutch midfielders Arnold Muhren and Frans Thijssen, Ipswich were a delight to behold. They played richly entertaining football but had a strong backbone, and had the cash been available to build a deeper squad they surely would have become champions.

They did have their moments, however, winning the UEFA Cup in 1981, though for the sheer joy it brought, even that could not equal their heady victory over Arsenal in the 1978 FA Cup Final. Before the match the press patronisingly dubbed the Suffolk side as country cousins; in fact, they were a talented and superbly drilled band of professionals and did their manager proud as they outplayed the Gunners to record a massively popular win.

An operator of Robson's calibre was bound to receive periodic offers. After all, he was established as a coach with flair, a firm disciplinarian, a man who could succeed on a small budget by unearthing promising youngsters and transforming them into stars. But as the chances to leave Portman Road came in, so he spurned them. He could have gone to Derby (1973), Leeds (1974), Newcastle (1975), Everton (1977, and he was close to succumbing), Barcelona (1978), Athletic Bilbao (1979), Manchester United and Sunderland (both 1981). Instead he remained loyal to Ipswich and the Cobbolds, treating them as they had treated him, and it did him huge credit.

However, there was one temptation from which Robson could not walk away. He had been interviewed for the England post when Don Revie upped sticks in 1977 and had run the international 'B' team between 1978 and 1982. Understandably, when the opportunity of the top job came his way in 1982, he accepted.

Thus critics who had accused him of shrinking from soccer's most daunting challenges were proved wrong, and he got off to a solid start, despite early vilification for the axing of Kevin Keegan. But, predictably in view of England's failure to reach the 1984 European Championship finals, his 'honeymoon' was woefully short. After one Wembley defeat by Russia he was spat on and showered with beer but that was nothing compared to what certain newspapers had in store.

Chief persecutors were *The Sun*, which produced badges proclaiming 'Robson Out, Clough In', though that, in its turn, was mild compared with what would follow later letdowns. Around this time Robson was head-hunted once more by Barcelona, who offered vast financial inducements, but he demonstrated his strength of character by refusing the Spaniards for a second time.

In the short term he was rewarded by one of the finest results England have ever managed, victory in Brazil, but by now all attention was centred on the 1986 World Cup. England duly qualified, then stuttered in their early matches in Mexico before recovering, thanks largely to Gary Lineker's hat-trick against Poland, to reach a quarter-final against the eventual champions, Argentina.

That day Robson's men were undone by Diego Maradona, the world's premier player, who scored twice in his side's 2-1 win. The first was the infamous 'Hand of God' goal, when Maradona's blatant handball went unpunished, and the second was a work of pure genius. England played well and threatened a draw, but couldn't quite achieve it; they had been unlucky but Robson deserved praise for orchestrating a noble effort.

It wasn't quite like that in 1988 when, despite the presence of world-class players such as Lineker, John Barnes and Bryan Robson, England lost all their games in the European Championship finals and returned home from Germany in disgrace. Now Bobby Robson's relations with the press hit a new low. He was castigated mercilessly and without the slightest modicum of taste, being told to 'Go in the name of God'. Then, after a drab showing against Saudi Arabia, this was amended to 'Go, in the name of Allah'. Very droll. He was accused at various stages of inept selection, excessive tactical caution and failure to get the best out of some brilliant individuals, notably Glenn Hoddle. Not surprisingly, the strain began to tell, particularly when allegations surfaced about his private life and his care-worn countenance became an ever more familiar feature of both front and back pages.

Clearly there was a limit to what one man could take and, after England scraped into the 1990 World Cup finals in Italy, Robson announced that he would quit after the tournament. The build-up games inspired little faith but the team progressed, admittedly unsteadily and with a measure of good fortune, to a semi-final confrontation with West

Germany. Here, for the first time, they played like potential champions, with the maverick Paul Gascoigne showing signs of realising his phenomenal potential.

But just as Robson was poised on the threshold of emulating Sir Alf Ramsey by reaching a World Cup final, luck deserted him. The Germans having taken a fortunate lead, England equalised through Lineker and proved the stronger side, only to die the most dreaded of soccer deaths, by penalty shoot-out.

At least, however, an emotional Robson could bow out on a decent note, with fans chanting his name to honour rather than to ridicule him. It was the least he merited after eight years in which he had presided over 47 victories, 30 draws and only 18 defeats, as well as carrying out vast amounts of unsung youth coaching work.

If there were ever any doubt about his ability, it was laid to rest emphatically in his subsequent career. After bidding a tired farewell to England, he led PSV Eindhoven to two Dutch titles, thus laying the championship bogey that had haunted him at Ipswich. Then came a move to Sporting Lisbon, which ended surprisingly in the sack because of European elimination, and a more successful spell with Porto, whom he guided to a European Cup semi-final in 1994 before winning two more titles.

After undergoing a second cancer operation in 1995 (the first had been in 1992), Robson recovered rapidly and turned down the chance of managing Arsenal. Still, though, his drive remained strong and a year later, aged 63, at last he accepted an invitation from Barcelona, signing a two-year contract with the Catalan giants.

In his first term, despite the recruitment of star Brazilian striker Ronaldo, the side made an uncertain start and as the pressure of colossal expectation mounted he ran into political problems with autocratic club president Josep Nunez. By New Year 1997 the Ajax coach Louis Van Gaal had been lined up to replace Robson at season's end, but the Englishman embarrassed his doubting employers by inspiring his men to double glory, Barcelona beating Paris St Germain to lift the European Cup Winners' Cup and Real Betis to take the Spanish Cup, also finishing close runners-up to bitter rivals Real Madrid in the championship race.

Now he was impossible to sack, so when Van Gaal arrived for 1997/98, Robson was shunted 'upstairs' to become director of recruitment, a glorified chief scout, little more than a sabbatical position which he held for a year before taking over once more at PSV.

During this 12-month sojourn in Eindhoven, holding the fort while Eric Gerets obtained his coaching qualifications, the 65-year-old Robson astonished the local press by playing in full-blooded practice games, and when he departed in 1999 his appetite for the fray was undiminished.

Thereafter he returned to England and accepted a Football Association offer to become mentor to the next generation of England coaches, but in September he got the call from the club he had loved as long as he could remember, Newcastle United. Robson had been offered charge of the Magpies in February 1997 but would not walk out on Barcelona; now, though, the time was right.

At St James' Park, where he replaced Ruud Gullit, he found a strife-torn club at the foot of the Premiership; morale was low, indiscipline was rife and there were wounds to heal. He began by restoring Alan Shearer, who had been dropped by the controversial Dutchman, to the side and the England centre-forward responded by scoring five goals in Robson's first home match, an 8-0 annihilation of Sheffield Wednesday.

Immediately the new boss had infused the place with his infectious enthusiasm, tapping into the fanatical loyalty of supporters who had been alienated previously not only by the Gullit regime, but also by the indiscretions of directors who had been caught on tape insulting both their womenfolk and their intelligence.

Soon he overhauled the coaching regime and began team-building, at first without much money to spend but eventually with a substantial budget. Despite being ridiculed widely for taking such an onerous job at a time when, his critics felt, he should have been subsiding gently into retirement, he transformed United's fortunes.

In that first campaign they reached the semi-finals of the FA Cup, enjoyed an enlivening UEFA Cup run and climbed to mid-table safety in the Premiership. Then, after another season of consolidation, they topped the table in December before finishing fourth in 2001/02, and in the following summer Robson, who had been appointed CBE in 1991, was knighted. Newcastle rose to third in 2002/03 and attained the second group phase of the Champions League; and in 2003/04 an appearance in the UEFA Cup semi-finals, where they lost to Marseille, offered compensation for dipping to fifth place in the League, still a respectable result given the colossal power and resources of the 'big four' ahead of them, Arsenal, Chelsea, Manchester United and Liverpool.

All the while Robson represented traditional and sensible sporting values while continuing to radiate his passion for the game, and at times he was understandably perplexed by the boorish or careless attitudes of some of the young millionaires in his charge.

Some observers doubted whether a septuagenarian was capable of controlling the volatile likes of Kieron Dyer, Craig Bellamy and Lee Bowyer, and virtually on the eve of 2004/05 his position was undermined by chairman Freddy Shepherd – one of the directors caught mocking the fans so disgracefully – who announced that the manager's contract would not be renewed in the spring.

After early results proved poor, at the end of August Robson was summarily sacked by Shepherd, but on the day of his poignant departure it was his and not the chairman's dignity which shone through the storm clouds gathering over St James' Park.

Even after that, after everything, Robson remained eager to be involved in football, and in January 2006, now aged 73, he was named as consultant to the new Republic of Ireland boss Steve Staunton. Soon there followed a third successful cancer operation, though his vulnerability was underlined that August when, after being appointed honorary president of Ipswich Town, he fell ill ten minutes into their home game against Crystal Palace and was taken to hospital.

Robson stepped down from his Irish role in November 2007 and in March 2008, as he launched a foundation to help in the fight against cancer, he spoke of battling the disease for the fifth time. He was aiming to raise £500,000 for the new charity, which would pay for a cancer trial and research centre bearing his name at Newcastle's Freeman Hospital.

Bobby Robson was a sensitive and decent man, and a truly accomplished manager who rose courageously above an army of petty tormentors. Though he never achieved his ultimate ambitions of lifting the World Cup or the English League crown, he came close enough to earn real and lasting honour in the game to which he devoted his life.

Robert William Robson, footballer and football manager: born Sacriston, County Durham, 18 February 1933; played for Fulham 1950-56 and 1962-67, West Bromwich Albion 1956-62; capped 20 times for England 1957-62; manager Vancouver Royals 1967-68, Fulham 1968, Ipswich Town 1969-82, England 1982-90, PSV Eindhoven 1990-92, Sporting Lisbon 1992-93, Porto 1993-96, Barcelona 1996-97 (head of recruitment 1997-98), PSV Eindhoven 1998-99, Newcastle United 1999-2004; died County Durham, 31 July 2009.

Bobby Thomson

By common consent, Ray Wilson is England's most accomplished left-back of the last half-century. But there was a time, a couple of seasons before he cemented his lasting pre-eminence through his peerless displays for the 1966 World Cup-winning team, that Wilson looked to have a serious rival for his place in Alf Ramsey's yet-to-be-settled combination.

That man, younger by nearly a decade, was Bobby Thomson of Wolverhampton Wanderers, a poised and polished six-footer whose pace, athleticism and composure appeared to mark him out for a glittering international future.

Certainly that was the initial view of Ramsey, who selected Thomson for his first full cap as a 19-year-old against Northern Ireland at Wembley in November 1963. Though the opposition, who succumbed 8-3, were not of the highest calibre, the rookie defender impressed with his self-possession and smooth all-round efficiency, and over the ensuing year he represented his country another seven times.

Not the least of the newcomer's assets was the ability to occupy either full-back slot, and he understudied effectively for both Wilson and the right-sided George Cohen during England's 1964 summer tour of North and South America. Further steady advancement appeared to be a formality for such an exciting prospect, yet Thomson's international career was over only four days after his 21st birthday, leaving perplexed observers to speculate on the reasons for such an unexpected loss of impetus at the highest level.

One major factor, perhaps, was that Wolves had ended their golden period of serial success under Stan Cullis and entered a phase of rapid decline, their relegation in 1965 depriving Thomson of top-flight competition at a crucial stage of his development.

Another was the continued excellence of Wilson into his thirties, and the consistency of other competitors, the likes of Liverpool's Gerry Byrne – who was allotted England's reserve left-back berth in the 1966 World Cup finals squad – and Keith Newton of Blackburn Rovers.

Still, international anti-climax did not prevent Thomson from completing a distinguished and fulfilling club career, notably with Wolves, for whom he played 300 league and cup games, then Birmingham City and Luton Town among others.

His first steps in the game were taken as a speedy winger, but he was given the opportunity to play at full-back during a trial for England schoolboys and found himself ideally suited to the new role. Thereafter he became the target of several big clubs in his native Midlands and he opted for Wolves, signing as an amateur in 1959, turning professional in the summer of 1961. Perhaps it was to the teenager's advantage, at first, that by 1961/62 the hitherto powerful Molineux club was on the slide, lingering dangerously close to the foot of the old First Division, the equivalent of today's Premier League.

Manager Cullis, the stern disciplinarian who had presided over two title triumphs and an FA Cup win in the space of the previous four campaigns, shuffled his pack vigorously in an attempt to reverse the ominous trend and in January he drafted Thomson into a left-back slot that had proved particularly problematical.

Performing creditably in a 2-1 debut defeat at home to West Bromwich Albion in the FA Cup, he revealed craft, determination and a cool head, enough to retain his place virtually uninterrupted for the remainder of that term. For good measure he helped Wolves to the final of the FA Youth Cup, in which they were beaten 2-1 by Newcastle United, and his future beckoned invitingly.

In 1962/63, his first full senior campaign, Thomson made remarkable progress, not missing a match and attaining levels of maturity and reliability unusual in one so young, contributing hugely to Wolves' marked temporary improvement – they rose to fifth place in the table – and making his breakthrough at England under-23 level.

Boldly rewarding these achievements, Ramsey duly promoted him to face the Irish and persisted with him even when, to the consternation of Cullis, the Black Countrymen plunged to 16th position in 1963/64.

Occasionally the manager, desperate at his team's slump, berated his left-back for not tackling more ferociously, but that was not Thomson's way; rather he was cultured, neat and intelligent, eschewing overt violence, preferring to win the ball by vigilance and shrewd anticipation. As Molineux matters slipped from dismal to disastrous (in sporting terms) in 1964/65 – unthinkably to most observers, Cullis was sacked in the autumn – Thomson dropped out of Ramsey's side after a mid-term friendly with Holland in Amsterdam, which at least enabled him to concentrate on Wolves' unavailing attempt to escape relegation to the second flight.

He remained a solid performer blessed with exceptional pace – fans reckoned he could back-pedal almost as fast as he could sprint forward – and Ramsey did not forget about him, continuing to honour him through the under-23s, for whom his 15 appearances constituted a record, and by including him in four Football League line-ups. Possibly, though, he was affected by the defensive strife around him at Molineux and no longer did he appear to be a credible challenger for Ray Wilson's England shirt.

Still in his early twenties, Thomson adapted ably to life in the second tier and was one of new boss Ronnie Allen's most influential players as Wolves gained promotion to the First Division in 1966/67 as runners-up to Coventry City. However, he did not remain long at the club after Allen was replaced by the strident Bill McGarry in November 1968, accepting a £40,000 transfer to second-tier Birmingham City in the following spring.

At St Andrew's – where he was reunited with his former mentor, Cullis – he put in a season of solid endeavour before losing his place. There followed a brief loan stint with Third Division Walsall in 1971/72 before the 28-year-old returned to the Second with Luton Town in June 1972.

He was ever-present as the Hatters earned a place among the elite by finishing second to Middlesbrough in 1973/74, but fell out of favour during a season of travail back in the First Division. By now his best days were behind him and his Football League sojourn ended with brief service for Port Vale in the third flight.

During the later stage of his career, Thomson spent summers in the United States, assisting Hartford Bicentennials (later re-branded Connecticut Bicentennials) and Memphis Rogues. Even then, he loved his football too dearly to bid it farewell, and he enjoyed spells with Worcester City, Stafford Rangers and several other non-League clubs while running a sports shop in Sedgley, in the heart of the Black Country.

Renowned for his extreme fitness into middle age and beyond, the amiable, self-deprecating Thomson continued to play for the Wolves All Stars, a side of former Molineux men which raises money for charity, in 2008 after his health had begun to fail, and he coached youngsters until shortly before his death.

Robert Anthony Thomson, footballer; born Smethwick, West Midlands, 5 December 1943; played for Wolverhampton Wanderers 1961-69, Birmingham City 1969-72, Walsall on loan 1971-72, Luton Town 1972-76, Port Vale 1976-77; capped eight times by England 1963-64; died Dudley, West Midlands, 19 August 2009.

Norman Curtis

They used to call him 'Cannonball', and with good reason. When Norman Curtis took penalties for Sheffield Wednesday during the 1950s, a team-mate would place the ball on the spot and the combative left-back would start to charge from deep inside his own half, steadily at first but building fearsome momentum as he neared the opposition's box. Then, without breaking stride, the energetic marksman would unleash a shot of pulverising velocity, and on 19 occasions out of 24 the strength of the goalnet underwent a stringent examination. On the other five, it is said, the woodwork took the blow and shivered accordingly.

Inevitably, such a spectacular routine earned Curtis a timeless niche in Hillsborough folklore, but it should not be allowed to obscure his all-round competence at his primary function, that of defending to a consistently lofty standard throughout what was, for the Owls, an unnervingly chaotic decade.

Indeed, three times they were relegated from the top flight, but on each occasion they bounced back immediately as Second Division champions, with the Yorkshireman integrally involved in his yo-yo club's every emotional extreme.

Curtis hailed from the small coal-mining town of Dinnington, where he started his working life as a butcher's boy and might have expected to make his living in the local pit but for his footballing ability. After the war, during which he served as a navigator with the Royal Navy's air fleet in the Far East, he became a part-timer with Gainsborough Trinity of the Midland League while working as an engineer in the town.

He shone as Trinity won their league title in 1949, so brightly that in January 1950 he was sold to Sheffield Wednesday of the old First Division, the equivalent of the modern Premier League, for £1,250. Come November he was plunged into regular top-flight action in a struggling side, and although he made a favourable impact there was nothing he could do to prevent demotion the following spring.

During 1951/52 Curtis vied for the number-three shirt with Vic Kenny and continued to perform reliably as the Owls lifted the Second Division crown, though understandably most of the newspaper headlines were hogged by the prodigiously prolific young centre-forward Derek Dooley, who struck 46 times in 30 outings.

Back among the elite in 1952/53, Curtis became ever more prominent, taking over the spot-kick duties in his own inimitable manner – he converted six that term, including two each in encounters with Portsmouth and Derby County – but also maturing as a full-back. Waspish in the tackle, quick to recover if beaten and versatile enough to switch to the right flank at need, he proved an abrasively tenacious marker who, as the decade progressed, coped admirably with the best right-wingers in the business, including the great Stanley Matthews.

In a season marred by an horrendous injury to Dooley which resulted in the amputation of his right leg, Wednesday managed narrowly to preserve their new-found status, as they did again in 1953/54, a campaign in which Curtis demonstrated his courage and adaptability in characteristically enterprising fashion.

When the Owls' goalkeeper Dave McIntosh suffered a broken arm ten minutes into a match at Preston, the sturdy left-back stepped up as emergency custodian – this was in the era before the use of substitutes was permitted – and although he conceded five of the goals in a 6-0 defeat, he managed to save two penalties, one by Tom Finney and the other by Jimmy Baxter.

That term, too, Curtis featured in Wednesday's run to the semi-final of the FA Cup, turning out at right-back as they lost 2-0 to Preston at Maine Road, Manchester.

Alas, such a whiff of success was illusory as the Hillsborough club went down in 1954/55, but long-term boss Eric Taylor led them back up as champions in 1955/56, only to take the plunge yet again two seasons later.

The rollercoaster ride continued in 1958/59, during which Curtis belied his near-veteran status by playing in every game as Wednesday, now guided by new manager Harry Catterick, claimed the Second Division crown for the third time in eight seasons.

Back among the elite, the Cannonball continued to fire, converting what was to prove his last spot-kick for the Owls in a home victory over Luton Town shortly after his 35th birthday, but then soon made way for a formidable young challenger, Don Megson.

When he left Sheffield in August 1960 to become player-boss of Fourth Division Doncaster Rovers, with a £1,000 transfer fee changing hands, Curtis had made 324 senior appearances and scored 21 goals for Wednesday and earned plaudits as one of their most loyal servants.

At Belle Vue he enjoyed one vigorous campaign, playing 40 times and shepherding his new charges to a safe mid-table position which was an improvement on the club's showing during the previous term. However, though he was a quiet fellow away from the action, he was a strong-minded individual and after a bitter disagreement with the chairman over youth policy, he resigned in the summer of 1961.

After leaving Doncaster he spent four years as player-manager of non-League Buxton and continued to demonstrate his all-round prowess by playing Minor Counties cricket as a wicketkeeper-batsman for Lincolnshire.

Also he ran a sports shop in Gainsborough and later he worked as a sales representative for Carlsberg.

William Norman Curtis, footballer and manager; born Dinnington, Yorkshire, 10 September 1924; played for Sheffield Wednesday 1950-60, Doncaster Rovers 1960-61; managed Doncaster Rovers 1960-61; died York, 7 September 2009.

Terry Bly

When football fans with elephantine memories gather together and the talk turns to prolific goal-scorers, the likes of Dixie Dean and Arthur Rowley, Jimmy Greaves and Alan Shearer, crop up as a matter of course. But if mention is not made of Terry Bly, there is something seriously lacking in the company's collective awareness of the most prolific sharp-shooters to grace the English professional game.

Peterborough United entered the Football League for the first time in 1960/61 and hit that somewhat staid institution like a blue-and-white tornado. Sweeping the opposition before them, they charged to the Fourth Division championship at the first attempt, and the tall, rangy East Anglian at the potent apex of their attack rattled in an astonishing 52 goals, a figure which still stands as the most in one League season by any post-war marksman. Indeed, only four men in the competition's history have surpassed his mark, with Dean's 60 for Everton in 1927/28 being the highest total.

Bly was not blessed with delicate skills, but he was strong, brave and overwhelmingly enthusiastic, and he had a god-given instinct for being in the ideal position at the optimum time to execute that most basic but most infinitely demanding of sporting tasks, that of depositing a bouncing, spinning, elusive leather sphere between the opponents' posts.

During that gilded campaign at London Road, he scored goals with his head, with both feet and with various other parts of his anatomy, his energy and determination proving far too taxing for most defenders in the basement tier to handle. Some critics called him cumbersome and inelegant, but the rampaging centre-forward, his team-mates and his manager Jimmy Hagan were not bothered. They were laughing all the way to the Third Division. Bly's achievement was all the more remarkable given that after joining Norwich City straight from school, soon he was rejected by them as not good enough. However, he impressed at a lower level with Bury Town, and was welcomed back into the Canaries' fold in 1956.

His impetus was interrupted again by a knee operation, but then he sprang to national notice in January 1959 by scoring twice as Third Division Norwich dumped Manchester United out of the FA Cup, beating Matt Busby's team 3-0 on a hard, snow-dusted surface at Carrow Road.

True, United had been devastated by the Munich air disaster which had claimed the lives of eight players only 11 months earlier, but they had just completed a sequence of eight successive top-flight victories and, with Bobby Charlton enjoying what was to prove the most bountiful scoring term of his career, still presented formidable opposition.

The result was greeted by one newspaper with the headline 'Bly, Bly Babes', which was tolerably witty if possibly a trifle tasteless in view of United's recent bereavements.

Meanwhile for the Canaries and their callow spearhead, the FA Cup adventure had barely begun. In the next round Bly struck twice more as Cardiff City were dispatched, then he contributed the only goal of a fifth-round replay with mighty Tottenham Hotspur, and added two more as Sheffield United were overcome in the last eight.

All seven of his goals had been plundered at Carrow Road, and when asked to continue his spree against Luton Town in the semi-final at Villa Park he was unable to oblige, and Archie Macaulay's plucky side bowed out 0-1.

Thereafter Bly's progress as a Canary was steady rather than meteoric and he managed only seven strikes in 25 games as Norwich earned promotion in 1959/60, then that summer the 24-year-old was sold to League newcomers Peterborough for £5,000.

Soon he embarked on the season of his life, commencing with a goal in his first game for the Posh, at home to Wrexham, and finishing with his seventh hat-trick of the campaign as Barrow were beaten on the final day, when the title was clinched.

An immensely modest fellow, he attempted to deflect much of the credit for his individual feat in the direction of his team-mates, particularly wingers Billy Hails and Peter McNamee, who had kept him so well supplied with the crosses from which he fed so voraciously.

Inevitably Bly was never so prolific again, though in 1961/62 he did excel at the higher level, his 29 League hits helping Peterborough to a creditable fifth-place finish in the Third Division table, which attracted the attention of a bold young manager named Jimmy Hill, who took him to Coventry in a £12,000 deal in June 1962.

Hill was in the process of transforming City into an upwardly-mobile and family-friendly club, launching what was dubbed the 'Sky Blue Revolution' in an atmosphere of showbiz razzmatazz. He believed Bly could provide the goals to lift them out of the third tier, but after the striker had weighed in with a commendable 25 in 32 appearances, his new boss lost faith in him and replaced him in April 1963 with his former Peterborough colleague, George Hudson.

Though Hudson was an instant success, netting a hat-trick on debut, many Coventry fans were livid at what they saw as the unfair demise of their hero, who was sold to Notts

County for £13,000 in the following summer. In fact, Hudson was a more cultured all-round operator than Bly and the shrewd Hill had gauged that the new man was a better long-term bet for a club on the rise.

As Bly never truly sparked at Meadow Lane, where he was deployed alongside future England centre-forward Jeff Astle, and was allowed to move on to Grantham Town as player-manager in 1964, Hill could be said to be vindicated, though some Highfield Road regulars never forgave him for the transaction.

It says much for Bly that dropping down from the Football League at the age of 29 did nothing to lessen his overwhelming passion for the game, and over the next decade and a half he became a folk idol at the Lincolnshire club.

Before laying aside his boots in 1970, he scored 125 goals in 199 outings for Grantham, and went on to manage the Gingerbreads in 719 games, then stepped aside in 1978 to concentrate on running a sports shop in the town. During his reign he led his men to four Midlands League crowns, two Midlands League Cup triumphs, a victory in the Lincolnshire County Cup and to FA Cup wins over Rochdale and Stockport County of the Football League. Terry Bly will be remembered most widely for his never-likely-to-be-emulated tally in his Peterborough prime, but this amiable, unassuming but fiercely dedicated football man will never be forgotten at humble Grantham, either.

Terence Geoffrey Bly, footballer; born Fincham, Norfolk, 22 October 1935; played for Norwich City 1956-60, Peterborough United 1960-62, Coventry City 1962-63, Notts County 1963-64; died Normanton, near Grantham, Lincolnshire, 24 September 2009.

Alex McCrae

Fabrizio Ravanelli, Alen Boksic and Ayegbeni Yakubu are just three of the vaunted international marksmen who have attempted to emulate him in the modern era, but Alex McCrae, who touched his footballing pomp midway through the 20th century, remains the last man to score 20 League goals for Middlesbrough in a top-flight season.

In fact, the slim, elegant Scot hit the target 21 times in 1950/51, when the Teessiders finished sixth in the old First Division table and his lethal link with the sumptuously talented England inside-forward Wilf Mannion constituted one of the most inventive attacking combinations in the land.

The unassuming McCrae was a delightfully subtle operator, physically resilient enough to cope with opponents of a brutish disposition when the need arose, but preferring to engage in the deft skills which he had been perfecting since boyhood.

Versatile enough to play in any forward position but favouring the inside-left slot alongside a dedicated spearhead, he brought to his work an appealing fusion of flair and enthusiasm, specialising in crowd-pleasing dribbles and quick-fire interchanges of short passes of the type purveyed so beguilingly by the maestro Mannion.

McCrae was a predatory finisher, too, especially with his left foot, which proved particularly potent during that exceptionally prolific campaign at Ayresome Park. He had plundered three hat-tricks before Christmas, and when he netted in a 3-3 draw at home to Burnley just before the turn of the year he had registered 20 times in 24 outings.

Alas, that was also the day Middlesbrough surrendered their leadership in the title race and, with their sharpshooter-in-chief sidelined by injury for most of February and March, they never regained either their winning momentum or that coveted top spot.

Born in the central Scottish village of Stoneyburn, McCrae played his early football for local teams Parkhead Thistle, Murrayfield Rangers and Haddington Juniors and began making his living as a coalminer, which he continued to do after signing for Heart of Midlothian in the summer of 1941. Exempt from military service because of his job, he played for the Edinburgh club throughout the remainder of the war, and was part of the side which triumphed 3-2 over the British Army of the Rhine in Germany in 1946.

By then in his mid-twenties, McCrae shone for Hearts when peacetime competition resumed, attracting the attention of a clutch of top-tier English clubs, eventually moving to Charlton Athletic in May 1947 in exchange for £7,500 and the proceeds of a friendly game between his old and new employers.

Many of the Tynecastle faithful were outraged by the sale of such a favourite, but manager Davie McLean bade them be calm, predicting that a lad just starting out in the game would prove to be an ideal replacement. He wasn't wrong; the boy in question was Jimmy Wardhaugh, who by the end of the 1950s had become the most prolific scorer in Hearts' history, a record he would hold for some 40 years.

McCrae, meanwhile, struggled to settle south of the border, switching to Middlesbrough for £10,000 in November 1948 but still not replicating the impressive level of his Scottish League performances during his early weeks beside the Tees. He was dropped and must have feared the worst, but then Mannion, who had been missing from the team due to a bitter wages dispute, was restored to action. Soon the newcomer was recalled and gradually the pair struck up a rewarding rapport.

The full fruits were not apparent, however, until 1949/50, when McCrae began to find the net on a regular basis, his 14 strikes helping a hitherto lacklustre side to a comfortable mid-table position in the First Division.

Come 1950/51, during which he celebrated his 31st birthday and was therefore approaching the veteran stage, he struck the form of his life, and Middlesbrough supporters were mortified when he fell prey to fitness problems.

After that McCrae was never quite the same force again, though by the time a £4,000 deal took him to Falkirk in March 1953, he had scored 49 goals in 130 competitive games for 'Boro, a more than respectable tally.

At Brockville, too, he performed with a zest that belied his advancing years, his goals proving a key factor in the Bairns clinging on to their top-division status. There was one crushing disappointment, however, when injury kept him out of the side which beat Kilmarnock, after a replay, to lift the Scottish Cup in 1957. Thus he missed what would have been his first major honour at the age of 37.

That autumn, still bursting with characteristic commitment, he took over as player-coach of Ballymena United, guiding them to Irish Cup glory in his first season, and to defeat in the final of the competition a year later. During just over two terms in Ulster he made one appearance for the Irish League, but such was his burgeoning success as a coach that soon he was in demand once more in his homeland.

Duly he accepted the reins of Stirling Albion in January 1960, then only two months later succumbed to the lure of his former club, Falkirk. Though they were a relatively small operation with severely limited resources, McCrae preserved their place among the elite for the next half-decade, which was no small achievement.

In 1966 he left the full-time professional game, but maintained his contact as a scout for Middlesbrough in Scotland, also turning his gaze to Northern Ireland. It was there that he made his most valuable discovery in the person of Jim Platt, a rookie goalkeeper with Ballymena United who went on to make more than 500 appearances for the Teessiders.

In addition McCrae, who was possibly the oldest surviving former Hearts footballer, worked for British Leyland at Bathgate, near Livingston, until his retirement in 1985.

Alexander McCrae, footballer; born Stoneyburn, West Lothian, 2 January 1920; played for Heart of Midlothian 1941-47, Charlton Athletic 1947-48, Middlesbrough 1948-53, Falkirk 1953-57, Ballymena United 1957-60; managed Ballymena United 1957-60, Stirling Albion 1960, Falkirk 1960-65; died Livingston, West Lothian, 8 October 2009.

Ray Charnley

There have been Blackpool footballers who have played more games for the club than Ray Charnley; and there have been men who have contributed more League goals to the Bloomfield Road cause than the tall, rangy Lancastrian centre-forward. But on both counts, from faithful fans of the Seasiders whose memories stretch back half a century and beyond, there would have to come the heartfelt and grateful rider: not many.

Charnley was Blackpool's leading marksman in senior competition for nine consecutive seasons between 1958/59 and 1966/67. Every one of those campaigns was in the top flight of the English game and in several of them it was his goals which effectively preserved their place among the elite.

His Blackpool tally is exceeded only by Jimmy Hampson's between the wars, when often the club was in the second tier where goals were easier to plunder, and, very narrowly, by Stan Mortensen's in the decade after the second global conflict, when he was supported by a collection of stellar talents, notably the great Stanley Matthews. True, Charnley benefited from the wing maestro's service for four terms, but by then Matthews, though still potent, was well into his forties and passing his incomparable peak.

Overall then, Charnley was a gem, albeit of the rough-hewn variety. Though his style was more practical than pretty, he was considerably less indelicate on the ball than many of his front-running peers from that era. He was adept at controlling long dispatches from his own defenders while fending off the close attentions of aggressive opponents, he was a titan in the air and he was a powerful finisher who occasionally surprised even his most ardent admirers with a shot or a pass of unexpected subtlety.

Yet for all the sterling attributes revealed in ample measure in schoolboy and youth football, in which he sampled inside-forward and wing-half roles before settling as an attacking spearhead, there was a time in his teens when Charnley's future in the professional game was in serious doubt. When the likes of Middlesbrough, Huddersfield Town and even Blackpool expressed interest in his talent, he was persuaded by his father to continue with his apprenticeship as a painter and decorator.

Meanwhile he played his football for Preston North End's 'B' team until it disbanded, Bolton-le-Sands and finally Morecambe, for whom he struck 43 goals in 53 matches, which persuaded the Seasiders to make a new approach.

By this time he was 22 and with a trade behind him, so when Blackpool boss Joe Smith proffered a £775 cheque to Morecambe in May 1957, Charnley was ready to take the plunge. At this point Blackpool were a major footballing force, having finished second and fourth in the old First Division in the two previous seasons, and the newcomer, although plainly raw, was deemed promising enough to make his debut in his first autumn at Bloomfield Road.

Initially his progress was tentative, and even after netting twice in a 7-0 home demolition of Sunderland which remains Blackpool's highest winning margin – he looked a decent bet for a hat-trick until forced to leave the action with a severely gashed head – he was in and out of the team. But after returning in a mid-term reshuffle which saw the previous number-nine, Jackie Mudie, switch to inside-right, Charnley was back to stay.

Boosted by the backing of new boss Ron Suart, he thrived in 1958/59, missing a handful of games because of a broken collarbone but striking 20 times in the League and adding six more on the way to the League Cup quarter-finals, in which the Seasiders were beaten by Luton Town after a replay.

Gradually Blackpool were slipping from their eminent perch of the previous decade – a process accelerated by the abolition of the maximum wage, which caused relatively small-town clubs to suffer at the hands of wealthier big-city rivals – and in 1960/61 they relied even more heavily than usual on Charnley's goals, a late winner from a pinpointed Matthews cross against fellow relegation battlers Newcastle United proving crucially important.

He was rewarded by a place on the FA's summer tour of the Far East before finding the form of his life in 1961/62, accumulating 36 hits in 50 games – a quartet in the 7-2 Bloomfield Road annihilation of Wolverhampton Wanderers was particularly memorable – and Suart was quietly outraged when he continued to be overlooked by his country.

Charnley's international call-up finally arrived in October 1962 when he faced France at Hillsborough in the European Nations Cup, but really England manager Walter Winterbottom might have known better than to name a forward line containing four debutants – the others were Mike Hellawell, Chris Crowe and Alan Hinton – and it was hardly surprising that they failed to gel. A woefully poor game finished 1-1, and although Charnley did earn the penalty by which Ron Flowers equalised, he had little chance to shine and was never picked again.

In the famous tangerine shirt of Blackpool, however, the goals continued to flow. He was particularly menacing when operating in tandem with the inspirational young firebrand Alan Ball in mid-decade, after which there was an encouraging rapport with Alan Suddick, a gifted acquisition from Newcastle.

Charnley was versatile, too, able to deputise effectively in central defence when the need arose, and his genial, easy-going nature increased his popularity with the public. Indeed, once when he was omitted from the team – he wasn't dropped too often, but it did happen occasionally – when Suart opted to experiment with centre-half Roy Gratrix as leader of the attack, Charnley turned up on the Bloomfield Road Kop, wearing a flat cap and exchanging banter with the fans.

By 1966/67 he was approaching the veteran stage, but still managed 14 League goals for a side which had declined so comprehensively – despite the presence of evergreen full-back Jimmy Armfield, and the young Emlyn Hughes – that it finished well adrift at the foot of the table.

By now the old Blackpool goal hero Mortensen was occupying the managerial seat, and it was ironic that it should be during his watch that Charnley, his long-term successor, should bow out of Bloomfield Road in December 1967, a fee of £12,500 taking the 32-year-old to Preston, who were also languishing in the Second Division.

Most Blackpool regulars felt that the man who had netted 222 times in his 407 appearances for their club should not have been sold, especially after he scored against his former employers, albeit in a 4-1 defeat for North End, only nine days after his move.

However, he did not tarry long at Deepdale, joining Fourth Division Wrexham in July 1968, then enlisting with Bradford Park Avenue and ending his League days when the hard-up Yorkshire club was not re-elected in 1970.

There followed a brief stint back at Morecambe before Ray Charnley gave up the game to concentrate on his painting and decorating business back in Blackpool, a town he had come to love – and where the feeling was mutual.

Raymond Ogden Charnley, footballer; born Lancaster, 29 May 1935; played for Blackpool 1957-67, Preston North End 1967-68, Wrexham 1968-69, Bradford Park Avenue 1969; capped once by England 1962; died Blackpool, Lancashire, 15 October 2009.

Ray Lambert

Ray Lambert played his football for Liverpool in times both gloriously uplifting and downright wretched for the Anfield Reds during the middle years of the 20th century.

His decade in the limelight began triumphantly, with an integral part in lifting the first post-war League title, and ended in dire frustration, with the club languishing in the second flight of the domestic game.

Through it all, under golden skies and stormclouds alike, the Welsh international full-back was utterly steadfast, the trustiest of defensive bulwarks, a team man with every fibre of his being.

Decidedly more practical than elegant in style, Lambert was muscular, courageous and composed, his prematurely balding head standing out like a beacon of solidity in the Reds' rearguard. He was endowed with a canny positional sense, too, and was versatile enough to patrol either defensive flank with equal effectiveness.

Lambert qualified for an early taste of sporting renown in 1936 when, at the age of 13 years and 189 days, he was reported to be the youngest player ever to join a Football League club, having impressed as a dominant centre-half for Flintshire and Wales Schoolboys.

He signed a professional contract on his 17th birthday in July 1939, but then lost the first flush of his prime to the Second World War, during which he played for the Army against Portugal, guested for Reading and New Brighton and made four appearances for Wales in unofficial competition.

Following conversion to full-back, Lambert made his senior entrance in an FA Cup encounter with Chester at Sealand Road in January 1946, his fellow debutants including Billy Liddell, who developed into one of the finest players in Liverpool's history, and Bob Paisley, who remains by far their most successful manager in terms of honours garnered.

That November he earned the first of five full caps, featuring at right-back in the Welsh team that defeated Scotland 3-1 at Wrexham – he finished on the losing side in his other four outings for his country – then rounded off a terrific season by contributing with characteristic consistency as Liverpool won the 1946/47 League championship, shading a taut race with Manchester United and Wolves by a single point.

But for the enduring excellence of Arsenal's Walley Barnes and Alf Sherwood of Cardiff City, it seems likely that Lambert would have enjoyed a lengthy international career, but as it was he never played again for Wales after May 1949, when he remained at the peak of his powers.

In 1950 he was ever-present as manager George Kay's Reds reached the club's first Wembley FA Cup final, only to lose 2-0 to Arsenal. His direct adversary was Denis

Compton, the majestic England batsman who also showed a clean pair of heels to plenty of full-backs in his role of the Gunners' left winger. However, on a damp afternoon beneath the old stadium's twin towers, with the lush, slippery grass making it awkward for defenders to turn, Lambert jockeyed his tantalising opponent valiantly, emerging with honours even from their personal duel.

Thereafter he remained a regular in a team which had passed its peak and, under new boss Don Welsh, declined gradually towards the ignominy of relegation in 1953/54.

Lambert, whose only two goals for Liverpool both came from the penalty spot, helped to acclimatise to life in the second flight – Liverpool finished the 1954/55 campaign in a disappointing 11th place – but having entered his 34th year during the following summer, soon he was replaced by the younger John Molyneux in the late autumn.

A faithful one-club man, Lambert deserved better than to see out his Football League days in such a comparatively humdrum side, but the fact was that a career which had commenced with the dual highs of international recognition and the League crown had ended in poignant anti-climax, albeit through no fault of his own.

When Bill Shankly, who arrived to take on the messianic role of Liverpool's saviour in 1959, looked back over the Anfielders' recent history, he might have wished that the sturdy Welshman had been young enough to take a part in the Anfield revolution which was about to begin.

Lambert, whose son Wayne was once on the books of Manchester City, went on to become a newsagent at Queensferry, in his native Flintshire.

Raymond Lambert, footballer; born Bagillt, Flintshire, 18 July 1922; played for Liverpool 1939-56; capped five times by Wales 1946-49; died Flintshire, 22 October 2009.

Keith Kettleborough

With his balding head, pallid features and scuttling gait, Keith Kettleborough didn't cut a glamorous figure on the football pitch, even during his prime with Sheffield United in the first half of the 1960s.

No matter: the slim Yorkshireman was one of the game's true craftsmen, a subtly constructive midfield general who brought to his work an appealing cocktail of artistry and industry which, during mid-decade as plans were being laid to capture the World Cup, prompted England manager Alf Ramsey to call him into his training squad.

Kettleborough never made the final cut, despite shining brightly for Newcastle United and contributing significantly to their escape from relegation in the spring before his country's supreme triumph in 1966, but he had done enough to prove that if he wasn't quite in the international bracket, he didn't lag far behind.

For all that achievement, encompassing more than 400 games for five League clubs, he embraced cricket more enthusiastically in his early teens, playing at schoolboy level for both Yorkshire and the North of England.

However, after succeeding at the winter game during his National Service in the RAF, Kettleborough found himself on the radar of numerous talent scouts. A trial with Grimsby Town proved inconclusive, but in December 1955 he was signed by his home-town club, Rotherham United, and graduated rapidly to the first team.

By 1957/58 he had earned a regular berth with the Merry Millers, who were struggling in the lower reaches of the old Second Division (now the Championship), and soon it became clear that he was an uncut gem. Operating as a deep-lying link-man between defence and attack, Kettleborough proved to be a passing master who could stroke the ball accurately over long distances and short, always probing for openings.

He was endowed with remarkable stamina, too, revelling in his box-to-box remit, and he was a feisty tackler, leaving his imprint on any uninformed adversaries who deemed, perhaps from his somewhat studious appearance, that he was easy prey.

Come 1959/60, Rotherham were a much-improved side in the top half of the table and Kettleborough was a major influence, notably in that term's FA Cup third round second replay against Arsenal, in which he scored a beautiful goal in the Millers' 2-0 victory over the Gunners at neutral Hillsborough in front of 56,000 fans.

With his profile duly heightened, a transfer to Sheffield United was arranged in the following December, but he did not bow out quietly. In his last match at Millmoor before his £15,000 move to Bramall Lane, he was booed by his own crowd after rounding the opposing goalkeeper but then missing an open goal. His response was to run to the main stand where, fleetingly but unmistakably, he dropped his shorts.

Despite being hampered by a knee injury which limited his appearances, Kettleborough proved an important factor in the Blades' rise to the top flight, as runners-up to Ramsey's Ipswich Town, at the end of his first half-season at his new club. As a bonus he was prominent as they reached the semi-finals of the FA Cup, subsiding only after three fiercely contested encounters with First Division Leicester City.

More impressively still, Kettleborough touched fresh peaks as United finished fifth at the end of their first campaign in the elite tier, not finding the net frequently himself, but proving an astute provider of scoring opportunities for predatory centre-forward Derek Pace and fellow attacker Billy Russell. However, Kettleborough was a modest character, and always insisted on due credit being paid to a doughty rearguard in which 'keeper Alan Hodgkinson, central stopper Joe Shaw and full-back Graham Shaw (no relation) were outstanding.

Thereafter United consolidated their place in the premier grade without rising again to such heights and, while attracting the eye of the England boss, Kettleborough was invaluable in nurturing such promising rookie forwards as Mick Jones, later to earn fame with Don Revie's Leeds United, and Alan Woodward, who would go on to play more than 600 times for the Sheffield club.

Strong-minded and never afraid to stand his corner, Kettleborough did not always see eye to eye with the Blades' equally steely boss, the Glaswegian John Harris, and in January 1966 he was sold to Newcastle United for £22,500.

At that point the Magpies looked to be likely candidates for demotion to the Second Division, but the 30-year-old's creativity, energy and experience did much to transform Joe Harvey's side, which escaped the drop with something to spare.

Kettleborough's sojourn at St James' Park was unexpectedly brief, as in December 1966 he placed his foot on the management ladder by accepting a player-boss role with Doncaster Rovers, newly promoted to the Third Division, with a fee of £12,000 changing hands.

It was to prove a testing time as the Belle Vue club were already struggling and when they were relegated at season's end, Kettleborough was dismissed as manager but remained as a player.

Having already incited opprobrium for dropping local hero Alick Jeffrey, the ex-boss became something of an aunt sally to disappointed fans and it was hardly a shock when he moved on to Division Four Chesterfield, who paid £6,000 for his services in November 1967. While at Saltergate he became one of the few men to play against a club he had once managed, no doubt irritating his former critics at Doncaster by performing with undiminished skill.

In August 1969, aged 34, he became player-manager of non-League Matlock Town, after which he left the game.

Kettleborough's cricketing prowess, which enabled him to play professionally for both Rotherham Town and Rawmarsh in the high-quality Yorkshire Leagues, subsequently continued to find expression with the Whiston Parish Church club, for whom he starred as a high-scoring batsman.

Away from sport, for many years he ran a milk business in south Yorkshire, and later he was clerk of works for a private preparatory school in Sheffield, his duties including the coaching of both football and cricket. Not surprisingly given his undying enthusiasm, Kettleborough excelled in the work, attracting plaudits from parents who credited him with imbuing their offspring with his own enduring affection for both sports.

Keith Frank Kettleborough, footballer; born Rotherham, Yorkshire, 29 June 1935; played for Rotherham United 1955-60, Sheffield United 1960-65, Newcastle United 1965-66, Doncaster Rovers 1966-67, Chesterfield 1967-69; managed Doncaster Rovers 1966-67; died Rotherham, 2 November 2009.

Archie Baird

Any contemplation of the life of Archie Baird must attach colossal significance to the game of football, as Aberdeen fans of the 1940s and early 1950s will testify with unstinting enthusiasm and affection. But all that achievement and derring-do in the Pittodrie cause, exhilarating and ground-breaking though unquestionably it was, doesn't begin to tell the full story of a remarkable individual whose intrepid, intensely harrowing experiences as a prisoner of war place mere sporting issues in their proper context.

Baird, a tall, stylish, creative inside-forward, was a key figure as the Dons lifted the first major trophies in their history during the seasons immediately following the cessation of global hostilities, by which time he was no longer looking at the world through the eyes of the callow, excitingly promising rookie who had been the target of eminent clubs on both sides of the Scottish border in 1938.

At that point the likes of Blackpool, Motherwell, Partick Thistle and St Mirren were vying for his signature, but the 19-year-old's mother was so impressed by the honest approach of Aberdeen manager David Halliday that the boy heeded her advice to head north-east from his Lanarkshire home to enlist with the Dons.

Baird, who had starred for Strathclyde Juniors alongside future Rangers luminary Willie Waddell, was an intelligent fellow who nursed ambitions to be an architect, but his football skills had proved impossible to ignore and now he planned to train in the mornings and study for his future career in the afternoons.

However, he made a slow start at Pittodrie, struggling for an impact in this new competitive environment, and he was still featuring for the reserves when the conflict broke out in 1939.

Now, all too soon, the youngster who had viewed joining the Dons as a great adventure was to find himself caught up in an expedition of an altogether more daunting nature, one on which failure surely must have carried fatal consequences.

While serving in the medical corps for the ill-fated British Expeditionary Force, he missed the evacuation at Dunkirk but managed to board the last ship out of St Nazaire when France fell in the summer of 1940.

Awaiting his return to the war, Baird was stationed at Headingley, Yorkshire's cricket headquarters, and while he was there he guested for Leeds United, facing top performers of the day such as the Everton trio Tommy Lawton, Joe Mercer and Cliff Britton.

The respite was brief, though, and he was dispatched to North Africa, where he was part of the force which confronted Rommel in the Western Desert. When Tobruk was taken in the summer of 1942, his field ambulance was surrounded by German tanks and he was captured, then handed over to the Italians, who placed him in a prisoner-of-war camp near Rimini on the Adriatic coast.

Many of his fellow detainees died in what he described later as 'a filthy hell-hole' but Baird, who beguiled some of his time by day-dreaming about his earlier life as a footballer, remained resilient and in 1943, after 18 months of incarceration, he and a comrade, Harold Smith, managed to escape.

Knowing that the Allies had landed in Italy and aiming to join them, the pair headed south into the lower reaches of the Apennines. They lived off the land, helped on their way by sympathetic Italian farmers, and when severe winter weather set in Baird was sheltered for some months by a compassionate family, the Pilottis, who found other safe billets for Smith and another fugitive who had joined the pair on their trek towards freedom.

With his sharp and lively mind, Baird picked up Italian quickly, enabling him to pose convincingly as the son of his courageous benefactors, to whom he became devoted and with whom he embarked on a lifelong friendship. Speaking many years later, he said: 'They were real heroes. They looked after me despite knowing the Germans would have shot them if they had found out.'

Eventually, as Hitler's forces pulled out of Italy, Baird rejoined the Allied ranks and returned to Britain, guesting as a footballer for Aldershot and non-League Falmouth before returning to Aberdeen following his demob in September 1945.

Vastly matured by his recent experiences, he was now a far more confident character than the tentative youth he had been during his initial Pittodrie sojourn, and he became established rapidly in the Dons' first team.

Operating as an incisive prompter alongside his close pal and fellow inside-forward George Hamilton and diminutive spearhead Stan Williams, Baird proved hugely influential as Aberdeen won the Southern League Cup, an emergency wartime competition and the precursor to the soon-to-be-launched Scottish League Cup. They beat Rangers 3-2 in a see-sawing final in front of 135,000 fans at Hampden Park in May 1946 to claim the first big prize since the club's formation in 1903.

There was reward on a wider front, too, with an appearance for Scotland in the Victory international against Belgium that January, the game finishing 2-2. Because it was classed as an unofficial wartime encounter, no cap was awarded, and that proved to be his sole outing for his country. He was immensely unfortunate because he had excelled against the Belgians, keeping his feet deftly in thick snow on a foggy Hampden afternoon, and had been selected for the next fixture, against England, only to be forced out through injury.

A season later Baird was prominent again as the Dons beat highly-fancied Hibernian 2-1 to win the Scottish Cup, thus securing their first senior trophy and emphasising the progress they had made in finishing third in that term's title race behind Rangers and Hibs.

They reached the inaugural League Cup final, too, losing 4-0 to Rangers, and faced the future on a tide of optimism.

Baird, with his clever passing, neat ball skills and happy knack of contributing important goals, was seen as a major plank of Halliday's entertaining side, but he was hampered cruelly by knee problems which demanded three operations, and also he suffered a fractured leg.

His best extended run was in 1950/51, when he netted ten times in 40 league and cup appearances, but after barely figuring in 1952/53, the 34-year-old – whose overall record of 37 goals in 144 games for Aberdeen would have been far more extensive had he been blessed with fitness on a consistent basis – accepted a transfer to second-tier St Johnstone.

At McDiarmid Park Baird enjoyed a fruitful Indian summer, moving back to wing-half and missing only a handful of matches as the Saints twice finished in upper mid-table, then narrowly missed promotion to the top flight in 1955/56, his last campaign.

After leaving the game, Baird – who until his death was believed to be Aberdeen's oldest surviving player – embarked on a fulfilling and packed life as a sports writer for the *Scottish Sunday Express* and a PE teacher who rose to become assistant head of Hilton Academy in Aberdeen by the time he retired in 1979.

Somehow he even chiselled out the necessary time from his crowded schedule to qualify as a glider pilot.

Baird believed passionately in education, achieving degrees in English and Italian through the University of London by correspondence course in the 1960s, then teaching his second language at evening class. A warm, gregarious and charming man who had come to love all things Italian, he moved to Italy for a year from 1980, along with his wife Nancy, to teach English there.

His attachment to journalism was equally deep – many of his family members were practitioners, including brother-in-law Magnus Magnusson and Magnusson's daughter Sally – and he became a popular columnist on the Aberdeen-based monthly magazine *Leopard*.

Archie Baird was an author, too, penning a moving autobiography, *Family Of Four*, which was published in 1989. It was a book in which his love of football was abundantly evident, but which illustrated eloquently his appreciation of its rightful place when he came to consider the more profound values of life.

Archibald MacKechnie Baird, footballer, journalist and teacher; born Rutherglen, Lanarkshire, 8 May 1919; played for Aberdeen 1938-53, St Johnstone 1953-56; died Cove, Aberdeen, 3 November 2009.

Neil Dougall

Scottish international Neil Dougall was a jack of most footballing trades and a master of several as he helped Birmingham City and Plymouth Argyle to a trio of divisional titles in the decade and a half after the Second World War.

During a professional career spanning 19 seasons, he appeared in every outfield position except the left wing, though he is remembered most vividly in the Midlands as an elegant, sparkily creative inside-forward, and on the South West coast in a deeper-lying role as a solid, often inspirationally canny wing-half.

Dougall's instinctive mastery of virtually all the game's individual skills was acclaimed by team-mates at both clubs, and his remarkable versatility was viewed as an invaluable insurance policy by a succession of managers in an era before substitutes could be employed to plug gaps caused by injuries.

Football was in the Dougall genes. His uncle, James, had played for Preston North End and Scotland, and his father, Billy, represented Falkirk and Burnley before joining the training staff at Turf Moor, where he launched the Clarets' youth development scheme.

That connection brought Neil to the club as a schoolboy in 1935 and he made promising progress through the junior ranks, turning professional in 1940. However, the outbreak of war produced a dramatic change in priorities and he joined the RAF.

Still, there was time for him to guest with Oldham Athletic, Watford, Coventry City and Walsall, then when hostilities ceased in 1945 Dougall was transferred to Birmingham City for £2,750.

In his first season he excelled at inside-right, his combination of pace, passing skills and intelligence helping the Blues to win the Football League South, an unofficial wartime competition. In addition, he made his senior debut in the FA Cup, earning the approbation of St Andrew's regulars by chipping in with three goals as City reached the last four, where they bowed out only after a replay to Derby County, the eventual winners.

The newcomer proved to be the final, melding constituent in a dashing forward line assembled by the shrewd manager Harry Storer and comprising right-winger Ambrose Mulvaney, Dougall himself at inside-right, centre-forward Charlie Jones, Harold Bodle at inside-left and George Edwards on the left flank.

So resplendent was the Scottish play-maker's form in the autumn of 1946 that he was called up for his only full cap in his country's first official post-war fixture, which ended in a 3-1 defeat by Wales in Wrexham.

With Dougall continuing to torment opponents, Birmingham finished that term a creditable third in the Second Division table, a prelude to their promotion as champions a year later, a triumph to which he contributed only five goals but in which he was vastly influential.

In 1948/49 he never seemed out of place among the elite, but in the spring, with the team looking increasingly weary and new boss Bob Brocklebank wanting to rebuild, he was sold to Second Division strugglers Plymouth Argyle for £13,000.

At 27 Dougall was still in his prime, but he was slow to re-settle in the lower flight and it was not until his conversion to right-half midway through 1949/50 that he began to attain the consistent excellence that would sustain him throughout the new decade.

Sadly for the Pilgrims, Dougall's personal renaissance was not enough to keep them from slipping into the Third Division South at season's end, but their new-found bulwark did prove immensely instrumental in their bouncing back as champions in 1951/52.

During the following campaign the Scot was at his imperious best, missing only one game as the men from Home Park equalled the highest position in their Football League history, climbing to fourth place in the Second Division.

Such elevation didn't last, however, and Argyle slumped in the mid-1950s, culminating with relegation in 1955/56. Despite suffering a succession of injuries, Dougall remained undaunted, and it was fitting that he provided sterling input as the Pilgrims became the first winners of the newly consolidated Third Division, taking in the former North and South sections, in 1958/59.

Operating at left-back, he managed the first half of that triumphant effort before stepping aside, not long after entering his 38th year, to join the coaching staff. But turbulent times lay ahead at Home Park. In March 1960 manager Jack Rowley departed after a boardroom dispute. By then the side was labouring dangerously near the foot of the second tier and Dougall was called in alongside former Argyle team-mate George Taylor to steer them narrowly clear of demotion that spring.

Such joint management responsibility rarely works smoothly, however, and soon, after the club failed in an attempt to recruit former West Bromwich Albion boss Vic Buckingham, Dougall took sole control, espousing an attractive brand of free-flowing football in which front-men Wilf Carter and George Kirby and constructive wing-half Johnny Williams were prominent.

But after a top-half finish in 1960/61, results declined dismally in the following autumn, and after Argyle conceded five goals on three consecutive Saturdays, Dougall was replaced by one of his staff, Ellis Stuttard.

There was a feeling that the affable Scot was simply 'too nice' for the abrasive business of football management and he returned to a backroom role with the club until 1968.

After leaving the game he ran a fitness club in Plymouth until his retirement in 1986.

Dougall, who scored 44 goals in nearly 400 senior appearances for his two clubs, died in his adopted home-town following a lengthy illness.

Cornelius Dougall, footballer; born Falkirk, Stirlingshire, 7 November 1921; played for Birmingham City 1945-49, Plymouth Argyle 1949-59; capped once by Scotland 1946; managed Plymouth Argyle 1960-61; died Plymouth, Devon, 1 December 2009.

Alan A'Court

It was difficult to miss Alan A'Court on a football field. The dashing, blond left-winger, who featured for England in the 1958 World Cup finals and shone for Liverpool as they returned to the top flight of the domestic game in 1962, was an effervescent individual, bubbling with verve and exuding an engagingly obvious enjoyment of his work.

Indeed, he performed with such unstinting commitment and concentration that it was not unknown for him to sprint to the Anfield byline at maximum velocity, dispatch a cross at full stretch and then, oblivious to the close proximity of the low boundary wall to the touchline, plunge headlong into the Kop. The fans, well accustomed to the flying flankman's neck-or-nothing style, would hold out their arms, palms-upwards, to break his fall.

The only disappointing aspect of the popular A'Court's 12-year Liverpool tenure, during which he made nearly 400 senior appearances and scored more than 60 goals, was that his pomp coincided with the lowest point in the Reds' modern history, during which they slid ignominiously from the elite division and then spent eight seasons battling to get back.

A'Court was a jovial, mischievous character, a practical joker who worked wonders for dressing room morale, but there was steel in his make-up, too, as evidenced when he made waves in his rugby-loving family by choosing soccer as his sport in his early teens.

However, as the extent of the young Merseysider's talent began to emerge with local sides Prescot Celtic and Prescot Cables, it became apparent that he had opted wisely, especially when Bolton Wanderers and Everton began to show a lively interest.

It was Liverpool, though, who convinced him to forsake his job as a trainee supervisor with the Littlewoods mail order company in the summer of 1952, and the following February, aged 18, he made his senior debut, wearing a number-nine shirt in a First Division encounter at Middlesbrough.

For the remainder of that season, and through the next, A'Court made periodic appearances on the Liverpool left wing, playing alongside survivors of the 1946/47 championship side, such men as Bob Paisley, Laurie Hughes and the great Billy Liddell.

By then, however, the team was distressingly threadbare and was relegated in 1954, a circumstance rendered all the more unbearable to Kopites as local rivals Everton replaced them in the top tier.

Undaunted, A'Court earned a regular berth during 1954/55 and, under the selfless tutelage of Liddell – who instilled into the promising rookie his own Corinthian values concerning team spirit and the work ethic – he began to mature into an impressively dynamic performer, bringing to the table explosive pace, a modicum of fire and a consistency not always evident in young wingmen. In addition, he packed a savage shot, though he was never a prolific scorer, his seasonal tally only once reaching double figures.

But although A'Court was clearly a man on the rise, his brio persuading successive managers to accommodate Liddell on the right flank or at centre-forward rather than on his previously preferred left-touchline beat, it proved a long time before the same could be said of Liverpool.

From 1955/56, their finishing positions in the Second Division table read like a litany of excruciating frustration to arguably the most passionate body of supporters in the land: third, third, fourth, fourth, third, third, when the minimum requirement for promotion was second.

This tortuous sequence claimed the jobs of bosses Don Welsh and former club captain Phil Taylor, but through it all A'Court's personal development continued apace, as reflected by an inquiry about him by Arsenal. He didn't investigate the approach because he believed that soon Liverpool would rise again, but later he regretted not pressing his case, as such a move would have placed him in the limelight and might have enabled him to reach loftier heights.

Still, as the decade wore on he was selected for the Football Association, the Football League and England under-23s, for whom he was capped seven times.

Full international recognition arrived in November 1957, when A'Court was called up to replace the injured Tom Finney against Northern Ireland at Wembley. The visitors won 3-2 but the Liverpool man scored what was to be his only goal at the top level, helping to secure his berth in Walter Winterbottom's squad for the 1958 World Cup finals in Sweden.

Once again the 'Preston Plumber' was sidelined and A'Court deputised in the goalless clash with eventual winners Brazil, taking the eye as he ran boldly at Nilton Santos, one of the most feted of all full-backs. With Finney still indisposed, he kept his place for the next two games, a draw with Austria and a 1-0 defeat in a play-off with the USSR which saw England eliminated.

Thereafter A'Court was granted only one more opportunity for his country, possibly because he didn't gel effectively with the influential midfield schemer Johnny Haynes, who lined up alongside him and whose place was considered inviolate.

At club level, though, A'Court continued to prosper, especially after the single most momentous event in Liverpool's history, the appointment as manager in December 1959 of one Bill Shankly.

The inspirational, hugely demanding Scot took over a club that reposed in a moribund comfort zone, with a shabby stadium, an under-equipped training ground, a mediocre team and a complacent board of directors. He lost little time in launching his revolution, rapidly dumping players he deemed to be dead wood, but he identified A'Court – who scored the Reds' first competitive goal of the Shankly era – as a key man in the struggle to rise from the Second Division.

Duly the winger starred as Liverpool narrowly missed achieving that initial ambition in both 1959/60 and 1960/61, but it was in the next campaign that the renaissance gathered irresistible impetus following the summer acquisition of the pugnacious and skilful Scottish centre-forward Ian St John, and his colossal countryman, the stopper centre-half Ron Yeats.

Now, at last, Liverpool romped away with the Second Division title with A'Court, an ever-present that term, often meshing dazzlingly with 'The Saint' and his front-running partner Roger Hunt, another relative newcomer.

Hunt and A'Court became close pals off the field and demonstrated equal empathy on it, with the marksman who would go on to earn imperishable glory as one of England's World Cup winners in 1966 proving a ruthless converter of the flankman's pinpoint dispatches.

Back in the First Division in 1962/63, A'Court held his own as Shankly's Reds consolidated their status, but a series of niggling injuries in the second half of the season jolted his momentum and saw him competing for the number-11 shirt with Kevin Lewis.

Liverpool finished in a commendable eighth place, but the insatiable Shankly had his eyes on more glittering prizes, and to that end that summer he recruited young flankman Peter Thompson from Preston North End for a club record fee of £40,000.

Though A'Court was still only 28, the arrival of such a precociously gifted rival sounded his Anfield death knell. In 1963/64, as the newly buoyant Liverpool lifted their first League crown for 17 years, the man who had toiled so faithfully in the Reds' cause through the wilderness years was not picked for a single match, a supremely frustrating experience for a performer who believed he still had plenty to offer.

Thus, after making one last appearance – on Anfield's first night of European football, as Liverpool completed the formality of a second leg victory over Reykjavik of Iceland – A'Court accepted a £9,000 transfer to neighbouring Tranmere Rovers of the Fourth Division.

At Prenton Park it was a case of deja vu, as in consecutive seasons his team missed promotion by a whisker. By then he was in his thirties and, with his fitness and form beginning to suffer – though he did score the only hat-trick of his career, against Bradford City in the spring of 1966 – he retired as a player at the end of his second campaign as a Rover. Determined to remain in the game, he coached at Norwich from 1966 to 1969, then fleetingly at Crewe before embarking on a seven-year stint with Stoke City, during which he contributed to the Potters' first (and still only) major honour when they won the League Cup in 1972.

Towards the end of his Victoria Ground sojourn, A'Court served as assistant manager to George Eastham, then took charge as caretaker boss for two matches early in 1978 before the appointment of Alan Durban.

After that he worked briefly in New Zealand before settling happily into a coaching and administrative post with Keele University, his characteristic enthusiasm burning as brightly as ever.

Alan A'Court, footballer; born Rainhill, Lancashire, 30 September 1934; played for Liverpool 1952-64, Tranmere Rovers 1964-66; capped five times by England 1957-58; died Nantwich, Cheshire, 14 December 2009.

Jack Brownsword

If ever one man embodied the history, the tradition, the very ethos of a football club, then it was Jack Brownsword at Scunthorpe United.

As a performer once described by no less acute a judge than the revered Liverpool manager Bill Shankly as the finest full-back operating outside the top division, he made nearly 600 League appearances for the Iron and scored 50 goals, all but one of them from the penalty spot.

As a character he was the very best kind of sporting hero, a modest fellow celebrated by his local community partly for his immense deeds on the field, but also because he was accessible, invariably referring to his job in engagingly matter-of-fact terms, as if he were about to clock on for a shift at the local steelworks.

He was embraced, too, for an infectious sense of fun which enlivened the dressing room, for an unswervingly Corinthian approach which ensured that he was never booked, and for his loyalty when bigger clubs, such as Manchester City, expressed interest in plucking him away from the homely atmosphere of the Old Show Ground. Such hopeful head-hunters never quite grasped how deep was his bond with United, or that it was unbreakable.

In retrospect, though, it is easy to recognise. Brownsword signed for Scunthorpe three years before they entered the Football League in 1950, he was in his prime as they became the last champions of the Third Division North before it was amalgamated with its southern equivalent in 1958, and in 1962 he continued to excel when they finished fourth in the second tier, behind Shankly's newly rampant Anfield Reds, who romped away with the divisional title.

Thereafter Brownsword soldiered on as a formidable flank defender into his forties, then became club trainer at the Old Show Ground before cash-strapped Scunthorpe had no choice but to make him redundant during the 1970s.

Still, though, he marched under the Iron's banner and two decades later he was honoured as a vice-president. Now, having absorbed the shock of his death, fans and directors alike are debating the need for some lasting memorial to the man whose name became synonymous with their club.

After leaving school not long before the Second World War, Brownsword worked at a coal-mine in the Doncaster area and played his football for the Midland League side Frickley Colliery. In 1946 he joined Hull City, but after making only minimal impact in a handful of senior outings for the Tigers he returned to Frickley, his future in the professional game appearing decidedly precarious.

But a watershed in the wiry Yorkshireman's fortunes was imminent. In July 1947 he switched to Scunthorpe, then in the same league as Frickley, and he had become a bulwark of their rearguard by the time they graduated to the senior competition in 1950.

At 27, Brownsword was a late starter on a Football League career, but he was fiercely determined to make up for lost seasons and was admirably equipped to do so. A brave and incisive tackler, he was pacy, an attacking overlapper ahead of his time and shrewd in the key art of positional play.

Then there was his trademark skill of dispatching penalties. Brownsword was a goalkeeper's nightmare because of his composure and his accuracy, his method being a smooth approach to the ball and a clinical left-foot finish low to the net-minder's right hand.

Opponents knew exactly what he was going to do, but still couldn't stop him, as Charlton Athletic's Willie Duff discovered to his cost during one tense confrontation. Seeking to force Brownsword into a change of plan, Duff stood much closer than normal to his right-hand post, believing that the Scunthorpe man would opt for the yawning gap thus created. Accordingly the cunning custodian plunged to his left, but the kicker was unfazed, simply slotting a slide-rule delivery along his customary trajectory fractionally inside the vacated upright.

As the 1950s wore on, Brownsword became recognised as one of the top talents in the League's lower reaches, being selected five times for the Third Division North side to face the southern section, though club commitments limited his appearances to three. He played a colossal part in lifting the divisional crown under boss Ron Suart in 1957/58, and, earlier in that momentous term, performed mightily as Newcastle United were evicted from the FA Cup on their own turf. Then commenced six years in the Second Division, the highlight of which was that fourth place in 1961/62, when the Iron were only six points short of ascending to the top flight and might have made it but for the controversial sale of prolific centre-forward Barrie Thomas at the turn of the year.

But for all that League enterprise, the majority of it during the management reign of Dick Duckworth, the contest which remains most vivid in the club's folklore is the 6-2 FA Cup thrashing of Blackpool in January 1961.

That famous day at the Old Show Ground, Brownsword's direct opponent was the incomparable Stanley Matthews, who mesmerised most left-backs around the world but was humbled by Scunthorpe's finest, at one point even changing his boots in a vain attempt to make an impact.

However, the Iron's eminence would wane all too soon as the lifting of the players' maximum-wage regulation led to many small-town clubs struggling to stay afloat. Still the veteran Brownsword pulled his weight but could not prevent relegation in 1963/64, soon after which, aged 41, he retired as a player, staying on as first-team trainer through the second half of that decade and into the next until United's financial travail forced him to leave. During his time as sponge-man he remained remarkably fit, prompting irreverent cries from the terraces that he was faster than the players he tended, though that was manifestly not true about one of his young charges, name of Kevin Keegan.

Brownsword had spotted the future England captain playing junior football in Doncaster, then mentored him as he shone with the Iron before tipping off Liverpool about his precocious emerging talent.

Fittingly, in 1989 Brownsword, who had ended his working life as a salesman for a window company, was the guest of honour when Scunthorpe played their last game at the Old Show Ground before moving to Glanford Park, their current home.

In 2007, having been voted the all-time favourite of Iron fans, he was elected to the Professional Footballers' Association Hall of Fame.

Nathan John Brownsword, footballer; born Campsall, Yorkshire, 15 May 1923; played for Hull City 1946-47, Scunthorpe United 1947-64; died Burton-upon-Stather, Lincolnshire, 18 December 2009.

Albert Scanlon

Albert Scanlon was the most enigmatic of Manchester United's Busby Babes, the group of young, extravagantly talented athletes who were pushing back the boundaries of what was hitherto deemed possible on the English football scene when their world was shattered by the Munich air disaster.

Eight players lost their lives in the tragedy – which happened following a refuelling stop on the way home from a European Cup encounter with Red Star Belgrade in February 1958 – and two more were maimed so that they never kicked another ball.

When Scanlon survived, and recovered from his injuries to show coruscating form on his return to action on the Red Devils' left wing, it seemed certain that he, like Bobby Charlton and a handful of others who escaped death on that slushy German runway, would be a key bulwark in the stricken club's reconstruction.

But somehow, after advancing to the fringe of full international recognition, with five appearances for the England under-23 side and one for the Football League in the wake of the crash, the brilliant but mercurial crowd-pleaser lost impetus and his career petered out in comparative anti-climax.

Scanlon was a fascinating character, streetwise and popular with his team-mates but possessing a wide whimsical streak, sometimes leading those who knew him best to suggest he hailed from another planet.

In fact, he was a Mancunian born and bred, and the notion that he possessed the potential for greatness gained currency from his earliest days at the Old Trafford club, which began when he signed amateur forms in 1950.

Though markedly light in physical stature, the 15-year-old with the winsome air was never lacking in the crucial commodities of pace and skill, and although he found himself one of no fewer than ten gifted flankmen at the club, duly he progressed through the junior teams.

Even at that age, Scanlon was capable of embarrassing any opponent, no matter how accomplished, and after one practice match in which he was confronted by the ruthlessly formidable Bill Foulkes, a regular United first-team defender and an England international, he was informed gleefully by coach Bert Whalley: 'You're doing well, young Albert, you had Bill in two minds – he didn't know whether to kick you over the stand or into the dressing room.'

Off the pitch he made an impact, too, enthralling his contemporaries with lurid tales of a tearaway existence, such as how a steering wheel had pierced his stomach after he and his friends had crashed a stolen car – and he had the scar to prove it. For all this bravado, though, some saw him as insecure, an essentially shy young man in need of constant reassurance.

Most importantly to United boss Matt Busby, Scanlon – or Joe Friday as he was dubbed, after the slick-talking hero of the contemporary TV detective series *Dragnet* – continued to impress as a footballer, turning professional in December 1952, helping to win the FA Youth Cup in two successive seasons, making his senior entrance against Arsenal as a 19-year-old in November 1954, then finishing that term as the first choice number 11.

However, there was a black cloud on the Scanlon horizon, and it went by the name of David Pegg. During the two championship-winning campaigns of 1955/56 and 1956/57, and for the first half of 1957/58, the Yorkshireman's enchanting input relegated Scanlon to the sidelines.

The two left-wingers offered a distinct contrast in styles: Pegg was an intricate manipulator of the ball who would befuddle defenders with his trickery and who tended to drift inside, while Scanlon was piercingly direct, a specialist at leaving his marker for dead with searing acceleration before dispatching a cross.

When his confidence was soaring, he could scorch past opponents as if they barely existed and he could shoot powerfully with either foot. The fans loved his verve, his high-velocity, panic-inducing dashes, but he was inclined to be unpredictable, and there were days of intense frustration when he lingered infuriatingly on the contest's fringe.

Still, his basic quality was undeniable and his chance came again in December 1957. The side had suffered a collective slump and Busby dropped Pegg and three others, the replacements including Scanlon and the emerging Charlton.

It was a typically bold stroke by the perceptive United manager and the Red Devils embarked on an 11-game unbeaten run, immediately prior to the Munich calamity. Throughout that exhilarating interlude – which included the starring role in a remarkable 5-4 victory over Arsenal at Highbury, the Babes' final game on English soil – Scanlon lifted his game to a new level, now seemingly a fixture for the foreseeable future.

Then came the accident, in which Pegg perished but which Albert escaped with a fractured skull and a broken leg, but with profound psychological scars which would remain with him for the rest of his days.

While his physical wounds healed, he missed the depleted United's emotional progress to the FA Cup final, where they lost to Bolton Wanderers, and even when he was passed fit to resume his duties, he was reluctant to do so. Somehow it didn't seem right to pull on the red shirt without his fallen friends.

Inspirational assistant boss Jimmy Murphy convinced him to resume his career, however, and in 1958/59 Scanlon produced the most spellbinding football of his life.

Operating on the left of a prolific attack which also included Warren Bradley on the opposite flank and the sumptuous inside trio of Albert Quixall, Dennis Viollet and Bobby Charlton, he was ever-present and struck 16 goals as a patchwork team confounded the pessimists by finishing as title runners-up to Wolverhampton Wanderers.

Representative honours followed but his prospects suffered an unexpected setback in the spring of 1960 when Busby, seeking to maximise the still-developing genius of Charlton, switched the England man to the left flank. Suddenly Scanlon had been marginalised, and in November 1960 he was sold to Newcastle United for £18,000.

Pundits who had seen him as part of the nucleus of Busby's reconstructed team were astonished, though they might have been less so had they been privy to difficulties the player had been experiencing away from the game, personal matters of which the manager is said to have taken a dim view.

Still only 25 at the time of his transfer, much was expected of him on Tyneside, but he never settled, perhaps overawed at joining a squad of 53 professionals. There followed a brief unhappy stint with Lincoln City and a slightly more fulfilling one with Mansfield Town, but Scanlon's skills did not flourish in the League's lower reaches and in 1966 he departed the first-class game, poignantly unfulfilled.

Later he took jobs in bakeries and a bolt factory before finding a happy niche as a stevedore on Salford Docks, where he relished the sense of community, and he was bitterly upset when that way of life disappeared in the early 1980s. There followed more than a decade as a security officer in Manchester before retirement.

There might have been a flaw in his make-up which prevented him from attaining the glory his ravishing ability appeared to warrant, or he might have been a victim of the trauma of Munich. But the personable Scanlon always remained a Red Devil at heart, viewing his illustrious past with a singular mixture of sharp-edged realism and dreamy nostalgia.

He wasn't blind to human frailties or footballing shortcomings among his fellow Busby Babes, yet on an occasional Friday evening after finishing his shift at the docks, he would stroll to Old Trafford and fancy he could hear the roar of the long-ago crowd. Then, dipping into the squad of comrades who had perished at Munich, he would select his team for the next day's game.

Albert Joseph Scanlon, footballer; born Manchester, 10 October 1935; played for Manchester United 1950-60, Newcastle United 1960-62, Lincoln City 1962-63, Mansfield Town 1963-66; died Salford, Lancashire, 22 December 2009.

Allen Batsford

Allen Batsford was the manager who led Wimbledon into the Football League in 1977 after inspiring the Plough Lane club to lift three consecutive Southern League titles and guiding them on one of the most compelling of all FA Cup giant-killing adventures.

In 1975 Burnley became the first top-flight victims of a non-League side in more than half a century, and mighty Leeds United were given the fright of their lives before edging past Batsford's gutsy team only after a replay.

But that bald outline of his headline achievements, impressive as it is, barely begins to do justice to the lifelong commitment and remarkable expertise of one of sport's unsung artisans.

Batsford was a football man to the very core of his being, embracing the game with heart and mind and sinew, approaching his task with a meticulous professionalism immensely rare in non-League circles.

Those who came within his ambit, such as Dave Bassett – who was destined eventually to take Wimbledon all the way from the League's basement to its top flight on a shoestring budget – learnt all they needed to know about shaping a collection of disparate individuals into a tight, efficient unit.

Deeply thoughtful and utterly pragmatic, Batsford based his method on a well-drilled defence and a relentlessly industrious midfield. He believed that if his players kept the game simple, eschewing expansive flourishes but doing the ordinary things well, then ultimately his opponents would make mistakes on which his own men could capitalise.

A lot of people paid lip service to such a code, but Batsford stood out at that level in that he was not merely a physical trainer – although certainly he demanded of his charges a fearsome degree of fitness – but a genuine coach. He told them what to do and how to do it in game situations; he didn't merely din the rudiments into their heads, he was eloquent enough to make the majority of them understand.

Batsford found he had to be a stern disciplinarian, but he was a shrewd psychologist, too, knowing which characters needed an arm around their shoulders, and which, such as the lively and forthright Bassett, responded to a more astringent approach. To all of them, though, he displayed loyalty and warmth and, almost invariably, he received respect in return.

As a boy, Batsford made his first mark at county level with Middlesex and believed he was on the verge of a breakthrough at the age of 17 when he turned professional with Arsenal. However, although he graduated to the Gunners' reserves, the callow inside-forward cum wing-half failed to make the grade at Highbury and soon was forced to make his living outside football.

Still he was besotted by the game, and he played for Folkestone Town, Ramsgate and Margate before entering part-time management with Feltham Town of the Surrey Senior League in 1963.

Gradually Batsford became ever more fascinated with tactics and strategy, and in 1967 he stepped up to take charge of Walton and Hersham, where defensive midfielder Bassett became one of his key performers.

Serial success followed. Walton took the Athenian League crown in 1969, soon graduating to the more prestigious Isthmian League, in which they finished as runners-up in 1973. There was heady consolation for the near miss, however, as they beat Slough Town in the Wembley final of that term's FA Amateur Cup and also overcame Fourth Division Exeter City in the first round of the FA Cup.

A season later Batsford scaled his loftiest peak yet when, after holding Brian Clough's Brighton to a goalless FA Cup draw at Walton, his team romped to a 4-0 replay victory at the Goldstone Ground. Before the tie Clough had talked of a clash between his own 'thoroughbreds' and Batsford's 'donkeys', but afterwards the great man was magnanimous in defeat, admitting that the non-Leaguers fully deserved their win and behaving graciously to his conquerors.

In 1974 Batsford moved on to Wimbledon, taking a group of Walton players with him, including Bassett. Immediately he moulded the newcomers, together with the handful of survivors from the previous Plough Lane regime, into a potent machine and they finished the campaign as Southern League champions.

Gloriously, too, they dumped Burnley out of the FA Cup at Turf Moor, neutralising the international likes of Leighton James and Bryan Flynn to win 1-0. Then, even more sensationally, they defied the formidable power of Leeds – who would finish that season as European Cup finalists – by drawing 0-0 at Elland Road, thanks in considerable measure to goalkeeper Dickie Guy's penalty save from Peter Lorimer. Still unbowed, Batsford's plucky part-timers stuck to their work ethic in the replay at Selhurst Park, where they were defeated only by Bassett's unlucky own goal.

Thereafter the Dons completed their hat-trick of Southern League crowns before being elected into the Football League's Fourth Division, at the expense of Workington Town, in 1977.

Ironically now, with the club having scaled the loftiest peak in its history, the script began to go awry for the manager. He had never been enamoured of new owner Ron Noades, a dynamic but controversial businessman, and when results were poor during that first Football League autumn, the relationship deteriorated apace.

Batsford, who had been working for a concrete company in the mornings as well as steering his team, grew increasingly frustrated with what he saw as dreadful organisation – he reckoned there were no paid talent scouts, there was no one to vet opponents and there was no one to help him with the coaching.

Noades did bring in Dario Gradi to run a youth system, but Batsford didn't mesh comfortably with the new man and, after being infuriated when the players had to drive their own cars to an away match at Rochdale over Christmas because no team bus was provided, the manager walked out in early January 1978.

While Gradi became the new boss at Plough Lane and, with Bassett as his assistant, led Wimbledon away from the relegation zone, Batsford returned to non-League circles, first enduring an unhappy stint with Hillingdon Borough before thriving once more with Wealdstone, whose squad included future England star Stuart Pearce.

In 1981/82, Batsford led the Stones to success in both the Southern League's championship, which secured promotion to the Alliance Premier League (equivalent of the modern Blue Square Premier League) and its challenge cup, then to third place in their first season in the Alliance.

Subsequently he suffered heart trouble and left Wealdstone, but he recovered to coach at Queen's Park Rangers, then serve as general manager of Dulwich Hamlet before running the Millwall youth team and acting as a talent scout for Bassett during his former protégé's managerial stints with Watford, Sheffield United and Nottingham Forest.

Batsford remained dedicated to football until the last, and it was on his way home from watching Chelsea play Fulham in late December last year that he collapsed and died at Fulham Broadway tube station.

Allen Batsford, football club manager; born London, 9 April 1932; managed Feltham Town, Waltham and Hersham, Wimbledon, Hillingdon Borough, Wealdstone; died Fulham Broadway, 28 December 2009.

Alex Parker

Alex Parker was that comparatively rare football being, a full-back and a folk hero. Renowned as a poised and stylish yet formidably combative performer while excelling in Everton's confident charge to the League championship in 1962/63, he was revered no less passionately at his previous club, Falkirk, with whom he was awarded all but one of his 15 caps for Scotland. Accordingly, he occupies a berth in the Toffees' Hall of Fame and was considered an automatic selection for the Bairns' team of the millennium, both honours which were not assigned lightly.

Further afield, too, professional regard for the amiable Ayrshireman was virtually boundless, with no less an authority than his exalted countryman Matt Busby, the founding father of the modern Manchester United, declaring that during Parker's prime he knew no peer in his position, anywhere in the world.

One of the secrets of the stockily built Scot's success was an extraordinarily well-honed sense of timing. On the field, he elevated the sliding tackle into something not far short of an art form. Though by no means a sluggish mover, he was no greyhound, either, a circumstance which habitually he rendered irrelevant by choosing the precise moment at which to make his challenge. So often a dashing flankman might surmise that he had eluded the stretching Parker, only for the ball to be whisked away to safety at the last split-second.

Crucially given this method, he was adept at positional play, invariably choosing his ground with care, jockeying his opponent so that their clash would occur near the touchline to avoid the risk of conceding penalties. In truth, so precise was his technique that, even inside the box, that hazard was negligible.

Meanwhile off the field, the Parker timing was equally effective in his delivery of droll one-liners. For instance, during his spell at Falkirk, goal-line clearances became a speciality, and he gloried in describing his good friend, the net-minder Bert Slater, as the best goalkeeper he had ever played behind.

However, there was far more to Parker's contribution than doughty defending and quick wit. He was an accomplished all-round footballer who passed the ball with the elan of a play-maker and whose sense of adventure – he was one of the first overlappers in the Scottish game – reflected the fact that as a boy he had been an attacker.

He was immensely consistent, too, and although his aerial work was no match for the majestic likes of the Welsh giant John Charles, generally he was solid enough in that area, an asset he attributed jokingly to a garden practice session supervised by the enthusiastic wife of his manager at Falkirk, Bob Shankly.

After attracting widespread attention as a teenager with the Dumfriesshire junior club Kello Rovers, Parker was recruited by Falkirk, newly promoted to Scotland's top tier, in 1952. Initially he was employed by Shankly at inside-forward, then switched to wing-half, but it was not until he was moved to right-back in 1954/55 that he gained a regular place. Thereafter he thrived, emerging as a key figure in the Brockville club's regular successful battles to avoid relegation, and in 1957 he was voted Scotland's player of the year. That season he had shone as the Bairns won the Scottish Cup, overcoming Kilmarnock in a replayed final, and appeared to be consolidating a full international career which had begun two years earlier with selection against Portugal at Hampden Park three months short of his 20th birthday.

For such a precocious talent at an unfashionable club a transfer was inevitable, and it materialised in June 1958 when he joined Everton, valued at £18,000 in a package deal which also took winger Eddie O'Hara to Merseyside.

That summer Parker, who had already collected six under-23 caps and regularly represented the Scottish League, became the first Goodison Park man to appear in the World Cup finals but, perversely for a thoroughbred operator on the threshold of his pomp, his outing against Paraguay proved to be his last for his country.

In truth, he was below his best in the dispiriting 3-2 defeat by the South Americans in Norrkoping, Sweden, but it was perplexing in the extreme that he was never to be called up again. True, his long-term replacement on the right flank of defence was the polished Eric Caldow of Rangers, but earlier the pair had struck up a promising partnership with Caldow at left-back, and with all due respect to others who wore the number-two shirt – the likes of Dunky MacKay, Bobby Shearer and Alex Hamilton – they did not appear to be in Parker's class.

Thus supporters of the Evertonian's cause were not to be swerved from their belief that the selectors were discriminating against him because of his 'Anglo' status, a common enough perception in the cases of many fine players who crossed the border during that era.

At Goodison, however, after he was forced to delay his debut because his National Service commitments with the Royal Scots Fusiliers took him to Cyprus until November, his merit was recognised as handsome.

Parker and O'Hara had arrived thanks to the growing influence of pools magnate and future club chairman John Moores, who had persuaded the hitherto parsimonious board to loosen their pursestrings and provided them with the means to do so. It was the club's first major signing for years and although O'Hara was a disappointment, Parker flourished apace. He was taken aback when the idealistic Carey was sacked in 1961, despite guiding an improving side to fifth place in the top division, but the appointment of new boss Harry Catterick, a stern disciplinarian, proved to be an inspired decision.

Two years later the Toffees were champions, finishing a comfortable six points clear of runners-up Tottenham Hotspur and playing a compelling brand of football which fused elegance with power.

Catterick's team boasted admirable balance, with Parker meshing immaculately with two right-wingers, Billy Bingham in the first half of the campaign, Alex Scott in the second.

The marquee names were the strikers, the subtly artistic Alex Young and the venomously darting Roy Vernon, but there wasn't a weak link anywhere in the line-up.

At that point Parker was in his prime at 27 but, sadly, soon he fell prey to recurring hamstring problems and during 1964/65 he lost his place to Tommy Wright, a flintily committed local boy who went on to play for England.

Thus stymied, the Scot stepped out of the top flight that autumn, accepting a £2,000 switch to Fourth Division Southport, where his former Goodison comrade Bingham was now the boss. Using his experience to compensate for loss of pace, he slotted in effectively at Haig Avenue, and was prominent as the Sandgrounders earned promotion as runners-up to Stockport County in 1966/67.

Having reached the veteran stage, in January 1968 Parker became player-manager of the Northern Ireland club Ballymena United, where he remained for nearly two years. There followed a brief stint with Drumcondra of Dublin before he returned to Southport as a coach early in 1970.

At season's end the Sandgrounders were demoted and Parker replaced Arthur Peat as boss, leading his team to a creditable eighth place in the basement division before leaving the game in 1971 to enter the licensed trade.

He proved a popular landlord of the Swinging Sporran in Runcorn, always ready to yarn about his playing days but invariably referring to his own achievements with characteristic modesty.

Later Parker returned to his homeland to live in Gretna and in 2009 he suffered the amputation of his left leg. Still he relished a joke, though, chuckling delightedly when his compatriot and old Goodison chum Alex Young remarked: 'At least it's not the one you tackle with.'

Alexander Hershaw Parker, footballer; born Irvine, Ayrshire, 2 August 1935; played for Falkirk 1952-58, Everton 1958-65, Southport 1965-68, Ballymena United 1968-69, Drumcondra 1970; capped 15 times by Scotland 1955-58; managed Ballymena United 1968-69, Southport 1970-71; died Gretna, Dumfries and Galloway, 7 January 2009.

Gil Merrick

When England's ludicrously misguided notion of itself as the world's premier footballing power was eviscerated by the rampaging Hungarians in the early 1950s, utterly ruthlessly and yet with a compelling beauty to all who cherished the fundamentals of the game above blind patriotism, it was the humbling task of goalkeeper Gil Merrick to retrieve the ball from his net 13 times over the course of two fearfully unequal contests.

Inevitably as a result, he was ridiculed as a scapegoat in some quarters, but such treatment was shamefully unfair to a characteristically reliable performer who was no more to blame than the rest of a shell-shocked rearguard, which included the lionised skipper Billy Wright. In fact, Merrick deserved his status as his country's regular custodian during the first half of a decade in which all with eyes to see came to understand that England had a huge amount to learn, not only from the 'Magnificent Magyars' but also from other teams who had eclipsed the nation which had given football to the world.

Meanwhile at club level, the tall, dapper Midlander, whose personal trademark was a neatly clipped moustache in an era when the vast majority of sportsmen were clean-shaven, went on to become the most influential figure in the history of Birmingham City, compiling a Blues record of 551 competitive appearances and managing them to their only major trophy to date, garnered by triumph over local rivals Aston Villa in the 1963 League Cup final.

At least Merrick was well equipped personally to cope with any flak which flew his way in the wake of the Hungarian debacles. He was a confident, charismatic, impeccably groomed individual, strong both physically and mentally, fastidious about his fitness and meticulous in all aspects of his work. He could be spiky on first acquaintance, but while his judgements could be hard, invariably they were deemed to be honest.

As a 'keeper Merrick offered a vivid contrast to his main rival for the England jersey, Bert Williams of Wolverhampton Wanderers. Where the Molineux man tended towards the flamboyantly acrobatic, Birmingham's net-minder was never intentionally spectacular. Invariably calm, he was adept at positional play, continually calculating angles of attack and working out how to frustrate opponents with the minimum of fuss.

A fervent believer in catching crosses rather than punching the ball – clearly a sound approach, but far easier to suggest than to accomplish – Merrick was blessed with a pair of large, seemingly prehensile hands and exuded a reassuring presence which bred a sense of security in his fellow defenders.

As a boy he had excelled at most sports, winning school prizes as a runner and demonstrating such cricketing prowess as a young man that he played for Warwickshire Seconds as a batsman and opening bowler.

But goalkeeping was his passion – surprisingly for a lad growing up in Birmingham, his idol was Everton's Ted Sagar rather than local hero Harry Hibbs, whom ultimately he would replace as the Blues' long-term last line of defence.

Nearly every night when his football-loving father returned from his shift as a sheet-metal worker in the Sparkhill area of the city, the six-year-old Merrick would throw himself into a make-believe derby clash staged in the family kitchen, with the dad representing Villa, the son Birmingham.

There was little or no formal coaching, but his aptitude for the game was exceptional and after excelling for a succession of junior teams he graduated to City as a 17-year-old in 1939, not deterred by their recent relegation from the Football League's top division although taking the precaution of maintaining an apprenticeship at the metal works.

Then came the war, but the progress of the ambitious, intelligent rookie continued apace. While serving in the Army's PT Corps he ran a gym in Oswestry, but also played more than 170 games for Birmingham in unofficial emergency competitions, helping to win the Football League South title in 1945/46, as well as making guest appearances for Northampton Town, Nottingham Forest and West Bromwich Albion.

When peace resumed, Merrick was established firmly as his club's number-one, a status he was to hold for the next decade and a half. He thrived, initially under the forthright leadership of manager Harry Storer, enhancing his burgeoning reputation as the Blues finished third in the Second Division table in 1946/47, then burnishing it as they were promoted as champions a season later, conceding only 24 goals in 42 games.

Though the Blues struggled among the elite, being relegated as bottom club in 1949/50, Merrick's personal star remained in the ascendancy and in November 1951, not long before his 30th birthday and in his home town at Villa Park, he was called up for his full international debut against Northern Ireland.

Though it proved a dismally scrappy game, he performed efficiently in a 2-0 victory and thereafter, despite his Second Division status, he consolidated his place, collecting 23 caps and missing only one England game over the next three years.

One of the highlights of Merrick's international tenure was a commanding display in what was seen as the unofficial championship of Europe against Austria in May 1952. Inside the last ten minutes, having made a series of fine saves and with the score at 2-2, he plucked a cross from the air, robustly fended off the aggressive challenge of centre-forward Robert Dienst, and threw out to Tom Finney. 'The Preston Plumber' duly passed the ball to Nat Lofthouse, who charged through the Austrian ranks to score the winner to the uproarious approbation of a large contingent of British soldiers in the crowd, thus inscribing his name indelibly into sporting folklore as 'The Lion of Vienna'.

Having conceded only 15 goals in his first 13 internationals, Merrick looked secure between England's posts, but then came the Hungarian trauma; a 6-3 reverse at Wembley in November 1953, the first to continental opposition on home soil, was followed by a 7-1 humiliation six months later in Budapest, and suddenly Merrick found himself under intense scrutiny.

Perhaps as a result, he was unusually shaky as England went down 4-2 to Uruguay in a World Cup quarter-final in Basle, Switzerland, in June 1954 and never played for his country again.

Back with Birmingham after that poignant England exit, there was considerable consolation as Merrick, who also made 11 appearances for the Football League, helped City to another Second Division crown in 1954/55, then retained superb form as they enjoyed arguably the finest season in their history in 1955/56. By then bossed by Arthur Turner, the Blues finished sixth in the First Division and reached the FA Cup final, which they lost 3-1 to Manchester City, that game being best remembered for another goalkeeper, the German Bert Trautmann, playing on with a broken neck.

After three more campaigns of competence behind a notably tight defence, in the spring of 1959 the 37-year-old Merrick stood down to become reserve team coach at St Andrew's. Twice during 1959/60 he returned to senior duty as emergency cover before formally retiring as a player, then taking over from Pat Beasley as manager that June.

By then the Blues were a poor side once more, but the dynamically industrious Merrick – who taught PT at a local school during much of his playing career, only ceasing when he became boss – was dedicated to turning them round.

One of his first duties was to lead Birmingham into the second leg of the final of the Inter-Cities Fairs Cup, destined eventually to become the UEFA Cup. At the time it was spread over two years, and the Blues now faced Barcelona in the Nou Camp after drawing their home leg 0-0. They lost 4-1 but Merrick was undismayed, guiding them back to another final of the revamped competition a year later, this time bowing 4-2 on aggregate to AS Roma. Such European adventures, however, could not mask the difficult task facing Merrick on the domestic scene and though he blooded some terrific youngsters such as wing-half Terry Hennessey, inside-forward Johnny Vincent and 'keeper Colin Withers, and brought in the experienced likes of schemer Jimmy Bloomfield and feisty attacker Bertie Auld, he presided over four successive relegation battles.

He won all of them, albeit narrowly, and there was also the high point of lifting the League Cup in 1963, when Aston Villa were defeated by a 3-1 aggregate in the two-legged final. His reward, however, was the sack, delivered abruptly in the spring of 1964, a decision which left him heartbroken as he believed he had laid the foundations for a successful future.

As a manager, Merrick had been a stern disciplinarian who had a sharp way with those he considered to be fools. But both his integrity and his dedication were unimpeachable, he was a deep thinker who introduced new coaching ideas and medical improvements, and was respected widely throughout the game.

Putting his disappointment behind him, he spent 35 years working as head of personnel for a leisure and household goods company in Birmingham, being responsible at one point for 200 people and maintaining his prodigious work ethic until his retirement, at the age of 75.

Since then he has been honoured both by Birmingham City and their fans. Last year the club renamed their Railway Stand after him, he was the first man to be inducted into the Blues' Legends XI and he was the supporters' choice to represent the club on the Broad Street Walk of Stars in Birmingham city centre.

Gilbert Harold Merrick, footballer and manager; born Birmingham, 26 January 1922, played for Birmingham City 1939-60; capped 23 times by England 1951-54; managed Birmingham City 1960-64; died Birmingham, 3 February 2010.

Brian Godfrey

Welsh international Brian Godfrey was a footballer both tough and clever, and as a manager he was a shrewd, hard-bitten operator, albeit not at the rarefied level widely envisaged for him when he took his first job as a boss in the mid-1970s.

First as a penetrative and prolific goal-scoring inside-forward, and later as a thoughtful, creative, occasionally abrasive wing-half, Godfrey made more than 600 senior appearances during an 18-year career which embraced six clubs, yet only the first of those outings – for Everton at Fulham in January 1960 – was made in the top division of the Football League.

What characterised the sturdy Deesider above all was his passionate enthusiasm and abiding love for the game, which saw him playing at parks level into his fifties and for Aston Villa All Stars, made up of the club's former players, into his sixties.

Football was in Godfrey's blood, absorbed at the knee of his similarly zealous father, who played as an amateur in North Wales and once scored 16 goals as his team recorded a 21-0 victory. Such ruthless single-mindedness was to be a determining factor in the progress of the son.

Godfrey rose to local prominence with his home-town club, Flint Alexandra, then signed amateur forms with Everton as a 17-year-old in 1957, turning professional at Goodison Park a year later.

At a time when enterprising manager Johnny Carey was fashioning the nucleus of an exciting side which would go on to greater things under Harry Catterick, it was a period of opportunity, but the young left-winger, as he was then, failed to make a sustained breakthrough.

Thus, after his solitary senior opportunity as a Toffeeman, in June 1960 Godfrey joined Second Division Scunthorpe United, whose boss Dick Duckworth lost little time in converting him from flankman to inside-forward.

The newcomer settled rapidly at the Old Show Ground, impressing with his ball skills, strength and the power of his shooting, and soon he forged a productive partnership with the high-scoring centre-forward Barrie Thomas, their goals contributing mightily to the Iron's feat in finishing fourth in the second tier in 1960/61, still the highest placing in their history.

Godfrey was rewarded with an under-23 international call-up and, in October 1963, with a £9,750 move to Preston North End, a fellow Second Division club but one with deeper resources and therefore more plausible ambition of rising to the top flight.

At Deepdale he was to strike the form of his life, mostly in tandem with that dreadnought of a spearhead Alex Dawson, and he went on to score 52 League goals in 127 appearances for the Lilywhites, but before truly hitting his stride he was to endure bitter disappointment.

In his first season there, Godfrey played four games in Preston's FA Cup campaign, which led all the way to Wembley. However, after netting in the quarter-final triumph over Oxford United, the Welshman lost his place to Alec Ashworth and was not selected for the final, one of the most thrilling ever staged at the old stadium, in which North End lost 3-2 to West Ham United. He was absent, too, for much of the springtime struggle for promotion, which ended in third place and narrow failure, and he was not happy about it.

Thereafter, though, he shone, notably in 1964/65 when he struck 25 times and on the last day of 1965/66, when he contributed a five-minute hat-trick – Preston's quickest ever – in the 9-0 annihilation of Cardiff City at Deepdale.

By then he was a full international, having earned three caps and contributed two goals, one on debut in a 3-2 defeat by Northern Ireland at Swansea in April 1964, the other in a 4-1 reverse to Italy in Florence in May 1965, his farewell appearance for his country.

In September 1967, with North End stuttering, Godfrey moved to another struggling Second Division outfit, Aston Villa, in a package deal along with Brian Greenhalgh. He scored in his opening game, but found himself in a poor team which in 1970 suffered the ignominy of being relegated to the third grade for the first time in Villa's history.

Against a background of boardroom turbulence, and with Godfrey emerging as an influential captain after dropping back to a midfield role, they went close to promotion at the first time of asking and astounded most observers by beating Manchester United over two legs in the semi-final of the League Cup.

At Wembley they lost 2-0 to Tottenham Hotspur, but the ceaseless industry, imaginative prompting and inspirational leadership displayed by Godfrey made him an ideal capture for Third Division rivals Bristol Rovers at season's end, when he moved to Eastville as a makeweight in the £35,000 transaction that took the dashing young winger Ray Graydon to Villa Park. The Welshman was an ideal addition for the Pirates, who needed an *eminence grise* to preside over a pool of talented youngsters, of which the schemer Wayne Jones was the most talented.

He embraced the challenge vigorously, maybe a tad cussedly at times, setting a stalwart example as Rovers embarked on two rousing League Cup sequences, bowing out gloriously to eventual winners Stoke City at the quarter-final stage in 1971/72, then ousting Manchester United in an Old Trafford replay a year later, before losing to Wolverhampton Wanderers. Between the two there was silverware to cherish as Rovers defeated Wolves, Burnley and Sheffield United to lift the pre-season Watney Cup, with Godfrey at the heart of a sterling team effort.

Off the pitch, too, he developed, proving a persuasive spokesman for the players in their dealings with management before falling out with boss Bill Dodgin over tactics and departing to Fourth Division Newport County for £10,000 in June 1973.

There followed three seasons of intense endeavour at Somerton Park and a brief stint with Portland Timbers in Oregon before, as a 36-year-old in the summer of 1976, he took the next logical step, that of becoming a player-manager.

His first stop was at Southern League Bath City, for whom he performed with unreduced gusto for one season before laying aside his boots and guiding his charges to the 1978 Southern League title.

At this juncture Godfrey looked a certainty to thrive as a boss in the Football League, and duly he stepped up to take the reins of Third Division Exeter City in January 1979.

Optimistic predictions appeared to be justified as he kept the Grecians in the top half of the table for three seasons, and also took them into the FA Cup quarter-finals in 1980/81, beating both Newcastle United and Leicester City after replays along the way. In the last eight their progress was halted by Tottenham Hotspur, who went on to lift the trophy, and Godfrey's star was firmly in the ascendancy. But then came two nerve-shredding escapes from relegation and in June 1983 he resigned with a year of his contract still to run.

Surprisingly he never returned to the Football League, instead doing a competent job for Alliance/Football Conference club Weymouth between 1983 and 1987, then he brought about a renaissance for Gloucester City, inspiring them to the Southern League Midland Division championship in 1988/89 and to the second round of the FA Cup a season later.

In 1991 he was sacked when the club was desperately short of cash, but he was back in 1992, leaving again in 1994. There followed service with Shortwood United and Cinderford Town before a second return to Gloucester, where he worked as assistant under Chris Burns, one of his former players, in the early years of the new millennium.

In 2003 Godfrey moved to Cyprus, where he died after a lengthy battle with leukaemia.

Brian Cameron Godfrey, footballer and manager; born Flint, North Wales, 1 May 1940; played for Everton 1958-60, Scunthorpe United 1960-63, Preston North End 1963-67, Aston Villa 1967-71, Bristol Rovers 1971-73, Newport County 1973-76; capped three times by Wales 1964-65; managed Exeter City 1979-83; died Nicosia, Cyprus, 11 February 2010.

Petar Borota

It was difficult to be neutral about Petar Borota, the Chelsea goalkeeper between 1979 and 1981, a generally glum period of under-achievement at Stamford Bridge.

Undeniably he was a born showman, a flamboyant entertainer who could, momentarily at least, divert attention from the serial trials of a frustratingly poor side. But beyond that basic premise, opinions on the Yugoslavian international diverged sharply.

Some saw him as an engaging eccentric who brought panache, colour and a streak of welcome unpredictability to an increasingly regimented English game; others had him down as ruinously erratic, an irresponsible clown who could undo the worthy graft of less frivolous colleagues while driving his coaches to distraction.

Certainly Borota was unorthodox. In an era before the influx of exotic talents from all over the world, when goalkeepers tended to restrict their activities to their own penalty areas, the swashbuckler from Belgrade was ready to indulge in a whole range of extravagant manoeuvres.

Often he would dash from his box to make a clearance; sometimes he would attempt to dribble past an onrushing opponent, not always with marked success; he was known to head crosses clear instead of catching or punching them; he would swing on his crossbar, admittedly when the ball was at the other end of the field; he would indulge in feverish goal celebrations, the like of which had never been seen in England; occasionally he might storm forward when Chelsea won a corner, long before such a practice was anything like standard; and one particularly provocative party-piece was deliberately bouncing the ball off his own bar when he judged the proceedings to be a trifle dull.

Once, in a cup encounter with Southampton, Borota darted out of his area with the apparent purpose of making a hefty clearance, only to execute a sudden and unexpected backheel to his dumbfounded centre-half, the man-mountain Micky Droy. Later, when asked to explain this disconcerting ploy, the Yugoslav grinned disarmingly and replied that he had wanted to enliven the crowd, who had thus far been starved of entertainment in a notably drab contest.

But all this apparently whimsical derring-do should not detract from the fact that, essentially, Borota was an immensely accomplished performer who had excelled for two home-town clubs. First he served OFK Belgrade, for whom he made some 130 appearances between 1969 and 1975, and then Partizan Belgrade, for whom he enjoyed 77 League outings from 1976 to 1979 while rising to international status and earning four full caps.

Standing a fraction under six feet tall, Borota was muscular, courageous and brilliantly acrobatic, one of the most spectacular shot-stoppers of his day. For all his adventurous antics, he took his craft seriously, preparing for games with impeccable rigour, and an incident for which he was famous in Yugoslavia – in which he had dropped his cap over his goal-line, then gone to pick it up while carrying the ball, thus conceding a goal – was wholly untypical of his professionalism.

He arrived at Stamford Bridge from Partizan in March 1979 as a £70,000 purchase by Danny Blanchflower, who had been recently drafted in to stop the rot at a club foundering dismally at the wrong end of the old First Division table.

In truth the eloquent, idealistic Irishman, who had enjoyed such a glorious playing career with Tottenham Hotspur but who had been out of day-to-day contact with footballers for 15 years, was an odd choice for such a muck-and-bullets assignment and neither he, nor the similarly quixotic Borota, had much hope of preventing Chelsea's relegation from the top flight as bottom club that spring.

But although Blanchflower resigned during the following September in despair at what he saw as the cynical values of the modern game, Borota won a regular place under new boss Geoff Hurst, and for the next two seasons was voted the Blues' player of the year.

For all his foibles, that offered a telling token of consistent competence which helped Chelsea to fourth place in the Second Division in 1979/80, missing out on promotion only on goal difference. More impressive still, in 1980/81, during which the team declined into mid-table mediocrity, he returned 18 clean sheets, beating the club record held by his eminent predecessor Peter Bonetti.

However, at season's end Hurst was replaced as manager by the pragmatic and experienced John Neal, who was not enamoured of Borota's style. Thus it came as no surprise in November when the 29-year-old Yugoslav, who had made more than a century of appearances for Chelsea, was dropped in favour of teenager Steve Francis and soon was dispatched to Third Division Brentford, for whom he never played a League game. There followed service with several Portuguese clubs through the middle years of the decade before he left the game.

A warm, genial character and a popular figure with his Stamford Bridge team-mates, even those occasionally stunned by his off-the-wall interludes, Petar Borota will be remembered as a man who polarised opinion, but who was never dull.

Petar Borota, footballer; born Belgrade, Yugoslavia, 5 March 1952; played for OFK Belgrade 1969-75, Partizan Belgrade 1976-79, Chelsea 1979-82, Portimonense 1982-83, Boavista 1983-84; died Genoa, Italy, 12 February 2010.

Charlie Crowe

Charlie Crowe was an effervescent bundle of footballing fervour who gave his all for Newcastle United when the Magpies were a buoyant power in the land during the decade immediately following the Second World War.

The highlight of the diminutive Tynesider's career was helping to lift the FA Cup in 1951, and while he had fallen out of favour temporarily when they recorded a second successive Wembley victory a year later, in 1955 he was selected for their third final in five years, only to cry off through injury.

His death leaves Vic Keeble, Newcastle's centre-forward in that game, as the sole survivor of the famous trio of triumphs, which still stand as the Magpies' most recent successes in major domestic competition.

There was nothing of the artist about Charlie Crowe. Rather he was a defensive wing-half without the slightest pretension to grandeur. He relished the midfield rough-and-tumble, habitually hurling himself into challenges on far brawnier opponents with astonishing gusto, frequently winning the ball against improbable odds and then delivering it, simply and sensibly, to a colleague of more subtle inclinations.

The regular beneficiaries included the left-flank trickster Bobby Mitchell, the pacy and prolific marksman Jackie Milburn and the crafty schemer Ernie Taylor, each one a far more gifted individual than the yeoman Crowe, but each also touchingly eager to acknowledge wholeheartedly the honest and crucial contribution of their doughty provider.

As a character, too, Crowe was widely appreciated. He was warm and witty, full of stories and even inclined to banter with fans during a match, cheerfully fielding enquiries about his beer intake the previous night or what he might have for dinner when he went home.

Once, while doing his National Service at a local colliery, he suffered a slight accident to a finger and soon afterwards, as he took a throw-in, a wag in the crowd roared: 'How's your finger, Charlie?' It became a familiar catchphrase, to be repeated in thunderous unison for several years on the terraces at St James' Park.

Crowe was raised in the working-class district of Walker-on-Tyne, playing his schooldays football for Victoria Jubilee and Newcastle Boys, then stepping up to youth level with Wallsend St Luke's and the Heaton and Byker Boys' Club.

After leaving school in the late 1930s he worked as an office boy for a local shipping company and as a pattern-maker in a factory before turning professional with Newcastle United in 1944, making his first-team entrance in an emergency wartime encounter with Stoke City in September 1945. That day the Magpies triumphed 9-1, with the rookie Crowe shining in direct opposition to Stanley Matthews, the most famous footballer in the world.

His senior debut followed later that season in an FA Cup clash with Barnsley, but then his progress stalled, partially through a succession of niggling injuries. Thus he barely featured as Newcastle were promoted to the top flight as runners-up to Second Division champions Birmingham City in 1947/48, but he ousted Norman Dodgin to become established at left-half in 1949/50, then enjoyed his most successful campaign in 1950/51.

By the spring of that term the Magpies had fashioned a golden opportunity to become the first club in the 20th century to win the League and FA Cup double, but once a place at Wembley was secured, their form fell away disastrously and they finished fourth in the

First Division table. Some believed the players were distracted by the prospect of playing in what was then the biggest game in the football calendar, but certainly the commitment of the ebullient Crowe never seemed to waver.

Come the big day, when Blackpool were the opponents, he was faced once more by the hero Matthews, by now a veteran and seemingly carrying the hopes of every neutral supporter in the land. Totally unfazed, the indefatigable Geordie was hugely instrumental in frustrating the great man, and Crowe's close friend Milburn scored both goals – one of them as spectacular as any witnessed at the stadium, before or since – in a stirring 2-0 victory.

After returning home to a rapturous reception from some 200,000 followers – 'Welcome hyem, canny lads!' proclaimed a banner at Newcastle Central Station – Crowe asked permission to borrow the trophy to show it to some fans. United agreed, assuming the precious silverware would be restored within hours, but he kept it for a two-week tour of Tyneside pubs and clubs, the risky jaunt being discovered only after a picture of Crowe and former Magpies idol Hughie Gallacher displaying the cup near Gateshead was published in the local newspaper.

As he prepared for the next season, the 26-year-old midfield dynamo was looking forward to further success as a member of Stan Seymour's thrilling team, but a rude jolt was in store. Soon he lost his place to Ted Robledo, thus missing out on the 1952 Wembley showpiece, in which Arsenal were beaten 1-0.

At first Crowe was nonplussed and requested a transfer, but Seymour was anxious to keep him, eventually reaching agreement after promising him 100 tickets for the final and a guaranteed berth on that summer's tour of South Africa.

Thereafter Robledo went home to Chile and the local man returned to the line-up, though vying for his place with Irishman Tommy Casey. During 1953/54 he enjoyed a spell as captain following a ballot of the players after regular skipper Jimmy Scoular was injured, and in 1954/55 he returned to something like his best form.

But after the Magpies reached the FA Cup final yet again, Crowe experienced what he described as 'the most disappointing day of my life.' A week before the Wembley meeting with Manchester City, he sprained his ankle during a League clash with Tottenham Hotspur at White Hart Lane. Milburn urged him to play in the final, promising that the rest of the lads would 'carry' him if he broke down – substitutes were not permitted in those days – but he knew that would be unfair on his club, so he withdrew and was replaced by Casey.

Recognising Crowe's devotion, and the major part he had played in getting the Magpies to Wembley, Newcastle struck a special medal for him, which offered some consolation for missing the 3-1 victory and illustrated the esteem in which he rejoiced.

However, in February 1957, aged 32, he was freed to join Mansfield Town, and he thrived briefly at Field Mill, skippering the Stags and earning selection for the Third Division North representative side before injury precipitated his retirement in the summer of 1958.

Later that year he was offered a coaching job back at his beloved St James' Park by new Magpies boss Charlie Mitten, but he rejected the pay on offer and decided to continue guiding the fortunes of non-League Whitley Bay until 1960.

Previously qualified as a coach, Crowe worked for the FA and in 1967 was offered the reins of a club in Cairo, Zamalek, only for the arrangement to be scuppered by an escalation of the Arab-Israeli conflict.

Outside the game, he ran a pub in Longbenton on Tyneside, represented a building firm, was a manager for Scottish and Newcastle Breweries, and finished his working days as an accommodation officer for the DHSS at Longbenton.

He compiled two books, *A Crowe Amongst The Magpies* (1998) and *Charlie Crowe's Newcastle United Scrapbook* (2001), and in 2009, after he had fallen prey to Alzheimer's Disease, they were re-published to raise money for a scanner appeal, spearheaded by his daughter Lesley. The equipment is needed by the Newcastle Magnetic Resonance Centre for research into the illness which claimed the life of one of the best-loved of all Tyneside footballers.

Charles Alfred Crowe, footballer; born Walker, Newcastle-upon-Tyne, 30 October 1924; played for Newcastle United 1944-57, Mansfield Town 1957-58; died North Shields, Tyneside, 27 February 2010.

Adam Blacklaw

Adam Blacklaw was the bold, fearless, sometimes spellbindingly brilliant last-ditch bastion of the Burnley rearguard as the team from the East Lancashire cotton town of around 80,000 inhabitants defied the big-city battalions to lift the Football League championship half a century ago this spring.

When the pressure on the Clarets' goal was at its most intense, the Scottish international goalkeeper appeared to loom larger, seeking to command his entire penalty box, let alone his recognised domain immediately in front of his posts.

A burly six-footer, he would hurl himself into the action, ready to clatter his way through his own defenders as well as opposition attackers, if that's what it took to claim the ball in his capacious hands.

Dependability and consistency were his watchwords – he missed only two League games in six seasons during his pomp, once through an international call-up and once when he was rested ahead of a European Cup tie – but Blacklaw was no mere stolid bulwark. In addition, he offered remarkable agility for such a big man, exceptional reflexes and a sound positional sense which made some of his shrewdest interventions appear deceptively simple.

As a character he was jovial and forthright, excellent for dressing-room morale, which tended to be high anyway during his time at Turf Moor. Quietly inspirational manager Harry Potts fostered, and his players embraced enthusiastically, an indomitable one-for-all-and-all-for-one ethos.

Blacklaw spoke of this team spirit in Tim Quelch's splendid account of the title triumph, *Never Had It So Good* (Know The Score Books, 2009): 'We had no real stars, but we worked hard for each other. If any of us was having an off day, everyone else would dig in even deeper to help him through it. We played for each other – that was the secret of our success.'

In fact, the notion that Potts' side was devoid of stars was debatable, with the sublimely creative Northern Irish inside-forward Jimmy McIlroy, dashing England winger John Connelly and influential wing-half Jimmy Adamson among their number, but the relevance of the togetherness factor was impossible to exaggerate.

The son of a ship's carpenter, Blacklaw grew up playing football on the cobbled streets of Aberdeen and turned out for his home-town's schoolboy team as a bustling centre-forward. But a far-sighted teacher believed he could shine between the sticks, he accepted the advice and soon he was representing Scotland schoolboys and the Banks O' Dee club in his new position.

Talent scouts from a clutch of high-ranking English clubs noted his progress, and in that era before the oil boom he concluded that he would have to leave Scotland to make his living. Leicester City expressed particular interest, but it was little Burnley who prevailed, even though he had no idea where the town was located. Blacklaw turned professional at Turf Moor in 1954, serving an apprenticeship as a bricklayer as insurance against failing to make the grade as a footballer, while honing his skills as a rookie custodian.

At first he had to be patient about making further strides as the Clarets were blessed with one of the finest goalkeepers of the day in Colin McDonald, but eventually, when the England international was injured, the Aberdonian made his senior debut as a 19-year-old in a 6-2 home victory over Cardiff City on a foggy Turf Moor afternoon in December 1956. There followed a lengthy interlude as understudy, but then McDonald, who was nearly seven years Blacklaw's senior, suffered atrocious misfortune, his career ended by a broken leg sustained while playing for the Football League in March 1959.

Now Blacklaw stepped into the breach, performing so securely that he became an automatic selection throughout the most illustrious half-decade in the Clarets' history.

In 1959/60, during which he rose to Scotland under-23 status, he missed only one game as Burnley pipped mighty Wolverhampton Wanderers to the title on the last day of the season. Next came the challenge of the European Cup, and after he did well as the French club, Reims, were overcome, he excelled against the German champions, Hamburg, making one save from Uwe Seeler that was so sensational that the great centre-forward was moved to join in the crowd's rapturous applause.

In 1961/62 Burnley went agonisingly close to emulating Tottenham Hotspur, who had just become the first club during the 20th century to win the League and FA Cup double. They finished as runners-up in the championship race to Alf Ramsey's surprise packet Ipswich Town, then lost 3-1 to Spurs at Wembley.

On the way to that final, Blacklaw had been in wonderful form, notably against Sheffield United at Bramall Lane in the last eight. The game finished 1-0 to Burnley, one of countless narrow victories down the years in which he was as much the match-winner as the men who supplied the goals at the other end.

Like any 'keeper Blacklaw suffered his embarrassments, never more excruciating than when he cannoned a clearance into onrushing Liverpool centre-forward Ian St John during extra-time in a 1963 FA Cup encounter, then pulled down his fellow Scot, thus conceding the penalty which resulted in the Clarets' elimination.

That summer, though, his customary efficiency was rewarded by a full international call, though the occasion was marred for him by a 4-3 defeat by Norway in Bergen, suffered despite a hat-trick from his fellow Aberdonian Denis Law.

There followed appearances against Spain, the 6-2 triumph still Scotland's heaviest away success in Europe, and a 3-0 defeat by Italy in a World Cup qualifier in 1965, his lack of further opportunities proving a mystery to all at Turf Moor.

However, in the spring of that year he had been unseated at club level by his countryman Harry Thomson following a 5-1 reverse at Leeds, and he could never count on his place again, the pair battling for the jersey over the next two campaigns.

Still Blacklaw remained a Burnley loyalist, as he demonstrated when rescuing Thomson, who had just starred in a goalless draw in a bruising European Fairs Cup contest in Napoli in February 1967, from an aggressive opponent at the final whistle.

Blacklaw, once a promising amateur boxer, ended up in a six-man scuffle, throwing one assailant down a flight of steps and being confronted by a gun-toting policeman before finding refuge in the dressing room.

That summer, in his thirtieth year and accepting that he was now in Thomson's shadow, he was transferred to local rivals Blackburn Rovers, performing competently for three Second Division seasons before finishing his League career with a single outing for Blackpool, where once again he found himself vying with Thomson, in October 1970.

Thereafter Blacklaw played for non-League Great Harwood Town, alongside former Blackburn luminaries Ronnie Clayton, Bryan Douglas and Roy Vernon, before managing Clitheroe Town, with whom he once demonstrated his undiminished passion for the game by running on to the pitch to grab the referee.

After leaving professional football, Blacklaw worked as a newsagent in Burnley, as steward of Burnley Cricket Club, ran the Cross Keys pub at Barnoldswick near the town, and had a spell as a caretaker at Nelson and Colne College. In 2009, when dealing with the onset of both Alzheimer's and Motor Neurone Disease, he was delighted to travel to Hampden Park to receive a Scotland cap. Oddly by modern standards, before 1975 the ceremonial headgear was awarded only for British Championship matches, but lobbying by friends secured this much-deserved honour in his 73rd year.

Adam Smith Blacklaw, footballer; born Aberdeen, 2 September 1937; played for Burnley 1954-67, Blackburn Rovers 1967-70, Blackpool 1970; capped three times for Scotland 1963-65; died Barnoldswick, Lancashire, 28 February 2010.

Ken Barnes

The debate about who is the finest of all uncapped English footballers is a futile one, yet it remains irresistible to seasoned observers of the game who combine a whimsical turn of mind with a keen sense of sporting injustice.

Their thoughts might reasonably turn to Manchester United stopper Steve Bruce; to Howard Kendall, the elegant Everton wing-half; to Arsenal's workaholic wingman Geordie Armstrong or, perhaps most persuasively of all, to Jimmy Greenhoff, the silkily subtle Stoke City and Manchester United striker.

But followers of the outstanding Manchester City side of the middle and late 1950s, when the Light Blues reached consecutive FA Cup Finals but tended to be overshadowed by their sparkling neighbours, the Busby Babes, are likely to look no further than Ken Barnes. An imaginative, inventive, boldly adventurous wing-half, the skinny, bandy-legged Barnes represented the heart and the mind of an attractive side of which imposing German goalkeeper Bert Trautmann, powerhouse half-back Roy Paul, deep-thinking attacker Don Revie and skilful inside-forward Bobby Johnstone were the acknowledged stars.

Consumed with passion for football in general and City in particular, he returned later to Maine Road as a scout, working under 17 managers over a 30-year span, during which he spotted millions of pounds worth of talent for the frequently cash-strapped club.

Renowned for his vehement opposition to modern coaching methods, which he blamed for stifling youngsters' flair and freedom of expression, Barnes was a stridently honest, often provocative personality who peppered his sentences with expletives and was nothing loth to excoriate those who held high office.

Directors, most of whom he perceived to be ignorant about the game, were a particular target for his ire, and occasionally he was heard to urge long-time City chairman Peter Swales to 'f*** off, you know nothing about football.' Players past and present, loved him, though, and his office became a revered inner sanctum, a smoke-filled den to which they could retreat and talk, to their hearts' content, about their communal obsession.

As for Barnes' lack of international recognition, his forthright personality might have had more to do with that than any perceived lack of ability on the field. He didn't get on with Walter Winterbottom, the donnish England boss during his 1950s prime, and he was vitriolic in his scorn for the committee which picked the national team.

As it was he veered close to selection, making three appearances for an FA XI against forces sides, being a reserve for the Football League in 1957 and actually being called up for another League encounter, only to miss the game with a broken toe.

The son of a railway worker, Barnes was born at Small Heath, almost in the shadow of St Andrew's, the headquarters of Birmingham City. Mad about football from early childhood, he played constantly in the surrounding streets, then almost completely free of cars, and revealed exceptional natural ability, joining Moor Green, the Midlands' top amateur club, when he was 15.

There followed junior appearances with both Birmingham and Bolton Wanderers, but after working for the Post Office assembling switchboard components for less than £1 a week, then completing his National Service as a storeman at RAF Stafford in the late 1940s, he surprised friends and family by signing for Stafford Rangers.

Predictably for such a gifted performer, Barnes flourished for his non-League employers, and after being courted by a posse of leading clubs, he joined Manchester City as a 21-year-old in a £900 deal in May 1950.

At Maine Road, however, he faced fierce competition for a senior berth and played in only one League game in his first four seasons. He did well on that debut outing in January 1952, but he was dropped immediately afterwards and asked for a move, spending several months on the transfer list.

Being held back behind rivals of inferior ability proved monumentally frustrating for the voluble, sociable Barnes, who never gelled with manager Les McDowall, a remote figure who held himself aloof from the banter which the wing-half relished.

The turning point arrived by accident when inside-forward Johnny Williamson, playing as centre-forward for the reserves, drifted into a deep-lying role, taking on creative duties alongside Barnes and dragging the opposing defenders out of position.

This was a ploy soon to be used successfully by the superlative Hungarian international side and in August 1954 McDowall had City's first team trying it, with Don Revie as the withdrawn spearhead. However, the system flopped until Revie told the manager, with some asperity, that Barnes was needed to make it work. Duly the Midlander was promoted, with gratifying results, and he remained as arguably the key component of the side for the next seven years.

At last, given the responsibility his talent merited, the 25-year-old Barnes was revealed in his full glory. He wasn't much of a tackler, he was ineffective in the air, he used his left foot for little more than standing on and defending was not his forte, but in every other respect he was a footballing thoroughbred.

His prime instinct was to get the ball down and pass it, which he did with vision, perception and consistent accuracy. The timing of his missives, often squeezed through gaps in opposing rearguards which barely existed, was exquisite, which made him a dream to play alongside.

Barnes wasn't pacy but he could run forever, and such was his enthusiasm for swashbuckling attack that sometimes he would gallop forward even when the other side had possession; then, when City won the ball back, he would be free and in space to make mayhem with his destructive skills.

Before long it became apparent that when Barnes played well, then City played well, which they did throughout most of 1954/55, when they finished seventh in the old First Division and reached the FA Cup final. Throughout that run Barnes was irrepressible, never more so than in the third-round defeat of Derby County when he notched his first goal for the club, carrying the ball from one penalty box to the other before netting with a clever shot. At Wembley City lost 3-1 to Newcastle United, conceding a goal in the first minute and losing full-back Jimmy Meadows to injury, a crippling blow in the days before substitutes were allowed.

Undaunted, they bounced back even stronger in 1955/56, even nursing turn-of-the-year ambitions to become the first team in the 20th century to win the League and FA Cup double. In the event they finished a creditable fourth in the First Division table, well adrift of champions Manchester United, but triumphed in the knockout competition, then far more prestigious than it is today, beating Birmingham City 3-1 at Wembley.

Barnes was prominent in that victory, uncharacteristically devoting the first period to subduing the dangerous Peter Murphy, but then surging forward to launch a series of devastating second-half raids which carried the day.

It was a match which entered football folklore for the heroic exploits of goalkeeper Trautmann, the former German paratrooper and prisoner-of-war, who played the last 17 minutes with a broken neck, although the full horror of his injury was not realised for several days.

Everyone connected with Manchester City expected the lifting of the trophy to be a platform for sustained achievement. Instead it proved a pinnacle, and soon began a slide into collective mediocrity – the result of top players moving on and not being adequately replaced – which was not mirrored by Barnes' continued excellence.

Made captain after the departure of Roy Paul in 1957, he remained a dynamic presence, driving or cajoling the men around him depending on their characters, all the time ruing the creeping decline. Still, there were highlights, such as his hat-trick of smoothly stroked penalties against Everton in December 1957 and, best of all, the productive link he forged with the coruscatingly brilliant inside-forward Denis Law, signed from Huddersfield Town in March 1960.

By then the club's senior professional, 'Beaky' Barnes – so dubbed for his aquiline profile – took the young Scottish star under his wing, teaching him to drive and helping him to settle into big-city life.

In May 1961, approaching the veteran stage and with nearly 300 senior appearances behind him, Barnes moved to Wrexham as player-boss and led the Welsh side to promotion from the Fourth Division at his first attempt. However, they were relegated two years later, and his increasing lack of diplomacy with directors made his dismissal virtually inevitable; duly the sack arrived in February 1965.

That traumatic experience decided him he wasn't cut out for League management and he rejected the overtures of Rochdale to become a sales representative for a steel company.

The siren call of football proved irresistible, though, and in 1965 he became player-boss of non-League Witton Albion while selling insurance by day, then took the reins of Bangor City before succumbing to his heart's desire by returning to Maine Road in 1970.

This time he had been persuaded by Manchester City chief Joe Mercer to look after the club's reserves, which led to a further three decades of service to the Light-Blue cause, much of it as chief scout. During that roller-coaster period for City, in which their fortunes lurched repeatedly and often melodramatically between joy and despair, Barnes was irrepressible, his enthusiasm, wisdom, irreverent humour and spiky refusal to bow the knee to self-important officialdom proving an inspiration, no matter how turbulent the times. He was ousted twice, temporarily by Peter Reid in 1992 and finally by Joe Royle in 2000, but remained a Maine Road institution, one of the most influential figures in the club's history.

Barnes, whose son Peter was a mercurially brilliant winger – starring for City, playing for many other clubs and winning 22 England caps between 1977 and 1982 – co-operated with broadcaster Jimmy Wagg in the publication of his life story in 2005.

On the cover of *This Simple Game* was the appropriate warning that it contained explicit language. For all that, it was a warm, thought-provoking memoir in which the home truths directed at the deluded men who complicate his beloved football were far more compelling than the sprinkle of profanities.

Kenneth Herbert Barnes, footballer: born Birmingham, 16 March 1929; played for Manchester City 1950-61, Wrexham 1961-65; managed Wrexham 1961-65; died 13 July 2010.

Brian Clark

The sublime header which condemned Real Madrid to a shock defeat by Cardiff City in a European quarter-final stands as the shimmering pinnacle of Brian Clark's career.

Yet certainly in terms of glamour and publicity, it offered a vivid contrast to his routine experience as a courageous and supremely dedicated striker who served six Football League clubs, totalling 220 goals in more than 600 appearances throughout the 1960s and 1970s.

Clark was always going to play the game for a living, following in the footsteps of his father, Don, who had been a prolific marksman for Bristol City in the seasons immediately after the Second World War. Having skippered an exceptional Bristol Boys team in the late 1950s, the sharp-shooting 17-year-old enlisted at Ashton Gate in the spring of 1960, making his senior debut a year later.

For another season Clark burnished his skills in the reserves before making a sustained breakthrough in 1962/63, forming a potent dual spearhead with the former England centre-forward and local folk hero John Atyeo. With Bobby 'Shadow' Williams completing an inside trio of immense enterprise, it was disappointing that Fred Ford's side wallowed in mid-table in the old Third Division, but that didn't obscure Clark's eye-catching personal progress.

That term he topped City's scoring chart, netting 26 times in all senior competitions and becoming a crowd favourite, not only for his goals but also for his unselfish and fearless approach. Standing just under six feet tall and sturdily built, the blond Bristolian was adept at shielding the ball under intense physical pressure, though he wasn't overtly aggressive, which would have been alien to an essentially amiable nature.

Clark was a glutton for sustained toil, which made him a perfect foil for the ageing but still mightily effective Atyeo, and he was a deft passer of the ball, excelling at quickfire interchanges with his classy partner. Best of all, he was a fine finisher, powerful in the air just like his father, and packing a savage shot in either foot.

Inevitably, as the decade wore on and the goals continued to flow, Clark was the subject of transfer talk – a possible £35,000 switch to top-flight West Bromwich Albion was mentioned – but nothing came of it, nor did he receive the England under-23 recognition which many observers believed was the least he deserved.

For the Robins, though, he continued to thrive, top-scoring as they earned promotion to the second flight in 1964/65, he and Atyeo both registering in the climactic last-day home victory over Oldham Athletic, and then doing well as City finished a creditable fifth in their first season at the higher level.

But then came a lean spell at the outset of 1966/67 and manager Ford dismayed the majority of the Ashton Gate faithful by dispatching the 23-year-old to Huddersfield Town in exchange for veteran Scottish schemer Johnny Quigley and £2,500.

The easy-going West Countryman never really settled in Yorkshire and after only 16 months with the second-tier Terriers he was sold to Cardiff City of the same division for £8,000 in February 1968. At Ninian Park he blossomed anew, registering twice on his debut in a 4-3 victory at Derby, averaging a goal a game for his first six outings, and striking up a productive front-line understanding with the young John Toshack.

Meanwhile the Bluebirds flirted with material improvement, particularly in 1970/71 when they finished third in the table, only three points off a promotion place, though that term was most significant for the European Cup Winners' Cup campaign for which they had qualified by lifting the Welsh Cup. With Clark a pillar of the attack, especially after the mid-season departure of Toshack to Liverpool, City cruised past Larnaca of Cyprus and the French club, Nantes, before confronting Real Madrid in the last eight.

Though given little hope outside the Principality, they confounded the Spanish thoroughbreds in the first leg at Ninian Park, with Clark's adroit nod, from a cross by rookie winger Nigel Rees, securing a 1-0 win which was greeted tumultuously by the 47,500 supporters who had crammed into the ground.

A 2-0 reverse in the second leg at the Bernabeu saw them eliminated, but they had fought bravely and Clark's goal became the second most famous in Cardiff's history, behind Hughie Ferguson's winner against Arsenal in the 1927 FA Cup final.

In 1971/72, during which the Bristolian was City's leading scorer for the third successive term, the team fell away badly, avoiding demotion only narrowly, but still it came as a surprise when he was sold to Third Division Bournemouth, valued at £70,000 in a package deal which also took midfielder Ian Gibson to Dean Court in October 1972. However, he didn't tarry on the south coast, switching to second-flight Millwall in September 1973 before returning to Cardiff in May 1975, assisting the Bluebirds' rise from the Third Division a year later.

There remained a two-and-a-half-year sojourn as a part-timer with Fourth Division Newport County, while working as a sales representative for a firm selling industrial safety equipment, before Clark retired from League football, somewhat battered physically but eternally cheerful, in his mid-thirties in 1978.

Later he served as player-manager with non-League Maesteg, AFC Cardiff and Bridgend Town, still displaying the same combination of big-hearted commitment and estimable expertise that had stunned Real Madrid all those years earlier.

Brian Donald Clark, footballer; born Bristol, 13 January 1943; played for Bristol City 1960-66, Huddersfield Town 1966-68, Cardiff City 1968-72 and 1975-76, Bournemouth 1972-73, Millwall 1973-75, Newport County 1976-78; died Cardiff, 9 August 2010.

Jackie Sinclair

Scottish international Jackie Sinclair was that rare and cherished footballing commodity, a winger who could be counted on to score plenty of goals. At least, that was the case during the mid-1960s with Dunfermline Athletic and Leicester City, for whom the effervescent little Fifer found the net on average once every two games, a ratio of which even the majority of specialist strikers would have been justly proud.

Yet perplexingly, after he joined Newcastle United as a 24-year-old seemingly on the threshold of his prime in December 1967, the Sinclair tally nosedived dramatically. However, he did play an influential role in lifting the European Fairs Cup, which remains the perennially under-achieving Magpies' only front-line trophy in more than half a century.

Brimming with brio and self-belief, Sinclair was, at his best, a direct and penetrating raider capable of flourishing on either flank. He could accelerate explosively over short distances, his characteristic high-velocity darts a potent menace to the most organised of rearguards. In addition, he was plucky and industrious, he could reach the byline and then cross or cut inside with equal facility, and he possessed a stinging shot in either foot.

As a boy he shone for a local amateur side, Blairhall Colliery, before becoming one of the first recruits for Dunfermline Athletic by a rookie manager called Jock Stein, who was destined one day to guide Celtic to the game's most exalted peaks.

Sinclair signed professional forms shortly after his 17th birthday in the summer of 1960 and lost little time in making his senior debut before returning to the reserves to hone his craft. His first major impact came with two goals in a home victory over Airdrie in November 1961, after which he matured rapidly under the inspirational Stein, emerging as a key performer in the Pars' most glorious era to date.

In 1962/63 Sinclair starred in a remarkable fightback from a 4-0 first-leg Fairs Cup deficit against Valencia, netting twice as Dunfermline triumphed 6-2 at East End Park, only to lose 1-0 in the subsequent play-off.

But his finest campaign was 1964/65, in which he scored 20 times under new boss Willie Cunningham and set up countless opportunities for a promising centre-forward named Alex Ferguson as the Pars finished only a point adrift of League champions Kilmarnock, and lost 3-2 to Celtic in the final of the Scottish Cup.

That was enough to secure the dynamic 21-year-old, who had netted 33 times in 61 League outings, a £25,000 move to Leicester City, then a significant power in the English top flight.

After scoring in his first match for the Foxes, a 3-1 home reverse to Liverpool, the diminutive Sinclair forged an occasionally comical-looking but superbly effective pairing with the lanky Irish striker Derek Dougan which was hugely instrumental in City remaining entrenched in the top half of the First Division for the next two seasons. To the surprise of many, it was the Scot who top-scored in both campaigns, returning 22 and 21 goals respectively and missing only a single game in the process.

It was during this bountiful interlude that Sinclair earned his only full cap, when Portugal visited Hampden Park as part of their warm-up for the 1966 World Cup finals in England. Eusebio and company prevailed 1-0, but Sinclair had done enough to earn selection for Scotland's next game, against Brazil, only to be forced out through injury.

He continued to thrive at club level, though, and most Leicester fans were nonplussed in December 1967 when the flankman who had notched 50 goals in 103 appearances was sold to top-flight rivals Newcastle for £67,500. In those days that was a sizeable sum, but as he had been on target to top the club's scoring charts for the third term in succession, it appeared to be a perverse decision by his fellow Scot, manager Matt Gillies.

Still only 24, Sinclair was expected to light up Tyneside as a prolific foil for marksmen such as Wyn Davies and Bryan 'Pop' Robson, but somehow the chemistry was not quite there. The 5ft 6in attacker remained a thrustful competitor, but he seemed less inclined to shoot than in his Filbert Street days, and sometimes he found it difficult to resist pressure for his place from rivals such as Jim Scott and Alan Foggon.

Still, nothing could detract from Sinclair's sparky contribution to the Fairs Cup triumph of 1968/69, during which he scored in the 2-0 aggregate victory over Rangers in the semi-final, then performed brightly in the final, in which the Hungarian side Ujpest Dozsa were bested 6-2 over the two legs.

Thereafter he failed to do himself justice at St James' Park and in December 1969 he moved to Sheffield Wednesday in exchange for striker David Ford. At Hillsborough Sinclair competed manfully in a poor team which was relegated that spring, and which never rose above mediocrity in the Second Division over the next three campaigns.

Thus it was hardly surprising when he was loaned to third-tier Chesterfield in the spring of 1973, then spent a brief stint with Durban in South Africa before returning to his first League club, Dunfermline, that August. Though 30 by then, he brought much-needed experience to a Pars squad which only narrowly avoided demotion in both of the next two seasons. There followed a final term with second-flight Stenhousemuir in 1975/76 before he left the League, later working for the National Coal Board, Stirling University and Dunfermline Golf Club.

Sinclair, whose older brother Willie played professionally on both sides of the Scottish border, and whose uncle, the Scottish international Tommy Wright, served Sunderland in the 1950s, continued to maintain a close interest in the game, not least because his son Chris played for four Scottish clubs, including Dunfermline, for whom he featured in the 1991/92 Scottish League Cup final. The family love affair with football was reflected also by his cousin, another Tommy Wright, who appeared for Leicester and five other clubs in the 1980s and 1990s.

John Evens Wright Sinclair, footballer; born Culross, Fife, 21 July 1943; played for Dunfermline Athletic 1961-65 and 1973-75, Leicester City 1965-68, Newcastle United 1968-69, Sheffield Wednesday 1969-73, Chesterfield on loan 1973, Stenhousemuir 1975-76; capped once by Scotland 1966; died 2 September 2010.

Bobby Smith

Bustling buccaneer or crude, uncomely battering ram? Both descriptions of Tottenham Hotspur and England centre-forward Bobby Smith might carry persuasive weight with those who saw the beefy, rampaging spearhead in his early 1960s prime, but arguably the truth was rather more complimentary than either of them.

While hardly renowned for his delicacy, and though his on-field demeanour ran a vast gamut between tempestuous aggression and flat-footed indolence, the ebullient Smith could treat a football with unexpected subtlety and his positioning, when he was on his game, was sharply intelligent.

Those underrated attributes apart, he merited vast credit for his sheer bravery, often taking the pitch with severely swollen ankles, the legacy of past conflicts. Smith soaked up constant painful punishment, but he was willing to dish it out, too, frequently creating physical mayhem on which more artistic colleagues capitalised heavily.

To snooty critics who recognised that the broad-shouldered son of a Yorkshire miner had his uses, but wailed about his perceived lack of class, he had the perfect answer. In his first five years at White Hart Lane he became the top goal-scorer in Spurs' history at that time, and it was a fact that Bill Nicholson's beautifully fluent side, the first in the 20th century to win the coveted League and FA Cup double, was never more effective than when Bobby Smith was at the vanguard of its attack.

He grew up in the close-knit mining community of Lingdale, and after leaving school he started work in the local pit as an apprentice blacksmith, shoeing the ponies which pulled the wagons of coal, a life of toil to which his bull-like build appeared to be ideally suited. At that point a career in football, which he played purely for recreation, appeared to be the remotest of possibilities, but the game was to provide an unexpected escape route.

In his early teens Smith was a prodigiously strong but otherwise unremarkable full-back with Redcar Boys. Then one day the team's centre-forward didn't turn up for a game, the rookie anvilman volunteered to replace him in the front line and he scored twice in a 3-2 victory. Thereafter he never played in defence again, impressing so vividly as leader of the line that he was recruited as an amateur by Chelsea in 1948.

Still, though, there were obstacles to be overcome. At first the young Yorkshireman felt homesick in London and he returned to Lingdale after a month. His father, anxious that the boy should avoid a lifetime of drudgery in the pit, was not unduly sympathetic, hurrying him back to Stamford Bridge with the imprecation that he should show Chelsea what he was made of.

So he did, turning professional in 1950 and graduating to the Pensioners' First Division line-up as a 17-year-old in September, his seven goals in 16 games helping to preserve the struggling Londoners' top-flight status that term.

However, even after the ambitious Ted Drake replaced Billy Birrell as manager in 1952, Chelsea continued to dice with relegation and, while fitting his football around two years' National Service as a storeman for the Army's medical corps, Smith found it hard to become established. In the circumstances, his 23 goals in 74 League outings for the club was hardly a risible return and there was one memorable performance which staggered pundits who tended to write him off as just another blunt instrument. In an FA Cup replay against Leeds United at Villa Park in March 1952 he plundered a magnificent hat-trick, one of his strikes involving a mesmeric dribble past the brilliant John Charles.

By mid-decade, though, with the youthful Chelsea combination known as Drake's Ducklings having metamorphosed from weedy under-achievers to League champions (in 1955), Smith was languishing in the shadow of the far more stylish Roy Bentley and he didn't play enough games to earn a title medal.

With his prospects thus dimmed, he accepted an £18,000 transfer to Tottenham in December 1955, settling initially into Jimmy Anderson's rather lacklustre team at inside-left and suffering cruel terrace jibes that he was a mere carthorse. Still, he performed creditably in the number-ten shirt, supplying goals which lifted Spurs clear of the demotion zone by the end of that campaign, but it was when he replaced veteran Len Duquemin at centre-forward that Smith truly blossomed as a free-scoring spearhead.

Over the next five years at White Hart Lane he ran amok, notching seasonal totals in all senior competition of 19, 38, 35, 30 and 33, and eclipsing the club record set by George Hunt in the 1930s.

In 1956/57, at the business end of a vastly improved attack prompted by the creative midfield duo of Danny Blanchflower and Tommy Harmer, Smith excelled as Tottenham finished as title runners-up to Manchester United and supporters who had ridiculed him previously now took him to their hearts.

A dazzling highlight of the following season was a hat-trick against the Busby Babes at Old Trafford, shortly before that wondrous young team was devastated by the Munich air disaster, and his exemplary personal form even survived the dip in the club's fortunes which saw them sink to 18th place in the League table in 1958/59.

With new manager Bill Nicholson having commenced his inspirational rebuilding of the side, Spurs rose to third place in 1959/60 – Smith was exceedingly hard on himself in declaring that his brief springtime scoring drought cost his side the championship – but in 1960/61, everything gelled as Tottenham became the first club in the 20th century to complete the League and FA Cup double.

Clever schemers Blanchflower and John White, dynamic wing-half Dave Mackay and Cliff Jones, one of the world's most penetrative wingers, attracted most of the plaudits, but Smith's bountiful input deserved every bit as much recognition. The team flowed exquisitely, but without the doughty warhead at the end of their sumptuous moves, all those intricate skills would have been wasted.

Occasionally, too, the former blacksmith supplied his own moments of enchanting footwork, such as the deft flick and unerring volley which undermined chief challengers Sheffield Wednesday during the title run-in. His strike in the FA Cup final victory over Leicester City was an underrated gem, too, needing as it did a wily dummy to gull a marker, a sure touch to control the ball and a coolly dispatched shot. There was a similar goal as Spurs retained their trophy at Wembley against Burnley a year later, but arguably the sweetest finish of his life was a delectable chip for England against Spain at Wembley in October 1960, an effort which made a mockery of his so-called clumsiness.

Smith's international career had started only a month earlier with a goal against Northern Ireland, and he netted in his first five games for his country, being part of coach Walter Winterbottom's exhilarating 1960/61 combination. He led a fabulous forward line which also included Bryan Douglas and Bobby Charlton on the flanks and inside-forwards Jimmy Greaves and Johnny Haynes, but they peaked between World Cup tournaments, thus not threatening to lift the game's top prize.

Indeed, Smith had little luck where the World Cup was concerned, not playing a game after travelling to the 1958 tournament in Sweden and narrowly missing selection for the Chile competiton four years later, though his record of 13 goals in 15 England outings suggests that he was treated harshly.

Back at club level, having been joined at White Hart Lane by the even more prolific Greaves during 1961/62, and with the worthy Les Allen still on the scene, Smith found that his place was not always inviolate. However, the canny Nicholson tended to use him for the biggest games, for which he had an instinct.

Thus he remained a major figure as Spurs became the first British winners of a major European trophy, thrashing Atletico Madrid 5-1 in Rotterdam to lift the Cup Winners' Cup in 1963. But in May 1964, aged 31 and increasingly ponderous for the top flight, he was replaced as Greaves' partner by the young Frank Saul and transferred to Fourth Division Brighton for a peppercorn £5,000 fee.

Always a relaxed character – he had been judged too easy-going to captain Tottenham following a trial in the job during the late 1950s – Smith was an habitual frequenter of racecourses and dog-tracks who had not provided handsomely for the time when he would have to leave the game.

As a poignant result, he departed White Hart Lane aggrieved by his lack of funds, and when reminded of his glittering achievements as a Spur, he declared bitterly that memories would never pay his bills.

It sounded ominously like the end of the road, but there was one more footballing hurrah left in the former idol. When Brighton announced his arrival at the Goldstone Ground, the sales of season tickets soared and more than 20,000 fans packed the stadium for the season's opener against Barrow.

Smith responded regally with two goals in a 3-1 win, then struck another 17 as the Seagulls went on to become the 1964/65 Fourth Division champions. Not only was he a regular scorer, but also he proved himself a play-maker, too, his experienced promptings helping five team-mates to reach double figures as more than a century of goals were racked up by manager Archie Macaulay's enterprising side.

Now a productive Indian summer seemed possible, but it was not to be. Smith, always a bulky individual, reported back for pre-season training weighing 15 stone, and was suspended for two weeks while he lost a stone. Once the confrontational tone had been set, the situation deteriorated rapidly and soon he was sacked for breaking club rules by contributing articles to a newspaper.

After that he moved into non-League circles, serving first Hastings United and then Banbury United, but his weight ballooned and, away from football, he hit hard times.

While working as a painter and decorator he fell down a manhole and suffered a serious foot injury, and he was troubled increasingly by old football wounds. There followed a series of labouring and driving jobs, nothing steady, and his periodic financial hardship was exacerbated by betting unwisely. As Smith himself put it, he spent too many of his post-football days ducking, diving and gambling, and though he offered a cheerful front at dinners and other functions, much of his retirement was spent in regretting his profligacy during his glorious pomp with Spurs and England.

Robert Alfred Smith, footballer; born Skelton, Yorkshire, 22 February 1933; played for Chelsea 1950-55, Tottenham Hotspur 1955-64, Brighton and Hove Albion 1964-65; capped 15 times by England 1960-63; died Enfield, Middlesex, 18 September 2010.

Eddie Baily

Eddie Baily personified both the quicksilver style and the exuberant soul of the Tottenham Hotspur side which lifted the Second and First Division titles in successive football seasons midway through the 20th century.

A nimble and imaginative inside-forward blessed with assured mastery over a moving ball, the loquacious little Londoner was a gleeful executioner of Arthur Rowe's push-and-run method, exemplifying the manager's catchphrase of 'make it simple, make it quick'.

But it was not only Baily's one-touch wizardry which made him a darling of the White Hart Lane faithful during the first decade after the Second World War. They embraced him, too, for the infectious warmth of his personality – his tendency to cavort with untrammelled joy on scoring a goal or to clutch his head in despair at a missed opportunity was novel in an era when few players were prone to extravagant displays of public emotion.

With his heart on his sleeve, the club's distinctive cockerel crest on his chest and, frequently, a colourful profanity on his lips, the 5ft 7in midfield general radiated pride in the Tottenham cause, and he was a key constituent of the social cement which bonded the team spirit of Rowe's exhilarating creation.

An outstanding performer as a schoolboy, Baily was snapped up by Spurs as an amateur and sent to develop his game with non-League Finchley, then being used by the north Londoners as a nursery club.

During the war he served with the Royal Scots Fusiliers and although he emerged unscathed from the conflict, news filtered back to White Hart Lane that he was missing in action. Thus his registration was allowed to lapse.

On returning to civvy street, hearing nothing from Tottenham and unaware of the administrative bungle, the disappointed Baily, fresh from excelling for the British Army team on the Rhine, was still determined to forge a career in football and signed amateur forms for Chelsea.

The misunderstanding was revealed only after he dropped into the Spurs ground to meet a friend, after which the Stamford Bridge club, reacting with impeccable honour, released him from his obligation, and in February 1946 he was back at the Lane.

By now in his early twenties, he progressed rapidly, soon turning professional and making his senior debut at inside-left in the home Second Division encounter with West Bromwich Albion in January 1947. Manager Joe Hulme did not offer him a regular place until the following autumn, but thereafter he was a fixture in a promising side which didn't take flight fully until Rowe became boss in May 1949.

Under his enlightened guidance Tottenham romped to the Second Division crown in the next campaign, with Baily a prominent factor in the success. Meshing effectively with the dynamic, prodigiously strong wing-half and captain Ron Burgess, and striking up a productive left-wing partnership with underrated flankman Les Medley, the diminutive play-maker was at the hub of a free-flowing, hugely entertaining unit.

Oozing flair and football intelligence, he was a distributor both perceptive and precise, and the quickness of mind was matched by fleetness of foot, his sudden bursts of acceleration often startling opponents who were expecting a trademark pass.

He was a goal-scorer, too, packing a shot in either foot that was remarkably powerful for such a small fellow, the secret of his high-velocity dispatches being down to exquisite timing rather than brute force. Indeed, Baily was not a hard man in the physical sense – barnstorming tackles were left mainly to the irrepressible Burgess – but he was a relentless and voluble competitor whose animated imprecations to team-mates were frequently discernible above the roar of the crowd.

In 1950, deservedly, his excellence at club level earned international recognition, with three outings for England 'B' followed by a full call-up for the World Cup finals in Brazil that summer.

Fortunately for Baily, he was not selected for the confrontation with the United States, which ended in a humiliating 1-0 defeat in Belo Horizonte, but afterwards he helped to lift the party's morale with his quips for every occasion and by leading a consolation sing-song at the team hotel.

Three days later he was handed his first cap, being preferred to the immensely gifted Wilf Mannion for the clash with Spain, in which he performed creditably but was unable to prevent another 1-0 reverse and elimination from the tournament.

He had done his prospects no harm, however, and went on to make nine appearances for his country over the next two years, scoring five goals, including two each in successive matches against Northern Ireland and Wales.

Thus it was frustrating when he was discarded at the age of 26, on the threshold of his prime, though still he was considered worthy of representing England against Young England, a game for which caps were not awarded, in mid-decade.

Happily, as a Spur, Baily continued to make a mammoth contribution, shining as Rowe's team lifted the League championship in 1950/51, their first season back in the premier flight, and finished as runners-up to Manchester United in 1951/52.

That term, when Tottenham entertained lowly Huddersfield Town, he was at the centre of a controversial incident which caused a national sporting debate. With the scoreline blank, Baily took a corner, the ball slamming into the referee and knocking him flat. It bounced back to the inside-forward, who crossed for spearhead Len Duquemin to nod the only goal of the game, which was wrongly allowed to stand by the official, perhaps still collecting his wits after his fall.

The rules state that another player must touch the ball before the taker can make contact again, and the ensuing furore was magnified by the circumstance that the decision affected both top and bottom of the table. There were even calls for a replay, but they were rejected by the Football League. In the end Spurs finished four points adrift of the champions and Huddersfield were relegated by a margin of three, so there were no major consequences. Baily, of course, was innocent of any wrongdoing, but it amused him greatly and he recalled the incident with hilarity for many years afterwards.

Over the next few seasons, though Baily remained a force, the team declined into mid-table mediocrity as Rowe fell ill and influential figures such as Burgess, full-back Alf Ramsey (destined to lead England to World Cup glory in 1966) and wing-half Bill Nicholson (who would be at the Tottenham helm as they won the League and FA Cup double in 1961) reached the veteran stage.

In January 1956, aged 30 and with more than 300 appearances for Spurs behind him, Baily was sold to Port Vale for £6,000, then moved on to fellow Second Division club Nottingham Forest nine months later.

He made a slow start at the City Ground, but he remained a classy operator and helped secure promotion to the top flight in 1956/57 before going on to end his playing days with Leyton Orient, whom he assisted in their escape from relegation to the third tier in 1958/59. After playing his final game in October 1959, he became a coach at Brisbane Road, participating in their rise to the First Division in 1962 before, following the Os' first-time demotion, returning to White Hart Lane as assistant manager to Nicholson in October 1963.

Baily re-entered the Spurs story just as the great double-winning side was beginning to break up, and he strove passionately alongside his former team-mate to ensure that the club remained a potent power. Thus his was a telling voice as Tottenham won the FA Cup in 1967, then the League Cup in 1971 and 1973, and reached the 1974 UEFA Cup final.

The Baily style of motivation was not a tranquil one, and he upset many an expensive charge by his sometimes near-hysterical raving on the training pitch or from the bench, but there was a general acceptance that every high-decibel rant was delivered with the good of Tottenham Hotspur at heart.

When Nicholson left following a sequence of poor results in the autumn of 1974 – surprising many by his exit at the age of 55, but not those privy to his disenchantment with modern trends in football – Baily went too, the Spurs board not heeding the departing manager's advice that they should appoint his assistant in his place.

Briefly Baily found work as a football and cricket coach at a school in Enfield, and did some talent-hunting for Chelsea before becoming chief scout with West Ham United.

It was a role in which he both revelled and excelled, one of his most memorable coups being the procurement of future England international Alan Devonshire from non-League Southall for £5,000.

He retired in 1992, much honoured at Upton Park, still revered at White Hart Lane, the last surviving regular member of Arthur Rowe's lovely side.

Edward Francis Baily, footballer; born Clapton, London, 6 August 1925; played for Tottenham Hotspur 1946-56, Port Vale 1956, Nottingham Forest 1956-58, Leyton Orient 1958-59; won nine England caps 1950-52; died Welwyn Garden City, Hertfordshire, 13 October 2010.

Malcolm Allison

Brian Clough called him 'the Errol Flynn of football, who was too handsome for his own good.' Don Revie dismissed him as 'an embarrassment to the game.' Yet despite the drinking, the gambling and the womanising — his lovers included Christine Keeler, the woman at the heart of the Profumo scandal — Malcolm Allison was arguably the finest, deepest thinking and most innovative soccer coach England has known.

'Big Mal' offered plenty of evidence on that score during a sublime partnership with Joe Mercer at Manchester City in the late 1960s and early 1970s. When they were together, with Mercer's wisdom and maturity moderating the excesses of his charming but headstrong protege, almost everything they touched turned to gold.

But subsequently, when Allison launched his own career as a boss, the Midas touch was reversed dramatically, providing ammunition for those who reckoned the flamboyant, impetuous swashbuckler was among the worst man-managers of modern times.

He could be ruthless, was boorish at times and was possessed of a cruel tongue when riled, yet Allison was honest and generous, and blessed with a messiah-like knack of inspiring loyalty, even love, among his followers.

But what made him special, at least in sporting terms, was his visionary ability to communicate his creed of positive football to the young men in his charge. When everything else was stripped away, when the cares and responsibilities of high office took second place to his pure passion for his calling, Malcolm Allison was magnificent.

The son of a Bexleyheath electrician, he signed for Charlton Athletic as an amateur in 1944, returning to play in earnest after National Service, which began a year later. However, there was to be no breakthrough at The Valley for the stylish and outspoken young centre half, who was disgusted by what he saw as the club's outdated coaching methods, and said so.

Not surprisingly, perhaps, he played only two League games before departing to West Ham United in February 1951, where he became a first-team regular for the next six years. Throughout that period, Allison's obsession with coaching took hold, fostered by his attendance of summer courses held by England manager Walter Winterbottom, and his conviction grew that Continental-type tactics and reliance on skill had the edge over more basic traditional British methods. He became the fulcrum of a 'brains trust' of senior Hammers, who would meet daily in a cafe near the ground to debate and theorise over the game; many of that group – including John Bond, Frank O'Farrell, Noel Cantwell and Dave Sexton – went on to become managers.

But it was Allison who stood out as the most rebellious, forever questioning the existing order, while impressing club manager Ted Fenton enough to be allowed input into training sessions. That West Ham side, renowned for its thoughtful, almost scientific approach, won promotion to the First Division in 1958; but Allison was to miss out on a medal, having lost a lung to tuberculosis at the age of 29. Thus he was forced into premature retirement, having never played a game in the top flight.

Later he was to declare that the only time in his life that he suffered illness was when, in his playing prime, he went early to bed and didn't concern himself unduly with drinking, smoking and women. His reaction on recovering from TB was to 'at least give myself a reason for being sick' by embarking on a series of wild sprees.

Now Allison's whole lifestyle changed. He became immersed in betting to the extent that he spent two years as a professional gambler. Then followed a brief and unsuccessful spell as a car salesman and a time-marking, booze-soaked period running a nightclub off London's Charing Cross Road. Fortunately, both for his own health and for the contemporary soccer scene, his addiction to the game was to reclaim him.

Against medical advice, Allison found himself unable to resist playing for non-League Romford, and from that followed coaching work with Cambridge University and Sutton United. As he became re-established, so his name began to be considered for various jobs, and in April 1963 he became manager of the Southern League club Bath City.

Allison enjoyed himself in the refined surroundings of the Georgian city, and did well enough to land the boss's seat at Second Division Plymouth Argyle a year later. His new responsibilities were discharged with a characteristic swagger, but with mixed results. He brought in a wave of youngsters and although League form was patchy, there was the consolation of a League Cup semi-final appearance. However, differences arose with the board, who wanted to interfere in team selection and disapproved of his lifestyle, and he was sacked after a year.

A few months later Allison accepted the most important job of his life, working alongside Joe Mercer at Manchester City. The wily, experienced Mercer was not in the best of health and needed a bright young thing at his shoulder, while Allison was bursting with ambition and ideas, but required a restraining hand. It was a partnership forged in heaven.

Their new club was in a woeful state, marooned in the Second Division and overshadowed depressingly by their all-conquering neighbours, Matt Busby's United. They knew City possessed vast potential, however, and set about effecting a transformation – with immediate success.

New players were acquired and at the end of the management duo's first season at Maine Road, the Blues were Second Division champions. They consolidated their berth among the elite during 1966/67 and then – joy of joys – pipped none other than United for the League title in 1967/68. The side, which starred the gifted forward trio of Francis Lee, Colin Bell and Mike Summerbee, played exciting, flowing football which received universal acclaim, as did Allison their coach.

He revelled in the limelight, though he was irked by the fact that no matter what City achieved, and no matter how low United's star fell (very low after their European Cup win of 1968) the Red Devils always attracted greater support and were perceived as Manchester's top club. That apart, Big Mal was supremely happy, and while sipping champagne and puffing at a massive cigar, he predicted that his team would 'murder everyone on the planet' and 'scare Europe to death'. Such boasts were typically extravagant and Allison was ridiculed widely when City bowed out of the European Cup to unfancied Turks at the first hurdle.

But despite such ill-advised posturing, the team was an outstanding one, going on to win the FA Cup in 1969, and both the European Cup Winners' Cup and the League Cup in 1970. One aspect of that success, for which the coach was responsible, was the astonishing contribution of skipper Tony Book, who had played for Allison at both Bath and Plymouth, followed his mentor to Manchester, then took a prominent part in all City's triumphs during his middle 30s, completing the fairytale by sharing the Footballer of the Year award with Derby County's Dave Mackay in 1969.

Among those most impressed by Allison's acumen were the Italian giants, Juventus, who offered him a fortune to join them that same year. He came close to accepting, but in the end could not walk out on his and Mercer's lovely creation, which was still at its peak.

Yet despite the success, signs of strain began to appear in the relationship as the 1970s got under way. As trophy followed trophy, so Mercer's health improved and earlier intimations that he would make way for Allison to assume sole control proved unintentionally misleading. Thus Big Mal, who yearned for the top job, became frustrated and was involved in an attempted boardroom coup. The situation became confused and Allison was close to dismissal. Eventually, though, he got the position he craved when Mercer moved uneasily into an 'upstairs' role in October 1971, before leaving, sadly disillusioned by behind-the-scenes politics, to join Coventry at the end of the season.

Around this time the extent to which Allison needed the elder statesman's cool judgement and discretion was thrown into sharp relief. With City apparently on course for the 1972 title, he bought the gifted but inconsistent Rodney Marsh, disrupting the side's system and arguably costing them the championship, which they missed by a point.

Thereafter Allison became increasingly disenchanted by boardroom manoeuvring and in March 1973 he surprised many observers by leaving Maine Road to accept the challenge of reviving Crystal Palace, already doomed to demotion from the top flight.

It proved to be the first step on a turbulent, unfulfilling 15-year odyssey, taking in 15 jobs in five countries. At Palace, he presided over the anticipated relegation in 1973, but then shocked fans by taking the Eagles straight down to the Third. Then he signed his friend and fellow student of the game, Terry Venables, as player-coach and together they guided Palace to the FA Cup semi-finals in 1976.

Along the way there was plenty of time for high jinks in London's bright lights, including a well-documented plunge in the team bath with actress Fiona Richmond. By May 1976, though, there was an inescapable feeling that Allison was treading water career-wise, too, and he resigned, thereafter working for Galatasaray of Turkey, Memphis in Tennessee and Plymouth for a second time before he was unable to turn down the chance of a return to Manchester City.

Back in the big time, money burnt a hole in his pocket as never before as he paid massive transfer fees for unproven players such as Steve Daley and Michael Robinson. After City suffered FA Cup humiliation at the hands of Halifax, then struggled in the League, the joke was that Allison would become the first man to spend a million on a corner flag. His stock was low, but sunk lower after failing to register a victory in the first dozen games of 1980/81. Inevitably, he was sacked. There followed a second sojourn with Crystal Palace, lasting 55 days, before he took his coaching skills to Sporting Lisbon, winning for them the League and Cup double before being dismissed for alleged indiscipline.

Cash-strapped Middlesbrough lured Allison back to the Football League in 1982, but he was ousted yet again for refusing to sell his best players. The remainder of the decade saw him occupy six further posts before accepting his last position, that of Bristol Rovers' caretaker manager in 1992. Though he had hit hard times financially, and was unable to afford his former luxurious trappings – the local newspaper bought him a new fedora, always his trademark headgear – the old charisma was undimmed.

Still he preached the gospel of skilful football, still young men were entranced by his opinions, but the Rovers job proved too hard for the twice-married 65-year-old, who had a two-year-old daughter by his current partner, and he couldn't prevent relegation.

After that – and before a destructive decline in his health which confined him to a nursing home for many years – one of the most colourful and expansive characters in football history lent himself to a touring chat show with Tommy Docherty, a rather sad footnote to a brave, if bumpy career. Had he been content to stick to what he did best – coaching rather than management – there was no limit to what he might have achieved. As it was, Malcolm Allison brought far more light than darkness to the English game.

Malcolm Alexander Allison, footballer and football manager; born Dartford, Kent, 5 September 1927; played for Charlton Athletic 1944-51, West Ham United 1951-58, Romford (non-League) 1960-62; manager, Bath City (non-League) 1963-64, Plymouth Argyle 1964-65, Manchester City (coach and assistant manager) 1965-71 then manager to 1973, Crystal Palace 1973-76, Galatasaray of Turkey (coach) 1976-78, Memphis (coach) 1977-78, Plymouth Argyle 1978-79, Manchester City 1979-80, Crystal Palace 1980-81, Sporting Lisbon 1981-82, Middlesbrough 1982-84, Willington (non-League) 1984; Kuwait (national coach) 1986, Vitoria Setubal of Portugal 1988, Farense of Portugal 1989, Fisher Athletic (non-League) 1989, Bristol Rovers (caretaker) 1992-93; died 15 October 2010.

Mel Hopkins

A sickening, albeit accidental clash of heads cost Mel Hopkins his likely place in one of the most lionised football teams of the 20th century.

When the Tottenham Hotspur and Wales left-back went up for an aerial challenge with Scotland's diminutive but unfailingly pugnacious centre-forward Ian St John at Hampden Park in November 1959, both men had eyes only for the ball.

But St John's forehead made high-velocity contact with Hopkins' face, shattering his nose and breaking his jaw, forcing him out of immediate first-team contention and allowing his English rival Ron Henry to usurp his club place in the long term. Thus the Welshman was confined to the sidelines as in 1960/61 Spurs became the first side in modern times to win the coveted League and FA Cup double.

In fact, although he resumed his international career and remained at White Hart Lane until mid-decade, Hopkins never regained regular custody of the club's number-three shirt from the immensely efficient Henry, instead switching to Brighton and Hove Albion, whom he helped to lift the Fourth Division championship in 1964/65.

The son of a coal-miner, Hopkins grew up in the rugby heartland of the Rhondda Valley, yet he was always so keen on the round-ball game that as a teenager he formed his own team and before long he was reaping the benefit of his single-mindedness.

After moving up to the Ystrad Boys' Club, he was spotted by a Tottenham scout, and although at that time he had never travelled further from South Wales than to Bristol Zoo, he accepted a trial in north London. The upshot, after spurning interest from Matt Busby's Manchester United, was a Spurs contract as an amateur in May 1951, duly followed by a professional deal a year later.

This was a period when Arthur Rowe's exhilarating push-and-run combination, which had lifted the championships of the Football League's top two tiers in 1950 and 1951, was beginning to decline so there was ample opportunity for promising rookies to make their mark.

Accordingly Hopkins made his senior debut as a 17-year-old at Derby in October 1952, soon emerging as a natural successor to the two men who had previously contested the left-back berth, the ageing Arthur Willis and Charlie Withers.

By 1954/55 Hopkins was the regular incumbent and when he earned his first cap for Wales, against Northern Ireland at Ninian Park, Cardiff, in April 1956, he was hailed as one of the best young flank defenders in Britain. Immediately he became an automatic selection for his country, embarking on a sequence of 23 consecutive appearances, including five in the World Cup finals of 1958 in Sweden, where Wales bowed out at the quarter-final stage to eventual winners Brazil.

That day in Gothenburg Hopkins shone against his direct opponent, the brilliant but bewilderingly unorthodox winger Garrincha, known in South America as 'The Angel with Bent Legs', a bamboozling dribbler with a deformed spine of whom the Welshman remarked: 'His legs went one way and his body went the other. It was difficult to know whether you were coming or going.'

Jimmy Murphy's gallant side, shorn of their own star player John Charles through injury and also facing the teenage genius Pele, lost by the game's only goal but covered themselves in glory for their spirited display.

Now Hopkins, who had helped Tottenham to finish second and third in England's top flight during the previous two League campaigns, while resisting what proved to be an ominously persistent challenge from the erstwhile understudy Henry, was at his zenith.

Standing an inch under six feet and with a loping, almost spidery gait, he could appear awkward, but that was deceptive. In fact, he was an accomplished all-round footballer, quick and tenacious, strong in the air, a perceptive passer and a brisk tackler.

Certainly Hopkins was rated highly by both his international boss Jimmy Murphy and new club manager Bill Nicholson, but then came that fateful collision with St John, then of Motherwell but destined for lofty heights with Liverpool, and his career impetus was halted in cruel fashion.

Thereafter he regained his regular slot for Wales, but never for Tottenham, a colossally frustrating circumstance for a classy performer who would have walked into most teams in the top division. Several transfer requests were rejected, but when young Cyril Knowles was recruited from Middlesbrough in the summer of 1964 and quickly proved his mettle, the picture changed and Hopkins was dispatched to Fourth Division Brighton for £5,000 in the following October.

At the Goldstone Ground, where his former Tottenham team-mate Bobby Smith – who died last month – was in prolific scoring form, the 30-year-old demonstrated all his old poise in helping the Seagulls to become divisional champions in his first season on the south coast.

That medal was the least he deserved after his ill fortune at White Hart Lane, but there were to be no more gongs for Hopkins, who was unable to hold his place in the Third Division and in July 1967 he departed to non-League Canterbury City.

There followed a stint with Ballymena in Northern Ireland before in January 1969 he returned to England with Bradford Park Avenue, remaining with the Yorkshire club while they twice finished bottom of the basement division before being voted out of the League in favour of Cambridge United in 1970.

Next came a spell with Wimbledon during their Southern League days, then he scouted for Derby where former Spurs comrade Dave Mackay was the manager, and made his living as a sports officer and coach for local authorities in Sussex.

Melvyn Hopkins, footballer; born Ystrad, Glamorgan, 7 November 1934; played for Tottenham Hotspur 1951-64, Brighton and Hove Albion 1964-67, Ballymena of Northern Ireland, Bradford Park Avenue 1969; capped 34 times by Wales 1956-63; died Worthing, Sussex, 18 October 2010.

Ronnie Clayton

Ronnie Clayton was the embodiment of an era in football history which could hardly contrast more vividly with today's game, in which his modern equivalents become multi-millionaires with one stroke of a pen. At the end of the 1950s, when Clayton was captain of England, on the morning of a match for his club, Blackburn Rovers, he was to be found walking the streets of the town, delivering newspapers. The industrious, unassuming Lancastrian judged his early shift to be necessary to help make a success of the newsagent's shop he ran with his wife in order to provide for his eventual retirement as a professional sportsman. The thought of the current England skipper, Rio Ferdinand, similarly employed is too surreal even to contemplate.

Though his tenure as an international captain lasted only five games before he was discarded for good at the age of 25, Clayton was a high-quality performer, a dynamic, driving wing-half – a midfielder in today's parlance – and a loyal one-club man at a time when such a breed proliferated. Throughout his two decades with Blackburn, during which he made nearly 700 senior appearances but never collected a medal in a major competition, he was a monument to integrity and sportsmanship, a courteous and dignified ambassador for his club, his country and the wider game.

As a boy Clayton was rejected by his home-town club, Preston North End, receiving the common but illogical and often misguided snub: 'Sorry son, you're too small. Come back in a year or two.' The disappointed but still ambitious 15-year-old decided not to wait for a growth spurt, instead accepting a trial with Second Division Blackburn along with his older brother and fellow wing-half, Ken, in 1949.

That was to prove a providential decision for both player and club, but not before a scare when the car in which the Claytons were travelling broke down on the way to Ewood Park. Undeterred, they hitched a lift on a beer lorry and both exhibited sufficient promise on the training field that day to secure amateur contracts.

Clayton Junior had been a left-winger for his school team, and had also played at centre-forward and centre-half, but after his conversion to wing-half at the age of 16, he had Blackburn boss Jackie Bestall purring about an international future.

Accordingly he made his senior debut in a home victory over Queen's Park Rangers on the last afternoon of 1950/51, turned professional the following August and made a significant impact during the subsequent term, not least in helping Rovers to an FA Cup semi-final which they lost, gallantly and only after a replay, to eventual winners Newcastle United.

Now Blackburn became established as a rising power in the second tier, but Clayton's gathering impetus was slowed temporarily by his National Service, during which he played for the Army and fretted about his club future to the extent that he requested a transfer.

Arsenal were among the leading clubs who pricked up their ears but the dispute, which also involved brother Ken, was settled and in 1954/55 Clayton became a Blackburn regular, a status he would retain for the next 15 years.

As his star rose he fulfilled Bestall's prediction, soon earning England honours at under-23 and 'B' level before winning his first cap, against Northern Ireland at Wembley in November 1955, replacing Bill McGarry of Huddersfield Town at right-half.

That season and the next he was in magnificent form for both club and country. As Rovers pushed hard for promotion, narrowly missing out on both occasions, it was a particular joy for Ronnie that his brother was usually alongside him at left-half, and a sickening blow when Ken's career was virtually ended by a broken leg in the spring of 1957.

At international level an exceptional display in a stirring 4-2 victory over Brazil at Wembley in May 1956 signalled the start of an uninterrupted 18-match sequence, with the half-back line of Clayton, veteran skipper Billy Wright of Wolverhampton Wanderers and youthful Manchester United prodigy Duncan Edwards emerging as a potent force.

Clayton's attributes were legion. Wirily athletic, he was a powerful and expert timer of tackles, his aerial work was crisp and precise, he seemed to draw on a bottomless pit of energy and his ball skills, while not of the extravagant variety, were by no means negligible. He was adept, too, at delivering sudden long-distance throw-ins which caught many a defence unawares and his distribution was invariably sensible, occasionally perceptive.

At Blackburn, where by now he was sharing star billing with the dazzlingly talented winger Bryan Douglas, to whom he would remain close for the rest of his life, his influence became all-pervading and he was a colossal factor when Rovers finally claimed a place among the elite as Second Division runners-up to West Ham United in 1957/58.

Having become captain, Clayton was the heartbeat of an attractive team now managed by Johnny Carey, and he led by courageous example, being ready to play through injury at need. On occasion, however, that very willingness worked against Clayton. He soldiered on gamely while struggling with a gammy knee and consequently gave a handful of below-par performances, which cost him his place in the England line-up for most of the 1958 World Cup finals in Sweden, the Wolves tough-nut Eddie Clamp being preferred. Clayton was recalled for the group play-off showdown with the USSR, which ended in a mortifying 1-0 reverse.

Club-wise, though, he settled easily in the First Division, his reliability the perfect rock around which his colleagues rallied, and at the outset of the 1959/60 campaign there wasn't a cloud on the Clayton horizon. He had been installed as England captain following the retirement of Wright, Blackburn got off to a flyer which took them to the top-flight summit in the autumn and he had regained all his former poise.

But the second half of the season was to represent the nadir of Clayton's career. Rovers tumbled down the table, though they took considerable consolation from their run to the FA Cup final, in which they faced Stan Cullis' formidable Wolves.

It turned out to be a dreadful game, with Blackburn reduced to ten men in those pre-substitute days when full-back Dave Whelan – destined to become a millionaire and the owner of Wigan Athletic – sustained a broken leg shortly before the interval. Already a goal down, they could achieve little more than damage limitation in the second period, and Wolves won 3-0.

Clayton, cruelly debilitated by tonsillitis, was not at his best, and he was criticised heavily for not rousing his men. The tenor of the occasion was sullied further when some Blackburn fans, feeling Wolves had been over-physical, showered the victors with orange peel and other rubbish. Consequently what should have been the season's gala occasion was labelled 'the dustbin final' and Clayton's personal stock plummeted.

Four days later, and still not well, he led out England at Wembley to face Yugoslavia and gave a notably poor display in a thrilling but, as far as the home support was concerned, disappointing 3-3 draw. One newspaper described his showing as one of the poorest ever by an England captain. Other headlines demanded that 'Clayton must go' and he did, replaced by Bobby Robson and never picked again for his country.

It was a bitter pill for a player who, at 25, should have been on the threshold of his prime. Now, having collected 35 full caps and made ten appearances for the Football League, his representative days were over.

However, he was a resilient character, making light of his misfortune and resuming his stalwart service at Ewood Park, excelling as a team now bossed by Jack Marshall became solid members of England's elite league throughout the first half of the 1960s.

Indeed, in 1963/64, with twin marksmen Fred Pickering and Andy McEvoy scoring freely and Douglas prompting beautifully from midfield, they led the table around the turn of the year. There were such triumphs as 7-2 over Tottenham Hotspur, 5-1 against Wolves and 8-2 at West Ham on Boxing Day. But then Pickering's wish for a move was granted and the side declined dramatically, finishing in seventh place.

Worse was to follow. In 1965/66 Blackburn were woeful, finishing bottom of the table 13 points adrift of their closest rivals, Northampton Town. Through it all Clayton remained a beacon of stability, often an inspirational figure, giving everything to the cause he had espoused throughout his career.

Having reached his thirties he was less mobile, and he dropped back into central defence, still reading the game as shrewdly as ever, yet again demonstrating his leadership qualities as the team almost bounced straight out of the Second Division at the first attempt, finishing in a creditable fourth place.

Clayton's last hurrah as a Rover came in 1968/69 when creaking knees limited his appearances, as his beloved club almost sunk to the third tier.

There followed a brief stint as player-manager of non-League Morecambe before a happy interlude playing with Great Harwood alongside old Ewood Park comrades Bryan Douglas and Roy Vernon.

Later came work as an area manager for a tyre company, but Clayton was still in love with football. He remained devoted to the club and to championing the cause of the local grass-roots game, and the Blackburn public never ceased to treat him as an icon. This kind and gentle man, who had captained his country and who would surely have been whisked away by more fashionable employers had he been born half a century later, had garnered no medals during his professional lifetime, but his harvest of admirers was bountiful, indeed.

Ronald Clayton, footballer; born Preston, Lancashire, 5 August 1934; played for Blackburn Rovers 1949-69; capped 35 times by England 1955-60; died Blackburn, Lancashire, 29 October 2010.

Ralph Coates

Ralph Coates is revered at Turf Moor as one of the finest of all Burnley footballers, and while the sturdy, endlessly industrious little flankman-cum-midfielder's star did not gleam quite so incandescently later with Tottenham Hotspur, he recovered from a shaky start in north London to play a telling part in lifting two major trophies in the 1970s.

The excellent Coates was an England international, too, yet he never quite sustained the early notion that he might be destined for greatness. One or two fanciful pundits even expounded the theory, when he was in his claret-and-blue pomp during the late 1960s, that he might go on to emulate his fellow north-easterner Bobby Charlton. Yet such a proposition was always preposterous, relating more to a similarity in hair-do – both men sported long, trailing wisps combed carefully over a bald pate – than to actual ability with the ball.

In fact, one was that very rare bird, a bona fide footballing genius; the other was a journeyman, ever steadfast, occasionally scintillating but essentially worthy, and none the worse for that.

At his best the pacy, indefatigably energetic Coates was a thrilling performer, all explosive bursts of acceleration and flowing body-swerves which left defenders leaden-footed in his wake. But at his worst he could appear anxious, even clumsy, a frustrating enigma. On such occasions his shot, which could be a fearsome weapon even though he was never a prolific goal-scorer, invariably fizzed wildly wide, like a bullet from the handgun of a blindfolded cowboy. Perversely, too, sometimes his crossing was more accurate when he was under heavy challenge than when he had time and space to spare.

But always there was honest effort, a saving grace in times of tribulation, and the fans sensed the good heart of an appealingly self-deprecating individual who was as faithful a team player as it's possible to be.

Coates had been serving an apprenticeship as a fitter when he arrived at Burnley as a dashing 15-year-old centre-forward from his local amateur side, Eppleton Colliery Welfare, in 1961, the latest of a stream of north-eastern recruits to the club. He turned professional two years later and made his senior debut as a stand-in for the rugged Andy Lochhead alongside twin spearhead Willie Irvine in December 1964, when the Clarets were ensconced comfortably midway in the top division.

In the following season, having been shifted to the left wing, he earned a regular berth as Harry Potts' enterprising team finished third in the title race, behind Liverpool and Leeds. The dynamic Coates offered a vivid contrast to the trickier, more flamboyant Willie Morgan on the opposite flank, the pair complementing one another ideally as they fashioned countless scoring opportunities for Irvine and Lochhead.

As a person Coates remained becomingly modest despite his rapid ascent, although on New Year's Day 1966 there was an out-of-character incident during a Lancashire derby with Blackburn Rovers at Ewood Park. With the visitors in control near the end, the Burnley man sat on the ball during open play, a provocative move which infuriated rival players and supporters alike. Later he explained that he had been attempting to take the heat out of a stormy contest with a touch of humour but, not surprisingly, it had the opposite effect.

Still, his career continued to gather impetus, especially after he switched roles to become a creative inside-forward, but that did not prevent Burnley from declining, imperceptibly at first, towards lower-table mediocrity. There was some consolation in reaching the quarter-finals of the European Fairs Cup in 1966/67 and the last four of the League Cup in 1968/69, though the latter achievement was marred by the fact of elimination by Third Division opponents, the eventual winners Swindon Town.

Come 1970 Coates hit new heights, collecting the first of his four full England caps in a 3-1 victory over Northern Ireland at Wembley in April, shortly before his 24th birthday. But during the subsequent campaign the fortunes of Burnley, with new boss Jimmy Adamson at the helm, headed at speed in the opposite direction and they were demoted.

Now a transfer for the versatile and often inspirational Coates seemed inevitable and so it proved as he was sold to Tottenham Hotspur for £190,000, then a British record for a cash deal, in May 1971.

Ironically, that was the month in which he played his last game for his country, a consequence of a succession of disappointing displays during his early tenure at White Hart Lane.

On arrival he was 25 and seemingly on the threshold of a golden prime, but most of his performances in 1971/72 appeared hesitant and error-strewn. It did not help that Tottenham manager Bill Nicholson returned him to a wing position, where he felt peripheral and where his obvious pace and strength were not always matched by the necessary finesse. Also, on joining a side which included the stellar likes of Martin Chivers, Alan Gilzean and Martin Peters, he had to adjust to no longer being the focal point of the attack, as he had become at Turf Moor.

But Coates was no quitter and after a brief rest from the limelight he bounced back as a midfield workhorse, relishing the added responsibility for chasing back to help his defence, impressing with his application, delighting with the occasional shaft of brilliance.

He featured in both legs of the UEFA Cup final victory over Wolverhampton Wanderers in 1971/72 and emerged as the hero of the 1973 League Cup final, scoring the only goal of the contest against Norwich City. That was after joining the action as a substitute for John Pratt, his absence from the starting line-up partly due to a nagging injury and partly to his still-fluctuating form.

Happily, by 1973/74 he had settled, appearing less tense, and he scored four times during Spurs' progress to another UEFA Cup final, which was lost to the Dutch club Feyenoord. For three seasons after that, under successive new bosses Terry Neill and Keith Burkinshaw, he played more games than he missed, often courageously masking the pain of nagging injuries which nevertheless decreased his effectiveness.

In 1976/77 Coates was part of the lacklustre team that finished bottom of the old First Division, then featured only fleetingly in the second tier before being loaned to the Sydney-based St George's for six months, eventually being freed to join Orient as a 32-year-old in October 1978.

At Brisbane Road, in the Second Division, he flourished anew, helping the Londoners to mid-table respectability over two campaigns, including 1979/80, which he began with a smart brace of goals against former employers Burnley and in which he netted nine times, the best seasonal return of his long career.

Coates made his final senior appearances at the outset of 1980/81 before suffering injury, then withdrawing to bolster and coach Orient's reserves. After retiring from the professional game in 1982, he continued to coach for a time before managing a leisure centre in Hertfordshire while playing Sunday league football until he was 59.

More recently he worked in corporate hospitality for Spurs, whose current manager Harry Redknapp, on hearing of Coates' death, summed up the essence of the genial north-easterner to perfection. 'Ralph', he said, 'was just a great guy, one of life's nice fellas.'

Ralph Coates, footballer; born Hetton-le-Hole, County Durham, 26 April 1946; played for Burnley 1961-71, Tottenham Hotspur 1971-78, St George's of Sydney 1978, Orient 1978-82; capped four times by England 1970-71; died Luton, Bedfordshire, 17 December 2010.

Bill Jones

Bill Jones was at the core of everything that was admirable about Liverpool Football Club in the middle years of the 20th century. Versatile, accomplished and loyal, an indefatigable workaholic with a great fighting heart, he was a bastion of the side which became the first post-war League champions in a pulsating denouement on the last day of the 1946/47 campaign.

He remained a key part of the Reds' backbone, usually in a defensive role, as they reached their first Wembley FA Cup final in 1950 and he was still at Anfield four seasons later, battling courageously and selflessly, if unavailingly, to avoid the hitherto unthinkable fate of relegation from the top division.

Mention of Jones' bravery in a mere sporting context is not to trivialise his true valour, displayed during the Allies' crossing of the Rhine as Hitler's home defences were breached in 1945, and for which the rookie footballer received the Military Medal.

Having joined Liverpool as a 17-year-old from the Derbyshire amateurs Hayfield St Matthews in 1938, Jones was one of a whole generation of players who lost their early prime to the conflict. However, he did manage to make his first-team entrance for his new club in unofficial emergency competition and there was also time during the war to make guest appearances for York City, Leeds United and Reading.

But it was not until August 1946 that he achieved his senior debut, lining up at centre-forward against Sheffield United at Bramall Lane in a tight contest settled by a single strike from his fellow debutant, Len Carney. Jones' first goals, two of them, came a week later in a 7-4 home victory over Chelsea, but then his career direction was altered irrevocably by Liverpool's signing of the prolific marksman Albert Stubbins from Newcastle United.

To accommodate the illustrious newcomer, initially manager George Kay shifted Jones to inside-left, but soon he slipped out of the side, reappearing midway through the season, first at left-half, then at left-back, centre-half and right-half, so that when the championship crown was finally claimed, he had appeared in six different positions.

The title race climaxed in classic fashion with the two top teams, Liverpool and leaders Wolves, facing each other in a showdown at Molineux. The Black Countrymen were firm favourites, being a point better off and having thrashed the Reds 5-1 at Anfield a few months earlier, but the visitors confounded the odds to win 2-1 and take the prize. That day Jones – standing in at right-half for his indisposed skipper, the cultured Phil Taylor – performed beautifully, his passing crisp and creative, his tackling fierce and determined, his reading of the game impeccable, but such was his adaptability, a precious commodity to any side, he never settled to a dedicated long-term role.

Over the next few years Liverpool, for whom Stubbins and the brilliant Scottish forward Billy Liddell were the most prominent performers, slipped back to become solid mid-table citizens, but there was a bonus in 1950 when they faced Arsenal in the FA Cup final.

Jones had spent most of that season in the number-five shirt, but he found himself at the centre of bitter controversy when it was announced that he would occupy the left-half berth at Wembley, replacing the popular, flintily indomitable Bob Paisley, who had played in every round and scored in the semi-final triumph over local rivals Everton.

The two players were close pals and Jones, though a totally innocent bystander to the decision, felt mortified for Paisley and embarrassed when some fans declared they would never watch the Reds again as a protest at the omission of the north-easterner.

It was hardly the ideal preparation for a showcase occasion, and unfortunately for Liverpool the normally consistent Jones turned in a poor display as the Gunners triumphed 2-0, with his immediate opponent Jimmy Logie proving highly influential in the outcome. Jones had one chance to salvage the day when the score was 1-0, but he headed against the Arsenal crossbar and the moment had gone.

Two weeks later, though, his customary prowess was recognised when he was called up by England to replace centre-half Neil Franklin of Stoke City, who was dropped after decamping to Colombia – then outside the umbrella of FIFA and therefore outlawed – in search of a pot of gold.

Poor Franklin's dream died all too soon and he returned to England disillusioned, but his suspension afforded Jones a precious opportunity. He didn't fail, featuring in successive victories over Portugal in Lisbon and Belgium in Brussels, but the centre-forwards he was marking both scored and he was discarded, never to play for his country again.

The undaunted Jones, who had also appeared for the Football League, continued to serve Liverpool with doughty resolution in his variety of rearguard and midfield slots, but come 1952/53 the Reds, by now bossed by Don Welsh, were in serious decline.

In 1953/54 they finished bottom and were demoted. The 33-year-old Jones was released, having played 278 games and scored 17 goals for his only professional club, although there was no shortage of shrewd observers who reckoned the Reds had made a premature decision, and that the veteran still had plenty left to offer as a still-ailing team strove to make an early comeback from the second tier.

Thereafter he became player-boss of non-League Ellesmere Port before returning to Liverpool as a talent scout during the late 1950s and beyond, listing among his discoveries the two top goal-scorers in the club's history, Roger Hunt and Ian Rush.

Jones, a gifted all-round sportsman who might have made a living as a cricketer had he not been committed to the winter game, was immensely gratified by the footballing success of his grandson, Rob Jones, who featured as a full-back for Liverpool and England during the 1990s before injury brought his career to a premature end.

William Henry Jones, footballer; born Whaley Bridge, Derbyshire, 13 May 1921; played for Liverpool 1938-54; capped twice by England 1950; died Chester, Cheshire, 26 December 2010.

Avi Cohen

The pundit who described Avi Cohen as 'the Beckenbauer of the Middle East' might have been a trifle fanciful in his assessment, but Liverpool fans of a certain age will appreciate the image thus conjured of the poised, smoothly stylish Israeli international defender who played a small but telling part in the Merseysiders' League championship triumph of 1979/80.

In only his second outing for the club, Cohen, the first player from his country to feature in the English top division, scored for both sides as the Reds clinched the title by beating Aston Villa at Anfield. After conceding an unlucky own goal to gift the visitors an equaliser, Cohen wished the ground would swallow him up, but soon he sent the Kop into paroxysms of glee by netting to put Liverpool on the way to a comfortable and decisive victory.

Inevitably, the tall, exotic newcomer – performers from overseas were still comparatively rare birds in the English game at the time – was clasped to the fans' collective bosom and, given his appealing cocktail of easy elegance on the ball, shrewd anticipation of the unfolding action and abundant physical courage, it seemed that a lasting new folk hero was born.

However, Cohen lost his battle for the left-back berth with the enduringly admirable and distinctly more pacy Alan Kennedy, and after making a minor contribution to Liverpool's progress to the 1981 European Cup final – in which the Reds prevailed thanks to Kennedy's brilliant late strike – the Israeli returned to his homeland, where he spent the prime years of his career.

Cohen, who was versatile enough to fill any defensive or midfield position, had first risen to prominence with Maccabi Tel Aviv, making his entrance in 1975 and earning the first of his half-century of international caps a year later. He was a star performer as the club became Israeli champions in 1976/77 and 1978/79, his class and assurance attracting the attention of Liverpool manager Bob Paisley, who took him to Anfield in a £200,000 deal in the summer of 1979.

That September Cohen made his senior debut for the Reds, rising from the bench to replace injured midfielder Ray Kennedy at Leeds, but he seemed off the pace and out of his depth and it was not until six months of rigorous training had prepared him for the frenetic rigours of the English game that Cohen re-entered the fray in such memorable fashion against Villa.

An affable and intelligent fellow, he became popular with fellow footballers and supporters alike, not least because of his strenuous and successful efforts to learn the language. One story about Cohen's linguistic enterprise has entered Anfield folklore. When he found himself changing at the next dressing-room peg to Kenny Dalglish, the newcomer declared repeatedly to his Scottish team-mate: 'You and me – the same!' In his customary broad Glaswegian, Dalglish asked the Israeli what he meant, and Cohen reiterated: 'You and me – the same. We both (need to) learn English!'

When he left Liverpool in November 1981, having made 23 appearances for the Merseysiders and collected two FA Charity Shield winner's medals, he went back to Maccabi in a £100,000 deal.

Thereafter he flourished in Tel Aviv for six years before making a fleeting return to Britain, being recruited to Rangers by Graeme Souness, a former Anfield colleague who had become player-boss at Ibrox. By then into his thirties, Cohen was hampered by injuries and made scant impact in Glasgow, enjoying only a handful of senior outings. However, one of them earned him a major honour, a League Cup winner's gong for his substitute appearance in October 1987 in the 3-3 Hampden Park draw with Aberdeen, the game being settled by a penalty shoot-out.

In 1988, the year in which the one-time international captain was awarded his 51st and final full cap, Cohen went back to Israel, where he spent two seasons assisting Maccabi Netanya before retiring as a player in 1990. Later he coached extensively, worked as a television and radio pundit and for the last eight years had been chairman of the Israeli Professional Footballers' Association.

Cohen, whose son Tamir plays for Bolton Wanderers and Israel, sustained head injuries in a motorcycle accident on December 20 and died nine days later in a Tel Aviv hospital.

Avraham Cohen, footballer; born Cairo, 14 November 1956; played for Maccabi Tel Aviv 1975-79 and 1981-87, Liverpool 1979-81, Rangers 1987-88, Maccabi Netanya 1988-90; capped 51 times by Israel 1976-88; died Tel Aviv, 29 December 2010.

Nat Lofthouse

If visitors from another planet, intrigued by the devotion of earthlings to their curious game of soccer, should hear the phrase 'traditional, old-fashioned English centre-forward' and want to know more, they would be well advised to study film of Nat Lofthouse in action. Better still, should these aliens have the facility of time travel and were able to return to the 1950s when the 'Lion of Vienna' was in his roaring prime, they could experience the real thing, a true working-class hero in all his vigorous glory.

As talismanic and constant a figure to his beloved Bolton Wanderers as was his friend and England colleague Tom Finney to fellow Lancastrians Preston North End, Lofthouse embodied football's most simple virtues. Whether wearing the white shirt of club or country, he toiled mightily, the archetypal human battering ram who plundered his goals – hundreds of them down the years – through prodigious strength, aggression and courage, his dynamic aerial power backed up by a savage shot in either foot.

Of course, though Lofthouse himself was far too modest to admit it, there was more to it than that. What marked him out from the typical hard-running English workhorse was an instinct for making the absolute most of his yeoman qualities. Muscle and sweat might have taken Nat Lofthouse a long way in his chosen profession, but not to the heady peaks he ascended, including 30 goals in 33 international appearances.

Significant, too, in the creation of a widely revered persona, was his down-to-earth attitude. Essentially a humble man who felt privileged to be paid for pleasure – his own view of his working contract – he was born in Bolton and lived his whole life there. Lofthouse loved the local community; indeed, he took such an active part in it while performing his various roles with Wanderers – first player, then trainer, coach, manager, scout, fund-raiser and president – that he came to epitomise it.

Though the town was famous for wool and cotton, it was coal that loomed largest in the Lofthouse household in the 1920s. Nat's father delivered the stuff with a horse and cart, and when the youngest of four boys was old enough to earn a living, he did so pushing tubs in the local pit. But football had always been his passion, from the days when he had played truant from school to shin up a drainpipe at Burnden Park to snatch a free view of his heroes in action.

Ironically his first organised game was as a goalkeeper – the very breed of which he would one day become a scourge – and he conceded seven goals, injury being added to insult as he received a hiding from his mother for scuffing his new shoes in the process. Soon, though, he found his spiritual home at centre-forward, later observing cheerfully that he didn't have the brains to be anything else, and scored seven times on his debut for the Bolton schools team.

In 1939 his prowess was recognised when he joined Wanderers as an amateur and, with so many footballers away at war, he played his first senior match a year later at the tender age of 15. However, as he grew towards maturity there was very little tender about the Lofthouse physique. Though he stood only a shade over 5ft 9in, he was blessed with a burly, four-square frame hardened by labour below ground, and before he turned professional in 1942 – on wages of £1.10s (£1.50p) per week – he needed ever ounce of stamina. A typical match-day schedule for the Bolton Bevin Boy was to rise at 3.30am, take the 4.30 tram to work, spend eight hours down the pit, then turn out for the Trotters in the afternoon.

Yet at first, despite earning respect as a trier and contributing a creditable goal tally, Lofthouse suffered terrace criticism for lack of technique. Though admitting disarmingly to natural clumsiness, he persevered and as soccer resumed normality after the conflict he matured gradually into one of the country's top spearheads.

Reward came in November 1950 with his first England cap, and he responded with two goals in a 2-2 draw with Yugoslavia at Highbury. That was but a foretaste of international success to come, none more lauded than the 1952 performance that earned him the Lion of Vienna sobriquet. Austria had a wonderful side at the time and expected to beat England soundly, but late in the second half of a tempestuous encounter the score was 2-2, Lofthouse having netted once.

Then, with the home side pressing for a winner, Tom Finney put the centre-forward through on goal; with a pack of defenders on his heels and the crowd baying wildly, he kept his head to clip the ball into the net even as he was clattered by the charging goalkeeper.

Such was the impact of the collision that he was stretchered off, returning later to share in the final moments of a 3-2 triumph before being chaired around the ground by an ecstatic contingent of British troops, then stationed nearby.

That year Bolton turned down an approach for his services from the Italian club, Fiorentina, who offered a deal that would have made Lofthouse rich beyond his dreams. Such was the one-sided nature of club-player relationships in that era that he was never offered the chance to decide for himself, though he maintained that the iniquitous situation never bothered him – it was just a fact of life and, as he felt himself to be immeasurably better off than the average working man, he was not going to make waves.

So Lofthouse continued to serve the Burnden Park cause nobly, and was their most eye-catching performer in two memorable FA Cup finals. First in 1953, as the reigning Footballer of the Year, he gave Wanderers a two-minute lead over Blackpool, then saw his side draw 3-1 ahead, only for the great Stanley Matthews to turn the contest on its head and inspire a late victory for the Seasiders.

That year Bolton had been very much the 'other' team, most neutrals longing for Matthews to pocket a winner's medal at the third attempt, and they were to occupy the same unenviable position in 1958 when a Manchester United ravaged by the Munich air disaster were the opposition.

This time, Lofthouse, now the captain, was not to be denied. Refusing to be affected by sentimentality, he scored both goals in a 2-0 victory, including a controversial second which many believed should have been disallowed after the rumbustious marksman had barged United goalkeeper Harry Gregg and the ball into the net.

Having played in the 1954 World Cup finals, Lofthouse was overlooked for the 1958 tournament, though he was recalled later that year and equalled Finney's England scoring record, since eclipsed by Bobby Charlton. In addition, he once netted six times for the Football League against the League of Ireland, realising the classic boyhood fantasy of a hat-trick in each half.

Come 1960, aged 35 and bothered by niggling knee and ankle injuries, he retired to become Wanderers' reserve team trainer. Having been very much the main attraction, with 285 goals in 503 club outings, he did not relish the prospect of sweeping floors and cleaning boots, which the job entailed, but so loth was he to leave Burnden that he accepted it.

In 1968, with Bolton short of money and having slipped out of the First Division, Lofthouse took over as manager. It was a move he was to regret, later declaring: 'I was the worst manager in the world.'

Though he got on well with his players, he was a natural worrier and was not good at taking the tougher decisions, and in November 1970 he stepped aside to take a purely administrative role. Amazingly, before the season's end he had served two more stints as caretaker boss, first Jimmy McIlroy and then Jimmy Meadows shifting quickly from the hot seat.

As loyal as ever, Lofthouse became Bolton's chief scout in May 1971, glad to be shot of the cares of top office and happy to retain an important job. However, he was not judged successful in the post and a year later came the rudest shock of his life to date – he was sacked.

Then for six years, his only connection with the club he symbolised was as a supporter, before he returned to take on the task of fund-raising figurehead, running the Burnden Executive Club. Surprisingly, December 1985 brought another spell as caretaker boss – albeit for only one match – and in 1986 he was elevated to the status of club president.

Distraught at the loss of his wife Alma in 1985, Lofthouse needed to keep himself busy, and did so in his new position, forever willing and able to promote the club's good name. He did so to the last and how appropriate that was; after all, to countless fans all over the world, Nat Lofthouse was Bolton Wanderers.

Nathaniel Lofthouse, footballer and football club manager: born Bolton, Lancashire, 27 August 1925; played for Bolton Wanderers 1939-60; capped 33 times for England 1950-58; manager Bolton Wanderers August 1968-November 1970, November 1970-January 1971, April-May 1971, December 1985; OBE 1994; inaugural inductee into Football Hall of Fame 2002; died Bolton, 15 January 2011.

Norman Uprichard

Northern Ireland goalkeeper Norman Uprichard was a courageous performer, even to the point of foolhardiness some observers reckoned, ready to dive head-first where many men would hesitate to hazard even a foot.

That valour, combined with not a little natural ability, was instrumental in securing his country a place in the quarter-finals of the World Cup in Sweden in 1958 and contributed to his status of folk hero at Portsmouth for the better part of a decade.

Internationally he operated mostly in the shadow of his slightly younger, even bolder and more talented pal, Harry Gregg, but at his club he was the top dog, his popularity enhanced by a willingness to engage in banter with the fans behind his net.

Standing only 5ft 9in, Uprichard was small for a goalkeeper, even in the post-war years when the average height was lower than today, but he compensated for lack of stature by remarkable agility. He didn't charge from his line to command his area in the manner of the imperious Gregg, but the lithe Ulsterman was a spectacular shot-stopper who entertained royally.

As a teenager Uprichard had shone equally at Gaelic football and soccer, earning a medal at the strictly Irish code only to be denied his prize and banned for life by the sport's ruling body because he had signed for Glenavon FC of Lurgan. The Gaelic association's rules at the time prohibited adult members from playing – or even watching – so-called foreign games, and more than half a century was to pass before finally he was awarded his medal, in 2004. Undaunted by such narrow-mindedness, the young Uprichard worked to develop his skills with Glenavon, with whom he had played as a right-winger until one day he stepped between the posts in an emergency and saved two penalties. Thereafter he flourished as a 'keeper, switching to Distillery – then a Belfast club, now located in Lisburn – and making his senior debut in March 1947.

Although second choice to Billy Smyth, with whom he would later vie for a place between Northern Ireland's posts, he excelled sufficiently for Arsenal to take him across the Irish Sea for a fee of £1,500 in June 1948. It was a golden opportunity but the daunting competition at Highbury – veteran George Swindin, the experienced Ted Platt and rising star Jack Kelsey – proved too much for Uprichard and in November 1949, having never represented the Gunners at League level, he was sold for £750 to Swindon Town of the old Third Division South.

In the comparatively modest surroundings of the County Ground, his career took off. Indeed, such was his club form with the Wiltshiremen that in October 1951 he was awarded the first of his 18 full caps in a 3-0 defeat by Scotland at Windsor Park, Belfast.

Northern Ireland were a poor team at the time, so Uprichard had plenty of chance to impress, and he played seven straight games without a win. His athleticism, sharp reflexes and bravery began to attract widespread attention, though, and a fabulous display in a 1-1 draw with Scotland at Hampden Park in November 1952 induced Portsmouth – then a powerful member of the elite division, albeit on the verge of gradual decline – to acquire his services for £6,000 the following day.

Such was Uprichard's intrepid approach to his work that injuries were inevitable and he damaged a hand in only his second outing for Pompey in a 4-3 victory over Sheffield Wednesday at Hillsborough. It happened in a collision with the Owls' prodigiously prolific centre-forward Derek Dooley for whom calamity was lying in wait only three months hence, when he was to have a leg amputated in the wake of another footballing accident.

Uprichard was more fortunate. Though broken knuckles kept him on the sidelines for most of 1953/54, he returned to become Pompey's regular custodian for the next four and a half seasons. On the day of his comeback, in a 3-1 triumph over Manchester United at Old Trafford in August 1954, he was in such fine fettle that he earned a glowing tribute from the Red Devils' boss Matt Busby, who waxed lyrical over both his courage and his professional prowess.

That term Portsmouth temporarily arrested their slump, finishing third in the table, only four points behind champions Chelsea, but then struggled ever more desperately in subsequent campaigns, culminating in relegation in 1959. Throughout that process, Uprichard found himself under protracted pressure, to which he reacted with serial excellence until the depressing final season, during which he was dropped at the midway point by toiling manager Freddie Cox, then released in the summer to join Third Division Southend United.

Meanwhile on the international front, he had fallen behind the exceptional Gregg but still, as the Manchester United man's deputy, Uprichard wielded key influence on two of the most crucial occasions in his country's footballing history.

First, when Gregg was fogbound in Manchester, the eager reserve performed with characteristic pluck and competence in the 2-1 besting of mighty Italy in Belfast in January 1958 which earned Northern Ireland a place in the World Cup finals in Sweden that summer.

Then, when Gregg was nursing an injury which kept him out of the play-off against Czechoslovakia in which a quarter-final place was at stake, Uprichard performed heroics in another vital 2-1 win. Despite smashing his hand against a post while saving a shot from Jan Dvorak, so that he was in agony every time he grasped the ball, and also twisting his ankle, he soldiered on – remember, no substitutes were allowed in those days – and ended the contest grimacing with pain but still magnificently defiant.

For the last-eight clash with France, manager Peter Doherty faced an impossible dilemma: did he go with Gregg and his gammy leg or Uprichard with serious hand and ankle issues? In the end he chose Gregg and France won 4-0, through no fault of the handicapped net-minder, who went on to be voted the top 'keeper in the tournament and therefore the world. That was a glowing and deserved accolade for the first-choice man, but also a vivid illustration of Uprichard's status as a more-than-adequate number-two in the greatest of all Northern Ireland teams, which contained the illustrious likes of Danny Blanchflower, Jimmy McIlroy, Peter McParland and Billy Bingham.

That November Uprichard played in his last international and after spending season 1959/60 with the Shrimpers, he left the Football League, going on to assist Hastings and Ramsgate before laying aside his gloves.

Later he worked as a pub landlord in Sussex and as a barman in Belfast before retiring to live in Hastings. Meanwhile back at Portsmouth he was still revered, both as a high-quality goalkeeper and as such an accessible character that he was willing to sign autographs for young fans who knocked on the door of his home, just along the road from Fratton Park. Rather a lot has changed in professional football since then.

William Norman McCourt Uprichard, footballer; born Moyraverty, Lurgan, Northern Ireland, 20 February 1928; played for Glenavon 1944-47, Distillery 1947-48, Arsenal 1948-49, Swindon Town 1949-52, Portsmouth 1952-59, Southend United 1959-60; capped 18 times by Northern Ireland 1951-58; died Brighton, Sussex, 31 January 2011.

Les Stubbs

Les Stubbs was a salt-of-the-earth type of footballer, short on artistry but long on strength, commitment and physical courage, sterling qualities which helped Chelsea to the League title of 1954/55. It was the first major trophy in their history and a triumph which destroyed forever the club's unfair image as a music-hall joke.

Although the energetic front-runner supplied a mere five goals in 27 appearances during the campaign and lost his place periodically to a precociously gifted young amateur, Seamus O'Connell, he proved an admirable and unselfish foil to Roy Bentley, the elegant England international marksman who prospered at his side.

Ever the stout cudgel to Bentley's stylish rapier, Stubbs typified the indomitable spirit of Ted Drake's modestly assembled but impeccably drilled combination, which defied widespread expectations that the more fashionable Wolverhampton Wanderers or Manchester United would prevail. True, the men from Stamford Bridge suffered ten defeats and garnered what was to remain the lowest championship-winning points total (52) since the war, but still they finished the equivalent of two wins better off than their nearest rivals, Wolves.

As a teenager Stubbs had shone for Great Wakering Rovers, the club which carried the name of his home village in Essex and which still flourishes today, before joining neighbouring Southend United of the old Third Division South, in May 1948.

The powerful rookie thrived at Roots Hall, weighing in with 40 goals in 83 outings for the Shrimpers, an impressive tally which attracted the attention of Drake, who was renowned for plucking emerging talents from the League's lower reaches.

Accordingly Stubbs moved to Stamford Bridge for £10,000 in November 1952, but made a slow start to life in the top flight, appearing only five times and failing to score as the Blues only narrowly avoided relegation in the following spring.

An appealingly unassuming individual, he had been a trifle apprehensive about making the step up, but gradually, as the shrewd Drake massaged his confidence, Stubbs blossomed at the higher level, earning a regular berth and netting nine times as the team rose to the top half of the table in 1953/54.

That set him up for his telling contribution to the title-winning term, during which his ceaseless industry and willingness to chase apparently lost causes in the team's interests endeared him to the Stamford Bridge fans and suited the make-up of Chelsea's forward line. His fearless foraging in all attacking areas created plenty of space for the wily Bentley and deep-lying inside-forward Johnny McNichol to exploit, while he linked effectively, too, with wingers Eric Parsons and Frank Blunstone.

Often Stubbs excelled in taxing away fixtures, such as at Sheffield United, where he struck the winner, and at Sunderland, where he registered in a 3-3 draw, but his most memorable hit came at Wolverhampton in December. That afternoon in the Molineux mud Chelsea were facing the reigning champions, who led 3-2 near the end before Stubbs eluded England skipper Billy Wright to equalise, then Bentley plundered the decisive goal in stoppage time. Crucial though such contributions were, however, none were as spectacular as his 40-yard effort in a 4-1 demolition of Portsmouth at Stamford Bridge, where regulars talked about the raking trajectory of his shot for years afterwards.

Yet just as Stubbs' star appeared firmly in the ascendancy, there came the challenge of O'Connell, who never turned professional, choosing instead to help his father in a cattle-dealing venture, and that despite scoring a hat-trick on debut in a 6-5 defeat at Old Trafford. He was more of a natural predator than the Great Wakering man and it frustrated Drake mightily that he could not persuade the youngster to commit himself to the game.

Despite O'Connell's refusal to forsake the family business, after the championship campaign Stubbs could never quite cement his claim to the number-ten shirt, and as the decade wore on he was engulfed by a rising tide of young talent, the likes of David Cliss, Ron Tindall, Peter Brabrook and the incomparable Jimmy Greaves.

They were tagged Drake's Ducklings by the newspapers, a nod in the direction of the Busby Babes, and although only one of them might have been expected to thrive with Manchester United before the Munich air crash of 1958 – Greaves would have walked into any team, in any era – the Stamford Bridge door was gradually being closed in Stubbs' face.

Still, he played for a London representative side in the inaugural Inter-Cities Fairs Cup – set up in 1955 to promote international trade, later becoming the UEFA Cup, now the Europa League – and was never less than wholehearted when offered a first-team run.

By the time of his transfer back to Southend in November 1952, along with wing-half Alan Dicks for a joint fee of £12,000, Stubbs had accumulated 35 goals in 122 senior appearances for Chelsea, a respectable total from a valued journeyman.

He remained with the Shrimpers for a season and a half before leaving the League, initially to serve Bedford Town, finally returning to his roots with Great Wakering. Still a vigorous performer, he played on for Rovers until he was 53, latterly in a pair of spectacles secured by an elastic band.

In 2005, half a century on from Chelsea's first League crown, he was one of the survivors of Drake's team to attend the Stamford Bridge celebration of the club's second title, secured that year under Jose Mourinho.

Away from the game Stubbs, a delightfully modest family man, worked as a civil servant for the Atomic Weapons Research Establishment at Foulness Island off the Essex coast, where he became leading fireman.

Leslie Levi Stubbs, footballer; born Great Wakering, Essex, 18 February 1929; played for Southend United 1948-52 and 1958-60, Chelsea 1952-58; died Great Wakering, 1 February 2011.

Neil Young

The most successful and entertaining period in Manchester City's history to date, the late 1960s and early 1970s, has entered football folklore as the Lee, Bell and Summerbee era. It's a convenient tag paying tribute to three exceptional and highly contrasting footballers, but it does scant justice to their elegant fellow attacker Neil Young, who was at the heart of all their most glorious triumphs under the inspirational guidance of manager Joe Mercer and coach Malcolm Allison.

The lanky, long-striding left-footer, who belied his willowy build with a shot of fearsome velocity, was City's top scorer both when they won the Second Division title in 1966 and then lifted the League championship two years later, clinching it with a dramatic last-day victory at Newcastle to which Young contributed two scintillating strikes.

In 1969 he lashed home the only goal of the FA Cup final victory over Leicester City. Then in 1970 he netted twice as the Blues beat Schalke in the semi-final of the European Cup Winners' Cup, and was on target yet again as the trophy was claimed by defeating Gornik Zabrze of Poland in the final on a soaking night in Vienna.

Francis Lee, Colin Bell and Mike Summerbee played mightily, too, of course, but to exclude such a talismanic performer as the popular local boy Young from the widely accepted definition of that fabulous sequence seems more than a tad perverse.

Young always maintained stoutly that he was unfazed by the omission, but he was a sensitive soul who encountered hard times after retiring from football, and it is difficult to believe that he wasn't hurt by the lack of overt recognition. He could, and did, take consolation, however, in the certain knowledge that he was never underrated by his team-mates and supporters at Maine Road. They understood the full worth of Neil Young; they knew it was immense.

Always taller than his contemporaries, Young was a central defender as a lad growing up in Fallowfield, but as he progressed to represent Manchester Boys his talent as an athletic front-running maker and taker of goals came naturally to the fore.

Duly he signed amateur forms for City as a 15-year-old in 1959, working as a trainee electrician until he turned professional in February 1961. Thereafter he rose rapidly, making his senior debut in a 2-1 defeat at Aston Villa ten months later, shining so brightly that he retained the right-wing berth for the remainder of the campaign and stayed a regular in the side for a decade.

At that point, however, as Young's star ascended, City's headed in the opposite direction and they were relegated from the top flight. The team had declined into mediocrity and beyond under the management of Les McDowall, a process which continued under another old-fashioned boss, George Poyser, but which was reversed spectacularly by the arrival at Maine Road of Mercer and Allison in the summer of 1965.

That pair transformed the club, with the genial Mercer's wisdom and man-management skills complemented perfectly by the visionary coaching methods of the flamboyant Allison.

Young's confidence burgeoned accordingly, and in 1965/66 he scored 14 times, mostly from the left wing but also as a central marksman, as City lifted the Second Division crown with plenty to spare.

There followed a season of mid-table consolidation among the elite, during which Young laid lasting claim to the number-ten shirt in which he was to enjoy his pomp. He relished his maturing alliance with the clever, combative right-winger Summerbee and the creative, prodigiously industrious inside-forward Bell, and when the bustling Lee arrived in the following autumn a potent front five of Lee, Bell, Summerbee, Young and left-winger Tony Coleman was complete.

Now Young – dubbed affectionately as 'Nelly' by some admirers who reckoned he didn't relish a full-blooded physical challenge – gave full rein to his repertoire of pace and grace. He was quick-footed in controlling the ball, a lovely, artistic passer and an expert finisher as he roamed to all attacking areas, scoring 19 times in 40 games, topped by a ripping volley and an acute-angled shot at St James' Park as the championship was wrested deliciously from neighbours United on the season's final afternoon.

If 1968/69 was marred by shock capitulation to Fenerbahce of Turkey in the European Cup, and a disappointingly humdrum First Division record, it was garnished by the FA Cup triumph, the enduring memory of which was Young's fulminating left-foot drive from a typically cute Summerbee set-up.

He missed the 1970 League Cup final victory over West Bromwich Albion to be present at the birth of his third child, but by season's end his European heroics had emphasised once more his place among City's most influential performers.

But lying in wait was a hammer blow from which the 26-year-old's still-climaxing career would never recover. Early in 1971 he was devastated by the death of his elder brother Chris, to whom he had been exceedingly close, and although he helped the Blues to reach that term's Cup Winners' Cup semi-final – which was lost to Chelsea – he would never regain prime form.

Thus drained emotionally, he slipped out of contention in 1971/72, yet still when he was sold to Second Division Preston North End for £48,000 in January 1972, having scored 108 goals in a little more than 400 appearances, he was demoralised to be deemed surplus to requirements by the club he had adored since childhood and which had been his only employer.

On arrival at Deepdale he was struggling for fitness, and Preston never saw anything like the best of him. Still, for three seasons, first under Alan Ball Snr and then with Bobby Charlton at the helm, he offered craft and experience and a few goals to a poor side, which was demoted to the third tier in 1974.

That summer he moved to Rochdale, freshly relegated to the basement division, where their struggles continued. So, too, did Young's, and after one miserable year he retired from the game, something of a lost soul.

It was a poignant exit by the former England youth international, whom many sound judges had tipped for a place in Sir Alf Ramsey's World Cup squad in 1970, but for whom the call never came.

Now Young embarked on a lengthy period of personal torment. With no job to go to after leaving Rochdale, he signed on the dole, and felt degraded by the experience. In time he worked as removal man, sports shop manager, milkman, supermarket shelf-stacker and insurance salesman. He went through two divorces, first from the mother of his three children, then to another woman with whom he had a daughter, eventually returning to live with his mother. His health declined – back problems and deep-vein thrombosis proved particularly debilitating – and at one point he attempted suicide through an overdose of painkillers.

But redemption was at hand. In 1988 Young met Carmen, who would become his third wife, and with whom he remained happily for the rest of his life. With his fortunes now on an upward trajectory, he found fulfilment coaching boys to play football. Also he made a return to the Manchester City community – from which he had been split since leaving Maine Road, partly because he had never been allotted the testimonial match which he felt to be his due and which he maintained had been promised him by Malcolm Allison – and he was warmed by the esteem in which he was still held by former comrades and fans.

In December 2010 he was diagnosed with terminal cancer and when the FA Cup draw pitted Manchester City against Leicester – the opponents vanquished by Young's goal in the 1969 final – the Eastlands club dedicated the match to him. Some 3,000 scarves were produced in the red-and-black colours worn on that memorable Wembley occasion, and were sported at the recent game by City fans as well as manager Roberto Mancini. Proceeds from their sale was split between Young and the cancer unit at Wythenshawe where he was being treated.

Neil James Young, footballer; born Manchester, 17 February 1944; played for Manchester City 1961-72, Preston North End 1972-74, Rochdale 1974-75; died Manchester, 3 February 2011.

Eric Parsons

Eric Parsons was a diminutive winger who made a colossal contribution as Chelsea became Football League champions for the first time in their history in 1955. Nicknamed 'The Rabbit' for his remarkable pace and distinctive bobbing gait, he overcame initial scorn from an over-critical faction of the Stamford Bridge crowd, following his 1950 arrival from West Ham United, to become one of the Blues' most popular performers.

And well he might. During the title-winning campaign Chelsea made nonsense of the music-hall wiseacres who lampooned them cruelly and undeservedly by outstripping, comfortably in the end, the much more fancied likes of Wolverhampton Wanderers and Manchester United, and throughout that glorious process Parsons was a constant star.

He played in every game, scoring 11 goals – including two on the afternoon the prize was clinched by a 3-0 home triumph over Sheffield Wednesday – and catapulting himself from comparative obscurity to the fringe of the England team. Indeed, but for the incomparable quality of Stanley Matthews and Tom Finney, surely Parsons must have earned full caps to go with the two outings for his country's 'B' side which were to remain his sole international honours.

The 5ft 7in flankman was both a maker and taker of scoring opportunities. At his peak during that championship term he maintained a stream of inviting crosses on which classy centre-forward Roy Bentley capitalised expertly, while when the goal tallies were finalised he lagged behind only Bentley himself (21 strikes) and inside-right Johnny McNichol (14).

Parsons, a prodigiously promising athlete during his schooldays, was spotted by West Ham playing for Worthing Boys and recruited by the Upton Park club in 1943. After Army service in North Africa during the war, he made his senior debut for the Second Division Hammers in January 1947, quickly establishing himself as a regular and not missing a match in either of the next two seasons.

As well as being quick, Parsons was tricky, intelligent and industrious, the last-mentioned quality being comparatively rare among wingers of that era, many of whom merely hugged the touchline waiting for the ball to be delivered to their feet.

He was ready to chase back and assist his wing-half, even his full-back, at need, foraging tirelessly for the ball, clearly unafraid of the consequent physical effort and risk.

After two years in the upper reaches of the second tier, West Ham fell away badly in 1949/50, narrowly avoiding demotion, and it seemed unlikely that such an emerging jewel on the threshold of his pomp would remain with a struggling club. Duly, in December 1950, Parsons was sold to Chelsea for £23,000, an immense fee at the time and a club record for the Blues. Expectations were vast but he didn't hit his best form immediately, partly due to a series of debilitating knee problems, and despite frequently working himself to a standstill he was jeered by some of his new 'supporters'.

He was tried at inside-forward but that didn't help. Even a return to his favoured right-flank berth didn't pay immediate dividends, and it was not until Ted Drake replaced Billy Birrell as manager in 1952 that his fortune changed.

The new boss nursed a high regard for Parsons and by praising him lavishly in public he massaged the wingman's hitherto fragile confidence. In fairness, the fans had always recognised him as a trier, and now they warmed to his re-awakening skills, too, as in 1952/53 and 1953/54, while Chelsea improved markedly as a team, his personal performance level soared.

But it was in the next momentous campaign that Parsons fulfilled his maximum potential, linking beautifully with his fellow forwards, particularly McNichol, whose perceptive passes inside opposing full-backs offered endless opportunities for the dapper flankman to shoot or to dispatch precise deliveries to the predatory Bentley.

On the penultimate Saturday of the season, when the championship was secured, Parsons was the hero, netting against Wednesday with a smart header from left-winger Frank Blunstone's cross and a hooked shot.

Afterwards, as the Stamford Bridge pitch was invaded by celebrating spectators, they feted him royally, chants of 'We want the Rabbit' issuing from the same folk who had condemned him so roundly a few years earlier.

Though by then in his thirties, Parsons remained a potent operator but after another season he gave way to young Peter Brabrook – one of 'Drake's Ducklings', as Chelsea's evolving side was now dubbed in the press – and in November 1956 he accepted a free transfer to Brentford of the Third Division South.

Like the dedicated professional he was, Parsons buckled down to life at the lower level, putting in four terms of dedicated service at Griffin Park, during which he suffered a broken leg.

Having played more than 450 games and scored close to a century of goals in senior football, he moved on to non-League Dover Athletic in the summer of 1961.

Later Parsons worked as a grocer, then ran a cigarette supply business. His death came only a week after that of Les Stubbs, a fellow attacker in the Chelsea side which had made the comedians eat their words.

Eric George Parsons, footballer; born Worthing, Sussex, 9 November 1923; played for West Ham United 1943-50, Chelsea 1950-56, Brentford 1956-61; died Worthing, 7 February 2011.

Dean Richards

BBC football pundit Alan Hansen knows a thing or two about centre-halves, having been one of the finest the British game has ever seen during his playing days with Liverpool, so it was worth listening in 1996 when he described Dean Richards as the most promising young central defender in England.

The tall, commanding Yorkshireman, who combined brawn and elegance to an unusual degree, became the costliest player in the land without a full international cap when he switched from Southampton to Tottenham Hotspur for £8.1 million in 2001.

Arguably Richards never quite scaled the lofty peaks predicted for him during his earlier days with home-town club Bradford City, then Wolverhampton Wanderers, though his record of more than 400 senior appearances spread over a dozen years is highly creditable.

Poignantly, any shortfall in achievement might be ascribed to the injuries which plagued him for much of his career, followed by the onset of a cruel illness which caused dizzy spells and severe headaches, forcing his premature retirement at the age of 31 in 2005 and probably leading to his death five years later.

After rising through the youth ranks at Valley Parade, Richards made his League debut for Bradford City as a 17-year-old in the autumn of 1991, developing rapidly to become a regular member of the third-tier Bantams' rearguard.

So impressive was his form that he represented the Football League against the Italian League, and in 1994/95 he was selected by his peers in the Professional Footballers' Association for his division's team of the season. That spring he joined Wolves on loan, the deal being made permanent at the end of the campaign for a fee of £1.85 million.

With the Black Countrymen in the second flight, Richards began to truly blossom. Muscular and broad-shouldered, he was aggressive in the tackle and formidable in the air, but there was far more to his game than sheer power. He was cooler and more composed than most rookies and he was comfortable in possession of the ball, which he delighted in carrying out of defence in much the same cultured style as Hansen in his Anfield heyday. Admittedly there were occasional lapses of concentration but there was every reason to believe that any flaws would be eradicated through experience.

But, sadly, at this point Richards – who had earned four England under-21 caps and been deployed as skipper – began to fall prey to injuries. First his burgeoning impetus was checked by a fractured cheekbone and then, while driving home to Bradford following a majestic performance in a drawn FA Cup tie with Spurs in January 1996, his car hit black ice on the M62 and he damaged a knee in the resultant smash.

He bounced back but further fitness problems accrued, and shortly after cementing his status as a Molineux hero by returning from one absence to score with a thunderous header in a 2-0 victory over local rivals West Bromwich Albion, he then exacerbated the knee condition caused by the road accident and was sidelined for virtually all of 1997.

Still, having been honoured twice more by the PFA in its team selections for both 1995/96 and 1996/97, Richards' star continued to ascend, and he was prominent in Wolves' invigorating FA Cup run of 1998, which was ended only by Arsenal at the semi-final stage.

During the subsequent term his indication that he might have to leave Wolves if they didn't gain promotion upset some fans, but it was evident that he deserved top-flight football and in July 1999 he attained it by joining Southampton on a Bosman-style free transfer.

Proving an effective replacement for the redoubtable Ken Monkou, soon he formed a fine central defensive partnership with Claus Lundekvam and in 2000/01 the Saints achieved their best League finish – tenth in the premier division – for almost two decades, with only two goals being conceded in the first three months of the new year.

That spring, amid media talk of a move to a bigger club, Richards signed a contract extension and the supporters relaxed, but come the following September many of them were outraged by his big-money switch to north London. The mood was all the more resentful because the centre-half was following manager Glenn Hoddle from St Mary's to White Hart Lane, and Spurs' popularity on the south coast plunged to a new low.

Richards was very much Hoddle's type of player, classy, constructive and seen as an ideal replacement for Sol Campbell, recently departed to Arsenal. Duly the newcomer made a stunning initial impact, scoring with a stooping near-post header only 15 minutes into his debut at home to Manchester United. By half-time Spurs were three up and, with their latest acquisition looking unflappably excellent, the Lane faithful were enraptured. Alas for them, United hit back with five second-half goals, the first three of them through headers, and Richards' entrance was thus tarnished.

Still, in subsequent games he meshed encouragingly with the less experienced Ledley King and soon his all-round abilities prompted comparisons with Gary Mabbutt, one of the most popular Tottenham players of recent times. At this point he might have been expected to kick on to an even more exalted level, but there were niggling injuries, and then he began experiencing unnatural tiredness, loss of balance and pain.

In 2004 Richards underwent a brain scan, which suggested that the likelihood of a brain tumour was extremely low, but in March 2005 he was advised that to continue playing could harm his health, so he retired. He returned to Bradford City to coach young players in 2007, but tragedy was lying in wait.

Dean Ivor Richards, footballer; born Bradford, Yorkshire, 9 June 1974; played for Bradford City 1992-95, Wolverhampton Wanderers 1995-99, Southampton 1999-2001, Tottenham Hotspur 2001-05; died Leeds, 26 February 2011.

Johnny Morris

The fiery, irreverent little Lancastrian inside-forward Johnny Morris was the multi-talented 'baby' of Matt Busby's first wonderful side, which established the modern tradition of Manchester United.

That lovely team, ever daring to attack so that it might entertain and win but never afraid to risk valiant defeat, finished as championship runners-up in the first three post-war seasons, but applied enchanting balm to the fans' serial frustrations by lifting the FA Cup in 1948 with a sublime exhibition of fluent, sweet-passing football.

At the time of that Wembley victory over a potent Blackpool combination illuminated exquisitely by Stanley Matthews, Morris was 24 and revealing comprehensive all-round ability. Soon, it seemed certain, he would ascend to parity with an exalted company of inside-men then adorning the English game, the likes of Raich Carter, Wilf Mannion, Len Shackleton and Morris' own clubmate, the endearingly modest Stan Pearson.

These were stars who bestrode the turf like sporting emperors, accustomed to dictating the course of the action which swirled around them, making goals and taking them with equal facility.

Morris was the youngest of their number and by no means the least gifted. The accuracy of his passing, over both long distances and short, was exceeded only by its astuteness; he was courageous, often way beyond the call of duty, tackling with a flinty ferocity which made much bigger opponents quail; he was a fine finisher with either foot, particularly his right; and he was unfailingly industrious, scampering to ever corner of the pitch from first whistle to last.

But even as he stood at the threshold of his prime and thrived at the heart of United's burgeoning dominion, so there occurred a rift with Busby, outwardly so benign but an awesomely hard man when crossed.

Thus in March 1949 a British record fee of £24,500 was agreed with Derby County and, to the considerable chagrin of most Red Devils' supporters, Morris was on his way to the Baseball Ground, where he would flourish enough to earn three England caps, but without ever quite scaling the heady heights once predicted for him.

Johnny Morris had emerged with the MUJACs, the Old Trafford club's former junior team, and while still in his teens he attracted widespread attention during a wartime spell on loan with Bolton Wanderers before turning professional with United in 1941.

All too soon, his career impetus was interrupted by the war and he headed for Europe as a member of the Royal Armoured Corps' tank regiment, being one of the first to cross the Rhine as the Allies closed in on victory.

When the conflict ended, Morris returned to Manchester, where instantly he captivated the Red Devils' new manager, Matt Busby, with his exceptional ability. By the autumn of 1946, he had graduated to the first team, with the adaptable Pearson switching from inside-right to inside-left to accommodate the precocious newcomer.

The effect was invigorating as Morris forged a brilliant right-wing partnership with veteran Scottish flankman Jimmy Delaney and also linked sumptuously with Pearson, spearhead Jack Rowley and left-winger Charlie Mitten.

Many of United's most irresistible attacks emanated from the stocky, curly-haired schemer, who was adept at timing his dispatches precisely, so that his colleagues could rampage into space behind opposing defenders.

Morris was in his element at Old Trafford, happy and fulfilled both professionally and socially, and there seemed no limit to what club and player might achieve together. However, an unexpected parting of the ways was imminent.

It was an era of post-war boom for the game, with the entertainment-starved masses flocking to fill the grounds, and with the coffers of the big clubs overflowing. Meanwhile the players were paid a comparative pittance by employers who operated the monstrously unjust retain-and-transfer system, which made footballers into virtual slaves, unable to move on even when their contracts had ended.

To the fiercely independent Morris, this was utter anathema, and he wouldn't accept it. Accordingly he stood up stridently for his rights at every opportunity and, having got nowhere with a succession of forthright requests for a benefit which he believed was owed to him, he asked for a transfer. He was met by a flat refusal by Busby, who told him: 'While I am here you will never leave the club.'

But Morris was as shrewd and combative off the field as he was on it, and he devised a wily strategy to escape from Old Trafford.

He was a magnificent all-round sportsman and recently he had demonstrated his golfing prowess by winning a tournament for United players and staff. Now he demanded his employment cards, declaring his intention of leaving football to make his living as a golfer.

Had he carried out this ingenious threat – and he might just have done so – United would have lost a major talent without banking a penny and so, exceedingly reluctantly, they agreed his switch to Derby.

Eventually United won that elusive League title, in 1952, but most contemporary pundits assert that far more honours would have ended up at Old Trafford had Morris and Busby not clashed over a point of financial principle.

With County, then in the top division, the spiky midfield general continued to play well, but he was no longer surrounded by such high-calibre colleagues as his old mates in Manchester and soon he receded from the international scene.

In 1952, still aged only 29, Morris joined Leicester City, with whom he experienced mixed fortunes, his two Second Division title medals of 1953/54 and 1956/57 being punctuated by relegation in 1954/55.

He left the League in 1958 to become player-boss of Corby Town, then filled a similar role for Kettering Town before laying aside his boots to guide Rugby Town, Great Harwood and Oswestry Town, work he combined with a job as a tyre salesman, plenty of time on the golf course and a full family life.

Away from the action, the effervescent Morris was an effortless spinner of yarns, as entertaining in the bar as he was on the field. He relished his time in football, adoring the cameraderie, especially at Old Trafford, and he understood perfectly that he might have achieved more had he compromised his beliefs and remained in Manchester in 1949.

But Johnny Morris was not one to harbour regrets. What might have been? It never bothered him in the slightest.

John Morris, footballer; born Radcliffe, Lancashire, 27 September 1923; played for Manchester United 1941-49, Derby County 1949-52, Leicester City 1952-58; capped three times by England 1949; died Bolton, Lancashire, 6 April 2011.

Billy Gray

Billy Gray was an energetic, endlessly enthusiastic, all-purpose football man. The diminutive north-easterner thrived with five clubs as a player, first as a winger, then as a deep-lying schemer and eventually as a full-back. Though not quite of full international quality, he earned a cap for England 'B' in 1950; he exerted vast influence as Nottingham Forest won the FA Cup in 1959; he managed Millwall to successive promotions in the mid-1960s, and he bossed two other League clubs; finally he returned to Forest as groundsman in the 1980s, during the era of Brian Clough.

Yet for all his commitment and his abundant natural ability, Gray – an all-rounder who also excelled at tennis and golf – did not find an easy path into the professional ranks. Though his post-war efforts in the Newcastle and District League for his local club,

Dinnington Colliery, earned him trials with top-flight Wolverhampton Wanderers and Gateshead of the Third Division North, neither took him on and it was not until May 1947, at the age of 20, that he was recruited by his first Football League employer, Leyton Orient.

At Brisbane Road he made a brisk initial impact, scoring in his second game, and although he didn't command a regular berth with the Third Division South side, in December 1948 he demonstrated his prodigious appetite by turning out twice in one day, for the reserves in the morning and the first team in the afternoon.

Despite making only 20 appearances for Orient, Gray was snapped up by Chelsea for a modest fee in March 1949 and commenced to play the best football of his life to date. Featuring on either flank, he sparkled as the Pensioners staved off relegation from the old First Division in three successive seasons in the early 1950s, under first Billy Birrell and then Ted Drake, and he was suitably rewarded with his England 'B' call-up. He made the most of it, too, scoring in a 5-0 victory over the Swiss in January 1950, but was never summoned again.

Gray shone, also, as Chelsea reached FA Cup semi-finals in 1949/50 and 1951/52, falling to Arsenal both times after replays, all four games being played at White Hart Lane. In the first he gave a particularly torrid time to the Gunners' Welsh international full-back Walley Barnes while linking slickly with classy centre-forward Roy Bentley, and in the third he contributed Chelsea's goal in a 1-1 draw.

The Stamford Bridge fans warmed to the chunky Gray's eagerness, they admired his pace, trickery and dexterity at crossing the ball, and they marvelled at his stamina as he sprinted up and down his touchline, putting in considerably more physical effort than many wingers of his day.

Accordingly, they were aghast in August 1953, when he was sold for £16,000 to Burnley, whose supporters were in a similarly outraged frame of mind over the recent departure to Sunderland of a favourite attacker, Billy Elliott. The signing of Gray, who inherited veteran Jackie Chew's number-seven shirt, was seen as a coup for Turf Moor boss Frank Hill, especially when the newcomer scored seven times in an autumn spell of six games, including a hat-trick in a 4-2 home victory over Spurs.

That term Gray was ever-present, forming a potent partnership with the inspirational Irish inside-forward Jimmy McIlroy and topping the Clarets' goal chart with 20 strikes in senior competition. It was a remarkable achievement, given that he had notched only 13 in his entire career before joining Burnley, and he was a major factor in the club's creditable seventh-place finish in the First Division and their elimination of Manchester United from the FA Cup.

Gray continued to excel as the Clarets remained in the top half of the table during the next two campaigns, but in 1956 he lost his place to the younger Doug Newlands, which led to his transfer to Nottingham Forest, newly promoted to the elite level, in June 1957.

In 1957/58 Gray, who had just turned 30, was workmanlike as Forest consolidated their status, but it was in 1958/59 that he blossomed anew after the shrewd City Ground manager Billy Walker converted him from flankman to midfield general.

Meshing smoothly with cultured wing-half Jeff Whitefoot and fellow inside-forward Johnny Quigley, he shone as a creator and also scored five goals, including three penalties, during Forest's progress to the FA Cup final. At Wembley, where Forest beat Luton Town 2-1 – despite losing the scorer of their first goal, Roy Dwight, to a broken leg and battling on with ten men in those pre-substitute days – Gray was in tremendous form. He had a hand in Dwight's effort and then, having dropped even deeper than usual following the accident, he set up his side's second goal for centre-forward Tommy Wilson.

As the years crept up on him, Gray switched successfully to full-back and was part of Forest's first foray into Europe, in the Inter-Cities Fairs Cup in 1961/62. Alas, they perished in the first round, 7-1 on aggregate to Valencia.

Having made his last appearance in the top flight only shortly before his 36th birthday, he joined Millwall as player-boss in November 1963, taking over a team in dire straits and which was relegated to the Fourth Division at the end of that season.

However, Gray, a deep-thinking, ceaselessly industrious character, reacted positively, laying the foundations of a youth policy which was to reap rich dividends later in the decade and blending his rookies with experienced performers such as Len Julians and Jimmy Whitehouse.

With a side including goalkeeper Alex Stepney, who was later to star for Manchester United, popular full-back Harry Cripps and striker Hugh Curran, he led Millwall to second place in Division Four in 1964/65. Then, with a few tweaks, he guided them towards runners-up spot in Division Three a year later, a colossal achievement rendered more remarkable by the fact that they remained unbeaten at the Den throughout both promotion campaigns.

Sadly for a man who had wrought such a dramatic transformation, Gray never took his creation into Division Two, having departed following a rift with Millwall directors in the spring of 1966.

That summer he took over at Brentford and, despite a shortage of cash which almost put them out of business during his tenure, he kept them in the top half of Division Four. In September 1967 he moved on to Notts County, another impecunious club from the same grade, and although they were bottom of the table when he resigned a year later, he had made several canny signings, including future Scotland international play-maker Don Masson and long-serving forward Les Bradd. Later he coached at Fulham before his stint in charge of the City Ground pitch.

In May 2009 Gray and his old comrade Whitefoot, who is now the only survivor of Nottingham Forest's FA Cup triumph of 1959, led the official celebrations of its 50th anniversary.

William Patrick Gray, footballer and manager; born Dinnington, County Durham, 24 May 1927; played for Leyton Orient 1947-49, Chelsea 1949-53, Burnley 1953-57, Nottingham Forest 1957-63, Millwall 1963-65; managed Millwall 1963-66, Brentford 1966-67, Notts County 1967-68; died Aspley, Nottingham, 11 April 2011.

Allan Brown

Allan Brown was dubbed the unluckiest footballer in the land after being invalided out of the FA Cup finals of 1951 and 1953 during an era when the Wembley showpiece was truly the gala day of the English game.

At the time the burly but deceptively deft Scottish international inside-forward was wearing the tangerine shirt of Blackpool, then one of the most powerful clubs in British football, and his plight seemed all the more excruciating because on both occasions he had played a major part in ensuring the Seasiders' presence beneath the twin towers of the famous old stadium.

In '51, having made his customary assertive impact in every round up to and including the semi-final, he suffered a serious knee injury in a League game at Huddersfield three weeks before the big day. Two years later his plight was perhaps even more poignant when he broke his leg in the act of scoring a late winner in the cup quarter-final against Arsenal at Highbury.

It was a sickening blow to a high-quality performer in his pomp, one who could hold his own in the company of such star Bloomfield Road team-mates as the incomparable flankman Stanley Matthews, prolific England marksman Stanley Mortensen and the shrewd little midfield schemer Ernie Taylor.

Known as 'Bomber' Brown for his high-velocity shot, he was strong, quick and courageous, but also was a beautiful passer of the ball, being capable of arrowing penetrative long-distance dispatches to his fellow attackers, or taking part in quickfire close-range interchanges which could be hellishly difficult to combat, especially when they involved the two Stanleys.

At international level, he both climaxed and concluded his service by appearing in Scotland's two games in the 1954 World Cup finals in Switzerland, both defeats, and it seems reasonable to conjecture that he would have collected more than his 14 caps had it not been for a depressing catalogue of injuries.

As a teenager, Fifer Brown played for Kennoway, the team bearing the name of the mining village where he was born, before entering the professional ranks with East Fife in 1944. He made his senior debut in 1947, but it was not until he had completed his National Service that he earned a regular berth in 1948/49, by which time the club had reached the top flight of the Scottish League.

He helped them to finish a creditable fourth that term, and again in the next, but their highlight of 1949/50 was in winning the League Cup, Brown scoring in the semi-final victory over Rangers, before shining in the 3-0 cuffing of Dunfermline Athletic in the October final. Then, to prove it was no fluke, they reached the final of the Scottish FA Cup in the spring, but this time lost to the Ibrox giants.

Brown's meteoric progress was recognised by an international call-up and he scored in each of his first three outings for his country, in victories over Switzerland at Hampden Park that April and Paris in France a month later, sandwiched by a draw with Portugal in Lisbon.

An ambitious and determined individual, now he eyed a move to England, and when East Fife demurred he went half the next season without wages, taking part-time jobs to earn cash and remain fit. In a bid to end the bitter dispute, East Fife spoke to Liverpool, Portsmouth and Manchester City about a possible transfer before selling their prime asset to Blackpool in December for £27,250, then the record fee received by a Scottish club. Brown settled quickly at Bloomfield Road, no doubt helped by a Scottish enclave which included George Farm, Jackie Mudie, Hugh Kelly and Ewan Fenton, and he made a dramatic impact on his debut, creating all three goals in a 3-2 win at Charlton.

Thereafter, despite a miserable injury record, he became a key figure for the next half-decade, during which he netted 74 times in 185 games for the Seasiders, without ever being their principal spearhead. His most bountiful campaign was 1952/53, during which he struck 17 times in 34 appearances, a comparable ratio with the sharp-shooting Mortensen.

For Brown it was a season which culminated in heartache, his collision with the Arsenal goalkeeper, Jack Kelsey, condemning him to watch on crutches what would enter folklore as 'The Matthews Final', in which Blackpool defeated Bolton 4-3. His form at the time of the accident had been scintillating, prompting Clifford Greenwood of *The Green* to report: 'If Allan Brown was not the best inside-forward in the country on the day he broke his leg at Highbury, I have never seen a footballer.'

By the mid-1950s, mostly due to a variety of wounds, he began to find himself in and out of the side and in February 1957, despite having registered 13 hits in a mere 17 League games that term, he was sold to First Division rivals Luton Town for £8,000.

Though by now in his thirties, Brown proved immensely influential at Kenilworth Road, and in 1959 finally made it to an FA Cup final, having scored five times on the Hatters' road to Wembley, including the winner in a quarter-final replay at home to Blackpool. It was ironic that he was his former club's executioner, but at least it allowed the Seasiders' more charitable fans to congratulate a former hero on his change of luck.

At Wembley Luton met Nottingham Forest, whom they had recently drubbed 5-1 in a League game with Brown scoring four times, but as a portent for the main event it could hardly have been more misleading. Forest, reduced to ten men by a mishap to Roy Dwight, won 2-1, and Brown missed a late chance to take the contest into extra time.

After enduring relegation with Luton in 1959/60, the veteran Scot was sold to second-tier Portsmouth for £4,000 in March 1961, but was unable to prevent their demotion a few weeks later. However, having been converted to wing-half as he had slowed down, he proved a bulwark of the Pompey team which lifted the Third Division crown in 1961/62.

After one more season at Fratton Park, Brown left the Football League in his 37th year to become player-boss of Wigan Athletic, then a Cheshire League club. He was an immediate success, guiding his new charges to a bevy of trophies, including four in one term, and to one remarkable sequence of 53 games without defeat.

Come 1966, frustrated that there seemed to be little likelihood of Wigan attaining League status at that point, Brown took over at Luton, who by then were in dire straits near the foot of the Fourth Division. Displaying all his characteristic single-mindedness, and administering stern discipline, he transformed the Hatters so radically that they won their championship at the end of his first full season. Then, astonishingly, while Luton were on their way to another promotion, he was sacked in December 1968 for applying for a job with Leicester City, then struggling in the top flight.

Unsurprisingly Brown wasn't unemployed for long. In January 1969 he took the reins of Torquay United, leading them to sixth place in the Third Division that season, then to two mid-table finishes before being dismissed following a poor start to 1971/72.

There followed a stint as Bury boss between April 1972, during which he helped to lead the Shakers out of debt for the first time in years by trading at a profit in the transfer market, then he set them on the way to promotion from the basement tier before becoming manager of Second Division Nottingham Forest in November 1973.

At the City Ground, where he nurtured the precocious talent of Duncan McKenzie before angering fans by selling him to Leeds, he saw Forest to seventh place in the table and to the quarter-finals of the FA Cup in 1973/74, but then was sacked in the middle of 1974/75 – and replaced by Brian Clough – following a dismal run of results culminating in an inept display in the local derby with Notts County.

Next came a fleeting and unrewarding spell in charge of Fourth Division Southport before he took control at Blackpool, the scene of his greatest achievement, in May 1976.

He arrived at Bloomfield Road with all the advantages of a much-loved former player and in his first campaign, with an attractive team featuring the free-scoring Mickey Walsh, the Seasiders missed out narrowly on promotion to the First Division.

They were favourites to make it next time, but in February 1978 there were differences with the board and Brown was axed, much to the consternation of supporters.

After that he enjoyed a coaching engagement with Quadsia of Kuwait, before he made a second return to Blackpool in March 1981 in the wake of Alan Ball's acrimonious departure. At that point they were a hard-up club in freefall and he couldn't prevent them dropping into the fourth grade that spring. In 1981/82 he steered them to a mid-table position before leaving the game.

Allan Duncan Brown, footballer and manager; born Kennoway, Fife, 12 October 1926; played for East Fife 1944-50, Blackpool 1950-56, Luton Town 1956-60, Portsmouth 1960-62; capped 14 times by Scotland 1950-54; managed Luton Town 1966-68, Torquay United 1969-71, Bury 1972-73, Nottingham Forest 1973-75, Southport 1976, Blackpool 1976-78 and 1981-82; died Blackpool, Lancashire, 19 April 2011.

Eddie Lewis

When Manchester United manager Matt Busby was seeking a long-term replacement for centre-forward Jack 'The Gunner' Rowley, as that prolific powerhouse of the Old Trafford attack began to show signs of ageing during the 1952/53 campaign in which the Red Devils saw their championship crown slip away to Arsenal, there was a brief but enthralling interlude when teenager Eddie Lewis looked capable of stepping up to the mark.

The burly Mancunian scored only seven minutes into his debut against West Bromwich Albion at the Hawthorns in November, then embarked on a post-Christmas spree of eight more goals in ten matches. He was gorging himself on the pinpoint deliveries of wingers Johnny Berry and David Pegg while linking promisingly with the shrewd veteran inside-forward Stan Pearson, and there were optimistic observers on the Stretford End who believed they were witnessing the birth of a star.

Alas for Lewis, his manager, although impressed by the rookie's progress, was not quite convinced. Accordingly, he signed the strapping young leviathan Tommy Taylor from Barnsley for the then-colossal fee of £29,999 – Busby handed the odd pound to the tea lady because he didn't want to encumber his new recruit with a £30,000 tag – and thereafter the local boy was given scant opportunity by the brilliant newcomer.

When it became clear that any Old Trafford future for Lewis would be as a reserve, he elected for a fresh start and in December 1955, after inquiries from Sunderland and Wolverhampton Wanderers had been knocked back, he accepted a £10,000 transfer to Preston North End, at the time a formidable force on the domestic scene.

Having contributed 11 strikes in 24 appearances for United, Lewis arrived at Deepdale carrying considerable expectations, but he failed to settle there and in November 1956 he moved on to second-tier West Ham United in a swap deal which saw Irish international wing-half Frank O'Farrell travel in the opposite direction.

At Upton Park his tally of 15 goals in 36 games was better than respectable, but he could not claim a regular berth in the side which lifted the divisional title in 1957/58 and that summer he switched to Leyton Orient, where finally he found a hugely productive niche. Following one largely ineffective term in the Orient front line, Lewis was converted into a left-back, a role in which, after a couple of seasons of acclimatisation, he flourished superbly.

A watershed in the fortunes of both Lewis and the Brisbane Road club came with the arrival as manager in August 1961 of Johnny Carey, who had been captain of Manchester United when the young spearhead had made his entrance nearly a decade earlier.

Now Carey, who praised Lewis as an all-round footballer and did much to boost his confidence, transformed Orient from strugglers into a buoyant combination which clinched promotion to the top flight as Second Division runners-up to Bill Shankly's Liverpool in 1962.

As part of a trusty defensive unit which included fellow full-back Stan Charlton, centre-half Sid Bishop and wing-halves Malcolm Lucas and Cyril Lea, Lewis performed with admirable consistency and missed only one game during that glorious campaign.

Sadly, though, critics who maintained that the east Londoners were being promoted above their station were proved correct, as they floundered dismally among the elite and finished bottom of the First Division in 1962/63, ten points adrift of the pack.

With first Les Gore and then Benny Fenton having replaced Carey as boss, Orient laboured back in the Second Division and in 1964 Lewis – who had been judged surplus to requirements by the Os, for whom he had made 164 senior appearances – entered non-League circles with Folkestone Town.

Lewis went on to manage clubs in the Greater London League before emigrating to South Africa in the 1970s. At first he worked as an insurance salesman, then he became a successful coach, and eventually one of football's most prominent figures in his adopted country.

During the era of apartheid he ran two major clubs in different leagues, guiding Wits University on a Saturday and the Kaizer Chiefs on a Sunday. In time he passed on his wisdom to many more teams, including Manning Rangers, Free State Stars, Sharp Highland Park, D'Alberton Callies, Giant Blackpool, AmaZulu and Moroka Swallows, of whom he became technical advisor in 2007, a post he occupied until his death.

A strong, forthright personality recognised as one of the pioneers of the professional game in South Africa, Lewis was also a respected analyst on television. He died after a long battle with cancer, demonstrating remarkable resolution as he refused to bow the knee to the disease, continuing with gymnasium sessions until a short time before the end.

Edward Lewis, footballer and coach; born Manchester, 3 January 1935; played for Manchester United 1949-55, Preston North End 1955-56, West Ham United 1956-58, Leyton Orient 1958-64; died Johannesburg, South Africa, 2 May 2011.

Tommy Wright

When Sunderland's extravagant spending in the decade after the Second World War earned them a slightly raffish reputation as 'the Bank of England club', their headlines tended to be generated by the likes of Len Shackleton, Trevor Ford and Billy Bingham. Yet few men did more to further the Wearsiders' cause during that colourful but ultimately unfulfilling phase of their history than the stellar trio's dashingly direct fellow attacker Tommy Wright.

The Scottish international right-winger, who contributed punch and penetration, ceaseless industry and not a few goals, was ever-present as the Roker Park club finished third in the top flight in 1949/50, the only time they have scaled such rarefied heights since they were champions of England in 1936, during the early heyday of the revered Raich Carter.

Wright, who could also perform with distinction in any other forward position, was consistent, too, his tally of strikes reaching double figures in four out of his five full seasons in the north-east, the fifth term being sabotaged by injury.

After being spotted playing for one of his local clubs, Blairhall Colliery in Clackmannanshire, Wright was taken to Glasgow by Partick Thistle in 1945. He made his senior debut in 1947/48, his skill and brio contributing impressively to the Jags finishing the campaign third in the elite division behind Hibernian and Rangers, and when he commenced the following term in similarly effective form, it became obvious that his tenure at Firhill would be short-lived.

Accordingly, in March 1949 an £8,000 bid from Sunderland was accepted and Wright inherited the Rokerites' number-seven shirt from Len Duns, a veteran of the title triumph 13 years earlier. After bedding into the side that spring, the newcomer shone throughout the following campaign, in which Sunderland finished only a point adrift of champions Portsmouth and runners-up Wolverhampton Wanderers.

Forming a productive right-flank combination with Ivor Broadis, and also linking smoothly with the other inside-forward, the dazzling but eccentric Shackleton, Wright became a stalwart of Bill Murray's entertaining team, his personal highlight a hat-trick in a 4-2 home victory over Everton in the penultimate game of the season when the big prize was still at stake.

During 1950/51 the fearsome physical presence of spearhead Trevor Ford was added to the mix, and Wright became one of the abrasive Welshman's chief providers, his crosses and through-balls resulting in countless goal-scoring opportunities.

Fitness problems cost him most of the subsequent term, but he was back in both peak condition and form for 1952/53, during which he earned his three Scotland caps, helping to beat Wales 2-1 at Ninian Park and featuring in draws with Northern Ireland at Hampden Park and England at Wembley. His settling-in at the higher level could not have been helped by being paired with a different inside partner each time – first Allan Brown, then Jimmy Logie and finally Bobby Johnstone – but he gave an acceptable account of himself and some observers reckoned he was unfortunate to be discarded thereafter.

Wright was edged off the international stage by a succession of rivals – including Rangers' powerful Willie Waddell, big John McKenzie of Partick Thistle and Hibernian's elegant Gordon Smith – but he continued to thrive at club level, enjoying his most prolific season in 1953/54 when his 18 goals in 38 appearances were hugely influential in Sunderland escaping relegation to the Second Division.

However, having reached his middle thirties, and with the excellent Bingham laying unarguable claim to the right-wing slot, in January 1955 Wright returned to his homeland to join East Fife as the makeweight in the deal which took the prolific marksman Charlie 'Cannonball' Fleming to Roker Park.

Back in the Scottish League's top tier, he looked comfortable, clearly one of the classier members of the Bayview staff, and his 18 goals in 36 games were an admirable addition to the 55 in 180 outings achieved in more demanding circumstances on Wearside.

Wright surprised many observers by re-crossing the border to join Oldham Athletic of the Third Division North in March 1957 – the fee was £700 – but he sojourned only briefly at Boundary Park, leaving the Football League that summer to join North Shields.

Thus he completed a commendable career, setting the example for several family members to follow a similar path. His son, also Tommy Wright, played for five English clubs – most notably Leeds United, Oldham and Leicester City – in the 1980s and '90s and was a Scotland under-21 international; one nephew, Jackie Sinclair, who died last year, excelled for Dunfermline Athletic, Leicester and others, and was capped once by Scotland; and another, Willie Sinclair, played for Falkirk, Huddersfield Town and several more.

Thomas Wright, footballer; born Blandhill, Clackmannanshire, 28 January 1928; played for Partick Thistle 1945-49, Sunderland 1949-55, East Fife 1955-57, Oldham Athletic 1957; died Sunderland, 5 May 2011.

Frank Upton

When fans of Derby County were regaled with lurid tales of tough nuts at rival clubs in the late 1950s, they would grin knowingly. To them there were plenty of common or garden hard men scattered through the four divisions of the Football League – and then there was Frank Upton.

Not for nothing was the tall, angular Midlander, who later helped Chelsea to earn promotion to the top flight and to lift the League Cup, known as 'Frank the Tank'.

Whether operating in his customary role as a defensive wing-half, or slotting in at full-back or even as an emergency centre-forward, Upton relished a tackle, to put it mildly, his bone-crunching style beloved of regulars at the Baseball Ground and then at Stamford Bridge, not quite so popular among opposition supporters.

Not that the Tank, who also packed a howitzer of a shot, was a dirty player, rather he was fair and fearless and utterly committed to the cause. Subtle he was not, however, his passes often delivered with such sharp velocity that his other nickname, 'Stroker', was wickedly ironic.

Whatever else, Upton was an endlessly enthusiastic worker, who in his early days as a part-timer with Derby toiled also in a blacksmith's shop, getting up at 5am, making an arduous journey to his anvil by foot and by bus, then knocking off at the end of a demanding shift before, on two nights a week, bussing it to the Baseball Ground for training.

It was a routine which left him, he recalled, 'a bit shattered', although fundamentally he enjoyed it, and his opinion on Fabio Capello's lament about his England stars' summer fatigue after their recent lacklustre display against Switzerland would surely have been both trenchant and entertaining.

After leaving school, Upton featured for non-League Nuneaton Borough before signing for Northampton Town of the old Third Division South in March 1953. That spring the 18-year-old rookie played in the last four games of the campaign as the Cobblers missed out on promotion only on goal average, the absurdly complicated precursor to goal difference as a means of separating clubs level on points.

A few more promising appearances during the following term preceded a move to second-flight Derby County in June 1954, but although he missed only the final match of the season Upton couldn't save the Rams from relegation as bottom club, well adrift of the pack.

Soon, under the strict but expert tutelage of manager Harry Storer, Upton matured into a redoubtable and consistent performer, but after missing out narrowly on promotion in 1955/56 he made only nine appearances during 1956/57 as Derby won the Third Division North title, his serial absences explained by his National Service.

Thereafter he shone as Storer's side consolidated in the Second Division, his flinty endeavours almost securing a move to Liverpool at the end of the decade. At that point Bill Shankly had just assumed the Anfield reins and was seeking to stiffen the resolve of a team which had failed repeatedly to regain its berth in the top tier.

The inspirational Scot saw in Upton exactly the steel he required, but an illness in his family made the player reluctant to move so he remained at the Baseball Ground until a £15,000 transfer to Chelsea in August 1961.

Bought by Ted Drake, who was soon to be replaced as Stamford Bridge boss by Tommy Docherty, Upton once again suffered demotion with a new employer as the Pensioners ended that season at the foot of the First Division.

However, after taking time initially to pin down a specific role, Frank the Tank emerged as a key factor in Chelsea's successful attempt to bounce back at the first attempt, finishing as runners-up to an enterprising Stoke City side for which Stanley Matthews was enjoying a remarkable Indian summer as he neared his fiftieth birthday.

Playing at left-half, Upton proved a steadying influence in a precocious young side featuring the likes of Peter Bonetti, Terry Venables and Bobby Tambling, his experience effectively tempering the gleeful impetuosity of the talented boys around him.

Upton remained a key factor as the west Londoners soared to fifth in the elite tier in 1963/64, but he had fallen behind a more youthful hard case in the muscular person of Ron Harris. Thus he managed only three outings in the next campaign, during which Chelsea pushed Manchester United for the League championship, eventually finishing third.

There was compensation, though, as Docherty called him into the side for the second leg of the League Cup final against Leicester City at Filbert Street, with Harris moving to right-half in place of the indisposed John Hollins and Upton donning his customary number-six shirt. Having prevailed 3-2 in the first leg, Chelsea took the trophy with a goalless draw and Upton had bagged his only senior medal.

By then approaching the veteran stage, he returned to Derby in September 1965, spending a year in the Second Division and extending his Rams record to 272 games before joining Notts County for a brief stint in the Fourth. There followed six months with Worcester City before re-entering the Football League as player-boss of Workington in January 1968.

It proved to be a difficult task at Borough Park, and when the north-westerners finished second from bottom of the basement division that term, being forced to apply (successfully) for re-election, Upton was sacked.

Still dedicated to the game, and particularly accomplished when working with young players, he went on to a long and varied career as a coach, during which he served fleetingly as caretaker manager of Chelsea, following Ken Shellito's departure in 1978.

His other billets included Northampton, Aston Villa, Randers Freja of Denmark, Dundee, El-Arabi of Kuwait, Wolverhampton Wanderers, Bedworth United (manager), Coventry City, Keflavik of Iceland, Burton Albion, Northwich Victoria, Cheltenham, Derby and Leicester. There were also stints in Borneo and Malaysia, and he ran a sports injury clinic in Derby during the 1990s.

Frank Upton, footballer and manager; born Atherstone, Warwickshire, 18 October 1934; played for Northampton Town 1953-54, Derby County 1954-61 and 1965-66, Chelsea 1961-65, Notts County 1966-67, Workington 1968; died Findern, Derbyshire, 16 May 2011.

Mike Doyle

It's not easy to imagine a footballer being more passionate about a club than Mike Doyle was about his beloved Manchester City. The fiercely loyal, jaggedly combative Mancunian, who contributed mightily during the most successful interlude in the Blues' history to date – under Joe Mercer and Malcolm Allison in the late 1960s, then on into the following decade – was warrior, talisman and richly accomplished all-round performer rolled into one.

Yet even that collection of compelling attributes did not encompass the full extent of Doyle's appeal to the Maine Road faithful. As a bonus to City fans infuriated by the perceived superiority complex of their illustrious neighbours, he hated Manchester United with a vengeance. Better still in the eyes of his admirers, he was always ready to trumpet that loathing of the Old Trafford institution, a mindset which was entirely genuine and stretched back to childhood.

Certainly, when Doyle was in his prime, no build-up to a local derby was complete without a rash of inflammatory outpourings from the vituperative City loyalist. However, it would be shameful if Doyle's reputation as a rabid United-baiter was allowed to obscure his considerable talent as a player. Whether operating in midfield or, later in his career, as a central defender, he wielded immense influence. There was courage and commitment aplenty – he was once voted City's hardest ever footballer in a supporters' poll – but there was skill, audacity and remarkable consistency, too.

Doyle was a central figure as the Blues won the League title in 1968, the FA Cup in 1969, and the European Cup Winners' Cup and League Cup in 1970, then he skippered the side which lifted the League Cup again in 1976. It was a time of glittering achievement, often referred to as the Lee, Bell and Summerbee era in tribute to the team's extravagantly gifted attacking trio, but the work of cult hero Doyle and other doughty bulwarks such as Tony Book and Alan Oakes should never be underestimated.

Doyle, a policeman's son who was taught unarmed combat as a youngster so that he could look after himself in a tough city, was always determined to become a professional footballer. When he was nine he outlined his ambition in a letter to the *Manchester Evening News*, an earnest declaration of intent which was tucked away in the filing system of City's chief scout Harry Godwin.

A few years later, after Doyle had impressed as a defender for Stockport Boys, Godwin dug out the cutting, found his target's address and soon, in May 1962, the young City fanatic joined the Blues' groundstaff.

At Maine Road the tall, slim but physically resilient rookie made rapid strides as a footballer, but there was no disguising an emotional, even confrontational side to a personality which had been rendered even more prickly by enduring taunts from crowing United fans for as long as he could remember.

He was confident, too, as illustrated by an incident involving City's talismanic goalkeeper Bert Trautmann which has passed into club folklore. The giant German had just conceded eight goals against Wolverhampton Wanderers and as he was getting changed, young Doyle, who was sweeping the dressing-room floor, inquired into the condition of the great man's back, implying that it must be aching after bending down so frequently to retrieve the ball from the net. The precocious kid paid for his cheek, being sentenced to wash Trautmann's car for the rest of the season, but a colourful character had made the first of many indelible marks with his new employer.

After launching a lasting mutual enmity with George Best in an FA Youth Cup semi-final which was lost to Manchester United in the spring of 1964 – the pair just rubbed each other up the wrong way – 18-year-old Doyle made his senior debut, as a wing-half, in a Second Division clash at Cardiff in March 1965 and by season's end was laying claim to a regular berth.

That summer City's world was turned upside down by the arrival of Mercer and Allison, whose inspirational approach rapidly lifted the Blues from mid-table mediocrity to promotion at the head of the second tier in 1966. During that campaign, and in the one that followed consolidating among the elite, Doyle was never quite a fixture in the side, but did more than enough to underline his potential, usually in midfield but occasionally, and successfully, as an emergency centre-forward.

But it was in 1967/68, which climaxed with City pipping reigning champions United to the League title on the last afternoon of the season, that Doyle made the number-four shirt his own. Aggressive in the tackle, effective in the air and capable of joining in smoothly with the flowing movement of a wondrously entertaining team, he shone brightly, his lustre particularly noticeable as United were cuffed aside at Old Trafford in a crucial springtime encounter.

The glory continued with Doyle prominent as Leicester were beaten 1-0 in the 1969 FA Cup final; then he scored an equaliser as West Bromwich Albion were overcome 2-1 in the 1970 League Cup final, and he was a dominant figure as City defeated the Polish side Gornik Zabrze by the same score to lift the European Cup Winners' Cup a few weeks later.

Soon afterwards Mercer stepped aside, albeit uneasily, to leave Allison in control. City seemed to be on course for another title in 1972 until the signing of the gifted but enigmatic Rodney Marsh appeared to disrupt the balance of the side and they fell away to finish fourth, although only one point behind champions Derby County. Doyle never liked Marsh, seeing him as a flashy southern poser, and didn't trouble to hide his feelings, which was typical.

In 1973 there came a watershed in the Doyle career when he switched to central defence, initially alongside Tommy Booth and then in partnership with newcomer Dave Watson. He proved majestic in the new role, which he occupied as City lost the 1974 League Cup final to Wolves, and on the last Saturday of that season he was on top form and utterly exultant as a City win at Old Trafford confirmed the relegation of what had become an extremely poor United side.

A year later Doyle was handed the task for which he might have been born, the captaincy of Manchester City, by former team-mate Tony Book, by then the Blues' boss. He proved a splendid leader and was practically bursting with pride after leading his charges to League Cup final triumph over Newcastle United in 1976.

Such was his command and reliability that term that Doyle earned what the Maine Road faithful maintained was woefully overdue full international recognition, England manager Don Revie calling him up to face Wales at Wrexham. However, his top-level tenure was to be short-lived, his final game for his country ending in dismal defeat by Holland in February 1977, when he was one of three centre-halves fielded by Revie against opponents with no recognised centre-forward.

Still, Doyle had collected five caps to add to his eight under-23 appearances and two outings for the Football League, and might have gained further senior honours had he not been forced to withdraw from England's provisional World Cup finals squad in 1970 because his wife was seriously ill.

For most of 1976/77 Doyle remained at his best, but he was never quite the same again after being sidelined by an ankle injury in the spring. City missed him, then, in a series of crucial games, which might have been a decisive factor in another tense championship race, the Blues finishing as runners-up, this time a point adrift of Liverpool.

Thereafter he struggled for fitness and in July 1978, having entered his thirties and played more than 550 times for the Blues – more than anyone else except Joe Corrigan and Alan Oakes – he was sold to second-tier Stoke City for £50,000. At the Victoria Ground, despite often playing through pain, Doyle gave magnificent value for money as the Potters were promoted in 1979 and he was voted the club's player of the year.

After helping Stoke adjust to life in the First Division, he stepped down a level with Bolton Wanderers in January 1982, then gave the last season of his career to Rochdale of the Fourth Division in 1983/84. Later Doyle, who worked as a representative for a sports equipment company after retiring from football, drank heavily and in 2007 he spent a spell in the Sporting Chance clinic, set up by Tony Adams through the Professional Footballers' Association. Thereafter he shunned alcohol for 18 months but the problem resurfaced and his premature death, at the age of 64, was due to liver failure.

Michael Doyle, footballer; born Manchester, 25 November 1946; played for Manchester City 1962-78, Stoke City 1978-82, Bolton Wanderers 1982-83, Rochdale 1983-84; capped five times by England 1976-77; died Ashton-under-Lyne, 27 June 2011.

Willie Fernie

Conjure an image of a typical top-quality Scottish inside-forward – a breed which proliferated in the two decades after the Second World War but now, sadly, seems all but extinct – and Celtic's Willie Fernie springs irresistibly to mind.

Quick and clever, an inspired dribbler blessed with the most beguiling of body-swerves, the elegant Fifer with the loping stride was an instinctive finder and exploiter of space, a perceptive passer and a beautifully balanced athlete as sure-footed on the mud and ice of midwinter as he was on the lush green grass of late summer.

Some critics reckoned he was prone to hang on to the ball too long, and he was the first to acknowledge that sometimes he did, but Parkhead's 'Wizard of the Weave' was a truly enchanting entertainer during his 1950s pomp. Indeed, such was his mastery over a football while travelling at speed that, despite operating as an infield attacker far more frequently than he appeared on the wing, Fernie earned another expansive sobriquet, 'Scotland's Stanley Matthews', the ultimate compliment to any player in an era when the Englishman's name was a byword for soccer excellence in every corner of the globe.

Fernie sported the dark blue of Scotland in the World Cup final tournaments of 1954 and 1958, and surely would have accumulated far more than his 12 senior caps but for the plethora of competition for his position from such creative thoroughbreds as Bobby Johnstone, Bobby Collins, Allan Brown and Jackie Mudie.

While enjoying his football as a teenager with a local Fife club, Leslie Hearts, Fernie revealed a combination of artistry, industry and physical resilience which attracted scouts from far and wide. However, trials with Aberdeen and Raith Rovers came to nothing before Celtic talent-hunter Pat Duffy impressed the rookie by visiting him in hospital, where he was being treated for a broken jaw, and he enlisted with the Bhoys in October 1948.

Though Fernie's potential was evident, he was not yet ready for Celtic's first string and initially he was loaned to Kinglassie Colliery, a side based in his home village. Duly he sparkled at that level and in March 1950 made his senior debut for Celtic in a 1-0 victory over St Mirren at Love Street.

By 1952/53 he had staked a persuasive claim to a regular place and he climaxed that breakthrough campaign with a rousing show on the left wing – he was versatile enough to perform on either flank as well as in any midfield slot – in the Coronation Cup final against Hibernian at Hampden Park in May. Deputising that day for the revered Irishman Charlie Tully in a reshuffled side, he set up the goals for Neil Mochan and Jimmy Walsh which secured a 2-0 victory over Hibernian.

Fernie carried that scintillating form into 1953/54, which was to prove the most fulfilling season of his career. Gelling enthrallingly with an array of fellow attackers which included John Higgins, John McPhail, Sean Fallon, Bertie Peacock (when he ventured forward from wing-half), Collins, Tully, Walsh and Mochan, he was a key man as Celtic lifted the League and Scottish Cup double, contributing a dozen goals in the process.

He loved to run at defenders and one deathless highlight came in the cup final triumph over Aberdeen when he embarked on a typical lung-bursting foray deep into opposition territory before delivering smoothly for Fallon to convert.

Duly his efforts were rewarded that May with a first full international call-up, building on earlier selections for Scotland 'B' and the Scottish League. First he helped to defeat Finland in Helsinki, then he featured in both of Scotland's reverses in the summer's World Cup finals, 1-0 to Austria in Zurich and a humiliating 7-0 to Uruguay in Basle.

Back at club level, Celtic were not the dominant force they would become in the years ahead, and Fernie's only subsequent honours were as part of League Cup-winning sides in 1956/57, when Partick Thistle succumbed 3-0, and 1957/58, when he gave arguably the most dazzling display of his life as Rangers were butchered 7-1. Lining up at right-half, the inspired Fifer orchestrated wave after wave of flowing attacks which utterly flummoxed the leaden-footed 'Gers and it was fitting that he should complete the rout with a clinical spot-kick in the dying minutes.

Though never an automatic choice for his country, he travelled to Sweden for the 1958 World Cup finals, appearing on the left wing in a 3-2 defeat by Paraguay. Once again the Scots failed to progress beyond the group stage and Fernie was never selected again.

By then approaching 30, and not viewed as indispensable by manager Jimmy McGrory, Fernie was transferred to Middlesbrough of the English second tier in December 1958, the £18,000 fee going a long way towards paying for Parkhead's new floodlights.

At Ayresome Park the experienced prompter was charged with priming the bullets for a thrustful, assertive young centre-forward named Brian Clough to fire, and the pair meshed productively, with the voluble (even then) Teessider averaging around a goal a game for his season and a half in harness with Fernie. Still, it was not enough to secure promotion and in October 1960 the Scot was sold back to Celtic for £12,000, the hope being that his accumulated nous would benefit an emerging generation of young hopefuls.

This time Fernie didn't settle, and after stretching his statistics to 74 goals in 317 senior games for the club, in November 1961 he moved on to St Mirren in a £3,000 deal. Though increasingly ponderous of movement as his years advanced, he scored on his first outing for the Buddies, then garnered the deep satisfaction of supplying the opener in a 3-1 victory over Celtic in a Scottish Cup semi-final in the spring of 1962. The final was lost to Rangers, but at least Fernie had made a telling mark before leaving Paisley a year later.

A trial with Partick Thistle came to nothing, then the veteran featured briefly for Alloa Athletic, Fraserburgh of the Highland League and the Northern Irish clubs Coleraine and Bangor before laying aside his boots in 1965.

Still, though, he was keen to remain in the game which he had adorned so handsomely and in June 1967 he returned to Parkhead as a coach, at the invitation of Jock Stein, who had just guided the Celts to their ultimate glory, becoming the first British club to lift the European Cup.

Fernie proved to be excellent at his new job, demanding high levels of fitness, enthusing his charges with the freshness of his approach and playing a telling part in the development of future stars such as Kenny Dalglish, Lou Macari and Danny McGrain.

He appeared to be ideal management material and, sure enough, soon after taking over as boss of Second Division Kilmarnock in October 1973, he presided over a 16-match unbeaten sequence. Killie missed the title, finishing two points adrift of Airdrieonians, but promotion was secured and under normal circumstances his side would have consolidated a berth in the top flight during 1974/75. However, the Scottish League was under reconstruction, moving from two divisions to three, which meant only the top ten would remain among the elite and Kilmarnock were two points shy in 12th position so they took their place in the middle grade for 1975/76.

Nothing daunted, Fernie continued to champion his favoured brand of entertaining football and his side finished the campaign as runners-up to Partick Thistle, thus rising to the new Premier Division. As a team of part-timers, and with little cash to splash, Kilmarnock were always going to face an uphill struggle to survive at that rarefied level and it came as no surprise when they were relegated as bottom club in 1977.

There followed a disappointing start to the following term and, predictably but sadly, the Rugby Park board lost patience with Fernie and sacked him in the October.

Immensely disillusioned, he left the professional game to become a taxi driver and he never returned to it, an unfitting end to an illustrious career.

William Fernie, footballer and manager; born Kinglassie, Fife, 22 November 1928; played for Celtic 1948-58 and 1960-61, Middlesbrough 1958-60, St Mirren 1961-63, Alloa Athletic 1963, Fraserburgh 1963-64, Coleraine 1964, Bangor 1964-65; capped 12 times by Scotland 1954-58; managed Kilmarnock 1973-77; died Glasgow, 1 July 2011.

Frank Munro

Once described unforgettably by a Wolverhampton Wanderers fan with an inspired turn of phrase as 'an E-type Jaguar inside a Sherman tank', Frank Munro was not only a redoubtable bulwark of the Black Countrymen's defence during the late 1960s and most of the 1970s, but also a classy and occasionally audacious entertainer.

Scottish international Munro was an imperious cornerstone of the accomplished Wolves side which reached the UEFA Cup final in 1972, then won the League Cup two years later, and after they were relegated in 1976 he skippered them back to the First Division – the equivalent of today's Premier League – at the first attempt.

The rock-like six-footer from Broughty Ferry was strong enough to slug it out with the most physical of centre-forwards when required, never yielding an inch. When not tackling ferociously or soaring combatively into aerial duels, Munro could control the ball assuredly, pass it perceptively and even embark on a deft dribble which was clearly a legacy of his earlier days as an inside-forward. Invariably, too, he radiated confidence and composure, precious qualities at the heart of any rearguard, and beyond that, for all the raw physical endeavour demanded of any top-flight defender, somehow his play was infused with his own personality, which was sunny. He loved playing football for his living, the Molineux fans picked up on that happy circumstance, and they adored him for it.

The Munro career, which yielded four caps each at youth and under-23 level, and then a further nine for the senior team, got off to a false start when he headed south to join Chelsea as a promising teenage forward in 1961. He failed to make the grade and never turned professional at Stamford Bridge, instead heading back to his home city to sign for Dundee United in July 1963.

Now his star began to rise so rapidly that soon he was spoken of as 'the Scottish version of Duncan Edwards', a memorably daft and unrealistic tag of which he made light to become established at Tannadice as an attacking midfielder in 1964/65.

Somewhat surprisingly, in October 1966 Munro was sold to top-tier rivals Aberdeen for £10,000 and made a rapid impact at Pittodrie, appearing in that season's Scottish Cup final defeat by Celtic. That qualified the Dons for the European Cup Winners' Cup, as that term Jock Stein's Bhoys won every major trophy available to them, and thus in 1967/68 were attempting to retain the top prize, the European Cup.

Munro made the most of the opportunity, netting a hat-trick – including the club's first goal in continental football – as the Dons kicked off the campaign with a 10-0 home annihilation of the Icelandic side Reykjavik in their opening match.

By then, however, the young Taysider's footballing destiny had been decided by an eye-catching display, and another hat-trick, during a tournament that summer in the United States. While playing for Aberdeen, in the guise of the Washington Whips for the purpose of the competition, he shone against Los Angeles Wolves (actually the men from Molineux) in the final, in the process riveting the attention of their manager, Ronnie Allen, and the upshot was a £55,000 transfer to Wolverhampton in January 1968.

Mirroring his previous under-achievement in England, at first he struggled to make a mark, and it was not until he was converted from midfielder to centre-half by Allen's successor as boss, Bill McGarry, that he began to excel.

First partnering John Holsgrove and then, for three-quarters of a decade, John McAlle, Munro became a key figure in an exhilarating side featuring the likes of midfielders Mike Bailey, Kenny Hibbitt and Jim McCalliog, winger Dave Wagstaffe and forwards Derek Dougan and John Richards.

In 1970/71 they finished fourth in the League title race and picked up the low-key Texaco Cup at season's end. In the following spring Munro starred and skippered as Juventus were overcome in the quarter-finals of the UEFA Cup, then he scored in both legs of the semi-final triumph over Ferencvaros and put in a mighty shift as Wolves lost the final, 3-2 on aggregate, to Tottenham Hotspur.

However, his best-remembered goal that term arrived in its closing night in a 2-1 victory over Leeds United which meant Don Revie's men missed out on the championship, and thus a League and FA Cup double. In 1972/73 Munro and Wolves suffered the mortification of semi-final defeat in both domestic knockout competitions, but there was a major trophy to brandish at last in 1974 when Manchester City – Law, Lee, Bell, Summerbee et al – were beaten 2-1 in the League Cup final at Wembley.

Meanwhile Munro's exertions for his club had earned him full international honours, with four caps in 1971, the first being as a substitute for Frank McLintock in a 1-0 reverse to Northern Ireland at Hampden Park. In truth, his Scotland career never really ignited

411

and there followed a hiatus until he was picked five more times in 1975, his frustration highlighted by the fact that he finished on the winning side for his country only once, again against the Ulstermen in Glasgow. There were those who believed he deserved to be an international regular throughout his prime, but given that his competitors for a central defensive berth included Billy McNeill (at first), Martin Buchan, Gordon McQueen, Jim Holton, Bobby Moncur and Colin Jackson, that was never likely.

Still Munro remained a potent force for Wolves, even when they were demoted in 1975/76, and after a fleeting loan stint with fellow Second Division club Hereford United he returned to Molineux to captain the West Midlanders to promotion as champions at the first attempt.

Differences arose with new manager Sammy Chung, however, and in October 1977 he was loaned to Celtic, the club he had idolised as a boy. After being made temporary skipper for his debut, at home to St Mirren, his day turned rapidly sour as he scored an own goal in a 2-1 defeat. Still, manager Jock Stein saw enough in the 30-year-old to pay £20,000 for his services that December, thus ending a contribution to the Wolves cause of 371 games (with 19 goals) which leaves him 20th in the club's all-time appearance list.

Munro, the last signing of Stein's illustrious Parkhead reign, was seen as a natural replacement for the seriously injured Pat Stanton, but at a time when the Celts were struggling – they finished fifth in the league table, 19 points behind champions Rangers – he never quite gelled and the peak of his tenure was playing in the losing team against their bitter Glasgow rivals in that term's League Cup final.

In the spring he was given a free transfer and enlisted with South Melbourne Hellas, managed by former Wolves goalkeeper Dave MacLaren, combining his football with a job as an airport traffic officer. Later he coached briefly with Albion Rovers before guiding the fortunes of several Australian clubs.

Munro, who returned to Wolverhampton in 1991, suffered a stroke in 1993, after which his health continued to deteriorate, but despite being wheelchair-bound he was a regular attender at Molineux and an active member of Wolves' former players' association. An effervescent character, he bore his incapacity with remarkable courage, retaining his infectious sense of humour to the last.

Francis Michael Munro, footballer; born Broughty Ferry, Dundee, 25 October 1947; played for Dundee United 1963-66, Aberdeen 1966-68, Wolverhampton Wanderers 1968-77, Celtic 1977-78; capped nine times by Scotland 1971-75; died Wolverhampton, 16 August, 2011.

Stan Willemse

When Tom Finney, as brave and brilliant as any winger the domestic game has known, was asked to name the most physically formidable opponent he had faced, his reply was instant and unequivocal. The great man's verdict went to Stan Willemse, left-back in the Chelsea side which won the League title in 1954/55, a pacy, immensely brawny athlete yet also a footballer of poise and considerable quality.

Willemse tackled like a runaway tank and was the rock on which so many illustrious flankmen foundered, particularly during that memorable campaign in which the Stamford Bridge club became champions for the first time in their history.

As befitting a former Royal Marine who survived a shrapnel wound at Dunkirk, he was not a man to be carried away by sporting triumph, even cutting short his celebrations on the day the crown was confirmed by a home victory over Sheffield Wednesday so that he might watch his greyhound run at Brighton.

After shining at schoolboy level, Willemse joined his local club, Brighton and Hove Albion, and made his first-team entrance as a 16-year-old in emergency wartime competition. Then came his military contribution in France before his first senior games, as an inside-left during a quartet of FA Cup encounters early in 1946.

That summer he signed professional forms, soon after which he was converted to left-back and became a fixture in the number-three shirt, excelling even as the Seagulls finished bottom of the Third Division South in 1947/48, then helping them rise to sixth place in the table a season later.

Duly Willemse's consistent excellence attracted the attention of top-flight clubs and in July 1949 he was transferred to Chelsea for £6,500, the cash helping to pay for much-needed improvements to the Goldstone Ground, which had been damaged by German bombs. Unthinkably in today's climate, most of the locally-based players were employed by the club's builders during the close season, thus going on to perform in front of a stand they had helped to erect. Willemse, delighted that his fee – the highest ever received by Brighton at the time – had proved so useful to a club which always retained his affection, scratched his initials into the wet concrete footing of the new edifice.

He took a little longer to make his mark at Stamford Bridge, at first finding himself in the shadow of veteran Billy Hughes before the Welsh international was injured. Willemse seized his opportunity, impressing in several lengthy spells for Billy Birrell's First Division strugglers, though it was not until the arrival of Ted Drake as manager in 1952 that he claimed a regular berth.

Having survived the major changes instituted by the new boss, the tall, powerful defender began to thrive. Effective in the air and an accurate passer as well as being unceremoniously forceful at need – though it should be asserted that he was essentially fair in his application of the rules of the game – he became a favourite with the Bridge faithful and played a telling part in the Pensioners' remarkable transformation from perennial relegation battlers to champions in 1955.

Certainly, while England marksman Roy Bentley was the side's acknowledged star, the left-flank link between the full-back, wing-half Derek Saunders and winger Frank Blunstone was integral to the team's success.

Willemse proved versatile, too, taking over the number-eleven spot when Blunstone was injured in the spring, scoring in a win over Sunderland and acquitting himself admirably in a victory at Tottenham.

Chelsea clinched the prize with 52 points – still the most meagre total since the war, taking into account the later switch from two points for a win to three – but still the side deserved enormous credit for overcoming the likes of Stan Cullis' Wolves and the emerging Busby Babes of Manchester United.

Although Willemse never earned a full international cap, he played for England 'B' against Switzerland in 1953 and for the Football League against the Scottish League in 1954, then represented London twice in a new European competition, the Inter-Cities Fairs Cup (forerunner of the current Europa League), in 1955.

Willemse's lack of top-level recognition could be ascribed to the vast accomplishment of United's Roger Byrne, who had just broken into Walter Winterbottom's England set-up when Chelsea lifted their title, and by the time the Mancunian had perished in the Munich air disaster of February 1958, the older man was well past his prime.

Indeed, having made 221 senior appearances for the west Londoners, Willemse had been sold to Leyton Orient for £4,500 in June 1956, but not before featuring, albeit almost indiscernibly, in one of the most famous of all football photographs. As he hurled himself into a typical high-velocity challenge on Tom Finney at a saturated Stamford Bridge, the defender was virtually submerged in spray while the 'Preston Plumber' somehow managed to retain his balance. That was no mean feat given the identity of his opponent, and the resultant image was truly memorable.

Willemse, judged surplus to requirements at Chelsea due to the rise of a new generation – dubbed 'Drake's Ducklings' by the press – did well for Orient, who were newly promoted to the second tier. His experience was hugely valuable as he helped them to consolidate over two seasons before he retired in May 1958.

Thereafter he was landlord of a Brighton pub, then ran a betting shop before working as a security officer for the University of London.

When Chelsea claimed their second League championship, in 2005, Willemse and his old comrade Bentley carried the trophy on to the Stamford Bridge pitch prior to its presentation to modern captain John Terry.

Willemse is the third member of the 1955 team to die this year, following the demise of forwards Les Stubbs and Eric Parsons in February.

Stanley Bernard Willemse, footballer; born Hove, Sussex, 23 August 1924; played for Brighton and Hove Albion 1946-49, Chelsea 1949-56, Leyton Orient 1956-58; died 5 August 2011.

Laurie Hughes

Laurie Hughes scaled the loftiest peak available to a club footballer in 1947, helping Liverpool to lift the first post-war League championship. But three years later in the World Cup finals he plumbed a barely imaginable depth in the shirt of his country as England were humbled by rank outsiders, the United States of America.

The lanky Merseysider was a remorselessly effective central defender – one contemporary report had him heading the ball away 'with the persistence of a mechanical ramrod' – but he was far from being a typical muscle-bound stopper in an era when subtlety did not feature prominently among the qualities of most number-fives, even in the top flight of the Football League.

'Big Lol' was something else, a stylish, positionally perceptive and skilful centre-half, and if there were occasional moments when his apparent nonchalance in possession of the ball when surrounded by marauding attackers caused palpitations on the Kop, it did nothing to lessen the lasting affection in which he was held by most Anfield regulars in times both triumphant and troubled.

He was brave, too, once leaving the field in a game against Arsenal to have stitches inserted in an ugly head wound, then returning to carry on the battle and not shrinking for an instant from neck-or-nothing aerial challenges.

Yet for all his attributes, after starring in schoolboy football Hughes had been initially rejected by Liverpool, deemed too small and slight to make his mark in the dauntingly physical professional game, and so he signed instead for Tranmere Rovers as an amateur.

However, a sudden growth spurt and a series of richly promising displays for the Birkenhead club brought about a rapid change of heart at Anfield, and in February 1943 he re-crossed the Mersey to enlist with the Reds. Though still in his teens Hughes bedded in quickly, earning a regular place in the first team for the last three years of the war and making his senior debut in an FA Cup tie against Chester in January 1946.

Hugely significant in his continued development, and his emergence as a trusty bulwark at the core of Liverpool's rearguard when League competition resumed in the following autumn, was the pre-season tour of the USA and Canada.

While their homeland was gripped in post-conflict austerity, Hughes and his team-mates were treated like royalty throughout their trip, built up on a diet of steak, pancakes and fresh orange juice, and thus returned in fine fettle for the new campaign.

Still, with manager George Kay having to field an ageing team, expectations around Anfield were not high, but the prophets of doom were to be confounded comprehensively as Liverpool won the title in one of the most dramatic finishes in Football League history.

Ahead of the last round of matches, any one of three teams – Wolverhampton Wanderers and Stoke City were the other hopefuls – could have taken the prize. The Merseysiders duly beat Wolves at Molineux to overhaul one rival, but then faced an agonising two-week wait for Stoke to play their final game, the delay due mainly to the depredations of a savage winter but partly, also, to the government's discouragement of midweek games on the basis that travel to matches might fuel absenteeism from work at a time when high productivity was needed. In the event the Potters lost at Sheffield United and Liverpool were crowned in mid-June.

The lion's share of the credit tends to reside with attacking stars Billy Liddell and Albert Stubbins, but Hughes and his fellow half-backs, skipper Phil Taylor and the redoubtable Bob Paisley – destined to become one of the all-time great managers when he replaced Bill Shankly at the Anfield helm in 1974 – were also vastly influential in a remarkable team effort.

The still-slim but feistily resilient centre-half had matured into a vastly accomplished all-round performer, strong enough not to shrink from combat with the rumbustious spearheads of the day – such dreadnoughts as Tommy Lawton and Trevor Ford – but also constructive, intelligent and invariably composed even under the most intense pressure.

Having earned his championship medal in his first full term, Hughes became a long-term mainstay of a Liverpool side which began to creak unexpectedly over the next few years, but although he would never again be involved in a title race, he did shine on the way to the 1950 FA Cup final. After injury sidelined him from the semi-final victory over Everton, he was back in time to face Arsenal at Wembley, acquitting himself creditably against the fluent Gunners' attack but unable to prevent a 2-0 defeat.

So splendid was Hughes' form at this point that he was selected for England's first World Cup foray, in Brazil that summer, his country's need rendered urgent by the suspension of regular centre-half Neil Franklin, who had opted controversially to seek his fortune in Colombia, then outside the umbrella of the Federation of International Football Associations.

On debut against Chile in Rio de Janeiro, the Liverpool man was assured and confident alongside captain Billy Wright as Walter Winterbottom's side eased to a 2-0 victory, but the most seismic of sporting shocks was in store.

Four days later Hughes and England lined up against the USA in Belo Horizonte, with every expectation of swiping the unconsidered minnows imperiously from their path. But a combination of freakish ill fortune, some bizarre refereeing decisions and, it must be admitted, an under-par showing by a team featuring the stellar likes of Tom Finney and Wilf Mannion, brought about a 1-0 reverse which still stands as the most debilitating debacle England have suffered since international football kicked off a little after the midway point of Queen Victoria's reign.

Hughes didn't play badly, and he retained his place for the next game, a 1-0 defeat by Spain which saw the nation which gave football to the world ejected ignominiously from a competition it had entered in distinctly condescending fashion. Several years would pass before two annihilations at the hands of the sublime Hungarians would pound home the message that England had masses to learn from the continentals, but for the blameless Hughes that would not have direct significance. His international career had started and ended in the space of eight days.

Though cast aside by the FA's selection committee, he continued to excel for Liverpool, bouncing back from two lengthy absences through injury, but he could do nothing to halt what became the Reds' steady decline, culminating in relegation from the top flight in 1953/54.

Handed the captaincy by boss Don Welsh for 1954/55, he presided over a mediocre mid-table campaign, but retained personal consistency, which was replicated in the next two seasons, both of which ended with Liverpool narrowly missing out on promotion.

However, in 1957/58, by now a veteran, Hughes was supplanted by the younger Dick White, making his final senior appearance in a 5-1 drubbing at Charlton that September. Five months later, with Manchester United scouring the land for emergency recruits in the wake of the Munich air disaster in which eight of their players perished, there were rumours of a move to Old Trafford. Nothing materialised, however, and Hughes took on the role of *eminence grise* in Liverpool's reserves, helping young players to develop, until he retired in 1960.

After that he remained in his home city, becoming a newsagent, then running a fish-and-chip business before working in the betting industry.

Lawrence Hughes, footballer; born Waterloo, Merseyside, 2 March 1924; played for Liverpool 1943-58; capped three times by England 1950; died Liverpool, 9 September 2011.

Florian Albert

Florian Albert, the 1967 European Footballer of the Year, was a sporting aristocrat. Not by any mere accident of lineage – he was born the son of a farmer/blacksmith on the Hungarian side of the border with the former Yugoslavia – but by dint of a decade and a half of oozing class and elegance in the shirts of his sole club, Ferencvaros, and his country, where they know a thing or two about exceptional players.

Albert grew up idolising the prolific sharpshooter Ferenc Puskas, the unarguable star of the hallowed 'Magnificent Magyars', who taught England a thing or two about the game by annihilating them twice in the early 1950s, yet he became more naturally the heir of the Galloping Major's infinitely subtle team-mate, Nandor Hidegkuti.

As the Football League's finest were put to the sword so ruthlessly, 6-3 at Wembley and 7-1 in Budapest, it was the deep-lying centre-forward Hidegkuti who pulled the strings, and later Albert would succeed him as a goal-scoring schemer sublime.

The younger man, who netted 32 times in 75 internationals between 1959 and 1974 and created countless opportunities for the likes of Lajos Tichy, then later Ferenc Bene, was a destructive attacking wanderer capable of dictating the tempo of play. His ball technique was exquisite, the accuracy of his passing was matched by its incisive intelligence, he could shoot ferociously with either foot, he dribbled divinely and he was a shrewd tactician.

Admittedly, Albert's temperament was not perfect. There were days when, perhaps exasperated by the attentions of a close marker who prevented him from expressing himself, he could appear moody, drifting on the fringe of the action. Then his deceptively languid gait could give the false impression that he didn't care – a parallel might be drawn with the seemingly insouciant style of the current Manchester United marksman Dimitar Berbatov – but when he dominated a contest, he offered unalloyed delight.

Albert, who lost his mother when he was two, then later moved to Budapest from the small town of Hercegszanto, was an outstanding performer from boyhood and was associated with Ferencvaros, the capital's most successful club, from the age of 11. His rise was meteoric, playing for Hungary's junior team on his 16th birthday, making his senior debut for Ferencvaros a year later and earning his first full cap in a 3-2 victory over Sweden in his adopted city only a week after completing his school exams in 1959.

Soon Albert became an irresistible force in the Hungarian League, helping to win the championship in 1963, '64, '67 and '68 and the main domestic knockout competition in 1972, and topping the national scoring charts in three seasons. In 1964/65 he shone as the Green Eagles beat Juventus in the final of the Inter-Cities Fairs Cup, the forerunner of the current Europa League, having disposed of the Manchester United of George Best, Denis Law and Bobby Charlton over three games in a replayed semi-final.

Internationally, too, he was a colossal achiever, emerging as a central figure in the rebuilding of Hungary's team after an exodus of top players in the wake of the nation's bitter uprising of 1956 against Soviet-imposed policies.

He collected a bronze medal at the Rome Olympics in 1960, and he was joint top marksman (netting four times, as did five others) as the Magyars reached the World Cup quarter-finals in Chile in 1962. He touched his most opulent form in attaining the last eight again in England in 1966, and he was influential as his country finished third in the European Nations Cup in 1964, then fourth in 1972.

But Albert is best remembered in England for his sumptuous display in the 3-1 beating of champions Brazil, albeit minus the injured Pele, in a group match at Everton in July '66. On a sodden Merseyside afternoon, the tall, slim play-maker glittered in the Goodison gloom, playing a part in all three goals, most unforgettably in the second when he freed Bene to set up Janos Farkas for a savage volleyed finish.

With all due deference to Charlton's majestic effort for England against Mexico, it might be judged the goal of the tournament, certainly to the local fans who chanted 'Albert, Albert' in broadest Scouse as he walked off the pitch at the end.

In recognition of his sustained splendour, he beat the holder, that same Charlton, to the Ballon d'Or of 1967, and remains Hungary's only winner of the award. Albert retired in 1974 after scoring more than 250 goals in some 350 league outings for Ferencvaros, and in 2007 the club named their stadium after him.

At the end of his playing days he briefly managed Al-Ahly Benghazi in Libya, then later returned to Ferencvaros in several capacities, including technical director and honorary chairman. His son, Florian Jnr, also played for Ferencvaros and Hungary.

Albert died of complications following heart surgery three days earlier.

Florian Albert, footballer; born Hercegszanto, Hungary, 15 September 1941; played for Ferencvaros 1958-74; capped 75 times by Hungary 1959-74; died Budapest, Hungary, 31 October 2011.

Jimmy Adamson

It's a question which can never be answered, but it's a compelling one in any meaningful examination of Jimmy Adamson's life and work. Would England have won the World Cup in 1966 if the unobtrusive but authoritative north-easterner had accepted the Football Association's invitation to become manager of the national team some three and a half years earlier?

After he rejected the opportunity, the job of replacing Walter Winterbottom as international mentor to Bobby Charlton, Bobby Moore and company went to Alf Ramsey instead, and the result was the most glorious triumph in the history of the British game.

The reigning Footballer of the Year in 1962, Adamson rejoiced in mammoth respect for his inspired long-term captaincy of Burnley and he was establishing a reputation as an enterprising coach. But at the time he had no experience of management, and it was debatable whether he possessed the ruthless drive and determination of Ramsey, who had proved his mettle by lifting humble Ipswich Town from the old Third Division South to become the unlikeliest League champions of the post-war era.

Adamson's apparent reasons for not heeding his country's call were understandable. Still fit and ambitious as a 33-year-old who had just missed leading the Clarets to the League and FA Cup double – they had been pipped to the First Division crown by Ramsey's Ipswich and lost at Wembley to Tottenham Hotspur – he was not ready to lay aside his boots, and his employers were reluctant to release their influential skipper.

In addition, he pondered the wisdom of cutting his managerial teeth on such an onerous post, he was not enamoured at the prospect of spending long periods away from home, and he might not have been impressed by the cavalier manner in which his predecessor had been treated by interfering FA officials and committee members.

Also, having travelled to the 1962 World Cup finals in Chile as coach and assistant to Winterbottom – he was expected to play on the trip, too, though that didn't happen and eventually he retired without a cap – he had witnessed at first hand the media pressure faced by the manager.

In comparison to the often hysterical criticism meted out to later incumbents, the flak aimed at the future Sir Walter was mild, indeed, but Adamson found it distasteful and would not have relished the thought of stepping into the firing line.

Finally, the job was hardly given added lustre by handsome material rewards, Winterbottom having been paid approximately £40 per week. Overall, it was a situation summed up neatly by Jimmy Greaves, one of England's finest footballers of the era, who felt Adamson did himself a massive favour in spurning the opportunity, reckoning that he was too nice for the job – a description that few would have applied to the taciturn, habitually spiky Ramsey.

Hailing from Ashington in Northumberland, the same enormous pit village as World Cup heroes Bobby and Jackie Charlton, Adamson was the sixth son of a miner and toiled briefly below ground himself as a teenager, also working for a tailor.

However, he had been imbued with the ethos of football throughout childhood in countless fiercely fought contests in the alleyways between Ashington's sprawling terraces of colliery cottages. Thus the game was always his preferred means of expression.

Having been spotted by a Burnley scout as he excelled in a friendly kickabout, Adamson enlisted as a junior at Turf Moor in October 1946 and, after shrugging off a bout of homesickness, he turned professional three months later.

Tall and composed, he had been a centre-half at school, but soon the Burnley coaches, impressed by his assured ball control and measured passing, converted him into an inside-forward.

Unexpectedly he proved no more than a plodder in that advanced role and it was not until a second positional switch, this time to wing-half following his return from National Service in the RAF, that he began to realise his full potential.

Now he progressed apace, making his First Division debut at Bolton in February 1951 and taking the eye with a decisive tackle which prevented Wanderers' England spearhead Nat Lofthouse from scoring the winner. Thereafter he made the right-half slot his own, forcing aside the highly regarded Reg Attwell, who eventually returned to the team at left-half.

Though he was an unassuming individual, there was an unyielding strength and lively intelligence about Adamson which marked him out as a natural leader, and soon he was captaining the Clarets, who were moulded into a solidly efficient top-half-of-the-table side by manager Allan Brown in the mid-1950s.

During that period of steady building, Adamson returned to centre-half, and also featured at left-half, before reverting to his favoured right-half berth towards the end of the memorable 1959/60 campaign.

What made that spring so momentous was that small-town Burnley were battling for the League title with reigning champions Wolverhampton Wanderers and the north London giants Tottenham Hotspur.

Now bossed by former Turf Moor inside-forward Harry Potts, the Clarets had developed into a terrific side, prodigiously industrious and well drilled, but dusted with flair, too, notably in the shape of Irish play-maker Jimmy McIlroy, England winger John Connelly and the cultured Adamson himself.

Most pundits predicted that either Wolves or Spurs would prevail on the run-in, but it was unfashionable Burnley who lifted the crown by a single point on the season's final day, thanks to a stout rearguard action which secured victory over Manchester City at Maine Road.

It was a phenomenal achievement for all concerned, but few played a more integral part than the skipper. Operating as a deep-lying midfield anchorman, he was adept at reading the game, winning the ball and using it perceptively, combining to particularly devastating effect with the superbly inventive McIlroy.

Beyond that, he radiated composure, poise and reliability, giving his team-mates a stable platform on which to build, and though he was not a shouter of the odds, he was both an effective motivator and a shrewd tactician.

In 1960/61 Adamson led Burnley proudly into the European Cup, where they beat Reims of France before bowing out, 5-4 on aggregate, to the West German champions, Hamburg.

Back on the domestic scene they remained a major force, and in 1961/62 went close to winning the League and FA Cup double, finishing as First Division runners-up to Ipswich Town and losing to Spurs at Wembley.

At this point Adamson was renowned among his contemporaries as one of the best uncapped players in the land and the Scots, especially, could not fathom how he was serially ignored by the England selectors. However, he had to be content with appearances for the Football League and England 'B', though that spring brought some consolation in the Footballer of the Year accolade, for which he narrowly beat clubmate McIlroy.

After making his decision not to take charge of the England team, Adamson played on for two more seasons despite suffering a troublesome knee injury, amassing nearly 500 appearances for the Clarets before stepping aside to become club coach in 1964.

It was a role he embraced successfully and it seemed a natural progression in February 1970 when Potts 'moved upstairs' to become general manager, making way for Adamson to take over as team boss.

He talked enthusiastically about Burnley becoming 'the team of the '70s' with such gifted young performers as Dave Thomas, Leighton James and others, but the well of talent did not prove as deep as he had surmised and they were relegated in his first full term at the helm.

However, the Turf Moor board retained faith in their long-time servant and were repaid when Adamson led the Clarets back to the top flight as Division Two champions in 1972/73, then consolidated among the elite with an marvellous sixth-place finish in 1973/74.

Soon, sadly, the cash constraints which haunt most clubs of Burnley's size dictated the sale of star player Martin Dobson and other promising rookies, and Adamson departed, a disillusioned man, in January 1976, four months before his side was demoted again.

There followed a fleeting spell in charge of Sparta Rotterdam before he replaced Bobby Stokoe as manager of a lacklustre Sunderland team in November 1976. He could not reverse the slide quickly enough to prevent relegation at season's end, but began a reconstruction programme which resulted in a decent sixth-place Second Division showing in 1977/78.

Next, to the surprise of some observers who reckoned his record did not justify such a prize, he was handed the reins of mighty Leeds United, who were seeking a steady hand following the rapid arrival and departure of Jock Stein.

At Elland Road Adamson began encouragingly, leading his new charges into Europe at the end of his first campaign, but then came a limp UEFA Cup exit in 1979/80. Fans were disgruntled at the sale of favourites such as Tony Currie and Frank Gray; new signings Alex Sabella, Brian Greenhoff and Derek Parlane didn't work out, and the team became excruciatingly ordinary.

Attendances dropped, there were repeated calls for his head – he needed a police escort after one horribly dull draw with Coventry City – and in October 1980 he bowed to popular demand by resigning.

Though still only 51, Jimmy Adamson never returned to the professional game. It was an exit as poignant as it was premature.

James Adamson, footballer and manager; born Ashington, Northumberland, 4 April 1929; played for Burnley 1947-64; managed Burnley 1970-76, Sparta Rotterdam 1976, Sunderland 1976-78, Leeds United 1978-80; died 8 November 2011.

Gary Speed

From the time he riveted attention as the brilliant baby of the beautifully balanced Leeds United midfield which was so integral to the Yorkshiremen's League title triumph of 1992, right through until he presided inspirationally over the unexpected renaissance of Wales as a force in international football in recent weeks, Gary Speed barely put a foot wrong.

As a player for Leeds, Everton, Newcastle United, Bolton Wanderers and Sheffield United, and for his country – between 1990 and 2004 he earned 85 caps, a record for an outfield man and second only to goalkeeper Neville Southall – invariably he was a colossally influential and versatile all-round performer.

As one of the most promising young managers in the world game, his potential for long-term success appeared to be limitless; and as a character he was widely cherished as a down-to-earth, loyal, industrious, good-humoured individual, one of the most popular figures in Welsh sport.

After rising through the youth ranks at Elland Road, Speed made his senior debut as a 19-year-old left-sided midfielder during 1988/89, then earned a regular place towards the end of the following season, which Leeds finished on top of the old Second Division, the equivalent of today's Championship.

Undaunted by elevation to the elite grade, the Welsh rookie rapidly became a key part of a superb centre-field quartet which also included the experienced and gifted Scottish duo Gordon Strachan and Gary McAllister, and the vigorous young local boy David Batty. They gelled together fluently, with Speed based on the left flank, majoring on pace and athleticism, a prodigious work ethic and a stupendous aerial ability which was seen to maximum effect through his priceless knack of arriving late in opposing penalty boxes to direct powerful headers towards goal.

In 1991/92, when Leeds deservedly outstripped Manchester United to become the last English champions of the pre-Premier League era, Speed contributed seven League strikes, missed only one match and was named by manager Howard Wilkinson as his player of the season.

Clearly one of the outstanding prospects on the British scene, and a key member of the Wales team after making his full international entrance against Costa Rica in August 1990, Speed could contemplate the future with unbounded optimism, not least because at need he could fill virtually any position bar goalkeeper.

But with Leeds failing to keep pace with the gathering force of Alex Ferguson's Old Trafford empire, a sense grew that the exhilaratingly talented Welshman's career could do with some fresh impetus, and it seemed that might be achieved when he was sold to Everton, the club he had adored all his life, for £3.5 million in July 1996. It seemed to be a dream move as he was greeted rapturously by the Goodison fans, and he was made captain at the outset of 1997/98, but while Speed did well enough personally, the Toffees toiled collectively and soon he outraged his erstwhile admirers by demanding a transfer.

Duly in February 1998 he was sold to Newcastle for £5.5 million, and at St James' Park he continued to mature into one of the finest midfielders in the land, especially after moving from the left to a central position. Now he shone whether deployed as an anchorman or with a more attacking brief.

His control, distribution, shooting, stamina and courage, his spring-heeled excellence in the air, his reading of the game, his composure under pressure and his leadership qualities, everything was impeccable and the Magpies always looked a far better side with Speed than without him.

He spent six years on Tyneside, experiencing FA Cup final defeats to Arsenal in 1998 and Manchester United in 1999, and sampling a taste of the Champions League, before switching to Bolton for £750,000 in July 2004. Yet again he contributed consistently, in 2006 becoming the first man to reach 500 Premier League appearances.

Early in 2008, by now in his 40th year, Speed joined second-flight Sheffield United, initially on loan, and featured regularly for the Blades – scoring a League goal for the 20th successive season – till laid low by back trouble in November 2008. He announced his retirement as a player in 2010, having made nearly 700 League appearances in his 22 years as a professional, and had served only four months as Bramall Lane boss when he was made manager of Wales that December.

At that point expectations were low, but Speed proceeded to confound them comprehensively. Though he would always be honoured for his international service on the pitch, which included captaining the side 44 times and netting seven goals, few if any observers believed that he would bring about a swift and dramatic upturn in his nation's fortunes.

But he did. In the ten games before his shocking death, he oversaw five victories, culminating in three in quick succession, the most recent being a 4-1 drubbing of Norway in a friendly at Cardiff earlier this month.

In the process Wales climbed into the world ranking list's top 50, and suddenly the Principality's footballing future looked dazzlingly bright. It was a stunning development and it was all down to Gary Speed.

Gary Andrew Speed, footballer and manager; born Mancot, Flintshire, 8 September 1969; played for Leeds United 1988-96, Everton 1996-98, Newcastle United 1998-2004, Bolton Wanderers 2004-08, Sheffield United 2008; capped 85 times by Wales 1990-2004; managed Sheffield United 2010, Wales 2010-11; MBE 2010; died Huntington, Chester, 27 November 2011.

Johnny Williams

Johnny Williams cut a majestic figure as he bestrode the Plymouth Argyle midfield for 11 seasons from the middle 1950s, surging forward with a dignity and style which called to mind some Atlantic-bound ship in full sail departing the city's historic harbour.

It was perceived widely, and by such shrewd judges as Manchester United manager Matt Busby and Wolves boss Stan Cullis, that the tall, upright Bristolian was tailor-made for the upper echelons of English football, but Williams never tasted life in the top tier, instead remaining loyal to the Pilgrims throughout his prime and later serving Bristol Rovers in the city of his birth.

He was renowned for the power and accuracy of his long-distance shooting, and for all his admirable defensive solidity it was that attacking instinct which made him such a favourite with the Home Park faithful. Indeed, they selected him for Argyle's team of the 20th century, an accolade which his 448 appearances and 55 goals for the club thoroughly merited.

After leaving Bristol for Plymouth with his family as a boy, Williams began an apprenticeship as an electrical fitter at Devonport dockyard, but his father believed passionately that his son had the makings of a professional footballer so he asked Argyle to give him a trial.

Manager Jimmy Rae agreed, was duly delighted by what he saw on the practice pitch and Williams left his local works side, EEM Department, to make a provisional agreement with Plymouth as a 17-year-old in October 1952.

Soon he turned professional and in September 1955 he made his senior debut at inside-left in a 1-0 home victory over Blackburn Rovers in the old Second Division, the equivalent of the modern Championship. Three weeks later he netted his first goal, a consolation effort in a 4-1 defeat by Liverpool at Anfield, and that term he played frequently in various forward positions.

However, Plymouth were a struggling side and they were relegated at season's end, with young Williams having lost his place. He was back in at the outset of 1956/57 only to be axed after Argyle made a dismal start, but that proved to be but a temporary blip in his progress.

During a brief autumn interlude in the reserves, it became evident that Williams' natural power and the crispness of his tackling made him a natural wing-half and it was in that role in which he made a swift return to first-team duty. Thereafter he never looked back, becoming a fixture in the senior side for the next decade, his athleticism and strength matched by his ease on the ball, his passing and shooting prowess and a calm demeanour which was invaluable in many a defensive crisis as Argyle fought to stave off a second successive demotion in the spring of 1957.

Unlike many promising youngsters, Williams was able to fit his National Service commitments around turning out for his club, and his game improved notably during his Army days, performing alongside such future luminaries as Manchester United's Bobby Charlton, and Cliff Jones, who would go on to shine for Tottenham Hotspur.

The standard of competition was high and Williams rose to the challenge, prompting Busby to remark after watching him in action one night in Scotland that, despite being in the company of several high-profile professionals, Williams was the finest footballer afield. Soon came his premier tangible achievement when he excelled as the Pilgrims lifted the Third Division title in 1958/59, and at this point he was being monitored by a posse of top-flight clubs, including Cullis's Wolves, then on their way to winning a second successive League championship.

However, Argyle were so desperate to keep their main man that they slapped a reported £40,000 tag on him, which deterred prospective purchasers at a time when the British transfer record stood at only £45,000.

Undaunted, Williams continued to excel for Argyle as they slid up and down the Second Division table during the first half of the 1960s, with the highlight an appearance in the League Cup semi-final of 1965. They lost to Leicester City over two legs, but Williams had the satisfaction of scoring past Gordon Banks, the goalkeeper who would star as England lifted the World Cup some 18 months later.

Having reached his 30s, Williams was left out in the cold by manager Derek Ufton in 1966 and that December he signed for Bristol Rovers. Though past his peak, he offered valuable experience to the Third Division Pirates, whom he served until 1969, when he left the professional game.

Later Williams made a fleeting return to Argyle as a coach under Billy Bingham, and enjoyed a stint as player-boss of non-League Bodmin Town. A man of integrity and an approachable individual, he went on to run a successful garage business in Plymouth.

John Stanley James Williams, footballer; born Bristol, 16 August 1935; played for Plymouth Argyle 1952-66, Bristol Rovers 1966-69; died Plymouth, 24 November 2011.

Socrates

The charismatic Brazilian giant Socrates, an icon of sporting cool in the 1980s when he enjoyed his regal pomp and his colourful personality was showcased in successive World Cup tournaments, was a footballing force of nature.

Hailed in some quarters as one of the finest players of all time, he was a visionary midfield general who could slice apart the most clamlike of defences with his incisive, imaginative passing. He was equally revered for his swashbuckling, yet somehow relaxed style, the sudden savage strikes on goal with either foot vying for attention with his delicious trademark backheel flicks and his piratical appearance, usually complete with beard, headband and flowing locks.

As befitted a man named Socrates, he was a noted intellectual, too, an eloquent espouser of left-wing causes, and a doctor of both medicine and philosophy. Then there was his much-merited reputation as a bon viveur – he was a famously heavy smoker and admitted to having had problems with alcohol, which he described as his 'companion', though he maintained that it never curtailed his effectiveness on the pitch.

Socrates began his professional career with the Botafogo club, based in the Brazilian town of Ribeirao Preto, serving them for four years from 1974. During that period he worked for his medical qualifications and although he was clearly endowed with colossal football talent, so determined was he not to compromise his studies that it was not until 1979, a season after he had moved to the Sao Paulo-based Corinthians club and having passed his 25th birthday, that he made himself available for his country.

Politics, and the lot of ordinary working people, had always been of immense importance to Socrates, whose early heroes were Fidel Castro, Che Guevara and John Lennon. Thus Corinthians, which had grown out of the pro-democracy movement, had been founded largely by immigrant labourers and had opposed the military dictatorship which ruled Brazil during much of his youth, was always an institution dear to his heart.

That year he made the first of 60 appearances for Brazil, which he adorned with 22 goals, and moved swiftly into his prime. In his 297 outings for Corinthians, he netted 172 times, but it was for his expansive displays in the yellow shirt of Brazil that Socrates earned global renown.

Captaining a fabulous team which included the likes of Zico, Falcao and Cerezo, he shone brightest of all during the World Cup finals in Spain, but after captivating audiences with sumptuous displays against the Soviet Union, Scotland, New Zealand and, especially, Argentina, the Brazilians succumbed unexpectedly to the ultimate champions, Italy. Supporters of that Brazil side, one of the most brilliant not to win the World Cup, were dismayed at their ejection, particularly bemoaning the absence from the last four of Socrates, whose combination of skill, intelligence and power had cultivated a devoted following in virtually every country in which the game was played.

Come the 1986 tournament in Mexico, by now not quite such a seductive force but still wildly popular, Brazil again failed narrowly to reach the semis, this time bowing out to France in a penalty shoot-out, with Socrates missing the first spot-kick. This was cruelly ironic as fans loved his seemingly casual stop-start method of addressing the ball, but on this occasion he miscalculated and was foiled easily by goalkeeper Joel Bats.

That year his international career ended, but he remained effective at club level. In 1984 he had joined Fiorentina, though he never settled in Italy, rebelling against what he saw as undue regimentation and preferring the freer lifestyle of his homeland, to which he returned after only one season.

Thus in 1986 he enlisted with Flamengo, then joined Santos in 1988, but by then he had reached the veteran stage and laid aside his boots in 1989, at the age of 35.

However, Socrates, whose honours included a place in Brazil's Hall of Fame and being voted South American Footballer of the Year in 1983, had not finished with the game. In 2004, somewhat bizarrely, he accepted a month-long assignment as player-coach of Garforth Town of the Northern Counties East League in England. He was 50 and made only one appearance in a game, for 12 minutes as a substitute against Tadcaster Albion, before returning to Brazil. Later he explained that Yorkshire had been a little cold for him, but added that he'd had tremendous fun.

For some years after leaving the professional game, Socrates – whose brother, Rai, was part of the Brazil squad which lifted the World Cup in 1994 – practised medicine in Ribeirao Preto, later becoming a philosopher and a television football pundit.

His judgement was sound, too. Once asked by journalist Andy Mitten for his views on the English game, he replied: 'English football? I think of Paul Scho-les. He's good enough to play for Brazil. I love to watch Scho-les, to see him pass, the boy with the red hair in the red shirt.' Coming from such a feted fellow midfielder, this was not the least of the many honours collected by Manchester's finest.

Socrates Brasileiro Sampaio de Souza Vieira de Oliveira, footballer, doctor of medicine and philosophy; born Belem do Para, Brazil, 19 February 1954, played for Botafogo 1974-78, Corinthians 1978-84, Fiorentina 1984-85, Flamengo 1986-87, Santos 1988-89; capped 60 times by Brazil 1979-86; died Sao Paulo, Brazil, 4 December 2011.

Len Phillips

Len Phillips was a consummate footballing artist, a play-maker of sumptuous touch and bewildering guile who could shred a defence with a single penetrating pass.

Yet although he played three times for England and was a huge factor in Portsmouth winning back-to-back League championships in 1949 and '50, he was never a household name. Within the professional game, however, he was honoured as a true thoroughbred, and the forthright Londoner was content with that.

The epitome of the loyal one-club man, Phillips was a perfect fit for the down-to-earth, industrious post-war Pompey side which tended to be damned by faint praise from pundits located a long way from the south coast, the majority of such observers seemingly seduced by the more glamorous big-city battalions.

The truth was that under manager Bob Jackson, Portsmouth were a magnificently drilled unit, one of the finest teams of their era, made up of talented individuals with no aspirations to personal stardom and certainly not fazed when confronted by it in the opposition ranks.

Phillips grew up in the capital, playing for Hackney Boys, then working in a wine distillery before being called to join in the global conflict. He enlisted with the Royal Marines while still a teenager in 1940, and as a crew member on an assault landing craft, he was one of the first ashore in Normandy on D-Day, the sixth of June, 1944.

He found time, also, to excel as a delightfully inventive inside-forward for the Marines, then in February 1946 he signed for Portsmouth, scoring five goals in 11 outings that spring in the wartime emergency competition for southern clubs.

He made his senior debut that December in a First Division victory at Blackburn, but then had to show patience before claiming a regular berth in the spring of 1948. At that point Pompey were an improving top-half outfit, then in 1948/49, with former manager Jack Tinn's creation having been further polished by his successor Jackson, they took a dramatic step forward by lifting the title, comfortably outstripping runners-up Manchester United, who finished five points adrift.

Phillips was in his element, missing only two games, netting 11 times himself – Pompey won every contest in which he scored – and laying on goals aplenty for the rest of a potent attack comprising the exhilarating winger Peter Harris, fellow inside-forward Duggie 'Thunderboots' Reid, forceful spearhead Ike Clarke, the versatile Jack Froggatt and, for much of the campaign, another inside man, Bert Barlow.

Invariably poised and composed, Phillips was their inspirational fulcrum, acutely aware of the ever-changing picture around him on the pitch, spraying incisive deliveries to all quarters, and sending connoisseurs into raptures with his deft manipulation of the ball.

In 1949/50 Portsmouth did it again, retaining their crown by pipping much-fancied Wolverhampton Wanderers on goal average, the infernally complicated method which preceded goal difference as a means of separating teams with the same number of points. Once more Phillips wielded colossal influence, this time contributing only five strikes in his 34 outings, but shining more brightly than ever as a schemer.

International recognition was overdue and finally it arrived in November 1951 – around the time he was briefly transfer-listed by Pompey over a disagreement which was quickly resolved – when he featured in England's 2-0 win over Northern Ireland at Villa Park.

Disappointingly, there followed a three-year gap before he was summoned again to his country's colours, by which time he had been converted from inside-forward to wing-half. In this new deeper-lying role, Phillips performed well enough in Wembley victories over Wales and West Germany towards the end of 1954 to remain in the plans of national boss Walter Winterbottom, but a bitter blow was imminent.

While training with England in March 1955 ahead of their annual encounter with Scotland, he suffered a severe knee injury which precipitated the end of his professional career.

He did make one more appearance for Portsmouth, in an FA Cup tie with Grimsby Town in January 1956, but suffered a recurrence of his problem and left the club, for whom he had enjoyed more than 250 senior outings and contributed a half-century of goals, at season's end.

By then Phillips was a veteran in his 34th year, but still it was an anti-climactic departure from Fratton Park for such an accomplished technician who had been central to Pompey's golden age, and had worn an England shirt in the company of such luminaries as Stanley Matthews, Tom Finney and Nat Lofthouse.

He demonstrated his undiminished enthusiasm for the game by playing non-League football well into his forties, serving Poole Town, Chelmsford City, Bath City, Ramsgate Athletic and Waterlooville. Later he worked as a lathe operator for the De Havilland aircraft company in Portsmouth.

In 2010 Phillips, the last surviving regular member of Pompey's two championship sides, was entered into the club's Hall of Fame.

Horace Leonard Phillips, footballer; born Shoreditch, London, 11 September 1922; played for Portsmouth 1946-56; capped three times by England 1951-54; died Portsmouth, 9 December 2011.

George Robb

It was George Robb's cruel misfortune to be in at the twilight of England's footballing gods on the biggest day of his career. The Tottenham Hotspur left-winger, a powerful, industrious and skilful performer in a top-level domestic context, earned his only full international cap on the dank Wembley afternoon in November 1953 when his country stumbled to its first defeat by foreign opposition on home soil.

In truth, it was not just the loss of a match. The 6-3 hammering by Hungary represented humiliation for the misguided patriots who maintained that the nation which gave football to the world still reigned supreme, and, for those with eyes to see, it signalled a forward path, a new way which involved quickfire passing allied to dazzling movement off the ball to a degree never witnessed previously within these shores.

For Robb, whose selection in the number-11 shirt ahead of the infinitely superior Tom Finney baffled just about everyone except the southern pressmen who had lobbied long and loud for the worthy Londoner to replace the magnificent 'Preston Plumber', such gilded opportunity would never knock again.

However, he rendered noble service to Spurs at a time of transition from Arthur Rowe's masterful push-and-run unit which lifted the League championship in 1950/51 into the sublime combination which, under Bill Nicholson in 1960/61, became the first club in the 20th century to win the League and FA Cup double.

Robb, a young inside-forward before blossoming as a winger, first made his mark as a teenager with non-League Finchley, and his form was impressive enough to commence a collection of 18 England amateur caps.

In 1944 he became associated with Spurs as an amateur, but when he was not offered full-time terms he trained as a teacher, then worked at a primary school in Crouch End.

However, it was clear that the dashing, dark-haired raider had the ability to make the grade in the Football League's top flight and in December 1951 he returned to White Hart Lane, still as an amateur. That Christmas Day he made his senior debut, scoring in Spurs' 3-0 victory over Charlton Athletic at the Valley, but it was not until he turned professional in June 1953 – by which time he had represented Great Britain in the 1952 Olympics in Helsinki – that he nailed down a regular place in the first team.

During the campaign that followed, despite Rowe's declining side languishing in the bottom half of the First Division table, Robb flourished, scoring 16 goals and missing only a handful of League outings. An unfailingly vigorous and aggressive attacker, he was at his most effective when cutting inside from the flank to shoot at goal with either foot, and at his best he combined delightfully with the imaginative inside-left Eddie Baily.

That season, too, he played for the Football League and endured his traumatic experience at Hungarian hands, then made three appearances for England's 'B' side. Thereafter Robb gave staunch service to Rowe and his successor Jimmy Anderson, and was particularly prominent in Spurs' run to the last four of the FA Cup in 1956.

After scoring against Boston United, Middlesbrough and West Ham, he was on the point of pushing the ball into the net of Manchester City for a late equaliser in the semi-final at Villa Park when the great German 'keeper Bert Trautmann appeared to drag him down by grabbing his legs. However, no penalty was given, Spurs were out of the competition and Robb was never to win a major professional honour.

He came close again in 1956/57, when Spurs were runners-up to Manchester United in the title race, but then lost his place in the spring of 1958 to the brilliant young Welshman Cliff Jones, who had been signed from Swansea Town.

Shortly after Anderson was replaced as White Hart Lane boss by Bill Nicholson in the following autumn, Robb suffered a serious knee injury from which he never recovered, and he left the game in 1960.

Having taught at Christ's College, Finchley, throughout his time at Tottenham, he retained that post until 1964, then moved to Ardingley College, near Haywards Heath in Sussex, where he remained until his retirement in 1986.

George Robb died on Christmas Day, exactly 60 years after making his first competitive appearance for his only professional club.

George W Robb, footballer and teacher; born Finsbury Park, London, 1 June 1926; played for Tottenham Hotspur 1951-59; capped once by England in 1953; died 25 December 2011.

Gary Ablett

Gary Ablett was a polished and imperturbable utility defender who helped Liverpool to win two League titles and the FA Cup between 1988 and 1990, then became the only man to lift the famous old knockout trophy with both the Reds and their Merseyside rivals, Everton.

Gaunt and gangly of appearance, the personable Liverpudlian was wirily resilient, an excellent timer of challenges both aerial and on the ground, a safe and sensible passer of the ball with his favoured left foot, and an intelligent breaker-up of attacks through shrewd positional play and decisive interception. He preferred to operate in the centre of the rearguard, but was equally effective at full-back, his versatility proving a boon to his managers throughout his career.

Though marginally short of true international class – he played once each for England's 'B' side and the under-21s – Ablett never looked out of his depth at the top club level, holding his own for several seasons in the last Liverpool side to claim the domestic game's principal prize.

On leaving school in 1982 Ablett enlisted at Anfield as an apprentice, turning professional in November 1983. There was to be no immediate senior breakthrough, but he impressed so mightily on loan with Third Division Derby County in January 1985 that the Rams made a six-figure offer for him, an approach which manager Joe Fagan rejected firmly.

Ablett did well on a second loan stint, this time at second-tier Hull City, in the autumn of 1986 before finally making his first-team entrance for Liverpool that December when an injury to centre-half Alan Hansen gave him his chance in a goalless draw at Charlton. Thereafter Ablett returned to the reserves until the spring, when he scored his only goal for Liverpool on his first Anfield start, against Nottingham Forest.

It was during the second half of 1987/88 that Kenny Dalglish, then in his first spell at Liverpool's helm, gave the young Merseysider a protracted run in the team, which had received brilliant fresh impetus that term through the arrival of John Barnes and Peter Beardsley. Ablett emerged as a dependable performer in both full-back slots during the second half of a campaign which the Reds finished as runaway champions, only to be thwarted in the FA Cup final by underdogs Wimbledon.

During 1988/89 he became a regular member of the side which underwent the trauma of the Hillsborough disaster, which resulted in the deaths of 96 fans who were crushed during an FA Cup semi-final against Forest. In purely footballing terms, which took second place at the time, Ablett continued to flourish, making up for his previous Wembley disappointment by taking part in the 3-2 final triumph over Everton. However, there was bitter disappointment in store as Arsenal pipped Liverpool to the League crown through a dramatic last-minute victory at Anfield on the season's concluding day.

Now Ablett appeared to be on the threshold of his prime, but the development of youngsters Steve Staunton and David Burrows, together with the acquisition of Glenn Hysen, cost him his berth for much of 1989/90, though he did make sufficient appearances to qualify for his second title medal. With the competition for places increasing, new manager Graeme Souness accepted a £750,000 offer from Everton and in January 1992 Ablett embarked on the second phase of his career on the opposite side of Stanley Park.

He excelled as a Blue, proving inspirational as relegation was narrowly avoided in 1994, then coolly dependable as Joe Royle's men stunned favourites Manchester United by beating them 1-0 in the 1995 FA Cup final.

Soon Ablett was eased out by young rivals, and after a loan to Sheffield United he was sold to second-flight Birmingham City for £400,000 in July 1996. He excelled for three-and-a-half seasons at St Andrew's before finishing his English playing days in the Blackpool side which was demoted to the basement division in 2000.

However, Ablett loved the game far too much to leave it, and in 2002 he returned to Everton as a youth coach. Four years later he re-crossed Stanley Park to Anfield, taking charge of Liverpool reserves, whom he guided to their national title in 2008.

Keen to manage, he took over at cash-strapped Stockport County in 2009, but was unable, through no fault of his own, to prevent their relegation to League Two and he left after one term. He was on the verge of joining Ipswich Town as a coach in 2010 when he was diagnosed with the blood cancer which was to claim his life.

Gary Ian Ablett, footballer and coach; born Liverpool, 19 November 1965; played for Liverpool 1983-92, Derby County on loan 1985, Hull City on loan 1986, Everton 1992-96, Sheffield United on loan 1996, Birmingham City 1996-99, Wycombe Wanderers on loan 1999, Blackpool 2000; Long Island Rough Riders, USA, 2001; managed Stockport County 2009-10; died 1 January 2012.

Ernie Gregory

There can hardly be any footballer, from any age, who gave more loyal service to one club than did Ernie Gregory to West Ham United.

As a big, dominant, charismatic goalkeeper he was a linchpin of the Upton Park side for a dozen seasons in the middle years of the 20th century, a reassuring and often inspirational influence as the Hammers won the Second Division title in 1958.

Later he served West Ham as a coach, offering sage guidance to fine custodians such as Phil Parkes and Mervyn Day, and even after his 1987 retirement brought an end to his remarkable 51-year official tenure at the club, he was a regular visitor at the Chadwell Heath training ground, keeping an eye on the new generation of young 'keepers and delivering typically shrewd scouting assessments.

Though necessarily athletic, Gregory wasn't an overtly spectacular performer, rather he specialised in canny positioning and safe, unshowy handling to deal with raids on his goal. He was unfailingly courageous, too, in an era when referees offered net-minders scant protection from fearsomely brawny centre-forwards, the likes of Trevor Ford, Derek Dooley and Nat Lofthouse, who seemed to bounce off him like lightweights when they encountered his muscular frame.

As a boy Gregory was a promising boxer, and on the football field he was a defender, but one day his goalkeeper brother Bob broke his leg and Ernie took his place between the sticks. Thereafter he progressed to the West Ham Boys side, for whom he was playing in the English Schools Trophy final in 1936 when he was spotted by Hammers boss Charlie Paynter. He was approached, too, by Arsenal and Sunderland, but he was an east Londoner to his boots and never contemplated joining anyone but West Ham, which he did that year. While still unpaid he helped local amateurs Leytonstone to win the Isthmian League title in 1938, then turned professional with the Hammers in 1939.

Aged only 18 at the outbreak of the Second World War, Gregory served in the Essex Regiment, also finding time to make half a century of appearances for the Hammers in unofficial emergency competition. Having lost the first half of his twenties to the conflict, he made his senior debut in a 4-1 second-tier victory over Plymouth Argyle in December 1946, and by season's end he was the club's first-choice 'keeper, a position he retained, injuries permitting, until 1959.

For much of that period West Ham, bossed from 1950 onwards by Ted Fenton, were a moderate Second Division side, despite the presence in their rearguard of such luminaries as Malcolm Allison, Noel Cantwell and John Bond, and they owed plenty to the heroics of Gregory for keeping them buoyant.

There was no shortage of observers, especially in the East End, who maintained that he should be rewarded by full caps, but he was unable to oust such formidable rivals as Manchester City's Frank Swift, Bert Williams of Wolves and the Birmingham City man, Gil Merrick, though he was granted one outing for England 'B', against France in 1952.

In 1957/58, during which he entered his 37th year, Gregory was still at the top of his game as the Hammers lifted their divisional title, and he remained a major force as Fenton's men performed wonders by finishing sixth in the premier grade in the subsequent term. However, that spring he lost his berth to the talented young Irishman Noel Dwyer and he made the last of his 406 senior appearances in a 2-1 home defeat by Leeds United in September 1959.

At that point, extraordinarily, Gregory was less than halfway through his tenure with the Hammers, whom he served as a coach for the next 28 years, through the managerial regimes of Ron Greenwood and John Lyall, helping with the development of, for example, the club's trio of World Cup heroes, Bobby Moore, Geoff Hurst and Martin Peters. He offered experience, continuity and wisdom to wave after wave of Upton Park hopefuls, while setting a peerless example of integrity and simple dignity and, frequently, entertaining them with his infectious brand of humour. Ernie Gregory was summed up admirably by one of his star pupils, the England goalkeeper Phil Parkes, who described his mentor as the greatest servant West Ham have ever had.

Ernest Gregory, footballer and coach; born Stratford, London, 10 November 1921; played for West Ham United 1946-60; died 21 January 2012.

Syd Thomas

There wasn't much of Syd Thomas, the Welsh international winger who helped Fulham rise to the top flight of English football in 1948/49, but on his day he was a captivating entertainer.

Standing only 5ft 6ins and slight of build, he looked as if he might be eaten alive by some of the brawny full-backs plying their trade in the immediate post-war era, but often his sleight of foot and sudden bursts of acceleration, allied to a fierce determination which belied his diminutive stature, would leave them toiling impotently in his wake.

Sadly for Thomas, his Craven Cottage prospects were blighted by the substantial presence of his rival for the Fulham number-seven shirt, the far more prolific goal-scorer Arthur Stevens, and then, shortly after a promising fresh start with Bristol City, his playing days were terminated by tuberculosis.

Thomas, a former baker's boy in the small Welsh market town of Machynlleth, Montgomeryshire, built a local reputation as an outstanding teenage footballer and played for Wrexham reserves in 1937/38, but was not offered a contract.

However, his breakthrough was not long delayed. In August 1938 he was invited to take part in a trial game by Fulham of the English Second Division and so impressed the Cottagers' watching manager, Jack Peart, that he was signed from Welsh League club Treharris at half-time, thus completing the first 45 minutes as an amateur and the second period as a professional.

Now a thrilling future beckoned, only for the Second World War to intervene. At either end of the conflict he made a handful of appearances for Fulham in unofficial emergency competition and he played frequently during his RAF service as a driver at an airport construction site in Africa's Gold Coast, but his senior debut was delayed for eight years.

It finally arrived in a home draw with Tottenham Hotspur in November 1946, but soon he drifted to the fringe of the team, occasionally making fleeting returns as an inside-forward, a role in which his precise passing stood out.

Thomas's most consistent first-team run came in 1947/48, when he played 35 times, including in an FA Cup quarter-final defeat by Blackpool, and that term, too, he made his full international entrance against England at Ninian Park, Cardiff. The visitors, boasting arguably the finest forward line in their history – Stanley Matthews, Stan Mortensen, Tommy Lawton, Wilf Mannion and Tom Finney – cantered to a 3-0 win, but Thomas was retained for the next three games, two defeats by Scotland and a victory over Northern Ireland, before losing his place to Tottenham's Ernie Jones.

In 1948/49, which Fulham finished as Second Division champions, he took up his favoured right-wing berth in the autumn when Stevens was switched to centre-forward, only to lose it again when the dashing Londoner moved back to the flank following the arrival of Arthur Rowley, who was on his way to becoming the top scorer in English football history.

Still languishing in Stevens' shadow, Thomas was selected only three times in the First Division, and in June 1950 he was sold to Bristol City of the Third Division South for £9,000.

At Ashton Gate he made a positive early impact, gelling instantly with skilful German inside-right Alous 'Alec' Eisentrager, a former prisoner-of-war who remained in England after his release to become a Robins favourite. Soon, though, Thomas fell victim to TB and never played professionally again, his eventual enforced retirement giving rise to a dispute over his fee between Fulham and City.

Thomas, who returned to his home-town to work in the family bakery business, was recently reported to be the oldest surviving Fulham footballer, but this has not been confirmed.

David Sidney 'Syd' Thomas, footballer; born Machynlleth, Montgomeryshire, (now Powys), 12 November 1919; played for Fulham 1938-50, Bristol City 1950; capped four times by Wales 1947-48; died 19 January 2012.

Tom McAnearney

Tom McAnearney was a beacon of calmness and consistency at the heart of Sheffield Wednesday's midfield, first in the Owls' yo-yo years between the top two divisions of English football in the late 1950s, and then, during his personal prime, as the men from Hillsborough enjoyed half a decade among the leading six clubs in the land.

That the slim but wirily resilient wing-half never won a cap for his native Scotland was due not to any shortcomings in his own game – which was of the unspectacular variety, though relentlessly efficient – but to the presence of such illustrious contemporaries as Dave Mackay, Paddy Crerand, Jim Baxter and Frank McLintock, all exceptionally gifted players who understandably dominated the thinking of successive national bosses.

McAnearney was never more effective than in 1960/61, when Bill Nicholson's wondrous Tottenham Hotspur became the first club during the 20th century to lift the League and FA Cup double, and Wednesday were their nearest challengers, finishing as runners-up in the top flight and reaching the quarter-finals of the knockout competition.

The red-haired Dundonian was recruited by the Owls from his local junior club, Dundee North End, as an 18-year-old in October 1951, and within a year he had made his First Division debut in a 2-0 home defeat by Liverpool.

However, by the time he earned a regular place in 1955/56, having completed an apprenticeship as a bricklayer while rising through the ranks, Wednesday had been relegated and were much in need of his youthful vigour and enthusiasm. Duly he provided it in spades and by season's end he was rewarded with a Second Division championship medal.

That term he had emerged as an intelligent, perceptive passer who read the game shrewdly, and a solid tackler, but for the next two seasons McAnearney found himself in a side which struggled among the elite, culminating in another demotion in 1958.

During the following summer Eric Taylor was replaced as team boss by the rising management star Harry Catterick, who established the Scot alongside the towering centre-half Peter Swan and the feisty Tony Kay – both of whom were destined to be disgraced in the bribes scandal of the early 1960s – as a high-quality half-back line which was hugely instrumental in the Owls taking the divisional title for the second time in four seasons.

Now McAnearney was on the verge of his pomp, having linked beautifully in recent years with fine attackers such as Redfern Froggatt, Albert Quixall, Alan Finney and the prolific Johnny Fantham, and duly he shone as Wednesday became firmly established in the First Division. Over the next five campaigns, first under Catterick and then guided by Vic Buckingham, they finished fifth, second and then sixth three times in succession, with the Dundonian their captain for some of that period. As well as demonstrating his quiet but uplifting leadership, he became a coolly competent penalty taker, never more memorably than in the 1-0 FA Cup victory over Manchester United at Old Trafford in February 1960 – eventually they lost to Blackburn Rovers in the semi-finals – and in the 4-3 away win against Burnley, one of their main rivals for the runners-up spot, a year later.

McAnearney's poise was invaluable, too, as Wednesday made their first forays into European competition, reaching the quarter-finals of the Inter-Cities Fairs Cup – the forerunner of today's Europa League – in 1961/62, although he was sidelined by injury ahead of the last-eight elimination by Barcelona.

In the autumn of 1964, aged 31, he lost his place to the immensely promising young Peter Eustace and in November 1965 he was sold to Third Division Peterborough United for £5,000, having made nearly 400 senior appearances for the Owls.

McAnearney didn't linger long at London Road, accepting the post of player-coach at Fourth Division Aldershot, who paid a similar fee for his services in March 1966. He laid aside his boots in 1968 during a spell as player-boss before returning to Hillsborough as a coach later that year.

Subsequently he became caretaker manager of Sheffield Wednesday after Jack Marshall was sacked in March 1969, then stayed to assist new boss Danny Williams before accepting the reins of Bury in November 1970. It was too late to prevent the struggling Shakers' demotion to the basement tier that season, but he remained at Gigg Lane until May 1972, when he became manager of Aldershot.

McAnearney led his new charges to promotion to the Third Division at the first attempt, but they went back down in 1975/76. Thereafter they stabilised in the top half of the Fourth and reached the last 16 of the FA Cup in 1979, a stirring effort, ahead of his exit in January 1981. McAnearney – whose younger brother Jim also spent most of the 1950s with Wednesday but never thrived and went on to enjoy greater success with Plymouth Argyle and Watford – later coached briefly with Chelsea, then became a postman in Aldershot before retiring to Sheffield.

Thomas McAnearney, footballer and manager; born Dundee, 6 January 1933; played for Sheffield Wednesday 1951-65, Peterborough United 1965-66, Aldershot 1966-68; managed Aldershot 1967-68 and 1972-81, Sheffield Wednesday as caretaker 1969, Bury 1970-72; died 14 February 2012.

Ray Barlow

Ray Barlow was a footballing artist, the sweet-passing midfield fulcrum of Vic Buckingham's delightfully free-flowing West Bromwich Albion side of the mid-1950s, and it was not only Baggies loyalists who scratched their heads in perplexity that the stylish wing-half was awarded only a single England cap.

Certainly there was no shortage of shrewd observers within the game who reckoned the tall, rangy Wiltshireman preferable to Jimmy Dickinson, the splendidly consistent and defensively ultra-solid Portsmouth stalwart who kept Barlow out during his prime, Dickinson wearing his country's colours 48 times in the process.

As befitted a former inside-forward, Barlow was primarily an attacker, and a gloriously entertaining, endlessly subtle one at that. His speciality was threading exquisite deliveries through the tiniest of gaps in opposing rearguards, seeming to sense openings which appeared only fleetingly and of which more mundane operators were not even aware.

Often he was the most striking figure afield, dictating the tempo of a game with an imperious authority which contrasted vividly with his engagingly unassuming character away from the action. Yet for all the elegance of his work on the ball, Barlow was a powerful presence, too, his dynamic box-to-box surges and his strength in the tackle being notable features of his all-round excellence.

Having joined West Bromwich from amateur football in his home county as an 18-year-old in 1944, he was pitched immediately into emergency wartime competition, then made his senior debut in September 1946, scoring from inside-left in a 7-2 victory at Newport County. Midway through 1948/49 Barlow cemented a regular position in the side and, still operating mainly as a forward, scored in the 3-0 triumph at Leicester in the campaign's penultimate match which was to clinch Albion's promotion to the top flight as runners-up to Second Division champions Fulham.

Among the elite, Barlow's poise and polish were all the more evident, especially when he settled in his most effective role of left-half, although such was his versatility that sometimes he was pressed into service at centre-half, inside-forward and even centre-forward. His input was never more effective than in 1953/54 when the Baggies were within four points of becoming the first club in the 20th century to lift the coveted League and FA Cup double, finishing as runners-up to West Midlands neighbours Wolverhampton Wanderers in the old First Division and beating Preston North End in the knockout competition.

Barlow, who was the last Albion survivor from their Wembley line-up, shone brightly in defence and attack under the twin towers, both linking up with left-back and captain Len Millard to nullify the potent threat of Preston's fabulous Tom Finney, the newly-crowned Footballer of the Year, and surging forward to earn the penalty from which Ronnie Allen equalised on the way to a dramatic 3-2 triumph.

Internationally, though, there was less satisfaction. There were two outings for England 'B', four for the Football League and an FA tour of South America, but it remained inconceivable to all who placed a high priority on skill and imagination – particularly in an era when England were twice humiliated by the magnificent Hungarians – that Barlow should be limited to 90 minutes in the full national team, the one which beat Northern Ireland 2-0 in October 1954.

That day in Belfast he was part of an experimental side containing seven debutants, of whom Johnny Haynes was the only one who would carve a regular niche, yet it seemed to many in attendance at Windsor Park that Barlow and the brilliant Fulham schemer might have forged a fruitful long-term combination on the football fields of the world.

Happily for Albion, his club form was not affected by his country's cold shoulder, and he continued to thrive at the Hawthorns, meshing particularly smoothly with fellow wing-half Jimmy Dudley, deep-lying centre-forward Allen and, as the decade wore on, the attacking midfielder Bobby Robson.

In the late 1950s he succeeded Millard as captain, leading them to fourth and fifth in the First Division table in successive seasons before, having reached the veteran stage, he accepted a move to second-tier Birmingham City in August 1960. Not surprisingly given the accumulation of physical knocks taken during more than 450 competitive outings for the Baggies, Barlow didn't last long at St Andrew's, moving on to non-League Stourbridge in 1961 after only a handful of appearances for the Blues.

A devoted family man, he went on to run a tobacconist's and sweetshop in West Bromwich, then a post office in Stourbridge, always retaining his connection with the club he had served with such distinction and which accorded him a signal honour during its 125th anniversary celebrations in 2004, when he was included in Albion's best-ever 16-man squad.

If further proof of Ray Barlow's eminence were needed, it came from Sir Bobby Robson, who not long before his death in 2009 described his former Hawthorns comrade as one of the finest players he had ever worked with. Considering that Robson had played for and managed England, then bossed Barcelona and Newcastle United among others, that was a meaningful tribute, indeed.

Raymond John Barlow, footballer; born Swindon, Wiltshire, 17 August 1926; played for West Bromwich Albion 1944-60, Birmingham City 1960-61; capped once by England 1954; died Bridgend, South Wales, 14 March 2012.

Barry Kitchener

With his rugged looks, flowing locks and immense physical presence, Barry Kitchener was the epitome of the warrior centre-half, and from the middle 1960s to the early 1980s he embodied the indefatigable spirit of Millwall Football Club.

Exuding strength, defiance and a certain unflappable dignity that somehow remained intact no matter how tempestuous the action which raged around him, and into which he hurled himself fearlessly and with inspirational relish, he was a pillar of reliability, exactly the sort of team-mate every professional loves to play alongside when the going gets tough.

Kitchener compiled a club record of some 600 senior appearances for the Lions, an astonishing 244 of them in consecutive contests, and it wasn't only regular attenders at The Den who reckoned he was unfortunate never to test himself in England's top division.

As it was he shone consistently in the middle tiers, suffering relegation to the Third in 1974/75, then captaining the side which bounced straight back to the Second at the first attempt, only to experience the trauma of demotion again three seasons later.

Through all the ups and downs, as managers Benny Fenton, Gordon Jago, George Petchey and Peter Anderson came and went, the quiet, craggy Kitchener was a constantly reassuring factor.

Spotted in Essex by a shrewd Millwall scout, the Dagenham-born defender was recruited from Newbury Park Youth Club as a 16-year-old. He signed professional forms in 1965, turned out at left-back for the youth team and reserves, then made his senior entrance in the number-three shirt, deputising for Den idol Harry Cripps in a 2-0 defeat at Birmingham in February 1967.

But with the exuberant and popular Cripps in his pomp, with many seasons on the left flank of the Lions' defence still ahead of him, and stalwart stopper Brian Snowdon reaching the veteran stage, the rookie Kitchener was seen as an ideal replacement at the heart of the rearguard.

So instantly successful was his conversion that he was ever-present over the next five Second Division terms, reaching new heights of dominance in 1971/72 as Fenton's team finished third in the table, only a point adrift of promoted Birmingham.

Kitchener was commanding in the air, not prone to over-elaboration when the ball was on the ground but capable of safe and sensible distribution, and ready to hurl his body into the way of anything that threatened the Millwall net.

Apart from spending the summer of 1979 on loan with Tampa Bay – he excelled in the United States, helping to reach the Soccer Bowl final, in which the Rowdies were beaten by Vancouver Whitecaps – he played all his senior football for the Lions, his loyalty never in question.

By the early 1980s, feeling the inevitable wear-and-tear of a decade and a half in the professional game, Kitchener was supplanted as a regular in the side, first by Tony Tagg and then by Sam Allardyce, who would also see service with Tampa Bay.

After finishing as a player in 1982, he coached the club's reserves and youngsters, and when Anderson was sacked as manager that November there were plenty of Millwall fans who reckoned their old favourite should take the reins. In the event he did so for a handful of matches as caretaker before George Graham was appointed.

Thereafter he did not remain for long in the professional game, but went on to run a souvenir business in Norfolk with his wife.

He remained a regular visitor to The Den, where he will always be revered, his lasting stature emphasised in 2007 when he was chosen as Millwall's entry in the Professional Footballers' Association Hall of Fame, which was set up to commemorate the union's centenary that year.

Barry Raymond Kitchener, footballer; born Dagenham, Essex, 11 December 1947; played for Millwall 1965-82; died 30 March 2012.

Eddie May

Burly, affable Eddie May looms large in the modern history of Welsh football.

During his playing prime in the first half of the 1970s he cut an imposing figure at the heart of the Wrexham rearguard, totalling some 400 senior appearances.

Later the most successful stint in his long, varied and eventually globetrotting coaching and managerial career came at the helm of Cardiff City, whom he guided to the double of Third Division title and Welsh Cup glory in 1992/93. He also served Swansea City as a player and, fleetingly, Newport County as a coach, thus becoming one of the few men to be associated with all four of Wales' most famous clubs.

Essex-born May's first League employers were Southend United, whom he joined from Dagenham in January 1965, making his debut for the Third Division Shrimpers that spring as a left-back.

Soon, though, the muscular six-footer found his natural position as a dominant centre-half, majestic in the air, powerful and unfailingly courageous, but his fine personal form could not prevent the Roots Hall club from sinking to the basement division in the spring of 1966.

In June 1968 May was sold to fourth-tier rivals Wrexham for £5,000 and he settled rapidly at the Racecourse Ground, playing an influential role as the Robins were promoted in 1970 as runners-up to Chesterfield.

Thereafter he became skipper, leading John Neal's enterprising side to Welsh Cup success in 1972 and in two other rousing knockout campaigns. In 1973/74 Wrexham reached the last eight of the FA Cup, beating soon-to-be-crowned Division Two champions Middlesbrough and top-flight Southampton before bowing 1-0 to Burnley, then among the top six clubs in the land.

Then in 1975/76 May was an inspirational part of the side which made it to the quarter-finals of the European Cup Winners' Cup, where they went down 2-1 on aggregate to the illustrious Belgians, Anderlecht.

The following August, aged 33 and having missed only 34 League outings in his eight seasons in North Wales, he was freed to join Fourth Division Swansea City, whom he helped to earn promotion in 1978, after which he retired as a player.

May loved the game far too much to leave it, though, and he became a coach at Leicester City, contributing to the Foxes' Second Division title campaign of 1979/80, then spending three years as assistant boss to Lennie Lawrence at Charlton Athletic between 1983 and 1986.

Next came coaching berths in Saudi Arabia, Kenya and Iceland, a month in charge of cash-strapped Newport County in the wake of their 1988 demotion from the Football League, a spell as number-two with Lincoln City and more coaching in Norway before he accepted the reins of Cardiff City in the summer of 1991 following a stint helping the club's youngsters.

May's drive and enthusiasm were exactly what the bottom-tier Bluebirds needed, and after one term of consolidation he led them to both the title and Welsh Cup triumph in 1993, thus becoming only the second Cardiff boss to lift a divisional crown, the other being Billy McCandless, who achieved Division Three (South) success in 1947.

In 1993/94, with precious little money at his disposal, he did well to avert relegation and to preside over one of the most joyous afternoons in Ninian Park history when visiting Manchester City were ousted from the FA Cup.

However, the club's finances were in a mess, the team struggled following a difficult takeover and in November 1994 he was sacked. So loyal was May, though, that when his replacement, Terry Yorath, was also dismissed in the spring, he returned until season's end, which brought inevitable relegation and his second exit.

Thereafter came brief stints in charge of Torquay United, Dundalk in the Republic of Ireland and Brentford, followed by coaching assignments around the world, including jobs in Finland, Zimbabwe (where he led the Highlanders club to two league championships), South Africa, Uganda and Malawi.

The honest, down-to-earth May's enduring popularity at Cardiff was illustrated by his invitation to manage one of the two sides which played the inaugural match at the club's new stadium in 2009.

Edwin Charles May, footballer and manager; born Epping, Essex, 19 May 1943; played for Southend United 1965-68, Wrexham 1968-76, Chicago Sting on loan 1975, Swansea City 1976-78; managed Newport County 1988, Cardiff City 1991-94 and 1995, Torquay United 1995-96, Dundalk 1997, Brentford 1997; died 14 April 2012.

Arthur Bottom

Folk idol, saviour, sharp-shooter – all descriptions which have been applied, and with impeccable justification, to Arthur Bottom.

The Sheffield-born inside-forward, as engagingly unassuming off the football field as he was spikily aggressive on it, was a bustling, free-scoring marksman who enjoyed his roaring pomp with York City in the mid-1950s, when he was integral to the lowly Minstermen's romantic progress to the semi-final of the FA Cup. In those simpler, some might say more wholesome days, when the professional game's most venerable competition still represented the pinnacle of ambition to the majority of its players, Bottom was feted generously for his derring-do, albeit in the restrained manner of the times.

Then, when he was granted a fleeting opportunity to test himself at the top domestic level, he grabbed it avidly, contributing a rush of springtime goals which did much towards keeping a wobbly Newcastle United side in the First Division in 1958.

All too soon, it seemed, he was back in the obscurity of the lower leagues, but his name was not to be forgotten within the football community, hence the title of an enduringly popular York City electronic newsletter – 'There's Only One Arthur Bottom'.

The Bottom career commenced in April 1947 when he turned professional as a 17-year-old with Sheffield United, having been recruited from the local YMCA club.

He made his senior entrance in a 2-2 draw at home to Stoke City in October 1948, but as it was his sole outing that season he was not implicated in the Blades relegation from the elite tier. Still, he could not claim a regular berth over the next few years and when United won the Second Division title in 1952/53 he remained mostly in reserve.

Thus Bottom's June 1954 move to York City of the Third Division North was hardly greeted with euphoria on the terraces of Bootham Crescent, but by season's end he was being hailed as a hero.

He started the term with a debut hat-trick in a 6-2 win at Wrexham and went on to total 39 hits in 46 appearances, a colossal factor in York equalling their best-ever League effort by finishing fourth in the table. But it was their feat of becoming the first Third Division club to reach the last four of the FA Cup which riveted national attention on the Happy Wanderers, as they were dubbed temporarily in reference to a current pop song.

Bottom contributed eight goals to a storming campaign, the highlights of which were richly deserved victories over Blackpool (complete with the great Stanley Matthews) and Tottenham Hotspur, then two semi-final matches against Newcastle United.

In the first encounter at Hillsborough, the local boy equalised an early Magpies goal with an exquisite chip, then almost forced a late winner, only for 'keeper Ronnie Simpson to scoop his header to safety with a desperate lunge. City fans swore the ball had crossed the line, though honest Bottom later revealed that it hadn't, but he did cavil at the referee giving a free-kick against him, meaning that the 'goal' wouldn't have stood anyway.

Newcastle prevailed 2-0 in the Roker Park replay and went on to lift the Cup against Manchester City at Wembley, but the York striker had well and truly arrived, continuing his prolific form into subsequent seasons.

So impressed had been the Geordies by Bottom that when they were in dire straits near the foot of the First Division in January 1958, they turned to the man who had plundered 105 goals in 158 games for the Minstermen.

After leaving Bootham Crescent for St James' Park in a £4,500 deal, Bottom did not disappoint, announcing his arrival with the brace which secured the points at Everton and scoring seven times in eight games as the Magpies clawed marginally clear of relegation.

At this point, quick, strong and skilful, and in his prime at 28, Bottom might have been expected to thrive long-term with Newcastle, but the purchase of expensive Welsh star Ivor Allchurch forced him out of the reckoning and he was sold to Third Division Chesterfield for £5,000 only 11 months after moving to Tyneside.

In 1960 he entered non-League circles with Boston United, then served Alfreton Town, and took a job as a silversmith in a cutlery company. By then Arthur Bottom had left the game, but his niche in its annals was secure.

Arthur Edwin Bottom, footballer; born Sheffield, 28 February 1930; played for Sheffield United 1947-54, York City 1954-58, Newcastle United 1958, Chesterfield 1958-60; died Sheffield, 18 April 2012.

Alfie Biggs

He was known as 'The Baron' and he once described his footballing domain of Eastville, now sadly obliterated by a sprawling furniture store, as 'some kind of paradise'. In the Bristol of the 1950s and 1960s, Alfie Biggs, local hero and celebrated man about town, was in his element.

He played for the Rovers, who were styled as the homelier, more down-to-earth of the two clubs struggling for sporting supremacy in the West Country capital. Without being disrespectful to Bristol City, always wealthier and in some intangible way just a trifle more up-market, it was a fair assessment.

Tall, blond and dashingly handsome, Biggs was a free-scoring forward – his final Rovers tally was 197 goals in 463 appearances – and he was blessed with almost every attribute required to scale the loftiest peaks of the English game.

He was quick, courageous and bullishly powerful, and his aerial work was majestic, but where he differed vividly from so many contemporary front-men was in the sheer variety of his gifts. For instance, his touch on the ball with both feet was invariably smooth and assured; his shooting could be savage or subtle depending on need, and his distribution was deft, perceptive and usually precise.

But if such was the Biggs cocktail, then why did he spend the whole of his lengthy career outside the top flight? The answer is to be found in his character.

Though locally he was a famous socialiser, certainly relishing bar and betting shop, dancefloor and snooker hall, he was never seriously attracted to the bright lights of any city but the one in which he was born. Biggs was a Bristolian to his core, and if he lacked the kind of professional ruthlessness and single-mindedness which might have secured stardom on a more glittering stage than his beloved Eastville, Rovers fans rejoiced in their easy-going marksman's contentment.

Indeed, he was an engagingly modest individual with no delusions of grandeur, who earned his high-faluting nickname partly through the sharpness of his dress-sense at the dawn of the rock'n'roll era, but also because he played the game with a buccaneering, stylish flourish which chimed so fittingly with his club's nickname, the Pirates.

Crucially, too, though he never disguised his appetite for nightlife, it was not his way to lead team-mates astray, and often he advised impressionable youngsters to head home to their beds, even as he was eyeing his next entertaining port of call. Equally, he was an impeccable trainer, frequently amazing more abstemious team-mates by running them into the ground on the morning after an evening of enthusiastic indulgence.

Thus Biggs became revered as one of the most colourful characters in Rovers history, and it is ironic to reflect that he might easily have made his name in the red shirt of Bristol City, rather than the Pirates' distinctive blue-and-white quarters.

Hailing from the City heartland of Knowle West, he was courted assiduously by the Robins as a vastly promising teenager, but when he turned up at Ashton Gate to sign a contract he was kept waiting so long that he lost patience, hopped on a bus and joined the Rovers instead. It was a snap decision which he was never to regret.

After making his first-team entrance in a friendly against Manchester United in 1953, Biggs gradually carved a niche for himself as a deep-lying inside forward, scoring a few goals but mainly foraging to create opportunities for spearheads such as Barrie Meyer and Geoff Bradford. It was in 1955/56 that he claimed a regular berth with the Second Division Pirates, and during that term, when still only 19, he experienced what he described as the pinnacle of his career. Once again Manchester United provided the opposition, but this time the contest was in deadly earnest.

In January 1956 Matt Busby's brilliant Babes were champions-elect, romping away at the head of the First Division, and now they descended on Bristol to complete what seemed like the formality of victory in the third round of the FA Cup. But despite fielding all their top players except the injured Duncan Edwards, the incomparable young leviathan of English football, they met their match in the Eastville mud.

The Rovers team had been assembled by manager Bert Tann for a mere £110 – the price of 11 signing-on fees – and when they humbled the Old Trafford giants 4-0 it was greeted as the sporting upset of the age. Meanwhile Biggs, who contributed two memorable goals to the club's most glorious hour, had announced his credentials as a rookie attacker with limitless potential.

There followed elimination by Doncaster Rovers in the next round, but Biggs continued to shine as Bert Tann's men finished sixth in the division, only four points short of the promotion places. For the remainder of the decade he was hugely influential, excelling in harness with fellow marksmen Bradford and Dai Ward, and exhilarating wingers George Petherbridge and Peter Hooper.

There was another sixth-place finish in 1958/59 and Rovers were never out of the table's top half, but money remained short and when Preston North End offered £18,000 for the Baron in July 1961, Tann could not afford to refuse.

At the time the experienced Deepdale boss Jimmy Milne was cock-a-hoop, describing his capture as the best player he had ever bought, and no less an authority than Stan Cullis, the iron hand at the helm of then-mighty Wolverhampton Wanderers, called the deal the transfer coup of the season.

However, although Biggs thrived on the field in far-off Lancashire, netting a creditable 22 goals in 48 League outings for the Second Division Lilywhites, he pined for Bristol. He missed the familiar smell of the gasholders which loomed, grimly but somehow hospitably, over Eastville; he missed the flowerbeds which adorned either end of the pitch; and he missed his mates. Thus he was delighted when Tann paid £12,000 to take him home to captain the newly-relegated Pirates in October 1962. Now aged 26 and in his pomp, Biggs moved to centre-forward and although he never led his charges to promotion from the third flight he became more prolific than ever before.

His most bountiful campaign was 1963/64, during which he plundered 37 goals and linked beautifully with fellow raider Ian Hamilton, and as he entered the veteran stage it seemed a given that he would complete his playing days as a Pirate.

But a £10,000 bid from Third Division Walsall in the spring of 1968 produced a surprise move to the Midlands, where he sojourned only briefly before ending his career with an even more fleeting stint for Swansea Town of the Fourth.

After retirement in 1969 he returned to Bristol, initially to work as a car salesman while playing non-League football for Taunton Town. There followed jobs as a postman, a baker, a delivery man and a security officer but, before a late-in-life move to Poole in Dorset, he retained close links to Rovers, being a faithful patron of the Eastville Club, the watering hole which continued to sit rather forlornly in the corner of the car park after the stadium was demolished.

In there, as he held court in a swirl of cigarette smoke and recalled his Pirates pomp, Alfie Biggs was the Baron again.

Alfred George Biggs, footballer; born Bristol, 8 February 1936; played for Bristol Rovers 1952-61 and 1962-68, Preston North End 1961-62, Walsall 1968, Swansea Town 1968-69; died Poole, Dorset, 20 April 2012.

Bobby Black

Bobby Black was a master craftsman who looked after his tools. The goal-scoring winger stuck to the same pair of football boots throughout his entire professional career, opting for repair over replacement whenever the trusty leather showed signs of wear and tear.

It was a policy which paid off handsomely for both his clubs, East Fife and Queen of the South. The Fifers enjoyed the most successful period in their history when the tenacious attacker was patrolling their right flank in the first six seasons after the war, then he sparkled for the Doonhamers for nearly a decade from the early 1950s.

Black could, perhaps, be considered unfortunate never to win a full international cap, particularly after he scored twice on his only major representative outing, for the Scottish League in their 3-1 victory over the League of Ireland at Dalymount Park, Dublin, in 1954. However, it was never going to be easy getting past the formidable likes of Willie Waddell of Rangers and Hibernian's Gordon Smith, his main rivals for his country's number-seven shirt.

After shining for an amateur team, Connell Park Rangers, the teenage Black made a few appearances for Queen of the South, his local Scottish League club, in unofficial wartime competition and it seemed likely that he would forge a professional future at Palmerston Park. But he cast his employment net wider, and in 1945, after trials with Blackburn Rovers and Huddersfield Town had led nowhere, he signed for East Fife, then a force to be reckoned with in Scotland's second tier.

In the spring of 1948 manager Scot Symon, who would go on to untold glories as the boss of Rangers, called Black into an enterprising side which had just clinched both their divisional championship and the League Cup, and the rookie impressed in the season's last two games.

Thereafter his career took off as he became a regular for the Methil men as their golden era gathered pace. Blending potently with star performers such as shrewd inside-forward Allan Brown and explosive marksman Charlie 'Cannonball' Fleming, Black was a key contributor as East Fife finished fourth in the top flight in 1948/49.

That was a mammoth achievement for the unfashionable Fifers, but they exceeded it in 1949/50 by not only retaining their top-four berth but also winning the League Cup for the second time, beating Rangers 2-0 in the semi-final, then Dunfermline Athletic 3-0 in the final, both games being played at Hampden Park.

That term Black was in magnificent fettle, but when East Fife returned to headquarters in the spring for the Scottish Cup final they were beaten 3-0 by Rangers, the reverse at least partially explained by recent injuries to their two main goalkeepers.

By now he was approaching his prime, a gifted ball-player whose twinkling skills were spiced by a feisty edge in the tackle, a shrewd positional sense which brought him plenty of goals and apparently boundless energy. Thus the leg injury which sabotaged his season in 1951/52 was a bitter blow to East Fife, whose admirable third-place finish might have been even better but for Black's lengthy absence.

However, in the following summer Symon decided to part with the ebullient 25-year-old, who was delighted to return to his roots with Queen of the South. At first his form was indifferent as he struggled to overcome the effects of his injury, but gradually he asserted his class, going on to forge productive links with inside-forwards Jimmy McGill and Wattie Rothera, and centre-forward Jim Patterson.

Highlights for Black were his call-up for the Scottish League and a barnstorming effort in 1955/56, when he scored 14 times as the Doonhamers came sixth in the top division.

After that the team began to struggle, suffering relegation in 1958/59, and in 1961 the veteran flankman was released. By then, though, he had etched his name indelibly into Queen of the South folklore, his 120 goals in 346 games making him the second most prolific marksman in the club's history, behind his old mate Patterson.

Later Black crossed the border to play non-League football for Bath City and Bridgwater Town, while earning his living as an accountant and analyst for a footwear company. A natural all-round sportsman who still relished the buzz of high-level competition, he also excelled at bowls, playing for Somerset alongside many-times world champion David Bryant, helping to lift national titles on several occasions.

It might be said that Black founded a football dynasty as both his sons played for a living, Bobby for Queen of the South and Russell for Sheffield United, Dundee and Halifax Town. Next came grandsons Toby and Jamie Paterson, who both turned professional, and then two great-grandsons – Brodie Paterson has been capped for Australia's youth team and Denny Johnstone is on the verge of breaking through at Celtic.

Robert Black, footballer; born Thornhill, Dumfries and Galloway, 1927; played for East Fife 1946-52, Queen of the South 1952-61; died Bristol, 4 June 2012.

Alan McDonald

There was nothing fancy about the football of Alan McDonald, but for more than a decade he was a mightily effective centre-half for Queen's Park Rangers in the top domestic flight of the English game, and he earned half a century of caps for Northern Ireland along the way.

The rangy 6ft 2ins Ulsterman was commanding, combative and, crucially for his longevity, admirably consistent. He was never the paciest of performers but he read the unfolding action intelligently and when the ball was at his feet he was not inclined to risk losing it, thus tending to opt for long-distance punt over delicate dispatch.

His characteristic authority, confidence and loyalty gelled with courage, determination and a fierce pride in his work to render him a natural and inspirational captain of both club and country.

Having been spotted by a Rangers scout in Ireland, McDonald enlisted at Loftus Road as a 17-year-old apprentice in August 1981, bedding in gradually and learning from the first-team likes of Glenn Roeder, Terry Fenwick, Steve Wicks and Bob Hazell.

The former schoolboy and youth international didn't break through in time to contribute to the Second Division title triumph in 1982/83, but manager Terry Venables wanted his promising rookie to gain senior experience and so loaned him to struggling Charlton Athletic, whom he helped to escape relegation to the third tier that spring.

Thus bolstered, McDonald made his Rangers entrance while still in his teens in the following September, playing solidly in a 4-0 drubbing of Wolves at Molineux. There followed a clutch of efficient displays before he was replaced for the remainder of the First Division campaign by the older Wicks.

In 1984/85 his appearances became more frequent as Rangers gradually consolidated their position at the higher level, but it was in 1985/86 that McDonald, who was also an able full-back, truly made his mark. That season he was ever-present in the League and featured prominently as the west Londoners reached the League Cup final, particularly in the quarter-final replay victory over Chelsea at Stamford Bridge, in which he scored, and the semi-final defeat of Liverpool which denied Kenny Dalglish's team the chance to become the first to lift the domestic treble.

Rangers under-performed at Wembley, losing 3-0 to Oxford United, but that term, too, he arrived on the full international scene, excelling on debut in a tense 1-0 win over Romania in a World Cup qualifier in Bucharest. Proving that was no fluke, he shone again a month later at the heart of a hectic rearguard action in the goalless draw with England at Wembley which secured Billy Bingham's men their berth at the 1986 finals in Mexico.

In that tournament he battled gamely against the high-quality likes of Spain's Emilio Butragueno and Zico of Brazil, playing in all three group matches, which produced only a single point against Algeria.

Thereafter McDonald continued to improve. Combining productively with the smaller, nippier Paul Parker, he was hugely influential as Rangers climbed to fifth place in the First Division under Jim Smith in 1987/88, a feat equalled by Gerry Francis's fine side of 1992/93, the first season of the Premier League. The big stopper's poise and encouragement were of immense benefit to the development of Darren Peacock, his younger central-defensive partner in the early 1990s who was eventually sold to Newcastle United for £2.7 million, and McDonald remained a Loftus Road bulwark into his thirties.

He was devastated by the club's demotion in 1995/96, but stayed at Loftus Road for one more season before being freed – after playing nearly 500 games for the club – to join second-flight rivals Swindon Town in the summer of 1997.

A year later he retired, going on to sample coaching with Northern Ireland under-21s before entering management with Glentoran in his home city of Belfast in June 2007.

He took to the task with alacrity, swiftly bringing in new faces and leading the Cock'n'Hens to triumph over Crusaders in the final of the prestigious County Antrim Shield in his first full season.

Boss McDonald tasted even sweeter success in 2008/09 as Glentoran became Irish Premier League champions, pipping their local rivals Linfield by a single point, but then sampled the other side of the coin, resigning in February 2010 after his side had slumped.

McDonald, a popular character renowned as a dressing-room practical joker, owned a trophy shop in Bangor, Northern Ireland, which had been run previously by his international team-mate Billy Hamilton. His death, shockingly premature at the age of 48, happened while he was playing golf on a course near Lisburn in County Down.

Alan McDonald, footballer and manager; born Belfast, 12 October 1963; played for Queen's Park Rangers 1981-97, Charlton Athletic on loan 1983, Swindon Town 1997-98; capped 52 times by Northern Ireland 1986-96; managed Glentoran 2007-10; died Temple Golf Club, County Down, 23 June 2012.

Jimmy Tansey

As a tenacious, sharp-tackling, consistently competent full-back with Everton throughout most of the 1950s, Jimmy Tansey took his work extremely seriously. But that never stopped him having a laugh with the fans.

Once, after being dumped on the seat of his pants by the wizardry of an opposing winger – and there was a plethora of beguiling flankmen in his day, of which the incomparable Stanley Matthews and Tom Finney were the most renowned – the slightly bandy-legged Liverpudlian was subjected to a chorus of colourful ridicule from the massed ranks assembled on Goodison Park's Paddock terrace, now long defunct.

His reaction, rather than revealing unseemly bitterness or retreating into a shell of impotent hurt, was to round on his tormentors with an imaginary machine-gun, pretending to mow them down in waves, all the while wearing a grin as wide as the Mersey.

It was a typically spontaneous gesture from an engagingly warm character and it was greeted with uproarious delight, instantly disarming his erstwhile critics. For such moments, as well as for his general efficiency in a frequently toiling team, was Jimmy Tansey loved.

After joining Everton as a teenage wing-half, he was converted into a full-back during his rise through the junior teams and made his senior entrance for the Second Division Toffees as a replacement for the injured Jack Lindsay in a 2-2 draw at Notts County in March 1953.

However, it was not until 1955/56, by which time Everton had been promoted, that Tansey laid regular claim to their number-three shirt, initially at the expense of Republic of Ireland international Don Donovan.

That term, with the team ensconced in the wrong half of the league table but reaching the last eight of the FA Cup, the local boy impressed hugely with his dependability, the crispness of his challenges, his shrewd positional play and his subtle knack of jockeying his opponents away from the area of immediate danger.

Tansey peaked in 1956/57 when he was the only ever-present in manager Ian Buchan's hard-working but rather limited side, which finished 15th in the top tier. Playing at left-back, he struck up an effective understanding with Donovan, who was now operating on the right, and the commanding centre-half Tommy Jones.

One of his finest hours came that autumn, when reigning champions and current table-toppers Manchester United were humbled 5-2 on their own Old Trafford turf, with Tansey shackling Johnny Berry, the Busby Babes' quick and feisty little outside-right, thus cutting off a main supply line to the hosts' predatory strike-force of Tommy Taylor, Billy Whelan and a rookie named Bobby Charlton.

He retained his berth for another full season before yielding it to the younger John Bramwell early in the 1958/59 campaign. Thereafter, losing pace as he strove to recover from a series of niggling injuries, Tansey languished on the fringe of the team until, having entered his thirties, he joined Fourth Division Crewe Alexandra in the summer of 1960.

He had made 142 appearances for Everton, but only managed a handful more for the Gresty Road club before leaving the professional game.

Tansey, a gentle and engagingly affable character with a twinkling sense of humour, later worked as a fitter for British Leyland.

James Tansey, footballer; born Liverpool, 29 January 1929; played for Everton 1948-60, Crewe Alexandra 1960-61; died Liverpool, 7 July 2012.

Joe McBride

Joe McBride was the quintessential striker. Whenever he didn't know what else to do with the ball, he stuck it in the net.

So ran a tribute from the revered Celtic manager Jock Stein to one of his favourite charges during the late 1960s, when the Bhoys were sweeping all before them. Jimmy McGrory, another Celtic icon and the most prolific marksman in the history of the British professional game, reckoned his fellow Glaswegian to be the best centre-forward he'd ever laid eyes on, and Sir Alex Ferguson, who hailed from the next street to McBride in Govan, believed that, but for injury, his former neighbour's final tally would have been of prodigious proportions.

As it was, the much-travelled marksman didn't do badly during a bountiful 16-year career in which he served nine clubs, his aggregate of 221 Scottish League goals bettered only by Ally McCoist and Willie Wallace since the war.

Though fans of some of his other employers might beg to differ, McBride is remembered most vividly for his exploits in the green-and-white hoops, particularly in

1966/67, the season in which Celtic capped their domestic treble by becoming the first British club to lift the European Cup.

Agonisingly for the chunky sharp-shooter, he missed the climactic triumph over Internazionale of Milan, and eternal anointment as one of the 'Lisbon Lions', through an injury sustained in a Christmas Eve clash with Aberdeen. A measure of his form at the time is that even though he didn't play again that term, still his tally of 35 hits made him the leading scorer in the land in all competitions.

One surprising statistic is that although he was picked four times for the Scottish League, he played only twice for his country, against Wales and Northern Ireland in 1966, the paltry haul of caps the result of being the contemporary of such top-quality operators as Denis Law, Ian St John, Alan Gilzean, Wallace and Colin Stein.

McBride was born only some 200 yards from Ibrox, the home of Rangers, but he would never play for Celtic's great rivals, instead being recruited as a young right winger by Kilmarnock. After being loaned out to a junior club, Kirkintilloch Rob Roy, he turned professional in 1956 and made his senior debut in a top-division encounter with Dundee on Christmas Day 1957.

Thereafter he progressed rapidly as a central attacker at Rugby Park, scoring so regularly that he attracted the attention of leading English clubs, eventually joining reigning champions Wolverhampton Wanderers for £12,500 in November 1959.

Unexpectedly McBride floundered at Molineux, proving unable to unseat Wolves' splendid front pair of Jimmy Murray and Bobby Mason, and the Scot was sold to struggling Luton Town for £12,000 in February 1960 without being granted a senior outing in the famous gold shirt.

Though he netted six times in 13 games that spring, he could neither prevent the Hatters' relegation to the second tier, nor settle south of the border, and in November 1960 he was transferred to Partick Thistle.

For two years, he flourished at Firhill, which earned him a £5,000 switch to Motherwell in November 1962, and at Fir Park the McBride career really took off as he finished as 'Well's leading marksman in three consecutive terms ahead of his £22,500 move to Celtic as new boss Stein's first signing in June 1965.

It was at Parkhead that McBride became a star. In 1965/66 he was Scottish football's joint top-scorer – along with his old chum Ferguson, then of Dunfermline Athletic – with 31 goals as Celtic were crowned as League champions. He featured in consecutive League Cup final victories over Rangers, and despite his injury he contributed hugely to the retention of the title in 1966/67.

McBride cut a powerful, pugnacious figure on the pitch. Quite brilliant in the air for a man of medium height, and packing a fierce shot, he was also deceptively skilful, being adept at controlling long passes out of defence and laying them off to predatory team-mates Bobby Lennox and Steve Chalmers.

However, despite plundering a hat-trick against Morton at Cappielow in December 1967 in his first full League appearance for a year, McBride was never again central to Stein's plans. The quicker, slightly younger Wallace had been acquired from Hearts, the veteran Chalmers remained potent and the darting Lennox was in his prime, so in November 1968 – having contributed 86 strikes in a mere 94 games for Celtic – McBride was dispatched to Hibernian as a £15,000 replacement for departing hero Colin Stein.

The Easter Road newcomer was an instant sensation, striking eight times in his first three matches, and continuing to score freely over the next two years. Then, having entered his thirties and cutting a slightly bulkier figure, he was sold to Dunfermline for £4,000 on Christmas Day 1970, thus outraging the Edinburgh fans who had come to adore him.

In October 1971 McBride joined his seventh and final Scottish top-flight club, Clyde, serving them for the remainder of that campaign before retiring in April 1972.

In recent years he became a familiar figure at Parkhead once more, working as an ambassador for the club.

McBride's son, also Joe, was a Scottish under-21 international winger who played for Everton and Hibs among others before taking up coaching. He is currently working with the first team at Cardiff.

Joseph McBride, footballer; born Govan, Glasgow, 10 June 1938; played for Kilmarnock 1956-59, Wolverhampton Wanderers 1959-60, Luton Town 1960, Partick Thistle 1960-62, Motherwell 1962-65, Celtic 1965-68, Hibernian 1968-70, Dunfermline Athletic 1970-71, Clyde 1971-72; capped twice by Scotland 1966; died Glasgow, 11 July 2012.

Eddy Brown

Eddy Brown was a centre-forward as prolific as he was eccentric – and that was saying something. A trailblazer of the goal celebration in the 1950s when such flamboyances were virtually unknown, he delighted in shaking hands with a cornerflag, indulging in an impromptu hug with a policeman, hopping into the crowd for a swift draught of lemonade, all with a piece of the sheer unadulterated ebullience with which he invested every area of his life.

But when it came to the business of hitting the net Brown was in deadly earnest. During a 13-year professional career taking in five clubs, most notably Birmingham City in the decade's second half, the charismatic Lancastrian racked up more than 220 strikes in a tad fewer than 450 appearances, a rough average of a goal every two games for which any modern manager would pay a king's ransom.

Yet all that infectious exuberance and athletic ability would have been lost to the game had Brown carried out his boyhood intention of entering the priesthood. From the age of 12 until he was 19 he studied at De La Salle Catholic College on Guernsey, from which he was evacuated to the mainland during the war.

But while deploying his keen intelligence to garner four A-levels, and discovering a passion for the works of Shakespeare which would remain with him all his days – he used to recite adapted passages to team-mates, opponents, referees, anyone who would listen, often in praise of his hero, Preston North End's Tom Finney – Brown realised that he wanted to play football for a living. So in March 1948 he turned up at Deepdale – like Finney, Brown was Preston-born – to offer his services. Duly the rookie impressed, turned professional five months later and made his senior debut that November.

Much inspired by the visionary footballing 'evangelist' Bill Shankly, then nearing the end of his playing days, Brown refused to be discouraged by Preston's relegation from the top flight that term and in 1949/50 he earned a regular berth.

Now the full scope of his prowess became apparent. A dynamic dasher who could leave most defenders trailing in his wake, he also possessed an explosive right-foot shot and was blessed with a goal-poacher's instinct for being in the right position at the right time. Measuring only 5ft 9ins, he was no more than average in the air, and he admitted that his left foot was employed merely for standing on, but he began to score heavily and his reputation grew.

Thus it was a surprise in September 1950 when he joined Second Division rivals Southampton as part of the deal which took Charlie Wayman to Preston. At first Brown felt uncharacteristically daunted at the prospect of replacing the sharp-shooting hero of The Dell, but he managed it well enough, even though he never settled on the South Coast.

Accordingly in March 1952 he accepted a £7,000 switch to Coventry City, whom he could not prevent from slipping out of the second tier that spring but for whom he netted plentifully over the next two and a half years.

Then, in October 1954, came the key transfer of his career when he joined Birmingham City in a £9,000 deal. His 14 hits in the remainder of that season, including a hat-trick in the 9-1 annihilation of Liverpool at St Andrew's, were crucial to the Blues lifting the Second Division title.

Better still, in 1955/56 Brown was an integral contributor to the most productive campaign in the club's history, spearheading the revered forward line of Gordon Astall, Noel Kinsey, himself, Peter Murphy and Alex Govan and scoring 29 times as City tasted rare success in both league and knockout competition.

As well as finishing sixth in the elite grade, they reached the FA Cup final, which they lost 3-1 to Manchester City on an afternoon of Wembley drama best remembered for the northerners' goalkeeper Bert Trautmann suffering a broken neck but playing on oblivious to his condition.

Brown also dazzled in the Inter-Cities Fairs Cup, a new continental competition, the equivalent of today's Europa League but spread over three years from 1955 to '58. Birmingham reached the semi-finals, where their leading marksman registered twice in a 4-3 first-leg home victory over Barcelona, only for the Catalans to triumph in a third match after an initial draw on aggregate.

During his St Andrew's stint, which ended with a switch to Leyton Orient in January 1959, Brown also enjoyed himself outside football, trying his hand as a male model and teaching part-time in Wolverhampton.

After maintaining his scoring habit for the Brisbane Road club, he left the Football League in 1961, going on to immense success as player-boss of non-League Scarborough. Later he worked for his family's carpet firm, taught PE at Preston Catholic College and managed an amateur side well into his seventies.

Even after that Brown remained irrepressible, telling one interviewer: 'I've got one foot in the grave and another on a banana skin.'

Edwin Brown, footballer; born Preston, Lancashire, 28 February 1926; played for Preston North End 1948-50, Southampton 1950-52, Coventry City 1952-54, Birmingham City 1954-59, Leyton Orient 1959-61; married two/four children; died Preston, 12 July 2012.